Antiquity Papers 3

MEGALITHS FROM ANTIQUITY

edited by

Timothy Darvill & Caroline Malone

Antiquity Publications Ltd
Cambridge 2003

ANTIQUITY, the archaeological journal founded in 1927, covers a wide sweep of the modern development of archaeology. The first edited volume of classic papers took the theme of landscape (Stoddart 2000), the second focused on the Celts (Carr & Stoddart 2002) and this, the third volume, explores the theme of Megaliths. The volumes share the same format — selected articles from ANTIQUITY's 76 years demonstrate the great range of archaeological thought and practice and cover the professional recognition of the discipline. The continued intention is to set the original articles within a modern context, but, as always with ANTIQUITY, to add a personal perspective.

Megaliths and their related monuments have been an abiding theme in ANTIQUITY, and the hundreds of papers, notes and editorials have revealed changing approaches, application of new archaeological methods, geographical range, interpretative schemes and much more. In this volume, 37 papers, focusing principally on European and British megaliths and monuments, are collected under four themes: funerary structures and barrows; Stonehenge and Avebury; circles and standing stones; and, finally, interpretative studies and other dimensions. The papers range across the decades of ANTIQUITY publication, to demonstrate the changes of both knowledge and approach, alongside the perpetual questions that continue to be posed about this important class of monument.

The articles have all been reproduced in the modern format of ANTIQUITY. In particular, footnotes have been replaced where possible by the modern bibliographic referencing scheme. However, each section is prefaced by a longer introduction to set context and outline subsequent developments, replacing the original short, personalized introductions begun by Glyn Daniel, and continued by later editors. All illustrations in the volume (and on the front cover) have been already published in ANTIQUITY.

We should like to thank the authors for allowing their articles to be reprinted. We should particularly like to thank Anne Chippindale and Libby Peachey for all their hard work in the production process and Short Run Press for their efficient printing.

Published in the United Kingdom in 2003 by Antiquity Publications Ltd
King's Manor, York YO1 7EP

© 2003 Antiquity Publications Ltd

All rights reserved. No part of this publication may be reproduced or transmitted in any form or by any means, electronic or mechanical, including photocopy, recording or any other information storage and retrieval system, without prior permission in writing from the publisher.

ISBN 0-9539762-2-X

Printed and bound in the United Kingdom by Short Run Press Ltd, Exeter

MEGALITHS FROM ANTIQUITY

Contents

1 Timothy Darvill & Caroline Malone   Introduction

1 Chamber tombs, long barrows and funerary structures
3 Timothy Darvill & Caroline Malone   Editorial introduction
9 G.E. Daniel   The megalithic tombs of northern Europe
19 Stuart Piggott   The long barrow in Brittany
33 Glyn Daniel   The 'dolmens' of southern Britain
47 Stuart Piggott   The tholos tomb in Iberia
55 P-R. Giot   The chambered barrow of Barnenez in Finistère
61 Colin Renfrew   Colonialism and megalithismus
77 Poul Kjærum   Mortuary houses and funeral rites in Denmark
87 Claude Masset   The megalithic tomb at La Chaussée-Tirancourt
93 Ian Kinnes   Les Fouaillages and megalithic origins
103 J.G. Scott   Clyde, Carlingford and Connaught Cairns — a review
109 Christine Boujot & Serge Cassen   A pattern of evolution for the Neolithic funerary structures of the west of France
125 T.G.E. Powell   Megalithic and other art: Centre and West
137 George Eogan   Knowth before Knowth
149 Mark Patton   Megalithic transport and territorial markers: evidence from the Channel Islands
153 Glyn Daniel   Some megalithic follies

2 Stonehenge and Avebury: past, present and future
159 Timothy Darvill & Caroline Malone   Editorial introduction
167 Stuart Piggott   Stukeley, Avebury and the Druids
177 R.S. Newall   Stonehenge: a review
183 Andrew J. Lawson   Stonehenge: creating a definitive account
191 R.S. Thorpe & O. Williams-Thorpe   The myth of long-distance megalithic transport
203 M. Parker Pearson & Ramilisonina   Stonehenge for the ancestors: the stones pass on the message
225 Christopher Chippindale   What future for Stonehenge?
237 Geoffrey Wainwright   The Stonehenge we deserve

3 Circles and rings; posts and stones
249 Timothy Darvill & Caroline Malone   Editorial introduction
253 Stuart Piggott   The excavations at Cairnpapple Hill, West Lothian 1947–8
263 G.J. Wainwright   Durrington Walls: a ceremonial enclosure of the 2nd millennium BC
275 Alex Gibson   The timber circle at Sarn-y-bryn caled, Welshpool, Powys: ritual and sacrifice in Bronze Age mid-Wales

285 Barrie Hartwell **A Neolithic ceremonial timber complex at Ballynahatty, Co. Down**
293 Grahame Soffe & Tom Clare **New evidence of ritual monuments at Long Meg and her Daughters, Cumbria**
299 Alasdair Whittle **A late Neolithic complex at West Kennet, Wiltshire, England**
307 Corinne Roughley, Andrew Sherratt & Colin Shell **Past records, new views: Carnac 1830–2000**

4 Beyond the megaliths
313 Timothy Darvill & Caroline Malone Editorial introduction
317 R.J.C. Atkinson **Neolithic engineering**
325 Alexander Thom **Megaliths and mathematics**
333 D.C. Heggie **Megalithic lunar observatories: an astronomer's view**
339 Clive Ruggles & Gordon Barclay **Cosmology, calendars and society in Neolithic Orkney: a rejoinder to Euan MacKie**
355 Paul Devereux **Three-dimensional aspects of apparent relationships between selected natural and artificial features within the topography of the Avebury complex**
361 Paul Devereux & Robert G. Jahn **Acoustical resonances of selected archaeological sites**
363 Aaron Watson & David Keating **Architecture and sound: an acoustic analysis of megalithic monuments in prehistoric Britain**
377 Henry P. Chapman & Benjamin R. Gearey **Palaeoecology and the perception of prehistoric landscapes: some comments on visual approaches to phenomenology**

381 References

Megaliths from ANTIQUITY: an introduction
by TIMOTHY DARVILL & CAROLINE MALONE

FROM ITS DISTINCTIVE megalithic cover image to its contents of hundreds of papers and notes on megaliths over 75 years, ANTIQUITY has nurtured a continuing, and indeed growing study. Megalithic monuments have formed an abiding interests in ANTIQUITY and reflect the foibles and passions of four of its editors, who have encouraged the publication of an immense variety of megalithic and monumental themes. The papers selected here focus on the megaliths of Europe, but megaliths from all over the world appear in ANTIQUITY. For example, even in the first decade of ANTIQUITY, some 25 papers were published including the then newly recognized sites in the Sudan (Evans Pritchard 1935), Kenya (Huntingford 1935) Kashmir (Gordon 1937) and southern Russia (Tallgren 1933). These showed that simple stone structures were widespread phenomena, constructed over a long span of history, capable of broad interpretations as well as individual analysis. Here, our selection of articles and notes has been chosen to demonstrate how methods, ideas and interpretations about megaliths and related monuments have changed over the life of ANTIQUITY. Indeed, the fact that these contributions were published in the journal, and the ideas placed in the public arena, meant that they were formative in the developing study of prehistory. Inevitably, space restricts what can be included here, so specific themes have been chosen from a rich array of British and European prehistory, to examine stone, earth and timber monuments.

We have arranged our selection of papers within a series of four key themes. The first explores the earliest megalithic structures in Europe — the great chamber tombs and long barrows of the 5th, 4th and 3rd millennia BC. The founding editor, O.G.S. Crawford, and his successor Glyn Daniel, were fascinated by these early monuments (see, for example, Crawford's work on long barrows (1927) and the stone cists of Scilly and Northumbria (1928), and Daniel's two papers on British and European Megalithic tombs (reprinted here), together with the papers and editorials they published. These collectively reflect the emergence during the 20th century of the objective discussions of megaliths as more than mysterious structures. Colin Renfrew's classic paper published in 1967 shows how the various groups relate to one another and how ideas of origins and diffusion have variously attributed date, style and influence. It is true to say that megalithic studies have never been the same since!

In the second section we turn to the most famous megalithic monuments in the British Isles: the great henge circles of Stonehenge and Avebury. Both have long and fascinating histories of study, investigation and interpretation, from the very emergence of prehistoric interests in the 16th and 17th centuries. Stonehenge is the universal icon of prehistoric archaeology, whether simply expressed as a trilithon, or in its entirety. For decades the two sites have become locked into an almost perpetual limbo because of the conflicting demands for public access, popular interpretation, conservation and the need to investigate the remains further in order to advance knowledge. The inability of earlier generations of archaeologists to publish their results promptly, following continuous digging and work during the 20th century at Stonehenge, is a problem tackled only in the last decade of the century (Lawson 1992). However, ANTIQUITY was able to extract considerable information from the excavators in the form of published papers and notes while they were still alive, and thus enable progress across prehistoric studies. Stonehenge and Avebury are in many ways just the most well-known examples of a whole series of circles, rings, rows, pairs and single standing stones that characterize the later Neolithic and Bronze Age of northwest Europe.

Indeed, some may well be very much earlier but have been consigned to such a general and broad period because of limited research and poor dating evidence. If ever there was an important research priority it is surely the proper documentation and dating of these monuments, which have only seen systematic study in a few regions.

The third section explores the issues raised by monuments built of materials other than stone, especially the henges and timber circles. Since the first issue of ANTIQUITY, a keen interest was shown in developing research strategies that examined the structural histories of monuments and the methods by which new evidence could be found. Stuart Piggott's Cairnpapple paper proved to be one classic. It is joined here by more recent research on other henge and timber sites such as Durrington Walls (Wainwright 1968), Sarn-y-Bryn-Caled (Gibson 1992), Ballynahatty (Hartwell 2002) and the West Kennet enclosure (Whittle 1991). In addition, new research of old stone megalithic sites has also proved rewarding, as the reports on Long Meg and her Daughters (Soffee & Clare 1988) and Carnac (Roughley *et al.* 2001) reveal, when new survey technologies and analyses are brought into play.

The fourth section examines alternative approaches to megalithic studies, and seeks to go 'beyond the megaliths' themselves to present papers which explore dimensions other than simply stone and earth structures and building sequences. Papers included here are representative of the range of approaches, from examinations of engineering principles and their limitations (Atkinson) to the much more rarefied worlds of archaeoastronomy and sensory archaeology. The poor preservation of so many megalithic sites, and their histories of modification, damage and 19th-century landscape romanticization have all had a toll on their present state, making scientifically objective study very difficult. However, as the papers selected show, there is no shortage of ideas, theories and research projects directed towards exploring and trying to explain these ever-enigmatic monuments. Over time there have been popular trends for research and debate; at one moment how the monuments were actually built, and attempts to assess the ethnography of prehistoric builders; at another, an obsession with the concept of the cosmos as hailed by the heady years of space travel and research in the 1960s and '70s. Despite the sometimes poor preservation of megalithic structures, their enhancement and modification in the 19th century to create better-looking landscape features, and the poor knowledge of date and original form, there has been much discussion of the factors taken into account in their construction, use and function. Archaeoastronomy has been at the core of many of the propositions and theories. And it was in the pages of ANTIQUITY that some of these ideas were first given wide expression. Glyn Daniel, editor between 1957 and 1986, had little time for such interpretations and often let his feelings show in editorials and the juxtaposition of articles. Strangely, as interpretative theories have come more to the fore over recent years it is matters such as alignment, orientation and landscape setting that have again come to prominence. Three papers give a flavour of the changing debates from Thom's original thesis, to comments on Hoyle by Heggie, to the recent appraisals by Ruggles & Barclay.

ANTIQUITY has always been important in presenting and promoting new ideas about megaliths and prehistoric monuments, and its editors have been quick to give novel ideas their first wide public airing, and also to provide comments (sometime less than enthusiastic) on the changing trends of megalithic research.

Post-processual archaeology is currently having an impact, and recent research has sought to go beyond the obvious to examine function and meaning through the sensory impact of monuments, as shown by papers on acoustics (Devereux & Jahn; Watson & Keating) and visibility (Devereux; Chapman & Geary). These are the themes which will no doubt take the presentation of megaliths in ANTIQUITY into its next phase.

1 Chamber tombs, long barrows and funerary structures

by TIMOTHY DARVILL & CAROLINE MALONE

THE CHAMBER TOMBS, long barrows and related funerary structures scattered across northern and western Europe are now well recognized as representing the oldest monumental traditions and architectural styles of their respective regions. Some elements, for example passage-graves, occur over wide areas while others, such as *allées couvertes*, are found within a far more restricted compass. When ANTIQUITY started, in 1927, academic debate about the origins and distribution of megalithic chamber tombs and long barrows was well established. The spread of what were believed to be related structures along the Atlantic seaboard and well inland was already mapped. The diffusionist dogma which insisted that the earliest examples were pristine structures in southern Europe and the Mediterranean northern coasts held sway; the northern European megaliths were viewed as degenerate examples representing the spread of a megalithic culture.

Of all the subjects covered in this collection of papers, it is the discussion of megalithic tombs of various kinds that has taken up the most pages in ANTIQUITY over the years, especially during the editorship of Glyn Daniel between 1958 and 1986, as this was his main field of research (see Evans *et al.* 1981: 72–190). More than 100 relevant papers are spread across the 75 volumes published up until 2002, and selecting the most significant or representative to include here has not been easy. Our approach has therefore been to focus on four aspects: the studies of megalithic tombs in the inter-war period; the post-war investigation of key sites and the recognition that the European examples were older than their supposed progenitors; regional studies of local sequences and characteristic traits; and the broader integration of megaliths into the landscape past and present. Along the way it has been necessary to omit a number of related debates that have spilled into the pages of ANTIQUITY over the years, including the question of bank barrows (Crawford 1938) and long mounds (Barclay *et al.* 1995); relationships between long barrows and the long houses of the *Linearbandkeramik* (Ashbee in Morgan & Ashbee 1958: 111; and see Bradley 2001); and the megaliths of the central Mediterranean and Mediterranean islands (Trump 1961; Whitehouse 1971).

A useful starting-point for any appreciation of megalithic studies in the inter-war period is Glyn Daniel's paper 'The megalithic tombs of northern Europe', reprinted here (Daniel 1938). Daniel provides a rounded account of the various classification systems developed in the late 19th and early 20th centuries, and discusses their merits and their role in trying to establish the origin and development of these structures across northern Europe, and especially in Scandinavia. His polygenetic theory of origins usefully sums up the difficulties of linking everything together, and in his penultimate paragraph we find him prophetically musing over the possibility that the sequence accepted at the time might in fact need to be turned on its head (Daniel 1938: 310). The paper needs, however, to be seen in the context of several others of the period, notably Stuart Piggott's 'The long barrow in Brittany' (1937) and Daniel's 'The "dolmens" of southern Britain' (1937), both reproduced here. The latter, based on Daniel's doctoral research which he did not publish in full until much later (Daniel 1950), begins to identify regional groupings of chamber tombs within England and Wales, paving the way for a great deal of work in the post-war period and beyond. Piggott, by contrast, starts with the prospect of cross-channel influences between Armorica and central southern England, emphasizing in particular the similarities in long barrow form and the early date of these structures in northern France on the basis of one barrow, the Manio Cairn, being stratigraphically sealed by the Kermario Avenues at Carnac (Piggott 1937: 444). Britain, France, and Scandinavia were not the only centres of interest at the time. Miles Burkitt suggested links between Iberia and Anglesey (1938), while 'The tholos tomb in Iberia' was the title of a review paper by Stuart Piggott, published in 1953 (this volume) (Piggott 1953). It covers the important work of documenting the megalithic monuments of Spain by the German husband and wife team Georg and Vera Leisner, published as a series of volumes in Germany mainly in the 1940s. Sadly, Piggott's plea (1953: 143) for megalithic surveys of the type pioneered by the Leisners for all European countries has met with only limited success (see Masters 1974; Daniel 1976), but that in itself has not slowed the output of site-based, regional and national studies.

The excavation of numerous chamber tombs on a previously unprecedented scale was one of the great achievements of megalithic studies between 1945 and 1970. It was happening all over Europe, and many projects were reported in ANTIQUITY either as full interim reports or notes. In northern France, the site at Barnenez, Brittany, was discovered as a result of stone-quarrying by a road-constructor. It proved to be a multiple passage grave with 11 separate chambers within a multi-phase rectangular stepped mound. An initial report was published by Pierre-Roland Giot that we reproduce here (Giot 1958). The early date of the site was suspected, but it was not until much later that its true antiquity was established (see Giot *et al.* 1994 with earlier references). Meanwhile, in southern Britain, ANTIQUITY reported excavations at two long barrows in Hampshire that started in 1957: the Nutbane long barrow and the Fussell's Lodge long barrow (Morgan & Ashbee 1958; see Morgan 1959 and Ashbee 1966 for final reports). Both of these sites benefited from radiocarbon dating of charcoal samples, both determinations being rather older than expected (Vatcher 1959; Ashbee 1964). Nearby, at West Kennet, Wiltshire, excavations in 1955–6 revealed previously untouched chambers and a complex sequence of deposits that spanned most of the Neolithic (Piggott 1958; see Piggott 1962 for full report). Other excavations of the period reported in ANTIQUITY included: a group of three apparently chamberless barrows around Avebury, Wiltshire (Ashbee & Smith 1960; 1966; Smith & Evans 1968); East Heslerton, Yorkshire (Vatcher 1965); Ringham Low, Derbyshire (Alcock & Alcock 1952); Wayland's Smithy, Oxfordshire (Atkinson 1965); and Dyffryn Ardudwy, Merioneth (Powell 1963). The two last-mentioned sites were shown both to be multi-phase structures which on the same spot revealed the development of monument form and structure in a way that was expanded upon elsewhere by John Corcoran (1972).

Increasing evidence for the early date of chamber tombs in northwest Europe naturally enough began to call into question the notion that they were derived from Mediterranean prototypes. A key plank in the argument favouring independent origins of the European megaliths was severing the links between the central Mediterranean (especially Greece, Malta and Sardinia) and the chamber tombs of the western Mediterranean (especially Spain and Portugal). This was very successfully done in a seminal paper by Colin Renfrew entitled 'Colonialism and megalithismus' published in 1967 and reproduced here (Renfrew 1967). This contribution to multilinear evolutionary thinking tried to move away from the 'tendency to lump all megaliths together as obviously related' (Renfrew 1967: 284). It was a process finally resolved a few years later, and usefully summarized in Renfrew's book *Before civilization* (Renfrew 1973: 120–46).

In the meantime, synthetic studies began to adopt more open, questioning, lines of inquiry, and approaches to the study of individual megalithic monuments also changed. A symposium entitled 'Megalithic studies in the west of Britain' was published by a group of scholars connected in various ways with Liverpool University (Powell *et al.* 1969) which provided Glyn Daniel with the opportunity not only to review the publication but also to look back at studies of megalithic tombs over the previous three decades or so (Daniel 1970). Amongst the themes picked out for comment is the straitjacket imposed by the use of conventional terminology (and see Daniel 1969: 170), the relationships between megalithic tombs and other contemporary structures, and the lack of clarity over the sub-division of the class as a whole and the origins of individual components of it. Overall, the piece reflects the spin that many scholars of megalithic monuments found themselves in as the implications of radiocarbon dating began to hit home, confusion that was already apparent in an earlier contribution from Glyn Daniel entitled 'Northmen and Southmen' (Daniel 1967).

Excavations from the late 1960s produced a wealth of new evidence to contribute to the on-going debate. In Denmark, excavations at Tustrup revealed the presence of mortuary houses amongst a group of three megalithic tombs, work reported by Poul Kjærum in a paper entitled 'Mortuary houses and funeral rites in Denmark' (this volume) (Kjærum 1967). Mortuary houses within or under earthen long barrows in southern Britain were also discussed extensively in ANTIQUITY in the light of different ways of interpreting structural elements within the Fussell's Lodge long barrow, Wayland's Smithy phase 1 oval barrow, and other earthen long barrows (Simpson 1968; Ashbee 1969). The suggestion that the timber structures under long barrows composed of earth and rubble were essentially alternative interpretations of the stone-built chambers within long cairns took a long time to find widespread acceptance. With the excavation of a well-preserved and perhaps partly burnt long barrow at Haddenham, Cambridgeshire (Hodder & Shand 1988), the penny finally dropped that long barrows across the British Isles represented a single class of structure manifest archaeologically through a series of regional traditions. Moreover, as more megalithic structures were examined through excavation, a series of revised taxonomic groups began to emerge in the way hoped for by Daniel (1970: 266).

In France, explorations in Picardy revealed a well preserved *allée couverte* of the later Neolithic Seine–Oise–Marne culture, excavated and reported by Claude Masset in a paper that is reproduced here (Masset 1972). This site extended the distribution of known examples of the *allée couverte* tradition which focuses on the Paris Basin, and suggested an early date for these structures around the beginning of the 2nd millennium BC. Other tombs excavated during the period 1967 through to 1990 include: in France, the sumptuously decorated passage grave at Gavrinis (Le Roux 1985) with its broken capstone bearing decorations that show it was once part of a large menhir, another part of which forms the capstone of La Table des Marchands 4 km away; in Ireland the developed passage grave at Knowth (Eogan 1969; 1983); in Scotland long barrows at Dalladies (Piggott 1973) and Lockhill (Masters 1973), and the developed passage grave at Quanterness (Renfrew *et al.* 1976; Molleson 1981); in Wales the long barrows at Penywyrlod (Savory 1973), Gwernvale (Britnell 1979; 1980), and Trefignath (Smith 1981); and in England the long barrows at Hazleton North (Saville *et al.* 1987) and Haddenham (Hodder & Shand 1988).

Relationships between tombs in different regions of northwest Europe continued to be a subject of great interest and the excavation at Les Fouillages on Guernsey, between 1979 and 1981, provided significant new information, reported by Ian Kinnes in a paper reproduced here (Kinnes 1982). The site is a multi-phase structure covered by a roughly triangular mound. Radiocarbon dates place its construction in the 5th millennium BC, and ultimate *Linearbandkeramik* pottery came from the mound.

With the results of the earlier of these excavations, and others, to hand, it became possible to develop detailed local sequences of preferred monument design and structure. Typically these emerged through a process of debate and study by groups of scholars, as with the long barrows of southwestern Scotland and northern parts of Ireland discussed by Corcoran (1960) and DeValera (1960), a debate usefully summarized for ANTIQUITY in a paper by J.G. Scott entitled 'Clyde, Carlingford and Connaught cairns' which we reproduce here (Scott 1962). Subsequent studies published by Scott (1973), Corcoran (1973) and Collins (1973) were all originally presented to the Third Atlantic Colloquium held in Moesgård, Denmark, in 1969 and take the debate further still. Lionel Masters's extended review of the two-volume study *The chambered tombs of Scotland* by Audrey Henshall (Henshall 1963; 1972) provides a useful critical summary of a series of schemes and classifications for the full range of Scottish monuments (Masters 1974). Strangely, discussion of one of the most widely recognized regional groupings, the Cotswold–Severn long barrows (see Daniel 1970: 262 for debate on terminology), never spilled over into the pages of ANTIQUITY, despite a series of detailed studies (e.g. Grimes 1960: 75–101; Daniel 1964; Corcoran 1969; Darvill 1982). One of the most detailed local sequences is, however, that by Christine Boujot & Serge Cassen published as 'A pattern of evolution for the Neolithic funerary structures of west France' that we reproduce here (Boujot & Cassen 1993). In it the astonishing range of monuments around the bay of Quiberon and the gulf of Morbihan provide the basis for a coherent and dynamic evolutionary sequence of funerary structures between 5000 and 3000 BC.

Dating is of course critical to megalithic studies within the regional context both to establish local sequences at individual sites and to confirm the contemporaneity or otherwise of key monuments. ANTIQUITY has proved to be one of the main outlets for the publication of radiocarbon dates for megalithic tombs so that they reach a wide interested audience quickly. Amongst the monuments covered by such notes, mention may be made of just a few. In England, dates from West Kennet, Wiltshire, determined by AMS confirmed the period of use as being centred on the mid 3rd millennium BC (Gowlett *et al.* 1986); others include: Lambourne long barrow (Wymer 1970) and Hazleton long barrow (Saville *et al.* 1987). For Scotland, Quanterness, Orkney (Molleson 1981). For Wales, Gwernvale (Britnell 1980). For Ireland, Michael O'Kelly summarized dates in the mid 3rd millennium BC for the construction of Newgrange, Ireland (O'Kelly 1969; 1972). For Jersey, Mark Patton detailed how the construction of the developed passage grave at La Hougue Bie dated to a century or so before 4000 BC while its blocking and final use happened around 2600 BC (Patton 1995). For northern France Chris Scarre and colleagues presented the most recent radiocarbon determinations from the passage graves at Bougon, near Poitiers (Scarre *et al.* 1993), while Pierre-Roland Giot and colleagues reported further determinations in the early 5th millennium BC for Barnenez and other simple passage graves in Finistère in western Brittany (Giot *et al.* 1994).

What the dating of monuments and the development of local and regional traditions show is that many kinds of monument display distinctive traits that are geographically, culturally, or temporally restricted in their distribution. Megalithic art is one such characteristic that has attracted considerable attention. In 1960 Terence Powell published a paper entitled 'Megalithic and other art: centre and west' which we have included in this selection (Powell 1960). In it he examines the rather neglected rock art of monuments in central Germany and examines its affinities with rock art elsewhere in prehistoric Europe. Subsequently, attention has tended to focus on the motifs included only on one kind of structure at a time, but useful progress has been made. Excavations at Knowth and Newgrange in the Boyne Valley of eastern Ireland increased the corpus of recorded passage-grave art by several orders of magnitude (see for example Eogan 1969; 1977; 1983; O'Kelly 1964; 1968) with the result that a series of new detailed studies became possible. One study by George Eogan entitled 'Knowth before Knowth' is reproduced here (Eogan 1998) because it shows how the detailed analysis of motif styles, and the methods by which they were executed, allows insights into the sequence and history of the monument that might otherwise be lost.

The decoration of stones within megalithic tombs highlights the links between these structures and the landscapes in which they sit because comparable rock-art panels occurs in many locations on natural boulders and rock surfaces too. The relationship between stone outcrops and the orthostats and blocks used in the construction of chamber tombs is one that has also been explored through scientific means and through the consideration of meaning and significance. That stone was brought considerable distances to be used in the construction of tombs has long been noted at West Kennet, Wiltshire (Piggott 1958: 237; 1962: 14) and Stony Littleton, Somerset (Donovan 1977), amongst other places. But one of the most vivid examples is reported by Mark Patton in a paper entitled 'Megalithic transport and territorial markers: evidence from the Channel Islands' which we reproduce here (Patton 1992). On Jersey, for example, it seems that at the largest passage-grave, La Hougue Bie, nine sources of stone from all parts of the eastern end of the island were used, while for smaller monuments fewer, more local sources were drawn upon.

Interpreting the selection of specific rock types for tomb building and the meaning of the motifs used to decorate the surfaces of stones inside and outside the monuments is far from easy. Conventional explanations focus on cultural relationships and the use of symbols to express identity, but in 1995 Jeremy Dronfield extended the traditional range of interpretations by considering the impact of altered states of consciousness and the role of entopic images in the development of motifs such as the zig-zag and spiral (Dronfield 1995).

Landscape aspects to the placement and distribution of chamber tombs has been the subject of a number of recent contributions to ANTIQUITY. Gabriel Cooney, for example, has examined the passage-grave cemeteries in Ireland and concluded that the development of each follows a series of formalized and repetitive spatial arrangements in which the largest mounds dominate the associated structures (Cooney 1990). Meanwhile, Felipe Criado Boado and Ramon Valcarce examined the megaliths in Galicia, northwestern Spain, not only in terms of sequence and form, but also in terms of social relations such as the treatment of individuals and community, and the preference for upland situations linked to good agricultural land (Boado & Valcarce 1989).

Megalithic tombs were not only conspicuous in the landscapes occupied by their builders and users, but many have remained so into modern times. Chris Evans (1994) takes this survival further with his consideration of way that megalithic constructions and natural features blur together in the popular imagination. He notes the role of the Tolmen in Cornwall in securing national legislation for the protection of monuments in England during the late 19th century.

Megaliths have also been popular with the visiting public over the years and this has often meant restoration and conservation works, a matter that has been covered in ANTIQUITY for Hetty Pegler's Tump, Gloucestershire (Clifford 1966), Kits Coty, Kent, (Saunders 1981), and Newgrange, Co. Meath, Ireland (O'Kelly1979; 1981) amongst others.

Even restoration is not especially new, and we end this section with a paper by Glyn Daniel entitled 'Some megalithic follies' (Daniel 1959). In this delightful tailpiece he draws together cases where megalithic structures have been created in modern times for adornment or amusement.

The megalithic tombs of northern Europe[1]
by G.E. DANIEL
ANTIQUITY 12 (47), 1938

DURING THE 19TH century conclusions of great value concerning the origin and diffusion of the megalithic tombs of Europe were arrived at by the study of a few tombs in various regions: Montelius' (1905) *Orienten och Europa* marks the culmination of research on these lines. In the last 25 years it has been gradually realized that before we can speak with assurance of the many problems which the megalithic tombs involve, before we can disperse what has aptly been called 'the murky fog surrounding the megalith question' (Hawkes & Hawkes 1934: 321), we must have accurate and detailed regional surveys of the prehistoric burial-chambers of southwestern, western and northern Europe. As is well known, such surveys have already been produced in many regions; for example those in Iberia by Obermaler, Vergileio Correia and Pericot y Garcia, and in Brittany by le Rouzic and Forde. In the British Isles we have been exceptionally fortunate in this respect: the work of Crawford and Hencken in England, of Hemp and Grimes in Wales, of Childe in Scotland, and of Estyn Evans in northern Ireland, has made the megalithic tombs of the British Isles better known than those of any comparable region in Europe.

In all these careful surveys, and in the many scientific excavations that have recently been conducted, we are obtaining the basis for a re-survey of all the problems associated with these prehistoric burial-chambers: but before such a survey can be carried out, it is imperative that not only parts but the whole of western and northern Europe should be covered with a network of surveys comparable with those we have mentioned. Until recently two large areas remained in which the 'murky fog' gathered thickest — the south of France, and Scandinavia and north Germany. The latter region comprises the megalithic tombs of Denmark, Sweden south of a line from Oslo to Stockholm, north Germany, and north Holland, which, since the early works of Montelius, Madsen, and Sophus Muller, have not been studied on a general basis with the care they deserve. Recently, however, van Giffen (1925) has provided us with a magnificent account of the Dutch megalithic material, while Schwantes (1934–39: 153*ff*) has described afresh the material from Schleswig-Holstein; and in the two books we are considering here, we are given a first-rate survey of the north European material by two archaeologists whose knowledge of the Scandinavian and north German tombs is unrivalled. These works not only provide a much-needed and readable account of northern megalithic culture for all interested in prehistoric burial-chambers, but they also deal carefully and clearly with the many complex problems involved in a manner which all specialists will value and admire. There can be no doubt that when future archaeologists come to assess the progress of megalithic research, they will give the highest commendation to these works of Nordman and Sprockhoff which do so very much to dispel the

---

1   A review of two recent books on the megalithic tombs of Scandinavia and Germany: Nordman (1935) and Sprockhoff (1938).

thick fog of ignorance which, as we have said, despite the publication of many isolated plans, until recently enveloped these northern tombs. (It still envelops, alas, the megalithic tombs of the south of France.)

Professor Nordman's work on northern megaliths is already well known to us through a number of excellent articles from his pen (for instance 1917; 1918); recently he was invited by the Society of Antiquaries of Scotland to give the Rhind Lectures for 1932 on the Megalithic Culture of Northern Europe and its connexions with that of the south and west, and his present work is, as he says in his preface, 'an unaltered reprint of the Rhind Lectures'. He has, however, added many bibliographical footnotes (which are in themselves of very great value), and a number of figures. In the first two of his six lectures, Nordman discusses the form, grave-goods and burial rites of the megalithic tombs of northern Europe: he confines his attention mainly to the Danish and Swedish material. In his third lecture he discusses the spread of the megalithic culture in northern Europe and its relations with other cultures in that area. His fourth and fifth lectures describe the origins of the Scandinavian megaliths and their relations with the megaliths of other parts of Europe while his last, and most valuable lecture, deals admirably with the chronology of the Scandinavian tombs.

Dr Sprockhoff, who gave us a few years ago (1930) a splendid summary of the megalithic tombs of northwest Germany, in this book extends his survey to cover all the megaliths of north Germany. His title is somewhat misleading for he does not discuss, save incidentally, the burial-chambers of Denmark and Sweden. Sprockhoff's work is divided into seven sections, the first six of which deal respectively with morphology and burial-rites, weapons, tools and implements, pottery, settlement sites, general cultural conditions, and the chronology of the tombs; while his final section is a short historical summary. The first three sections naturally constitute the main part of the book, and are illustrated with a splendid series of plans and photographs: in addition to this, there are six excellent maps showing the distribution of dolmens, of all megalithic tombs, of thin butted axe-heads, of early flint daggers, of the passage-grave groups, and of the globular amphorae culture (the *Kugelflaschkultur*) in Germany. There is no general index to the book, but there is an alphabetical list of all the sites and finds mentioned in the text. Sprockhoff's plans are especially valuable and we have no longer to turn up the crowded diagrams of Krause and Schoetensack for illustrations of the north German galleries.

Sprockhoff's book is not only of the greatest importance in the study of megalithic tombs and of northern prehistory in general: its publication is an important event in the archaeological world, for it is one of the first two volumes to be published in a new series of archaeological monographs edited by Dr Sprockhoff himself under the title of *Handbuch der Urgeschichte Deutschlands.* Sprockhoff's study of the German megaliths is the third volume in this series, Dr Buttler's (1938) on the Danubian and Western Neolithic cultures (no. 2 in the series) is the other published volume, and the whole series is to cover in 20 volumes the archaeology of Germany from the Palaeolithic period to the Vikings. The promised volumes include Schwantes on the Palaeolithic and Mesolithic, Sprockhoff on the German Bronze Age, Kraft on the Urnfields and von Merhart on the Hallstatt culture. The series is admirable in conception, and if all the volumes are as well written, as scholarly, and as well produced as the two already published, they will form a most remarkable contribution to the advancement of archaeological research. Is it too much to hope, in passing, that the example of this magnificent German series will cause a similar series to be conceived dealing with the archaeology of Great Britain? Surely we are not lacking in the initiative and financial support which is needed to carry through such a series to success?

One is perhaps inclined to estimate the importance of the various regions of western and northern Europe that possess megalithic tombs in terms of the literature on these tombs, and of the quantity of plans that have been published. We, in the British Isles, are inclined to regard our own megalithic tombs as of very great importance, but there can hardly be many more than 1500 prehistoric burial chambers existing in the British Isles in recognizable form at the present day. It comes, then, as a most salutary shock to realize the tremendous number of megalithic tombs in Scandinavia and north Germany. Shetelig (Shetelig & Falk 1937: 63) refers to 3600 megalithic tombs surviving in the Danish Isles: Almgren's maps (1934: figures 22 & 23) show over 400 dolmens and passage-graves in south Sweden: and now Sprockhoff (1938: see his maps I and IV) reveals the very great number of megalithic tombs in north Germany. This statistical evidence alone shows how important are the Scandinavian tombs, and how welcome must be these new analyses of the northern megalithic material. Sprockhoff has much of great interest to say of the destruction of megalithic tombs; and he publishes two highly instructive maps of the island of Rugen showing the distribution of megalithic tombs in that island in 1829 and again in 1929. In 1829 (1938: figure 62) there were no less than 229 megaliths on the island, yet a hundred years later (1938: figure 63) there were only 38. Of course some of the 229 are probably included on very doubtful literary references, but, even so, these maps provide a valuable commentary both on the destruction of megalithic tombs in general, and, if the destruction on Rugen is to be taken as fairly typical of the whole northern region, on the original numbers and importance of the megalith-builders in the north.

It would be easy and idle to criticize both the books of Sprockhoff and Nordman with which we are here concerned for not being what they never set out to be, namely, what may be called 'catalogue-surveys' of the megalithic tombs of northern Europe. Yet regional survey, before it can be satisfactorily accomplished, must be accompanied by lists of sites, and with a maximum number of maps and plans. In England we have been especially fortunate in this respect, and possess two excellent catalogue surveys of our megalithic monuments, the one done by the Megalithic Survey of the Ordnance Survey, and the other by the Research Committee on Rude Stone Monuments of the British Association for the Advancement of Science. Both these surveys are well on the way to completion, and an excellent series of maps and lists has been published by the Ordnance Survey embodying the results of its Megalithic Survey. In the north of Ireland a similar inventory of megalithic monuments is being prepared under Estyn Evans, and Miss Collum is preparing, with le Rouzic, an inventory of the burial chambers of the Morbihan. Then, of course, we have in van Giffen's great work, already mentioned, a catalogue survey of the Dutch megaliths which is beyond all cavil, save, perhaps, on the grounds of its size. In northern Europe no such catalogue-surveys exist (except on a very small scale such as that of Krause & Schoetensack in the Altmark (1893), and of Enqvist (1922) on Orust and Tjörn): and we have, for instance, to go back to the magnificent volumes of Madsen for our best plans of the Danish tombs. Sooner or later archaeologists in northern Europe must set about producing detailed lists and maps of their megalithic monuments, and must contemplate the publication of corpora of tomb plans. These are tremendous labours — we have already commented on the number of the Scandinavian megaliths; but they are as necessary as they are tremendous. No one is more fitted to undertake their direction than the two archaeologists whose analytical accounts of the northern megalithic tombs we are here discussing.

Both Nordman and Sprockhoff base their morphological analyses of the Scandinavian and north German megalithic tombs on the classifications of Montelius: Sprockhoff on the simple *dos-gånggrift-hällkist* classifications which Montelius first produced in 1874 at the Stockholm Congress, Nordman on the more elaborate division into nine types which Montelius detailed in his *Orienten och Europa* (1905). Both, however, introduce interesting modifications of these classifications. Thus Nordman prefers to classify as passage-cists sites such as Mönsted in Jutland, which Montelius described as passage-graves with the passage in line with the long axis of the chamber. Sprockhoff singles out for especial treatment what he calls *die westeuropäischen Steinkisten*: some of these (e.g. Züschen, Fritzlar) have a portholed septal slab. Sprockhoff is of course dealing only with the German sites: we must group with them the similar portholed galleries in Vastergotland, and the two well-known sites at Weris in southeast Belgium. Montelius insisted that only the cists or short galleries were ever completely covered in by barrows or mounds and this generalization is still often repeated nowadays; but Nordman shows quite clearly that this is not true and that almost all forms of megalithic tomb in northern Europe are sometimes found covered with barrows: 'it seems probable', he writes (1935: 16), 'that the actual passage-grave as well as the grave-cist was, as a rule, covered by the barrow'.

Even so, these modifications are not enough to make the Montelian classification a really workable typology. The Montelian scheme distinguishes very properly between the normal passage-grave with a round or polygonal chamber found all over Atlantic Europe, and the T-shaped passage-grave which, despite alleged parallels in many parts of western Europe, is generally agreed to be a Scandinavian development of the normal passage-grave ; but the classification does not recognize, nor does Nordman make this point, that there are a number of undifferentiated or V-shaped passage-graves in Scandinavia, that is to say, passage-graves such as Forslov, Ringsted, Söro, Sjaelland (Madsen 1896: no. 45), and Herslev, Langeland (Montelius 1905: 172, figure 169) in which there is little formal distinction between passage and chamber; and that some forms of these undifferentiated passage-graves (for instance Skåningegård, Horns, Frederiksborg, Sjaelland (Madsen 1896: no. 3)) correspond to the 'entrance graves' described by Hencken in the Isles of Scilly. While the evolution of the T-shaped passage grave is an exclusively Scandinavian development, the development of the undifferentiated passage-grave, and, finally, of the entrance-grave, is one which also occurs in Spain, Brittany[2] and the Channel Isles. There is no reason to suppose that these developments are connected with each other; we may regard the evolution of the V-shaped passage grave in Scandinavia as parallel to similar developments in southern and western Europe. Forms such as Skår, Stenkyrka on Tjörn (Montelius 1905: 147, figure 146), and Hjadstrup on Fyen (Montelius 1905: 172, figure 168), are probably intermediate between normal passage-graves such as Sjöbol on Bohuslan and Broholm on Fyen and the undifferentiated passage-graves.

It seems likely too that the Montelius dolmen class should be subdivided in greater detail than does Nordman. It is not enough to distinguish between dolmens in round and long mounds: distinction must also be made between rectangular and polygonal (or round) chambers. The polygonal dolmens[3] usually occur in round mounds and but rarely in north Germany, while the rectangular dolmens are most often found in long mounds

---

2   The Scilly tombs are probably derived from the Breton developments.
3   I use the word dolmen throughout here in the Montelian sense of a small single chamber, and when I say rectangular or polygonal dolmen I refer to the shape of the chamber and not to that of the surrounding barrow. The terms *runddysser* and *langdysser* I translate here as 'dolmens in round barrows' and 'dolmens in long barrows' and not 'round dolmens' and 'long dolmens' as do many archaeologists (e.g. Shetelig & Falk recently in their *Scandinavian Archaeology*, 1937).

and are very common in north Germany.[4] I am never clear on what formal grounds some of the rectangular dolmens are distinguished from the small cists: many of the rectangular dolmens are below the ground level[5] and are of roughly the same proportions as the cists.

Nordman emphasizes that the vast majority of the long barrows in Scandinavia and north Germany are not ovate or wedge-shaped, as are most of our British long barrows, but rectangular, i.e. they do not have one end wider than the other. Sprockhoff figures (1938: figures 42–44) some of the north German long barrows that are wedge-shaped: he shows that they are confined in the main to Rugen and Pomerania, and that the chambers are never placed at the broad end of the barrow, nor is there any formal element such as a forecourt. Indeed the German wedge-shaped long barrows must be regarded as variants of the normal rectangular long barrow of Scandinavia, and can have no connexion with the British wedge-shaped barrows. Some of the north German long barrows figured by Sprockhoff are excessively elongated: one at Visbecker Braut (1938: 39, no. 52) is about 12 times as long as it is broad, while the Putlos barrow (1938: 39, no. 53) is 375 feet long but its width is only 17 feet.

Nordman notes the presence of rectangular long barrows in south Brittany, and is inclined to connect the Scandinavian long barrows with these. We must distinguish at least four types of long barrow in Brittany:
1. the unchambered wedge-shaped long barrow such as Manio 1, 3, and 5 (this type of monument in Brittany has recently been described by Piggott 1937);
2. the wedge-shaped long barrow with a chamber at its broad end, such as Grah-niol in Rhuis;
3. the rectangular long barrow with closed chamber such as St Michel or, of a different kind, Kerlescan and Kerlearac; and
4. the rectangular long barrow with one or more chambers opening into one of its broad sides (e.g. Mané Lud, Mané Kerioned).

It is only with the two latter classes that the Scandinavian long barrows may be compared, and the great difference between the form of the closed chambers in the Breton and Scandinavian long barrows makes the fourth class the only valid parallel to the northern long barrows. Indeed such a monument as Mané Kerioned, which has two undifferentiated passage-graves opening into the broad side of a rectangular long barrow, compares very accurately with Herslev on Langeland. But I doubt whether there is any generic connexion between these two sites: W.C. Lukis suggested that the Breton long barrows of class 4 originated through adding chambers to already existing round barrows, and I think that a similar process may have given rise to the Scandinavian long barrows. Nordman himself, writing of the long barrows with several chambers, says they were 'obviously enlarged later in many cases' (1935: 18). Professor Childe (1933: 133–4) thinks that the evolution of the T-shaped passage-grave would naturally give rise to an elongated barrow, and this theory has a great deal to commend it; but highly exaggerated T-shaped passage-graves do occur in round barrows (e.g. the site near Sparresminde on Moen) (Madse 1896: no. 57). I think it is the building of more than one T-passage grave in a row that gave rise to the long barrow in Scandinavia, and that this long rectangular form, once standardized, was then built around other kinds of chambers.

---

4 Polygonal dolmens occur very rarely in long mounds. Rectangular dolmens occur more often in round barrows and are then confined mainly to Denmark.

5 Such as those recently figured by Schwantes (1934–39: figures 186–188). See also Sprockhoff (1938: figures 1–7).

In an earlier article, Professor Nordman (1922: 36) was inclined to agree with Montelius' first thesis, namely that dolmen, passage-grave, and long gallery formed an evolutionary series; but here he accepts Montelius' latest views (1905), expressed in *Orienten och Europa,* that the Scandinavian passage-graves represent a separate movement from western and southern Europe, and I think there can no longer be any doubt that this is so and that the northern dolmens did not develop in Scandinavia into passage-graves. There has, of course, been much argument as to which area of passage-grave culture in Atlantic Europe provided the origin of the Scandinavian graves: Childe has argued for north Scotland and Nordman here argues for Brittany, but it seems to me that the claims of southern Iberia are as strong as any. Sophus Muller first emphasized the connexions both in form and in decoration between the passage-grave pottery of Scandinavia and Iberia: the oculi and rayed sun ornament on some of the Scandinavian pots must surely imply Spanish connexions, and it should be remembered that amber (presumably Danish) was found at Los Millares and Alcala.

Since Fergusson in 1872 published his distribution map of megalithic monuments and indicated by a series of arrows the routes he imagined the megalith-builders had taken, it has been widely held that the movement from southwest Europe to Scandinavia which gave rise to the northern megaliths proceeded around the north of Scotland. Shetelig (Shetelig & Falk 1937: 58–9), however, seemed to favour the English Channel as the route taken by these early voyagers, and Nordman certainly does. He is sharply critical of the views of Fox and Rydheck, which suggest continuous land in the North Sea and no English Channel as late as the end of the 3rd millennium BC, when these megalithic migrations were taking place. There is no shadow of proof, he says, of the existence of continuous land in the North Sea during the period of megalithic culture, and I think that one must agree with him. Clark (1936: 239) has recently summarized very clearly the evidence for the date of the formation of the English Channel, and we can no longer argue that the Pentland Firth route was the one adopted by the megalith-builders because of the non-existence or dangers of the English Channel. The absence of strong Spanish affinities in the decoration of the pottery from the north Scottish tombs, and their presence in some Scandinavian megalithic pottery, would suggest that the movement from Spain (or by Brittany from Spain) to the north of Europe, did really take place through the Straits of Dover.

Nordman emphasizes in this book a point he made earlier (in 1917b), namely that the earliest Scandinavian passage-graves (i.e. those with round or polygonal chambers such as Sjöbol and Broholm) are found in east Jutland, the Danish islands in the sound, and the coasts of Bohuslan and Skåne. Sprockhoff however republishes a plan of the 'Denhoog' on Sylt (1938: 25, no. 27) and this tomb, together with Ulbersdorf in south Dithmarschen (planned by Schwantes 1934–39: 182, figure 196), suggests to me that there may have been another early centre of passage-grave culture in northern Europe, i.e. in western Schleswig-Holstein. Nordman and Sprockhoff agree in deriving all the Scandinavian passage-graves from these early types: the T-shaped passage-graves and the undifferentiated passage-graves are the most notable developments. In Sweden the T passage-graves become very large and angular — those in the Karleby–Luttra–Falköping area of Skaraborgslan are well-known. In Denmark side-chambers are developed and elaborated (Nordman republishes his plan of the remarkable monument at Alsbjerg), and double-passage graves developed. In north Holland and north Germany the passage to the T passage-grave becomes shorter and shorter, until in the end, as I believe, the long gallery was evolved by omitting the small passage. This line of development to the long gallery seems to me more likely than that suggested by Montelius, which is criticized by Nordman, although he does not suggest any alternative interpretation.

Sprockhoff shows very clearly that the portholed galleries of south Germany and Belgium represent a spread from the Paris basin, and it seems not unlikely that, as Kendrick argued in his *Axe Age* (1925), the Vastergotland portholed galleries derive from the same area via sites such as Weris and Züschen. Nordman, however, disagrees with this view, and would derive the idea of the porthole in the Vastergotland galleries from the Thuringian cists (such as Allstedt in Weimar) and ultimately from the Caucasus. Of course both theories are faced with the same difficulty: the complete absence of portholes in the megaliths in the area between south Germany and Vastergotland.

We in Britain are naturally most interested in the connexions between the British and north European megalithic cultures. It has frequently been argued that the Scandinavian dolmens derive from Great Britain, the ordinary passage-graves (such as Sjöbol and Broholm) from the north Scottish tombs, the T-shaped passage-graves from monuments such as Wayland's Smithy or Nympsfield in the Cotswold–Severn area, or from the curious Orkney monuments such as the Holm of Papa Westray, Unstan, Quoyness, and Quanterness, and that the Scandinavian portholed galleries must be connected with the portholed megalithic tombs of England. Nordman argues that all these relationships are very unlikely, and I agree with him that it is improbable that any of the elements of the northern megalithic cultures were derived from the British Isles. On the other hand it is likely that the Medway tombs represent a spread to Britain of a north European type: Sprockhoff's plans show that the Medway tombs are easily paralleled in north Germany.

There is one major criticism of the work of both Nordman and Sprockhoff to be made; it is that they do not discuss at length the problem of the origin of the Scandinavian dolmens. They accept the Montelian sequence of the priority of the dolmens over the passage-graves and of the passage-graves over the galleries, and they agree in the derivation of the Scandinavian passage-graves from western and southern Europe, but they pay scant attention to what is, in my mind, one of the major problems in modern megalithic theory, this problem of the antecedents of the northern dolmens. The problem is perhaps not so relevant to Sprockhoff's researches: he publishes a fine distribution map of dolmens in north Germany and derives the German dolmens from Denmark, and this is, no doubt, correct. But to Nordman's survey this matter is of the greatest and most vital importance and one could wish that he, with his intimate knowledge of the northern megalithic material, had devoted a whole lecture to its elucidation.

The dolmen complex in the north has four morphological elements: the round or polygonal chamber, the rectangular chamber, the round mound, and the straight-sided rectangular mound. Nordman fully recognizes that though some of these elements may be matched in western Europe (e.g. the chambers in Britain and the barrows in Brittany) we cannot point to one area outside Scandinavia and north Germany in which all these elements occur: so that, as he says (1935: 85), 'there is, therefore, a certain degree of probability in favour of the early dolmens in Denmark being a form that originated in that country'.

So far I am in complete agreement with Professor Nordman: indeed no impartial student of the comparative morphology of megalithic tombs in Europe can come to any other conclusion than that the northern dolmen did originate in the north. The problem is, in what way did it originate? Was it created, like a conjurer's trick, apparently out of nothing, or was it evolved from existing megalithic tombs in the north? Many early archaeologists favoured the conjuror's trick; Nordman suggests an ingenious but unconvincing compromise. 'I imagine' he says (1935: 85), 'that the actual idea of building large stone tombs penetrated to the North, and that there the problem was first solved in the way indicated by the early dolmens.'

To my mind it is very probable that the dolmen evolved in northern Europe out of various developments of the passage-grave. All the morphological elements of the dolmen complex in the north can be derived in northern Europe from passage-grave forms — I think there can be no dispute on this point. We have already said that it is confusing to speak of the 'northern dolmen': such a phrase conceals the variety of forms in this class. We have spoken of the four morphological elements in the dolmen complex: they are combined in northern Europe to give us four types of monuments;
1   the polygonal chamber in a round barrow;
2   the polygonal chamber in a long barrow;
3   the rectangular chamber in a long barrow, and
4   the rectangular chamber in a round barrow.

The rectangular dolmen in a round barrow was probably evolved by a shortening of the entrance graves we have already mentioned: sites such as Sonderskov (Madsen 1896: no. 43) and Vildsted, Flinterup (Madsen 1896: no. 47) (both in Söro, in Sjaelland) are probably intermediate between the entrance-graves and the short rectangular chambers or dolmens. The rectangular dolmen in a long barrow probably developed from a shortening of the closed long galleries so common in northern Europe. The round or polygonal chambers in round barrows probably developed out of ordinary passage-graves such as Sjöbol and Broholm, and the curious 'passage-dolmens' perhaps represent intermediate stages between passage-grave and polygonal dolmen. The polygonal chamber in a long mound is a very rare and unusual form and may be due to a late fusion of some of the morphological elements in the dolmen class: in any case, some of the normal passage-graves with round or polygonal chambers are occasionally found in slightly elongated long barrows. This polygenetic theory of the origin of the northern dolmens is set forth schematically in the accompanying diagram.

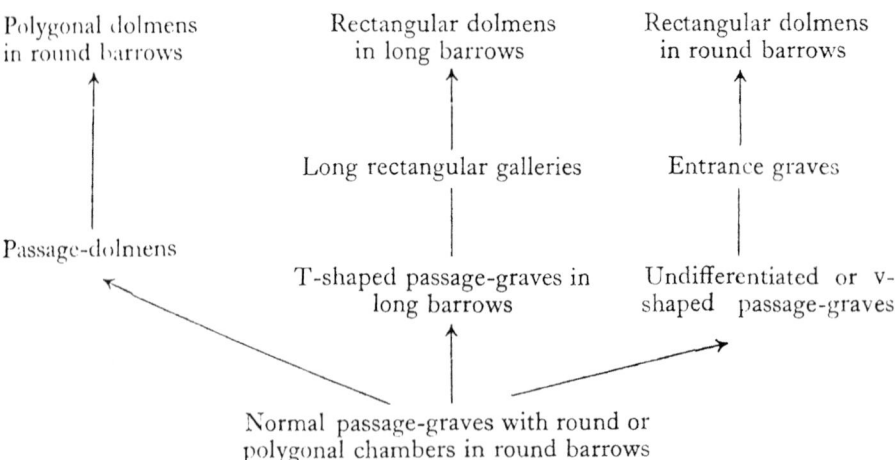

Such a theory of the origin of the northern dolmen as I have outlined clearly implies that all the dolmens must be later than at least a large number of the passage-graves, and this is, of course, in complete opposition to existing orthodox theory which upholds that doctrine of the priority of the dolmen in the north which Montelius (1874: 161–2) first expounded on inaccurate distributional evidence. Both Nordman and Sprockhoff maintain this priority, but, fortunately, I am in very good company in supporting this rankest of heresies, for Professor Forde (1930: 99), after discussing a number of Danish finds, wrote: 'Such finds throw doubt on the schematic view that the passage-graves are invariably later than the smaller tombs', and in his recently-published presidential address to the Prehistoric Society, Dr Mahr says (1937: 340), 'I think that both the scheme Montelius established for Scandinavia, and the one Bosch Gimpera still upholds for Iberia, are untenable'.

This is not the place to discuss the arguments for and against the priority of the dolmen in the north, nor is it, perhaps, fair to say that in Iberia, in Brittany, in Ireland, and in southern Britain, the priority of the dolmen has been argued to be a myth. As Estyn Evans and Miss Gaffikin say (1935: 5), 'the dolmen myth dies hard', and I suspect it will need a great deal of exposition and argument to show that even in northern Europe the dolmen priority is probably a myth. These are the horns of our present dilemma: if the sequence of grave-goods (which is alleged to develop with the dolmen–passage-grave–long gallery sequence) be correct, the dolmens must be the earliest forms of megalithic tomb in northern Europe; and we are then forced to the uncomfortable conclusion that the dolmen-complex originated out of nothing in Scandinavia — indeed we are back to the conjurer's bag of tricks. If, on the other hand, the dolmen did develop out of various passage-grave forms, as we have suggested, the grave-goods sequence cannot be correct. And in merely stating this problem I cannot refrain from wondering whether this grave-goods sequence is as correct and unshakable as usually alleged. I have never yet seen a satisfactory explanation of the occurrence of collared flasks, funnel-necked beakers and thin-butted celts (i.e. of allegedly early 'dolmenic' grave-goods), in the elongated T-shaped passage-graves of northern Germany and Holland, which must, on any theory, be late in the series.

I hesitate to develop here the fascinating problems involved in the origin of the Scandinavian dolmen. I want to do no more than indicate what neither Nordman nor Sprockhoff do, that there is a very vital problem involved in the Scandinavian dolmen, and that the accepted Montelian sequence of northern tombs is at present open to severe criticism. It is to be hoped that in the near future Professor Nordman and Dr Sprockhoff will increase our indebtedness to their researches — an indebtedness made very heavy by these present admirable surveys — by discussing in detail the manifold problems of the origin and date of the Scandinavian dolmens.

References
ALMGREN, O. 1934. *Sveriges Fasta Fornlämningar från Hednatiden*. 3rd edition. Uppsala.
BUTTLER, W. 1938. *Der donauländische und der westische Kulturkreis der jüngeren Steinzeit*. Berlin: W. de Gruyter.
CHILDE, V.G. 1933. Scottish megalithic tombs and their affinities, *Transactions of the Glasgow Archaeological Society* 8 (n.s. 7): 120–37.
CLARK, G. 1936. The timber monument at Arminghall, and its affinities, *Proceedings of the Prehistoric Society* n.s. 2 (1936): 1–51.
ENQVIST, A. 1922. *Stenåldersbebyggelsen på Orust och Tjorn*. Uppsala: Appelbergs Boktryckeri.
EVANS, E.E. & M. GAFFIKIN. 1935. Belfast Naturalists' Field Club Survey of antiquities, megaliths and raths, *Irish Naturalists Journal* 5(10): 242–52.
FORDE, C.D. 1930. Early cultures of Atlantic Europe, *American Anthropology* 32: 19–100.
HAWKES, C.F.C. & J. HAWKES. 1934. Prehistoric Britain in 1933, *Archaeological Journal* 90: 315–38.
KENDRICK, T.D. 1925. *The Axe Age*. London: Methuen.
KRAUSE, E. & O. SCHOETENSOCK. 1893. Die megalithischen Gräber (Steinkammergräber) Deutschlands, *Zeitschrift für Ethnologie* 25: 105–76.
MADSEN, A.P. 1896. *Gravhøje og Gravfund fra Stenalderen i Danmark*. Copenhagen: Gyldendal.
MAHR, A. 1937. New aspects and problems in Irish prehistory: Presidential address for 1937, *Proceedings of the Prehistoric Society* 3: 262–436.
MONTELIUS, O. 1874. In *Compte Rendu* of the 1874 (Stockholm) *Congrès d'anthropologie et d'archéologie préhistoriques*, 161–2.
    1905. Orienten och Europa, *Antiqvarisk Tidskrift för Sverige* (Stockholm) 13: 1–252.

NORDMAN, C.A. 1917. Jaettestuer i Danmark, *Nordiske Fortidsminde* II.
    1918. Studier öfver gånggriftkulturen i Danmark, *Aarbøger for nordisk Oldkyndighed*. Copenhagen.
    1922. Some Baltic problems, *Journal of the Royal Anthropological Institute* 1922: 26–43.
    1935. *The Megalithic Culture of Northern Europe*. Helsinki: Helsingfors. Suomen Muinaismuistoyhdistyksen Aikakauskirja (Finska Fornminnesföreningens Tidskrift) 39(3).
PIGGOTT, S. 1937. The long barrow in Brittany, *Antiquity* 11: 441–55.
SCHWANTES, G. 1934–1939. *Vorgeschichte Schleswig-Holsteins, Stein- und Bronzezeit*. Neumünster: Wachholtz.
SHETELIG, H & H. FALK. 1937. *Scandinavian archaeology*. Oxford: Clarendon Press.
SPROCKHOFF, E. 1930. Zur Megalithkultur Nordwestdeutshlands, *Nachrichten aus Niedersachsens Urgeschichte* (1930) 4: 1–55.
    1938. *Die Nordische Megalithkultur*. Berlin & Leipzig: W. de Gruyter.
VAN GIFFEN, A.E. 1925. *De Hunebedden in Nederland*. Utrecht: A. Oosthoek. (English translation, 1927–8).

The Long Barrow in Brittany
by STUART PIGGOTT
ANTIQUITY 11 (44), 1937

THE ENGLISH LONG barrows have for long been a fertile source of discussion, and since Thurnam's paper of 1868 there has been much speculation as to the precise Continental affinities of these tombs. It seemed clear from the outset that they were members of the complex family of megalithic tombs distributed from Iberia to Orkney, while Thurnam himself compared more detailed features such as the chamber at West Kennet with such Breton examples as Mané Lud. Subsequent writers, notably Forde (1930; 1934), have seen in the Breton many-chambered passage-graves of the type of Kerival the probable source of such long barrow chambers as Stoney Littleton, Parc Cwm or Wayland's Smithy; but it was difficult to provide convincing Continental parallels for the whole specialized English long barrow type. While certain elements (notably details of passage, antechamber and chamber) could be paralleled again and again in the megalithic series, the persistent and carefully constructed trapezoidal mound eluded search outside Britain. Furthermore, a study of the grave-goods, particularly in the light of a number of recent excavations of barrows in southern England, showed that the long barrows of Wessex, mainly non-megalithic and supposedly derived from the megalithic barrows in the Cotswolds or further west, were apparently contemporary with and an integral part of the earliest Neolithic culture of Britain (Neolithic A) and a similar cultural identity seemed probable in Sussex.

The problems thus presented were discussed by the writer in a recent paper (Piggott 1935), where it was claimed that since the long barrows of South Wiltshire and Dorset were on the evidence available the earliest members of the group, any search for origins must be directed to this region. In the face of the apparent absence of Continental prototypes the suggestion was put forward (leaving the writer, and doubtless most of his readers, unconvinced) of an indigenous origin of the type in southern England, although it was pointed out that, could convincing evidence be obtained from northern France, the distribution pattern certainly suggested a movement from Armorica to Dorset (Piggott 1935: 117).

It is clear that the requirements of any claimants for the position of proto-long-barrows are twofold: they must present the features of the angular (usually trapezoidal) mound, defined by a peristalith or dry walling in stone country and by palisades and revetments elsewhere, and they must belong to a culture chronologically early enough to allow of their appearance in southern England in Neolithic A times. In addition, the presence of earthen long barrows of types which, though containing multiple burials, structurally preclude successive interments in the strict megalithic tradition and are securely dated to the earliest phase, suggests that this successive burial practice may not be an original feature.

Field and museum work in southern Brittany early this summer left the writer with little doubt that there exists in this region a class of monument which has strong claims to be regarded as ancestral to the English long barrows: monuments which, although distinguished as a type by le Rouzic 15 years ago, and by him for long considered as the Breton equivalents of our long barrows, have not received the attention they deserve.

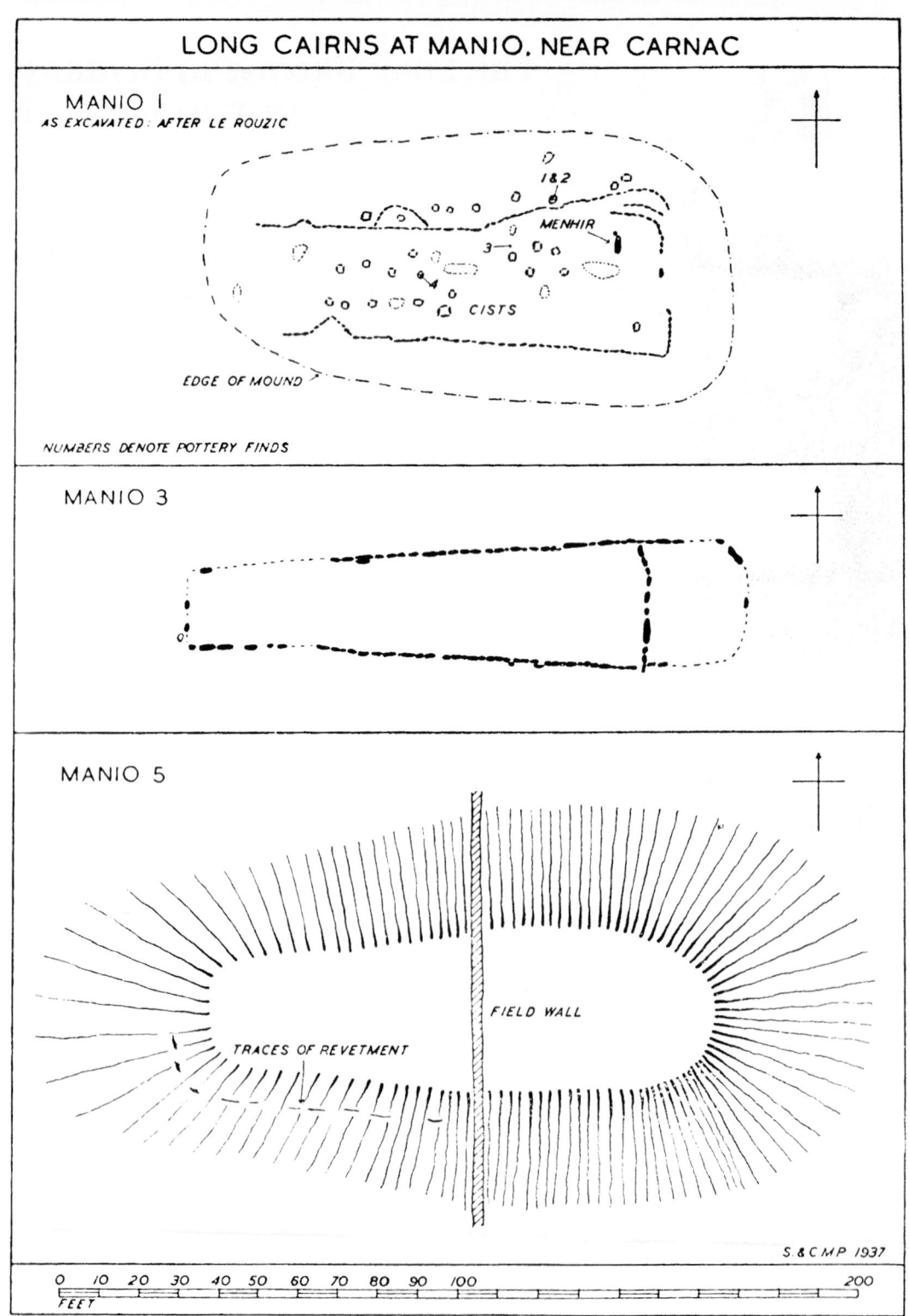

FIGURE 1.

FIGURE 2. *Manio 1 from the west showing menhir at eastern end. (Photo C.M. Piggott.)*

The tombs in question are best represented by a group of four on the plateau of Manio, to the northeast of Carnac, described by le Rouzic (1921; the excavation of Manio 1 is described in le Rouzic *et al.* 1922; a summary with plan is in le Rouzic 1933: 227–9, and photographs of the pots in le Rouzic 1934: 486). FIGURE 1 shows plans of the three best preserved, the numbering being that of his first paper. Of these, Manio 1 is the most important. Its features can best be appreciated from the plan: outwardly it appears today as a low oblong mound, nowhere more than 3 feet high, with a single standing stone, 12 feet high, in its eastern end (FIGURE 2). Le Rouzic's excavations revealed a sub-angular peristalith of small stones and a number of small cists or coffers, containing traces of burning, but apparently no actual bones, mostly within the peristalith, although eight and a possible ninth lay outside to the north, while one was enclosed by walling which formed a semicircle against the peristalith. Near the standing stone was a small dry-walled chamber with grave-goods to be described later, and the excavations further revealed the fact that the base of the standing stone was carved with serpent-like designs (*Corpus des Signes Gravées* (1927): plates 3–6). The most remarkable feature of the barrow however is the fact that it underlies the great Kermario alignments or avenues of standing stones, four lines of which pass directly across the barrow from west to east, the menhir described above standing at right angles to the stones of the alignments and overtopping them by several feet (FIGURE 3).

Manio 2 exists today solely as a badly preserved low long mound, some 250 feet long, with its axis (as in the other examples) east–west and a breadth of from 80 to 100 feet. Near its western end but outside the mound is a small standing stone.

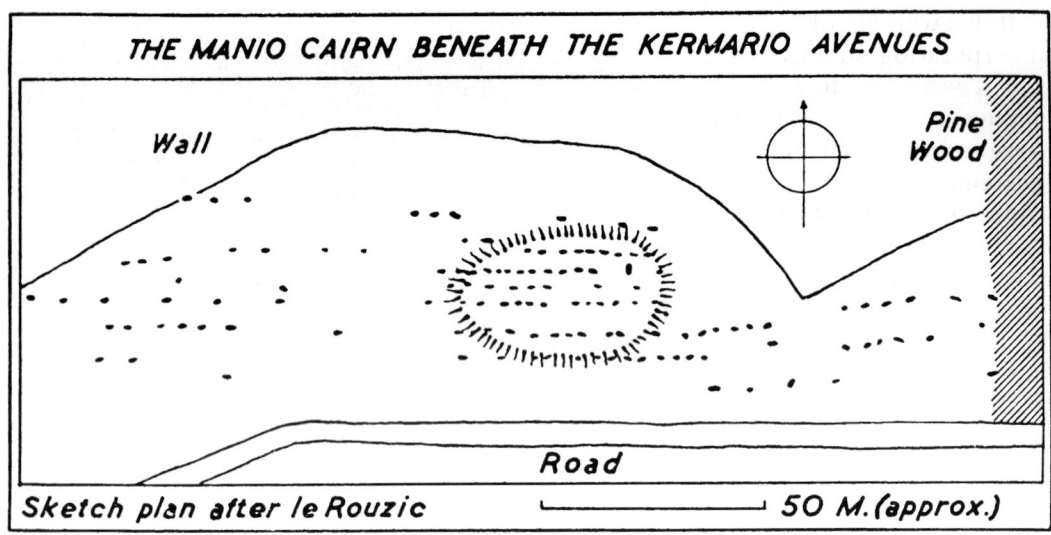

Figure 3.

Manio 3 consists only of a peristalith, of the trapezoidal form shown on the plan, from which every vestige of the mound has been removed. At the eastern end there are remains of a stone setting which may be the remains of some form of forecourt (Figures 4–5).

Manio 4 of le Rouzic's list is a low *round* cairn, unrelated to the series under discussion.

Manio 5 presents an outward appearance precisely similar to an untouched English long barrow, with slight traces of a peristalith showing through on the southwest. It was excavated by le Rouzic in 1916, and from his (unillustrated) report one gathers that a quadrilateral area, 49x13 m, was found enclosed by a peristalith and rough dry walling. Within this, a hearth was found in the southwest angle. Twelve metres from the west wall of the peristalith, and on the main axis, was found a roughly circular dry-walled structure some 4 m in diameter and 1·80 m in maximum height, the internal space measuring about 1·60 m in diameter and having a paved floor (Figure 6).

A similar group of three long cairns (Figure 7) was excavated by Miln near Crucuny in 1878 (Miln 1883, 36–49, with plans of the cairns but no illustrations of the finds. Two sherds however are illustrated in le Rouzic (1934: 495.) The first of these, known as Mané-Pochat-en-Uieu, was found on excavation to be a quadrangular mound enclosed

Figure 4. *Peristalith of long cairn at Manio (no. 3) looking northwest, with stones of forecourt setting on right. (Photo C.M. Piggott.)*

within a wall mainly of small stones, but incorporating standing stones of some size. The area enclosed by this wall is orientated nearly east and west, with the large end to the east. Within this area were the remains of two structures of piled-up stones covering black earth, while remains of burning with patches of charcoal were noticed at several points on the old surface within the wall.

Of the second cairn, Mané-clud-er-yer, little remained. The east wall, some 16 m long, was intact, while 32 m of the north, and 7 m of the south wall were traced. The plan, so far as can be judged from these fragmentary remains, would appear to have been similar (i.e. irregularly quadrangular) to the other two cairns. Mr Crawford has directed the writer's attention to a plan by W.C. Lukis, preserved among the Lukis MSS, of another

FIGURE 5. *Peristalith of Manio 3 looking along south wall eastward. (Photo C.M. Piggott.)*

long cairn of the type under discussion 'about 50 yards due N. of dolmen of Klud-er-yer'; 'explored by Abbé Collette, 1872'.

The third cairn was known by the name of Mané-Tyec, and as can be seen from the plan, was similar in general features to Mané-Pochat-en-Uieu, being surrounded by dry walling incorporating upright stones, but in addition having various earthfast stones standing within the enclosure. Remains of a circular structure were found towards the western end, and again traces of fire on the old surface. The eastern end of the structure was in a mutilated state.

Suspending discussion of the features presented by these cairns we come to a consideration of the grave-goods discovered in the recorded excavations. At the foot of the

FIGURE 6. *Long cairn at Manio (no. 5) from the south. (Photo C.M. Piggott.)*

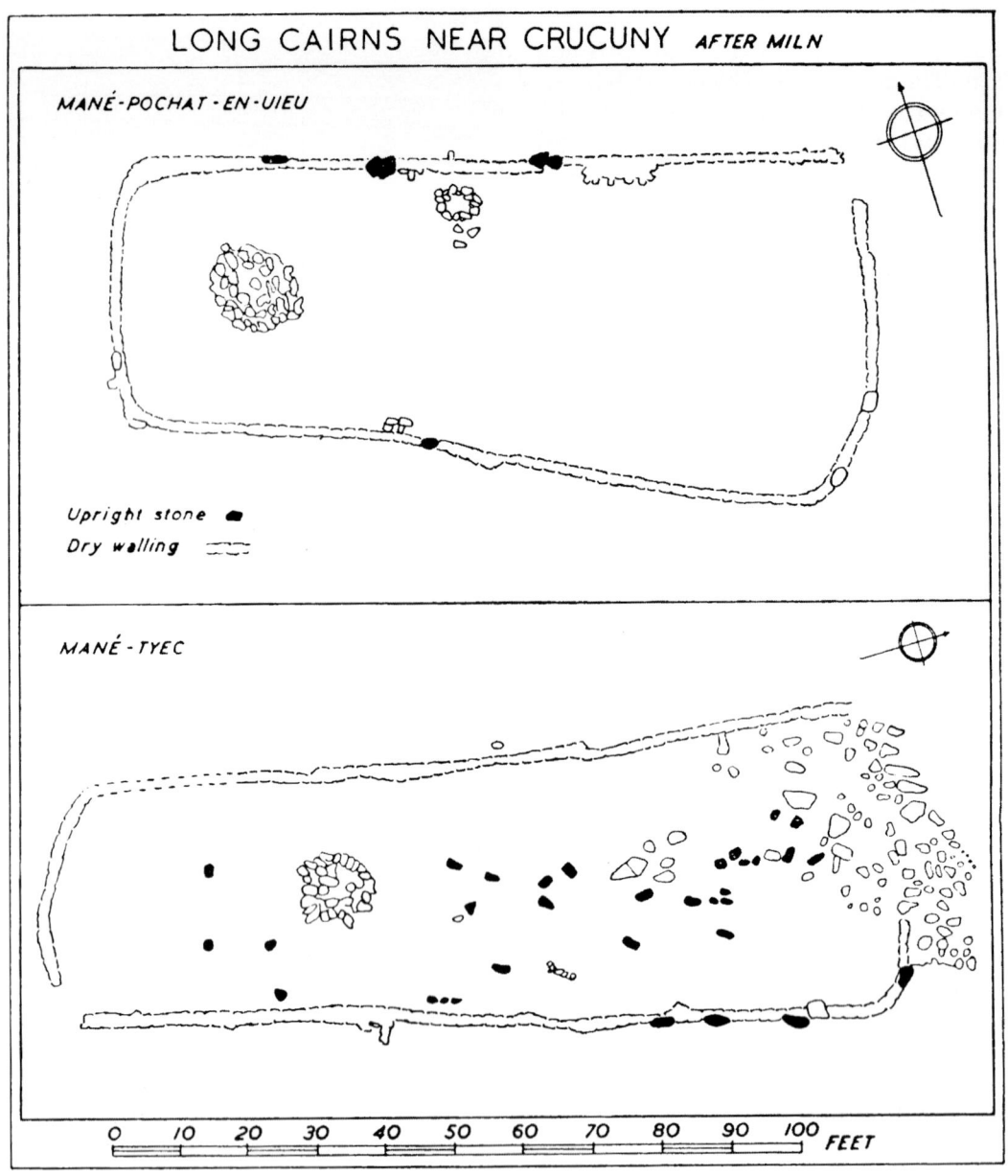

FIGURE 7.

menhir of Manio 1 was a votive deposit of four small axes of diorite and fibrolite, while a fifth was found near-by, together with a quartz pendant. Near the menhir was a cist with a large cover-stone, on the upper side of which was an engraving of a hafted axe (*Corpus*: plate 6). Fragments of pottery and flint flakes were found scattered throughout the cairn and in the 'cists', but in cist 52 of the original report, and as indicated on the plan in FIGURE 1, two pots were found (nos. 1 and 2, FIGURE 8), one within the mouth of the other, while in cist 17 was found vessel no. 3. Finally in cist 35 was found part of a flat-based pot, no. 4, illustrated in the original report.

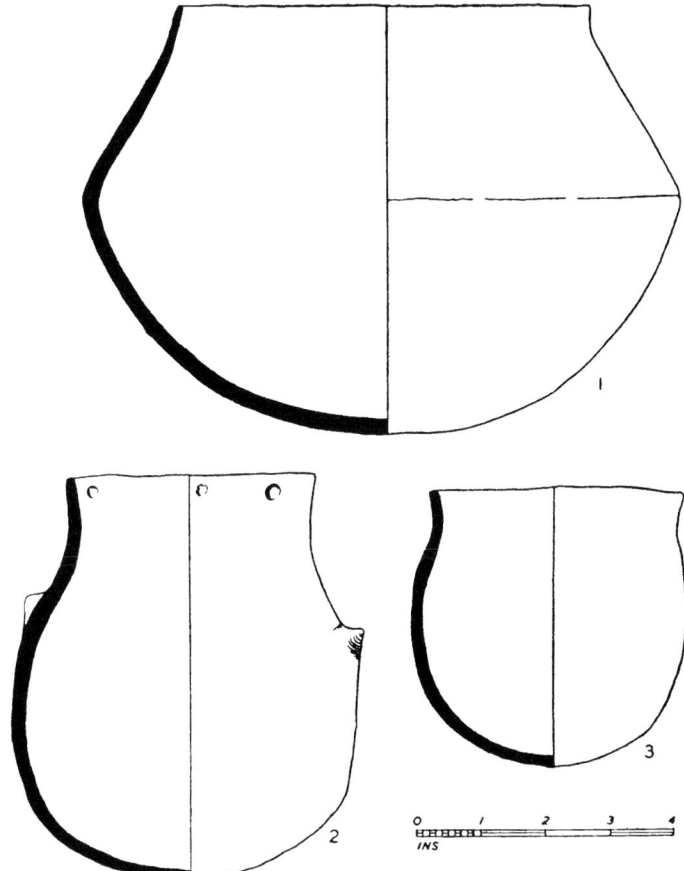

FIGURE 8. *Pottery from long cairn at Manio (no. 1). (Musée Miln, Carnac.)*

The scanty finds from Manio 5 seem to have included sherds with horizontally perforated lugs, one with a double row of small applied knobs just below the rim, and one with rough incised ornament, all from outside the revetment. A triangular arrowhead was found in the circular structure, and coarse sherds scattered elsewhere in the mound.

The somewhat indeterminate pottery from the Crucuny group was found mainly along and usually outside the walls, and included sherds of round-bottomed bowls, perforated lugs, and some sherds with ornament in incised and pointillé technique, illustrated in le Rouzic (1934: 495).

The material enumerated above — seven monuments and some exiguous grave-goods — seems little enough to work on, yet all the evidence points in the same direction. The structures are clearly not megalithic in the true sense, and it has been sometimes urged that the closed cists in the barrows represent a degeneration, and that they are at the end of a devolutionary series which begins with such tombs as Ile Longue. But it does not really seem necessary to assume that these cists were inspired by the great megalithic tomb series that comes to Brittany from Iberia. Making a box of small stones to contain the remains of the dead is an idea as obvious in a stony country as is digging a hole in regions of softer subsoil, and the practice may have developed independently of the complex ritual implied and the architectural technique demanded by intrusive cupola tombs. The cist implies a difference of ritual which is important: in such burials the grave cannot be

> ... broke up againe
> Some second ghest to entertaine

as can a passage-grave — this may be a degeneration, but (to continue the Donne quotation) may not such cists belong to a time in Brittany before

> ... graves had learnt that woman-head
> To be to more than one a Bed.

The position of Manio 1 under the alignments of Kermario is strong evidence for an early date for the type. The exact chronological position of the Carnac alignments is unfortunately uncertain, but on general principles 'we cannot', as Forde remarks, 'claim that the alignments are later than the megalithic culture as a whole'. It is hardly possible to dissociate the Kennet Avenue at Avebury from some ultimate connexion with the Carnac series, and here we have definite evidence for a date in the 'B' beaker phase — a period which chronologically cannot be far removed from the Breton bell-beakers, which may indeed, as Grimes hinted (1931: 348n), be the parents of our Wessex type of s-profile 'B' beaker (Abercromby's Type Bi). (The axes of jadeite and allied stones, Breton type, from various British sites may also be quoted. *Cf.* Crawford (1913: 643), and map in G. & R. MacAlpine Woods (1933–34: 354).) Were this in fact the case, we might see in Avebury evidence of Breton contacts, both in structure and ceramic, in the period of the Carnac alignments.

The pottery gives support to an early dating. In Miln's excavations in the Crucuny group sherds were found, as we have seen, along the walls of the cairns, some with ornament which might be compared with the style of the *vase-supports* (Chassey II), which would imply a date well within the main Breton megalithic period, but the circumstances of their discovery leave it possible to regard the sherds as secondary, though such an interpretation, uncorroborated by other evidence, would be dangerous. On the other hand the Manio material is susceptible of an earlier dating.

The vessels illustrated in FIGURE 8 stand apart from the general series of megalithic wares in Brittany by reason of their simple bag-like forms, their dark leathery smoothed surface, and their lack of ornament. They stand in fact nearest of the Breton pottery to the 'undifferentiated ancestral continuum' of the *Westischekeramik* postulated by Childe and equated by Mrs Hawkes with Vouga's *Néolithique Ancien* and the undecorated wares at the Camp de Chassey, and with our English Neolithic Ai. Indeed Vouga has himself expressed the belief that the Manio vessels are the equivalents of his earliest period in the Swiss lakes (le Rouzic 1934: 489).

It is hardly necessary to cite parallels to the Breton pots from Neuchâtel: even the flat-based vessel (le Rouzic *et al.* 1922: plate VII, 4) can be compared with an example from Port-Conty (Vouga 1928: 405, figure 6C), and the sherd from Manio 5 with applied knobs finds parallels in Vouga I at Port-Conty and Cortaillod (Vouga 1934: plate XIV, 6; 1928: 406. The close similarity of these illustrations however suggests that they may represent the same sherd!), although the type persists and flourishes in later periods.[1]

---

1   Middle Neolithic at Auvernier (Vouga 1928: 397); Chassey II at Nécropole de Canteperdrix (Curwen 1930: 33) and at Fort Harrouard (*Cinq Années:* 127, 129); with incised ware at Croh-colle (le Rouzic 1934: 496). The examples from Chassey itself (Déchelette 1908–1910 1: 555, nos. 35 and 20) are presumably late, and the same may be said of the vessel from Er Mar, Riantec (Du Chatellier 1897: plate 7, no. 9).

The triangular arrowhead from the same cairn is again a type of Vouga II, but two examples are known from the lower level.

It thus seems impossible to escape from the conclusion that we have here the Breton representatives of this early Neolithic culture: the simple types of which the carinated burnished bowls of the megaliths are the stylized descendants, the native ceramic persisting side-by-side with intrusive wares from the south and west. We may thus have to modify Mrs Hawkes' chronological table (1934: 41), and interpolate a Neolithic culture in Brittany before the carinated bowl–Chassey II complex — a culture which must stand in some fairly close relation to our Neolithic Ai, since both would be but slightly divergent specializations from the original stock. Mrs Hawkes, in discussing the spread of the Vouga I culture, brings it to Britain by an unspecified route across France which however in her view 'certainly did not touch upon Brittany' (1934: 40). If we are to attempt to connect our southern English long barrows (apparently of Neolithic Ai culture) with the long cairns of the Morbihan, some Breton connexion in pottery is obviously to be sought for, and while the writer agrees with Mrs Hawkes in her contention that the main stream of Neolithic culture reached England by some route eastwards of Armorica, yet there is evidence that it is to Brittany that we must look for certain features in our southwestern Neolithic culture.

Miss Liddell's five seasons' excavations at Hembury Fort in Devonshire, the last reports of which have just been published (Liddell 1930–35), have brought to light an extremely important Neolithic culture which at an early stage was seen to possess certain individual ceramic traits that distinguished it from the normal Neolithic Ai culture to which however it obviously belonged. First of these was a total absence of any ornament, even the simple pin-prick and scored decoration which occurs at the lowest levels of Windmill Hill being absent, but second and more important was the occurrence of a type of lug or tubular perforated handle with expanded ends, which the writer distinguished as a 'trumpet-lug' in 1932 (Childe 1932: 76). A single poor example of this type of handle was found at Windmill Hill, but at Hembury it was present as a recurrent feature, the finest example being on a bowl of fine burnished red ware, the grit in the paste of which was identified as of Dartmoor origin, some 20 miles west.[2] Although nothing comparable was found among the Neolithic pottery from the Legis Tor huts on Dartmoor, similar sites still further west, on the slopes of Carn Brea in Cornwall, yielded Neolithic pottery of Hembury type including a trumpet-lug (Peter 1896: 92).[3] No other sites in the extreme west are known, but turning eastwards we find at Maiden Castle in Dorset a Neolithic culture which so far as can be judged in advance of publication seems closely to resemble that of Hembury, and certainly includes trumpet-lugs. Axes of Cornish stones on this site emphasize its western connexions (Childe 1936: 266).

These sites, together with one or two others exhibiting less striking peculiarities but apparently culturally identical,[4] constitute a distinct sub-group within our Neolithic A culture, the type-fossil being the trumpet-lug. This is a form of handle which does not appear in the simplest Vouga I pottery: it is clearly a developed form. It occurs however with plain Neolithic ware at the Grotte de Saze, Gard (St Germain Museum; noted by the

---

2   Liddell 1931: 93; 1932: 175. The steatite bead, broken but apparently originally of a type characteristic of Vouga I at Neuchâtel, may be cited as another exotic feature at Hembury (Liddell 1932: plate XVI & p. 182. *Cf.* Vouga 1934: plate XVII, 17 & p. 48).

3   The sherds are at Truro, and the writer is grateful to Mr Lindsay Scott for directing his attention to their importance in this connexion.

4   E.g. Haldon, Devon (to be published shortly; *cf. Hembury Fort Exhibition* 1935: 33); Holdenhurst Long Barrow, Hants (Piggott 1937: 1–14), and probably Corfe Mullen, Dorset (Calkin & Piggott 1938).

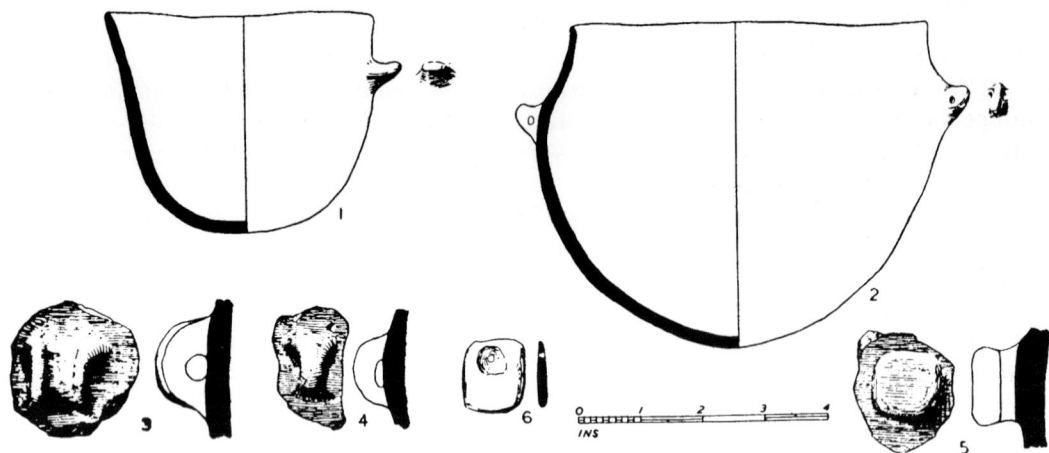

FIGURE 9. *Pottery (1–5) and stone pendant from cist at Castellic. (Musée Miln, Carnac.)*

writer in 1935) and at the Camp de Chassey (St Germain Museum; *cf.* Liddell 1935: plate XXXV), where the numerous examples are probably to be associated with the undecorated wares of the early phase distinguished by Mrs Hawkes. Its absence at Fort Harrouard again suggests that it is an early feature in the Chassey culture, and probably of central and southern French origin.

In the museum at Carnac is a group of pottery from a rectangular stone cist under a round cairn at Castellic (le Rouzic 1933: 228), north of Carnac (FIGURE 9). So far as the structure of the cairn is concerned, no connexion with the long cairn series described above can be claimed, and the place given it by le Rouzic in his typological scheme can only be regarded as illusory. The pottery, however, with its simple lugged pots, strongly suggests affinities with that from Manio rather than with any of the main megalithic series, and includes an excellent example of the trumpet lug. On the strength of this group we must, it seems, admit that the trumpet lug may form a feature of the earlier Neolithic pottery of Brittany, and a further connexion between this region and southern England becomes apparent.

We are, however, confronted by several difficulties. The Castellic tomb is anomalous, and typologically of uncertain date, unless one defines its chronological position by admitting the early character of the pottery, which seems almost an inevitable conclusion. It should be remembered too that, as noted by Schuchhardt (1926: 68–70), at least one low round barrow is overlaid by the Kerlescant alignments, and there are hints in England that Neolithic A round barrows may not be unknown, and not necessarily to be explained as the result of 'influence' from Early Bronze Age sources.

Again, on the present evidence, the distribution of 'Hembury Ware' and long barrows in southern England, although overlapping, is not wholly concordant, the more westerly pottery sites being in regions where long barrows are practically speaking absent (although low mounds of the type of Manio I may still be awaiting discovery in Devon by careful field-workers). The problem is therefore by no means solved, but the evidence does permit of a working hypothesis which appears to fit in with our present state of knowledge of the ceramic and megalithic sequence of northwest Europe.

If we admit the validity of placing the Manio and Castellic pottery as equivalent to Vouga I, we begin our Breton ceramic series earlier than Mrs Hawkes would allow in

1934. In the present writer's opinion such a basic culture may well have been established in Brittany at approximately the same time as the inception of the Neolithic A culture in England, and he would see in the Hembury ware evidence of cultural contact. The incised wares of Brittany, as Mrs Hawkes demonstrated, are related on the one hand to the south French ware *à cannelure,* and on the other to the west Scottish–north Irish group of decorated vessels. In south France this ware is Chalcolithic, but in one instance at least in Brittany, pre-beaker. While it survives in the Morbihan side-by-side with beakers, one should note in this connexion that not only is it pre-beaker in three sites in Scotland (Rudh' an Dunain, Skye, Anon. 1932: 398–9; Clettraval, North Uist, Scott 1935: 500–516; Unival, North Uist (unpublished, information from Mr Lindsay Scott)) and one in North Wales (Lligwy, Anglesey, Piggott 1933: 68–72), but in one tomb in North Uist is earlier than a cup ornamented in the Chassey II style (at Unival, see above); a type of ware which is itself pre-beaker at the Grotte de Bize, although in Brittany hardly anterior to and in south England represented by pottery which follows immediately upon the beaker phase. It seems probable that this unornamented Neolithic ware stands in Brittany as ancestral to the smooth burnished bowls which form ancillary grave-vessels to the beakers: indeed at Kervilor a bowl with incised pendant loop ornament in the style of Beacharra was associated with an unornamented bowl of fine polished grey ware with a diminutive and vestigial trumpet-lug.

The writer has elsewhere suggested that the typical English 'chambered long barrow' (e.g. Uley, Notgrove, West Kennet) may be a hybrid product resulting from the insertion of a passage-grave (or as Daniel has urged, more correctly a gallery-grave) into one end of a long burial mound. The Breton tombs described above bear structural affinities to the English long barrows without megalithic chambers; it is possible that the barrows usually placed at the end of the Cotswold typological series, with closed cists in the body of the mound (e.g. Eyford, Crawford 1925: 94–7) may have to be regarded as primitive rather than degenerate. (The grave-goods from Eyford could in fact be used to support an early dating, a Neolithic A bowl being found in cist F, and a beaker being demonstrably secondary in D. The jet bead from E is difficult to date, as its closest parallel, from Notgrove, was not in significant association, but the presence of a jet bead at Hembury (Liddell 1932: plate XVI, p. 181) should be borne in mind in this connexion). The circular structures in Manio 5 and at Crucuny may recall the somewhat analogous construction at Notgrove, while the menhir at the eastern end of Manio I can be paralleled at Gatcombe (Tinglestone) and possibly at Lyneham in the Cotswolds (Crawford 1925: 134, 163), and would appear to have had wooden representatives at Thickthorn (Dorset) (Drew & Piggott 1936), Durrington (Hoare 1812: 170)[5] and Wexcombe[6] (Wilts), and Badshot (Surrey) (Keiller & Piggott 1937; *cf.* also Clark 1936: 247; 1937: 173).

In Brittany it is perhaps possible to regard the insignificant cairns of the type of Manio as ancestral to the monstrous long cairns of Mané Lud, St Michel or Moustoir, which could be claimed as the survival of the long cairn tradition side-by-side with the

---

5 'On reaching the floor of the long barrow we found a circular cist like a little well, but it contained no interment; from this well-like cist, a tunnel, like a chimney, ascended nearly to the top' [of the barrow]. This clearly represents a circular post-hole, with the decayed post leaving a hollow in the packed rubble of the mound.

6 Excavated by Mr O.G.S. Crawford and Dr E.A. Hooton in 1914. The unpublished section of the barrow, which Mr Crawford has kindly shown me, presents a feature strongly suggesting a large upright post at one end of the mound.

30 MEGALITHS FROM ANTIQUITY

FIGURE 10.

great passage-graves, and influenced by the prevalent megalomaniac passion for huge size. The Manio type of long cairn may have a wider distribution than published examples suggest: among the Lukis MSS Mr Crawford has found a plan of an analogous cairn on La Grée de Cojou, St Just, Ile-et-Vilaine, surveyed by Sir Henry Dryden and W.C. Lukis in July 1867. In one instance, a fusion analogous to that postulated for England would seem to have taken place, for at Grah-niol le Rouzic's recent clearance of the site has revealed a gallery grave with one lateral chamber at one end of a long mound, the gallery only occupying one half of the total length. Since, as Forde and more recently Daniel have urged, the transeptal plan of the Notgrove type appears to have an origin in such chambers in Brittany as Keriaval (FIGURE 10), the suspected fusion may have taken place there, and these barrows in England may in fact represent a movement independent of, and probably a little later than, that producing the Dorset and south Wilts group, although the English evidence seems to run counter to any suggested line of approach (e.g. the Bristol Channel) which would make the long barrows of South Wales ancestral to the Cotswolds group.

References
Cinq Années.
Corpus des Signes Gravées. 1927.
ANON. 1932. Chambered cairns near Kilfinan, Argyll, Proceedings of the Society of Antiquaries of Scotland 66: 398–400.
CALKIN, J.M. & S. PIGGOTT. 1938. Neolithic 'A' habitation site, Corfe Mullen, Proceedings of the Dorset Natural History and Archaeological Society 60: 73–4.
CHILDE, V.G. 1932. The continental affinities of British Neolithic pottery, Archaeological Journal 88: 37–158.
CLARK, J.G.D. 1936. Archaeological distributions, Proceedings of the Prehistoric Society 2: 247–8
    1937. Earthen long barrows, Proceedings of the Prehistoric Society 3: 173–5.
CRAWFORD, O.G.S. 1913. Prehistoric trade between England and France, L'Anthropologie 24: 641–9.
    1925. Long Barrows of the Cotswolds. Gloucester: J. Bellows.
CURWEN, E.C. 1930. Neolithic camps, Antiquity 4: 22–54.
DÉCHELETTE, J. 1908–1910. Manuel d'Archéologie préhistorique, celtique et galloromaine. I. Archéologie préhistorique. Paris.
DREW, C.D. & S. PIGGOTT. 1936. The excavation of Long Barrow 163a on Thickthorn Down, Dorset, Proceedings of the Prehistoric Society 2: 77–96.
DU CHATELLIER, P. 1897. La Poterie aux époques préhistorique et gauloise en Armorique. Rennes: J. Plihon & L. Hervé.
FORDE, C.D. 1930. Early cultures of Atlantic Europe, American Anthropologist 1930, n.s. 32: 19–100.
    1934. The typology of the Breton megalithic tomb, in Proceedings of the First International Congress of Prehistoric & Protohistoric Sciences, London, 1932: 114–17.
GRIMES, W.F. 1931. The early Bronze Age flint dagger in England and Wales, Proceedings of the Prehistoric Society of East Anglia 6 (1928–31): 340–55.
HAWKES, J. 1934. Aspects of the Neolithic and Chalcolithic periods in western Europe, Antiquity 8: 24–42.
KEILLER, A. & S. PIGGOTT. 1937. Badshot long barrow, Surrey Archaeological Society Collections.
HOARE, R.C. 1812. The ancient history of Wiltshire I. London: William Miller.
LE ROUZIC, Z. 1921. Tumulus d'enceinte quadrilatère du Manio, commune de Carnac, Bulletin de la Société Polymathique du Morbihan 1921: 85–92.
    1933. Morphologie et chronologie des sépultures préhistoriques du Morbihan, L'Anthropologie 43: 225–65.
    1934. Les mobiliers des sépultures préhistoriques du Morbihan, L'Anthropologie 44: 485–524.
LE ROUZIC, Z., S. PÉQUART & M. PÉQUART. 1922. Carnac, fouilles faites dans la région: campagne 1921. Nancy: Berger-Levrault.
LIDDELL, D. 1930. Report on the excavations at Hembury Hillfort 1930, Devon Archaeological Excavation Society 1930: 39–63.
    1931. Report on the excavations at Hembury Hillfort second season, Devon Archaeological Excavation Society 1931: 90–120.
    1932. Report on the excavations at Hembury Hillfort third season, Devon Archaeological Excavation Society 1932: 162–90.
    1935. Report on the excavations at Hembury Hillfort fourth and fifth seasons 1934 & 1935, Devon Archaeological Excavation Society 1935: 135–75.
MACALPINE WOODS, G. & R. 1933–34. Excavations in a dry valley in Beer, SE Devon, Proceedings of the Prehistoric Society of East Anglia (1932–34): 354–65.
MILN, J. 1883. In Bulletin de la société polymathique du Morbihan 1883: 36–49.
PETER, T.C. 1896. The exploration of Carn Brea, Journal of the Royal Institute of Cornwall 12: 92–102.

PIGGOTT, S. 1933. The pottery from the Lligwy burial chamber, Anglesey, *Archaeologia Cambrensis* 88: 68–72.
    1935. A note on the relative chronology of the English long barrows, *Proceedings of the Prehistoric Society* 1: 115–26.
    1937. the excavation of a long barrow in Holdenhurst Parish near Christchurch, Hants., *Proceedings of the Prehistoric Society* 3: 1–14.
ROYAL ALBERT MEMORIAL MUSEUM. *Royal Hembury Fort Exhibition.* 1935. Exeter: Wheaton.
SCOTT, W.L. 1935. The chambered tomb of Clettraval, North Uist, *Proceedings of the Society of Antiquaries of Scotland* 69: 500–516.
SCHUCHHARDT, C. 1926. *Alteuropa: eine Vorgeschichte unseres Erdteils.* Berlin: de Gruyter.
THURNAM, J. 1868. On ancient British barrows, especially those of Wiltshire and the adjoining counties. Part 1, Long Barrows, *Archaeologia* 42: 161–244.
WHEELER, R.E.M. 1936. The excavation of Maiden Castle Dorset, recent interim report, *Antiquaries Journal* 16: 266–83.
VOUGA, P. 1928. The oldest Swiss lake-dwellings, *Antiquity* 2: 387–417.
    1934. *Le néolithique lacustre ancien.* Neuchâtel: Secrétariat de l'Université. Recueil de travaux, Université de Neuchâtel, Faculté des lettres fasc. 17.

The 'dolmens' of southern Britain
by GLYN DANIEL
ANTIQUITY 11 (42), 1937

'OBSERVATION NOT GUIDED by ideas, even hypothetical ideas', says Professor Wolf, 'is blind; just as ideas not tested by observation are empty' (Wolf 1928: 23). The student of megalithic monuments has as constantly to regret that early antiquaries were not more aware of the necessity of making accurate plans and of recording morphological and constructional details of the monuments — many alas, now ruined or vanished — which they visited, as he has to deplore their delight in formulating theories which they never tested by field-survey; but he has also to cope with evils more dangerous even than these, namely observation so dominated by false or imprudent hypotheses that it results in a distorted vision worse by far than mere blind observation or empty ideas.[1] Some of these hypotheses — like the Druids, the Ancient Egyptians, the metal-working Prospectors, the megalithic race, solstitial and clock-star alignments, to mention only a few — have been disproved by research and flourish today only among perverse and illogical archaeologists. Others — such as the concept of the Montelius dolmen here examined in its relation to southern Britain[2] — while just as inadequate and inaccurate, are the commonplaces of modern text-books.

The etymology of the word 'dolmen' is disputed. The word is apparently not known in that form before 1807 and seems to be a variant of a Low Breton word *dolmin* or *dolmine* (see Murray, *NED.*, *s.v.* Dolmen; Reinach 1893: 36–7; Déchelette 1908: 374–5). Corret observed that this word was used by the peasants of the Morbihan to describe certain megalithic burial-chambers near Locmariaquer, and he adopted it to designate all such monuments wherever found (Corret 1796: 24). Baron Bonstetten's classic definition (1865: 3)[3] is a development of Corret's suggestion; and throughout the 19th century the term is widely used in this sense, as, for instance by Bertrand, Barnwell, W.C. Lukis, Borlase, and Gowland. A later French usage distinguished two kinds of burial-chambers: (a) the dolmen, and (b) the *allée couverte*.[4] At first the term *allée couverte* was indiscriminately applied to passage-graves, to the approaching passage of passage-graves, and to gallery-graves; but gradually it came to mean only gallery-graves, and the terms '*dolmen à galerie*' and '*galerie d'accès*' were used for passage-graves and their approaching passages respectively.[5] Thus it is to denote all burial-chambers except gallery-graves

---

1   E.g. the theory that some burial-chambers are built on low artificial hills has led some archaeologists — even Montelius himself — to record *beneath* chambers such low mounds which have no objective existence. See Crawford (1925: 148–9).
2   'Southern Britain' here means Wales, and England south of Mersey and Humber.
3   In his *Essai sur les Dolmens*. This is a rare book and the definition is worth quoting: '*Le nom de dolmen s'applique à tout monument en pierre, couvert ou non couvert de terre, d'une dimension suffisante pour contenir plusieurs tombes, et formé d'un nombre variable de blocs bruts (les tables) soutenus horizontalement au-dessus du niveau du sol par plus de deux supports*'.
4   The word is first used by de Caumont (1863: 582). See also de Fondouce (1873).
5   The term passage-grave is used throughout this article to connote tombs such as Cunha Baixa, Kercado, New Grange, Falköping, etc.; the term gallery-grave tombs such as La Halliade, Kerlescant, Browndod, Carn Ban (Arran), etc. It is perhaps worth emphasizing here that these terms are technical and not descriptive; obviously in common parlance there is little difference between passages and galleries.

that Reinach, Déchelette, and le Rouzic use the word 'dolmen'. A further restriction in meaning was implicit in Montelius' classification, for he gave specific distinction to the *dolmen à galerie*, and used the term 'dolmen' to denote simple single-chambered megalithic tombs. Thus it will be seen that what may for convenience be called the Bonstetten dolmen, the Reinach dolmen, and the Montelius dolmen, differ fundamentally.[6] During the last 50 or 60 years the concept of the Montelius dolmen has dominated almost all morphological analysis of megaliths in the British Isles, in Germany, and in Scandinavia.

Oscar Montelius classified the megalithic graves of Scandinavia first into four classes, and later into eight ; but essentially his scheme distinguished three main types: (1) the dolmen, (2) the passage-grave, (3) the gallery-grave of various forms.[7] The Montelius dolmen is a rectangular, polygonal or almost circular tomb, walled with orthostats and roofed with one capstone. In plan it is entirely closed or has one side open, and in some of this latter type two low stones form a small passage outside the entrance. It stands either quite free or in the centre of a low rectangular or round mound, which never reaches up to the level of the capstone. Montelius' classification is not merely morphological: it implies a typological sequence and a relative chronology, for he held that the passage-grave evolved out of the dolmen and in turn gave rise to gallery-graves and cists. The following quotation sums up his argument: '*Les dolmens proprement-dits — c'est à dire les dolmens sans galerie — sont, à mon avis, les tombeaux les plus anciens que nous connaissons actuellement en Suède. La sepulture à galerie est une forme plus moderne, qui s'est développé du dolmen dans le Nord de l'Europe*' (Montelius 1905: 162). The implications of the Montelian theory of the dolmen are fivefold:

1 that it is a specific class of burial-chamber,
2 that it is not found incorporated in a barrow,
3 that it is earlier than other forms of megalithic graves,
4 that the passage-graves evolved out of it, and
5 that this evolution took place in Northern Europe.

The last two points need no discussion here. The northern origin of the passage-grave has been frequently disproved, and Montelius himself in his later work postulated two invasions of northwestern Europe, the one associated with dolmens, the other with passage-graves, and he derived the passage-graves of the Western Mediterranean from the *tholoi* of the Eastern Mediterranean, particularly those of the Mesará in Crete. But he still maintained the first three of the implications listed above, which may be called the three key-points in the theory of the Montelian dolmen.

The influence of this classification has been tremendous; but it has unfortunately led prehistorians to classify megalithic monuments not on the basis of their objective morphology, but insofar as they fit in with the Montelian classification. The Iberian peninsula affords the clearest example of this process. The early classifications of Iberian burial-chambers (as, for instance, those by Leeds, Obermaier, and Bosch-Gimpera) are almost entirely applications of the Scandinavian sequence to that area ; it is only in the last 10 years that Forde, Fleure, and Peake have described and classified the Spanish and Portuguese material as it exists. The burial-chambers of the British Isles have been similarly forced into the divisions of the Montelius system. Mainly through the work of

---

6   Dolmens have been defined in ways other than these three primary ones here discussed. A common usage is to describe all free-standing chambers as dolmens. See, for example, Windle (1904: 174–5).
7   A good summary of his earlier classification will be found in Montelius (1876: 152). His later classification is developed in Montelius (1905: 183).

Anderson and Thurnam the chambered cairns of Scotland and the long barrows of southern England have long been well known, but it has been customary to dismiss the remainder of the British material under the vague and convenient heading of 'dolmens'. According to the old text-books,[8] Ireland was particularly rich in dolmens, they were plentiful in Cornwall and Wales, some were to be found in Gloucestershire and Wiltshire, and a passing reference was always made to Kits Coty as a typical dolmen in eastern England. Nor is this picture out of date, for it is repeated in most modern books and papers.[9] One cannot do better than quote the following from an official handbook published in 1932, 'Chambers conforming to the usual definition of a dolmen are found in the West of England (especially Cornwall and Wiltshire), Wales, and Ireland'.[10] As Estyn Evans and Miss Gaffikin (1935: 5) have wisely remarked, 'The dolmen myth dies hard'.

FIGURE 1 shows the distribution of burial-chambers in southern Britain.[11] The work of Thurnam and Crawford enables us to distinguish a group of chambered long barrows which may be conveniently described as the Severn–Cotswold group. The distribution of this group is mapped in FIGURE 2, and includes south Glamorgan, Brecknockshire, Gloucestershire, north Wiltshire, west Oxfordshire and Berkshire, and Somerset. Many of the chambers in this group are small rectangular or polygonal structures (e.g. Randwick, Tinkinswood, Manton Down, Gatcombe Lodge) and, stripped of their long barrows, would be ideal Montelius dolmens. Within the region covered by the Severn–Cotswold group there do occur such chambers which are today free-standing. These free-standing chambers are distinguished on FIGURE 2; good examples of them are Gwernvale near Crickhowell, Pentyrch in the Vale of Glamorgan, the Devil's Den in Clatford Bottom, the Hoar Stone, Enstone, and the Whispering Knights — both in Oxfordshire. It will readily be seen how very few examples there are,[12] and that their distribution is coincident with that of the chambered long barrows, i.e., they do not occur in parts of Gloucestershire or Wiltshire or Glamorgan in which there are no chambered barrows. Despite this however, they have frequently been claimed to belong to a different and earlier class of megalithic tomb than the typical Severn–Cotswold chambered long barrow — in fact, that they are typical Montelius dolmens. Crawford however has argued that these 'dolmens' marked on FIGURE 2 are no more than the denuded remains of chambered long barrows.[13] The present writer is in complete agreement with this thesis; it is quite unjustifiable to speak of 'dolmens' as separate morphological entities in the area covered by the Severn–Cotswold group.

---

8   See Fergusson, Peet, Rice Holmes, etc. Montelius gives a characteristic account (1905: 25).
9   As, for example, Childe (1925: 287): 'Dolmens are common in Ireland, Cornwall, and Wales, and there are some on the coasts *(sic)* of Devon, Dorset, and Wiltshire, and perhaps one in Kent'.
10   *A Handbook of the Prehistoric Archaeology of Britain*: 25. (Produced in connection with the First International Congress of Prehistoric and Protohistoric Sciences, London, 1932). Note again the emphasis on Wiltshire.
11   Based on a field survey made during 1933–36. I take this opportunity of thanking Mr W.F. Grimes for his invaluable assistance with the Welsh material.
12   The Devil's Den in Clatford Bottom is the only example in Wiltshire existing at present and Goddard, Crawford, and Passmore have independently recorded the remains of a long barrow here.
13   Crawford 1922: 4; 1925: 21; *Map of Neolithic Wessex,* p. 6. Some have suggested alternatively that these free-standing chambers here discussed were covered with round mounds. Crawford has dealt with this suggestion. It would be indeed curious if all the chambered round barrows in this region (with the possible exception of Greenwell 217) had been denuded while so many of the chambered long barrows remained intact.

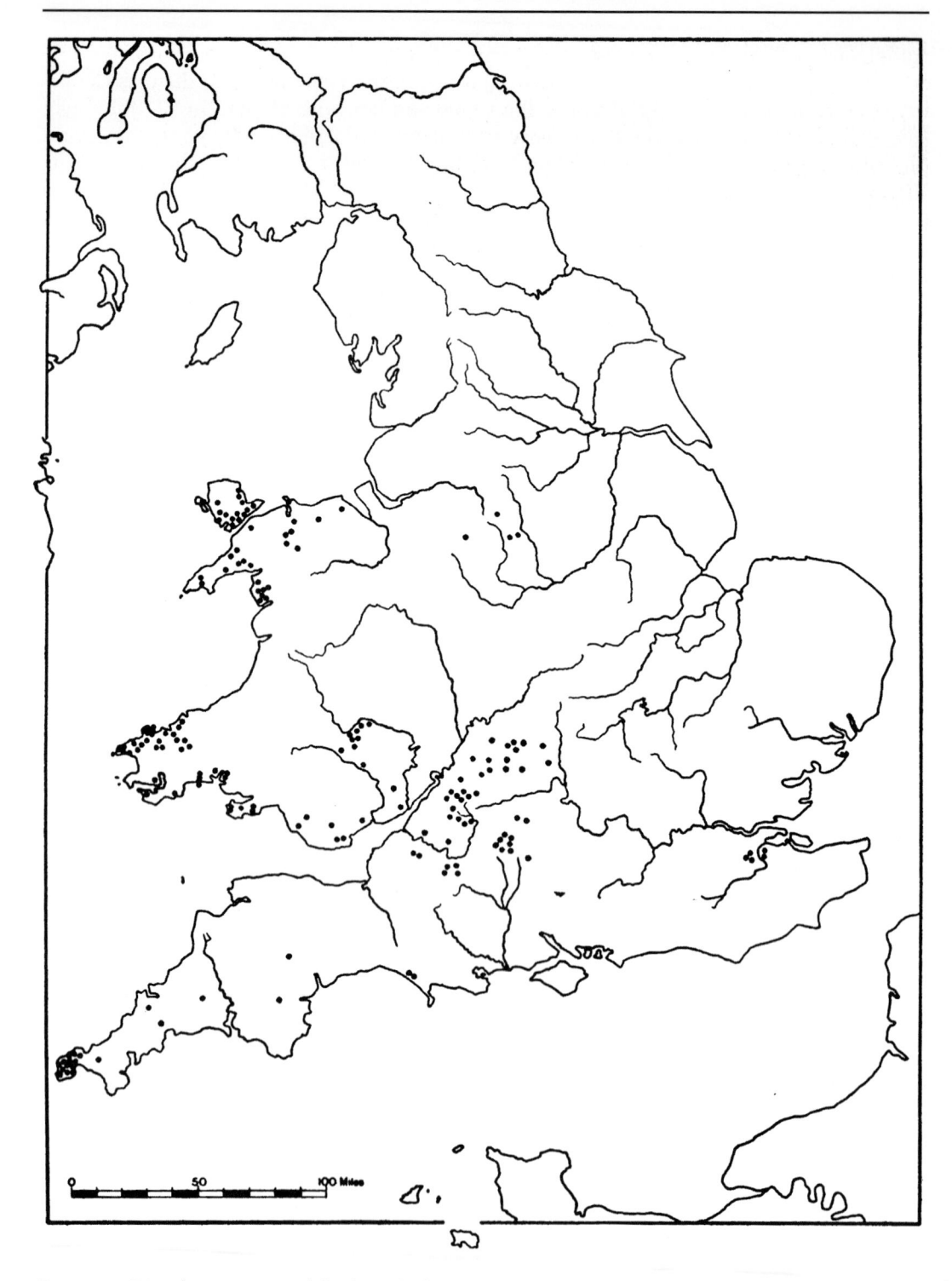

FIGURE 1. *Distribution map of the burial-chambers in southern Britain (Isles of Scilly not shown).*

FIGURE 2. *Sketch-map showing ther distribution of the Severn–Cotswold group. Solid dots = chambered long barrows. Open dots = free-standing chambers. Squares = chambers belonging to other morphological groups.*

Kits Coty and Coldrum in Kent were favourite text-book examples of Montelius dolmens. Crawford (1924: 3) has however drawn attention to the remains of the long barrow at Kits Coty, and suggested that this 'dolmen' may be no more than the false entrance or 'dummy portal' of a long barrow. He suggests moreover that the Medway group may be regarded as an eastward extension of the Severn–Cotswold group, in which case the remarks already made on the dolmens of that group would be equally applicable here. I think it more likely however that Kits Coty is the remains of a small rectangular chamber of the Coldrum type than of a false portal. The morphological affinities of the Medway group with certain burial-chambers in the Netherlands have been frequently pointed out;[14] the geographical isolation of the group from the Severn–Cotswold group, and its concentration on the Medway valley are all in favour of a Dutch origin. But whatever may be the origins of the group, it is clear that again we have no dolmens here; Kits Coty, Coldrum and Addington are long barrows with chambers at their eastern ends, and it seems probable that Lower Kits Coty and the Chestnuts at Addington are remains of similar structures.[15]

A third group of burial-chambers exists in southern Britain, which may be called the Scilly group, and which is characterized by small gallery-graves enclosed in round mounds. Dr William Borlase first recognized this type in the 18th century, and it has recently been studied in detail by Hencken (1932; 1933: 15*ff*). This group is concentrated in the Isles of Scilly, where over 40 typical examples still exist, but a few good examples such as Pennance, Treen (two), and Brane in Sancreed, exist on the mainland in Penwith.[16]

---

14   Fergusson first suggested a north-European origin for the Medway megaliths. See also Ward (1916: 242); Fleure & Peake (1930: 63).
15   But Piggott (1935: 22) thinks the Chestnuts site may have had a round barrow. There seems to me little evidence to support this suggestion.
16   Tregaseal, Chapel Carn Brea, Tregiffean Vean, and perhaps Carn Gluze probably represent degenerate gallery-graves of the Scilly type.

There are just a few passage-graves in North Wales. Bryn Celli Ddu in Anglesey is well known, while 10 miles west of it Barclodiad y Gawres at Trecastle Bay reproduces fairly accurately the cruciform plan characteristic of the central Irish passage-graves. A 17th-century drawing of Ystum-cegid-isaf in Lleyn, and the accompanying description, strongly suggests that it was originally a passage-grave.[17] These are the only undoubted passage-graves *(sensu stricto)* in southern Britain. Hemp (1935: 253) suggests that Plas Newydd may be another passage-grave, but the smaller of the two chambers, which he claims as an ante-chamber, may equally well be a side-chamber as at Rondossec III, near Plouharnel (Morbihan). There are also a few typical gallery-graves in England and Wales, apart from the groups already mentioned. Trefignath on Holy Island is a good example and is segmented; while Hen Drefor and Dindryfol on Anglesey are almost certainly similar monuments, as Grimes suggests (1936a: 119–20). The Bridestones near Congleton in Cheshire is another typical gallery-grave.

So far we have distinguished five morphological groups among the burial-chambers of England and Wales:
1   the Severn-Cotswold group,
2   the Medway group,
3   the Scilly group,
4   the passage-graves of northwest Wales, and
5   the gallery-graves in Anglesey and Cheshire.

It must be emphasized that this paper is not a constructive morphological analysis of the burial-chambers in southern Britain, but merely a criticism of the application of the Montelius dolmen theory to the megalithic tombs of that area. It is thus impossible to deal here with the fascinating problems presented by the morphology of sites such as Pant y Saer, Mininglow South, Greenlow, Five Wells and West Kennet, or with the group of North Welsh chambered long barrows such as Rhiw in Lleyn, the two Carneddau Hengwm in Merionethshire, Tyddyn Bleiddyn in Denbighshire and Capel Garmon in the Conway valley — all of which have, like the Severn–Cotswold sites in Thurnam's (1868: 215*ff*) class II, lost the importance of the broad end of the long barrow as a normal position for the chamber. These are all exceptional sites, the result probably of regional development in England and Wales, and they do not affect the primary issues here discussed. FIGURE 3 is redrawn from FIGURE 1 with the omission of the five groups distinguished above and of the exceptional sites mentioned. The superficial student of burial-chambers will confidently label all the sites on this map as Montelius dolmens. Yet do they fulfil the three requirements of the Montelius definition? Are they all of the same morphological type, and are they earlier than the monuments of the other five groups, and finally, are they all devoid of covering mounds? These three questions must be briefly discussed.

It is possible to distinguish two morphological types among the sites mapped in FIGURE 3, which may for convenience of reference be called the Longhouse and Zennor types. The first type consists of single polygonal chambers and is of rare occurrence, the best examples being Presaddfed in Anglesey,[18] and Longhouse, Llanrian in north Pembrokeshire, both of which are planned in FIGURE 4. Plas Newydd in Anglesey is

---

17   Richard Farrington, *Snowdonia Druidica,* 1769, opp. p. 175. This is an unpublished manuscript in the National Library of Wales, and I am indebted to Mr W.F. Grimes for drawing my attention to it.
18   C.A. Ralegh Radford has suggested to me that the group of megaliths to the north of the fine chamber at Presaddfed may perhaps be the remains of a passage leading south to the chamber. I am inclined however to agree with Baynes (1910–1911: 21–2) that they probably are the remains of a second chamber.

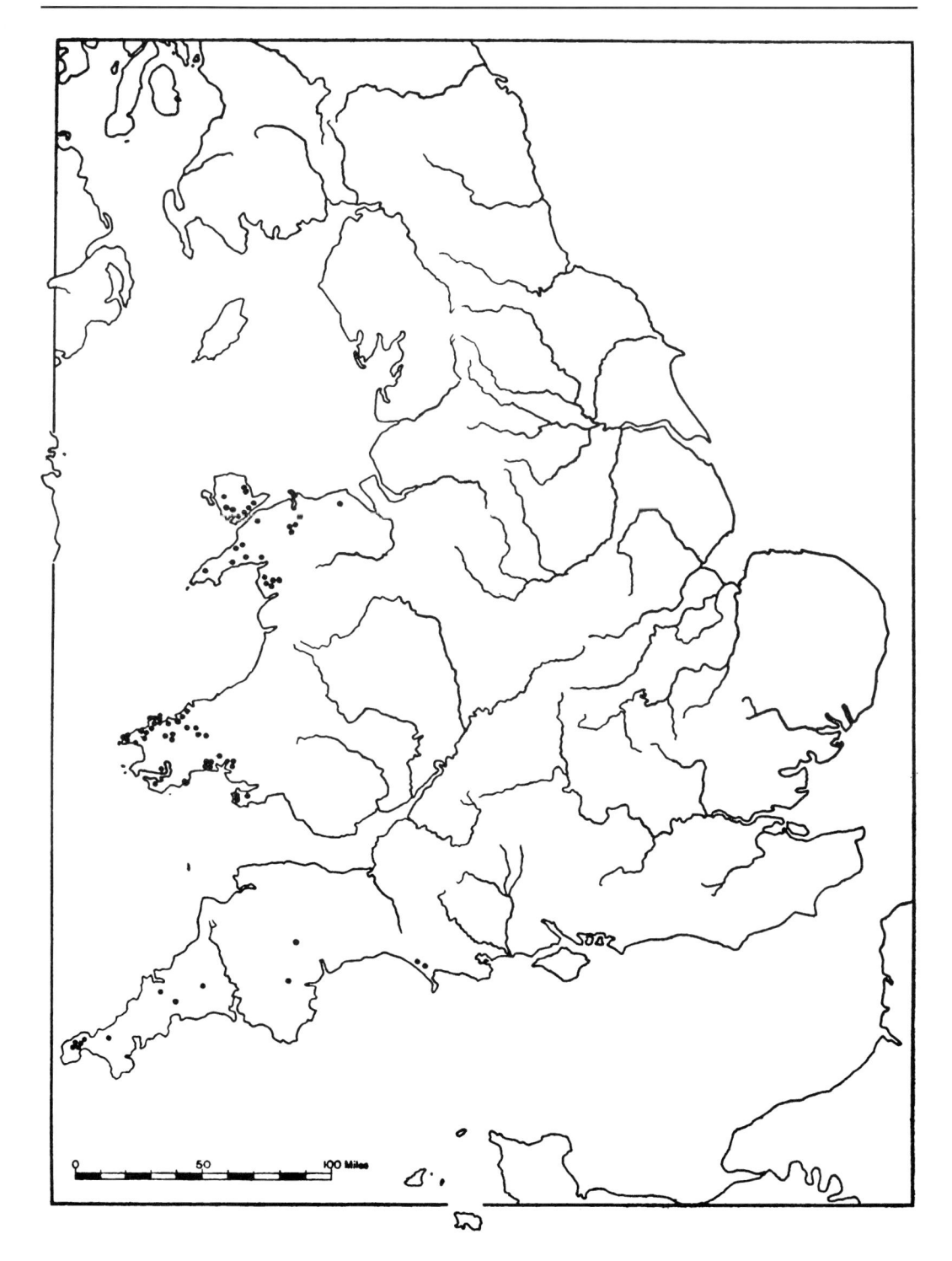

FIGURE 3. *Distribution map of sites belonging to the Longhouse, Zennor and the Longhouse–Zennor derivative groups.*

probably, as mentioned above, a member of this group with a side-chamber to the south.[19] The Hanging Stone near Burton in south Pembrokeshire is also probably of this type, as Grimes has pointed out (1936a: 131). The Zennor type consists of rectangular chambers and is much morewidely distributed. Its distribution falls into three groups:

1. southwestern England; good examples in Cornwall are Mulfra, Chun, Trethevy, Pawton, as well as Zennor itself, while the Grey Mare and her Colts near Abbotsbury in Dorset is very typical;
2. southwestern Wales; where Penrhiw, Treffynnon, Ebenezer (Llangynog), Penbont (Newport), and the southern of the four chambers on Pendine Head are normal rectangular chambers. The site between Newport and Dinas in north Pembrokeshire, variously referred to as Cerrig y Gof and Cerrig Atgof, consists of a number[20] of rectangular chambers arranged in a circle. Pentre Ifan and Carn Turne are almost certainly of this type;
3. northwest Wales; where Bryn yr Hen Bobl and perhaps Bodowyr in Anglesey, Four Crosses, Bachwen (Clynnog), Penarth (Clynnog), and Cefn Isaf in Lleyn, Gwern Einion, and the two chambers at Dyffryn in Merionethshire, and Hendre Waelod, Maes y Facrell (Llandudno) and the two chambers near Roe Wen in the Conway valley are typical examples of the Zennor type. Cist Cerrig (Treflys) near Portmadoc appears to be the end of another rectangular chamber.[21]

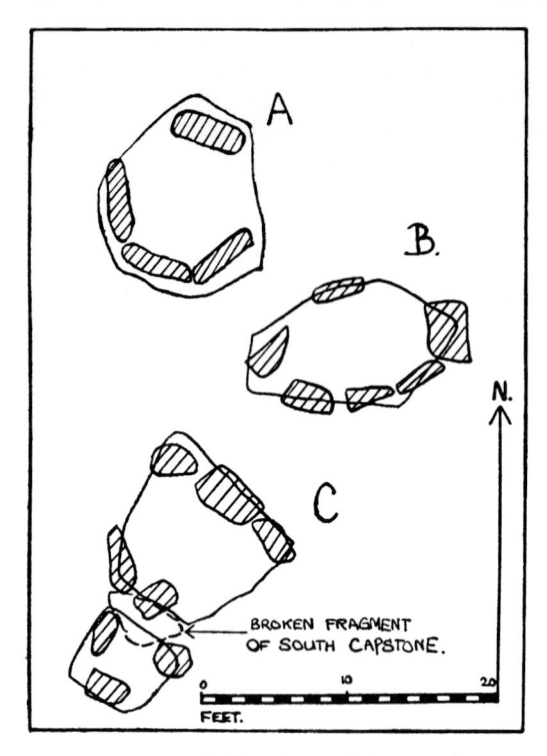

FIGURE 4. *Typical chambers of the Longhouse group. A Presaddfed, B Longhouse, C Plas Newydd.*

The distinction of the certain and probable examples of the Long-house and Zennor types still leaves many sites on the map (FIGURE 3) and these may be classified into two groups:
1. a group confined to west Wales here referred to as the 'sub-megalithic group';
2. a number of sites which are morphologically indeterminate or ambiguous.

The term 'sub-megalithic' is admittedly unsatisfactory but it is here used to designate a large number of tombs, obviously connected with the more normal burial-chambers of Wales, but which are not constructed in the usual way (i.e. with orthostatic walling and trabeate megalithic roof). Some of these (for example Sling (Llandegai) in Carnarvonshire, Cam Wnda and Cam Gilfach in north Pembrokeshire, two at Carn Llidi on St David's Head, Manorbier in south Pembrokeshire, and the two on Llangyndeirne Mountain in

---

19 As Grimes points out (1936a: 131), the stone separating the two chambers functions at present as a supporter, but there has clearly been much alteration at this site.
20 At present certainly four and originally probably five.
21 Though it may be, as W.J. Hemp has suggested to me, a false entrance or 'dummy portal'.

south Carmarthenshire), conform to the 'earthfast' type of Du Noyer, and consist of a megalithic capstone resting at one end on the ground and at the other on an orthostatic wall.[22] Others have extensive rock-cut elements such as Pant-y-Saer, Lligwy, and Glyn. Arthur's Stone, on Cefn Bryn in Gower, has an underpinned capstone, and in the southeastern of the two well-known caves at Gop, in Flintshire, is a curious burial-chamber which utilizes the cave walls in its construction. All these chambers present peculiarities of construction rare among the normal chamber-tombs of western Europe, and they do not present any coherence in their morphology. Some approximate closely, as far as the technical limits imposed by their construction allow, to examples of the Longhouse and Zennor types. It seems probable that the sites here referred to as 'sub-megalithic' are degenerate examples of the Longhouse and Zennor types,[23] and that their formal degeneracy is emphasized by a parallel decay in constructional technique.

A number of sites on FIGURE 3 are morphologically either indeterminate or ambiguous. Some, such as Mountain and Broomhill Burrows in Pembrokeshire or Ty Mawr in Anglesey, are so ruined that it is impossible to hazard an opinion as to their original form. Indeed some of them are so destroyed as to leave their very genuineness in dispute. Other sites again have been rebuilt and no adequate early plans exist; such are Drewsteignton, Pendarves Park, and the Hellstone near Portisham. The majority of these sites have a number of orthostats with a capstone resting on top, but the arrangement of the uprights is such that no reliable inferences can be drawn about original morphology. Good examples of this type are furnished by Mynydd Cefn Amlwch, Llech y Drybedd, Carn Llys and Lanyon. Classifications of free-standing chambers are sometimes based on the number of orthostats or capstones employed,[24] but there seems little purpose in such arrangements or in distinguishing such structures as 'tripod-dolmens' and 'lichavens', for these distinctions at best imply not original morphology but merely the extent of subsequent destruction. Chambers with only two or three orthostats at present can never, at least in the majority of cases, have been originally so erected. As W.C. Lukis and Barnwell used to point out, such structures could not have been functional chambers. They must surely represent partially destroyed chambers and the paucity of surviving orthostats makes their original plan ambiguous. It is impossible, for instance, to say whether typical 'tripod-dolmens' such as Mynydd Cefn Amlwch or Llech y Drybedd were originally rectangular, or polygonal, or almost circular. But it is most dangerous to assume that morphological ambiguity implies that the chambers concerned 'are of the simple form' (Grimes 1936b: 12); they are all varied in the formal evidence which they afford, and it is uncertain morphology rather than simplicity that characterizes them. It would be equally dangerous to suppose that these destroyed sites represent a distinct morphological type only persisting in decay. Crawford has suggested, as mentioned above, that the 'dolmens' of the Severn–Cotswold area are partially destroyed chambered long barrows: it is here suggested that this group of sites labelled 'morphologically indeterminate' are really partially destroyed examples of the other morphological groups already distinguished in the rest of England and Wales.

It will be seen that we suggest that the sites on FIGURE 3 belong essentially to two morphological traditions, but that many monuments reveal these traditions in a degenerate and decayed form. Grimes (1936b: 11–14) has argued against this view in his analysis of the burial-chambers in southwest Wales; he regards the rectangular chambers in this

---

22 For a short account with plans of the Welsh 'earthfast' types see Grimes (1936a: 132 *ff*).
23 Or even, perhaps, of passage-graves or gallery-graves.
24 Gardner-Wilkinson's is perhaps the best known. See also Macalister (1928: 115–16).

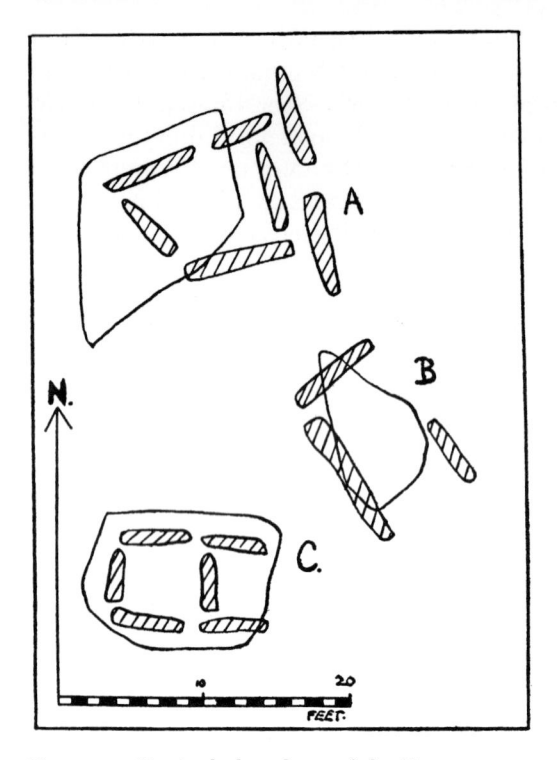

FIGURE 5. *Typical chambers of the Zennor Group:* A *Zennor,* B *Penrhiw,* C *Dyffryn, Merionethshire.*

area — citing Penrhiw, Treffynnon, and Ebenezer (Llangynog) — as a 'purely accidental variation' of his 'simple form' such as Llech y Drybedd, Newport, and Llanboidy, a variation moreover due to the use of 'flat slabs'. While we appreciate the influence which available material ever exercises on the form of burial-chambers, this view seems untenable.[25] The orthostats used in building chambers of the Zennor type are frequently identical with orthostats used in chambers of the Longhouse type or in passage-graves: they are certainly no 'flatter'. Again it must be emphasized that the Penrhiw, Treffynnon and Ebenezer sites — as well as many others in Pembrokeshire — can be closely paralleled in Cornwall and in North Wales and, incidentally, in Ireland. It would be difficult to believe that these widely distributed rectangular chambers can all be explained away as accidental variations, and moreover variations of a type whose validity we here deny.

The problem of the relative age of monuments of the Longhouse, Zennor and sub-megalithic types is a more difficult one than that of their morphology. There exists no unequivocal evidence derived from associated grave-goods: we have to rely entirely on formal considerations. It must be obvious that if a normal passage-grave has its passage subsequently destroyed, the resulting structure would be indistinguishable from an example of the Longhouse type. Baynes has shown (1912: 23 & figure 6)[26] that Bryn Celli Ddu with its passage destroyed would resemble Presaddfed. It seems to me highly probable that the Longhouse type of polygonal single chamber represents in fact partially destroyed passage-graves, and is therefore no earlier than the Bryn Celli Ddu–Barclodiad y Gawres group. But it may well be, although I deem it improbable, that these Longhouse chambers are still intact from the point of view of chamber morphology, i.e. that they never had approaching passages. It would then be possible to argue that they gave rise to the Welsh passage-graves, that they were degenerate passage-graves, or that they had no connexion with the passage-graves in North Wales — the first and third of these arguments would manifestly allow one to claim chronological priority for them, but the complexity of passage-grave morphology as well as the wealth of analogues for the Welsh passage-graves would suggest that the second of these possible arguments was the correct one. The adoption of this thesis again gives a late date to the Longhouse type of burial-chamber. Many burial-chambers of the Zennor type preserve features which un-

---

25   I have touched on some of these issues in Daniel (1936: 259).
26   It should be observed however that similarity of orientation does not necessarily support Baynes' argument.

ambiguously connect them with more elaborate monuments in the British Isles. Thus Dyffryn, Zennor, and Trethevy have traces of segmentation, while Pentre Ifan and Carn Turne have orthostatically walled semi-circular forecourts, and some sites such as Zennor, Trethevy, and the Grey Mare and her Colts at Abbotsbury (Dorset) have straight orthostatic façades flanking their entrances. All these features remind one of the segmented gallery-graves of northern Ireland, southwest Scotland and Man; and there can be little reasonable doubt that the Zennor group derives from these monuments or from similar derivations of them in other parts of Ireland (e.g. Gaulstown, Ballynageragh, and Knockeen, all in Co. Waterford). It seems therefore probable that gallery-graves such as Trefignath and the Bridestones in southern Britain, which are analogues of the Irish, Scottish and Manx monuments already mentioned, must be earlier than the Zennor group. There is therefore no evidence to support the chronological priority of the Longhouse and Zennor types over all the other burial-chambers in England and Wales.

The task of studying the morphology of the burial chambers of southern Britain is immensely complicated, as Wheeler has recently pointed out (1934: 332), by the paucity of evidence with regard to the form of the associated barrows, and this difficulty is most acute in dealing with the sites mapped on FIGURE 3. Fleure and Peake (1930: 63) doubt whether some of these sites 'were ever covered by a mound', and Fox and Bowen (1936: 42) say 'it is a remarkable fact that with one exception none of the "chambered tombs" of Carmarthenshire — or of the southwestern counties generally — show any trace of a mound or cairn: and it must be considered doubtful whether such ever existed'.[27] Some have gone to the other extreme and roundly asserted that these chambers are 'simply the exposed burial chambers of barrows' (Grimes 1936b: 5); while the Congress handbook already referred to claims that they 'are regarded by Crawford as merely the cists of ruined long barrows' (*Handbook* . . . 1932: 25).[28] The truth is that many of these chambers show very clear signs of covering or encompassing barrows, while others show none at all.[29] Unfortunately no example of the Longhouse type has any trace of a barrow, but, in view of the suggested affinity of this group with the passage-grave group we may, I think, safely assume that if the Longhouse type had barrows originally they were round ones such as passage-graves in Ireland, Brittany and Spain normally have. With regard to the Zennor type on the other hand, there is much evidence of the former existence of covering barrows, although this evidence is not consistent. Lanyon Quoit stands at the northern end of a low long barrow, Corringdon Ball in south Devon at the southern end of a very fine long barrow, the Grey Mare and her Colts at the east end of another, but Chun is set in a round barrow. In North Wales, Dyffryn, Cors-y-Gedol, Roe Wen North, and Maes-y-Facrell have normal long barrows,[30] and Grimes suggests another long barrow at Bron-y-Foel Isaf. Bryn yr Hen Bobl is however recessed in a round barrow which originally covered it completely, while in South Wales, Cerrig-y-Gof, the four sites on Pendine Head, as well as the two sites known as Sweyne's Houses on Rhossili Down in Gower, all have round barrows. If the affinities mentioned above of the Zennor type with

---

27 This statement is manifestly incorrect. *Vide infra*.
28 This is an iniquitous misquotation. Crawford says clearly (1925: 21), 'I repeat that I am dealing only with the district covered by Sheet 8 [of the Ordnance Survey Quarter Inch Maps — G.E.D.] where, as I believe, megalithic chambers were covered only by long mounds or cairns'.
29 Careful excavation and detailed air-photography may reduce the number of those with no barrows visible at present to the earth-bound field-archaeologists.
30 Even if Grimes's contention (1936a: 124) that the mound west of this chamber is natural, be correct (which I deem improbable) there is no doubt that the mound is functionally a 'long barrow'.

the Irish–Scottish gallery-graves be accurate, this would strengthen the existing evidence that the Zennor type has characteristically long barrows. But its occasional association with round barrows cannot be denied, nor, at present, easily explained. Any further discussion of the form of the barrows which the Longhouse and Zennor types may have had originally would involve us in the intricacies of the theory of the free-standing chamber. Suffice it to say here that argument by analogy affords no proof, and it cannot be demonstrated that chambers which are now free-standing were originally enclosed in a barrow. There are plenty of examples of burial-chambers which certainly never had barrows,[31] and it seems to me highly likely that the majority of the sub-megalithic type never had any barrows. It is just possible that those examples of the Zennor type that now have no barrows, and all the sites in the Longhouse group, never had barrows, but on the whole it seems improbable.

It should be clear from the foregoing that to talk vaguely of dolmens in southern Britain is to imply a non-recognition of the many morphological groups which may be distinguished in that region. Nor does any one of these groups correspond to the Montelius definition of the dolmen. In fact the theory of the Montelius dolmen is as inapplicable to England and Wales as it is to Iberia and Brittany, and also, I suspect, even to Scandinavia. As was said at the outset, the word dolmen can be, and is, used in a variety of ways: but it must be emphasized that as the Montelius definition is morphologically the most restricted that has ever been given to the word, other uses must connote even less morphological exactness. Apart from this it seems not unreasonable to ask that when archaeologists use the word dolmen with reference to the burial-chambers of western Europe, they should specify with what implications they do so. The French peasants of the Morbihan at the present day give the name dolmen to all megalithic burial-chambers, whether they be passage-graves, gallery-graves, 'lichavens' or 'simple' denuded chambers. This is Bonstetten's use of the word and it is a legitimate and useful one, which, were it not for the other varied and unfortunate uses of the word, could perhaps be recommended. The present writer however would prefer to see the word dolmen dying out of archaeological parlance, even as it is at present disappearing from the revised sheets of the Ordnance Survey maps.

References

A Handbook of the Prehistoric Archaeology of Britain. 1932. London: Congress of Prehistoric & Protohistoric Sciences.
BAYNES, E.N. 1912. The megalithic remains of Anglesey, *Transactions of the Honourable Society of Cymmrodorion* 1910–1911: 3–91.
BONSTETTEN, Baron. 1865. *Essai sur les Dolmens*. Geneva: Jules-Guillaume Fick.
CAUMONT, A. DE. 1863. *Bulletin monumental*.
CHILDE, V.G. 1925. *The dawn of European civilization*. New York (NY): Knopf.
CORRET, T.M. de la T. d'A. 1796. *Origines Gauloises*. Paris.
CRAWFORD, O.G.S. 1922. Notes on archaeological information incorporated in the Ordnance Survey maps, Part 1. Long barrows ... Southampton: HMSO. *Ordnance Survey, Professional Papers* n.s. 6.
1924. The long barrows and megaliths in the area covered by sheet 12 of the ¼-inch map (Kent, Surrey & Sussex). Southampton: HMSO. *Ordnance Survey, Professional Papers* n.s. 8.
1925. *Long Barrows of the Cotswolds*. Gloucester: J. Bellows.
1932. *Map of Neolithic Wessex*. Ordnance survey. London: HMSO. *Ordnance Survey, Professional Papers* n.s..
DANIEL, G. 1936. Map of South Wales showing the distribution of long barrows and megaliths (O.S.), reviews, *Proceedings of the Prehistoric Society* n.s. 2: 157–9.
DÉCHELETTE, J. 1908. *Manuel d'Archéologie préhistorique, celtique et galloromaine*. I. *Archéologie préhistorique*. Paris.
EVANS, E.E. & M. GAFFIKIN. 1935. Belfast Naturalists' Field Club survey of antiquities, megaliths and raths, *Irish Naturalists' Journal*, July (5) (1934–5): 242–52.
FLEURE, H.J. & H.J.E. PEAKE. 1930. Megaliths and Beakers, *Journal of the Royal Anthropological Institute* 60: 47–71.

---

31   Gor and Los Millares in southeast Spain, for example, or the Cretan *tholoi*.

FONDOUCE, C. DE. 1873. *Allées couvertes.*
FOX, C. & E.G. BOWEN. The New Stone Age, the Bronze Age, and the early Iron Age, in J.B. Lloyd (ed.), *A History of Carmarthenshire* 1. Cardiff: William Lewis.
GRIMES, W.F. 1936a. The megalithic monuments of Wales, *Proceedings of the Prehistoric Society* n.s. 2: 106–39.
GRIMES, W.F. 1936b. *Map of South Wales showing the distribution of Long Barrows and Megaliths.* London: HMSO. Ordnance Survey Professional Papers n.s. 13.
HEMP, W.J. 1935. The chambered cairn known as Bryn Yr Hen Bobl, near Plas Newydd, Anglesey, *Archaeologia* 85: 253–92.
HENCKEN, H.O'NEILL. 1932. *Archaeology of Cornwall and Scilly.* London: Methuen.
   1933. Notes on the megalithic monuments in the Isles of Scilly, *Antiquaries Journal* 1933: 13–29.
MACALISTER, R.A.S. 1928. *Archaeology of Ireland.* London: Methuen.
MONTELIUS, O. 1876. Sur les tombeaux et la topographie de la Suède pendant l'age de la Pierre, *Compte rendu, Congrés international d'Anthropologie et d'Archéologie Préhistoriques*: 152*ff.*
   1905. Orienten och Europa, *Antiqvarisk Tidskrift for Sverige* 13: 1–252.
PIGGOTT, S. 1935. A note on the relative chronology of the English long barrows, *Proceedings of the Prehistoric Society* n.s. 1: 115–26.
REINACH, S. 1893. In *Revue Archéologique* (series 3) 22: 36–7.
THURNAM, J. 1868. On ancient British barrows, especially those of Wiltshire and the adjoining counties. Part 1: Long barrows, *Archaeologia* 42(1): 161–244.
WARD, J. 1916. The St Nicholas chambered tumulus, Glamorgan. Part II, *Archaeologia Cambrensis* 71: 239–67.
WHEELER, R.E.M. 1934. London and the Grim's ditches, *Archaeological Journal* 91: 254–63.
WINDLE, B.C.A. 1904. *Remains of the Prehistoric Age in England.* London: Methuen.
WOLF, A. 1928. *Essentials of scientific method.*

The tholos tomb in Iberia
by STUART PIGGOTT
ANTIQUITY 27 (107), 1953

GEORG & VERA LEISNER. *Antas do Concelho de Reguengos de Monsaraz.* 1951. Lisbon: Instituto para a Alta Cultura.

CARLOS CERDAN MARQUEZ & GEORG & VERA LEISNER. Los Sepulcros Megaliticos de Huelva. 1952. Madrid: Com. Gen. de Excav. Arq. Inf. and Mem. no. 26.

AT THE END of the last war it became known to archaeologists in this country that there had been published in Germany in 1943 the first part, itself in two massive volumes, of a monumental survey of the Spanish chambered tombs by Dr & Frau Leisner. *Die Megalithgräber der Iberischen Halbinsel — I Der Suden* was sponsored and produced by the Römisch-Germanische Kommission, and for the first time the results of the excavations of Siret, Bonsor and others were presented to scholars in a manner which set a new standard in the publication of such material. The work is noteworthy not only for its detailed and informed discussion of the tombs and their contents, but for its scheme of total presentation of the evidence in visual form and to uniform conventions of scale and draughtsmanship, supported by photographs where necessary.

In the course of their work on the remaining areas of Iberian chambered tombs, the Leisners have produced a number of studies of individual sites or problems, and in the works under review, monographs dealing with the tombs of specific regions: with them should be taken their smaller survey of the Evora group of tombs (1949). In all, these three surveys record something over 330 tombs and much new evidence from their excavations carried out on the better preserved sites. The method of presentation follows that of *Die Megalithgräber,* and we are given a full series of plans and sections of the tombs, distribution maps, and a complete picture of the grave-goods. Everything has been done to facilitate the use of the volumes as source-books, with constant cross-references; the Reguengos volume is particularly well printed and produced.

The Reguengos region lies on the eastern edge of Portugal on the right bank of the Guadiana river. A total of 134 tombs are described, all of types which would be classed as passage-graves by British archaeologists, but of which only two are of *tholos* construction, the remainder being variants of orthostatic structures. The tombs are discussed first in terms of their architecture and ground-plan, and then in reference to their contained grave-goods; there follow sections on the finds divided into stone, pottery, schist idols (very fully discussed and classified), bone, ornaments, metal and so on, and on funeral rites. An important chapter of conclusions, and a full annotated list of monuments, completes the text.

The Leisners' conclusions expressed here and in the Huelva volume are discussed below, but out of the abundant objective detail presented to the reader we may select one or two points for emphasis. The two *tholoi* are in each instance a secondary feature inserted into the cairn of a pre-existing orthostatic passage-grave — a most remarkable arrangement. Most of the tombs had been badly plundered, but more than half the untouched burial deposit was found at Poço da Gateira I, enabling the deduction to be made that the normal accompaniment of a burial seems to have been a pot, a stone axe,

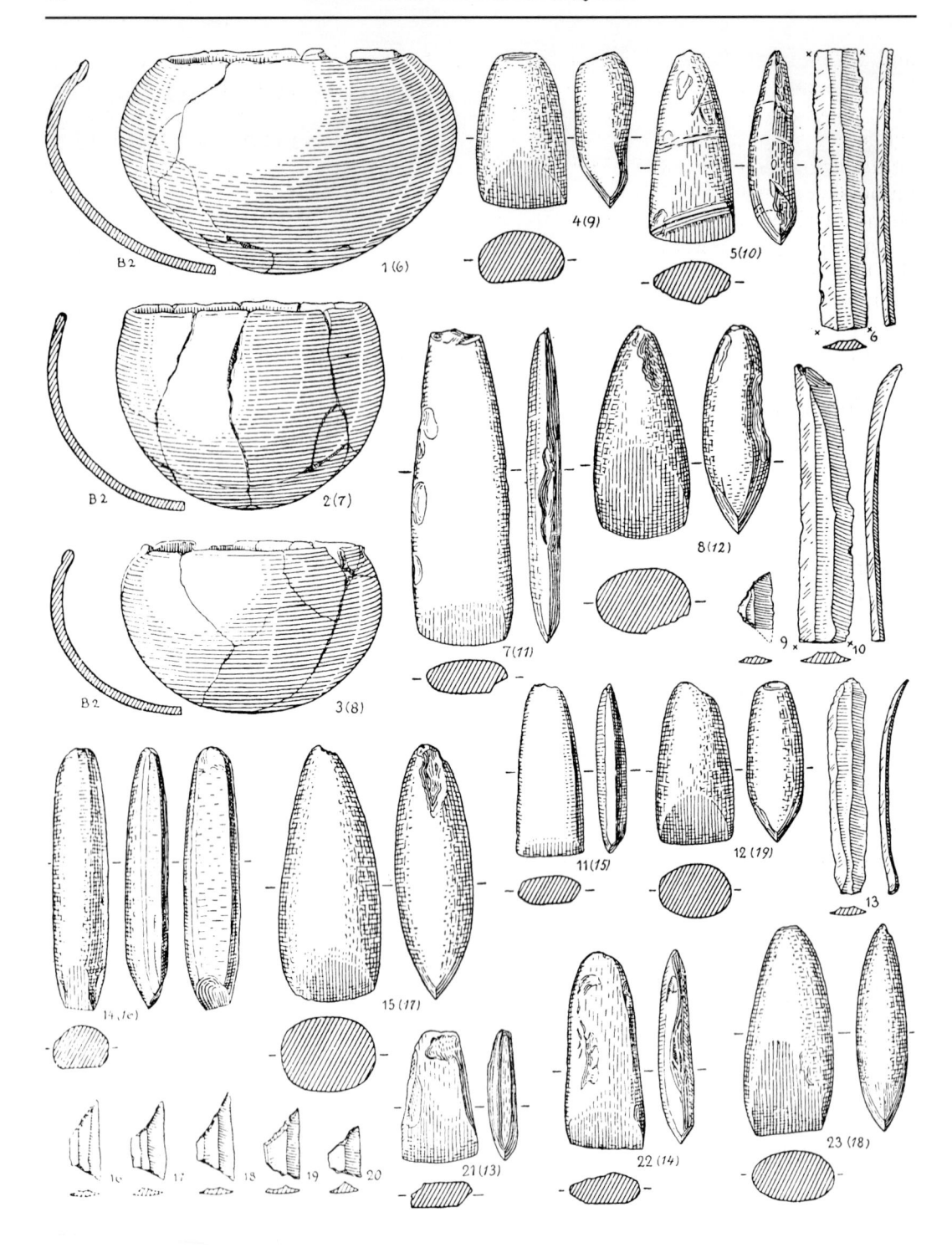

FIGURE 1. *Grave-goods from chambered tomb of Poço da Gateira I. (Flints c.$\frac{1}{2}$, remainder c.$\frac{1}{3}$.)*
(After G. & V. Leisner.)

and a stone adze (FIGURE 1). Some tombs must have contained a very large number of burials — at Olival da Pega the Leisners estimated that there may have been 200 burials, with surviving grave-goods including sherds representing at least 355 pots, and 134 schist plaques! The pottery of the Reguengos tombs included a large percentage of the *ceramica almagra,* or polished red-coated ware, which forms an important item in the authors' conclusions, but Olival da Pega produced typical Millaran pottery, including sherds of a bowl with 'oculi', as well as fragments of a form of *vase-support* (found again at Comenda I). Axes were normally round-sectioned, microliths of Neolithic type occur, the flint arrow-heads are triangular with flat or hollowed base, and from one tomb (Gorginos II), a copper or bronze arrow-point of Argaric type. Schist plaques and croziers were abundant (FIGURE 2).

As in the Los Millares tombs, the *symbolkeramik* from Olival da Pega included sherds with a decoration of incised triangles filled with a pointillé pattern. This form of ornament (often with white filling) is closely allied to that characteristic of the French Neolithic pottery (including *vase-supports)* of the Er Lannic style, and it seems likely that there may in fact be a close connection: in Charente, of course, the well-known Peu-Richard type of pottery has, as a frequent form of decoration, eye patterns closely comparable with those of the Millaran *symbolkeramik.* In Lipari, pottery with similar pointillé triangles and versions of the eye-pattern can be dated by associated Late Minoan (or Helladic) pottery to somewhere around 1550–1500 BC (Bernabo Brea 1952), and perhaps it is not then coincidence that the Wessex 'incense cups' of the Aldbourne type, independently dated by Mycenaean contacts to very much the same period, should employ precisely similar pointillé triangles as the main ornamental motif, while for eye-patterns in the British Isles we may look not only to carvings on the stones of chambered tombs but to the chalk 'drums' or idols from Folkton in Yorkshire. Such an overlap between the later building and use of passage-graves, and the development of the Wessex Bronze Age under mixed Central European and Mycenaean influences, would be in accord with other evidence.

In the Huelva volume we find a description of the tombs in a province of Spain adjacent to that of Reguengos, lying between the Guadiana and the Tinto with the main group (El Pozuelo) on the left bank of the Huelva river itself. Of the 50 tombs, 7 are *tholoi,* the remainder orthostatic; these are all described by Cerdan, Perez and the Leisners in the first part of the book, and there follows a discussion of the evidence by the Leisners, divided into that from the *tholoi* and that from the other types of tomb. While the former are of familiar types, the orthostatic tombs show some very curious variants of plan, with double or even triple elongated chambers opening from one passage, and a 'transepted' example (El Pozuelo 7) a plan of which had already been published by MacWhite, who compared it with similar tombs in West France and the Cotswolds: El Pozuelo 6 has another multi-chambered, but more rambling, plan. The Huelva pottery includes only a small proportion of the *ceramica almagra,* and plain globular bowls and shallow platters predominate. One of these, from the tomb of La Zarcita, has horizontal channelling on its vertical edge recalling that of the shallow bowls from Hebridean and Orcadian tombs, and the same richly-furnished tomb produced an oblong pottery trough on four legs and a vessel in the form of a bird. Cylindrical-section stone axes occur as at Reguengos, as well as a few schist plaques, and also finely flaked flint daggers or halberds, hollow-based barbed arrowheads, and a flat copper axe, all of Millaran forms and from the La Zarcita *tholos.*

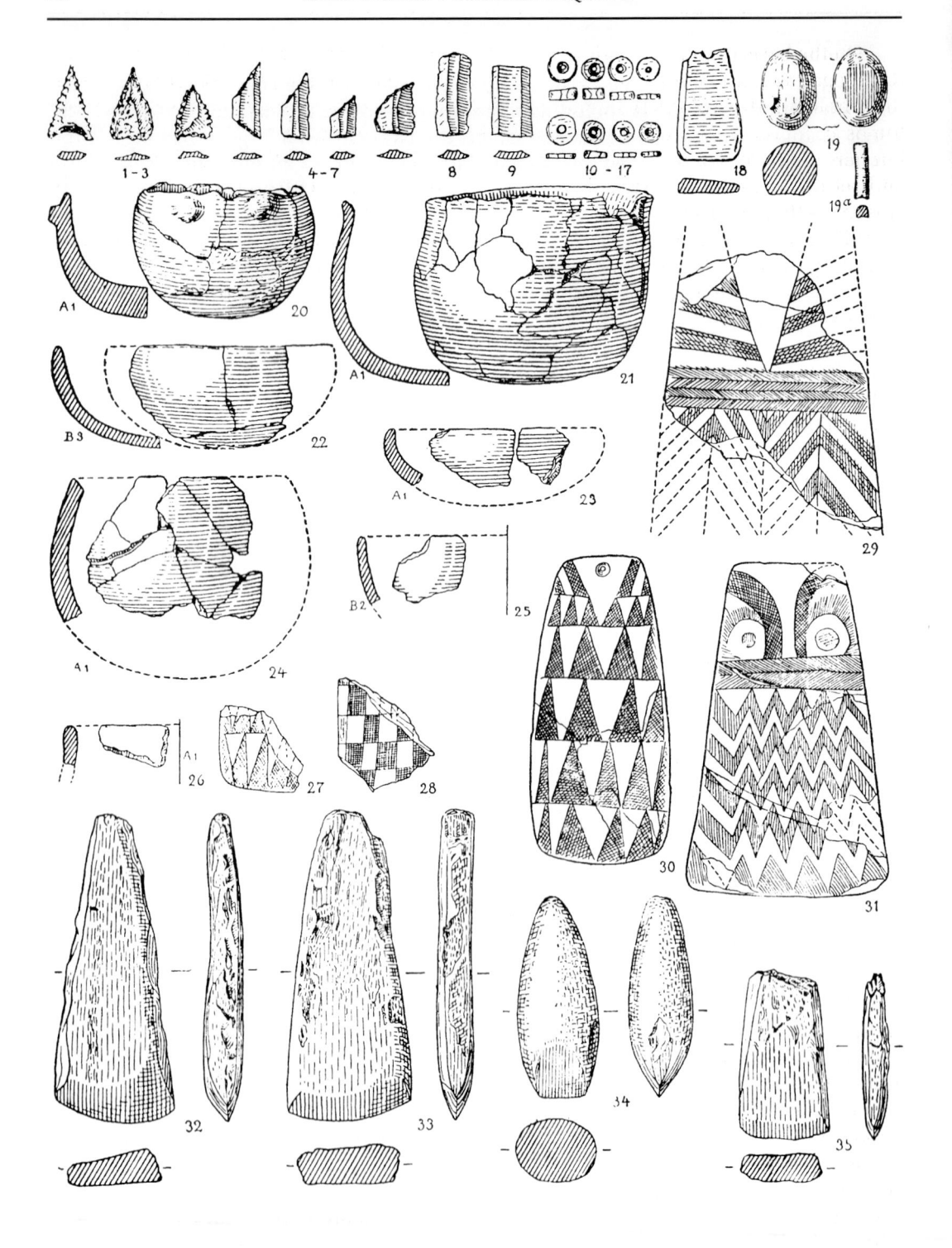

FIGURE 2. *Grave-goods from chambered tomb of Farisoa I. (Pottery, schist plaques and polished stone* c.$\frac{1}{3}$, *remainder* c.$\frac{1}{2}$.) *(After G. & V. Leisner.)*

On the basis of this new evidence from Spain and Portugal the Leisners have, in the Reguengos volume, undertaken a full-length discussion of the greatest importance on the whole question of the sequence and relationship of the various types of chambered tombs in Iberia: a foretaste of their views had indeed appeared in *Die Megalithgräber,* but here they are stated in the amplified form made possible by their more recent work, and set out with great clarity. They begin by stating the two opposed views generally current — that of Bosch-Gimpera, largely followed in Spain and by Aberg, that there was an indigenous evolution from the megalithic cist or 'small dolmen' to the passage-graves including those of *tholos* construction, and that originated by Forde, and supported by most British archaeologists, which would see a process of degeneration from a primary, intrusive, *tholos* tradition.

Supporters of the latter view have held that the 'Neolithic' character of the grave-goods from the orthostatic tombs is in fact a reflection of the impoverishment of the rich Millaran culture; the rarity of controlled excavations in the past has also enabled them to cast doubts on the recorded assemblages from such tombs. But our authors, with a mass of objective observations now before them, point out that there are significant differences in the types of pottery, tools and other objects from the coastal *tholoi* and the inland orthostatic tombs respectively: in the latter the stone axes are invariably circular in section and not square-cut, microliths are constant, and the pottery, especially the haematite or ochre-coated *ceramica almagra,* is something distinct from anything known in the Millaran culture. These elements they regard as representing a truly Neolithic culture distinct from, although persisting side-by-side with, the latter traditions.

They would see, in fact, a pre-Millaran, *pre-tholos* phase of Neolithic culture in Iberia, doubtless itself introduced from outside, with its burials either (as in south Spain) in the circular tombs without stone roofs, previously assigned by them (following Siret) to an early 'Almerian' phase, or, in the areas under discussion, massive stone cists or 'small dolmens' originally contrived for individual rather than for collective burial. They would distinguish the *tholos-tomb* as an intrusive accompaniment of the Millaran culture or its equivalents, and see in the orthostatic passage-graves the interaction of two architectural traditions, in which the less sophisticated techniques of the earlier group were employed to build collective tombs approximating in plan to the Millaran *tholos.* This, as they say, is Daniel's thesis of the dual character of chambered tomb plans re-stated with a difference — what primarily is significant is not the antithesis of gallery-grave and passage-grave, but that of the *tholos-tomb* as against the orthostatic tradition of the megalithic cist.

These views clearly merit the most respectful consideration from all students of chambered tombs. The reviewer, for one, finds himself in general convinced of their validity. The primacy of the megalithic cist as the antecedent of the gallery-grave series had already been suggested by Hawkes in his *Prehistoric Foundations of Europe* (1939), and outside Iberia the recognition, within recent years, of the true nature of the Scandinavian 'dolmens' as megalithic cists for individual burial has pointed to the likelihood that in Denmark too the orthostatic passage-graves may result from just such a fusion of architectural modes as the Leisners have postulated for western Iberia. The chambered tombs of Catalonia and the Pyrenees, with the development of the gallery-grave form, would show what would happen to the 'small dolmen' of Iberia if contact with *tholos*-builders was not made, and in the British Isles the distribution of passage-graves of *tholos* type as compared with those of orthostatic construction suggests that here, too, the latter form evolved from contact with the builders of gallery-graves. The

European material as a whole needs reviewing in this light, and in any such survey the distinction between a collective chambered tomb, and the stone-lined cist for individual burial, however massive, should be borne in mind at every turn.

So far as the Western Mediterranean is concerned, the crucial problem must still remain the origin of the collective tomb with a chamber of *tholos* construction. Apart from vague analogies of great antiquity in Arpachiyah or Egypt there appear to be no good prototypes for the typologically earlier *tholoi* as at, for instance, Los Millares, except for the little corbelled chambers in the Cyclades, themselves not very convincing. The circular tombs of the Mesarà plain in Crete can never have had corbelled roofs, and can hardly be invoked as the progenitors, and the most adventurously short chronology for the west could not make the Iberian *tholoi* descendants of those in Mycenaean Greece in the 15th century BC. The Aegean evidence, and indeed that of the Mediterranean as a whole, suggests that the rock-cut tombs which in Iberia may appear as parallel expressions of the passage-grave idea, side-by-side with *tholoi* and tombs of orthostatic construction, may be a primary form of collective burial-place, themselves closely linked to burial in natural caves, though it is difficult to date any west or central Mediterranean examples earlier than the earliest *tholoi* there, even though their prototypes in the east have a high antiquity.

In Sicily, the earliest rock-cut tombs of the Castelluccio and allied cultures are not likely to be much if at all earlier than the appearance of bell-beakers in the island, and their Maltese counterparts on the present evidence cannot be far removed in time. The Iberian rock-cut tombs in the Malaga region and round the mouth of the Tagus appear contemporary with the later *tholos* tombs and their orthostatic versions there; the same goes for the Arles and Sardinian examples (with bell-beakers), while the Balearic rock-cut tombs have produced Argaric material. Unless something new appears out of Africa we seem still to be left with the earlier Los Millares *tholoi* as the first examples of their type, themselves evolved before or concurrently with the appearance of the rock-cut tomb in the west Mediterranean.

Typologically, rock-cut tombs of the Alapraia–Anghelu Ruju–Arles plan, with a comparatively long *dromos* approach which differentiates them from the Castelluccio-Palmella type opening direct from a forecourt, would seem likely to be a parallel development, in the western Mediterranean area, to the lengthened passage of such *tholos*-tombs as, for instance, Romeral. The eastern Mediterranean evidence makes it clear that the chambered tomb with *dromos,* whether rock-cut or of *tholos* construction, is a type appearing there for the first time in Late Helladic times without convincing local antecedents. These facts (and others) would encourage me to support the thesis of a derivation of the Mycenaean chamber-tomb tradition from the west, even in the face of such an opponent as Sir John Myres. Mycenaean or Minoan traders had reached the western Mediterranean by the second half of the 16th century BC, as the Lipari evidence shows, and in L.H. III times this contact was intensified. Sardinia, where the Anghelu Ruju tombs have notably long *dromoi* in the Late Helladic manner, and where Mycenaean copper ingots have been found, would represent a stage in the journey from west to east. Until it can be shown that there is a convincing common origin for the *tholoi* of Iberia and for the chambered tombs of Late Helladic Greece, the archaeological evidence of an earlier date for the former must remain significant and suggestive. It is the more significant in that the development of the rock-cut or *tholos* tomb into forms having long passages or *dromoi* appears to have taken place in the west Mediterranean during just those centuries, around 1700–1500, which would bring them into an immediately antecedent relationship to the almost identically planned and constructed tombs of Late Helladic Greece. If these are to have a more or less local, Aegean, origin, we have to assume that, in some unexplored region there, the little Early Cycladic corbelled vaults and rock-cut tombs had developed into types startlingly like those of Iberia, even to the growth of the passage or *dromos,* during Middle Helladic and the first phase of Late Helladic times. While such parallel development is of course not impossible, until it is demonstrated by actual tombs of the requisite types dated to this intervening period in the eastern Mediterranean the case for a western origin cannot lightly be brushed aside.

The work of the Leisners points a final moral. What we want, for every area where chambered tombs were built, is a series of surveys on the comprehensive lines they have so splendidly initiated, and are so pertinaciously continuing, in Iberia. In this country only one such survey has been published, that of the Cotswold tombs carried out by the Editor of ANTIQUITY over 25 years ago. We need total annotated catalogues, maps, and illustrations not only of tomb-plans, but of every detail of their construction and of their grave-goods. The material to be comprised is by no means overwhelming; for England and Wales the foundations for such a survey have been laid by the Ordnance Survey, Mr Grimes and Dr Daniel. In Scotland, Miss Henshall, as Carnegie Research Fellow of the School of Scottish Studies of the University of Edinburgh, is undertaking a corpus of material (which is already well advanced) on lines closely modelled on those of the Leisners. Ireland is an obvious, if perhaps intimidating, field of study from which a magnificent survey might eventually come: Mr Ruadhri de Valera has made a beginning. When we have this basic evidence before us we may be able to see our problems a little more clearly, if not the solution of some of them.

References
BERNABÒ BREA, L. 1952. Civiltà preistoriche delle Isole Eolie, *Arch. Prehist. Levantina* 3: 69–93.
HAWKES, C. 1939. *Prehistoric foundations of Europe.* London: Methuen.
LEISNER, G. 1949. *Antas dos Arredores de Évora.* Évora: Nazareth.
LEISNER, G. & V. LEISNER. 1943. *Die Megalithgräber der Iberischen Halbinsel* 1: *Der Suden.* Berlin: de Gruyter.

The chambered barrow of Barnenez in Finistère

by **P-R. GIOT**

ANTIQUITY 32 (127), 1958

THE ESTUARY WHICH runs north from Morlaix in the department of Finistère in Brittany is flanked on the right or east side by the peninsula of Kerneléhen; on the northern end of this peninsula near the farms of the hamlet of Barnenez (Plouezoc'h) are two big barrows or stone cairns. Both of these are long barrows orientated from east to west, the northern one being shorter than the southern. Both the barrows of Barnenez North and Barnenez South have been known to archaeologists for more than a hundred years, but have not been excavated until now. A century ago local people dug into what were described as underground passages, and the same was done by local amateur archaeologists during the last war, but they did not appreciate what kind of monument they were dealing with and did not report their work.

Four years ago a road contractor, attracted by the easy supply of road metal afforded by these big piles of stones, bought from one of the owners permission to demolish them. He began attacking Barnenez North in November 1954, and completely destroyed a Passage Grave which seems to have had a passage dry-walled and roofed with megalithic capstones, and a circular chamber similarly walled and roofed with a single large stone at the height of about 2 m — the height of a man. On the site of the chamber the present writer and his associates discovered sherds of western Neolithic pottery. Part of Barnenez North, on the ground of another owner, is still intact. The whole barrow, which was oval, measured about 35 m in length by 20 m in breadth and 3 m in height.

Later, in the spring of 1955, the same contractor began quarrying into the northwestern end of the bigger barrow, Barnenez South, which is 85 m long by 25 to 35 m broad with a maximum height of 5 to 8 m. This huge artificial mountain was a good bargain for him. These new depredations resulted in the disclosure and partial destruction of four chamber tombs. But, at this moment, in spite of the fact that the contractor had not made the legal declaration to the authorities that French law requires in every case when antiquities are discovered, and in spite of the remoteness of the site, news of the robbing of Barnenez North got around; the present writer was informed *ex officio* and was able to set immediately in motion procedure which brought this illegal quarrying to an end.

Barnenez was then scheduled as a historical monument, and the State brought an action against the contractor which resulted in a sentence from the *Tribunal de Première Instance* at Morlaix, later increased by the Court of Appeal at Rennes. The contractor has not only been fined, but ordered to pay for the cost of the consolidation and restoration of the ruined burial chambers.[1] These sentences are of the very greatest interest and importance and create an excellent precedent for the application of the new French legislation on antiquities.

On the other hand, these unhappy events have, in the end, permitted the systematic excavation of the whole of the larger barrow, Barnenez South, with the help of grants

---

1   Cost fixed by expert's appraisement at 1,440,388 francs.

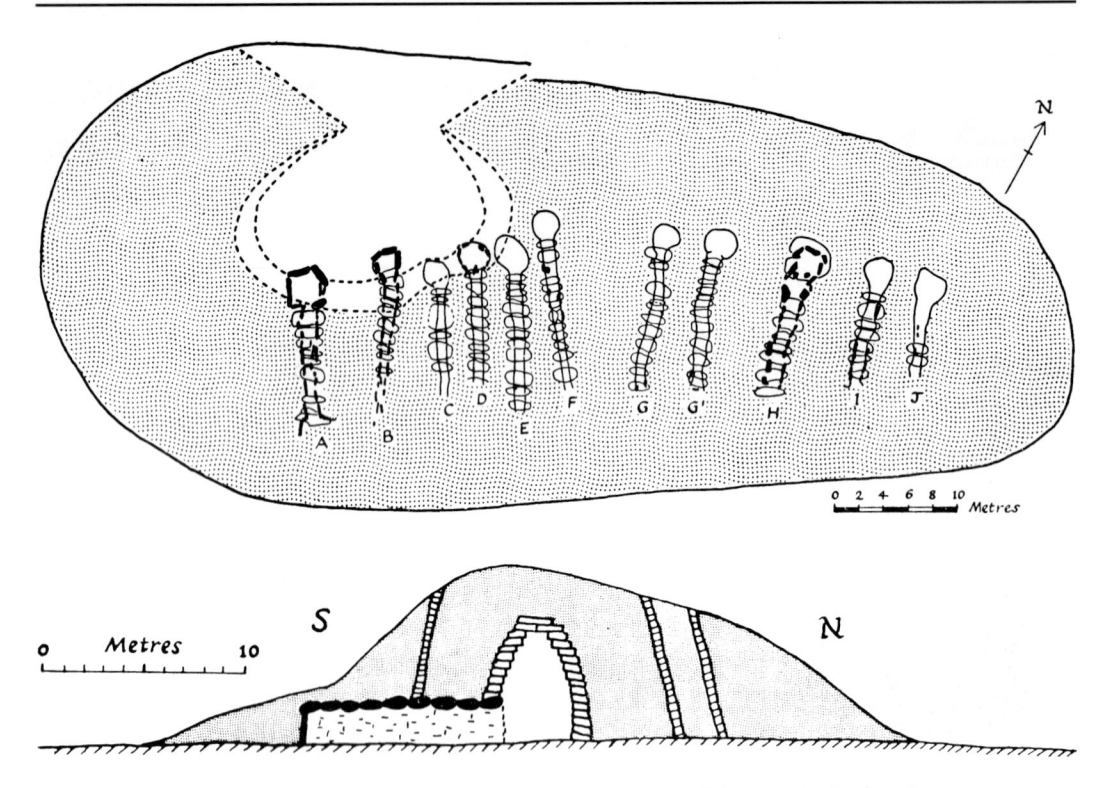

FIGURE 1. *Barnenez South.* (Top) *Plan of chambered cairn and* (bottom) *idealized section through one of the corbelled chambers.*

from the *Direction Générale de l'Architecture du Ministère de l'Éducation Nationale,* with the result that the site is revealed as of the greatest importance in the study of megalithic architecture. The barrow comprises and covers no less than 11 Passage Graves, set side by side, opening on to the south side of the barrow (FIGURE 1); these differ among themselves in their morphological and constructional details, and provide a unique collection of types. The present writer conducted the excavations at Barnenez in 1955, 1956 and 1957, with the assistance of J. L'Helgouach and J. Briard, both *Attaché de Recherches au Centre National de la Recherche Scientifique.* The propping up and strengthening of the chambers is being carried out under the direction of Monsieur R. Lisch, *Architecte en Chef des Monuments Historiques.* When at last accessible to the public, the burial chambers which have been cut open by the contractor will be without doubt more spectacular than the intact chambers, into which it will only be possible to penetrate by crawling along the passages. It is, of course, ironical that after a planned and systematic excavation one would never have dared to prepare such a spectacular and instructive exhibit as is provided by the contractor's slicing of the chambers (see FIGURE 2).

The barrow of Barnenez South is built of small stones kept in place by long revetting walls set obliquely and converging towards the centre of the mound. The stone used is locally obtained, and most of the material used in the construction of the barrow and the dry-walling comes from within a few hundred feet of the site. The volume of the mound is 6500 cu. m, which in itself indicates the enormous amount of labour involved in its construction. On the other hand, all the big stones used in the megalithic construction of the chambers and passages are of a type of granite which comes from the island of Sterec, a mile off the end of Kernelehen peninsula.

FIGURE 2. *Barnenez South. (Top) Contractors' lorries engaged in carrying away the mound. (Bottom) Section cut by contractor through Chambers B and C.*

The rescue excavation consisted of exploring Chambers *A, B, C* and *D;* the systematic excavation comprised the passages leading into these chambers from the south, and then the discovery of the remaining tombs, and their careful exploration. The seven new Passage Graves discovered have been labelled *E, F, G, G¹, H, I,* and *J.* We will now describe these 11 Passage Graves briefly (FIGURE 1).

A This is the most westerly of the 11 Passage Graves. The passage starts with an entrance defined by orthostats; on the eastern orthostat of the entrance are seven engraved 'wave' symbols. Many of the orthostats walling the passage are tilted and the way in is very narrow. The chamber is built of a corbelled vault of dry-stones resting on enormous orthostats; the top of the corbelled vault is 4 m above ground level. During the use of this tomb, and presumably to prevent some of the stones of the chamber and of the passage from tilting more than they do, large quantities of mud were brought in, and sherds of western Neolithic pottery were discovered under and on top of this layer of mud. The corbelled vault is now reduced to one-third by the depredations of the contractor's men.

B This monument is entirely built of megaliths. The chamber is roofed with a single capstone. The orthostats of the passage, set in front of dry-walling, are at the present day much tilted inwards and it is very difficult to get through the passage. Sherds of western Neolithic pottery and some fragments of human bones were found in the passage.

C The walls of the chamber and the passage of this Passage Grave are entirely built of dry-walling. The passage is roofed with capstones, and has collapsed in the middle. The top of the corbelled vault of the chamber was 4 m above ground level but has now been half destroyed. The finds from this chamber include sherds of western Neolithic pottery, bell beaker of local type, sherds of coarser ware, 12 transverse flint-arrowheads, a flint fabricator, and a western European tanged dagger of arsenical copper.

D This passage grave is of much the same type as Chamber *C,* but the lower part of the chamber consists of a wall of interbonded orthostats and dry-walling. Most of the corbelled chamber is destroyed, but the passage is excellently well preserved, and yielded stratigraphical evidence. The lower level — Barnenez South D I — yielded sherds of western Neolithic pottery, some decorated with incised festoons, sherds of bell beakers of the best red ware with decorated concentric bands of oblique lines of incised dashes, a superb barbed and tanged flint arrowhead, four transverse arrowheads, a fabricator and fragments of burnt human bones. The upper level — Barnenez South D II — consisted of a mixture of stones and sherds of coarse ware in the style of the secondary Neolithic 'flower-pot' style, with everted bases and finger-tip decoration on the rim or on applied lugs. Together with this coarse pottery were found three polished greenstone axes, a fabricator, and an unpolished flint axe.

The chamber tombs designated *E, F, G,* and *G¹* are of the same general style as *C,* but occasionally have orthostats walling parts of the passages. *E* has walls in perfect condition, but the top of the corbelled vault has collapsed. One sherd of uncertain ware was found in this tomb, which also yielded a few burnt oyster and limpet shells and a layer of burnt vegetable material, including grains of cereals, peas, bilberries and hazel-nuts. A radiocarbon date, kindly provided by Professor de Vries of Groningen, has shown that this vegetable layer is a medieval intrusion of only 750 years ago.

The passage leading to Chamber *F* ended in a collapsed structure so that we had to enter this monument, a perfectly preserved corbelled vault, through the roof itself, which was 4 m in height. No finds were made in this monument. The passage of Chamber *G* was filled up half-way with stones, among which filling was a human tibia. The chamber itself was thus completely sealed: it was a perfect corbelled vault 2 m 50 cm in height. No funerary material of any kind was found inside this tomb in spite of the care apparently taken in sealing off the chamber against intrusion. This surely proves that either nothing was put in the tomb or that what was put there was of a perishable character. Chamber G^1 is very similar to G; the passage is again blocked half way, and the chamber itself, the same size as Chamber G, is perfectly preserved, and empty.

H is a complicated monument. The passage is entirely megalithic in architecture; the chamber is very large, walled by big orthostats, and is separated by two septal slabs into an antechamber covered by a corbelled vault (the top of which has fallen in), and a main chamber covered by a huge capstone. One of the septal orthostats separating the antechamber and chamber, and four of the orthostats of the main chamber are engraved with 'wave' symbols and other signs, including triangular axes, hafted axes, and a bow. A few sherds of western Neolithic pottery were found in this remarkable monument; these were extremely small and are the sum total of the finds.

I has a passage which is half-megalithically and half-dry stone walled. The chamber is a dry-walled corbelled vault of which the top is collapsed. In the filling of the chamber were Iron Age sherds and horse bones.

J has a short passage which is badly ruined. It is roofed with capstones and on the underside of the first capstone there is an engraved representation of a motif classic in the megalithic art of southern Brittany — a stylized human figure of quadrangular form out of which splay, at one end, lines or 'hairs'. The collapsed corbelled chamber yielded Iron Age pottery.

Let us now turn from the description of these 11 Passage Graves to an interpretation of the monument as a whole. These 11 monuments are all contemporary, or very nearly so. C, D, E and F were built together from tangent bases: C was necessarily built after the building of the megalithic chamber B, on which its base rests. The primary grave goods common to six of the chamber tombs (though often there are very little) consist of western Neolithic round-bottomed undecorated vessels. Only two of the tombs, namely C and D, appear to have had a continuing use into Chalcolithic and Secondary Neolithic times.

Corbelled vaulted Passage Graves (referred to by some archaeologists as *tholoi*) are known here and there in Brittany, but are perhaps scarcer than capstone-roofed Passage Graves because they are more easily destroyed than megalithic monuments *sensu stricto*. Examples of such monuments in Brittany are Île Longue at Larmor-Baden, Morbihan, Île Carn at Ploudalmezeau, Finistère, excavated by the present writer in 1953 (Giot 1954: 404; 1955: 53), Roc'h Avel and Guennoc at Landeda, Finistère, and the famous Yvias in Côtes-du-Nord excavated and planned by Martin in 1900 (Martin 1900: 24). At Barnenez the intimate association of strictly megalithic architecture with corbelled vaults shows that both these technically different monuments are simply differing solutions to the same problem, solutions perhaps adopted according to the availability of material. The symbols engraved on some of the orthostats can be paralleled at once in the classic decorated tombs of the Morbihan.

On the whole, everything at Barnenez can be paralleled in Brittany, except the double chamber H, and this has no parallel at all in the whole of European megalithic architecture. But while every detail — or almost every detail — can be paralleled in Brittany, there is no parallel for the association of 11 Passage Graves in one barrow. The most that Brittany can show hitherto is five or six burial chambers in one mound, namely La Motte-

Sainte-Marie, Pornic (Loire-Atlantique). Of course, in Normandy, the chambered barrow of Fontenay le Marmion (Calvados) contains the remains of a dozen corbelled vaulted chamber tombs. Barnenez South has thus given us a most interesting contribution to our knowledge of the variety of megalithic architecture. What is also interesting and sobering to note is that there is, to the best of our knowledge, no other unexcavated barrow of such proportions in Brittany, so that the opportunity afforded to the present writer and his associates in the last few years may never repeat itself.

References
GIOT, P.-R.1954. Informations, 4ème Circonscription des Antiquités Préhistoriques, *Gallia* 12: 401–8.
    1955. Le cairn de l'Ile Carn en Ploudalmezeau, fouilles de 1954 (en collab. avec J. L'Helgouach), *Bulletin de Ia Société Archéologique du Finistère* 81: 53–62.
MARTIN, A. 1900. Le Tumulus de Tossen ar Run en Yvias (Côtes du Nord), *Bulletin de la Société Archeeologique des Côtes-du-Nord* (1900): 24–38.

Colonialism and megalithismus
by COLIN RENFREW
ANTIQUITY 41 (164), 1967

IDEAS AND THEORIES in prehistory often seem to have a life of their own, surviving and flourishing quite independently of the evidence upon which they might be supposed to rest. The biblical Lost Tribes, the Etruscan migrations of Herodotus, and the Phoenician merchants of Strabo, for example, served for centuries as a model for the explanation of Europe's remote past, unsupported in many cases by any evidence whatsoever.

It was perhaps natural then, when the brothers Henri and Louis Siret discovered in Almeria the first traces of the rich and exotic Chalcolithic culture of Spain (named now after its principal site at Los Millares), to see it as the work of Phoenician colonists. In this way they could explain the presence of such apparently 'civilized' features as built tombs of stone, female figurines, ivory combs, and axe and cuttlefish symbolism.[1] So they successfully launched the idea of colonists in Iberia, arrivals from the East Mediterranean and initiators of the Bronze Age in western Europe. The idea is still very widely accepted today.

While some later scholars completely rejected the notion of migration or influence from the east, preferring to see a purely local evolution, others, such as Wilke and Obermaier, modified it and strengthened it. They dropped the Phoenicians, and emphasized the Mycenaean similarities, especially of the Iberian corbelled burial chambers. These resemble the *tholos* tombs of Mycenae itself.

The view that any sophisticated features in Barbarian Europe (or indeed elsewhere) were of necessity derived from the Higher Civilizations, and in particular from Egypt, was taken over by Sir Grafton Elliot Smith and his 'heliolithic' adherents. European megaliths, especially Iberian megaliths, became the transformation of the Egyptian *mastaba*: 'When an important Egyptian colonist died abroad, his associates attempted to give him the rite of burial he would have had if he had died at home' (Elliot Smith 1930: 364). He ingeniously overcame the lack of any evidence for an intervening stage between the Egyptian *mastaba* and the European megalith by inventing for himself an intermediate form, appropriate both in plan and section (FIGURE 1).

This was an extreme case, and is today a discredited one, of what is now identified as a diffusionist kind of model,[2] with Egypt as the focal point. All inventions or cultural advances were explained as the result of cultural diffusion from there. Its magnificent absurdity was corrected in 1925 by Gordon Childe, who denied any direct Egyptian influence in western Europe. He saw too that the Spanish corbel-vaulted tombs must be earlier than the Mycenaean *tholoi.* One of his arguments (Childe 1932: 211) in correcting Nils Aberg's low chronology for the Neolithic of northern Europe, was that a more appropriate origin for the Spanish *tholoi* would be the Early Minoan tombs of southern Crete a millennium earlier.

---

[1] The list illustrated by L. Siret (1913: 34, figure 6) is: 1. cupola tombs; 2. funerary adzes; 3. axe symbol; 4. sign for water; 5. signs for rain or clouds; 6. sign for cuttlefish ('oculus motif'); 7. sign for the earth; 8. female statuettes; 9. worked flint; 10. hippopotamus ivory; 11. ostrich eggs; 12. alabaster vases.

[2] The value of examining the underlying principles for an archaeological theory, the model on which it is based, has been emphasized by Professor Stuart Piggott (1959: 3).

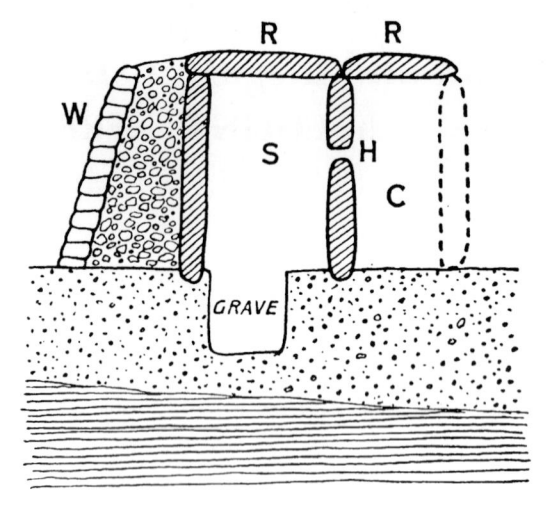

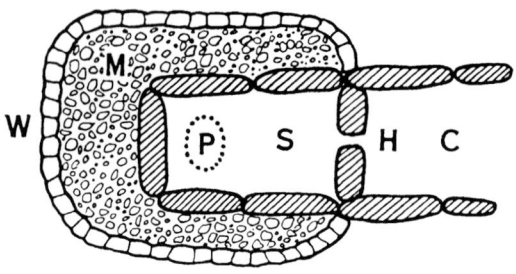

FIGURE 1. *Support by Elliot Smith for his 'heliolithic' theory (from* Human history, *1930). The caption read:*
'Fig. 55. A hypothetical tomb, such as might be made for an Egyptian in a foreign land, without craftsmen sufficiently skilled to make a proper mastaba tomb as is shown in Fig. 54.'

Childe has been termed a moderate diffusionist: all his arguments were based on careful and informed cross-cultural comparison, and he discussed also the theoretical aspects of diffusion (1956: 135). But it is important to realize that the whole of his chronology for Neolithic Europe rested upon two major *hypotheses*: that the east-central European Copper Age, and subsequently the Aunjetitz Bronze Age, were inspired by similar and *prior* developments in the Aegean and the Near East; and that the Chalcolithic/Early Bronze Age[3] cultures of Iberia, and at a further remove the entire megalithic movement in western Europe, were likewise preceded and inspired by developments in the Aegean world of the Early Bronze Age. Megalithic tombs in general, with collective burial, 'mother goddess' symbolism, spirals, metallurgy and other advanced features of Iberian and west European culture, owed their appearance in Europe to Aegean influence.

This hypothesis, as concerns Iberia, has recently been re-stated with great vigour and with a mass of careful documentation by Dr Beatrice Blance (1960, partly summarized in 1961: 192), and again in the recent important publication by Almagro & Arribas on Los Millares (1963).

This notion of major Aegean influence on Chalcolithic Iberia has become one of the traditional cornerstones of European prehistory, so that much of the European development, including both metallurgy and collective burial, is derived from the east. It has proved remarkably durable. Although much of the original evidence for it has been refuted — such as the supposed Mycenaean origin of the *tholoi,* or of the temples and spirals of Malta — the old parallels are resuscitated instead in Early Minoan or Early Cycladic guise, and the basic conclusions are unchanged. There is now a tradition of acceptance for the hypothesis of Aegean influence. It depends on a diffusionist model, rarely explicitly stated, that developments — such as those of prehistoric Iberia — are less likely to have developed there than to have been imported from outside.

No one can question that cultural diffusion, whether by the agency of migration or of stimulus diffusion, is an important factor which works towards cultural change everywhere. It would be difficult to doubt, for instance, that the transition throughout Europe to a Neolithic way of life took place under influences diffused from the Near East. The purpose of this article, however, is to question whether in this case the evidence is

---

3   The Los Millares culture and its contemporaries have been termed Eneolithic or Chalcolithic by some writers, or sometimes Early Bronze Age (= Bronce I). The term Chalcolithic is used here.

good enough to suggest that diffusion from the Aegean — let alone actual colonists — was a major factor in the inception of the Iberian Chalcolithic, or in the development of megalithic tombs in western Europe.

There are three main tasks: to examine the diffusionist case, as admirably set out by Dr Blance, to understand how it is that the Iberian evidence can give rise to such conclusions, and to suggest an alternative view.

The 'colonies'

The notion that there is no smoke without fire lends support to the colonist view: while individual parallels with the Aegean may not be impressive, in aggregate they often appear convincing. The dangers of this process, applied to the early American civilizations, have been succinctly illustrated by J.H. Rowe (1966: 334). All traits of exotic appearance are selected, in a somewhat subjective manner, from their cultural contexts, and labelled as foreign or imported. The 'Import Ware' of Vila Nova de São Pedro, for instance (do Paço & Sangmeister 1956: 222),[4] is in fact the defining ceramic characteristic of the Portuguese Chalcolithic culture of the Estremadura. Petrological examination has shown it to be of local manufacture. Pottery and other finds seem to be included in the colonist assemblage only if an Aegean parallel can be found for them, otherwise they are relegated as 'indigenous'. Richer sites (like Los Millares, Vila Nova de São Pedro or Almizaraque) are designated colonies, the remainder are native.[5]

In fact only a limited number of features link the different proposed 'colonies', each of which shows rich and striking local features. Three important features lie at the heart of the discussion.

1 *Fortified settlements, sometimes with semi-circular bastions.* Semi-circular bastions are known from three Aegean Early Bronze Age sites: Chalandhriani in Syros, Panermos in Naxos, and Lerna.[6] There are a few further fortified sites of the period, notably at Troy, Thermi, Poliochni, Phylakopi and Askitario. In a valuable article, Arribas (1959) lists no fewer than 24 fortified sites of the Iberian Bronze I (Chalcolithic), more than half of the total of settlement sites known. Some of these have not been excavated, and not all of these need in fact be as early as the Chalcolithic period. But it seems that there are more fortified sites known in Iberia than in the Aegean. Certainly the Iberian examples seem to amount to more than a few colonies. Surely the need for fortification requires a different explanation, in terms of the development of Iberian culture at the time and its growing complexity. The existence of bastions may likewise plausibly be explained functionally.[7] Similar bastions have in fact been found at Buhen in XIIth dynasty Nubia. They are almost certainly independent of the Aegean examples. Their independent invention does not appear a particularly remarkable one.

2 *Copper metallurgy, and the use of the two-piece mould.* Metallurgy is an important feature of the period, but there seems little to link it with that of the Aegean. The midribs on the Alcalá daggers (Leisner & Leisner 1943: plate 79, 5–8 (Alcalá tomb

---

4 Illustrated by Miss Blance (1960: plate 25). (The broad grooving also seen on the pottery has no parallel in the Aegean Early Bronze Age.)
5 Dr Blance started first with a careful and objective statistical analysis of the material, not published in her ANTIQUITY article. What is in question here is the explanation adduced to account for it.
6 The Aegean, and especially Cycladic, parallels are dealt with in greater detail in my Ph.D thesis (Renfrew 1965).
7 The concept of functional association of cross-cultural traits has been accepted since the remarks of Tylor in 1889 (Galton, *JRAI* 18: 270). It was central to Childe's concept of Urban Revolution that metallurgy and urbanization were functionally related.

FIGURE 2. *Late Neolithic grave at Kephala in Kea, Cyclades. (Photo A.C. Renfrew.)*

3) and plate 14, 1 (Los Millares tomb 57)) could well be the result of annealing and hammering-up, and there is no good evidence for the use of the two-piece mould in Iberia at this time (this point, arising out of discussion with Mr J.A. Charles, is mentioned in Renfrew 1967), so that this important piece of evidence disappears. The Alcalá dagger form is not closely similar to the Aegean ones, and the absence of such typically Aegean forms as double-spiral pins, spearheads and tweezers is more notable than the presence of such simple and functional objects as flat axes and awls, which are indeed ubiquitous in Europe. The early and sparing use of copper in the Vinča–Tordos and Boian cultures — before the development of metallurgy in the Aegean — and its early and sporadic occurrence throughout Anatolia and the Near East seem arguments for multiple independent discoveries of the use of copper, both by hammering and casting and its extraction from oxide and carbonate ores. Why not in Iberia?

3 *Collective burial in built tombs.* Collective burial in caves was already practised in Iberia in the Neolithic period (Castillo 1947: 506). Multiple burial in round tombs is seen in the Neolithic Almerian culture, and in the first Portuguese *antas* which may well be as early. These are very much earlier than the Mycenacan *tholos* burials (which were in any case not collective) and probably antedate the Early Minoan round tombs and graves of the Cycladic Keros-Syros culture. They do find a better parallel in the recently discovered Neolithic cemetery at Kephala (Caskey 1964: 314 & plate 45) in the Cycladic island of Kea (FIGURE 2). There seem however no compelling reasons to link the simple form of the Kephala tombs with those of Almeria. To do so would necessitate a pre-colonist incursion from the Aegean in the Neolithic period. This necessity was not felt by Childe, although accepted by Siret and Blance.

It may be felt that these three important features of Chalcolithic Iberia, fortification, metallurgy and built tombs, are not surprising in a proto-urban culture, founded as it was on a very flourishing Neolithic, with which there is no apparent discontinuity.

The second objection to Aegean colonization is the geographical and chronological dispersion, both in Iberia and in the Aegean, for the parallels cited, which themselves are not always impressive. The matter is made more difficult by the virtual absence of an absolute chronology (and disagreement over a relative one) for Iberia. So far the only fixed point is provided by a ^{14}C date of 2345±85 BC (H-204), apparently for the transition between Los Millares I and II, corroborated by the date of 2430±120 BC (KN-72) for Almagro & Arribas' Tomb 19 at Los Millares, a round tomb with passage, and by a date of 2210±110 BC for Praia das Maçâs in the Estremadura (west chamber) (Almagro & Arribas 1963: 158, 263 & plate 108; Leisner & Ferreira 1963: 360, 362). The early phase at Los Millares may thus well be earlier than the Aegean Early Bronze 2 period (that of Chalandhriani, Aghios Kosmas and Early Helladic II Lerna) where metallurgy and round bastions make their appearance. This objection applies equally to the painted ware of the Almeria district, which does not in any case resemble that of the Aegean.

Pattern-burnish ware was classed as 'colonist' by Blance on the basis of unstratified occurrence at Mesas de Asta and Carmona. It occurs also at Lapa do Fumo and Carambolo de Sevilla (Guerrevo 1945: 39 & plate 8; da Cunha Serrão 1959: 337; Bonsor 1899: figures 83, 84, 86, 87). Its chronological position in Iberia is not clear, while the closest parallel in the Aegean is in the Late Neolithic at the end of the 4th millennium BC. But a far closer parallel for the design has been indicated by Evans (1956: 60) and illustrated by Bray (1966: 102 & figure 3) from the painted ware of the Italian Ripoli culture.

The schematic female figurines again are seen in the preceding Neolithic of Iberia. And examples of the 'Cycladic' violin form are rare. The very wide range of varieties includes a majority with well-delineated extended arms. These have clear parallels in the rock painting of the time and have plausible prototypes in the earlier 'Levantine' art.[8] There is no need to seek an eastern source for a 'mother goddess' if such a person be found desirable. The very wide range of Chalcolithic figurines — flat in Portugal, often round in the Badajoz and carved on phalanges in Almeria — do not have good parallels in the Aegean, unless the emphasis of the eyes is taken alone as a significant feature, nor is *Symbolkeramik* found there. On the contrary, when the complete ceramic assemblages of Iberia and the Aegean are compared, they are notably dissimilar.[9]

The use of rock-cut tombs by some of the original 'colonists' can hardly be an Aegean feature, since they do not appear in the Aegean until the end of the Early Bronze Age. Most of the Iberian ones are in the Portuguese Estremadura, where they are notably associated with Beaker burials. The tombs at Alcaide, quoted by Childe, had Argaric grave goods (Reyna 1946: 52), but they do at least have a rather close parallel at Thapsos in Sicily (FIGURES 3, 4). (The Thapsos parallel was indicted by J.D. Evans (1956: 60).) But the context there is contemporary with the El Argar culture, and does not therefore bear on Chalcolithic Spain.

Other 'colonist' features cited by Miss Blance are the red monochrome and highly burnished grey wares, stone and bone containers, and herringbone masonry. There is no way of refuting or substantiating such generalized traits. The site of Vila Nova de São Pedro does present a somewhat more specific parallel in the form of a bird-headed pin of

---

8   See H. Breuil's work on Iberian rock art published in 1933 (II: figures 27 & 37; III: plates XXXIII, XXXVII, figure 38; IV (1935): plates XXVII, XXXV, etc.) Not all of these are earlier than the marble figurines, but they have earlier prototypes. Egyptian prototypes for megalithic art and paintings are again argued by L. de Albuquerque e Castro (1959: 251).
9   Childe, in more critical mood, actually dismissed this parallel, as well as those for the pottery and tombs, adding, 'Though much has been learnt about the Peninsula's prehistory and foreign relations in the past six years, reliable evidence for chronology based on an interchange of actual manufactures has not been achieved' (1953: 167).

FIGURE 3 (above). *Rock-cut tomb at Alcaide, Spain. (Photo A.C. Renfrew.)*

FIGURE 4 (left). *Rock-cut tomb at Thapsos, Sicily. (Photo A.C. Renfrew.)*

bone, but the form is not identical with the examples from Syros and Thermi, and indeed neither this nor the 'vase-headed' pin is strikingly original. Vila Nova de São Pedro is indeed among the richest of the Iberian Chalcolithic settlements, but some of its features may be later ones, connected rather with Beaker developments.

The strength of the colonist theory is that it explains not only the possible origin of some of the 'exotic' traits, but why they are there. The ingenious suggestion that the colonists were metal prospectors is weakened however by the relative abundance of copper in the East Mediterranean, by the location of the tin ores of Iberia in the northwest (where 'colonist' features are rare), and by the total absence of tin in the local metal artefacts (Junghans *et al.* 1960: analyses 297, 737, 825; do Paço & Arthur 1952: 31;

do Paço 1955: 27). This would be strange if Los Millares were an intermediary in the tin trade from Galicia.

It fails, however, to account for numerous other exotic features including decorated phalanges, baetyls, pressure-flaked flint daggers, concave-based arrowheads, pinecones, sandals, mattocks, ostrich egg beads, amber, ivory combs, copper arrowheads (Palmella points), *Symbolkeramik,* schist croziers, and schist and clay plaques. Moreover it can point to no single undoubted import from the Aegean: obsidian, for instance, is never found, although materials from Africa are. Indeed the earliest certain imports to the west Mediterranean from the east are the faience beads from Fuente Alamo (Childe 1957: 284), and the Middle Helladic pottery of Monte Sallia in Sicily (Taylour 1958: 54). There is no indication of Iberian maritime mobility over great distances: the amber is probably Portuguese rather than north European, and the callaïs is as likely to derive from north-west Spain as from Brittany.[10]

Professor Evans has suggested (1956: 67) how, in the Early Bronze Age, various cultural traits reached Iberia by the slow process of 'culture creep', and, as we have seen, there is sound evidence for contact, at least with Italy and Sicily during the El Argar period and later. There is no reason why various Aegean cultural traits should not have reached Iberia by stimulus diffusion, although perhaps no conclusive evidence that they did. But this process can hardly have brought about the revolutionary cultural change, with the simultaneous acquisition of metallurgy, fortifications and megaliths, which the colonists are supposed to have wrought.

Iberian development

It is interesting to enquire how such very different interpretations of the Iberian material are possible. The ambiguities appear to arise essentially from the complete absence of a reliable relative chronology. The consequent chronological freedom has allowed some scholars, such as Bosch Gimpera, to hold that the single polygonal chamber of inland Portugal was the ancestor of the Passage Graves, while others, such as Forde and Childe, saw them as late and crude imitations of the more sophisticated forms. So easily is the typology reversed.

Today there is broad agreement about the relation of the Chalcolithic to the Neolithic and to the Argaric Bronze Age. But within the period the position is chaotic. While the Almerian culture may be accepted as Neolithic, its subdivision by Siret, followed by the Leisners and by Blance, is entirely a typological one. Moreover it is not clear whether the divisions are of chronological significance (as broadly accepted by the Leisners) or of a cultural one (as suggested by Blance). Most writers today see the Portuguese simple chambers as Neolithic predecessors of the more elaborate Passage Graves, but their chronological relation to the Almerian graves is unknown.

At the other end of the Chalcolithic, the transition to the El Argar culture is equally vague. Clearly some Passage Graves (for example some of the Los Eriales group) were constructed, not merely re-used, in the Argar period. In the Tagus region there is mixing between Argaric and Chalcolithic materials, which are apparently not separated stratigraphically at Vila Nova de São Pedro. The copper or bronze Palmella points are sometimes found with Argaric material, and occur in many megalithic tombs at Los Millares and elsewhere.

---

10   Amber sources in Europe, including Portugal, are mentioned by C. Beck *et al.* (1965: 97). Siret suggested an Iberian source for callaïs (1913: 39).

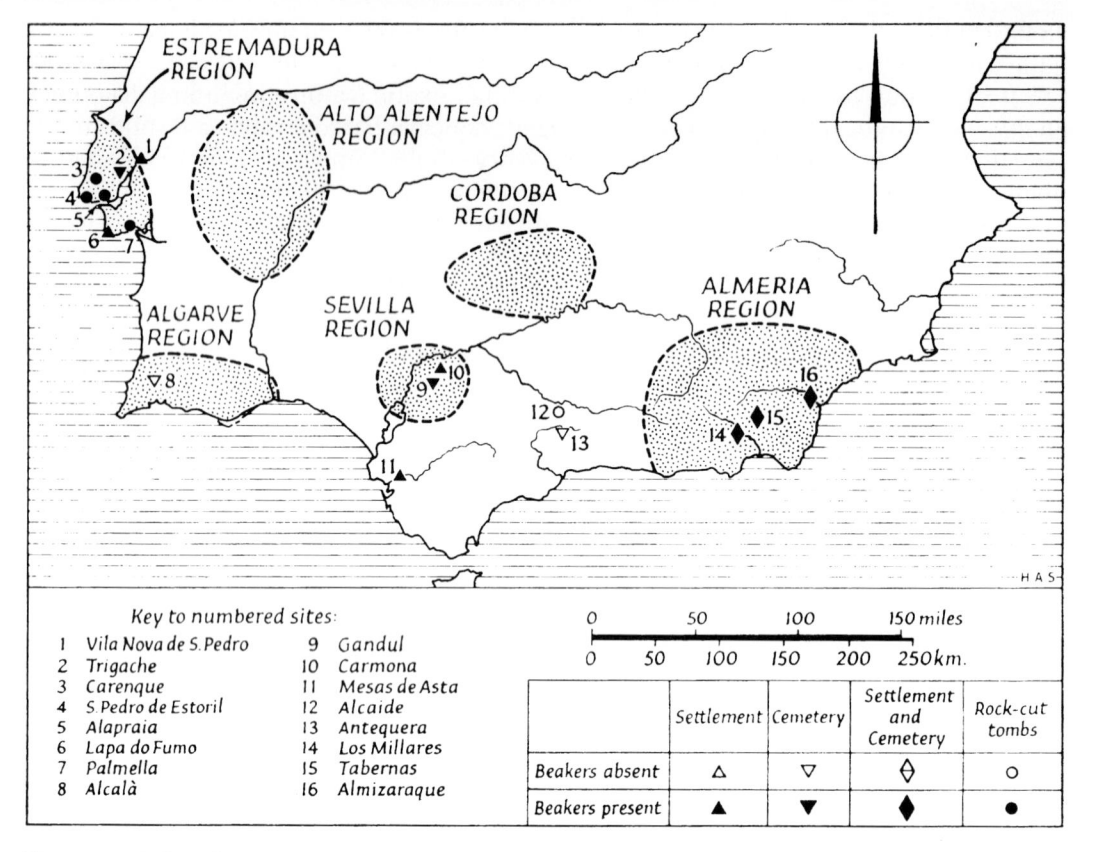

FIGURE 5. *Cultural regions in the Chalcolithic of southern Iberia, indicating important 'colonist' sites and the presence of Beakers at them. (Drawing H.A. Shelley.)*

Within the Chalcolithic the chronological position of the Beakers is totally confused. They occur at nearly every 'colonist' site (FIGURE 5) and at not one of these are they convincingly separated from 'colonist' material. At only two sites is there a chronological subdivision within the Chalcolithic. Los Millares is divided on typological, not stratigraphical grounds. Although Beakers are generally placed in the later phase there (Almagro & Arribas 1963: 236, they are apparently found in Los Millares I also (Leisner & Leisner 1943: 459, 566, 568, 590–91). At Vila Nova de São Pedro they are not found in the earliest level, but it seems that they may occur in the next, which is contemporary with the construction of the defensive wall (do Paço & Sangmeister 1956: 222). They are the principal ceramic feature of the Portuguese rock-cut tombs, and are mixed with 'colonist' material at Mesas de Asta, Carmona, Almizaraque and elsewhere. Among 'colonist' sites they are absent only at Alcala: they are absent too at Alcaide, but this is an Argaric site. The Iberian Beakers are closely associated with metal finds. Since sometimes they cannot be separated chronologically many 'colonist' traits may be due to Beaker influence, especially in Andalusia and the Estremadura.[11] Certainly one suspects that the V-perforated 'tortoise' buttons of Vila Nova de São Pedro and S Pedro de Estoril (Leisner *et al.* 1963: plate XIV) would have been classed as colonist had they not first been identified

---

11 It is not yet excluded completely that fortifications in Iberia may be a Beaker innovation. Apparently the fortified site (with circular bastions) at Lébous in the Hérault is of Beaker date (1930±250 BC, Gif-156; compare 2010±175 BC for La Grotte Muree, Montpezat, with Beakers, Gsy-116). *Cf.* Arnal *et al.* 1964: 191).

as Beaker (Bray 1964: 85, figure 8). M.A. Smith has indeed emphasized the inconclusive nature of Beaker contexts in much of Iberia (1953: 106), and her objection to the identification 'Beaker folk', like mine to the notion of 'colonists', is essentially that it involves an arbitrary division of the material.

There is a great need for further stratigraphic excavation in settlements, following the lead given by do Paço at Vila Nova de São Pedro. Amidst the present lack of sound evidence, it is not unduly surprising that to sort the material into 'colonist' and 'indigenous' at first seems progressive. But a systematic division into cultural areas might be more productive — to speak of Iberia as a whole is excessively general.

On the basis, principally, of the excellent distribution maps of the Leisners,[12] at least six major regional groups may be distinguished in southern Iberia (FIGURE 5) on the distribution of graves, and the variation of grave goods:

A   Estremadura Group (Tagus estuary area). Corbelled tombs, rock-cut tombs, many concave-based arrows, tanged arrows, round limestone idols, Beakers, grooved and incised pottery ('Import Ware'), metal objects, Palmella points.
B   Alto Alentejo Group (Inland). Few concave-based or tanged arrows, schist plaques, croziers.
C   Algarve Group (Alcalá etc.). Corbelled tombs, concave-based arrows, no tanged arrows, baetyls, metal objects.
D   Sevilla Group. Cupola tombs with long passages, concave-based arrows, no tanged arrows, Beakers, some pattern-burnished ware (not in tombs).
E   Cordoba Group (Inland). Few concave-based or tanged arrows, paintings of schematic figures with arms defined (usually not in tombs).
F   Almeria Group (Los Millares, etc.) Corbelled tombs, concave-based and tanged arrows, many transverse arrows, *Symbolkeramik,* painted pottery, Beakers, stone figurines with arms defined, bone idols, phalanges, metal objects.

All of these share four additional features, as well as possessing Passage Graves: simple undecorated pottery, stone axes, flat-based triangular arrowheads with fine flat-flaked working, and schematic anthropomorphic figuration. These are seen already in the Neolithic Almerian culture and in the Portuguese Neolithic graves, although there is an evolution in the arrowhead. The rather schematic representation of the human form has a longer ancestry. The Chalcolithic cultures were certainly the inheritors of the preceding Neolithic.

Another contribution can be indicated. The Leisners and their predecessors already pointed out certain North African and Egyptian parallels in the Chalcolithic period (Leisner & Leisner 1943: 558, 588), and Childe accepted the North African origin of the Almerian culture. It would be as extreme to derive the entire Iberian Chalcolithic from Africa as it is to do so from the Aegean. But at least there are some genuine African imports in Iberia (FIGURES 6 & 7), notably ostrich-egg beads (Grave 12 at Los Millares contained 800), and ivory, whether of hippopotamus or of elephant.[13] It seems likely that the magnificent flat-flaking of the daggers and arrowheads is of African inspiration, where there is a long tradition culminating in the Capsian Neolithic (McBurney 1960: 247). Flat-based, concave-based and tanged arrowheads are found there, and ostrich-egg shell beads are common (Forde-Johnstone 1959: 33; Camps-Fabrer 1966: 295). The remarkable Iberian sandals and ivory combs have no good parallels in Europe, but such things

---

12   Students of Iberian prehistory will always be indebted to the Leisners for their admirable collection and presentation of so great a quantity of primary material.
13   This is likely to be an import from Africa, although the possibility of fossil ivory cannot yet be excluded, *cf.* Leisner & Leisner (1943: 474).

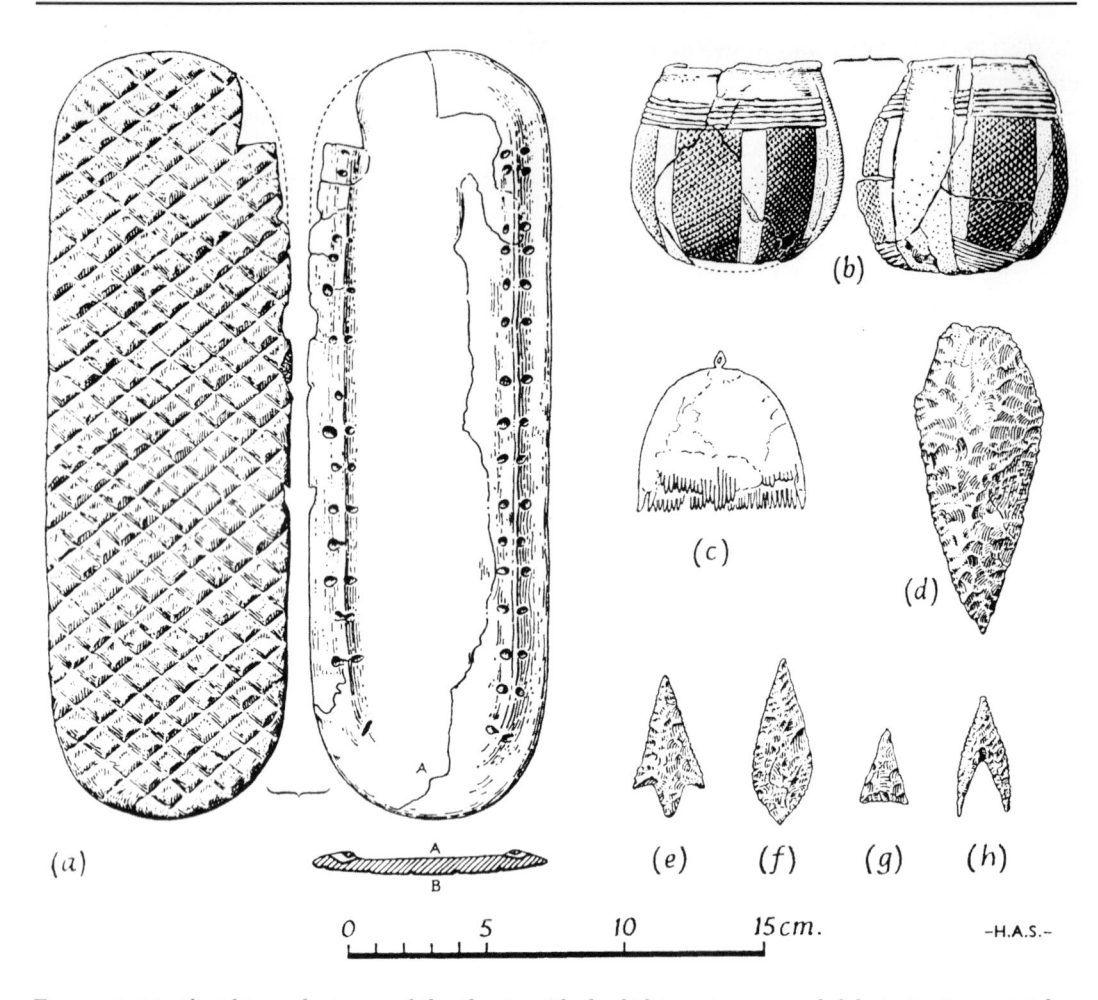

FIGURE 6. *North African features of the Iberian Chalcolithic:* a *ivory sandal;* b *imitation ostrich egg;* c *ivory comb;* d–h *flat-flaked flint work (after Leisner & Leisner 1943). (Drawing H.A. Shelley.)*

are known from Predynastic Egypt (Childe 1958: 59), and were perhaps used also in the Maghreb (Vaufrey 1955: 411; Camps-Fabrer 1966). The criss-cross decoration on some of the Iberian stone vessels as well as on the Monte do Cabeço seal (Leisner & Leisner 1959: plate 16, 1, 1) has parallels in the decoration of Capsian pottery. And finds of Iberian type at Gar Cahal (Mateu 1955: 13 & plate 2), including Beaker sherds, indicate that the straits of Gibraltar were also being crossed in the other direction in the Chalcolithic period.[14] The Capsian Neolithic combs, however, were apparently used for marking pottery, and are not here included in the distribution map (FIGURE 7).

The distinguishing features of the Iberian Chalcolithic may consequently be listed in a form which does not depend on massive cultural influence from outside, despite indications of contact with north Africa and within the west Mediterranean. They were at first limited to the coastal regions, for the Alto Alentejo and Cordoba regions retain a

---

14   Other Beakers have been recorded in north Africa (McBurney 1960: 255 (Beaker at Dar-es-Soltan); Camps-Fabrer 1966: 494).

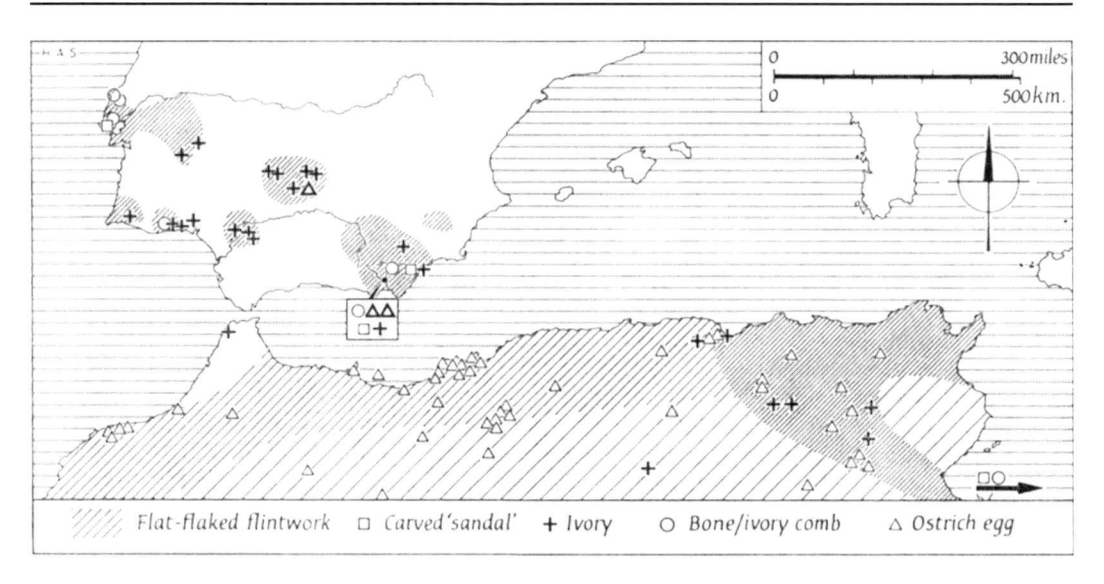

FIGURE 7. *Distribution of North African features in the Iberian Chalcolithic. (Drawing H.A. Shelley.)*

somewhat 'Neolithic' aspect until Argaric times. The following hypothetical processes may be suggested for the development from Neolithic to full Chalcolithic:

1 Full-scale passage graves developed from smaller local prototypes. The corbelled graves, of very limited distribution in Portugal, may have evolved in Almeria from the Almerian round tomb. From them developed in turn the Tagus rock-cut tombs and the magnificent graves with long passages of the Seville Group (Matarrubilla, Cueva de la Pastora) and of Antequera (Cueva del Romeral, FIGURE 8).
2 Iconographic elaboration led to separated developments in the different regions: schist plaques in the Alto Alentejo, stone figurines and decorated phalanges in Almeria, schematic rock painting in Cordoba.
3 Ceramic elaboration, possibly with some influence from north Africa and Italy, led to painted ware and *Symbolkeramik* in Almeria, channelled ware in the Tagus, pattern-burnish ware in Seville. Beakers are particularly common in this region and in the Tagus district. The Leisners believe those of Almeria to be intrusive.
4 Copper metallurgy originated independently of outside influence and developed gradually in the metalliferous regions. Doubtless native copper was used in the first place. Its diffusion was aided by maritime contact between the coastal regions, and by the same processes which disseminated the Beakers. For the first time there was a valuable trading commodity, and the increasing prosperity and cultural contact stimulated an increase in the size of community and perhaps in degree of specialization which is a first step towards urbanization. The result was a flourishing proto-urban culture with notable achievements in architecture and in the crafts. A very similar process may be seen in the Aegean at about the same time, a little earlier in Sumer and in Egypt, and rather later in the Americas and in Africa. There is no convincing *a priori* reason why these processes in the different cultural regions of the world should be interconnected. In fact some were, others were not.

This view of a local development of culture and metallurgy in Iberia is, let it be admitted, as much a hypothesis as the colonist view. But at least it avoids the early division of material into *a priori* 'colonist' and 'indigenous' categories. Ultimately, chronological evidence may be decisive against the colonist view, for ^{14}C dates towards the beginning of Early Helladic II (the proto-urban stage of the Aegean), of 2260±56 BC (P-217), 2120±65 BC (P-318), are not earlier than a developed stage of Los Millares. At present the Iberian chronology depends largely upon whichever of the current hypotheses for Beaker origins one accepts. If the Bell Beaker originated in Iberia, it must have done so before its appearance around 2200 BC in Holland. But there is at present no chronological evidence in Iberia to deny that some of the Beaker assemblage, such as the V-perforated buttons, may be much later. This may, of course, be part of a 'reflux' movement, but without better evidence from Iberia such a theory cannot receive very firm support.

The Iberian Chalcolithic may well have been under way by 2600 BC, comfortably before the inception of Aegean metallurgy (Renfrew 1967, and see Stuiver & Suess 1966: 539; Damon *et al.* 1966: 1055). But even if a shorter chronology be preferred, the Chalcolithic period must have lasted little less than a millennium. Within this period there is ample scope, geographical and chronological, for a gradual *process* of development, influenced by local factors in the various cultural regions and by their interrelation. This seems as likely as the overnight arrival of wisdom from the East.

FIGURE 8. *Corbelled burial chamber, Cueva del Romeral, Antequera. (Photo A.C. Renfrew.)*

Megaliths

As with Beakers or corded ware, the distribution of megalithic burial monuments has been and remains a central problem in European prehistory. There has been at times a tendency to lump all megaliths together as obviously related, the result of a single diffusionist movement, whether by colonization or through the agency of megalithic missionaries. Sometimes the typological similarities have been emphasized at the expense of the cultural contexts, and it is this tendency which is here stigmatized by the German term 'Megalithismus'. (The Spanish 'megalithismo' does not have the same pejorative overtones.) Daniel, on the other hand, has recently called for a more cautious and critical approach, with fewer initial and implied assumptions (Daniel forthcoming). The megaliths of Iberia have always been regarded by the colonialists as reflecting Aegean (or Egyptian) influences, which were then transmitted by the Atlantic route to the northwest. Other notable scholars have preferred a local evolution. And indeed the element in the colonialist theory that megaliths, especially corbelled Passage Graves, are derived from the east may well prove to be that theory's undoing.

Iberia has a wealth of varieties of megalithic collective tombs. But despite this range of types, the north European Gallery Grave, generally set in a long mound, is absent (except in Catalonia). A few striking tombs, such as the Cueva de Viera or the Cueva de Menga at Antequera, both in round mounds, cannot obscure this point. The standard form is the Passage Grave (Daniel 1941: 1). In France, both types are common, as in Ireland and north Britain, but in south Britain the Gallery Grave, whether Clyde–Carlingford or Severn–Cotswold in type, is more common. In Ireland the Passage Grave of the Boyne type is apparently later than the Gallery Grave. Indeed these arguments, the early ^{14}C dates for Wayland's Smithy and Monamore Cairn (3160±110 BC, Q-675) and for 'unchambered' long barrows, and above all the discovery that these often covered some structure, albeit of wood, perhaps a prototype for the chambered barrow, has led to a general feeling that Gallery Graves, and megalithic collective burial in general, owe little to Iberian influence.

With Passage Graves, especially those of dry-stone construction with a corbelled vault, the position is different. Some of the finest Breton examples, such as Île Longue or Île Carn (L'Helgouach 1965: 22 (Île Longue), 37 (Île Carn) and Barnenez G), show features, both in plan and construction, closely comparable with those of Iberia, notably the tombs of Los Millares, Seville and Alcalà (Leisner & Leisner 1943: plate 19 (Los Millares 47), plate 60 (Cueva del Vaquero), plate 62 (La Cañada Honda B) & plate 77 f (Alcalà cemetery), and again with the northwest, for example Corrimony, Maes Howe, Camster Round and tombs of the Boyne culture (Henshall 1963: figures 39, 114, 142; Piggott 1954: 193), so that there is a good *prima facie* case for some common origin or genetic relationship. It is of course supported by the fairly continuous distribution of megalithic tombs from Cadiz to the Shetland Isles, all broadly 'Neolithic' in date and with general similarities in grave goods (the so-called 'Western Neolithic' assemblage).

There are no megaliths in the Aegean. The orientalist approach has therefore been to regard the Iberian true megaliths (of orthostatic construction) as secondary to the *tholoi* or dry-stone corbelled tombs. These latter indeed have similarities in construction with those of the Mycenaean world, although the *dromos* is functionally conditioned by the necessity of an entrance passage into the mound. It became clear that the Iberian corbelled tombs were earlier than the Mycenaean *tholoi,* and Professor Piggott (1953: 137) neatly turned the tables by wondering whether the Mycenaean *tholoi* might not in fact be derived from Iberia, a suggestion that has not been warmly welcomed. *Nunquam ex Occidente lux!*

Of course some scholars derive the Mycenaean *tholoi* from the Minoan round tombs (Hood (1960: 166) discusses this question fully), although most of these seem never to have been vaulted. The Middle Minoan tomb at Kamilari (FIGURE 9), for example, does not seem to have had a corbelled vault. Whether or not these tombs, which began in the Early Minoan I period, might possibly have served as effective prototypes for the impressive Iberian tombs, the little graves of Syros and Kephala (FIGURE 2) are too small to carry much conviction, although they could conceivably have served as models for the Almerian round tombs. The Early Minoan round tombs are not likely to be much earlier than about 2400 BC (on a ^{14}C chronology; much earlier in calendar years).[15]

The radiocarbon dates for the Breton megaliths, including corbelled Passage Graves, provide something of a shock. Some are dated to about 3000 BC, notably Île Bono,

FIGURE 9. *Middle Minoan round tomb at Kamilari, Crete. (Photo A.C. Renfrew.)*

3245±300 BC (Gsy-64); Kerléven, 2785±125 BC (Gsy-111); Île Carn, 3030±75 BC (Coursaget *et al.* 1960: 147 n. 1). Here one must consider the validity of the French ^{14}C dates. That some material in megalithic tombs should be of much later date is not surprising, for it may well represent simply the continued use of a tomb of earlier construction, or the later construction of graves imitating earlier forms. This will be equally true in Iberia (*cf.* Anta dos Tassos, Portugal, 1370±200 BC (Sa-199) and the corbelled chamber of Praia das Maçâs, 1700±100 BC (17)). A ^{14}C date from a megalithic chamber should provide a *terminus ante quem* for its construction. But in the face of one or two extremely early dates in the 6th and 5th millennia BC (chiefly for cists within long mounds in Brittany) one is forced to fall back on the disappointing view that it is a *terminus post quem* for the death of the tree — the theory of bog oak. In such circumstances it might be argued that to accept any dates at all smacks of subjectivism. But it has to be emphasized that there now emerges a pattern for the Neolithic development of France and Britain (Clark & Godwin 1962: 10; Clark 1965: 58) as indeed for the spread of farming throughout Europe. Neolithic pottery may be dated from about 3200 BC in Britain and earlier in France, and these dates are in broad conformity with ^{14}C dates for similar finds in the Breton Passage Graves set around 3000 BC. The acceptance by L'Helgouach, Giot and other scholars of these ^{14}C dates seems reasonable.

There remains then only the general problem of the overall validity and accuracy of the radiocarbon method. All dates in the present article have been quoted in radiocarbon years, based on the 5568 half-life. It seems that any correction that has to be made to adjust these to calendar years will be on a world-wide basis, and will make them consistently several centuries older (Damon *et al.* 1966: 1055). This may affect synchronisms

---

15 A radiocarbon date of 2400 BC (on the 5568 half-life) may give a date in calendar years of around 3000 BC (*cf.* Stuiver & Suess 1966: 539).

with Egypt and the Near East, which have calendrical chronologies, but will apply equally to the Aegean as to the west European dates, on which the evidence here rests.[16] There seems little doubt that megaliths, including Passage Graves, were being constructed in northwest Europe by about 3000 BC (radiocarbon years) and hence perhaps by about 3700 BC (calendrical or true years).

The diffusionist is faced with a perplexing dilemma. The corbelled tombs of Spain resemble more closely the Breton Passage Graves than the Minoan round tombs. Either the Breton tombs derive from the Iberian ones, in which case the latter are 500 years earlier than the Aegean 'prototypes'; or the Iberian are later than the Breton, from which they might then be derived. In either instance the argument deriving them from the east collapses. At present the beginning of the corbelled tombs of Iberia might be set as reasonably at 3400 BC as at 2400 BC. Only further excavation can resolve between these widely differing alternatives.

There is something very disappointing about all this confusion. After more than half a century of research, we simply do not know what was the origin of the European megaliths, or more precisely whether they had a single origin. We do not know whether the Iberian megaliths began earlier than the Breton ones. To assert that they did is at present little more than to state a personal preference between inadequately substantiated theories.

Much the same is true of the Iberian Chalcolithic development. The belief that it was instituted by colonists from the East Mediterranean has become one of those foundations upon which much of European prehistory has been built. But this belief may be totally wrong, and certainly it seems exceedingly difficult to substantiate at present with detailed and independent documentation. The alternative upheld here, that the Chalcolithic of Iberia developed locally, with the local invention of metallurgy and a minimum of outside influence, must equally be ranked a possibility. I believe that this theory does less violence to the existing evidence than does the colonialist view.

But in any case, more evidence is required. The real need in Iberia today is for further careful settlement excavation of the kind so ably executed recently by Almagro, Arribas, do Paço, Sangmeister, da Cunha Serrão and other of their Iberian colleagues. Settlements rather than tombs should one day provide the sound relative chronology which is at present lacking. Until this is forthcoming, it is difficult to see how further analysis of the available evidence can resolve with certainty the various possible explanatory hypotheses. And until such evidence is forthcoming we shall not understand properly the development of the Early Bronze Age in Iberia or the possible role of Mediterranean influences in the prehistory of western Europe.

References
Actas e Memorias do I. Congresso Nacional de Arqueologia. 1959. Lisbon.
ALBUQUERQUE E CASTRO, L. DE. 1959. A arte megalithica e as escritas ideograficas, *Actas e Memorias . . .*
ALMAGRO, M. & A. ARRIBAS. 1963. *El poblado y la necrópolis megalítica de Los Millares.* Madrid.
ARNAL, J., H. MARTIN GRANEL & F. SANGMEISTER. 1964. Lébous, *Antiquity* 38: 191–200.
ARRIBAS, A. 1959. El urbanismo peninsular durante el bronce primitivo, *Zephyrus* 10: 81–128.
BECK, C.W., E. WILBUR, S. MERET, M. KOSOVE & K. KERMANI. 1965. The infrared spectra of amber and the identification of Baltic amber, *Archaeometry* 8: 96–109.

---

16   Many Aegean dates are given by Kohler & Ralph (1961: 357). The adjustment proposed by Stuiver & Suess will result in a 'long' Aegean chronology, and may bring Aegean dates into better adjustment with the calendrical dates of Egypt.

BLANCE, B. 1960. The origin and development of the Early Bronze Age in the Iberian peninsula. Unpublished Ph.D thesis, University of Edinburgh.
— 1961. Early Bronze Age Colonists in Iberia, *Antiquity* 35: 192–202.
BONSOR, E. 1899. Les colonies agricoles pré-Romaines, *Revue Archéologique* 35.
BRAY, W.M. 1964. Sardinian Beakers, *Proceedings of the Prehistoric Society* 30: 75–98.
— 1966. Neolithic painted ware in the Adriatic, *Antiquity* 40: 100–106.
BREUIL, H. 1933a. *Les peintures rupestres schématiques de la peninsule ibérique II*. Lagny.
— 1933b. *Les peintures rupestres schématiques de la peninsule ibérique III*. Lagny.
— 1935. *Les peintures rupestres schématiques de la peninsule ibérique IV*. Lagny.
CAMPS-FABRER, H. 1966. *Mature et art mobilier dans la préhistoire Nord-Africaine et Saharienne*.
CASKEY, J.L. 1964. Excavations in Keos 1963, *Hesperia* 23.
CASTILLO, A. DEL. 1947. In R.M. Pidal (ed.), *Historia de España*, 1. Madrid.
CHILDE, V.G. 1932. Chronology of prehistoric Europe: a review, *Antiquity* 6: 206–12.
— 1953. The Middle Bronze Age, *Archivo de Prehistoria Levantina* 4 Tom. 11: 167–85.
— 1956. *Piecing together the past*. London: Routledge & Kegan Paul.
— 1957. *Dawn of European civilisation* (6th edition). London: Routledge & Kegan Paul.
— 1958. *New light on the most ancient East*. London: Routledge & Kegan Paul.
CLARK, J.G.D. & H. GODWIN. 1962. The Neolithic in the Cambridgeshire Fens, *Antiquity* 36: 10–23.
CLARK, J.G.D. 1965. Radiocarbon dates and the expansion of farming culture from the Near East over Europe, *Proceedings of the Prehistoric Society* 31: 58–73.
COURSAGET, J., P.R. GIOT & J. LE RUN. 1960. C-14 Neolithic dates from France, *Antiquity* 34: 147–8.
DA CUNHA SERRÃO, E. 1959. Ceramica com ornatos a cores de Lapa do Fumo, *Actas e Memorias*.
DAMON, P.F., A. LONG & D.C. GREY. 1966. Fluctuations of atmospheric C14 during the last six millennia, *Journal of Geophysical Research* 71.
DANIEL, G.E. 1941. The dual nature of the megalithic colonisation of prehistoric Europe, *Proceedings of the Prehistoric Society* 7: 1–49.
— 1966. Carbon 14 dates and the chronology of European megaliths, *Actes du VIIme Congrès International des Sciences Préhistoriques et Protohistoriques*: 1–49.
DO PAÇO, A. 1955. Castro de Vila Nova San Pedro VII, Consideraçôes sobre o problema de metalurgia, *Zephyrus* 6: 27–40.
DO PAÇO, A. & M.L. COSTA ARTHUR. 1952. Castro de Vila San Pedro, *Zephyrus* 3: 31–40.
DO PAÇO, A. & E. SANGMEISTER. 1956. Vila Nova de Sao Pedro, eine befestigte Siedlung der Kupferzeit in Portugal, *Germania* 34: 211–30.
ELLIOT SMITH, G. 1930. *Human history*. London: J. Cape.
EVANS, J.D. 1956. Two phases of prehistoric settlement in the west Mediterranean, *Institute of Archaeology Annual Report* 13.
FORDE-JOHNSTONE, J.L. 1959. *Neolithic Cultures of North Africa*.
GIMENEZ REYNA, S. 1946. Necropolis de Alcaide, *Informes y Memorias* 12: 49–52.
GUERREVO, M.E. 1945. Excavationes de Asta Regia, *Acta Arqueologica Hispanica* 3.
HENSHALL, A.S. 1963. *The chambered tombs of Scotland*, I. Edinburgh: Edinburgh University Press.
HOOD, M.S.F. 1960. Tholos tombs of the Aegean, *Antiquity* 34: 166–76.
JUNGHANS, S., M. SCHRÖDER & E. SANGMEISTER. 1960. *Metallanalysen kupferzeitliche und frühbronzezeitliche Bodenfunde aus Europa*. Berlin: Gebr. Mann.
KOHLER, E.L. & F.K. RALPH. 1961. C-14 dates for sites in the Mediterranean area, *American Journal of Archaeology* 61: 357–68.
L'HELGOUACH, J. 1965. *Les sépultures mégalithiques en Armorique*. Rennes: Université de Rennes.
LEISNER, G. & V. LEISNER. 1943. *Die Megalithgräber der iberischen Halbinsel, Der Süden*. Berlin: de Gruyter. Römisch-Germanische Forschungen 17.
LEISNER, V., A. DO PAÇO, & L. RIBEIRO. 1963. *Grutas Artificialis de São Pedro do Estoril*.
LEISNER, V. & O. DO VEIGA FERREIRA. 1963. In *Revista de Guimaraes* 63.
LEISNER, V. & G. LEISNER. 1959. *Die Megalithgräber der iberischen Halbinsel, Der Westen*. Berlin: Walter de Gruyter.
MCBURNEY, C.B.M. 1960. *The Stone Age of North Africa*. Harmondsworth: Penguin.
PIGGOTT, S. 1953. The tholos tombs of Iberia, *Antiquity* 27: 137–43.
— 1954. *Neolithic cultures of the British Isles*. Cambridge: Cambridge University Press.
— 1959. *Approach to archaeology*. Cambridge (MA): Harvard University Press.
RENFREW, A.C. 1965. The Neolithic and Early Bronze Age Cultures of the Cyclades and their external relations. Unpublished Ph.D thesis, University of Cambridge.
— 1967. Cycladic metallurgy and the Aegean Early Bronze Age, *American Journal of Archaeology* 71: 1–20.
ROWE, J.H. 1966. Diffusion in archaeology, *American Antiquity* 21: 334–7.
SIRET, L. 1913. *Questions de chronologie et d'Ethnographie Ibériques*, I. Paris: P. Geuthner.
SMITH, M.A. 1953. Iberian Beakers, *Proceedings of the Prehistoric Society* 19: 95–107.
STUIVER, M. & H.F. SUESS. 1966. On the relationship between radiocarbon dates and true sample dates, *Radiocarbon* 8: 534–40.
TARRADELL MATEU, M. 1955. Die Ausgrabung von der Gar Cahal, Schwarze Hohle, in Spanish Marokko, *Germania* 23: 13–23.
TAYLOUR, W.D. 1958. *Mycenaean pottery in Italy*. Cambridge: Cambridge University Press.
VAUFREY, R. 1955. *Préhistoire de l'Afrique I: Le Maghreb*. Paris: Masson.

Mortuary houses and funeral rites in Denmark
by POUL KJÆRUM
ANTIQUITY 41 (163), 1967

IN 1954 A STONE and timber-built mortuary house belonging to the Funnel-Beaker (TRB) culture was excavated at Tustrup, in the county of Randers in Eastern Jutland (Kjærum 1955: 7). At that time such structures were unknown in the area of the Funnel-Beaker culture, but, five years later, a very similar mortuary house was found at Ferslev, just south of the Limfjord, in the neighbouring county of Aalborg (Marseen 1960: 36). From the archaeological evidence Tustrup dates from the very beginning of the period when Passage Graves *(Jættestuer)* were being built in Denmark. The structure and the ritual carried out in both the mortuary houses, as it could be deduced from the content and disposition of the grave goods, adds very considerably to our knowledge of the burial practices of the megalith builders of Denmark. Quite apart from this, the discoveries at Tustrup and Ferslev provide us with good fixed points in the relative and absolute chronology of the Funnel-Beaker culture since each house contained a large number of highly ornamented pots as well as charcoal from the walls and roofs of the houses, which could be dated by the ^{14}C method.

The Tustrup house was sited in the middle of a megalithic cemetery consisting of three chamber tombs: (a) a hexagonal burial chamber in a round mound with the entrance to the southeast, (b) a small Passage Grave with a short passage, in plan like the letter *q*, and (c) a Passage Grave with a chamber 10 m long with a side chamber off the back wall at the southwest corner (Kjærum 1957: 9). These three megalithic tombs were set in a semicircle with a radius of 50 m, centred on the mortuary house (FIGURE 1). All date from the period Ib of the Danish Middle Neolithic (Berg 1951; summary of the MN TRB periods in Bagge-Kaelas 1950/1952).

The mortuary house

The Tustrup mortuary house was constructed of a horseshoe-shaped, stone-built wall defining a nearly square room 5 m by 5·5 m opening to the northeast (FIGURE 2). The wall was 0·5 to 1·5 m thick and faced on the outside with stone slabs about one metre high, some of which had been dressed. Inside, the rear wall was faced with orthostats 1·6 m high, while the side walls were boarded with split oak trunks shaped like the segments of circles, the bark still preserved on the outside. These oaken planks were set up, as in a palisade, side by side in continuous foundation trenches packed with stones. The south wall was straight and unbroken for its full length, but the northern wall was broken by a niche 2 m wide and 0·8 m deep, lined by wattle. This niche contained a stone-filled pit about 0·8 m in depth.

In the opening of the horseshoe, to the northeast, there were no traces of a wall, but precisely in the middle there was a megalithic orthostat, carefully dressed and parallel-sided. As the upper part of this stone had been split and removed before the excavation, its original height is not known, but it might have been considerable as its socket had been dug to a depth of half a metre into the ground and was packed with stones. It seems reasonable to suppose that it was at least as high as the orthostats in the rear wall, *viz.* 1·6 m.

FIGURE 1. *The megalithic cemetery at Tustrup after restoration, viewed from the northwest. Foreground: freestanding Passage Grave chamber. Middle distance, left: mortuary house; right: Passage Grave covered by barrow. Background: round mound with hexagonal chamber. (Air photograph of the Tustrup complex taken 1966 by Dr St Joseph.)*

FIGURE 2. *The mortuary house at Tustrup after excavation (from the west). Foundation trenches for the timbers of the inner wall indicated by stones. Stones in the outer facing have been re-erected.*

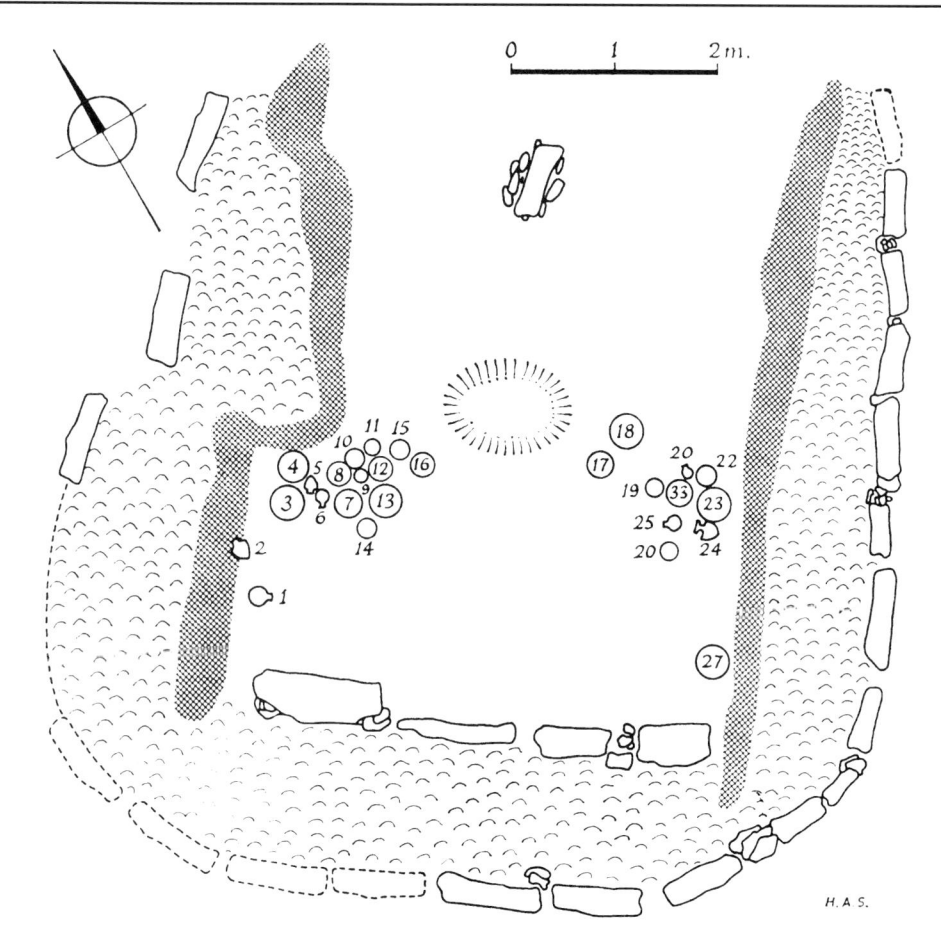

FIGURE 3. *Ground plan of the Tustrup house with the pottery vessels in their original position.*

The exact height of the side walls is of course unknown, but was at least over 1·5 m and possibly over 2 m. The house had been burnt and the walling posts were, when excavated, standing as charred stumps 20 cm high in the foundation trenches. In front of them and at right-angles to the line of the side walls were some beams laid side by side and parallel to each other, with the bark side upwards. These were preserved to a length of up to 1·5 m and to a distance of 2 m from the foundation trenches — which perhaps indicates the minimum height of the wall-boarding.

An oval pit was found exactly in the centre of the house. It was 1·2 m long, 0·8 m wide, and 0·6 m deep and, like the foundation trenches for the walls, was filled with sand — still loose when the house was destroyed.

Though no traces of a post were found in it, and its dimensions and shape are rather untypical for a post-hole, it seems possible that it did carry a central post supporting the roof. However this may be, the shape of the roof is unknown, but it does seem to have been covered with bark and turves. Under the charred wall beams were found small pieces of birch bark which, to quote our xylotomist, 'each consist of many layers pressed together while still in a plastic condition'. We have no doubt but that these 'layers' represent a roof of grass turves laid on sheets of birch bark, as is used in Scandinavia up to the present day.

A house constructed like the Tustrup mortuary house seems as though it were built for eternity: in fact it seems to have been burnt down soon after it was built. The oak trunks and even the willow branches in the wattle wall seem to have been still fresh when the house was burnt down; and the filling in the foundation trenches was still soft, if we may judge from the position of the bases of the wallposts — most of which had been thrown out of their original position by the destruction of the house.

An examination of the finds supports this view. Twenty-eight pots and spoons were found in two small groups in the southeast and southwest part of the house, and near the back wall. All the pots were broken, but the broken sherds were lying so close together that the only possible interpretation is that the intact pots were standing in two groups when the house collapsed (FIGURE 3).

All the pots were highly ornamented and comprised 10 pedestalled-bowls (8 of which were accompanied by a spoon), 6 Funnel-Beakers (one with a lid), 3 shouldered bowls, and one hanging-bowl. This is a typical inventory of period Ib of the Danish Middle Neolithic — the so-called *Klintebakken* stage (FIGURES 4 & 5) (Berg 1951; Bagge-Kaelas 1950/1952).

The ^{14}C date from the bark of the wallposts is 2470±80 BC (K718+K727B) (Mathiassen 1939; Bagge-Kaelas 1950/1952), and this is very important since the Tustrup find is hitherto the largest closed find of pottery from this short period and also has a very special relation to the megalithic graves, both because of the position of the mortuary house in the centre of a cemetery of megalithic tombs, and the fact that it was a mortuary house associated with megalithic tombs, and the presence of the pots — pedestalled-bowls and spoons — more often found in megalithic tombs than in settlements. Last, but not least, the pottery found at Tustrup is the earliest and most common type found in the earliest Danish and South Swedish Passage Graves, and seems to be contemporary with the introduction of this type of tomb into Jutland and apparently into Scandinavia as a whole. In Jutland the types of pottery found in the Tustrup house are so common in the Passage Graves of the area that one asks oneself if Passage Graves went on being built much later than this.

The Tustrup megalithic tombs

Before we discuss these matters of interpretation let us look at the results of excavating the megaliths around the Tustrup house as well as at some features from the other mortuary house from Ferslev. As we have already said, the finds from all the three megalithic tombs at Tustrup belonged to the same short period when the mortuary house was used — indeed some of the pots from the tombs are identical with those from the mortuary house, and are surely products of the same master-potter. And all this is in spite of the fact that the megalithic tombs belong to very different places in the traditional scheme of the evolution of megaliths. The finds made in the excavations, except for a few sherds from the chamber of the Passage Grave, were all found on both sides of the passage, in front of the façade of the Passage Grave and beside the kerbstones of the dolmens. Altogether about a hundred pots were found (50 in the Passage Grave, and 25 each in the dolmens). The find spots indicate that nearly all the pots had originally been deposited in the barrows, behind or upon the kerbstones on both sides of the chamber entrances. Only a few examples of the grave goods seem to have been deposited in the chamber and then cleared out of it. Deposits of this kind are, of course, typical of Danish and South Swedish Passage Graves, and although still only a few dolmen-barrows have been excavated thoroughly, these few seem to show that this special ritual had been followed in this type of tomb in the Middle Neolithic.

FIGURE 4. *Funnel beakers, one with lid found beside it. The ornament has been executed in incised and notch-stamped technique.*

FIGURE 5. *Four of the ten pedestalled-bowls and pottery spoons found in association with them — they would seem to have been made in pairs.*

The examination of the Tustrup cemetery seems to show that the same community erected different kinds of dolmens and Passage Graves at the same time, and carried out the same rituals in the various types of tomb.

When the Tustrup mortuary house was excavated it was, as we have said, the first structure of this type belonging to the Funnel-Beaker culture ever unearthed. When it was first discussed it seemed to me to be a ritual structure used in relation to the megalithic tombs in the cemetery around it — or possibly to the presumed grave in the pit under the northwest wall — a pit however in which nothing was found (neither remains of a skeleton nor any grave goods) and was therefore not with certainty a grave.

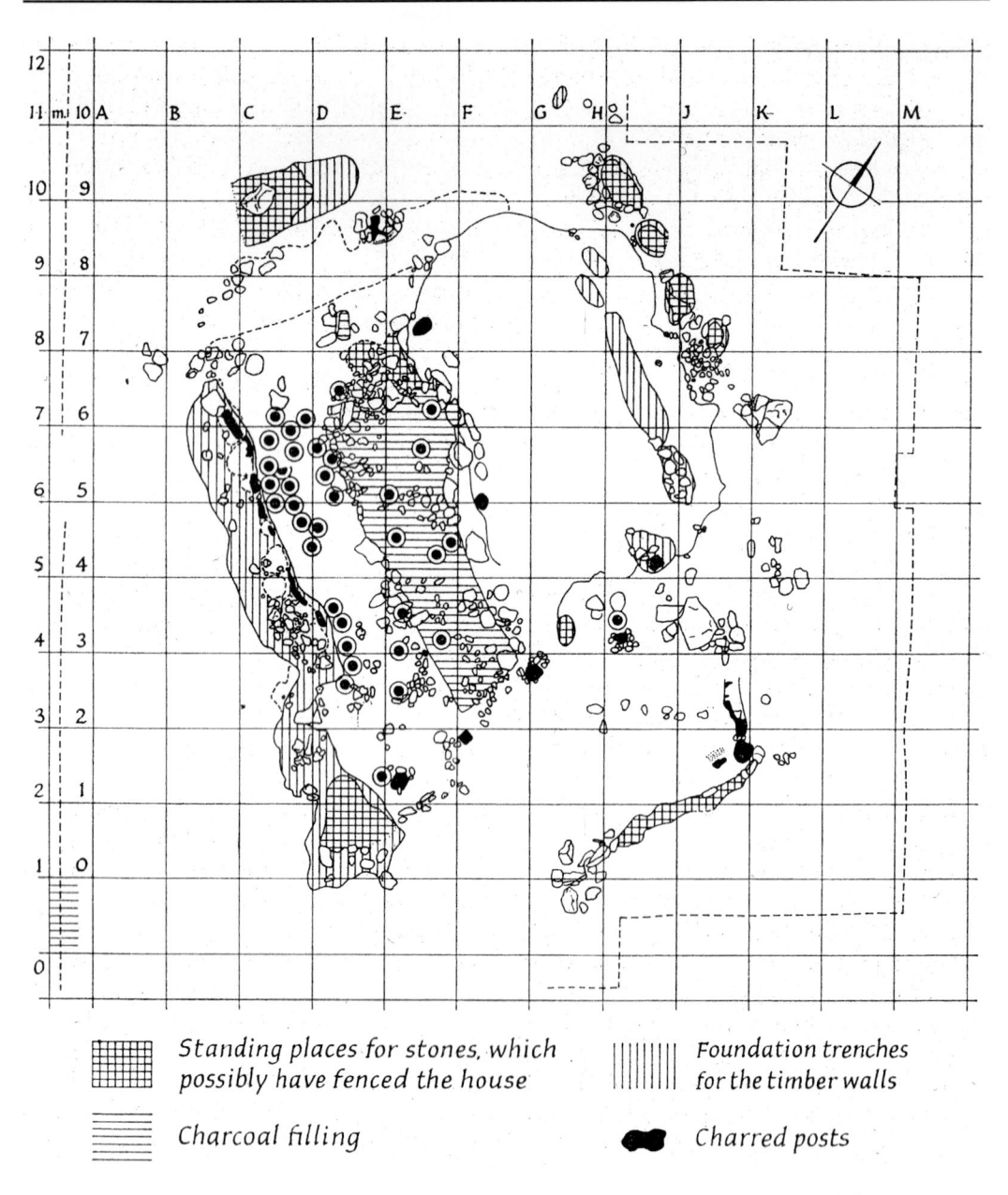

| Standing places for stones, which possibly have fenced the house | Foundation trenches for the timber walls |

| Charcoal filling | Charred posts |

FIGURE 6. *Ground plan of the Ferslev mortuary house: rings mark the positions of the pottery vessels.*

It now appears that the Ferslev house provides the solution to the Tustrup problem: whether the Tustrup house is
a   a mortuary house, i.e. a structure erected for ritual purposes connected with burial, or
b   a grave, or
c   both a grave and also an area for ritual and ceremony.

FIGURE 7. *Typical bowl from the Ferslev house with ornament in a notch-stamped technique.*

The Ferslev house
The ground plan and the size of the Ferslev house are about the same as the Tustrup house (FIGURE 6). It is nearly a square, 5x6 m with an inner wall lining of lime-wood *(tilia)* in the side walls built as palisades, while the rear wall was of bole construction, as indicated by grooved vertical posts, in which horizontal beams have been slotted. Along the northern and eastern walls were found vertical stone slabs, whereas none was found along the southern wall, though the area was specially examined with this in mind. These stones however do not seem to be an outer wall-facing, as at Tustrup; most probably they are no more than a boundary.

The roof of the Ferslev house seems to have been thatched, as a row of three posts was found along the centre-line of the house: one was standing just in front of the back wall, one was in the centre, and one exactly between the two outermost posts in the opening to the northwest.

The southwest part of this house had a rectangular setting of slabs 4x1 m but widening to the northwest end to 1·5 m. The slabs along the sides were about 0·25 m high, and at the northwest end about 1 m high, and the stone in the southeast, to judge from its socket, would have been of the same dimensions.

The interior of this stone setting was paved with burnt and crushed flint mixed with pieces of charcoal. In it were standing 7 nearly intact pots, and in the narrow passage between the stone setting and the southwest wall were 28 pots (FIGURE 6). One other pot was found by a post in the back wall: this may well be the only surviving member of a group spoiled by later disturbances, as sherds of at least 10 more pots were found in the secondary filling in a pit dug in the northeast half of the house.

Besides these 37 intact pots and the sherds of similar ornamented pots (FIGURE 7), which all belong to Period III of the Danish Middle Neolithic, there were sherds of about 25 pots ornamented in an earlier style trodden down in the floor and in the area just in front of the open end of the house. They belong to period II of the Danish Middle Neolithic. The radiocarbon determination, done in Copenhagen, is (K717) 2480±120 BC on limewood *(tilia)*.

Conclusions
When we consider the archaeological interpretation of the Tustrup and Ferslev houses, we see that their construction is the same, their inventory the same, as was their destruction — they were both burnt. There were differences. The Ferslev house had a stone-framed cist filled with crushed, burnt flint mixed with charcoal, whereas the Tustrup house had a stone-filled pit sunk under a niche in the wall. The Tustrup house seems to have been burnt soon after its erection, having served only one ceremony, whereas Ferslev had been standing for some time and had been re-used.

To explain these features we have to turn to the Passage Graves, in the floors of which are often found one or more sunken cists lined with stone slabs. The floors of chamber and cist are usually covered with a layer of burnt and crushed flint. There can be little doubt that these cists contained burials and presumably primary burials, but when found nowadays in burial chambers they are usually empty. In a few cases personal ornaments have been found in them: at Tustrup an amber spacer had escaped the clearing of the chamber.

By analogy with the cists in Passage Graves the cist in the Ferslev house is most probably a burial cist and the building a mortuary house. The Tustrup house has to be reinterpreted in the same way. Most probably both houses are grave houses — the actual graves the cist under the floor and the pit under the niche.

When the writer first published an account of the excavation of the Tustrup house he did not come to this conclusion as it seemed peculiar that if the burial was the primary reason for the building of a rather elaborate structure, it should have no grave goods, and be cut off from the interior of the house by a wall. And then the composition, quantity and deposition of the finds were different from the usual TRB graves. It is not usual to find large amounts of pottery in dolmens, Passage Graves or simple pit graves, while tools, amber ornaments and weapons are common. So the interpretation, at that time, of the house as a grave house seemed unconvincing.

When we turn again to the megalithic chambers we find complex problems of interpretation, particularly of the ritual areas. In the megalithic tombs of Western Europe the ritual areas seem to be structurally well-defined — such as forecourts. Forecourts are rare in Scandinavian megaliths, and here the rituals seem to have been performed in front of the façade of the barrow near the entrance to the chamber. It was here that mass offerings were placed. In contrast to the Dutch and Oldenburg megalithic chambers which are often packed full with pottery, only a few pots seem to have been deposited with each burial in Scandinavian megalithic tombs. But large quantities of pottery are found outside, alongside and upon the kerbstones or façade on both sides of the entrances, as was mentioned above for the Tustrup graves. In one site in Scania more than 50,000 sherds of pottery were found, representing the remains of more than a thousand pots (Forssander 1935: 16). In Jutland usually anything from 50 to 100 pots are found during the excavation of a megalithic tomb.

The meaning of these finds has been under discussion since the beginning of this century (Nordman 1917: 304; 1935: 29; Thorvildsen 1946: 73, with bibliography). It has been argued that they were either grave goods cleared out of the chamber to make room for fresh burials, or that they were offerings made at the tomb. The excavation of the

Passage Grave of Grønhøj near Horsens demonstrated that the bulk of the pots had been standing intact in front of and behind the kerbstones where they were found, before the tomb fell into ruin (Thorvildsen 1946). Later excavations have further confirmed this evidence, and in a still unpublished excavation it was possible to separate two layers in front of the kerbstones.[1] The upper layer contained material cleared out of the chamber — typical grave goods such as axes, arrowheads, amber beads and scattered sherds of a few pots. In the lower layer the sherds were lying in rows of small heaps concentrated under the topmost point of the sloping kerbstones, and immediately in front of the slabs originally set on top of the kerbstones, forming a platform all round the barrow. According to this evidence it seems beyond all reasonable doubt that the vessels used at the tomb were placed on this platform, and that when the barrow became ruined they fell down and were covered with stones, sand and broken flint from the barrow. Then, later, the burial chambers were re-used by intruders (in this case the Battle-Axe people), who cleared the grave of its primary burials. A detailed examination now shows that the pottery from deposits outside the Passage Graves is often more or less homogeneous: this is true at least for groups of pots, and by detailed excavation it has been shown that such homogeneous groups occur in restricted areas (Rosenberg 1933: 1 and Jordhøj, Mariager). The ritual of the builders of these megalithic Passage Graves would therefore seem to have involved offerings of large quantities of pots, and, or so it seems, pots of certain special types. Pedestalled-bowls, for example, are the most common type of vessel from the Passage Graves of Jutland, while, compared with other types, these are rare in the corresponding settlements.

Thus the evidence of these finds coincides in every respect with the evidence from Tustrup and Ferslev, and reciprocally they explain each other. Both houses seem to be grave houses, as burials certainly took place in them. But at the same time they were mortuary houses — consecrated areas corresponding to the role of the forecourts of the megalithic graves in Western Europe and façades of the Passage Graves in Scandinavia, since the funeral ceremonies also took place in them. In Tustrup only one ceremony took place: in Ferslev the house was standing for some considerable time, and here exactly the same thing happened as happened in the Passage Graves: the primary deposits and probably the primary burial as well were removed to make room for another burial and for the performance of new ceremonies and the depositing of fresh offerings — after which the house was burnt down.

We know of no exact parallels to the Tustrup–Ferslev structures in the TRB culture or among the megalithic groups of Western Europe, but in both areas there occur related mortuary and grave houses. From Kujawia in Poland there are two Kujawian long barrows with wooden buildings at the broad end of the long barrows, both of which date from late in the Early Neolithic TRB culture (Chmielewski 1952). Though nothing was found inside the houses their position indicates their ritual use. In the Saale area there are structures which can be interpreted as collective grave houses, or even burial chambers belonging to the Walternienburg–Bernburg culture, contemporary with Tustrup and Ferslev, and these too had been burnt down (Fischer 1956: 99, plate 25). Finally in the Western Megalithic area wooden-built grave or mortuary houses burnt down and covered by long barrows are well known (Piggott 1954: 50; 1967). It would seem then that the grave house/mortuary house idea is common to the megalithic builders, at least in the West, in Scandinavia and in Northern Europe.

---

1 Jordhøj by Mariager, Co. Randers, excavated by the author, 1963–4.

The evidence from Tustrup and Ferslev explains for us an important group of finds associated with megalithic graves, and quite apart from the ^{14}C dates — the first dating of the Middle Neolithic Funnel-Beaker culture from Scandinavia — shows the contemporaneity of Passage Graves in Scandinavia, in the continental Funnel Beaker area, and in the Western Megalithic area. The first Danish Passage Graves are of the same date or only a little later than the Dutch *hunebedden* — the Odoorn tomb, a TRB flat grave containing Funnel-Beakers, overlain by a Hunebed, was dated to 2640±80 BC (van der Waals 1964: 17, 52; van Giffen 1961: 1, 39), and the related graves in Western Germany; and are partly later, partly contemporary with the Breton and British megalithic structures (Giot 1963: 22).

References

BAGGE-KAELAS, L. 1950/1952. *Die Funde aus Dolmen und Ganggräbern in Schonen, Schweden I–II*. Stockholm.
BERG, H. 1951. Klintehakken, *Maddelelser fra Langelands Museum*. Rudkøbing.
CHMIELEWSKI, W. 1952. Zagadnienie Grobowcow Kujawskich, *Bibliotheka Muzeum Archeologicznego W Lodzie* 2. With French summary.
FISCHER, U. 1956. *Die Gräber der Steinzeit im Saalegebiet*. Berlin. Vorgeschichtliche Forschungen begrundet von Max Ebert 15.
FORSSANDER, J.E. 1935. *Skånsk megalitkeramik och kontinenraleuropeisk stenålder*. Lund. Meddelanden fran Lunds universitets historiska museum.
GIOT, P.-R. 1963. Les civilisations atlantiques du néolithique à l'âge du fer, *Travaux du Laboratoire d'Anthropologie Préhistorique de la Faculté des Sciences de Rennes*: 22.
KJÆRUM,P. 1955. Tempelhus fra stenalder, *Kuml* (1955): 7–35.
    1957. Storstensgrave ved Tustrup, *Kuml* (1957): 9–23.
MARSEEN, O. 1960. Ferslev-huset; en kultbygning fra Jaettestuetid, *Kuml* (1960): 36–55.
MATHIASSEN, T. 1939. Bundsø, *Arbøger for nordisk Oldkyndighed og Historie*.
NORDMAN, C.A. 1918. Studier öfver ganggriftkulturen i Danmark, *Arbøger*: 1–137.
    1935. The Megalithic Culture of Northern Europe, *Finska Fornm. Tidsskr.* (1935).
PIGGOTT, S. 1954. *Neolithic cultures of the British Isles*. Cambridge: Cambridge University Press.
    1967. 'Unchambered' long barrows in Neolithic Britain, *Palaeohistoria* 12 (1966): 381–94.
ROSENBERG, G. 1933. To Jættestuer, *Fra Nationalmuseets Arbejdsmark*.
THORVILDSEN, K. 1946. Grønhoj, *Arbøger*.
VAN DER WAALS, J.D. 1964. *Prehistoric disc wheels in the Netherlands*. Groningen: J.B. Wolters.
VAN GIFFEN, A.E. 1961. Een Vlakgraf van de Trechterbekerkultuur gesneden door een Standkuil van Hunebed D 32 te Odoorn, *Helinium* 1: 39–43.

The megalithic tomb of La Chaussée-Tirancourt
by CLAUDE MASSET
ANTIQUITY 46 (184), 1972

THE LONG MEGALITHIC TOMB of La Chaussée-Tirancourt is located 15 km west of Amiens (Somme). It was discovered in 1967 by deep ploughing. Since this date, excavations have been conducted each year. The definitive report on the site will be published in *Gallia Préhistoire* in due course. This monument, built of sandstone orthostats, is wholly subterranean: the floor is 1·70 m below present ground level. Despite the absence of capstones, it belongs to the well-known type of Seine–Oise–Marne *allées couvertes*. This type is well represented around Paris, but until the discovery of this site was unknown in Picardy. The artifacts discovered in the antechamber are characteristic of the SOM culture — perforated antler sleeves, coarse pottery, and an axe-amulet in green stone. The burial chamber itself yielded less characteristic grave-goods, of which the most interesting are two small copper beads. Radiocarbon dates are available because of violent fires at about the end of the period of use of the tomb. These will all be published in detail in due course, but it can be said here that these dates (uncalibrated) fall between 1750 and 1400 BC. Before these fires, the tomb seems to have been used over a very long period of time: bones, broken by the weight of prehistoric grave-diggers, already show the characteristic fractures of dried-out bone. Palynological studies have revealed changes in the surrounding vegetation from one burial layer to another. It seems likely, therefore, that the construction of this tomb can be placed at the beginning of the 2nd millennium BC.

At the very bottom of the monument, two transverse alignments of small sandstone slabs define three quadrangular compartments of different sizes. The smallest, located at the end of the burial chamber, was completely empty. In the second, seven skulls were found, and three whole skeletons were identifiable. One of these, well apart from the others, was isolated by an alignment of five small sandstone blocks. In the third compartment, in an excavated area equal in size to the second, 20, as compared with the 7, skulls were found — a statistical significance of 0·02. The position of the disordered bones of one individual might lead one to think that the corpse had been buried in a sitting position, leaning against a partition wall of some perishable material and that, eventually, after the flesh was gone, the bones had been pushed up against this partition in such a way as to take up as little space as possible (Ambroise & Perlès 1972). This partition wall left other signs of its existence: traces were picked up, parallel with the axis of the grave, from square D3, across square E4, until it disappears into the part of the tomb not yet dug.

Unfortunately the structure of Level V, the oldest in the grave, which we have just been describing, has been more or less obliterated by considerable changes as a result of the deposition of Level IV. Most of the bones of Level V were heaped together along the axis of the monument, then covered with a mixture of limon and fragments of chalk to a depth of 20 cm. Level IV consists of a filling of 6 to 8 tons of sediment. This was perhaps the reason why the prehistoric users of the tomb made a second entrance, discovered

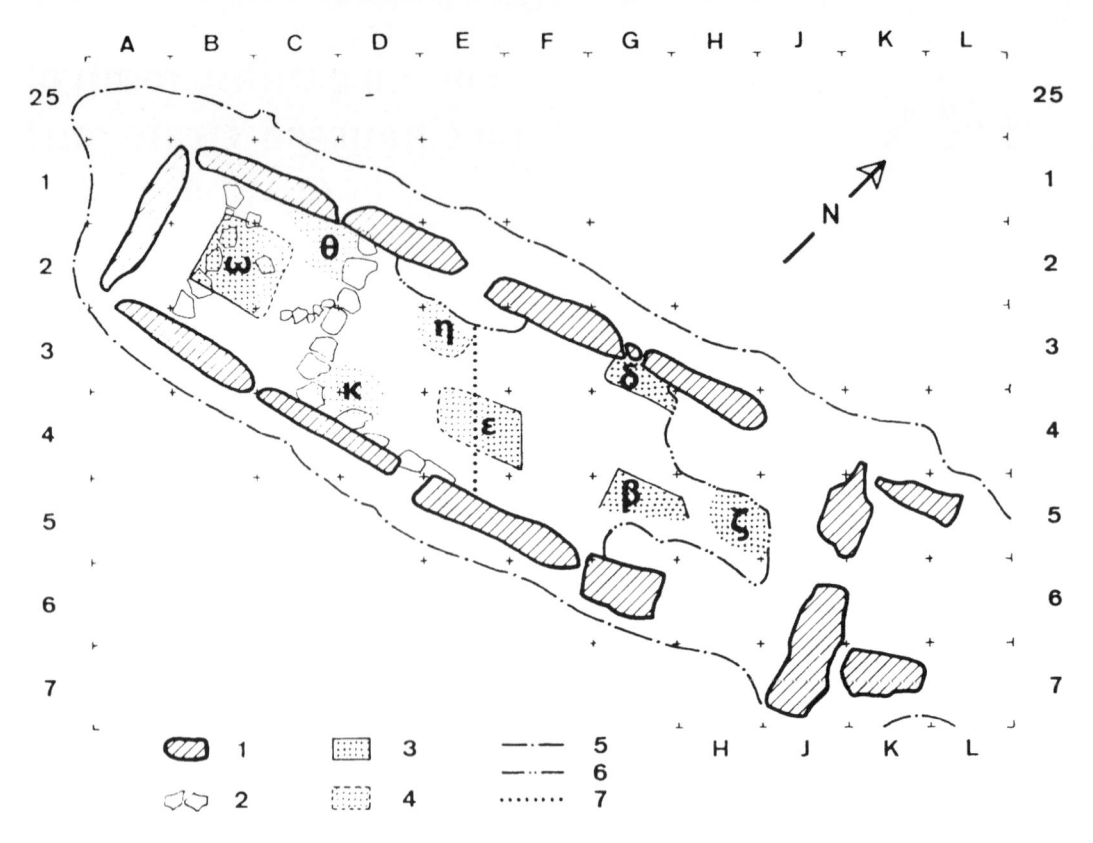

FIGURE 1. *Plan of the tomb of La Chaussée-Tirancourt:* 1 *orthostats;* 2 *sandstone slabs;* 3 *boxes observed during excavation (Level III);* 4 *boxes observed by survey and photography (C, D, E squares could be less precisely studied owing to previous excavations);* 5 *limit of the chalcolithic disturbance;* 6 *limits of the most deeply disturbed areas;* 7 *actual limits of the excavations: the front parts of Levels IV and V are not yet dug.*

only this season (1972), in square H7. An inclined plane made of chalk blocks, only very slightly crushed, sloped down as far as square J5, partially obliterating the principal entrance between squares J6 and K6.

On the top of Level IV were laid new burials, forming Level III which is much thicker than Level IV, and has complicated sub-divisions. To simplify these, three main periods can be distinguished. In the first, the bodies were laid neatly side by side along the length of the tomb, their legs drawn up and the knees all facing the same way — seen from the main entrance they all face to the right. Further modification took place, similar, though somewhat less radical, to that in Level IV: this resulted in a complete change in the internal organization of the tomb. Boxes, or cists, in which primary inhumations were made, now make their appearance. Between these boxes there are few bones and always disconnected ones. This system of boxes, or cists, was, in turn, partly obliterated by fresh modifications, then replaced by another system of boxes about which we know a great deal more — it is these boxes that are drawn in with dotted outlines on the plan (FIGURE 1). In this set of boxes the bones are usually in an undisturbed condition, and in a very few examples complete skeletons are found. For the greater part, however, the skeletons have been disturbed in varying degrees *post mortem:* long bones frequently

FIGURE 2 (right). *Skeleton at bottom of box β, disturbed after death. The pelvis and legs are missing as are the hands and one ulna. (Photo C. Masset.)*

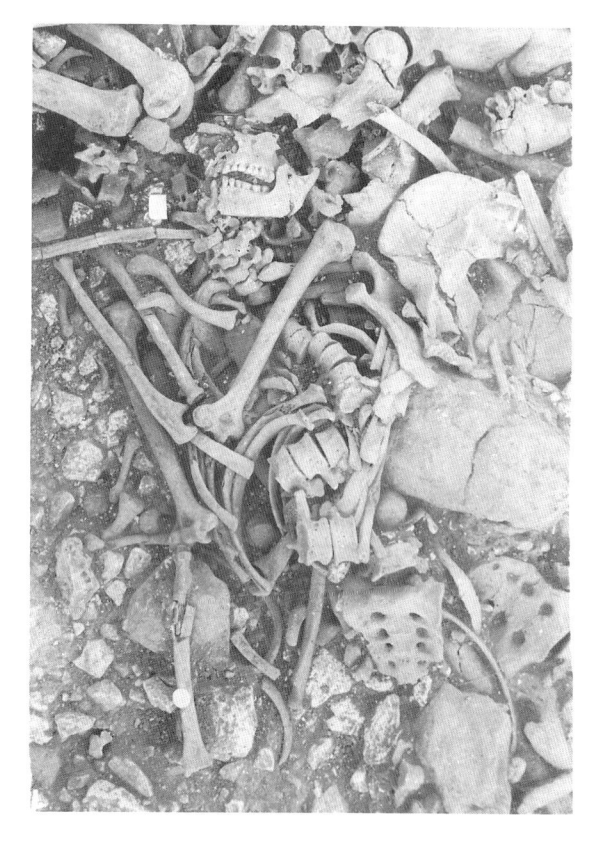

FIGURE 3 (below). *Edge of a box, in square B1, emphasized by long bones sloping outwards and by two skulls separated from their bodies and a lump of sandstone. Inside the box (left) the sediment is lighter in colour and is sticking to the bones which are in their anatomical position; orthostat A1 is in the background. (Photo C. Masset.)*

missing (FIGURE 2), and sometimes the skull. Frequently the sediment in the boxes is white, calcited, and full of very small bone splinters. Outside the boxes, the sediment is silty and the bones are never in their normal anatomical relationship: they are mainly represented by long bones and skulls. The latter usually assembled in groups of 20 to 30 along the orthostats and all round the box at the end of the tomb (ω). And so it is clear that, during the period represented by Level III, the tomb had in fact become a cemetery of seven or eight smaller collective tombs, each of them independent and separated from the others by areas containing later and secondary inhumations. Apparently the bones of these secondary burials come from the overspill of the bones in the boxes or perhaps from a deliberate tidying-up of the boxes.

The boxes show important differences: δ contained mostly children's bones, although these are rare at La Chaussée-Tirancourt: ω had a stratification of brown and white sediment; ζ was the only box not to have this white sediment, and, moreover, it was divided into two levels, separated by a bed of chalk fragments. This peculiarity is found only in ζ and β. The limits of the boxes, accentuated by long bones sloping outwards (FIGURE 3), are demarcated at times by small heaps of chalk fragments (ε), or, exceptionally, by a trench which cuts through some of the bones, leaving the rest in correct anatomical position (δ).

This discovery of boxes in an SOM collective tomb recalls older observations, of which Leuvrigny (1861) is the most interesting (Bailloud 1964: 270). At this site alignments of small stones delimited irregular compartments but did not go through to the bottom of the layer of human bones.

In some places, Level III is subdivided by very compact masses of chalk fragments, especially in the first half of the monument. The most important of these sterile sub-layers is Level III-2 which covered almost 4 sq. m in the areas G and F. Underneath the chalk filling, in an area of 2·5 sq. m by approximately 3 cm deep, was an air-pocket, and we supposed that the disappearance of some perishable material, which covered the bones before the chalk was laid, would account for this. As the chalk is extremely compact, it had probably quite often supported the weight of the prehistoric grave-diggers!

At Level III-3, the tomb is divided into two parts by a transverse trench which joins orthostats E5 and F3, between boxes ε and β. It is 10 to 15 cm deep and 50 cm wide and its sides are emphasized by bones lying obliquely. At both ends, near the orthostats, nearly 50 skulls were piled up in the trench. Beyond the limits of the trench and in the part of the tomb furthest away from the entrance, we found a surface where most of the bones were crushed: this could be an area where the grave-diggers had moved about a great deal.

Level III-1 corresponds to the top of the boxes, and note that it was called II-2 in an earlier publication (Masset 1971). Bones in anatomical position become rare in this level, and the uppermost part of a box is always occupied by groups of disordered bones which lay on a higher level than the disordered bones found between the boxes. These disturbed bones are more or less on the same level in all the boxes and could thus perhaps correspond to a deliberate removal of bones, similar to that observed in Level V. Here too, this re-arrangement would have preceded the deposit of a layer of silt mixed up with fragments of chalk which is Level II, but this level is found only in some areas.

The upper deposits of the tomb have suffered during the formation of Level I which is essentially composed of blackish silt mixed with wood charcoal, burnt earth, bones burnt after having been dried, and small slabs of sandstone split by fire. The top of the orthostats show very characteristic large burn marks. Two of the orthostats have been broken and large fragments removed: traces of them were clearly seen in the sediment together with small flakes of sandstone adhering to the orthostats. The Carbon 14 dates mentioned above come from this level, which corresponds not to one attempted single destruction, but to a series of limited attempts at destruction over a considerable period of time.

We have found, to date, that more than 300 people were buried in the megalithic tomb of La Chaussée-Tirancourt and this is a most impressive number, even for an *allée couverte*. It considerably exceeds the numbers of dead found in the rock-cut tombs in Champagne where the maximum number of corpses was a few dozen. This means that these tombs corresponded to one of our compartments in Level V, or to one of the boxes in Level III. The funerary rite throughout was inhumation, and the bodies were first laid to rest in this tomb. We have found no convincing evidence supporting any other kind of burial custom. Most of the skeletons have been greatly disturbed *post-mortem,* and some have even been moved away by (presumably) Chalcolithic grave-diggers. This is surely due to the fact that this tomb was overcrowded by corpses, but also to the disturbances that occurred at the end of each of the different periods of utilization.

References

AMBROISE, D. & C. PERLÈS. 1972. Étude de la position des ossements d'un squelette néolithique (sepulture collective de La Chaussée-Tirancourt, Somme). *L'Anthropologie* 76: 535–44.
BAILLOUD, G. 1964. *Le Néolithique dans le Bassin Parisien.* Paris: *Gallia Préhistoire.* IIième supplément.
DANIEL, G.E. 1966. The megalith builders of SOM, *Palaeohistoria* 12: 199–208.
MASSET, C. 1971. Une sépulture collective mégalithique à la Chaussée-Tirancourt (Somme), *BSPF* 68, CRSM no. 6: 178–82.

Les Fouaillages and megalithic origins
by IAN KINNES
ANTIQUITY 64 (216), 1982

THE ISLAND [OF GUERNSEY] has a fine series of surviving megalithic monuments with passage graves such as La Varde and outstanding examples of ornate statue-menhirs as at Catel (Kinnes 1981). There are distinctive local variants, as in the cellular elaboration of the Déhus tomb and the regional style of cist-in-circle monument. In terms of islands as laboratories of prehistory it is instructive to note that these structures survive only where protected from the ravages of agriculture, here on the sterile sand-drift of the north and the rocky promontories of the west coast. Sporadic records and the place-name evidence studied in detail by de Guérin (1921) indicate the extent and unevenness of destruction. Of some 70 monuments thus recorded only 12 survive in any recognizable state, and earlier density at about 1 per sq. km is an important corrective to attempts at territorial analysis based on extant distribution. Finds from the tombs, exca-

FIGURE 1. *Les Fouaillages: the site under excavation in 1980. (Photo W.F. Tipping.)*

FIGURE 2. *Les Fouaillages: the initial monument. (Photo W.F. Tipping.)*

vated mainly by the Lukis family, are prolific but lack contextual evidence for seriation or detailed analysis, and can be grouped only on general affinity with developments elsewhere. No Neolithic domestic sites have been excavated, and knowledge of settlement patterns depends heavily on largely undatable flint scatters.

In the circumstances the detailed investigation of a well-preserved site was desirable. At the very least it should amplify the insular picture and might conceivably shed light on the wider questions of Neolithic settlement and the phenomenon of chambered tombs themselves. The opportunity arose in 1977 with the discovery of a new and apparently intact site by members of the Société Guernesiaise. In a courageous and far-sighted decision, the States of Guernsey Ancient Monuments Committee agreed to sponsor total excavation on the site, now known as Les Fouaillages (Guernsey patois for 'gorse-brake').

Les Fouaillages

The site lies at 6 m OD on L'Ancresse Common (Vale parish, WV 335830), a sand-covered heathland tract at the north of the island (FIGURES 1, 2). Four other megalithic structures exist in the same protected environment (Kendrick 1928). Before excavation it appeared as an elongated mound some 2 m high, its profile and dimensions obscured by dune formation and the earthworks of a golf green on its northern side.

A small trial trench by the Société Guernesiaise in 1978 produced quantities of prehistoric pottery and flintwork in apparent association with a length of well-built boulder walling (FIGURE 3). There was no trace of previous intrusion and the site is not mentioned in the Lukis records. It seemed reasonable to assume that the context was intact and, initially, that it might be a small chambered tomb of familiar island type.

From the outset it was decided that the site should be totally excavated for maximum information recovery and to discount the common problems of chambered tomb studies caused by partial excavation. It is now clear that anything less would have led to major misinterpretation of the contexts and their sequence. Twelve weeks of excavation between 1979 and 1981 realized this aim and recovered a remarkable and complex sequence of activity from the early Neolithic onwards, associated with rich and important stratified assemblages. Unfortunately, acidic soil conditions precluded bone survival and environmental information therefore rests heavily on soil and pollen analysis now being undertaken as part of a major project for the islands by Dr D. Keen and Dr R. Jones of Lanchester Polytechnic (Coventry).

FIGURE 3. *Les Fouaillages: the unroofed chamber in course of excavation. (Photo W.F. Tipping.)*

The first structural stage of the monument has now been conserved for permanent display and is in the care of the Ancient Monuments Committee.

The outline phasing that follows may be varied slightly by post-excavation work but can be regarded as broadly accurate at this stage.

Phase 1
This is represented by a scatter of distinctive microliths, all found in derived contexts, but representing some form of later Mesolithic activity on site. They can be distinguished from the earlier Neolithic small blade industry but refinement of assemblages depends upon further detailed analysis.

Phase 2 (FIGURES 4 & 5)
Four stone structures were erected on an east–west line and enclosed by a triangular mound, length 20 m and width 10 m, built of stacked turves and stone-faced. At the west was a circular paved area of small slabs and boulders, 1·6 m in diameter. Close to this was a sub-rectangular cairn of tightly-packed boulders, length 1·9 m, width 1·8 m, and height 1 m, which enclosed a small domed cist with a single capstone. At the east end of the cairn stood a shouldered menhir or marker slab, perhaps chosen for its generalized anthropomorphic resemblance. Both structures were covered by the primary mound.

Further east was an unroofed double chamber, length 2·6 m, and width 1·7 m, of slab construction reinforced by drystone walling, defined at the rear by two massive marker slabs and with its entrance framed by two stone-packed postholes. At the east end was a small slab-built chamber with 3 capstones, its internal dimensions only 1·8 m

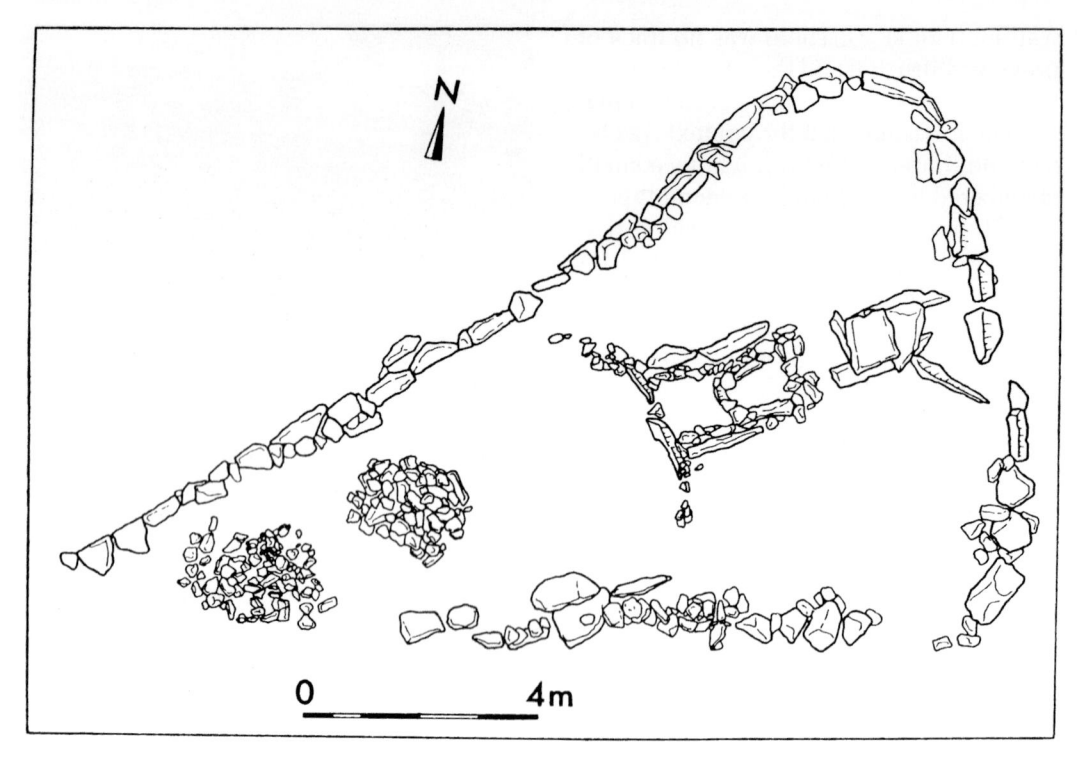

FIGURE 4. *The initial monument (Jenny Grant).*

long, 0·4 m wide and 0·4 m high. This lay at the rear of a small cuspidal forecourt area approached from one side by a gap in the façade line. These two chambers remained open and accessible after mound construction.

The lateral kerbs of variable boulder, slab and drystone build were constructed against the turf stack and the massive slabs of the façade leant against its near-vertical eastern face. Despite the concealment of two structures, no evidence was found for sequential mound construction and the whole monument must be regarded as a single planned complex.

Throughout the mound were considerable quantities of domestic debris representing an assemblage of ultimate Bandkeramik tradition. The narrow blade flint industry features few specialized tools, although small transverse arrowheads and scrapers improvised on nodule remnants are distinctive. The pottery covers a wide range of fabrics and vessel sizes, a significant proportion being decorated. Seven near-complete decorated vessels had been deposited at the base of the mound, in the unroofed chamber and on the western paved area. Fragments of fine stone *anneaux-disques* were common.

Radiocarbon dates for charcoal associated with one vessel at the base of the mound are 3640±50 BC and 3560±60 BC (BM-1892, 1893), confirmed by one for charcoal in the backfill of the unroofed chamber at 3330±140 BC (BM-1894).

This assemblage has broad affinities with material of latest Bandkeramik style in the Paris basin (Bailloud 1974) and compares closely with that from Jersey domestic contexts at Le Pinnacle (Godfray & Burdo 1950) and Mont Orgueil (inf. K.J. Barton). We can now visualize a distinctive regional grouping for this style. Little comparable material has yet been recovered from Normandy or Brittany. Sea-level changes over the last six

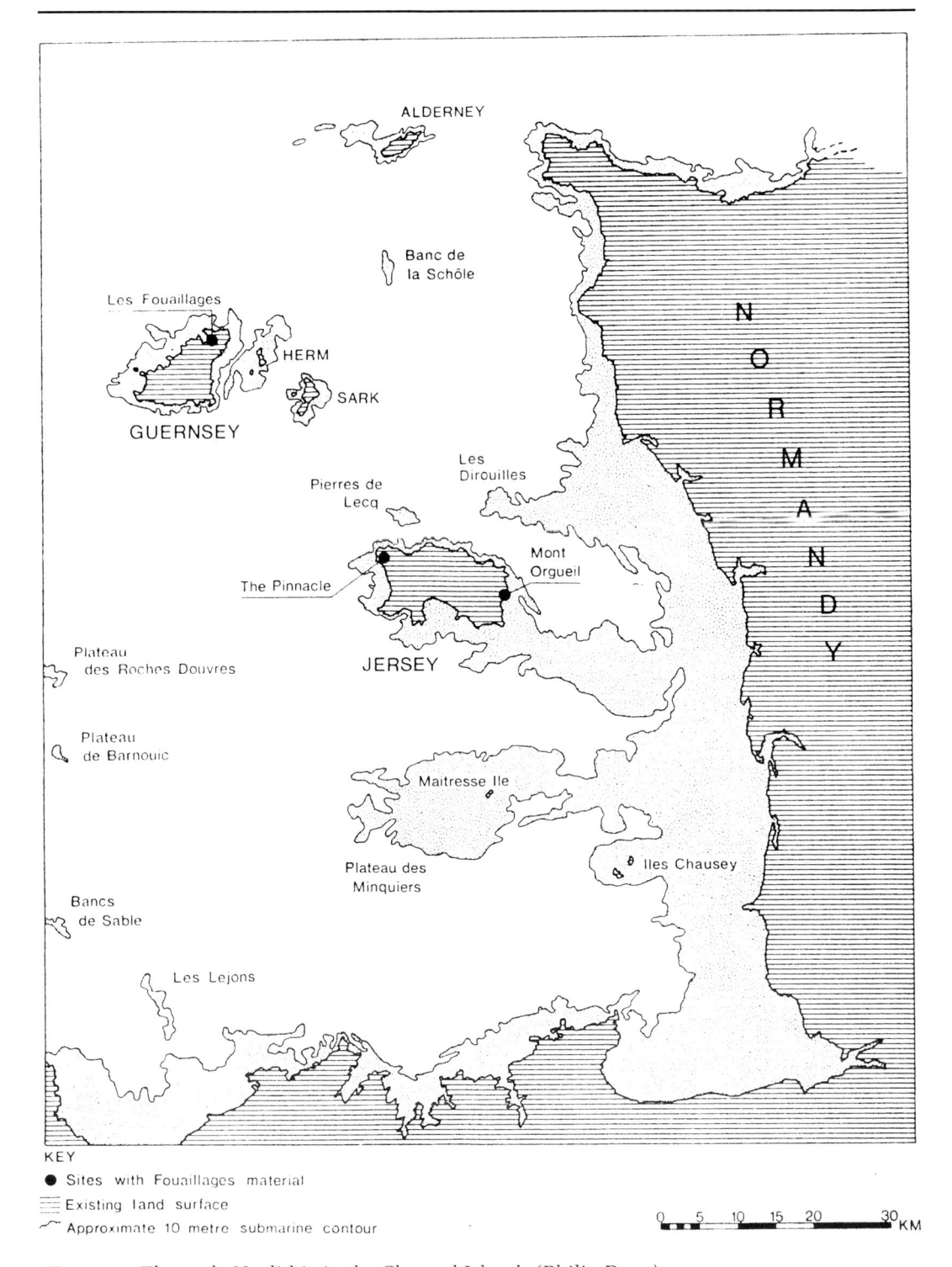

FIGURE 5. *The early Neolithic in the Channel Islands (Philip Dean).*

millennia are contentious but an average 10-m rise can be estimated (FIGURE 1), demonstrating the possibility of overland movement to Jersey. At present the Neolithic settlement of Guernsey seems to be an early example of sea-borne colonization, perhaps taking advantage of existing hunter–fisher networks.

The mound was therefore used and constructed by groups of direct Bandkeramik ancestry. Earlier interpretations had assumed that the material was an accidental incorporation from a pre-existing settlement site, but the discovery of near-complete vessels as formal deposits must discount this. The conjunction of domestic debris and formal deposits does echo a frequent Bandkeramik practice in flat-grave cemeteries. The monumental nature of this mortuary site is, therefore, of considerable importance. Individual components can be matched elsewhere: the triangular mound for the 4th millennium BC only in Kujavia (Chmielewski 1952), the 'platform' and cairn in the Manio-type long mounds of Southern Brittany (Giot *et al.* 1979: 212–18). The eastern chamber is of non-specific type and the unroofed chamber has no parallels known to the author.

The range of structures is a unique combination, with a functional basis reflecting both cultural choice and the different aspects of an elaborate mortuary procedure. Typologically and functionally the whole is suggestive of a formative stage within the long mound tradition (Daniel 1967). This tradition, largely, it seems, non-megalithic, is only slowly being realized across northern Europe and clearly the visible Kujavian and Manio elements are specialized aspects of its complexity.

Phase 2A

The unroofed chamber was backfilled with earth and successive layers of stone. The eastern chamber was filled nearly to roof level with clean beach-sand and the forecourt area blocked with earth and stones with rough coursing on the line of the façade.

Phase 3

After an hiatus perhaps of some centuries, the site was re-used for a new mortuary purpose. The eastern end of the existing mound was covered by a massive semicircular emplacement of successive layers of packed beach pebbles, earth and boulders. At the centre of this, on top of the existing mound and using the still visible marker slabs as a focal point, was a circle of recumbent boulders, 3·8 m in diameter, with two attached semi-circular enclaves. Within this two massive posts were erected, 2·4 m apart, defining a presumptive linear mortuary zone. The structure was long-lived, the posts being replaced once and the zone later redefined by a rectangular setting of small boulders, 2·8 m long and 1·5 m wide.

Within the massive foundation structure were large quantities of finds: plain bowl sherds, flint-work of broad flake technology and many stone tools including polished stone axes. Several *polissoirs,* up to half a ton in weight, had been incorporated. A middle Neolithic date for the construction is likely on the basis of associated finds, although a potential 1000-year life for the mortuary structure seems excessive. Unfortunately, radiocarbon samples from the appropriate levels were nonviable.

The structural affinities are diverse. The semi-circular foundation might normally be interpreted as standard 'forecourt blocking' but is here definitely functionally and chronologically distinct. Sub-division of linear mortuary zones has become a familiar feature in British contexts (Kinnes 1979: 59–60) and a rare hint of the same principle in mainland Europe is seen in the crematorium structure at La Hoguette (Caillaud & Lagnel 1972). Redefinition by a stone setting after original wooden delineation is again familiar from British sites such as Pitnacree (Coles & Simpson 1965).

The stone circle setting and use of the crest of an existing mound cannot be readily matched. Taxonomically the circle and annexes recall the ground-plan of the agglomerate cist-in-circle close by at L'Islet (Kendrick 1928: 168–71), but there seem good reasons to attach this form to the late Neolithic/Beaker period. Associated finds suggest contemporaneity with the insular passage graves such as La Varde, some 500 m to the north of Les Fouaillages, indicating a remarkable complexity of ritual observance and structural format in ill accord with typological explanations.

Phase 4

This mortuary structure went out of use at the end of the 3rd millennium, the final act being the votive deposit of a group of eight fine barbed and tanged arrowheads. These were made as matched pairs, and four were of imported Grand Pressigny flint. One had been damaged in manufacture, the tang breakage suggesting production for ceremonial rather than functional use (FIGURE 6).

FIGURE 6. *Les Fouaillages: barbed and tanged arrowhead of Grand Pressigny flint from the votive group. (Photo W.F. Tipping.)*

The visible monuments of phases 2 and 3 were then concealed by an oval mound, some 35 m long, of stacked turves laid on rammed beach-pebble foundations. There were no associated structures but the matrix was again prolific of finds. Among the pottery were fine and coarse ware Beaker sherds, including those of large cordoned storage vessels. The flint industry was of large blade and flake character. Two blanks for barbed and tanged arrowheads were notable finds in close association.

Sampling of an area in the southern lee of this final mound provided evidence for a contemporary domestic site. Features included post-holes, hearths and pits, and an extensive assemblage of flint and pottery was associated. Sherds of Jersey Bowl, the first such found outside that island, were recovered.

Radiocarbon determinations are available for the construction of the final mound and features within the settlement area. A charcoal deposit at the base of the final mound produced 1900±50 BC (BM-1891), and charcoal from the domestic site 2050±60 BC and 1880±50 BC (BM-1895 and 1897) for a hearth and post-hole respectively. A further date of 3140±50 BC (BM-1896) for another domestic hearth deposit cannot be reconciled with the associated Beaker-period material.

The opportunity to examine the chambered tomb of La Platte Mare, some 100 m to the north, provided a further component of this phase. This had been excavated by the Lukis family in 1837–1840, producing Beaker sherds and stone axes from the chamber

(Kendrick 1928: 122–6). The original form of the tomb was confirmed as cist-in-circle. The chamber fill had been completely removed but unabraded Beaker sherds were recovered from undisturbed mound material. It can be reasonably suggested that this formed the burial place for the community detected close by.

Later history
There was some evidence for plough-disturbance of the settlement area, and it is likely that agriculture should have been continuous and intensive on this rich loess-based soil. The area was newly defined by ditched boundaries, the mound of Les Fouaillages being reserved in the corner of one such field. Rare sherds of late Iron Age–early Galbo-Roman character provided sparse dating evidence for this episode. Ditch stratigraphy suggested frequent cleaning after limited sand blows but the length of use is unknown. Finally the upper part of the ditches and the land they defined were inundated by a massive blown sand incursion, ending all agriculture potential and creating the sterile heathland landscape familiar to the modern visitor.

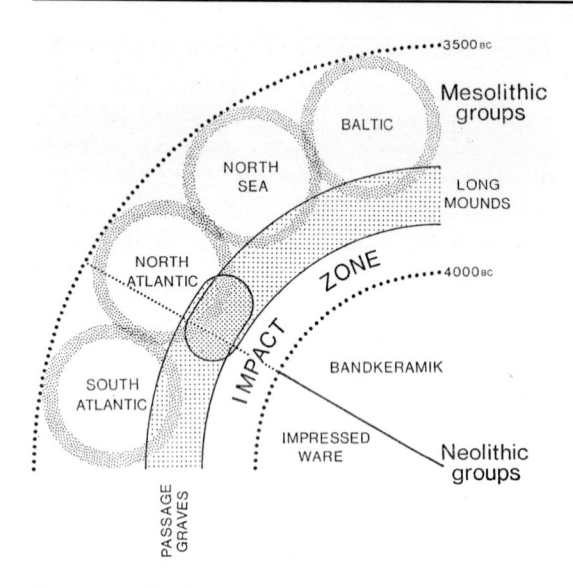

FIGURE 7. *The impact zone and tomb origins (Philip Dean).*

More recently the site was fortunate to escape the archaeological attentions of the Lukis family and the depredations caused by nearby quarrying during the Occupation, although slight exploratory traces from the latter were detected in superficial deposits. In summary, total excavation has revealed a remarkable sequence of ritual and domestic activity with the bonus of over 35,000 stratified finds. The yardstick status of the site is to some extent conditional on the degree of specific insular effects, but there can be no doubt that this knowledge will make a major contribution to the understanding of critical episodes in western European prehistory.

Megalithic origins
We have seen that the first monumental phase at Les Fouaillages with the cross-confirmation of radiocarbon dates, finds and structures must lie within the formative stage for chambered tomb origins. From elsewhere in northwestern Europe there is a scatter of earlier 4th-millennium BC determinations for passage graves (4 Breton, 1 Norman, 2 Centre-ouest and 1 Irish), a *grand tumulus* (St Michel) and a simple cist (in Loiret: Richard & Vintrou 1980). Some are of dubious quality, as dates gained from old material of uncertain coutext or by association (Chenion B1 with late Neolithic Artenac material: Guillien 1972). Only Bougon and Barnenez have produced more than one determination for the same structural phase and, on balance, there must be distinct reservations on the statistical basis for a megalithic florescence between 4000 and 3500 BC. Independent support is slight, but nevertheless present, with potentially early contexts for Carn pottery, a standard Breton early passage-tomb association, at Dissignac and, perhaps, Le Curnic (Giot *et al.* 1979).

The case must be regarded as non-proven until supported by detailed chronologies derived from a number of extensive excavations with closely-defined contexts dated in multiple by all available techniques. Whilst this might have the ring of idealism, it must be said that current syntheses are premature, being based on indifferent and even misleading evidence. Arguments for multiple independent origins in Western Europe are now common (Renfrew 1976), to the point of achieving an orthodoxy as widely accepted and acceptable as the *ex oriente lux* model of earlier decades (Renfrew 1967). It may be that the search for specific origins is not a right and proper area of enquiry. The nature of the evidence, common monumental solutions to different cultural problems or different solutions to common problems, might be non-susceptible to this approach.

The general outlines are clear. The centuries after 4000 BC saw the final impact of farming colonization across Western Europe, with major population movements and adaptations complicated by interaction with stable prosperous hunter–fisher groups around the rich marine basins from Biscay to the Baltic. Within this impact zone, defined temporally by the first half of the 4th millennium BC and spatially by the Atlantic margins, we can begin to discern the emergence of monumental tombs and even preferred formats (FIGURE 7). The resolution of fine chronologies, carrying as they do the implicit dangers of 'earliest' forms or specific origins, the creation of complex typologies and the definition of exclusive economic or cultural boundaries are, as an explanatory mechanism, inferior to an understanding of process.

References

BAILLOUD, G. 1974. *Le Néolithique dans le bassin Parisien*. Paris: CNRS. IIe supplément à Gallia Préhistoire.
CAILLAUD, R. & E. LAGNEL. 1972. Le Cairn et le crématoire néolithiques de la Hoguette à Fontenay-le-Marmion, *Gallia Préhistoire* 15: 137–85.
CHMIELEWSKI, W. 1952. *Zagadnienie Grobowcow Kujawisch W swietle ostatnich Badan*. Lodz.
COLES, J.M. & D.D.A. SIMPSON. 1965. The excavation of a neolithic round barrow at Pitnacree, *Proceedings of the Prehistoric Society* 31: 34–57.
DANIEL, G. 1967. Northmen and Southmen, *Antiquity* 41: 313–17.
DE GUERIN, T.W.M. 1921. List of dolmens, menhirs and sacred rocks, *Transactions de la Société Guernesiaise* 1921: 30–67.
GIOT, P.-R., J. L'HELGOUACH & J.-L. MONNIEr. 1979. *Préhistoire de la Bretagne*. Rennes: Ed. Ouest-France.
GODFRAY, A.D.B. & C. BURDO. 1950. Excavations at the Pinnacle, parish of St Ouen, Jersey (1930–36), *Bulletin de la Société Jersiaise* 15.
GUILLIEN, Y. 1972. Circonscription de Poitou—Charente, *Gallia Préhistoire* 15: 369–97.
KENDRICK, T.D. 1928. *The archaeology of the Channel Islands. Vol. 1: The Bailiwick of Guernsey*. London: Methuen.
KINNES, I.A. 1979. *Round barrows and ring-ditches in the British Neolithic*. London: British Museum. Occasional Paper 7.
  1981. The art of the exceptional: the neolithic statues-menhir of Guernsey in context, *Archaeologia Atlantica* 3.
KINNES, I.A. & R.B. BURNS. 1981. The Channel Islands: archaeology and early history, *Blue Guide to the Channel Islands*. London: A.C. Black.
RENFREW, A.C. 1967. Colonialism and megalithismus, *Antiquity* 41: 276–88.
  1976. Megaliths, territories and populations, in S.J. De Laet (ed.), *Acculturation and continuity in Atlantic Europe*: 198–220. Bruges: De Tempel.
RICHARD, G. & J. VINTROU. 1980. Les sépultures néolithiques sous dalles des Marsaules et de la Chaise à Malesherbes (Loiret), in *Préhistoire et Protohistoire en Champagne-Ardenne*, numéro spécial (Association d'études préhistoriques et protohistoriques de Champagne-Ardenne, Châlons-sur-Marne).

Clyde, Carlingford and Connaught Cairns — a review

by **J.G. SCOTT**

ANTIQUITY 36 (142), 1962

IN 1960 THERE APPEARED two important studies devoted to the Neolithic gallery graves of Ireland, hitherto considered to be part of the Clyde–Carlingford culture, as defined by Childe and Piggott (1954: 152*ff*). The first, by Professor de Valera (1960), is of unique importance: it records and discusses a mass of new evidence for the Irish gallery graves, and advances an entirely fresh theory for their origin and evolution. Dr Corcoran (1960) defines and isolates the elements of the Carlingford culture, and argues for its acceptance in its own right, as distinct from the Clyde–Solway culture.

De Valera's paper contains an inventory of 269 sites. No fewer than 152 are planned, of which 97 are new surveys. All the plans are to a small but uniform scale of 3/1000, which greatly simplifies comparisons. Most of the hitherto unrecorded sites are in Connaught, Sligo and Mayo, where de Valera has worked as Archaeology Officer to the Ordnance Survey.

De Valera advocates the term *court cairn* to describe the gallery grave with frontal façade, previously termed *horned cairn* where the façade was approximately semicircular, or *lobster claw cairn* where the façade extended almost to a full circle. For the latter type de Valera would use the term *full court cairn,* and the term *open court cairn* where the façade extends to less than a full circle.

Corcoran prefers to confine the term *court cairn* to those cairns where the court is fully enclosed, in other words to the *full court cairns* of de Valera. He would retain the term *horned cairn* for other gallery graves with forecourts. Corcoran lists 116 cairns in his Carlingford culture, and gives plans of 42, all at a uniform scale. Of these no fewer than 35 are not among those planned by de Valera. The two papers between them have thus plans of 187 cairns, and will be indispensable for the future study of the Neolithic period in Ireland.

De Valera differs at almost every point from established theories for the origin and evolution of gallery graves in Ireland and Scotland. He shows that the weight of distribution is no longer in the Carlingford region, as it had appeared when Childe and Piggott were writing, but in the west. Furthermore, he notes that the most massive of his whole court cairn series, and among them those with a very high standard of architectural design, are to be found among the full court cairns on the coastal belt. He therefore deduces a primary western entry for the court cairns, probably at Ballycastle in Mayo, with an eastward diffusion in three main directions — coastwards to north Donegal, across the Erne to the Tyrone uplands and across the central lakelands towards Carlingford.

De Valera fully realizes, accepts and indeed strongly advocates the obvious consequence of his theory, that the full court cairn must no longer be placed at the end but at the beginning of any evolutionary series. He would see the full court cairn with a two-segment gallery as the primary type, with degeneration showing in the increasing shallowness of the court, in the extension of the gallery to three or four segments and in the slackening of the rule of eastward orientation. He maintains that most of the chambered tombs on the east of the Irish Sea, with the exception of the passage graves and of the Severn–Cotswold group, derive from Ireland. He sees the main inspiration of the Clyde group in Ireland, though he admits that the lines of derivation are not clear, and that a likely place of origin in Ireland cannot be deduced.

The full results of de Valera's researches were not available to Corcoran, who favours the conclusion of Childe, Piggott and Mahr (1937: 348) that the full court, or lobster claw, cairn must be later than the horned cairn, and may have been derived from it. Corcoran also considers that in Ireland evolution of the horned cairn was marked by a reduction in the number of segments in the burial chambers, until the single-segment chamber, still generally retaining its forecourt, was reached.

Corcoran, however, seems unwilling to accept Piggott's derivation of the Irish series from the Scottish. He points to the significant differences in the segmentation of the Irish as compared with the Scottish burial chambers. He recalls that cairns with forecourts and façades are in a minority among the Clyde–Solway cairns. These considerations prompt him to reject the concept of a unified Clyde–Carlingford culture, and to suspect a common origin for the Carlingford and Clyde–Solway cultures, with contemporaneous periods of development for each.

It seems to me that to explain the Clyde–Carlingford culture in Ireland merely as a west to east, or an east to west, movement, with Scottish cairns commencing or concluding the series, is greatly to oversimplify the problem. There has been too great a readiness to assume that a spread into the interior, once begun, would keep pace with or even outstrip coastal diffusion. In addition, there are likely to have been successive external stimuli acting upon development, in both Ireland and Scotland, after this was already well under way. There are three points in the typological argument, two in Ireland and one in Scotland, which may be regarded as established, and around these all future discussion of the origin of Clyde–Carlingford cairns must turn.

The first point is implied by Piggott (1954: 160, 181), who saw a clear degeneration in tomb plan from a gallery grave with septal slabs to one with jambs and septals and finally to one with jambs alone, with a tendency for the segments to become oval in plan, and to be constructed of smaller stones than the massive flat slabs forming the angular segments found in Scotland and in some Irish monuments. Now the side slabs of burial chambers in Scotland are often imbricated, to use Childe's term — i.e. support for them is obtained by overlapping them from the back towards the front of the chamber, the inward thrust being contained by the septal slabs. Imbrication of a slightly different form is used in certain of the Irish burial chambers. Here the septal slabs are centrally placed between short side slabs running longitudinally, while against the outer sides of these lean the main side slabs, overlapping both to front and to rear. The tendency in Ireland seems to be for the short side slabs to give way to sturdy pillars, capable of supporting the main side slabs without the aid of septals, and so forming the characteristic jambs. Finally the jambs are placed transversely, and often cease to give much support to the main side slabs at all.

Now if one assumes that those burial chambers which retain short longitudinal side slabs and the principle of imbrication embody an older tradition, and if one isolates them, according to the plans provided by de Valera and Corcoran, the results are interesting. Of 36 examples no fewer than 23 are within 5 miles of the sea, occurring in Waterford, Louth, Armagh, Down, Antrim, Donegal, Sligo, Mayo and Galway, the sequence from east to west being broken only in Leitrim and Derry. These sites may well attest the initial diffusion of an early tradition of construction round the north coast from the east of Ireland to the west.

The second point is one which both de Valera and Corcoran note, and which seems to be the strongest argument in favour of de Valera's claim for an early development of full court cairns, though he makes little use of it. Probably six full court cairns, five in Mayo and one in Donegal, have shallow concave façades opening on to the entrances to the courts. An attempt will be made later to show how such a combination could come about, but surely it can only mean that by the time the shallow façade reached Mayo and Donegal, probably overland from the east, the full court had already been developed. The logical implication is that the full court developed early — indeed, was invented — in the west of Ireland, and that the deep semicircular forecourts of the rest of Ireland, and of Scotland and the Isle of Man for that matter, may ultimately derive from those of western Ireland.

The third point concerns the Scottish cairns, and is not noted by either de Valera or Corcoran. A survey of the 45 Clyde–Carlingford sites known in 1958 in Arran, Bute and Argyll showed that 17 certainly possessed façades. Of these only two were situated below 150 ft. above sea level, seven between 150 and 350 ft. and eight at heights of over 350 ft. above sea level (Scott 1956: 47–9). Childe in 1934 pointed out that in these areas the only soils adaptable to the agricultural methods of the immigrant Neolithic farmers would have been raised sea beaches and the alluvial gravels of the glens, in other words ground at less than 150 ft. above sea level. It would be reasonable to expect the primary settlements on such ground, and indeed 17 sites of cairns are known but only two can be shown to have façades. It may therefore be claimed that on distributional grounds in Arran, Bute and Argyll at least, cairns with semicircular façades are unlikely to be primary in the Clyde–Carlingford series.

It is possible, therefore, that during its primary phase the Clyde–Carlingford cairn in Scotland and Ireland was evolving from a simple burial chamber with entrance, perhaps with elementary imbrication of the sides on the lines of the portal dolmen.[1] The Scottish and Irish traditions in segmentation and imbrication may have diverged early, and the use of Piggott's *Beacharra A* ware in Scotland as opposed to *Lyles Hill* ware in Ireland may reflect the divergence. The two-segment chamber is likely to have been early, as stated by de Valera. In Scotland and in eastern Ireland the portal may have become an important and imposing feature, but probably only in the west of Ireland did a full court develop and perhaps begin to spread eastwards.

Corcoran points out that the problem of the relationship of the Severn–Cotswold to the Clyde–Carlingford cairns has been aggravated by the recognition of a concave forecourt at West Kennet in place of the cuspate plan normal to the Severn–Cotswold type. The relationship can hardly be denied, and although Corcoran may be right in explaining the West Kennet forecourt as the result of influences emanating from the North Channel area, yet there is little doubt that the weight of influence was in the other direction, from the Severn–Cotswold area towards the north. But the Clyde–Carlingford culture must already have completed the primary phase of its development when Severn–Cotswold influences impinged upon it. This seems to be the only way to explain the combination of Severn–Cotswold traits with others which are just as clearly not Severn–Cotswold in those Clyde–Carlingford cairns which appear typologically advanced and so chronologically late.

---

1   If, as A.E.P. Collins (1957) seems to imply, the slab-built cist in the round cairn at Knockiveagh, Down, is original, then a ^{14}C date of 3060±570 BC (D-37) must be admitted for this type of structure: Watts (1960: 112).

Since the cuspate forecourt seems not to occur in the northern cairns, the Severn–Cotswold traits must have been transmitted before that type of forecourt was developed in the south.[2] The traits which do appear in the north are the trapezoid cairn with flat façade, subsidiary burial chambers in addition to the main chamber and the use of drystone walling in cairn construction. These fuse to varying degrees with the native building tradition, producing a series of often imposing monuments in which sometimes the native and sometimes the incoming style predominates.

It would appear that in Scotland the flat façade was more readily adopted than in Ireland, where the deep semicircular forecourt may early have become an accepted part of cairn construction. Excavations in 1959 and 1961 at Beacharra, in Scotland, have shown that the cairn was in all likelihood trapezoid in shape, with an almost flat façade entirely built of drystone walling, and with sides probably similarly constructed. The burial chamber was of normal Clyde–Carlingford slab-built construction, but there were no other orthostats at all. At Crarae, on Loch Fyneside, a large trapezoid cairn again had an almost flat façade, in which both drystone walling and orthostats were used. Crarae in turn is linked by its complex entrance, consisting of two sets of portal stones, an outer and an inner, with the complex entrance site of Brackley, in Kintyre, in which part of a carinated *Beacharra B* bowl was found (Scott 1956: 22–54). Brackley is connected by a curious constructional trick in the burial chamber, where two of the side slabs rest not on the ground but on a foundation of boulders, with the double-horned, or dual court, trapezoid cairn of Audleystown, in Down, where drystone walling was used extensively, and some of the pottery shows *Beacharra* influence (Collins 1954: 7–56; 1959: 21–7). These cairns seem to form a nearly contemporaneous group, bearing witness not only to the influence of Severn–Cotswold traits upon the design of Clyde–Carlingford cairns on both sides of the North Channel, but also to the capacity of the Clyde–Carlingford culture, in its middle phase, to absorb and even to transmute those traits. The shallow concave façades at Audleystown, unusual in Ireland, ought probably to be regarded not as stages in the development of the flat façade into the deep semicircular façade, but rather as versions of the already evolved deep semicircular Irish façade which have been modified under Severn–Cotswold influence. It may have been this modified façade which was transmitted westwards across Ireland, eventually to combine in Mayo and Donegal with some full court cairns, as described above.

At Audleystown the trapezoid cairn implies that the front burial chamber is more important than the rear. Rear chambers may therefore be regarded as a peculiarly Irish interpretation of the Severn–Cotswold idea of subsidiary burial chambers. Now a comparison of de Valera's second map, showing the distribution of his dual court cairns (which must in origin be cairns with main front and subsidiary rear chambers), with his third map, showing the distribution of his court cairns with (other types of) subsidiary chambers, reveals a tendency for the two series to be mutually exclusive. This mutual exclusiveness is to some extent supported in the Clyde area. In Kintyre five of the eight certain Clyde–Carlingford cairns, including two with semicircular façades, have side chambers, but none has a rear chamber. In Arran, on the other hand, only one cairn has side chambers but four, all of which seem to have had main chambers with semicircular façades, seem also to have had rear structures. There is a strong hint here of a dichotomy in tradition, indirectly testifying to a renewal of cross-channel contacts, since it is dis-

---

2   De Valera sees a Severn–Cotswold connexion in five Mayo sites with transepted galleries; elsewhere, however, evidence for the transepted gallery in the north seems to be lacking.

cernible in Scotland as well as in Ireland. The link between the Irish and Scottish cairns during this phase is emphasized by the occurrence of pottery in the *Beacharra B* tradition of shape or decoration in both countries.

In his discussion of the pottery de Valera must be almost *contra mundum* in refusing to accept Piggott's distinction between *Beacharra B* and *Lyles Hill* ware, which he would apparently class together as Neolithic shouldered bowls. On the other hand one must accept de Valera's contention that the two open bowls from Cairnholy I cairn, in Kirkcudbright, are within the Irish range, and admit the Irish influence so implied. Indeed, it may well be that all Clyde–Carlingford cairns in Scotland having deep semicircular façades are Irish in inspiration, and belong to the final phase of the Clyde–Carlingford culture.

De Valera makes a valiant attempt to find a prototype for his full court cairn on the continent, but admits that the problem is unsolved. Recent opinion not only supports the Clyde–Carlingford Severn–Cotswold connexion, but in the absence of satisfactory prototypes for the Clyde–Carlingford group on the continent would derive it directly from the Severn–Cotswold group (Daniel 1960: 198). The reasons for thinking that this is too straightforward a solution *per se* have been set out above, and the genesis of the Clyde–Carlingford cairn has been sought in some simple imbricated megalithic chamber akin to the portal dolmen. De Valera records at least 100 portal dolmens, and notes that, though rare outside his court cairn province, they extend along the east of Ireland as far as Waterford. All of them he regards as degenerate and late offshoots of his court cairns, but with totally inadequate evidence from excavation an early date, at least for a proportion of them, remains a possibility. Surely the solution of this longstanding problem is a challenge to Irish archaeology.

Corcoran suggests that his Carlingford culture should include not only the typical megalithic monuments, evidence of a unifying religious influence among originally discrete social groups, but also the associated elements, pottery and flintwork, some of which may be Mesolithic in origin. While sympathizing with this suggestion one may pertinently ask whether the time has come to advance it, or whether his Carlingford culture would be a suitable subdivision, implying as it does a total separation of the Irish from the Scottish sites. Rather than prematurely to cast aside the term Clyde–Carlingford it would surely be better to risk alliterative ennui and refer to the Clyde–Carlingford–Connaught culture pending further work. It is a measure of the contribution of these two papers to megalithic studies in Ireland and Scotland that they have not only shown how much remains to be done, but have appreciably and permanently narrowed the limits within which such work should be carried out.

References
CHILDE, V.G. 1934. Neolithic settlement in the west of Scotland, *Scot. Geo. Mag.* 50: 18–25.
COLLINS, A.E.P. 1954. A stone circle on Castle Mahon Mountains, Co. Down, *Ulster Journal of Archaeology* n.s. 19: 7–56.
— 1957. Trial excavations in a round cairn at Knockkreagh, Co. Down, *Ulster Journal of Archaeology* n.s. 20: 8–28.
— 1959. Further work at Audleystown Long Cairn, Co. Down, *Ulster Journal of Archaeology* n.s. 22: 21–7.
CORCORAN, J.X.W.P. 1960. The Carlingford Culture, *Proceedings of the Prehistoric Society* 26 (1960): 98–148.
DANIEL, G. 1960. *The prehistoric chamber tombs of France*. London: Thames & Hudson.
DE VALERA, R. 1960. The Court Cairns of Ireland, *Proceedings of the Royal Irish Academy* 60c (1959–1960): 9–140.
MAHR, A. 1937. New aspects and problems in Irish prehistory. Presidential address for 1937, *Proceedings of the Prehistoric Society* 3: 261–436.
PIGGOTT, S. 1954. *Neolithic Cultures of the British Isles*. Cambridge: Cambridge University Press.
SCOTT, J.G. 1956. The excavation of the chambered cairn at Brackley, Kintyre, Argyll, *Proceedings of the Scottish Antiquarian society* 89 (1955–56): 22–54.
WATTS, W.A. 1960. C-14 dating and the Neolithic in Ireland, *Antiquity* 34: 111–16.

A pattern of evolution for the Neolithic funerary structures of the west of France

by CHRISTINE BOUJOT & SERGE CASSEN

ANTIQUITY 67 (256), 1993

FOR OVER HALF A CENTURY the 'invention' of the large megalithic structures of western France has regularly stimulated the minds and imaginations of French and foreign archaeologists. This has recently been demonstrated by the reactions of some archaeologists to the current debates on the purpose and age of the passage graves of Western Europe (Giot 1991).

In the course of seminars given in 1988–89 at the University of Paris I, we presented a study on the modes of transition, in Metropolitan France, from the individual to the collective tomb through their architecture and corresponding funerary practices during the 5th and 4th millennia BC. In particular, the assumption that passage graves derived from earlier funerary structures, by means of a coherent dynamic, led us to reassess archaeological associations (some of them unrecognized) and to reconsider some of the methods of construction. These lines of research appeared to supply evidence of a relative logic within the theoretical evolutionary process.

Typological classification and its foundation

The southern coast of Brittany is known to be particularly rich in megaliths, and one of the highest concentrations lies around the Gulf of Morbihan. As it has become one of the basic centres for research on 'Megalithism', it seemed logical to draw upon the documentary sources available (bibliographies as well as fieldwork) for this region to demonstrate the development of this architecture.

The history of Armorican archaeology was marked at first by Celtomania and the activity of antiquarians. Then, with the first plans drawn by Lukis and the first inventories compiled by Miln, Gaillard and Le Rouzic, it turned to more systematic forms of investigation. The density of megalithic remains and their astonishing diversity inevitably led to the formulation of increasingly sophisticated typological classifications, proposed successively by archaeologists such as Lukis, Montelius, Gaillard, du Chatellier, Le Rouzic, Ford, Daniel and, latterly, L'Helgouach.

Because of the ruinous state of many of these structures, most of which, stripped of their mounds, are now reduced to the remnants of their internal constructions, these first classifications were naturally restricted to the morphological features so revealed. It was not until some 30 years ago, thanks to excavation campaigns such as that in Barnenez, that French research on megalithism turned its attention to the tumuli (external structures) and thus made a major advance towards a fuller understanding of the monuments. Nonetheless, and despite the fact that L'Helgouach takes account, wherever possible, of any data concerning the form and/or technology of construction, typological classification of megalithic architecture still concentrates on the plan of the internal structures.

The evolutionary principle, which is acknowledged by several researchers and is considered to be dependent on changes in funerary rites during the late Neolithic period with more collective tombs, was translated into an extension of the chamber to the detriment of the passage (L'Helgouach 1973; Bailloud 1985). Thus the essential differentiation between these two characteristic parts of the internal space of the earlier passage graves disappeared with the gallery graves; in the latter, indeed, the walls of the chamber continue those of the passage which is sometimes compared in the case of Armorican monuments with some form of '*couloir résiduel évasé*' (L'Helgouach 1986: 191). The different stages of this transformation can be made out from the various architectural forms through a distinct regression of the access structure, which was gradually incorporated into the new space of the chamber.

The mechanism driving this evolution is based not only on the main components of the internal tomb, but also on those around it which make up its external envelope. Consequently, as a general rule the surface of the chamber is extended not only at the expense of the passage but also that of the mound that covers them: 'The search for a monumental aspect is given less priority, and eventually tends to disappear with location on low-lying ground, and the replacement of cairns by earth mounds just big enough to cover the tombs' (Bailloud 1985: 363).

From simple grave to passage grave: a working hypothesis

The Breton typological classification, which has been built up from a substantial amount of documents, remarkable for their quantity as well as for their quality, offers a coherent and above all dynamic evolutionary sequence. The functioning of this sequence then supplies the elements to permit the formulation of a pattern of development for these monumental structures.

If we start with a series of passage graves, some of which have chambers covered to a height of several metres by corbelled vaults, thus demanding a high mastery of building technique, this sequence appears to be lacking all the preceding stages. Our research on funerary structures, which should enable us to find the missing elements of the evolution, will therefore be based on a theoretical framework using the mechanical principle of this evolution to extrapolate backwards from passage graves with a single clearly differentiated chamber to the most elementary graves.

The choice of the simple grave as a starting point for this process is not determined by a wish to retain the traditional evolutionary pattern that seeks to demonstrate the increasing complexity of human societies by means of material structures. The intention is to follow a process of change which, starting with the most elementary type of tomb, develops through a variety of complex shapes to the simplicity and uniformity of the plans of the gallery graves (*allées couvertes*). This grave, as a place to deposit a deceased person, possibly enclosed in a protection (shrine, coffin, etc.) which is considered to be the most widespread funerary structure in Europe among the earliest Neolithic communities, represents a chronological landmark much earlier than the first passage graves.

In order to conform with the classification criteria established for megalithic burials, that is, the plan of their internal structures, the search for tombs that may complete our evolutionary sequence will be carried out firstly among those where the inner space is defined by a completely closed plan, such as a simple grave, leading to an open plan following a passage. Then, as the emphasis shifts from a subterranean tomb to a structure that is not only built above ground but also stands out in the landscape for its monumental cairns or tumuli, our field of investigation will be confined to the types of grave, showing different aspects of the transition from one to the other.

Simple graves, cists and *coffres*

Funerary constructions conforming with these conditions have frequently been attested from the Neolithic period. They are usually grouped together within a very large set of structures more or less accurately defined by a terminology limited to earth grave, cist and *coffre*, which only approximately describes their diversity. Whereas a single word (e.g. grave) is often used to designate realities such as the burial in the ground or in a perishable container (Mordant 1987; Duday 1985), the terms 'cist' or '*coffre*' are sometimes indiscriminately used to describe the same type of interment.

In fact there are many architectural particularities and/or ways of functioning which help in the differentiation between cists and *coffres*. It is possible to retain, from among the many propositions made so far (Bailloud 1985; Petrequin & Piningre 1976), some relevant invariable features to arrive at one definition. Thus, by 'cist' we mean a stone or wooden construction which forms a subterranean or sub-mound grave, intended to receive only one body or several individuals at the same time before being permanently blocked up. The *coffre* has the same structural characteristic, but access is from above, which permits the practice of successive burials.

Morbihan tombs

These tombs of the 5th millennium, which are common to all Europe, have also been listed around the Gulf of Morbihan; they were built during the Neolithic and into the Metal Ages. The existence of those tombs is still attested on the famous Mesolithic cemeteries of Teviec and Hoëdic: some burials that contained several individuals are usually plain graves, perhaps with internal structures, and so similar to cists or *coffres*, according to how they were used. Furthermore, because of the unusual appearance of some of them, which are covered by a structure resembling a small cairn, the tombs of Teviec and Hoëdic have been considered as the only representatives of the first expressions of Megalithism.

Yet, in our opinion, two classic types of monument known as *tertres tumulaires* and *tumulus carnacéens* could also lay claim to that status (FIGURE 1). *Tertres tumulaires* are traditionally long and low monuments in the shape of rectangles, trapezoids or, more seldom, circles, built of earth possibly mixed with stones and bordered by a line of slabs set close together in the ground or by drystone walls. They sometimes contain nothing but hearthstones; many other 'structures', more or less well-ordered and considered by Le Rouzic to be small *coffres*, could as well correspond to post-holes judging by observations made on the Table des Marchands (excavations by L'Helgouach and Cassen; Cassen & L'Helgouach 1992). True cists or *coffres* can also be found (FIGURE 2). *Tumulus carnacéens* designate a category of monuments usually of impressive size; the best-known example is Saint-Michel in Carnac (125 m x 60 m x 10 m). Besides some classic passage-graves set there during a later phase, they conceal vaults or crypts, where extraordinary archaeological material was discovered, consisting of hundreds of axes made from rare rocks, and also ornaments and food offerings. These two types of monument contain structures whose characteristics fit them into the theoretical evolutionary process from the simple grave up to the first passage graves. Their plans are usually completely enclosed (Manio V, Mané Lud, Mané Hui, Moustoir, Castellic) and yet begin to show side openings. Evidence comes from 19th-century descriptions of the Mané-Er-Hroëck (Locmariaquer), where the excavators noticed the existence of an entrance and even of a 'cork' (Galles & Lefèvre 1863). Further evidence has resulted more recently from clearing of a 'transitional access' to the vault inside the very long mound of Er Grah (Locmariaquer) (Le Roux *et al.* 1989). In elevation some of those structures are semi-

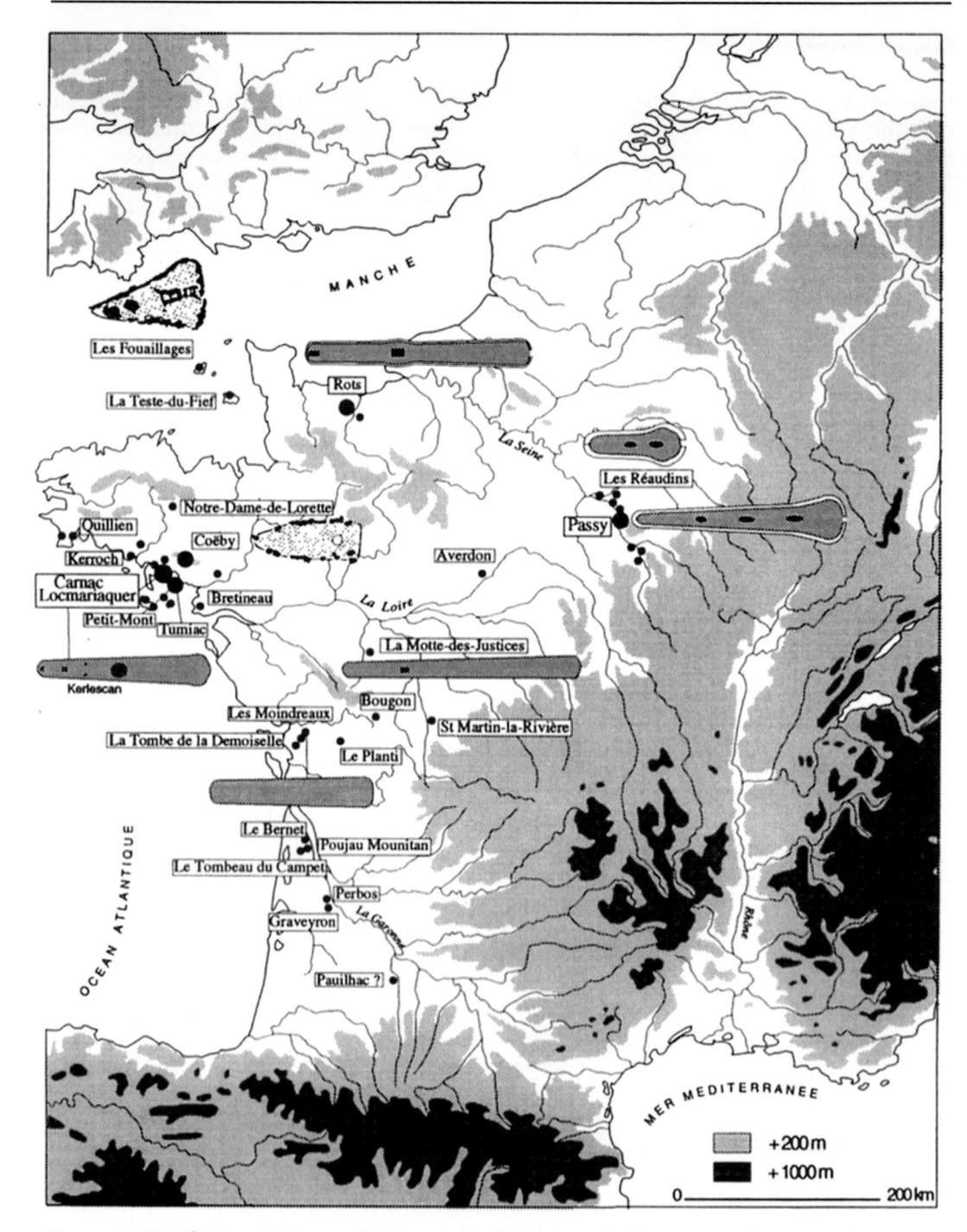

FIGURE 1. *Distribution in France of the main Neolithic tumuli (long or circular) quoted in the paper, which did not contain passage graves in their first stage of construction (end of 5th millennium BC).*

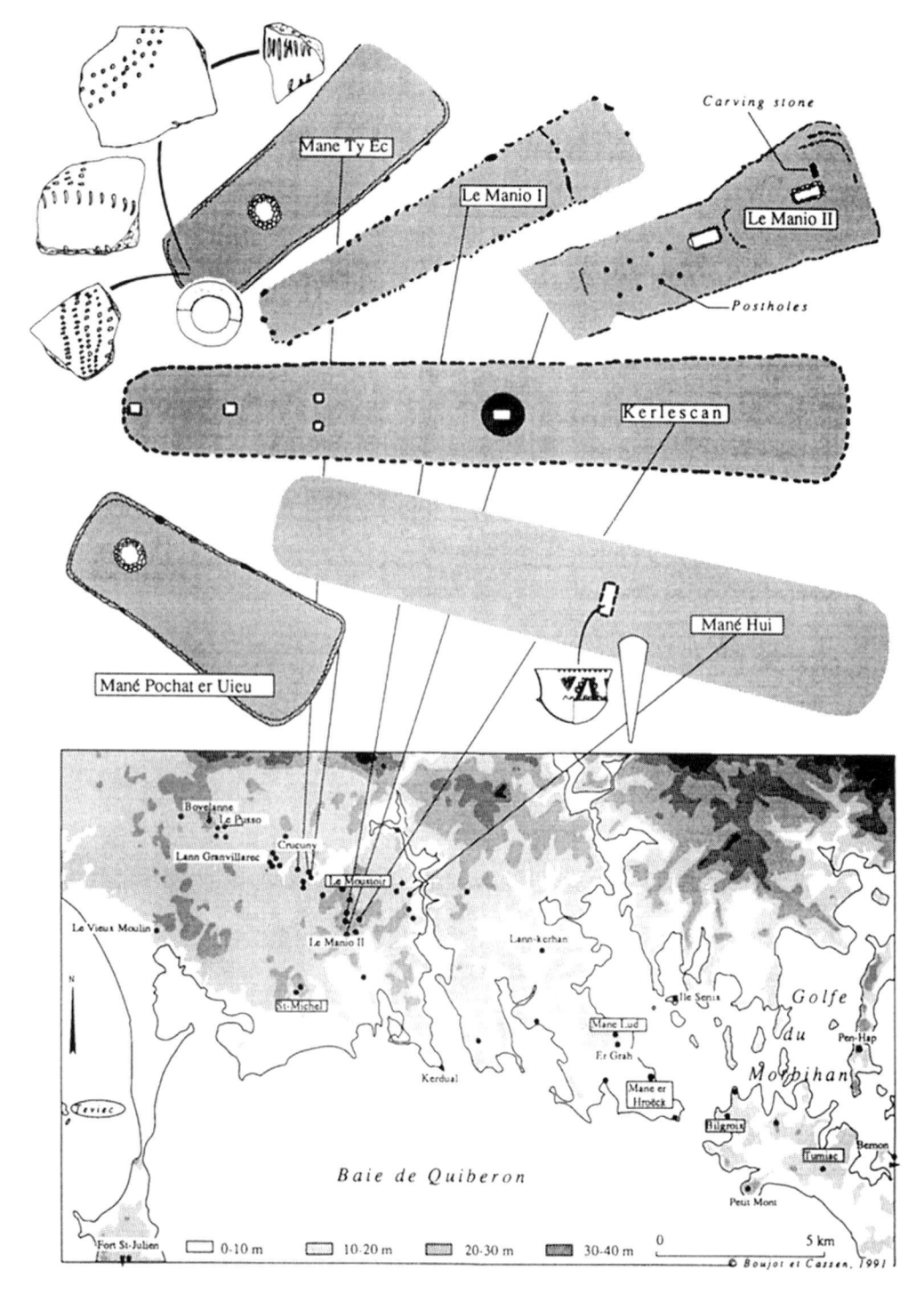

FIGURE 2. *Distribution in Quiberon Bay and Morbihan Gulf of Neolithic tumuli, long or circular, which did not contain passage graves in their first stage of construction. The sites underlined are the largest of these monuments covering sealed tombs. (Simplified architectural plans after Bailloud et al. 1955; Gaillard 1897; Le Rouzic et al. 1922; Miln 1883. Pottery drawings after Bailloud; stone ring after Miln.)*

buried, like Mane-Er-Hroëck or cist XI in the tumulus of Crucuny, Carnac (Le Rouzic & Pequart 1923). Finally if we take as the third parameter the evolution of the external envelope, which tends to get smaller in the later monuments, it can be said of the Carnacean tomb, by virtue of the fact that the mound is disproportionately large by comparison with the inner volume, that it favours the hypothesis of their being older.

Building techniques
In order to complete this argument, observations about the building technique of the tombs inside these low mounds or Carnacean tumuli establish new links with the oldest passage graves, which are often made of dry stones and corbelled. Descriptions of the internal structures of Manio V (Le Rouzic 1920), Mané-Pochat-er-Uieu, Mané-Ty-Ec (Miln 1883) and Castellic (Fontes 1881) reveal certain building similarities in the erection of dry-stone walls in the form of a vault. In this respect, the report on Manio V is even more significant, since it states that the mound contained 'a very odd, irregular monument, made up of large corbelled rocks' (Le Rouzic 1920: 5). This information on the size of the blocks used permits direct comparison with the methods used to raise the walls of the vaults in the large Carnacean tumuli. These consisted of utilizing elements that can be defined as megalithic, owing to their size, and putting them in place not vertically, but in horizontal layers that overlap one another so as to start a form of corbelled construction. This very distinctive building technique has been reported not only at Mané Lud (Galles & Mauricet 1865), but also at Moustoir (Galles & Mauricet 1865) and Tumiac (Galles 1878; Le Rouzic 1934–5). These walls in large superimposed blocks, also to be found in the crypts of Mané-Er-Hroëck (Locmariaquer) and Saint-Michel (Carnac), are characteristic of some other examples of the earliest passage graves with circular chambers, such as that of Parc Guren (Crac'h), and so can be considered to be a transitional stage.

Comparison with material culture and traditional absolute chronology
Once the principle of the evolution of funerary structures in the mid 5th millennium BC has been established, the next question is the extent to which comparison with other data concerning the material culture confirms the internal logic of the process and the architectural transformation dynamic. Furthermore, if this argument is to be pursued, a revision of the current chronology seems to be necessary, since the existing periodical division is not adapted to this pattern. It should be recalled that previous studies on some passage graves (among the best-known ones) considered that these monuments were in use a few centuries before the construction of the Neolithic *tumuli* containing cists, which contradicts the present hypothesis.

Stratigraphic connections
Stratigraphic links have been described for several megalithic monuments owing to cairns having been built which sealed chronologically earlier occupation areas. The best-known example is still unquestionably that of the potteries known as 'Danubian' in La Hoguette (Calvados). However, the relative antiquity of these ceramics, contemporary with early and late *Linearbandkeramik* (Jeunesse 1987; Lüning *et al.* 1989), is of no immediate help in this discussion.

On the other hand, Le Rouzic noticed early on that the layers of silt that overlie the primary cairn (with no passage grave) of Saint-Michel in Carnac continue beneath the pillars of the Eastern dolmen known as No. 2 (Le Rouzic 1932). It is also worth noting that a long, low mound, not yet excavated, was discovered in 1943 and that one of its extremities would be covered by the northeast side of the large tumulus. Similar connections have been observed in Le Petit Mont, since a part of the 40-m long earthen mound lies under the accumulations of the primary cairn A (Lecornec 1987).

In Carnac again, the *coffres* or cists of the Moustoir are included in the long narrow primary cairn, whereas in the western extremity a secondary quadrangular tomb with entrance is inserted into a sedimentary mound covering all the structures on the site. Moreover, the archaeological material found in the latter chamber is similar to assemblages from other regional passage graves (smooth ceramics with round bases and shoulders, circular *coupes-à-socle*) (Galles & Mauricet 1865).

At the Mané Lud in Locmariaquer, the passage grave on the western edge of the deposit is not integrated with the main cairn which includes the central sealed tomb (Galles & Mauricet 1864). New excavations would be necessary to check the stratigraphic position of the passage grave of Pen Hap (Ile aux Moines), which is set at the edge of an 80-m long mound; this would make it possible to confirm the assumption that the mound preceded construction of the dolmen with quadrangular chamber.

When considering the archaeological material discovered in the palaeosoils underlying some passage graves of different types, it should be noted that a Castellic/Mané-Hui assemblage has been reported in Dissignac (Loire-Atlantique) (L'Helgouac'h 1984). Under the Table des Marchand (Morbihan), *coupes-à-socle* are associated with the latest phase of the pottery style. In Normandy, at Ernes-Condé-sur-Ifs, vessels with impressions, repoussé buttons and finger-printed rims have been found together with a square-mouthed vase ornamented with a stamped sun-like motif. This stratigraphic level where schist bracelets also occur is dated 5560 BP (San Juan & Dron 1991). Not far away, under the tumulus of the Commune Sèche in Colombiers-sur-Seulles (Calvados), pottery that is also reminiscent of the Villeneuve St Germain (VSG)/Cerny backgrounds of the Middle Loire basin are also associated with schist bracelets (Chancerel *et al.* 1992).

Bracelets and stone rings
This type of stone object, which is relatively widespread in western France, is characteristic of the VSG/Cerny stages of the Parisian Basin, detectable as far as the boundaries of Armorica.

Despite the lack of evidence that they all date back to the Neolithic period, several individual or multiple graves located in Normandy as well as in the two Charentes contain schist or rare stone bracelets (Auxiette 1989; Gaillard *et al.* 1984). They are also to be found in Brittany in several sealed corbelled tombs (Giot & L'Helgouach 1955; Lefèvre & Galles 1863; Le Pontois 1929; Le Rouzic 1923; Marsille 1928), but they have never been found in passage graves.

By analogy with the Middle Loire Basin and thanks to the obvious connections with the assemblages from the palaeosoils of Norman passage graves, whenever the ceramic style can be identified, the chrono-cultural attributions to the Cerny Horizon (a practical provisional term designating this chronological subdivision common to several related cultural groups) become unquestionable.

Ceramic and lithic associations
One of the most reliable archaeological associations, directly connected with the funeral structures under consideration here, is undoubtedly that discovered in the cist of the long *tumulus* (90 m) of Mané-Hui in Carnac (Gaillard 1897; Bailloud 1975). This individual tomb built of granite slabs contained very interesting material, which is attributed to an early Castellic phase.

Two beautiful polished axes, one of which must have been about 30 cm long, are made of rare green stone (jadeite), and two other hatchets or adzes in fibrolite form an instructive collection, since it is known that no large 'ceremonial' axe has previously been found among the objects found in western France passage graves. Consequently a parallel is naturally drawn with all the other Neolithic funerary spaces without passages in which identical objects have been found (Mané-Er-Hroëck, Tumiac, Saint-Michel). In the same Mané-Hui cist a collection of sharp trapezoidal arrowheads permits the assumption that they were struck from the large light-coloured flint core discovered by Gaillard in a corner of the tomb, which must have been imported from some distance.

This closed unit of Mané-Hui provides some clues that tend to confirm our argument. The Fouaillages mound has permitted different researchers to establish a relationship between Cerny and the pottery discovered inside the monument (Kinnes 1982; Constantin 1985). This is probably a ceramic style characteristic of the Channel Islands, that of the Pinnacle, which chronologically belongs to the Cerny Horizon. Recent excavations on the Table des Marchands have confirmed that this style is relatively close to the Morbihan Castellic (Bailloud 1955; Cassen 1991a; Patton 1992). In the two geographical areas considered no evidence of the early phase of both styles has so far been found in the passage graves. Only remnants of recent Castellic (decorations in fluted semi-circles fitted into each other) have been discovered among the offerings placed in the typologically early tombs with corbelled circular chambers, such as Kerlagat in Carnac or Vierville A in Normandy (Le Rouzic 1930; Bailloud 1975; Verron 1976).

In Boisanne (Côtes d'Armor), a grave interpreted as the remains of a tomb has recently been dated to 5500 BP; it contained a vase of definitely Cerny aspect (Tinevez et al. 1990). In Ile-et-Vilaine the mound of Croix Saint Pierre is noteworthy for the presence of potsherds with repoussé buttons; the same characteristics appear again not far away at the alignment of standing stones of the Grée de Cojou (5560–5500 BP). On the southern coast of Brittany, the mound beneath the Petit Mont passage graves is contemporary with the palaeosoil of dolmen 2 (5550 and 5600 BP) and with Cerny-type ceramics found nearby. Elsewhere repoussé buttons always characterize pottery from the monuments of Quillien, Parc-Ar-Hastel (Finistère) (du Chatellier 1907; Giot et al. 1979) and Kerroch (Morbihan); the last-named is a rectangular architectural structure identical with those described in the region of Carnac (Le Rouzic 1965). More than a score of low mounds covering sealed tombs were identified in that Carnacean area and they always contain these same items (Le Rouzic 1938; Bailloud 1963; L'Helgouach 1971) (FIGURE 2).

In short, the existence of an original cultural assemblage is indisputable, despite the small number and the variability of the material elements defining it. This Cerny Horizon, which covers the Chambon, Castellic, Pinacle, Sandun etc. styles (at least in their early phases), seems to be identified or recognized with increasing certainty in some settlements in western France (Chancerel et al. 1992; Cunliffe 1984; Gallais 1987; Letterlé et al. 1991).

As regards the ceramic styles defined in the 1960s in the Armorican passage graves of different types, it seems that the typological differentiations (Carn, Le Souc'h, Chasséen, Kerleven, etc.) do not correspond with the connections observed in the field (Boujot et al. 1990). As a consequence, the Carn style appears to be considerably more recent and thus does not contradict our analysis (L'Helgouach 1989).

Absolute chronology
The main objection that is bound to be raised against our study will be based on the existence of famous sites (the passage graves of Bougon, Barnenez, etc.) at the same

period when we believe that we have detected constituent elements of the earliest monumental funerary architectures, structures which in our view should give rise to well-ordered succession of passage graves.

Apart from for a few reservations (Kinnes 1988), the hypothesis of the great antiquity of the dolmens of western France has been accepted by all researchers. We made an earlier attempt to relate our work to the isotopic analyses obtained from the French megalithic tombs (Cassen 1991b). Once again, in order to emphasize further the statistical problem of the representative nature of a series of physical measurements, and to shed light on the wide discrepancies between two dates for one or another ancient dolmen, which are summarily interpreted as reflecting different occupation phases (even though these are undetectable in the funerary offerings and personal belongings of the dead) we have selected an example from outside our own area of experience, but which should admirably illustrate our reservations.

By studying the monument of Hazleton (Gloucestershire), we shall take advantage not only of the exemplary excavation of two passage graves and distinct quadrangular chambers, but also of a series of 21 radiocarbon datings (on bones) covering the pre-megalithic phase (samples taken out from the palaeosoil) and megalithic phase (human bones in the chambers) (Saville 1983; 1984; Saville *et al.* 1987). Apart from recent work on the Petit Mont (Morbihan), which in any case supported our hypothesis, no French monument has such a radiocarbon dating sequence. In the case of Hazleton, it is only necessary to synthesize the dates to reveal the irrefutable discrepancies between the various analyses. Some results obtained in the southern chamber, for example, are a few centuries earlier than those of the pre-megalithic occupation soil. In spite of this discrepancy, it is important to remember that the series of dates actually progresses in the expected chronological order, the one given by the archaeostratigraphic sequence. In the Iberian Peninsula, some bold studies have also thrown light on the methodological problems associated with sampling in the mounds of megalithic tombs (palaeosoils) as well as the complications arising from laboratory analyses using different technologies and often supplying different dates for the same sample (Monge Soares & Peixoto Cabral 1984; Domingos da Cruz 1988).

Turning now to the series of dates established for the megalithic tombs of western France, which have to be compared with those ascribed to the Cerny Horizon on the Atlantic coast, it is obvious that, allowing on the one hand for the phenomenon of distortion and on the other for the subjectivity of sampling in construction soils, the historical succession actually evolved in the sequence that we propose. In other words, the Western Cerny Horizon, centred around 5500 BP, precedes the passage graves complex for which no contemporary settlement has produced a date earlier than 5300 BP.

Synthesis: perspectives of research

Many unknown factors remain, of course, in particular relating to monuments without passage graves (in their first stage of utilization), and about which our knowledge is still sketchy, as no research has been done in this field since the beginning of the century. Nonetheless, earlier reports on the subject are sufficiently rich in information to make up for this lacuna and contribute to the formulation of a pattern (FIGURE 3) which, despite its gaps, makes it possible to tackle the question of megalithism and its origins against the more general background of the appearance of monumental funerary structures in France as well as in the whole of Europe. Megalithism in western France cannot therefore be viewed only as the product of the inventive genius of local peoples, in contrast with the farming settlers of the Paris Basin farther east.

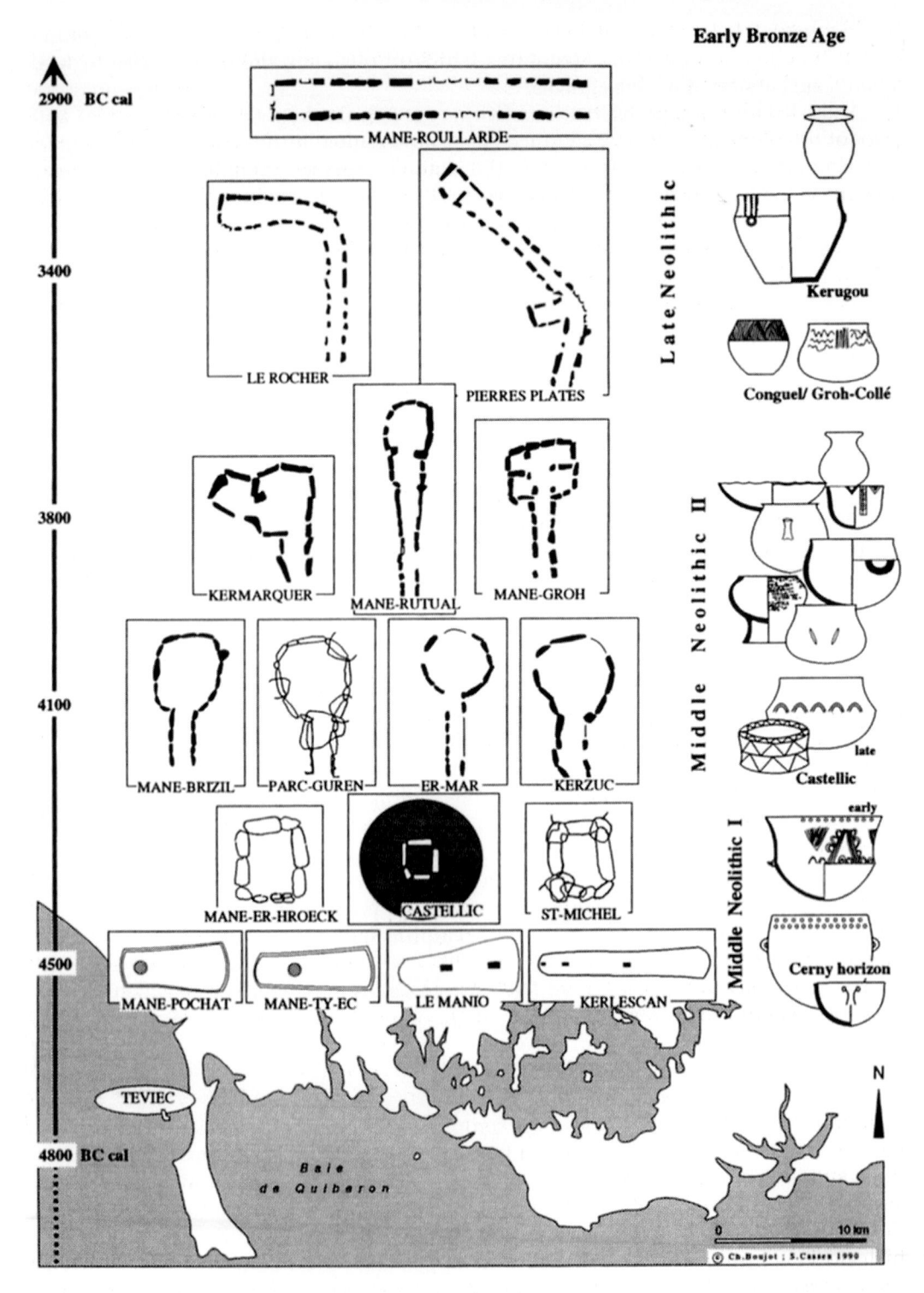

FIGURE 3. *Synthesis of the development of funerary structures (from simple grave to gallery graves, through mounds with cists and passage graves) and succession of the regional pottery styles.*

The emergence of monumentality is one of the many archaeological manifestations of the combination of new economic and social conditions resulting from the development of agricultural societies at the end of the 5th and beginning of the 4th millennium BC. This combination has traditionally been designated by the controversial term *chalcolithization* (pan-European terminology; Lichardus et al. 1985; *secondary products revolution* for Anglo-Saxon archaeologists). The changes brought about are perceptible in all fields by means of several clues, such as new ideas in breeding practices, with the use of animals for work and the stalling of cattle, the exploitation of raw materials with the development of mining, and diversification in the field of economic production, favouring increasingly specialized activities.

These transformations are associated with many technological innovations, among which the plough constitutes an important step. Its utilization for the exploitation of less fertile soils is clear evidence of the intensification of a domestic mode of production which, according to Meillassoux, entails a particular type of social organization, here summarized briefly. This mode of production is characterized by a long-term collective working investment on the land, and so its produce will not be shared immediately: it will be redistributed later after being stored. As a result, this redistribution continued over time, for generations, according to a process of hereditary redistribution of the wealth accumulated — a process legitimized by the institution of filial social relationship based on the control of women and the division of labour according to age and sex, and by the building-up of a genealogical memory founded on the cult of ancestors (Meillassoux 1979).

Although Testard's work (1982) questioned this social structure as a characteristic not only of agricultural domestic societies, but also of any form of society based on the stocking of resources, it seems to be suitable as a possible reference which would have favoured the social and economic conditions for the appearance of monumental tombs at the same time as an increase in social disparities, for example, resulting from the intensification of a mode of production begun in the Mesolithic period. The close correlation between this social structure and the architecture of the first passage graves appears all the more obvious if the function of these graves, as funerary structures, is to reproduce the social system through their ideological representation. In that respect, the feminization of megalithic tombs, mentioned by such writers as Flaubert (1880), as well as by prehistorians such as Cartailhac (1889), deserves reconsideration in that context. Indeed, with an internal structure symbolizing a womb inside a mound which suggests pregnancy, the architecture of the first passage graves illustrates the social pattern proposed by Meillassoux perfectly. Beyond the death/birth association common to many societies, where it is symbolized in the shape of the tomb, the structure of the passage graves thus very clearly represents this new social relationship of reproduction founded on the necessity to ensure descendants through the control of women. If the discovery of bodies in a foetal position in some of the earliest burials (e.g. La Hoguette) tends to support this point of view, the family ties between the individuals sometimes gathered together in the same chamber remain to be confirmed. Finally, the monumentality of these structures represents a further expression of this reproduction aspect of the social system by means of the durability that it imparts to them over several generations. Funerary gigantism, as a time and space landmark, thus appears to be the product of the historical evolution of a domestic mode of production rather than resulting solely from the necessity to define territories — a necessity ascribed by Renfrew (1983–84) to the only demographic pressure exerted by the stagnation on the Atlantic coast of the agricultural colonizing movement towards the west.

The expansion to the Centre-Atlantic coast
Although the strongest analogies have proved the identical nature of Cerny funerary architecture in the valleys of Yonne and Seine and in Normandy (FIGURE 1; Duhamel *et al.* 1991; Mordant 1991; Desloges 1989; Sherratt 1990) and that in the west of France, there are also similarities that lead to a reconsideration of several monuments in Poitou and Aquitaine, which have been incorrectly dated and often confused with passage grave cairns. In the same way, the tomb of the Demoiselle (Charente-Maritime) and the Motte des Justices (Deux-Sèvres) belong to those very long trapezoidal *tumuli* mostly made out of sediments and containing cists, which would fit perfectly with our pattern (Musset 1885; Germond 1989). In Gironde and in Gers, the same Neolithic corbelled vaults, devoid of any passage, incorporated within a huge tumular volume (Le Campet) (Devignes 1989–90; Larrieu-Duler 1971), are to be found.

The apparent contemporaneity of the appearance of monumental architecture over such vast areas recalls some long-distance connections, established on the basis of prestige objects accompanying the deceased in some Carnacean tombs.

Prestige goods and exotic connections
Nothing so far has contradicted the probable Alpine origin of the first large jadeite polished axes from Brittany and Normandy (Campbell Smith 1965; Schut *et al.* 1987; Ricq-de-Bouard *et al.* 1990). Among several identical objects found in Gers in the southwest of France, the famous *Sépulture de Chef*, a funeral deposit at Pauilhac, provides an example of a large 'ceremonial' axe made to a pattern specific to the Morbihan models (Bischoff 1865; Cartailhac 1889). These examples demonstrate that we are working towards establishing geographical relationships at a spatial level, something which seems to frighten modern archaeologists. It is, however, the study of these long-distance relationships and the underlying economic network that will help us to understand all the factors involved in the emergence of funerary gigantisism in the Europe of 5000 years ago.

The discovery of horse bones in the Gers tomb (Roussot-Laroque 1976) is puzzling. Their presence, of course, is surprising, but so also is the fact that such bones were identified in Brittany as well (obviously in a Neolithic context) in the vaults of the Moustoir and Mané Lud. In Jersey the central crypt of the huge cairn of La Teste du Fief, which exactly follows the same building pattern as that of the Mané-Er-Hroëck, also contained the remains of a horse which accompanied the deceased, found bent in a lateral position (Deyrolle & Mauger 1912). It is known that horses were very unusual and appeared quite late in the faunal diagrams of the Neolithic deposits on the French Atlantic coast, yet they became essential prestige goods among the peoples of the Pontic plains, and this at the very moment when the monumental structures mentioned above were being erected. Could that coincidence be pure chance? Particular attention should be paid to the large number of Neolithic horse bones in the Averdon region of central France (Cabard 1991), which are the only representatives of wild animals among the remains of many common domestic species.

However, these connections are not intended to revert back to the shaky ground of neo-diffusionism, even if we were to revive less than seriously the migration of symbols by drawing a comparison between the identical representations of Varna (Bulgaria) and Locmariaquer (Morbihan) (Cassen 1991b). In the same way, despite the hints that have often been dropped, critical discussion of the radiocarbon dates from the west of France does not lead to the restoration of Hülle's *ältere Langgrabkultur*. Once again this revision upwards by four or five radiocarbon centuries does not put in question the undeniable originality of the funerary architecture of western France. It is, moreover, no coincidence that the complex alignments, testimony to their knowledge of the rhythms of sun and moon which suggest likely connections with the sphere of religion, are located in just those places where not only the widest possible variety of funerary, sacred and symbolical structures, but also the most 'luxurious' *viaticum* are to be found. It would seem permissible, therefore, to imagine that the personalities buried and honoured there may have been related in some way to those exceptional religious demonstrations. Future research will be directed to an understanding of the factors — possibly in the economic sphere at the beginning of the Armorican Neolithic — that contributed to the accumulation of so much 'wealth' in the hands of so few people, such as perhaps the collection of sea salt or the exploitation of rare stones.

Whatever may happen to the model put forward, it should be given credit for recalling those among our predecessors who had an intuitive understanding of some implications of the mechanisms developed here. For instance Le Rouzic, as early as 1934, did not hesitate to allot the tombs of Teviec to the early Neolithic. The confusion he created between the 'richest', most massive Neolithic tumuli and those, very similar in structure, covering Early Bronze individual tombs, unintentionally highlighted what may be symptomatic of the phenomena and metamorphoses of a true cycle of human history, in the sense that each of the two architectural groups emerging at the beginning of their respective periods reveals a very distinct process of social differentiation.

A few years later, Christopher Hawkes gave a resolutely evolutionary interpretation of the same deposits by emphasizing all the links between the structured graves of Teviec and the cists in the mound of Manio II (Hawkes 1940). As for Stuart Piggott, he understood the need to draw comparisons between the British and the Morbihan mounds, and, later between all similar monuments in eastern Europe (Piggott 1954). Finally, G. Bailloud turned his attention to pottery products, previously disregarded, and deduced typological and chronological correlations between Brittany, the Channel Islands and the Paris Basin, and even the south of France.

Today the dynamism of Spanish and Portuguese excavations and research on the Neolithic period and associated funerary structures seems to demonstrate on the one hand the relevance of our pattern (Tarrus i Galter 1990) and on the other the fact that we shall reach a better undestaning of the problems through international collaboration that goes beyond linguistic and regional compartmentalization.

References

AUXIETTE, G. 1989. Les bracelets néolithiques dans le nord de la France, la Belgique et l'Allemagne rhénane, *Revue Archéologique de Picardie* 1/2: 13–65.
BAILLOUD, G. 1963. Les civilisations atlantiques du Néolithique à l'Age du Fer. *I° colloque atlantique, Brest*. Rennes: Université de Rennes I.
　1975. Les céramiques cannelées du Néolithique morbihannais, *Bulletin de la Société Préhistorique Française* 72: 343–67.
　1985. Le Néolithique et le Chalcolithique de la France, in J. & M. Lichardus, *La Protohistoire de l'Europe*: 516–568. Paris: Presses Universitaires de France (PUF), Nlle Clio.
BAILLOUD, G. & P. MIEG DE BOOFZHEIM. 1955. *Les civilisations néolithiques de la France dans leur contexte européen*. Paris: Picard.
BISCHOFF, E. 1865. Monuments de l'Age de la Pierre et de la période gallo-romaine dans la vallée du Gers, *Revue de Gascogne*: 389–96.
BOUJOT, C. & S. CASSEN. 1990. Le développement des premières architectures funéraires monumentales en France occidentale, *Colloque interrégional sur le Néolithique, Vannes*: 15. Vannes: Groupe Inter Néo. *Résumé des communications*.
　1992. Le développement des premières architectures funéraires monumentales en France occidentale. Colloque interrégional sur le Néolithique, Vannes, *Revue archéologique de l'ouest* sup. 5: 195–211.
CABARD, P. 1991. La faune néolithique de la région d'Averdon, vallée de la Cisse (Loir-et-Cher), *Actes du Colloque interrégional sur le Néolithique, Blois*: 221–32. Blois: Société Archéologique du Vendomois.

CAMPBELL SMITH, W. 1965. The distribution of jade axes in Europe, *Proceedings of the Prehistoric Society*: 25–9.
CARTAILHAC, E. 1889. *La France préhistorique d'après les sépultures et les ossements*. Paris: Alcan.
CASSEN, S. 1991a. Cerny-sud: précisions et réflexions autour de l'article de C. Constantin, *Bulletin de la Société Préhistorique Française* 88(4): 99–100.
  1991b. Les débuts du IV° millénaire en Centre-Ouest: l'hypothèse du Matignons ancien, *Actes du Colloque international de Nemours, Identité du Chasséen*: 111–20. Nemours: Musée de Préhistoire d'Ile de France. Mémoire 4.
CASSEN, S. & J. L'HELGOUACH. 1992. Du symbole de la crosse: chronologie, répartition et interprétation. Colloque interrégional sur le Néolithique, *Revue archéologique de l'ouest* sup. 5: 223–35.
CHANCEREL, A., J. DESLOGES, J-L. DRON & G. SAN JUAN. 1992. Le début du Néolithique en Basse-Normandie. Colloque interrégional sur le Néolithique, Vannes, *Revue archéologique de l'ouest* sup. 5: 153–73.
CONSTANTIN, C. 1985. *Fin du Rubané, céramique du Limbourg et post-rubané: le Néolithique le plus ancien en Bassin Parisien et en Hainaut*. Oxford: British Archaeological Reports. International series S273.
CUNLIFFE, B. 1984. Excavations in the Middle Wart, Mont-Orgueil, *Jersey Archaeological Journal* 141: 216–42.
DE LUMLEY, H. & J. GUILAINE (ed.). 1976. *La Préhistoire Française* Paris: CNRS.
DESLOGES, J. 1989. Découverte d'une nécropole néolithique au lieu-dit la Haute Bonny, commune de Rors, Calvados, *Journée Préhistorique de Bretagne*: 34–5. Rennes: Université de Rennes I.
DEVIGNES, M. 1987. Les monuments mégalithiques de la Gironde. Inventaire et analyse. Doctorat de III° cycle, Université de Bordeaux III.
  1990. Archives et mégalithes ou de l'utilité des études d'archives pour mieux connaitre les monuments mégalithiques, *Revue Archéologique de Bordeaux* 81: 151–73.
DEYROLLE, & MAUGER. 1912. Note sur le dolmen sous tumulus de la Teste du Fief de la Hougue-Boête (Jersey), *Bulletin de la Société d'Anthropologie de Paris*: 165–71.
DOMINGOS DA CRUZ, J. 1988. O megalitismo do norte de Portugal, *Trabalhos de antropologia e etnologia* 28: 15–49.
DUCHATELLIER, P. 1907. *Les époques préhistorique et gauloise dans le Finistère*. 2nd edition. Rennes, Quimper.
DUDAY, H. 1985. Observations ostéologiques et décomposition du cadavre: sépulture colmatée ou en espace vide? RCP 742, *Méthodes d'études des sépultures*, compte-rendu de la Table-ronde 1985, St Germain-en-Laye.
FLAUBERT, G. 1979 (1880). *Bouvard et Pecuchet*. Paris: Gallimard.
FONTS. 1881. Fouilles à Carnac. Tombe circulaire, *Bulletin de la Société Polymatique du Morbihan*: 120–23.
GAILLARD, F. 1883. Les cistes du Mané-Groh et de Bovelane en Erdeven, *Bulletin de la Société Polymatique du Morbihan* and unpublished ms.
  1897. Le dolmen du Mané-Hui à Kerléarec en Carnac, *Bulletin de la Société d'Anthropologie de Paris*: 34–8.
GAILLARD, J., J. GOMEZ, Y. TABORIN, C.T. LE ROUX, R. RIQUET & A. GILBERT. 1984. La tombe néolithique de Germignac, *Gallia-Préhistoire*: 97–117.
GALLAIS, C. & J.Y. 1987. Le Néolithique ancien à L'Organais en St Reine de Bretagne (Loire-Atlantique), *Etudes Pré- et Protohistoriques des Pays de la Loire* 10: 31–4.
GALLES, R. 1878. *Fouille du tumulus de Tumiac en Arzon*. Vannes.
GALLES, R. & A. MAURICET. 1864. *Etude sur le Mane-Lud en Locmariaquer*. Vannes.
  1865. *Fouille du tumulus du Moustoir-Carnac*. Vannes.
GERMOND, G. 1987. Thouars. La Motte des Justices, *Gallia Informations*: 288.
GIOT, P.R. 1991. De l'origine des sépultures mégalithiques, *Bulletin Société Préhistorique Française* 88(5): 140–41.
GIOT, P.R. & J. L'HELGOUACH. 1955. Le tertre tumulaire de la Croix-St-Pierre à St Just (Ile et Vilaine), *Annales de Bretagne* 42(2).
GIOT, P.R., J. L'HELGOUACH & L. MONNIER. 1979. *Préhistoire de la Bretagne*. Rennes: Ed. Ouest-France.
HAWKES, C.F.C. 1940. *The prehistoric foundations of Europe: to the Mycenaean Age*. London: Thames & Hudson.
JEUNESSE, C. 1987. La céramique de la Hoguette. Un nouvel 'élément non-rubané' du Néolithique ancien de l'Europe du nord-ouest, *Cahiers Alsaciens d'Archéologie* 30: 5–33.
KINNES, I. 1982. Les Fouaillages and megalithic origins, *Antiquity* 56: 24–30.
  1988. Megaliths in action: some aspects of the Neolithic period in the Channel Islands, *Archaeological Journal* 145: 13–59.
LARRIEU-DULER, M. 1971. Pauilhac préhistorique, *Bulletin de la Société Archéologique et Historique du Gers*: 418–46.
LECORNEC, J. 1987. Le complexe mégalithique du Petit-Mont, Arzon (Morbihan), *Revue archéologique de l'ouest* 4.
LEFÈVRE, M. & R. GALLES. 1863. Mané-er-H'roëk. Dolmen découvert sous un tumulus à Locmariaquer, *Bulletin de la Société Polymatique du Morbihan*: 18–33.
LE PONTOIS, G. 1929. Le Finistère préhistorique, *Institut International d'Anthropologie* 3.
LE ROUX, C.T., Y. LECERF, J.Y. TINEVEZ & D. LEROY. 1989. Locmariaquer, Er-Grah: tertre tumulaire néolithique, *Bulletin d'Informations Archéologiques, Rennes* 2: 64–5.
LE ROUX, C.T., J. L'HELGOUACH, S. CASSEN, E. GAUMÉ, Y. LECERF, C. LE POTIER, D. LEROY, J.Y. TINEVEZ. 1989. Fouilles récentes à Locmariaquer (Morbihan). *Pré-Actes du XXIIIe Congrès Préhistorique de France*. Paris: Congrès Préhistorique de France.
LE ROUZIC, Z. 1920. Carnac. Fouilles faites dans la région, *Bulletin de la Société Polymatique du Morbihan*.
  1930. *Dolmens à galerie sous tumulus de Kerlagat, commune de carnac*. Vannes.
  1932. *Tumulus du Mont St Michel*. Vannes.
  1933. Morphologie et chronologie des sépultures préhistoriques du Morbihan, *L'Anthropologie* 43: 225–57.
  1934. Le mobilier des sépultures préhistoriques du Morbihan, *L'Anthropologie* 44: 486–508.

1934–1935. *Carnac: fouilles et restaurations faites dans la région*. Vannes.
1938. Carnac. Restaurations faites dans la région. Unpublished report to the Beaux-Arts.
1965. Inventaire des monuments mégalithiques de la région de Carnac, *Bulletin de la Société Polymatique du Morbihan*. Numéro spécial.
LE ROUZIC, Z. & M & MME ST JUST-PEQUART. 1923. *Carnac, fouilles faites dans la région. Campagne 1922*. Nancy: Berger-Levrault.
LETTERLÉ, F., D. LE GOUESTRE & N. LE MEUR. 1991. La chronologie du Néolithique moyen en Armorique à la lumière du site de Sandun à Guérande (Loire Atlantique), *Actes du colloque interrégional sur le Néolithique, Blois*: 149–58.
L'HELGOUACH, J. 1966. *Les sépultures mégalithiques en Armorique*. Rennes: Université de Rennes I.
1971. Les débuts du Néolithique en Armorique au 4° millénaire et son développement au commencement du 3° millénaire, *Fundamenta* Reihe A (Band 3): 178–201.
1984. Une architecture prestigieuse, il y a 7000 ans: le tumulus mégalithique de Dissignac, à St Nazaire, 303, *Pays de Loire*: 20–33.
1986. Les sépultures mégalithiques du Néolithique final: architectures et figurations pariétales. Comparaisons et relations entre Massif armoricain et nord de la France. Colloque de Caen, *Revue archéologique de l'ouest* sup. 1: 189–94.
1990. De l'île Carn à la Table des Marchands, *Revue archéologique de l'ouest* sup. 2: 89–95.
LICHARDUS, J. & M. 1985. *Protohistoire de l'Europe*. Paris: Presses Universitaires de France (PUF), Nlle Clio.
LÜNING, J., U. KLOOS & S. ALBERT. 1989. Westliche Nachbarn der bandkeramischen Kultur: La Hoguette und Limburg, *Germania* 2: 355–93.
MARSILLE, L. 1928. Anneaux-disques du Morbihan, *Bulletin de la Société Préhistorique Français*: 90–98.
MEILLASSOUX, C. 1979. *Femmes, greniers et capitaux*. Paris: F. Maspero.
MILN, J. 1883. Exploration de trois monuments quadrilatères, *Bulletin de la Société Polymatique du Morbihan*: 30–49.
MONGE SOARES, A. & J.M. Peixoto Cabral. 1984. Datas convencionais de radiocarbono para estações arqueologicas portuguesas e a sua calibraçao: revisao critica, *O Arqueologo Portugues* series 4(2): 167–214.
MORDANT, D. 1987. Des inhumations en 'pleine terre'? L'exemple de la Petite Seine, in H. Duday & C. Masset (ed.), *Anthropologie physique et Archéologie*: 155–65. Paris: CNRS.
1991. Le site des Réaudins à Balloy (Seine-et-Marne). Premiers résultats, *Actes du Colloque interrégional sur le Néolithique, Châlons/Marne*: 33–43. Châlons-sur-Marne: Préhistoire et Protohistoire en Champagne-Ardennes. Numéro spécial.
MUSSET, G. 1885. *La Charente-Inférieure avant l'Histoire et dans la légende*. La Rochelle.
PATTON, M. 1990. Neolithic stone rings from the Channel Islands, *Société Jersiaise*: 347–52.
1992. Entre Cerny et Castellic: le groupe Pinacle/Fouillages. Actes du Colloque interrégional sur le Néolithique, Vannes, *Revue archéologique de l'ouest* sup. 5: 147–51.
PETREQUIN, P. & J.F. PININGRE. 1976. Les sépultures collectives mégalithiques de Franche-Comté, *Gallia-Préhistoire* 19: 287–381.
PIGGOTT, S. 1954. *The Neolithic cultures of the British Isles*. Cambridge: Cambridge University Press.
PRESTREAU, M. & P. DUHAMEL. 1991. La nécropole monumentale néolithique de Passy dans le contexte du gigantisme funéraire européen, *Actes du Colloque interrégional de Blois*: 103–18. Blois: Société Archéologique du Vendômois.
RENFREW, C. 1983. *Les origines de l'Europe*. Paris: Flammarion.
1984. Archéologie sociale des monuments mégalithiques, *Pour la Science* 75: 28–37.
RICQ DE BOUARD, M., R. COMPAGNONI, J. DESMONS & F. FEDELE. 1990. Les roches alpines de l'outillage poli néolithique de la France méditerranéenne, *Gallia Préhistoire* 32: 125–49.
ROUSSOT-LARROQUE, J. 1976. Les civilisations néolithiques de l'Aquitaine, in de Lumley & Guilaine (ed.): 338–50.
SAN-JUAN, G. & J.L. DRON. 1991. Ernes (Calvados). Une occupation néolithique scellée par un cairn à chambre ronde, *Actes du Colloque interrégional sur le Néolithique, Blois*: 69–80.
SAVILLE, A. 1983. Hazleton, *Current Archaeology* 4: 107–12.
1984. Preliminary report on the excavation of a Cotswold-Severn tomb at Hazleton, Gloucestershire, *The Antiquaries Journal* 64: 10–24.
SAVILLE, A., J.A.J. GOWLETT & R.E.M. HEDGES. 1987. Radiocarbon dates from the chambered tomb at Hazleton (Glos.): a chronology for neolithic collective burial, *Antiquity* 61: 108–19.
SHERRATT, A. 1990. The genesis of megaliths: monumentality, ethnicity and social complexity in Neolithic north-west, *World Archaeology* 22(2): 147–67.
SCHUT, P., H. KARS & J.M. WEVERS. 1987. Jade axes in the Netherlands: a preliminary report, *Helinium* 27: 71–87.
TARRUS I GALTER, J. 1990. Les dolmens anciens de Catalogne, in J. Guilaine & X Gutherz (ed.), *Autour de J. Arnal*: 271–90. Montpellier: Université des Sciences et Techniques du Languedoc.
TESTARD, A. 1981. *Les chasseurs-cueilleurs et l'origine des inégalités*. Paris: Société d'Ethnographie.
TINEVEZ, J.Y., T. CORNEC & P. PIHUIT. 1990. Une fosse néolithique au lieu-dit la Boisanne à Plouer-sur-Rance (Côtes-d'Armor), *Revue archéologique de l'ouest* 7: 31–9.
VERRON, G. 1976. Les civilisations néolithiques en Normandie, in de Lumley & Guilaine (ed.): 387–410.

Megalithic and other art: Centre and West
by T.G.E. POWELL
ANTIQUITY 34 (135), 1960

THE OCCURRENCE OF designs cut on the stone walling slabs of certain prehistoric tombs in Central Germany has led from time to time to a search for comparisons, even prototypes, in the mural art of megalithic tombs in Atlantic Europe. Within recent years, some new observations and discoveries of considerable interest have been made principally as a result of a re-excavation at the well-known Lohne (Züschen) megalithic tomb near Fritzlar, and through the excavation of a tumulus on the Dölauer Heide near Halle/Saale (FIGURE 1).

The first of these monuments is a large, megalithically constructed, collective tomb with a long rectangular chamber entered through a port-hole slab which is set between the main chamber and a short ante chamber. The whole monument is set in a trench so that the roof was approximately at ground level. This is one of a group of such tombs in Hesse; there is a neighbouring group in Westphalia, and these are related both to a group in Sweden, and, more particularly, to the classic tombs of this type in the Paris Basin (SOM). The Dölau tumulus is something quite different, for in it, amongst other things, has been found a stone-constructed grave for only one individual. The wall and capstones are of moderate size but not megalithic, and the grave can be likened in various respects to some three other stone-built graves, all in the Halle district, and of which the best known was that found at Göhlitzsch with its representations of bow, quiver and battle-axe, cut, with other decoration, on the wall faces.

The cultural, and even chronological, distinctions that might appear to separate Lohne (Züschen) and Halle/Dölau are complicated by the fact that both share a particular decorative motif: close-set pick-executed chevroning, and, further, this is rather different from anything found in mural art in the far west.

Lohne (Züschen) also displays schematic representations of horned animals yoked to sledges or carts, also not known in the west, but recalling some rock carvings in the Ligurian Alps. In fact, Lohne displays two kinds of mural art not known in any tombs of the Paris Basin group to which it is structurally related, nor anywhere in Atlantic Europe. Furthermore, there is nothing in the burial ritual, or material culture, of the Dölau/Göhlitzsch graves, themselves but an aspect of the Saale Single Grave/Corded Ware *(Saaleschnurkeramik)* Culture, to suggest that any influence had flowed eastwards from the cultures of the megalithic tomb builders in the far west assuming, indeed, that western chronology can allow a sufficiently early date for such a possibility. How, in either of the two cases under discussion, is the idea of sepulchral mural art, whether for ritual or decorative ends, to be accounted for? Has too much been made of apparant western similarities? The problem has, however, a further extension for at least one unequivocal *statue-menhir,* of the southern French sort, has been found close to the Saale, and that used as building material in a grave of Early Bronze Age type in that region.

Finally, account has to be taken of ordinary menhirs, or large standing stones, for these are widely distributed in Western and Central Germany, with a small group in Bohemia, and these monuments also have some claim for consideration in the present context.

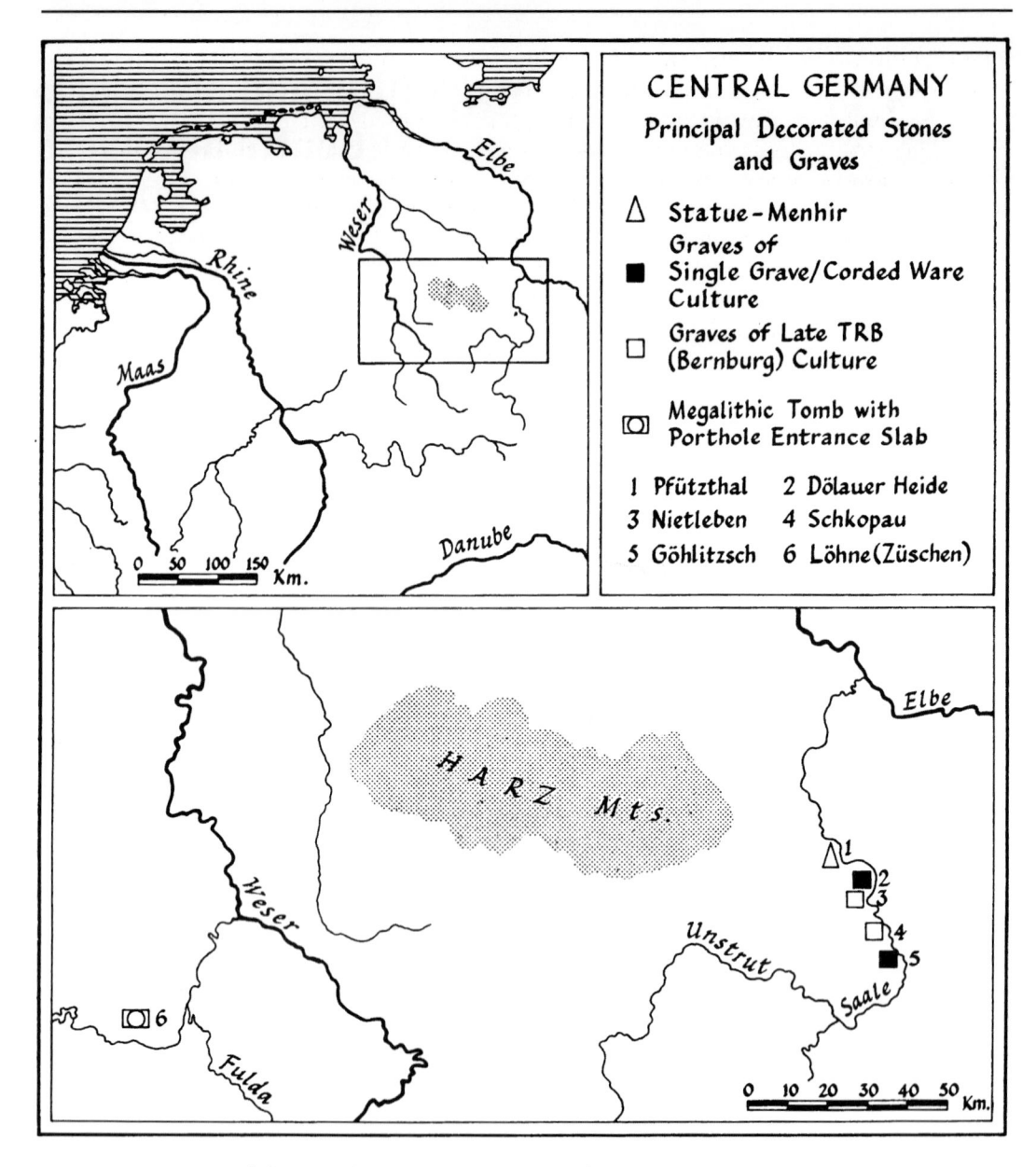

FIGURE 1. *Location of decorated monuments in Central Germany.*

It becomes clear that an explanation of the interplay of all these factors in Central Germany is no straightforward matter. The present notes are offered not so much as a solution of these problems as an attempt to clarify certain aspects of the available material, none of which is as well known to students in the west as it deserves to be. The writer has been so fortunate as to have been able to examine the Dölau and Göhlitzsch stones in the Landesmuseum at Halle/Saale, having already had some acquaintance with megalithic art in Atlantic Europe.

A beginning may be made with the tomb at Lohne (Züschen), and Dr Otto Uenze's excellent published descriptions and commentary merit close attention (Uenze 1956;

1958).[1] Here only some of the more salient points can be mentioned. At least some of the megalithic slabs, whether for walling or roofing, had had to be transported from distances of about four kilometres, and although capstones are rare at all the Hesse tombs, chiefly because of their removal in later times for agricultural or building purposes, Uenze makes the interesting point that wooden roofs may also have been employed on account of the scarcity of stone. The results of excavation of the tomb at Lohra, Kr. Marburg, where no capstones were in position, suggests that the decay of a wooden roof had allowed the low surmounting tumulus to collapse into the chamber and lie directly on the upper burial deposits (*Kurhessische Bodenaltertümer* 3 (1954): 27–48).[2]

The burial deposits at Lohne (Züschen) were removed in 1894, but very satisfactory evidence comes from the excavation of a similar *Steinkammergrab* at Altendorf, Kr. Wolfhagen, in which about 250 inhumations had taken place (*Kurhessische Bodenaltertümer* 3 (1954): 5–26). In all tombs of the Hesse group, as elsewhere, pavements of small flagstones had been laid on the chamber floor, and between various burial deposits as these rose from floor level. Skulls were often laid along the walls, and groups of bones enclosed in stone settings. These contrivances were for the purpose of making more room in the chamber for subsequent interments, and integrated skeletons near the entrance, but within the chamber proper, presumably represent the final use of the tomb by the community who erected it. Neither in Hesse, nor in Westphalia, is there evidence for any common ceramic tradition amongst the tomb builders, nor for pottery being an integral element in their material culture at all. Fragments of imported collared-flasks of the First Northern, Funnel-Beaker (TRB), Culture come from the Lohne (Züschen) and Altendorf tombs, but there are no rough pots with S-profile and modelled foot of the SOM kind, and Uenze makes the important suggestion that these pots in the Paris Basin should represent a late stage in the use of those tombs when the local inhabitants had come under the influence of intruders of the Single Grave *(Einzelgrab)* Culture, who possessed distinctive footed vessels. This point could best be resolved by more precise observations during excavations of Paris Basin tombs than has been the case heretofore. Furthermore, there is no known occurrence of Grand Pressigny flint in the *Steinkammergräber* of Hesse or Westphalia, but this flint does occur in Single Grave associations in these regions. The SOM-pot/Grand Pressigny flint horizon in the Paris Basin tombs should therefore be later than the primary use of the Hesse-Westphalia tombs. Both at Lohne (Züschen) and at Altendorf, sherds of true Single Grave pottery came to light, and the exact excavation technique employed showed that these sherds occurred only in the deposit immediately below the roof (Uenze 1956: 77–88, for further references and discussion). Intrusive Single Grave burials in these tombs may be likened to the way in which many megalithic tombs in Atlantic Europe were put to secondary use by the makers of Bell-Beakers, and in Britain and Ireland this practice continued to the time of Bronze Age 'food-vessels' whose makers were descended, at least in part, from Bell-Beaker and Corded Ware ancestors.

The art at Lohne (Züschen) may now be considered. Uenze has drawn attention to the horned animal art occupying the central position on the wall faces of such stones as are decorated in this manner. (Uenze (1958: 500–502) draws attention to small stone

---

1 This tomb is at Lohne, not at Züschen, which is a neighbouring town. I have therefore followed Dr Uenze's usage. I am indebted to Dr Uenze for various kindnesses, and for his stimulating writings on the subject.
2 Dr Daniel informs me of a completely wood-built tomb in the Paris Basin group: Bonnières-sur-Seine, see *Bull. Soc. arch., hist. et scientifique de la région de* Bonnières-sur-Seine *(S.-et-O.)*, 1953: 17–28.

(a) Lohne (Züschen)

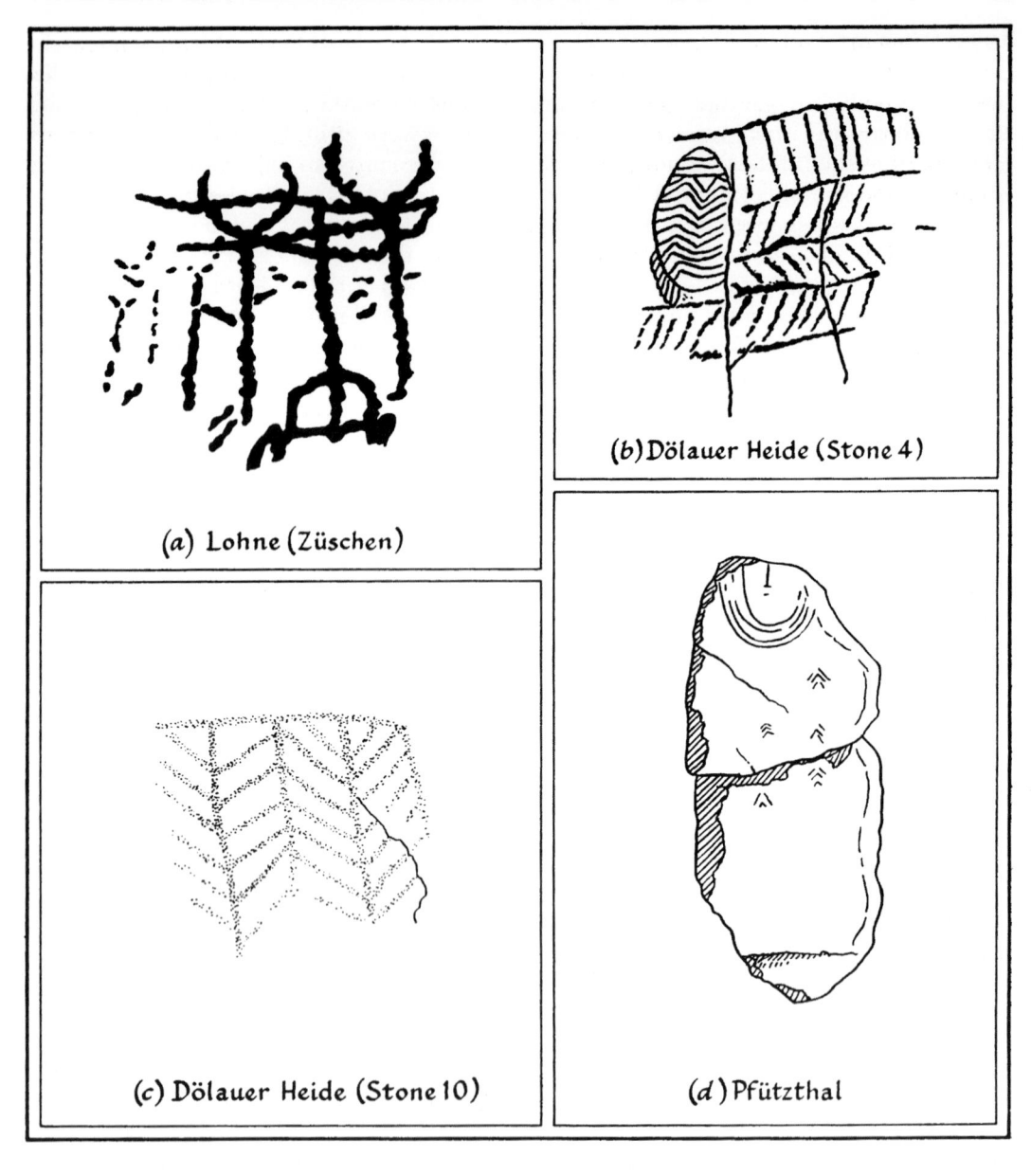

(b) Dölauer Heide (Stone 4)

(c) Dölauer Heide (Stone 10)

(d) Pfützthal

FIGURE 2. *Selected motifs from Central German monuments.*

slabs, found loose in the tomb deposit, with carvings. See our FIGURE 2a, from a slab of this kind which displays the detail of the animal art better than do any of the wall stones.) The designs certainly appear to represent a 'vertical view' of horned animals, probably oxen, that, in a number of cases, are yoked in pairs or threes, and draw some kind of vehicle (FIGURE 2a). This vehicle is represented as a straight line drawn at right-angles to the pole, each end terminating in a deep pit that might be interpreted as a wheel. In a few cases there is a semi-circular line drawn to join these pits crossing over the pole. It must again be a matter of conjecture as to whether these represent the body of some kind of vehicle, and, as Uenze points out, whether this art has any inference for the transportation of some of the blocks from a distance. A possible connection with rock art in the Ligurian Alps has already been mentioned (Bicknell 1911, especially plate III; also Louis 1950: figure 2), but these animals at Lohne (Züschen) should not be confused with the simple ox-horn designs found in some of the megalithic tombs in Brittany, although they may well have a common Mediterranean ancestry as proper subjects for portrayal in ritual art (Péquart & Le Rouzic 1927, especially plates 24, 46, 50).

The close-set chevroning, or herring-bone *(Fischgrätenverzierung)* at Lohne (Züschen) is executed in deep pick technique, and occurs only near the upper edge of two stones. Uenze very rightly draws attention to the close connection of this motif, both in pottery and grave decoration, with the Single Grave Culture, and deduces that its appearance at Lohne is in connection with the secondary use of the tomb when only the upper portions of the walling stood free. This chevron style in tomb art is best exemplified on the walls of Grave 7 in the tumulus excavated by Dr Hermann Behrens on the Dölauer Heide near Halle/Saale, in 1953 (Behrens *et al.* (1956) for original study of the decorated stones; Behrens (1958c) for excavation report on the tumulus, while 1958a & 1958b are convenient summaries). This tumulus is of particular interest for a number of reasons. It overlay a long rectangular post-built house of the Salzmunder phase of the Funnel-Beaker (TRB) Culture, and itself contained a wedge-shaped area, bounded by ditches, which together with several graves, all appeared to belong to this phase of the Funnel-Beaker Culture. The stone-built, decorated grave (no. 7), with an enlarged tumulus covering, were additions. The approximate measurements of the grave are: length 4 m, breadth a little over 1 m, and internal height 1 m. The walls comprise 11 stones, and the roof consists of six rather narrow slabs.

The proportions of the stones hardly allow the grave to be described as megalithic. At the inner end of the grave, and occupying about a third of the floor space, there had been constructed a wooden platform or floor. Apart from the actual remains of wood, the earth was darker in this area than elsewhere. Some disturbed bones of a man's skeleton were found scattered about the whole floor so that his original position cannot be determined, though the majority of such bones as survived lay in the centre of the grave, not at the floored end. There were no grave goods, but seven of the 11 wall stones were highly decorated; five had designs executed by the use of a sharp, deep-cutting pick, more possibly a punch used with a hammer stone, while on one stone the decoration had been effected in white colouring, and on another both picking and painting had been carried out. The good condition of the painted designs, and the tenacity of the material used, makes it improbable that the stones with pick-executed designs only had lost an original application of colour through atmospheric conditions.

For detailed description of this Dölau grave the original reports must be consulted, but here the first point to be noted is the general overall nature of the wall decoration, especially at the inner end of the grave. Both painted stones (nos. 5 and 8) are here, one of them (5) being the end stone (FIGURE 3). This end stone displays a general white painted scheme of a linear design in which hatched triangles and prominent reserved vertical zig-zags are conspicuous. Also portrayed are five axes standing vertically as if placed against the wall. These were picked and then painted after the linear scheme had been completed. Whatever may be thought of the significance of the other decoration at Dölau, the whole impression conveyed by this stone is the same as that of the Göhlitzsch slabs: it is the inside of the man's house with his weapons conveniently at hand.

The white-colour decoration on stone 8 is of the same pattern, reserved zig-zags, and hatched triangles, as the background scheme on stone 5. Coming to the stones with picked decoration, the inner face of stone 2 is entirely covered with a chevron pattern in

FIGURE 3. *Dölauer Heide, stone 5. (Photo Landesmuseum Halle/Saale).*

rather widely spaced picked lines, and stone 3 shows on the upper half of its face a simple linear pattern of horizontal and oblique lines. On the lower part of the face a large and shallow vertical groove had been picked out, and this may have had something to do with a timber which formed the outer edge of the wooden structure.

The two stones that perhaps lend themselves most to controversy are stones 4 and 10 (FIGURES 2b & 2c). Both stones have much rougher natural surfaces than the other slabs employed, and in both cases decoration is confined to an area covering more or less the upper half of the wall face. The main design on stone 4 consists, from the lower edge upwards, of three rows of alternating oblique lines set within a framework of single horizontal lines, and above these is a series of short vertical lines with some other less distinct picking including at least one small circle. Two horizontal lines terminate the upper boundary of the whole scheme. The most conspicuous feature on this stone is a more carefully pick-executed design which occupies the greater part of the left-hand side (as viewed) of the decorated panel. This problematical design has been usefully referred to by Professor Horst Kirchner as the Oval *(das 'Eirund')*, and this describes its general shape very well. The Oval is some 30 cm in height and 5 cm wide. The upper end is more pointed than the lower. The surface within the enclosing line is covered with a simple chevron design of picked lines except at the upper end where there are three horizontal lines. Depending from the enclosing line, where it curves upwards from the broad base on the outer side, are some 10 short lines with broader ends that look like a row of tassels. It would be possible to discuss this design at length, but it must suffice to say that while the views so far published tend to see in it a version of some anthropomorphic motif represented in western Passage Grave art, the present writer believes it to be a depiction of some kind of object, possibly a bag, or container of amulets, but of some sort that might have been normal in the dead man's house, just as were his weapons. Neither in execution, nor in detail of design, does he see any real likeness to West European megalithic art.

Stone 10 displays a pair of conjoined pentagonal frames in each of which is a 'pine branch' that has again been interpreted as a borrowing from western tomb art. The 'fir-tree man' is an uncommon, and evidently late, motif in a few Irish Passage Graves, and except for its basic linear construction, shares nothing in appearance with these balanced motifs at Dölau, nor with the smaller but comparable 'pine-branch' close to the axe-blade on one of the Göhlitzsch slabs (Behrens *et al.* 1956: plate III, and frequently illustrated elsewhere. The position of the handle near the butt of this axe, as in the Dölau examples, suggests that metal forms were intended). A possible interpretation, here put forward, is that these Central German motifs represent pelts, or dried skins of animals stretched on frames, hung on the walls, and so, with the other patterns whether representing textiles, painted plaster, or interwoven wattling, contribute to portray the interior decoration of a contemporary house of the living. It remains to mention stone 9 (FIGURE 4), for it displays a straightforward mural pattern in which the rows of close-set chevrons are almost identical with the 'secondary' chevrons at Lohne (Züschen). The discovery of this stone 9 at Dölau provides strong support for Dr Uenze's view as to the origin of the chevron art at Lohne, and similarly the two isolated stones from Ellenberg, Kr. Melsungen, in Hesse (Uenze 1956: plates 44 & 45; 1958: 105, figure 7), may be attributed more certainly, as Uenze suggested, to the westward expansion of the Single Grave people.

FIGURE 4. *Dölauer Heide, stone 9. (Photo Landesmuseum Halle/Saale).*

In connection with the use of colouring matter at Dölau, it should be said that the stones of the Göhlitzsch grave, when found, were coloured in red, black, and white. Some red colouring is still to be seen embedded in the picked lines. Another grave of the Saale Single Grave/Corded Ware Culture with coloured walls was that found at Stedten, but here the four walling slabs were specially selected from different rocks: red sandstone, white limestone, porphyry, and conglomerate (Childe 1929: 149).

Additional to Dölau and Göhlitzsch, two other stone-built graves in the Halle region are known to have possessed incised mural decoration. These were found at Nietleben, and Schopkau, but they present special problems. In the first place the decoration is of a fragmentary, indeed perfunctory, kind, but sufficient in its content to show its reliance on the art style exemplified at Dölau and Göhlitzsch. Secondly, the graves were distinctly wedge-shaped, the entrance being at the narrower end, and thirdly, both graves contained pottery distinctive of the Bernburg group which falls late in the Funnel Beaker (TRB) sequence, but which is generally regarded as ante-dating the appearance of *Saaleschnurkeramik*. In the inner part of the Nietleben grave, traces were found of a wooden platform or floor, and this feature would seem to provide a strong additional link with the rites and practices of the builders of Grave 7 in the Dölau tumulus. These points are all emphasized by Dr Behrens who believes that a distinction should be kept in mind as between the decorated graves containing Bernburg pottery and those, as yet without pottery, which display battle-axes and Corded Ware style motifs, on their walls. The chronological difficulty cannot be properly explored here, but it may be suggested that either the Bernburg pottery continued sufficiently late to be contemporary with the earlier phase of the Saale Single Gravel Corded Ware Culture, or that the perfunctory decoration at Nietleben and Schopkau was the result of influence from funerary practice through external contacts before the actual settlement of Single Grave people in the Halle region. Whatever the exact process, it may be noted that the pottery from the two graves in question is reported to belong to Bernburg II/III and II respectively.

It has already been proposed that in execution, content, and arrangement, the art of these Halle graves is something quite different from that of megalithic tombs in Atlantic Europe. Before attempting a brief statement of the different nature of the western art, something must be said as to an alternative origin for that found in the Halle graves. It is not necessary to put forward anything novel, for it has long been recognized that a tradition of 'house-graves' was of great antiquity, and of long endurance, throughout the grasslands lying north of the Caucasus, and, so far as Europe is concerned, extending well into the Pontic region north of the Black Sea.

These 'funerary parlours' were more often wood-built with floors and foundations of small stones, than constructed with stone slabs, but slab-built graves of the Globular Amphora *(Kugelamphora)* Culture are well known, and provide reasonable, and chronologically proximate, proto-types for the Halle graves under discussion.

Although no mural decoration has been reported from graves of the Globular Amphora Culture, the importance of its bearers for the initial transmission of ideas, and aspects of material culture, across the grasslands from the southeast has been fully recognized (Gimbutas 1956: 540–57 with bibliography). It is from the 'dolmens' of the western Caucasus that comes direct evidence for both painted and incised mural decoration, but unfortunately there appears to be nothing more definitive on this subject since Tallgren's (1934) invaluable summary of the old explorations. Tallgren compared some of the linear ornament to textile patterns, and suggested a connection between the Caucasian graves and Göhlitzsch, as well as with the later princely, wood-built tombs of Leubingen and Helmsdorf. Recently, Dr Marija Gimbutas has demonstrated clearly the relationship of the various central and north European grave forms, associated with the Globular Amphora and Single Grave/Corded Ware Cultures, to the Kurgan Culture of the Ukraine, and thence back to the parent culture of the Kuban-Terek and Caucasian region. Within the compass of the Kurgan Culture, the Hut-grave phase provides the closest analogies for the Central European graves. The Hut-graves, themselves, show direct evidence for wall hangings in the form of patterned rugs as in kurgan 7 at Tri Brata near Elista, northeast of the Caucasus (Gimbutas 1956: 74–80). The fashion for mortuary comfort, however, had already been set before the close of the 3rd millenium BC by such regal personages as the principal occupant of the great Maikop kurgan (Gimbutas 1956: 58).

From settlement sites, wall coverings of organic material have of course not survived, but decoration on plaster surfaces is well attested from a number of prehistoric cultures in central and eastern Europe. Childe drew attention to painted plaster at Lengyel and Ottitz, and at Arişud in the rectangular houses of the second phase (Childe 1929: 88, 99). In Hungary, houses of the Tiza Culture, excavated by Banner at Kopàncs, had plaster-covered walls with incised, and red and white painted, geometric designs (*Praehistorische Zeitschrift* 30 (1930): 584–93).[3] The incised panels of geometric ornament on the inner wall of the house model from the Tripolje settlement at Popudina may also be noted (Gimbutas 1956: figure 56, 2). More directly relevant to the present interest is the wall plaster painted in bands of rose-red, whitish-yellow, and grey, from the Tumulus Bronze settlement at Jiřikovice in Moravia (seen in Brno 1949); this culture having undoubted Single Grave/Corded Ware antecedents.

In seeking to compare the phenomenon of mural decoration as noted in certain Central German graves of various cultural associations with the art found in some groups of megalithic tombs in Atlantic Europe, it is quite insufficient to deduce connections on the strength of one or two approximations in motif discovered in individual western tombs. It must always be enquired where the tomb, and its mural art, may stand in relation to other tombs of the same group, and whether in the light of stylistic, geographical and chronological considerations, the art of a chosen western tomb might possibly represent a situation when this phase of the art could have been propagated in an easterly direction. So far as the present writer can see, the drawing of parallels between west and centre in this matter has been too largely the result of a mere hunt for individual motifs without regard to context, much less to precision in the things compared.[4] It is perhaps not sufficiently understood by many students of the subject that there is no general, overall family of western megalithic art. Such art as exists is highly peculiar to certain groups of tombs only, and each group has its own art style both in range of subject matter and presentation. Only in the most general way can the various groups be linked together, and that more through the recognition of a common ancestral tradition than through the sharing of precisely similar characteristics.

So far as Ireland is concerned, the art of the Boyne Culture Passage Graves is now known largely to represent a stage in disintegration of an originally coherent, but schematic, anthropomorphic style, so that 'fir-tree men', zig-zags and concentric arcs, amongst other patterns, can be recognized as stemming from more elaborate and explicable compositions (see Powell & Daniel 1956: 41–55, for discussion, with bibliography, of Boyne Culture tomb art). It is unjustifiable, therefore, to seek to relate these random motifs in Ireland with the Central German grave art. In any case, the possibilities in simple geometric design, as witnessed in prehistoric Europe generally, are so limited that recurrences over wide areas cease to have that kind of significance so often claimed.

In Brittany, the position about art in megalithic tombs is altogether more complicated. Here there is a predominant group of decorated Passage Graves, centred in the Morbihan, but with outliers. There are some tombs in the province, within the classification of Gallery Graves, that display examples of 'mother-goddess' art comparable to that found in some of the Paris Basin tombs and in some of the rock-cut tombs of the Maine-Petit Morin group (see Daniel 1958: 89–104 for France, with bibliography; Péquart

---

3   I am indebted to Professor Stuart Piggott for this reference, as also for much valuable discussion on the whole subject. The plaster is now exhibited in the museum at Hódmezövásárhely.

4   This is the chief fault in an otherwise valuable compendium of information by Dr Waldtraut Schrickel (1957). The West European claims are nearly all to be denied.

& Le Rouzic 1927 for illustrations of Morbihan tomb art, including Gavr'Inis and Le Petit Mont). The art of these tombs is unlike either of the two styles at Lohne (Züschen), and does not enter directly into the present discussion. In Brittany it is the art of the Passage Graves that is of present moment. In these, the schematized tomb-goddess is an important subject of portrayal, but the stylistic treatment is different than in Ireland, and would appear to derive more directly from a Mediterranean source parental also to the style of the southern *statue-menhirs,* and so with some affinity to the anthropomorphic figures of the Paris-Maine tombs. The Passage Graves in Brittany are also remarkable for some tombs with elaborate overall curvilinear designs, as in Gavr'Inis, and for pictographic symbols which may variously represent horns or ships, shrines, reaping or cultivation tools, and certainly hafted axes. In Gavr'Inis, the high relief sculptured axes, without hafts, clearly represent the well-known ritual jadeite axes. Only in the tomb of Petit Mont, now destroyed, were there walling slabs which showed markings that might possibly be compared to the chevron designs in Central Germany. The execution of the design was altogether less exact, and was looser and more broken in composition. These could hardly have stood as a prototype, and, on other ground, it may not be altogether inopportune to sound a word of caution as to the chronological position of such tombs as Petit Mont. Need its erection have been much earlier than the mid 2nd millennium BC, and what may have been the significance of the perforated stone battle-axe reported from its excavation? It would not be so impossible as to wonder whether, in the western expansion of some elements, the Single Grave Culture did not make an eventual contribution to tomb art on the shores of the Atlantic. A date for all of the Halle graves within the first quarter of the 2nd millennium BC, if not earlier, is much more probably established than the date of any decorated Passage Grave in Ireland or Brittany.

With regard to technique in treating the stone surface, it should be noted that the most usual method in the west was to produce a relatively broad line of rounded pockmarks by the use of a hard hammer stone, probably a hand-held pebble. The intended design was in fact not cut or punched on to the stone surface, but battered. There are, of course, some variations in technique in the west, and in some few instances a metal tool may have been employed. Painted designs are known with certainty only in western megalithic tombs south of the Pyrenees. In the northwest of the Iberian Peninsula, there are some few Passage Graves with both painted and pock-executed designs, and it is from this source that the Boyne Culture tombs almost certainly received their anthropomorphic art. Perhaps at Pedra Coberta, the highly stylized anthropomorphic pattern was extended to provide an overall scheme of true wall decoration, but this cannot be claimed with any certainty. (Powell & Daniel (1956: 50) collect references to painted tombs in Portugal, Galicia and Asturias.)

It remains to comment briefly on the other two kinds of stone monument in Central Germany mentioned at the beginning of this essay: a single *statue-menhir,* and a large number of plain standing stones, the ordinary kind of menhir.

The *statue-menhir* (FIGURES 1 (1) & 2d) was found at Pfützthal, Kr. Eisleben, in use as a cover slab for a grave that should fall, on indirect evidence, within the end of the local Neolithic or beginning of the Early Bronze Age (Kirchner 1955: 14, citing comparanda, and plate XXIX). The grave is unlikely to have been later than the early phase of the local facies of the Aunjetitz Culture.

It may reasonably be assumed that this stone had performed an earlier function as a free-standing cult figure in the manner of the classic southern French group. The anthropomorphic design consists of a very simple nose and mouth with necklace of four roughly concentric arcs. Further down the face of the stone are traces of some five arrangements of small oblique lines forming single chevrons. The rock is a fine-grained sandstone, and the design was apparently cut as to make continuous incisions, not either punched or pocked. The face and necklace of the Pfützthal stone show its close affinity to the classic French group, but whether its iconography was carried to the banks of the Saale from the Lower Rhône, or whether it came from a possible source in northern Italy, by way of the Alps, no opinion can here be ventured (Kirchner 1955: plate XXX, illustrates two of a number of decorated stones from Merano, Trentino, of close affinity to *statue-menhir,* and some Breton Passage Grave, art. See also Acanfora 1953). In view of the use of two *statue-menhirs* as building material in the roof of the Passage Grave at Collorgues, Gard, and that the economic background of the builders of this tomb appears to have been Early Bronze Age, the cultural background of the Pfützthal stone could well have been in the opening phase of the Aunjetitz Culture. Its chronological position *vis-à-vis* the art of the Halle graves must therefore be subsequent. The Pfützthal *statue-menhir* is probably not unique in the Saale region, but the carvings on the slab from Dingelstedt, Kr. Halberstadt (Schrickel 1957: Katalog, 76–78), and on the menhir at Seehausen, Kr. Wanzleben (Kirchner 1955: plate XXII(c)), are respectively too indeterminate and too divergent to merit discussion here.

For a full treatment of unadorned menhirs, reference must be made to Professor Kirchner's fine monograph (1955: *passim*). He points out that, in themselves, such menhirs can provide no direct archaeological evidence, and that the motives for their erection may have been many and equally valid over long periods of time. There are in fact examples of menhirs standing on both Bronze and Iron Age tumuli, but there are also large numbers unassociated with any known grave or ritual setting. Kirchner has thought it well to say that these appear to represent the spread of an idea, a ritual practice, and not the spread of a particular culture, in the ordinary archaeological use of the word, of which they might have been one manifestation. Simple menhirs are of course also well known in parts of Belgium, in northern France, and to a lesser extent in western Britain and Ireland. Again, indications for date point to a wide range in time, but in Brittany one or two menhirs, not seemingly part of a larger monument, can be shown, by random motifs of Passage Grave art cut on their flanks, to be at least as early as some Passage Graves.

As to whether the practice of erecting free-standing menhirs derives from the use of such stones in more complex settings, such as the menhir in the long tumulus at Manio, or in the Carnac alignments, no answer can here be attempted, but menhirs are unlikely to have been substitutes for megalithic tombs as ritual monuments. The kind of stone to be handled, with its method of erection, was generally different. In Belgium, De Laet (1958: 110) has pointed to the similar distribution of menhirs and the SOM Culture. For Hesse, Uenze (1956: 102–6) has argued against any connection between menhirs and *Steinkammergräber.* Uenze supports Kirchner's view that in Middle Europe menhirs were erected as the result of an independently moving idea. Presumably, however, the various communities who put up the stones must have already held certain magical concepts in common which would have been amenable to expression in this new mode. It is therefore not altogether unreasonable to look for some common cultural and economic background for these communities, and in this connection Kirchner's map of menhirs in Middle Europe should be compared with Irwin Scollar's recently published map of the provinces of the Michelsberg Culture (Scollar 1959: plate IX. Equally applicable to the Belgian menhir distribution, see Mariën 1952: figure 125).

In conclusion it may be said that the relative sequence in Central Germany of the various monuments discussed would appear to have been: first, the menhirs with a general western derivation not necessarily dependent on megalithic tombs. Second, two things:

a the animal art in the tomb at Lohne (Züschen), apparently of southern origin with affinities in the Maritime Alps; and

b the house-decoration art of the Halle graves, found also at Lohne as a final and intrusive embellishment. This art is an eastern characteristic in the Single Grave Culture.

Finally should have come the *statue-menhir,* a form of iconography again at home in the coastlands of the Ligurian Sea, related to, but not integral with, the art of the western Passage Graves, and possibly of somewhat greater antiquity.

My particular thanks are due to Dr Hermann Behrens for photographs of two of the Dölau stones he illustrated, and for facilities provided at Halle. To Mr J.L. Forde-Johnston I am indebted for the drawing in FIGURE 2.

References

ACANFORA, M. ORNELLA. 1953. *Le Statue Anthropomorfe dell'Alto Adige.*
BEHRENS, H. 1958a. Ein Neolithischer Grabhügel mit Darunterliegendem Hausgrundriss bei Halle (Saale), in Kramer (ed.): 93–8.
　　1958b. Reichverziertes Steinkammergrab und Trapezgrabenanlage unter einem neolithischen Grabhügel in der Dölauer Heide bei Halle/Saale, *Ausgrabungen und Funde* 3: 196–9.
　　1958c. Ein jungsteinzeitlicher Grabhügel von mehrschichtigem Aufbau in der Dölauer Heide bei Halle (Saale), *Jahresschrift für Mitteldeutsche Vorgeschichte* 41/42: 213–42.
BEHRENS, H., P. FASSHAUER & H. KIRCHNER. 1956. Ein neues innenverziertes Steinkammergrab der Schnurkeramik aus der Dölauer Heide bei Halle (Saale), *Jahresschrift für Mitteldeutsche Vorgeschichte* 40: 13–50.
BICKNELL, C. 1911. *The prehistoric rock engravings in the Italian Maritime Alps.* Bordighera: Gibelli.
BRNO, M. 1949. Barvené omítka z jiříkovic u Brna, (brief report), *Archeologické rozhledy* 1: 161–3.
CHILDE, V.G. 1929. *The Danube in prehistory.* Oxford: Clarendon Press.
DANIEL, G.E. 1958. *The megalith builders of Western Europe.* London: Hutchinson.
DE LAET, S.J. 1958. *The Low Countries.* London: Thames & Hudson.
GIMBUTAS, M. 1956. *The Prehistory of Eastern Europe* 1. Cambridge (MA): Peabody Museum.
KIRCHNER, H. 1955. *Die Menhir in Mitteleuropa und der Menhirgedanke.* Mainz: Akademie der Wissenschaft und der Literatur.
KRAMER, W. (ed.). 1958. *Neue Ausgrabungen in Deutschland.* Berlin: Mann.
Kurhessische Bodenaltertümer 3 (1954): 5–26, 27–48.
LOUIS, M. 1950. *Les gravures préhistoriques du Mont Bégo* (Guide Sommaire). Bordighera: Institut international d'études ligures.
MARIËN, M.E. 1952. *Oud België.* Antwerp: de Sikkel.
PÉQUART, M. & S.-J. & Z. LE ROUZIC. 1927. *Corpus des signes gravés des monuments mégalithiques du Morbihan.* Paris: Picard.
POWELL, T.G.E. & G.E. DANIEL. 1956. *Barclodiad y Gawres.* Liverpool: Liverpool University Press.
Praehistorische Zeitschrift 30 (1930), 584–93.
SCHRICKEL, W. 1957. *Westeuropäische Elemente im Neolithikum und in der Frühen Bronzezeit Mitteldeutschlands* 1. Leipzig: VEB Bibliographisches Institut.
SCOLLAR, I. 1959. Regional groups in the Michelsberg Culture, *Proceedings of the Prehistoric Society* 25: 52–134.
TALLGREN, A.M. 1934. Sur les monuments mégalithiques du Caucase occidental, *Eurasia Septentrionalis Antiqua* 9: 5–46.
UENZE, O. 1956. *Die ersten Bauern.* Marburg/Lahn: Kommissionverlag N.G. Elwert. Vorgeschichte von Nordhessen 2.
　　1958. Neue Zeichensteine aus dem Kammergrab von Züschen, in Krämer (ed.): 99–106.

Knowth before Knowth
by GEORGE EOGAN
ANTIQUITY 72 (275), 1998

A FEATURE OF Knowth is its megalithic art (Eogan 1986: 146–76). The large site contains at least 200 decorated stones, the smaller sites about 42. For the latter this is a minimal number as all have lost a large number of their stones due to land usage over the centuries, including removal during later Early Christian times, 9th–10th centuries AD, for souterrain building. It can be presumed that some of these were decorated. There are also 24 stones with decoration that had been removed from tombs and were lying around the site or built into souterrains. The stone basin in the Eastern Tomb is also highly decorated. On these figures at least 300 stones with art were used at Knowth; this constitutes the largest concentration of megalithic art known.

Recent discoveries

During the 1996 season, in the course of the excavations in the outer part of the passage of the Western Tomb, Site 1 (FIGURE 1), further stones with megalithic art emerged (FIGURES 2–9). Amongst these are seven stones which stand apart from the others, not only due to the character of the art and the fact that it is confined to two-thirds of the surface, but also due to their positioning. As a result of the latter the decorated surfaces are either wholly or partially hidden. Three of the stones, nos. C. 3, 5 and 10, served as capstones while nos. Or. 17, 18, 74 and 81 functioned as orthostats. Arising out of these discoveries a review of the already discovered stones in the Eastern Tomb was carried out. This has shown that four comparable examples exist in that tomb. These are capstones 20, 32, 43 and orthostat 2. In addition two corbels in the roof of the chamber are portions of similar stones (Co. 10F and 5D/6E) (FIGURES 10–13). It may also be noted that portions of two stones with angular picked decoration were found within the basal layer of the mound, each on the north side of the respective passage. These are narrower than the previously mentioned stones but yet they could have functioned as orthostats (FIGURES 2, 10: Dec. Stones A (Western) and B (Eastern)). Apart from these two portions all the other relevant stones are substantial pieces — they are palaeozoic green grits, they tend to be rectangular in shape and average 1·5 m in length and 70 cm in breadth. The art, applied by picking, is usually confined to one surface but a portion was left undecorated. Only one stone, West Tomb C.10, has decoration on two faces, the broad faces. On one face the art is poor and it is restricted to two limited areas with zig-zag motifs (not illustrated) but on the other face the composition is elaborate. On Western Tomb orthostat 17 there is a uniform composition which extends over the back and western side of the stone. The art on the stones described above consists of three separate compositions and the similarity between the decoration on some of these stones is striking:

Chevron West Tomb C. 3, 5 and Or. 17 and 74; East Tomb C.43, also the two pieces from the mound (Stone A and Stone B). Total 7

Chevron/Spiral West Tomb C.10 and Or. 18 and 81; East Tomb C.32 and Or.2, and two corbels, Co. 10F, 5D/6E. Total 7

Spiral East Tomb, C.20. Total 1

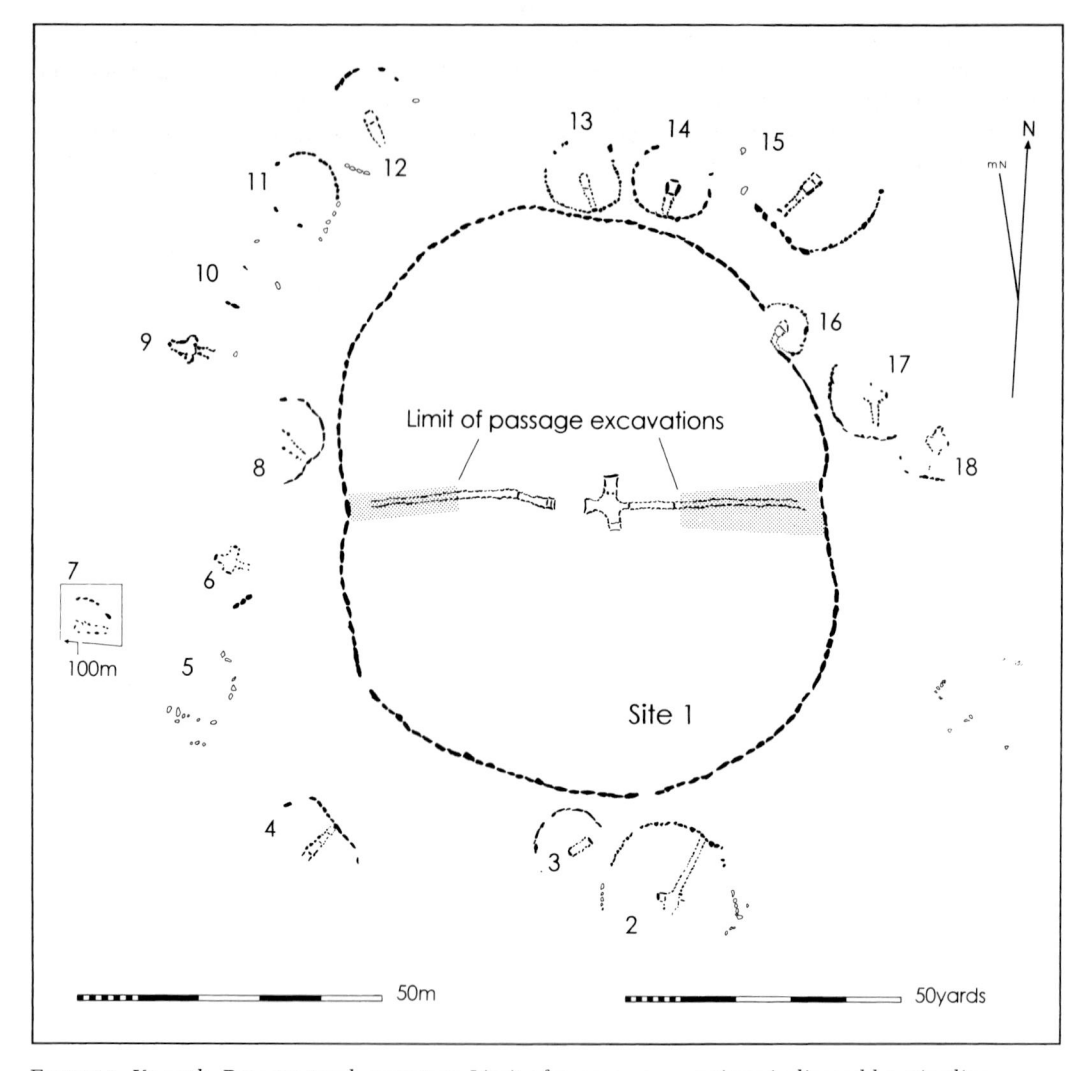

FIGURE 1. *Knowth. Passage tomb cemetery. Limit of passage excavations indicated by stippling.*

Except for East Tomb Or.2 the decoration was wholly or partially hidden. The art on West Tomb C. 3 and 10 and East Tomb C. 32 and 43 was on the under surface but, as these stones extended over the orthostats, portions were obscured. It was wholly obscured on Western Tomb C.5 and Eastern Tomb C.20 (being on the upper surface), on the back surface of Western Tomb Or.17, and on the two incomplete pieces (Stones A and B) from the mound. Parts of Eastern Tomb corbels 10F and 5D/6E were obscured. Portions of the decorated surfaces of Western Tomb Or. 17, 18, 74 and 81 were also hidden. With nos. 18, 74 and 81 the art was on the inner (passage) surfaces but the decorated end was inserted into the socket.

Apart from the foregoing group, decoration on hidden or obscured surfaces is not common at Knowth (the best example being the back face of orthostat 8 of Site 14, Eogan 1984: figure 66). Such art is more frequently found at Newgrange, for example on kerbstones 4, 13 and 18 (O'Kelly 1982: figures 25–27; see below). These stones seem to be in their original position, they were not recycled, the motifs are picked in the surface and are randomly placed. Accordingly, this art must have served a specific purpose and, therefore, constitutes a group in its own right. In addition, it contrasts with the art and the form of the stones already described from Knowth. As a result it may be suggested that the latter were all recycled, having previously been used in an earlier tomb. In Site 1, at Knowth, they seem to have been used simply as building stones at the convenience of the builders. For instance the decorated surface of a capstone may have been placed to the top or to the bottom. In view of the fact that the decoration did not extend all over the face, it may be assumed that they originally served as orthostats with the undecorated portions being in the socket. When they were re-used as orthostats, most were placed upside-down in relation to their former positioning. Furthermore, in re-use the stones were dispersed between the two tombs of Knowth 1 and also of Newgrange (FIGURES 2, 10, 14).

Earlier tomb
As has been pointed out there is variation in the art but, despite that, all may have come from the same tomb. Clearly it would have been a substantial and elaborate structure, probably the first of the great tombs. For an unknown reason this tomb became redundant. Its stones were removed and recycled but in their new positions their role and status were diminished by hiding the art, either by putting the decorated face upwards when used as capstones or, more usually, placing them upside down in the sockets, when used as orthostats. Did the plunder of this tomb indicate a ritual alteration and as a result became the victim of iconoclasm? The broken nature of the roof corbels in the Eastern Tomb suggests this; conversely, perhaps this earlier structure was a hindrance when it was decided to build Site 1. In order to facilitate that work its removal, and also that of portions of Sites 13 and 16, was initiated. Where this postulated tomb (or due to the contrast in the art, could there have been more than one?) stood has not been established. As stones from it have been found both at Newgrange and Knowth its location had to have been some place in Brugh na Bóinne, but as the greatest number occur at Knowth it may have been there that the tomb stood. Its location could have been on the hill-top; there would have been ample room to accommodate it in the area now covered by the large mound, extensive portions of which remain unexcavated.

Tomb alterations
As a result of this evidence it is appropriate to consider wider aspects of alterations to existing tombs, even destruction and reconstruction. It is likely that there was a sequence of tomb-building at Knowth. There is stratigraphical evidence to show that Sites 13 and 16, with their simple chambers and predominately incised angular art, could be amongst the earliest. Part of the mound of each was removed and the outer portion of the passage of Site 16 was realigned (Eogan 1984: 79, 109–13). The destroyed tomb, with curvilinear art in addition to angular art, could have been next in the series. This was followed by a stage of immense architectural and artistic exuberance. Site 1 with its preponderance of curvilinear motifs on the kerb may indicate that greater emphasis was now placed on outdoor ceremonies part of which might have been processions around the mound. The construction of Site 1 was not, however, the final building phase. Sites 17 and 18 appear to have been erected subsequently. This is indicated by the fact that Site 1 was built on top of a habitation layer; by the time that Sites 17 and 18 were constructed a natural sod layer had grown over this habitation layer. In addition a spread of

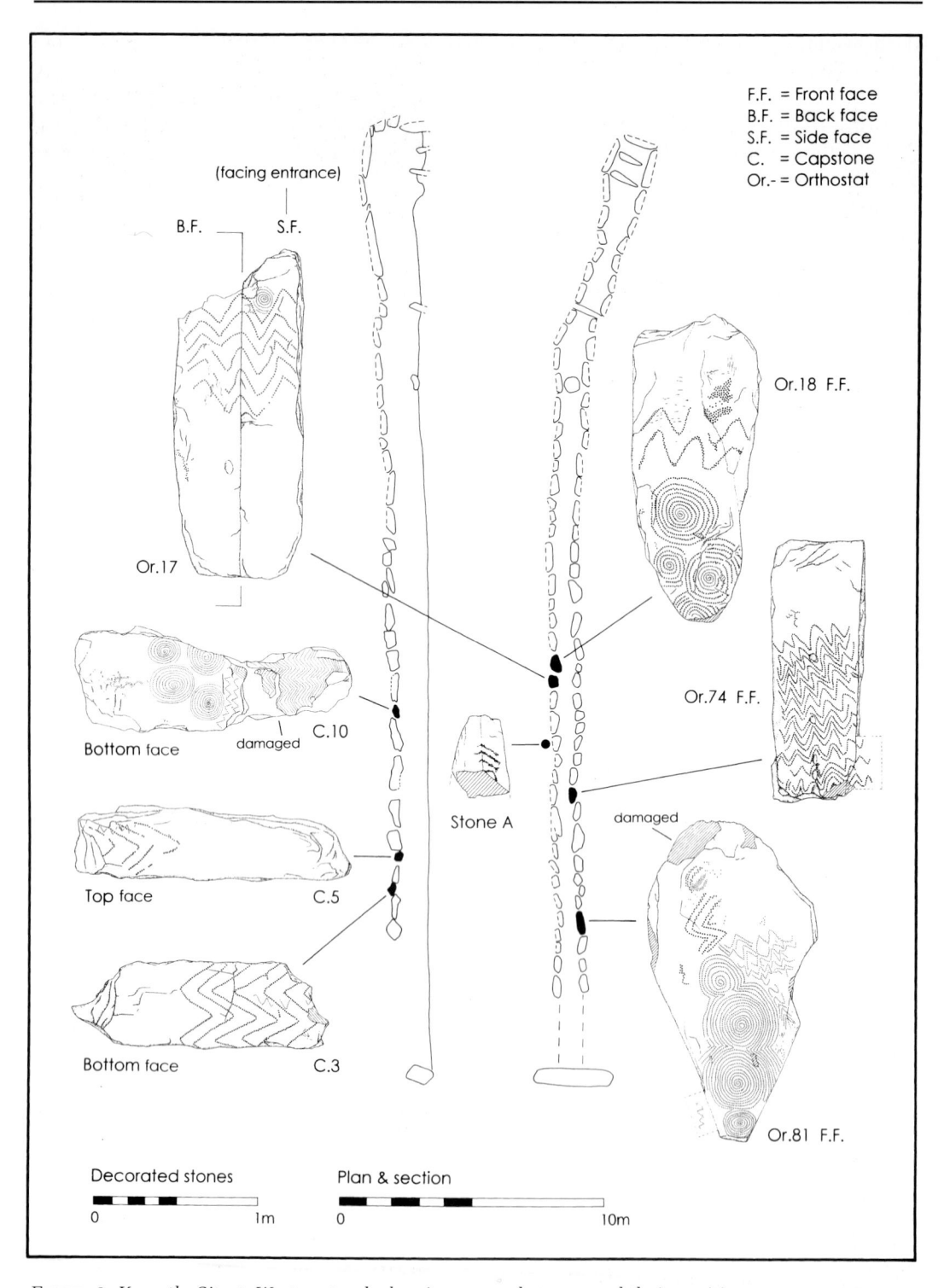

FIGURE 2. *Knowth. Site 1. Western tomb showing re-used stones and their positions.*

FIGURE 3. *Western Tomb, orthostat 17.*

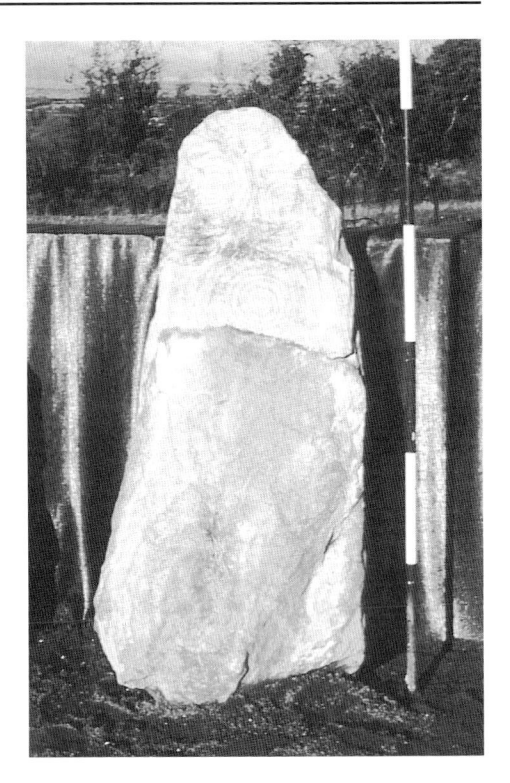

FIGURE 4. *Western Tomb, orthostat 18, position reversed to that in which discovered.*

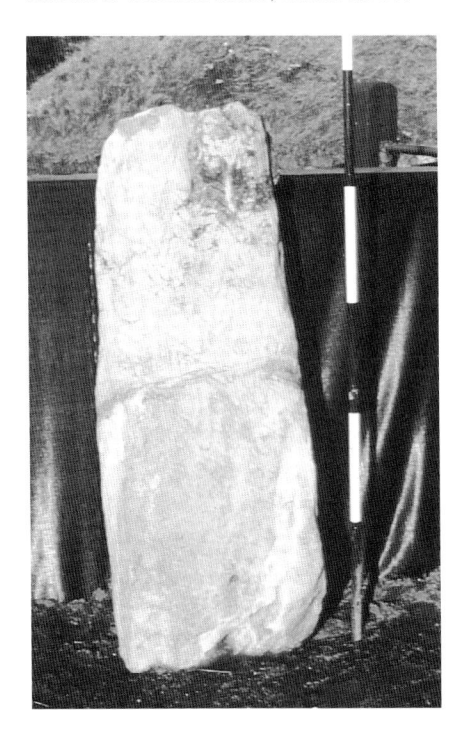

FIGURE 5. *Western Tomb, orthostat 74, position reversed to that in which discovered.*

FIGURE 6. *Western Tomb, orthostat 81, position reversed to that in which discovered.*

FIGURE 7. *Western Tomb, capstone 3.*

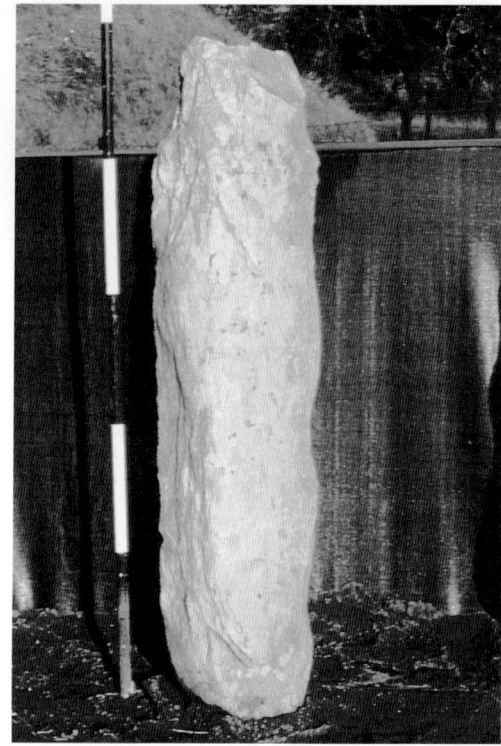

FIGURE 8. *Western Tomb, capstone 5.*

stones extended outwards from Site 1, with which it appears to have been associated. This spread underlies the mound of Site 17. Site 18 is earlier than 17 as part of its mound was overlain by a portion of the mound of the latter (Eogan 1984: 145–6; Eogan & Roche 1997: 87). The art also indicates successive changes. The broad ribbon art ('rectilinear style') overlies angular incised motifs in both the West and East Tombs of Knowth Site 1; while the close picking may be later still (Eogan 1990: 131).

Newgrange and Dowth
The work of O'Kelly and his collaborators at Newgrange indicates that a sequence of tomb-building and alteration also took place there (O'Kelly 1982: esp. 71–2; O'Kelly *et al.* 1978: 276–83, 343). In view of its simple chamber Site K is probably early. It has comparisons with Knowth 16 but it may be of a later date as its angular art is less rigid and

FIGURE 9. *Western Tomb, capstone 10.*

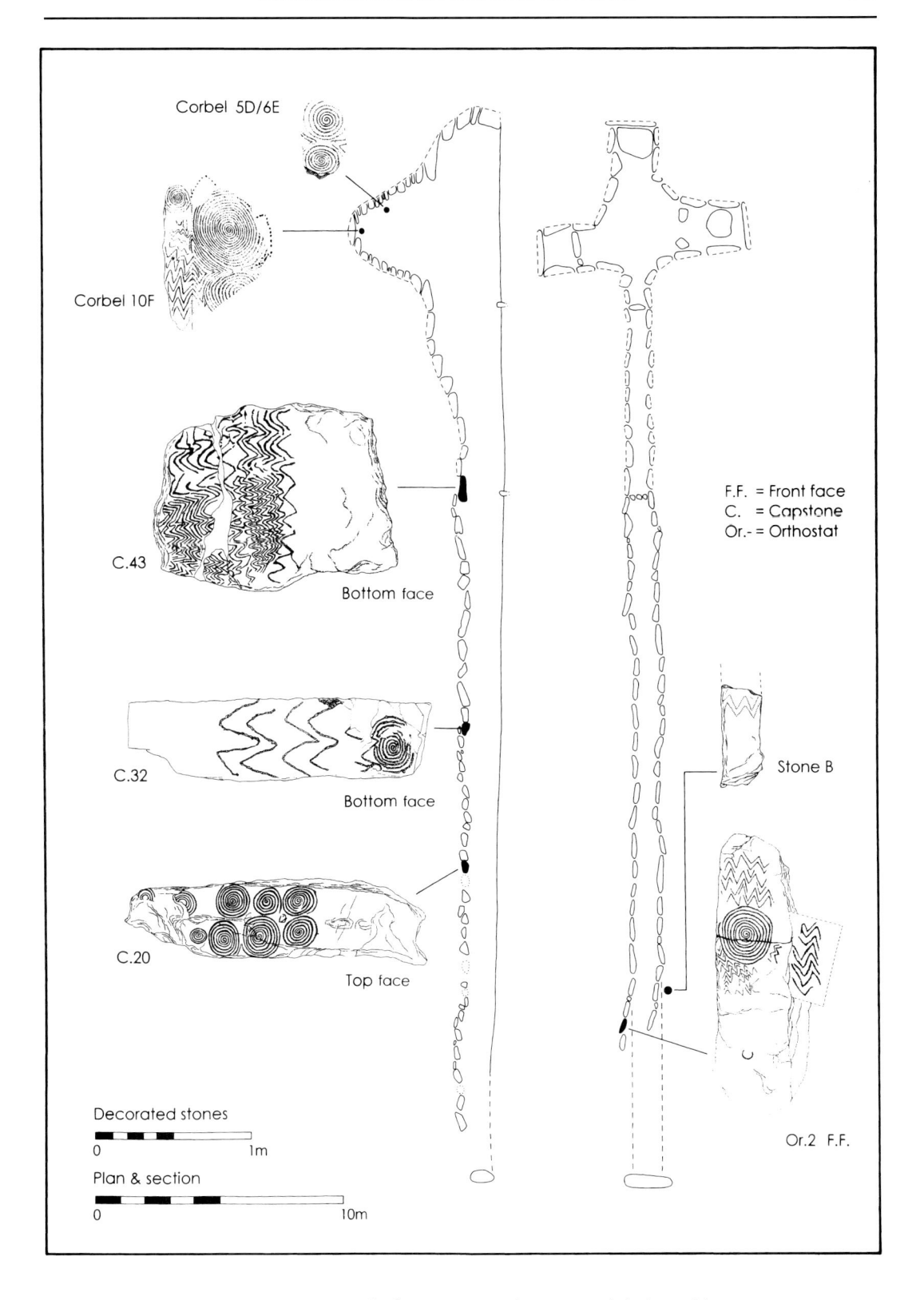

FIGURE 10. *Knowth. Site 1. Eastern Tomb showing re-used stones and their positions.*

FIGURE 11. *Eastern Tomb, orthostat 2 (left) capstone 32 (right).*

incision is rare. At least it is definite that that site is earlier than L, which has a cruciform chamber, as the kerb of the latter site was flattened on the adjoining side so as to avoid as much as possible the mound of Site K. This is equivalent to the situation at Knowth where the kerb of Site 1 curved inwards or was adjusted to avoid Sites 13 and 16. Under the large Newgrange mound the remains of a pre-cairn sod mound came to light, the kerb of the large site bulged outwards so as to avoid as much as possible of the existing structure. In order to establish if this contained a tomb, more extensive excavations would have had to be carried out but it would be unusual if a round mound at Brugh na Bóinne did not contain a passage tomb. In its construction the large mound also incorporated some previously used stones. In form and art orthostat L19 can be compared to orthostat 2 in Knowth East so the origin of both may have been similar (FIGURES 14 & 10). Orthostat R3 and possibly R18 may also have been recycled as at Knowth West; R3 was placed upside-down in its socket. Hidden art also features at Newgrange. Some of the corbels or

FIGURE 12. Eastern Tomb, capstone 43.

FIGURE 13. Eastern Tomb, corbel 10F in chamber.

roof support stones may have been the result of recycling, an example being stone Y in the passage roof with its angular incised art (O'Kelly 1982: plate 71, figures 41–42). On passage orthostats L19, 20 and R3 a portion of the decorated surface was hidden in the sockets. At Newgrange, as already noted, hidden art is best exemplified on the backs of kerbstones 4, 13 and 18 and on the front of K.6; on the last the decorated surface was almost completely hidden in the socket (O'Kelly 1982: figures 25, 26, 27 and 30). This art may have been deliberately hidden as part of the ritual process. It was part of the original art design of the tomb, therefore such stones were not the product of reuse.

At Newgrange tomb building continued after the construction of the large site. Site Z is considered to have been later. This view is based on the assumption that the surrounding area had been stripped of sod and that primary slip from the cairn lay on the stripped surface. Subsequently, natural sod renewed itself and it was on that surface that Site Z was built (O'Kelly et al. 1978: 343).

The precise chronological relationships between Newgrange Large and Knowth 1 are difficult to establish. There are close structural similarities between both but perhaps that can be attributed to conservatism in funerary architecture.

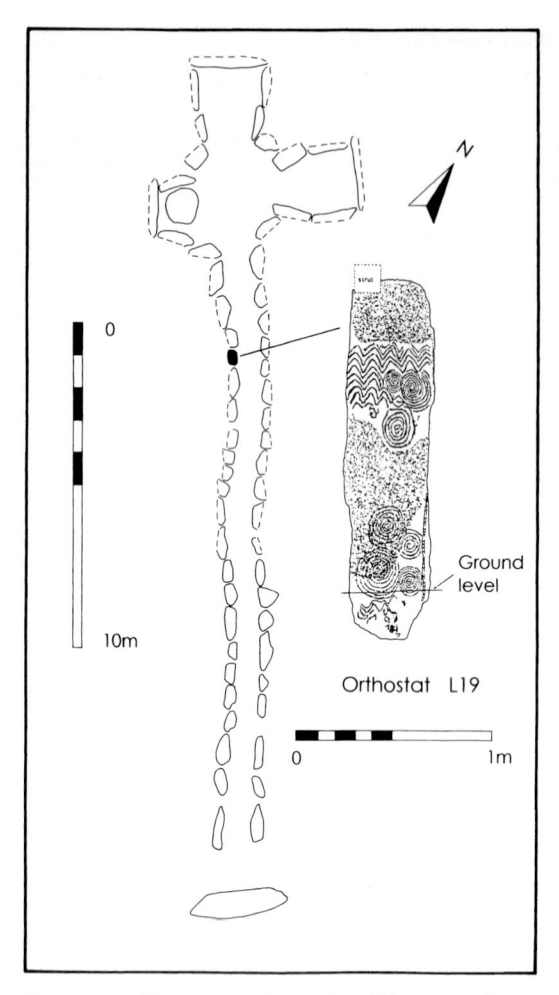

FIGURE 14. *Newgrange, large. Possible re-used stone, L19. From O'Kelly 1982: figure 41.*

However, it does appear that the builders of both sites extracted stones from the same passage tomb in the area and it is unlikely that such a source would have survived for several centuries. Furthermore, it should be recalled that ^{14}C dates from both centre around 2500 b.c., uncalibrated (Eogan 1986: 225–6), but in view of the restricted number of dates caution is required in that regard. Despite these factors it is unlikely that both monuments were constructed simultaneously as that would have placed an enormous burden and strain on society. Yet there need not have been a gap of many centuries. If that was so it indicates the presence in the Brugh na Bóinne region of a cohesive, resourceful and stable society that, over a few generations, constructed some of the greatest architectural creations of Neolithic Europe. Should that have been the case it appears that the passage-tomb complex reached and maintained the pinnacle of its achievements over what may have been a relatively short period and that afterwards it reverted to the building of less ostentatious tombs such as Knowth Sites 17 and 18 and Newgrange Site Z.

At Dowth South the circular chamber, as well as the art, suggests that this site is early in the sequence. In particular chamber orthostats 6 and 7 can be compared to Knowth

East Tomb orthostats 48 and 54 and West tomb orthostat 40. Orthostat C.12 has considerable overlay but there is evidence for some incised motifs (O'Kelly & O'Kelly: 1983: 174–8).

Some comparative evidence for stone recycling and tomb enlargements
Alterations of, or enlargements to, existing tombs have parallels elsewhere. In Ireland Site K at Newgrange is considered to have been a two-period site. The primary monument consisted of a short passage leading into an undifferentiated chamber. This was within a circular mound with the kerb and penannular ditch further out. Subsequently the passage was lengthened and the mound was enlarged (O'Kelly *et al.* 1978: 276–83). At Baltinglass, Co. Wicklow, three passage-tombs were constructed in sequence; each had its own covering cairn but eventually all were incorporated into the final enlargement (Walshe 1941; Herity 1974: 75, 259, figure 60:1).

Multi-period construction is known from passage tombs, and also other megalithic tombs, elsewhere in Europe. In Orkney and Brittany the cairns of passage tombs were often built in outwardly progressing stages, each of which had almost vertical uniface, the 'onion skin' structure (*cf.* Henshall 1963: 239–40; L'Helgouach 1965: figure 6). In Scotland one can cite Camster Long, Caithness (Masters 1981: 171) among British examples. In Brittany the primary trapezoidal-shaped cairn at Barnenez, Finistère, which contained five tombs was added to (Giot 1987: 12 102). At Petit Mont there were four stages of mound construction; the two initial mounds were unchambered but Cairns II and III contained passage tombs (Lecornec 1984). There are also parallels in Iberia. At Dombate, Galicia, a primary tomb was incorporated into a later enlarged structure (Bello Dieguez 1997).

The best evidence for the recycling of stones comes from Brittany (Le Roux 1985: 1992; L'Helgouach 1997). There, considerable destruction of standing stones and alignments took place and extensive re-use of such stones, either complete or partial, was a feature. These served in different capacities — as side stones, capstones or paving stones — in subsequently constructed passage tombs. This is clearly demonstrated by the fact that one stella was broken into three pieces and a portion was used as a roof stone in three separate passage tombs — La Table des Marchands, Gavrinis and er-Vinglé. The stella probably stood at Lochmariaquer as two pieces of it were re-used in that area, but the Gavrinis portion was located 5 km away and its transport would have involved a sea journey.

Discussion
This group of 15 distinctively decorated stones from Knowth, either whole or in part, indicates that a substantial and elaborate tomb stood in Brugh na Bóinne and that it pre-dates at least Knowth Site 1 and Newgrange Large as presumed stones from it were re-used at both of these sites. As Knowth has the largest number of re-used stones that may have been its location. Perhaps, as may have been the case in Brittany, its removal, in the words of Le Roux, can be attributed to the 'iconoclastic rage of the new generation of builders'. On the other hand it could simply be due to the need for greater space on the hill-top consequent to the building of the great mound. It is now clear that there was a sequence of tomb building at Knowth and also at Newgrange. Apparently the earliest tombs at Knowth had undifferentiated chambers and when art was present it was angular and in its application incision predominated. The plundered site was a substantial tomb and its art was more elaborate than that occurring on Site 16. The later Site 1, both artistically and architecturally, was an exceedingly impressive site. In particular in view

of architectural similarities, it and Newgrange are close. Art overlays suggest successive ritual change and there is also evidence that tomb building continued at both sites after the construction of the main mounds. At Knowth Sites 17 and 18 are later and so is Site Z at Newgrange. Not only do the new discoveries at Knowth indicate the presence of another pre-Site 1 tomb, they also indicate the emergence of the first elaborate funerary monuments. In addition they also suggest that when its successor (Site 1) came into use a change in ritual practices, which involved activities outside the chambers, were also a feature. Indeed, it is likely that at Knowth and Brugh na Bóinne as a whole, during the passage-tomb stage, that architectural, artistic and ritual changes were an on-going feature.

Acknowledgements. The excavations are being financed by the National Monuments and Historic Properties Service, Department of Arts, Culture and the Gaeltacht and I wish to thank that Service for all their assistance. I much appreciate the help of Gráinne Kelly, Niamh O'Broin and Helen Roche both in the field and with the preparation of the text. In addition, the line-drawings were prepared by Niamh O'Broin while the photographic work was carried out by Helen Roche. For secretarial assistance thanks are due to Niamh O'Callaghan.

References

BELLO DIEGUEZ, J.M. 1996. Aportaciones del Dolmen de Dombate (La Coruña) al Arte Magalitico Occidental, *Revue Archaéologique de L'Ouest* Supplément 8: 23–39.
EOGAN, G. 1984. *Excavations at Knowth I: Smaller passage tombs, Neolithic occupation and Beaker activity*. Dublin: Royal Irish Academy.
1986. *Knowth and the passage tombs of Ireland*. London: Thames & Hudson.
EOGAN, G. & J. ABOUD. 1990. Diffuse picking in megalithic art, *Revue Archéologique de L'Ouest* Supplément 2: 121–40.
EOGAN, G. & H. ROCHE. 1997. *Excavations at Knowth 2: Settlement and ritual sites of the fourth and third millennia BC*. Dublin: Royal Irish Academy, Department of Arts, Culture and the Gaeltacht.
GIOT, P.-R. 1987. *Barnenez, Carn, Guennoc*. Rennes: Laboratoire 'Anthropologie-Préhistoire, Protohistoire, Quaternary armoricains'.
HENSHALL, A.S. 1963. *The chambered tombs of Scotland* 1. Edinburgh: Edinburgh University Press.
HERITY, M. 1974. *Irish passage graves*. Dublin: Irish University Press.
LECORNEC, J. 1994. *Le Petit Mont, Arzon, Morbihan*. Rennes: Documents archéologiques de l'Ouest.
LE ROUX, C.-T. 1985. New excavations at Gavrinis, *Antiquity* 69: 183–7.
1992. The art of Gavrinis presented in its Armorican context and in comparison with Ireland, *Journal of the Royal Society of Antiquaries of Ireland* 122: 79–108.
L'HELGOUACH, J. 1965. *Les sepultures mégalithiques en Armorique*. Rennes: Travaux du Laboratoire d'Anthropologie Préhistorique de la Faculté des Sciences.
1997. De la lumière aux ténèbres, *Revue Archéologique de L'Ouest* Supplément 8: 107–23.
MASTERS, L. 1981. Chambered tombs and non-megalithic barrows in Britain, in J.D. Evans, B. Cunliffe & C. Renfrew, *Antiquity and man*: 161–76. London: Thames & Hudson.
O'KELLY, M.J. 1982. *Newgrange*. London: Thames & Hudson.
O'KELLY, M.J., F. LYNCH & C. O'KELLY. 1978. Three passage-graves at Newgrange, Co. Meath, *Proceedings of the Royal Irish Academy* 78C: 249–352.
O'KELLY, M.J. & C. O'KELLY. 1983. The tumulus of Dowth, Co. Meath, *Proceedings of the Royal Irish Academy* 83C: 135–90.
WALSHE, P.T. 1941. The excavation of a burial cairn an Baltinglass Hill, Co. Wicklow, *Proceedings of the Royal Irish Academy* 46: 221–36.

Megalithic transport and territorial markers: evidence from the Channel Islands

by MARK PATTON

ANTIQUITY 66 (251), 1992

IN A RECENT article, Thorpe & Williams-Thorpe (1991) have questioned the much-quoted evidence for the long-distance transport of megalithic stones in the European Neolithic. The best known example of supposed megalithic transport is the case of the Stonehenge bluestones, whose geological origin lies in the Preseli Hills of southwest Wales, 240 km from Stonehenge. Thorpe & Williams-Thorpe (1991) challenge Atkinson's (1979) assertion that these stones were transported from Wales by human action, suggesting very plausibly that the stones were deposited on Salisbury Plain as glacial erratics. There seems now to be little basis for the assertion that the Stonehenge bluestones were transported to Salisbury Plain by human action, and there is no good evidence for the transport of megalithic stones over very long distances (i.e. over hundreds of kilometres) anywhere in Europe (though Burl 1991 argues convincingly that the Stonehenge sarsens were transported from the Marlborough Downs by human action, over a distance of 38 km). Thorpe & Williams-Thorpe (1991) go on, however, to draw some more general conclusions which should perhaps be questioned. They assert, for example, that there is no evidence for the transport of megaliths from distances exceeding 5 km, that megalith builders invariably utilized 'the simplest & most obvious methods for stone selection, transportation and construction', and that consequently the locations of megalithic monuments are 'likely to reflect the local availability of building materials rather than the delimitation of contemporaneous tribal territories'. On a macro-regional level, it is almost certainly true that the distribution of megalithic monuments reflects the availability of building materials: this probably accounts for the absence of these monuments from areas such as the Landes (southwest France), the Sologne (north Central France) and East Anglia. The 'territorial marker' hypothesis, however, developed by Renfrew (1973; 1976) and elaborated in subsequent publications by Renfrew and others, does not depend on evidence for long-distance megalithic transport. The evidence from the Channel Islands outlined in this paper is not consistent with the claims of Thorpe & Williams-Thorpe, suggesting that there is more to megalithic distribution than simply the availability of building materials.

Megalithic petrology and distribution in the Channel Islands

In considering the question of megalithic transport, the evidence from the Channel Islands is particularly important. The islands have an important series of passage graves (Hawkes 1937; Patton 1987; 1990), dating to the Middle Neolithic period (c. 3000–4000 BC): these monuments are built of local igneous rocks, which are relatively easy to characterize, owing to the extremely varied nature of the islands' geology. The islands are also fortunate in having benefitted for over 50 years from the work of Dr Arthur Mourant, whose research interests span archaeology and geology. In a series of publications, Mourant (1933; 1937; 1963; 1977) has identified the geological sources of most of the

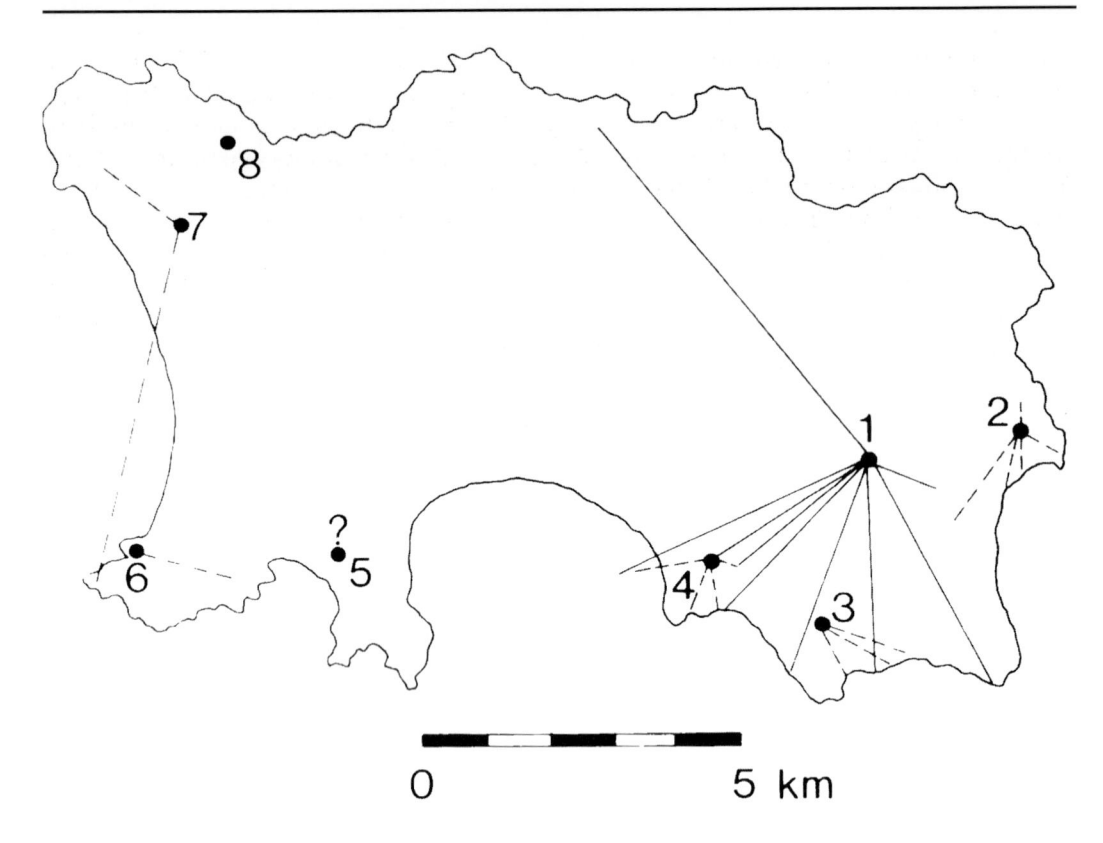

FIGURE 1. *Distribution of passage graves in Jersey, showing sources of stone used (after Patton 1991).*

1   La Hougue Bie
2   Faldouet
3   Le Mont Ubé
4   Le Mont de la Ville
5   Les Cinq Pierres
6   La Sergenté
7   Les Monts Grantez
8   La Hougue des Géonnais

site	diameter of mound	length of passage/chamber
Jersey		
Faldouet	33 m	14 m
Géonnais	20 m	9 m
Grantez	unknown	9 m
La Hougue Bie	55 m	6 m
Le Mont Ubé	unknown	3 m
Le Mont de la Ville	unknown	5 m
La Sergent	5 m	5·5 m
Guernsey		
La Creux-ès-Faies	18 m	10 m
Le Déhus	19 m	9·3 m
La Varde	18 m	3 m

TABLE 1. *Dimensions of passage graves in the Channel Islands.*

stones used for the construction of passage graves in Jersey. The results of this research are summarized by FIGURE 1. These results suggest that most of the island's passage graves are built of stones taken from the immediate area of the monuments themselves, within a radius of 2 km. The passage grave of Les Monts Grantez may incorporate stones from La Corbière, over 5 km to the southwest (Mourant 1937), though a closer source cannot be ruled out. The site of La Hougue Bie, however, is more interesting, since it incorporates stones from several points around the eastern half of the island, including sources also used by the builders of the passage graves of Le Mont de la Ville and Le Mont Ubé. These sources are between 1 and 7 km distant from the site of La Hougue Bie itself. The monument of La Hougue Bie occupies a more central position than the other passage graves of Jersey (FIGURE 1) and is also considerably larger (TABLE 1).

La Hougue Bie is located on high land, on a loess-covered plateau entirely devoid of stones. The stones of which the passage and chamber are built weigh up to 20 tonnes, and most have been transported up-hill (the sources of the stones are in most cases at sea-level, whereas the site is 86 m above sea-level). It is estimated (Kinnes & Hibbs 1988; Patton 1990) that a minimum labour force of 200 people would have been required to transport the largest stone to La Hougue Bie. Further calculations (Patton 1990) suggest that passage graves such as Faldouet, Le Mont Ubé and Le Mont de la Ville may have been built and used by individual communities consisting of 400–600 people. The largest stone at Faldouet, for example, weighs around 24 tonnes (Kinnes & Hibbs 1988) but, unlike the large stones at La Hougue Bie, has been transported along level ground. It is estimated (Patton 1990) that a team of 120 people would have been required to transport this stone: if we assume that most of the haulage work was done by adult men and (following Hedges 1983) that adult men constituted around 23% of the population, we arrive at a figure of 530 as the minimum size of the Neolithic community which built the Faldouet passage grave. The size and location of La Hougue Bie, together with the petrological evidence discussed by Mourant, suggest that this monument was a higher-order centre, serving several of the smaller communities (probably the communities represented by the passage graves of Faldouet, Le Mont Ubé and Le Mont de la Ville). Based on the figures cited above, we would estimate that the La Hougue Bie group consisted of 1500–2000 people. The location of La Hougue Bie is clearly not determined by the availability of building materials, all of which had to be brought to the site from a considerable distance and, in most cases, up-hill. It can be argued, however, that the monument was located at the centre of a larger territory (corresponding to the eastern half of Jersey) and that its location was partly determined by visibility factors (the monument, located on high land, was clearly meant to be visible and can even be seen from the adjacent mainland coast of Normandy). The stones of which the monument is built have not all been brought from the closest source, despite the abundance of granite and diorite at all of the sources used by the builders of the passage grave: the builders seem deliberately to have selected stones from all parts of their 'territory'. In a recent paper (Patton 1991) it is argued that the emergence of a larger ritual centre in the eastern half of Jersey represents a degree of centralization, possibly linked to the control of stone-axe exchange.

Discussion
Whilst accepting that there is no good evidence for the long-distance transport of megaliths in the European Neolithic, the Channel Island evidence outlined in this paper suggests that megaliths were transported over shorter distances on a regular basis, and that the distribution of megaliths within a region cannot be explained simply as a function of availability of building materials. If the builders of La Hougue Bie had utilized 'the sim-

plest & most obvious methods for stone selection, transportation and construction', as predicted by Thorpe & Williams-Thorpe (1991: 72), and located according to the availability of materials, the monument would have been built elsewhere. The fact that it was not built elsewhere implies that cultural factors outweighed practical considerations in this case. This appears also to have been the case elsewhere: if the location of megaliths was determined simply by the availability of materials, then the Grand Menhir of Locmariaquer would surely have been erected at source (on the banks of the Auray River) rather than transported 4 km in an operation that would have required an estimated workforce of 3800 people (Hornsey 1987). The technology required to transport a stone over a distance of 7 km is exactly the same as that required to transport it over 500 km, assuming that the terrain includes no steeper slopes. Even the number of people required would be the same; the task would simply take longer. Thorpe & Williams-Thorpe's debunking of the Stonehenge bluestones myth, therefore, important though it undoubtedly is, need not alter our understanding of European megaliths and their builders as dramatically as they seem to imply in their article.

Acknowledgements. I am particularly grateful to Dr Arthur Mourant, for his invaluable work on megalithic petrology in Jersey, and for discussing this research with me in detail. I would also like to thank Dr David Johnston for his helpful comments on a draft of this text: many of the ideas elaborated in this paper had previously been outlined by him in an unpublished paper read to the Prehistoric Society in 1975 and, although I had not seen that paper, our conclusions are in many respects remarkably similar.

References
ATKINSON, R.J.C. 1979. *Stonehenge*. Harmondsworth: Penguin.
BURL, A. 1991. Megalithic myth or man the mover, *Antiquity* 65: 297.
HAWKES, J. 1937. *The archaeology of the Channel Islands I: The Bailiwick of Jersey*. St Helier: Société Jersiaise.
HEDGES, J.W. 1983. *Isbister, a chambered tomb in Orkney*. Oxford: British Archaeological Reports. British series 115.
HORNSEY, R. 1987. The Grand Menhir Brisé: megalithic success or failure?, *Oxford Journal of Archaeology* 6: 185–217.
KINNES, I.A. & J.L. HIBBS. *The dolmens of Jersey*. Jersey: La Haule Books/Channel Television.
MOURANT, A.E. 1933. Dolmen de La Hougue Bie: nature and provenance of materials, *Société Jersiaise Annual Bulletin* 12: 217–20.
    1937. Notes on petrology, in Hawkes (1937): 205–7, 212–13, 225, 238–9, 244–5, 269.
    1963. The stones of the Mont de la Ville passage grave, Jersey, *Société Jersiaise Annual Bulletin* 18: 317–25.
    1977. The use of Fort Regent granite in megalithic monuments in Jersey, *Société Jersiaise Annual Bulletin* 22: 41–9.
PATTON, M.A. 1987. *Jersey in prehistory*. Jersey: La Haule Books.
    1990. Neolithic communities of the Channel Islands. Unpublished Ph.D thesis, University of London.
    1991. Axes, men and women: symbolic dimensions of Neolithic exchange in Armorica (northwest France), in P. Garwood, D. Jennings, R. Skeates & J. Toms (ed.), *Sacred & profane: archaeology, ritual and religion*: 65–79. Oxford: Oxford University Committee for Archaeology. Oxford Monographs in Archaeology 32.
RENFREW, A.C. 1973. *Before civilisation: the radiocarbon revolution and prehistoric Europe*. Harmondsworth: Penguin.
    1976. Megaliths, territories and populations, *Dissertationes Archaeologicae Gandenses* 16: 198–220.
THORPE, R.S. & O. WILLIAMS-THORPE. 1991. The myth of long-distance megalith transport, *Antiquity* 65: 64–73.

Some megalithic follies
by GLYN DANIEL
ANTIQUITY 33 (132), 1959

THE LATE EDITOR and Founder of ANTIQUITY had to deal with a difficult monument when he wrote his *Long Barrows of the Cotswolds* (1925). This was the Three Shire Stones which stand in an alcove in the wall on the west side of the Foss Way, two miles north of Batheaston, at the junction of Somerset, Gloucestershire and Wiltshire and the parishes of Batheaston, Marshfield and Colerne. Here are three uprights supporting a capstone. Inside is a broken boundary stone bearing the date 1736, and on the 2-in. manuscript map of the district at the Ordnance Survey (dated 1813–14) there is a note saying 'Shire Stones, erected 1736' (Crawford 1925: 227). As Crawford wrote, 'The present structure is evidently a modern imitation of a "dolmen"' (Jones 1953: 243).

If we all accept the Three Shire Stones as an 18th-century 'dolmen', as we must, it prompts us to wonder what other megalithic imitations or 'follies' were constructed in England.

In 1792 Lord Arundel employed Josiah Lane to make a grotto for him at Wardour Castle in Wiltshire. Lane was a celebrated constructor of rock-work and his grotto at Wardour is a most remarkable and charming structure. To quote Barbara Jones's (1953: 243) description of it: 'Built on a brick basis, it is of tufa and stone with the usual occasional ammonite, now covered with green moss and long ferns, for it is in a very sheltered and gloomy situation. The plan is most cunning, turning in and out with many views through jagged holes into other parts. The dark yews and the bank which it is built against, and the pattern-book construction, make it the most Gothic of grottoes.' Apparently Josiah Lane in his rock-work used part of a chamber tomb on Place Farm, Tisbury: three stones from this tomb were removed in 1792 and used at Wardour Castle (Arundel & Colt Hoare 1822–44: 529–30).*

In the very next parish to Wardour, at Fonthill, Beckford had an 'imitation cromlech' in the grounds, but this, as his house and tower and most of the curiosities in the grounds, are almost entirely destroyed. In 1814 the fifteenth Earl of Shrewsbury began the construction of a house and landscape at Alton in Staffordshire; after his death in 1827 the work was carried on by his nephew. Among other oddities it contains what is often described as an imitation Stonehenge, but more descriptively as 'The Druid's Sideboard'. This is an extraordinary construction of piled stones and megalithic slabs; to quote Barbara Jones again (1953: 120–1), 'the folly builders have found the Druids'.†

But the strangest and finest mock-megalith in Britain is surely the 'temple' on the Yorkshire moors at Ilton near Masham, of which two views are given here (FIGURES 1a & b). This was built in the 1820s by William Danby of Swinton Hall. He found the local people completely out of work and, wishing to help them, preferred to find them jobs rather than give them dole out of charity. He therefore got them to construct what he called a Druids' Temple and paid them each a shilling a day. The Masham Temple is a very remarkable structure with a grotto at the far end cut in the hillside, and several 'dolmens' and trilithons built outside the main enclosure in the surrounding country-

---

* I am indebted to Mr Geoffrey Grigson for this reference. He writes: 'One monolith is still there, so the rockwork is a meeting place of Druids, Chinese gardeners and the Cumaean Sybil.'
† The Park Place, Henley, monument should be mentioned here although it is not a folly. Originally the Mont de la Ville monument in Jersey it was moved to Henley in March 1788. See Hawkes (1939: 240).

side. One of these amusing mock-dolmens is seen in FIGURE 1b. It has been suggested from time to time that the Masham megaliths were rebuilt from, or partly from, existing prehistoric monuments, but there is no evidence to prove this, and indeed Yorkshire, apart from Boroughbridge and Rudstone, is not a megalithic county.*

It would now appear that Tibradden, in County Dublin, often acclaimed as a genuine Passage Grave, is in fact a 19th-century folly of a rather special kind. Before the excavation of the site by the National Monuments Branch of the Office of Public Works in Ireland, it was thought that the barrow on Tibradden Mountain contained a dry-walled Passage Grave of classic form, and that in the centre of the circular chamber there had been found, in 1849, a megalithic cist containing a food-vessel and cremated bones. Before the clearance work done by Mr Marcus O Hochaidhe three years ago the site had indeed the semblance of a filled-in Passage Grave, but now that it is open down to ground level this semblance is revealed as accidental. The whole construction of passage and chamber walls is uncharacteristic of the megalith builders, and around the inside of the chamber is a stone bench (FIGURES 1c & 2a). The excavator is of the opinion that passage and chamber were built in the mid-19th century, and we may imagine visitors then sitting on the stone seat admiring the central cist (H-Eochaidhe 1957: 221).†

When the scaffolding in Lensfield Road, Cambridge, was removed last year to reveal the new Chemistry Laboratory there was seen the remarkable megalithic panel shown in FIGURES 2b & c. It is decorated with the arms of the University of Cambridge and five chemical or alchemical symbols which, reading from left to right, mean *Talc, Iron, White Lead, Subacetate of Copper* (though this sign is indistinguishable from a prehistoric sun-disc ornament or a Chrismon sign), and *Precipitation.* Mr John Murray Easton, the architect, in a letter to the Editor, says: 'I am glad to know that you are interested . . . whether or not you approve of this 'megalithic oddity'. It arose from the usual mixture of reasons. Some sort of panel in this position was indicated, for no windows were wanted there . . . I have always been intrigued by the mysterious urge that compelled people to do what they did in megalithic times from Mycenae to the stone men of Malekula . . . Then I have a liking for stones *qua* stones. I made a sketch which has been pretty well adhered to and gave a roving commission to Miss Spencer Watson to go and find suitable stones in the Limestone belt. I wanted to get relief from the smoothness of brick and Portland stone by using these rough stones.‡

Of course it is not only the British Isles that can show megalithic oddities. The Church of Santa Cruz de la Victoria at Gangas-de-Onis near Oviedo is built on a chambered barrow and incorporates a Passage Grave which forms the crypt of the church; polygonal single chambers have been re-used as chapels at Alcobertas and Pavia in Portugal; and the Church of Les Septs Saints in the commune of Vieux-Marché, Lannion, Côtes du Nord in Brittany, has one transept built on top of a Gallery Grave which forms

---

*   See Arnold Jowett's study on the Masham Temple in *Country Life*, 17 August, 1945. In this article he states that in the 19th century the Earl of Darnley 'carted the sarsen stones of an entire cromlech to make a Merlin's Grotto in Cobham Park'. Is this so? Barbara Jones lists no folly of this kind. Information please.

†   A full report is in preparation. Meanwhile I have had the benefit of discussing this matter with Professor R. de Valera and Mr Liam de Paor.

‡   Mr Murray Easton co-operated very readily in telling me the history of the Chemistry panel, and I am grateful to him for his help and interest. In one of his interesting letters from which he has permitted me to quote, he says: 'I would like to have the chance of doing a free standing composition of "rude" stones.' Prevented as we are from doing what the *famille Piketty* did in France, those of us who wish for modern megalithic tombs may well, one day, satisfy Mr Murray Easton's desires. The symbols carved by Miss Spencer Watson were taken from *The Book of Signs*, the sixteenth book issued by the First Edition Club, in 1930, by Rudolf Koch (translated by Vyvyan Holland).

FIGURE 1. *Megalithic follies*
a *Masham: the temple*
b *Masham: one of the 'mock-dolmens' (the Editor provides the scale).*
c *Tibradden: the 'passage' looking east (note the stone bench).*

FIGURE 2. *Megalithic follies.*
a *Tibradden: the 'chamber' around the central cist looking west.*
b *Cambridge: the University Chemical Laboratories, panel on wall.*
c *Cambridge: the University Chemical Laboratories, panel on wall, detail.*

its crypt. The strangest megalithic monuments in France are at Confolens. On the island of Ste Marguerite, in the river Vienne, is a large capstone now supported by four columns of Romanesque design with 12th-century capitals. This monument was originally a rectangular single chamber which was turned into a Christian chapel. In the cemetery at Confolens is the re-erected Dolmen de Perissac which was bought for a hundred francs in 1892, and now has on top of it an extraordinary carved sarcophagus containing the remains of a lady much addicted to dolmens (Burnand 1896).

Visitors to Meudon, between Paris and Versailles, will know the odd megalithic structure that can now be seen on the Meudon terrace. It is built out of the remains of a Gallery Grave found in the 1840s, moved in 1861 and turned into a pyramid, upset by the Germans in 1870 after the Franco-Prussian war, and then rebuilt into the present 'dolmen' by a Monsieur Janssen after that war. A few miles away in the Cimetière des Essarts at Meudon is the reconstructed rectangular megalithic tomb that used to be the Dolmen de Kerhan in the Commune of St Philibert in the Morbihan. Dug by Gaillard in 1886, it was moved to Paris in 1896, and now forms the tomb of the family Piketty. A plaque on it commemorates the fact that since it was moved from Brittany it is still used as a collective tomb and that nine members of the Piketty family have been buried in the ground beneath it. It is difficult to know which is the most charming example of conscious megalithic antiquarianism - - the Pikettys still burying in a Gallery Grave, Mr Murray Easton designing a megalithic panel for a Chemistry Laboratory, or the Welsh Gorsedd of Bards performing their annual rites at the stone circles which they have been building in different parts of Wales for many years.

References
ARUNDEL, Lord & R. COLT HOARE. 1822–44. *History of Modern Wiltshire: Hundred of Dunworth*: 529–30.
BURNAND, F. 1896. Notes on French dolmens, *The Reliquary*.
CRAWFORD, O.G.S. 1925. *The Long Barrows of the Cotswolds*. Gloucester: John Bellows: 227
HAWKES, J. 1939. *The Archaeology of the Channel Islands:* II, *The Bailiwick of Jersey*. London: Methuen.
JONES, B. 1953. *Follies and Grottoes*. London: Constable.
H-EOCHAIDHE, M.O. 1957. Portal dolmen and Kiltiernan, Co. Dublin. *Proceedings of the Prehistoric Society* 23, 221.

2 Stonehenge and Avebury: past, present and future
by TIMOTHY DARVILL & CAROLINE MALONE

IN 1986 THE GREAT megalithic monuments of Stonehenge and Avebury (plus 42 square kilometres of land around them), in recognition of their outstanding universal value, were jointly inscribed as a single entry on the World Heritage List established by UNESCO. Although 40 km apart, the two sites have long been considered together, and were certainly built and used at around the same time. Whether they should be seen as monuments of the same community or, as Bernard Cornwall has it in his well-observed fictional tale *Stonehenge* (Cornwall 1999), the ceremonial centres for two quite distinct groups, is at present impossible to say. Both sites have figured in the pages of ANTIQUITY since the very first volume; Stonehenge in particular is probably the most frequently mentioned site across all subsequent issues, and has adorned the cover of every issue of ANTIQUITY since March 1927. Constraints of space allow us to offer only a small selection of what amounts to very extensive coverage, and accordingly we have chosen pieces that illustrate interest in four key themes: the antiquarian background; the investigation of the sites and their main features; placing the sites into a wider landscape context; and the matter of their on-going management and conservation.

The earliest accounts of Stonehenge and Avebury date back to medieval times, and are themselves the subject of academic study and debate in terms of what these sources actually tell us about the sites (Chippindale 1983a). Geoffrey of Monmouth wrote about Stonehenge in around AD 1136, and tells how the stones were re-erected on the present site after being brought from Ireland by the wizard Merlin in order to provide a memorial to those killed when Aurelius Ambrosius, king of the Britons, defeated the Saxons. Stuart Piggott presented a detailed analysis of the sources of Geoffrey of Monmouth in two papers published in ANTIQUITY, the second dealing specifically with Stonehenge (Piggott 1941). With characteristic scholarship he brings together the mythical traditions of the early literary sources with the available archaeological evidence.

Throughout the Middle Ages, both Stonehenge and Avebury were visible monuments and attracted the attention of travellers, writers and artists. One of the earliest available illustrations of Stonehenge is a 16th-century watercolour drawing by the Flemish artist Lucas de Heere. It is described and discussed by J.A. Bakker (1979), and provides an interesting insight on the preservation of the site in the late 1500s. John Aubrey worked at both Avebury and Stonehenge in the 1660s (Chippindale 1983a: 66–71), but it is probably William Stukeley who is best remembered for his descriptions and interpretations of the two sites (Stukeley 1740; 1743; Chippindale 1983a: 71–83). Although Stukeley's early life was dominated by an essentially scientific, highly structured approach to the world around him, after his move to London in 1717 his thinking changed and he became one of the main advocates of the Romantic movement in archaeology. Stuart Piggott, Stukeley's biographer (Piggott 1950), wrote a fascinating account of Stukeley's work at Avebury in 1720s and we reproduce it here: 'Stukeley, Avebury and the Druids' (Piggott 1935). Piggott later provided a wider context for this paper in his account of 'Prehistory and the Romantic movement' (Piggott 1937).

Soon after turn of the 20th century, new excavation programmes at both Stonehenge and Avebury were beginning to shed light on the date, structure and purpose of these monuments. At Avebury, St George Gray's work between 1908 and 1922 (Gray 1935) was too early to be reported in ANTIQUITY, but investigations by Alexander Keiller from 1935 to 1939 were reported in two papers (Keiller & Piggott 1936; Keiller 1939). O.G.S. Crawford, the editor, was a major supporter of the Avebury investigations, following his collaboration with Keiller in the 1920s in the production of the magisterial *Wessex from the Air* (Crawford & Keiller 1924). Keiller's work began outside the Avebury henge and examined the West Kennet Avenue, later moving within (the results were published by Isobel Smith (Smith 1965: 175–252)). Only relatively modest investigations have taken place within and around the henge since Keiller's work, although important discoveries continue to be made. In 1996 Bob Bewley and colleagues reported the discovery through aerial photography of a previously unrecognized mound to the west of the Red Lion in the northwest sector of the henge (Bewley *et al.* 1996). More recently, understanding of the medieval history of Avebury has been revolutionized by Andrew Reynolds' recognition of a late Anglo-Saxon *burh* and with much of the street plan still surviving in the fabric and structure of the present-day village (Reynolds 2001). Much still remains to done and there is much potential for the deployment of innovative techniques such as those reported by Nick Burton which combine terrain models and vertical aerial photographs (Burton 2000), or the high-resolution satellite imaging discussed by Martin Fowler (1996).

The year 1901 saw the first excavations of the 20th century at Stonehenge (Gowland 1902). A few years later, between 1919 and 1926, Lt-Colonel William Hawley carried out an extensive programme of excavations across the eastern part of the site for the Ministry of Works. These are summarized by R.S. Newall, who worked with Hawley, as a description of the site (Newall 1929). The coloured pull-out plan was one of the best published at the time. The next main phase of work was led by Richard Atkinson, and involved also Stuart Piggott and J.F.S. Stone. Starting in 1950 and continuing sporadically through to 1964, the excavation trenches were generally small and, like Gowland's and Hawley's before, were often targeted to assist in restoration and consolidation works as well as to provide new information about the monument. It was during this period of study that the presence of rock art on 11stones was noted and first documented (Crawford 1954). Part-way through the work, Atkinson published his classic popular work *Stonehenge* (Atkinson 1956). In this he set out a phasing of the site, based almost entirely on the one proposed five years earlier by Stuart Piggott (Piggott 1951), which endured down into the 1990s. R.S. Newall's extended review of Atkinson's book appeared in ANTIQUITY (Newall 1956), and is reproduced here because it provides a remarkable near-contemporary critique of the work by someone who was very close to Stonehenge and supremely knowledgeable about its archaeology and significance. Interestingly, Newall notes in his review (1956: 140) that:

> Mr Atkinson says that the earlier excavations of 1920–26 were not carried out as they should have been. As one who took a large part in them I freely admit this; but Colonel Hawley very often complained of the lack of interest shown. No advice was ever offered, and when he read his annual report his careful work was praised. One can never imagine that thirty years hence Mr Atkinson's work will be so criticized.

As it turned out, of course, just about 30 years after Atkinson finished digging a whole series of just such criticisms were offered, most notably the fact that neither his work nor that of Hawley (for which Atkinson had by this time taken responsibility) had been published. In the late 1980s English Heritage commissioned a series of projects in an effort to right this matter. The paper by Andrew Lawson included here ('Stonehenge — creating a definitive account') appeared in 1992 and provides a useful statement on the nature and character of the early and mid 20th-century excavations and the records made at the time (Lawson 1992). The full work was published as *Stonehenge and its landscape: the 20th century excavations* (Cleal *et al.* 1995), a volume reviewed in ANTIQUITY by Alasdair Whittle (1996). As at Avebury, small-scale excavations were carried out through the second half of the 20th century, and some of these produced remarkable finds, including the burial of a man shot in the back with arrows found in the ditch in 1978 (Atkinson & Evans 1978).

How Stonehenge was constructed and whether or not there are astronomical alignments embedded in its fabric are general matters that apply to many megalithic monuments, and we shall return to them in more detail in Section 4 below. What is rather unusual at Stonehenge is the extent to which stones whose source lies many kilometres away have been used selectively in its construction. The use of sarsen stones local to the chalklands has caused little comment, although the transport of these massive blocks weighing up to 50 tons perhaps from the Avebury area 45–50 km to the north is an enormous undertaking. Rather, attention has focused on the various stones (collectively known as 'bluestones' but in fact comprising several different lithologies) whose parent outcrops everyone accepts lie on and around the Presceli Hills of southwest Wales (Atkinson 1979: 105), where dolerite was used in the construction of monuments, crosses, gateposts, and many other things besides from prehistoric times through to the present day (Jones 1956; Darvill & Wainwright 2002). Compared to the sarsens, the Stonehenge bluestones are relatively small: the largest weighs about 4 tons, but many of the smaller ones could have been picked up and carried by a team of people or dragged along on a sledcar by oxen (see Fox 1931 for some sledcars from Wales). However, how exactly these stones got to Salisbury Plain is the controversial issue, and here two conflicting, and now rather entrenched, schools of thought can be seen.

Richard Atkinson summarized and enlarged the case for the human transportation of the bluestone in the first edition of *Stonehenge* (1956: 98–110), announcing boldly (1956: 99) that

> There can be no question of the stones having been carried even part of the way towards southern England by ice during the Pleistocene period, and their appearance at Stonehenge can only be explained as the result of deliberate transport by man. The question to be answered is therefore quite clear: by what route, and by what means, were these eighty-odd stones, weighing up to four tons apiece, brought from Prescelly to Stonehenge, a distance as the crow flies of some 135 miles.

No changes to this position were included in the second revised edition of the book (Atkinson 1979), although by this time the arguments for the natural forces as the agent of movement were gathering pace. Atkinson himself accepted that the bluestones were present on Salisbury Plain before the time that some were used in the construction of the first bluestone circles at Stonehenge (see Atkinson 1974), but this was not itself an argument for the glacial movement of bluestone boulders.

The developing case for natural geomorphic and geological processes being responsible for the movement of the bluestones was brought together in the powerful paper by R.S. Thorpe & O. Williams-Thorpe (1991) reprinted here. Their canvas was large in this review, although Stonehenge provides one of the main case-studies (1991: 71–2). When published it naturally provoked comment, and Aubrey Burl (1991) posed the question 'Megalithic man or man the mover?', preferring the argument that prehistoric people did move large stones very considerable distances. Mark Patton, meanwhile, used evidence from the Channel Islands to show that stones had been moved right across the island during the construction of megalithic monuments (Patton 1992). Olwyn Williams-Thorpe's reply (1993) simply re-stated the core of their case, but accepted that stones were moved anything up to 5 km or so during the construction of substantial monuments. In 1995 the movement of the Stonehenge bluestones was revisited in the pages of ANTIQUITY by Williams-Thorpe *et al.*, commenting on the results of Chlorine-36 dating (Williams-Thorpe *et al.* 1995). This technique can potentially reveal the length of time that a rock surface has been exposed to the atmosphere. Published estimates of between 5000 and 14,000 years for rock surfaces at Stonehenge and at bluestone outcrops in Preseli were rejected by Williams-Thorpe *et al.* on the grounds that it was impossible to tell where exactly the samples measured were from and what they related to. The debate is therefore far from over. Indeed, Aubrey Burl has recent shifted sides to favour the natural delivery of bluestones to Salisbury Plain (2000: 364–5), even though the majority of archaeologists probably still adhere to the idea that human action was the mechanism behind the movements.

There have been a number of experiments done to see how the stones of Stonehenge could be moved, amongst them Atkinson's use of canoes and rafts (1979: plate 22a) and, more recently, trials using concrete replicas (Richards & Whitby 1997). Ethnographic evidence is of value too, and here mention may be made of Garfitt's descriptions of the use of wooden rollers (Garfitt 1979).

On many occasions, Stonehenge and Avebury appear in the literature, the popular literature especially, as isolated monuments, icons of the prehistoric age. Yet both are simply the most well-known structures in landscapes chock-full of monuments built and used by successive communities. Some of the earlier structures, especially the long barrows, have been considered in Section 1. Contemporary monuments also abound, many of them discovered through aerial photography and fieldwalking. The first volume of ANTIQUITY carried reports on two important monuments connected with Stonehenge. First was the Stonehenge Avenue, traced using aerial photography from Stonehenge Bottom through to the River Avon, 2·2 km distant, and checked by trial trenching in June 1927 (Clay 1927). Second was the site of Woodhenge, discovered through aerial photography by Squadron-Leader Insall in 1925 (Insall 1927) and excavated by Maud and Benjamin Cunnington from 1927 through to 1929 (Cunnington 1927; and see Cunnington 1929 for the final report). Initially nick-named 'Woodhenge' because of its similarity to Stonehenge, the main difference was that instead of upright stones the excavations found postholes that had supported concentric rings of large timber uprights. Alex Gibson has developed earlier suggestions that in fact Stonehenge Phase 3 is simply a stone version of the timber structures found elsewhere (Gibson 1998: 119; but *cf.* Atkinson 1956: 176). Rather neatly, however, Stonehenge and Woodhenge together represent the main variation found within a range of free-standing and enclosed timber and earth circles across most of the British Isles (see Section 3 below). The site of Durrington Walls to the north of Woodhenge was also discussed in the late 1920s (Crawford 1929), later to be studied through excavations by J.F.S. Stone and colleagues (Stone *et al.* 1954) and Geoffrey Wainwright (see Section 3 below). But henges were not the only monuments to be considered. In 1960 Paul Ashbee and colleagues started excavating what they thought was a simple pond barrow on Wilsford Down, only to discover that it contained a 30-m deep central rock-cut shaft (Ashbee 1963). The bottom-most 3 m or so of the shaft was waterlogged and contained within the fill a remarkable range of well-preserved wooden objects and palaeoenvironmental material. The earliest object, securely dated by radiocarbon dates, is part of a wooden bucket of the late 4th millennium BC (Ashbee *et al.* 1989: 69). Much of the rest of the fill contains material of the second millennium BC, mainly middle Bronze Age, but the early date suggests that either very old equipment was occasionally brought into use or that originally the shaft was sunk in middle Neolithic times and that its use and perhaps periodic re-digging continued into much later times.

More recent discoveries near Stonehenge include a pit containing decorated stone plaques (Vatcher 1969), and in the summer of 2002 an exceptionally rich grave of the late 3rd or very early 2nd millennium BC was found near Amesbury. The decreased, a male aged 35–50 years, was accompanied by more than 100 items including three beakers, stone wristguards, flint arrowheads and gold earrings (Fitzpatrick 2002).

At Avebury, a similar story of continuing research and discovery unfolds in the pages of ANTIQUITY, although the timing of the work is generally slightly later, and perhaps for this reason its impact on our knowledge and understanding of the area seems that much greater. Maud Cunnington's work at the Sanctuary on Overton Hill (1931) showed that timber circles like those at Woodhenge occurred as free-standing monuments and connected with stone circles as well as within earthwork enclosures. Richard Atkinson's investigation at Silbury Hill in 1968–70, sponsored by the BBC, was perhaps one of the greatest disappointments of early television coverage of archaeological excavations. The media and, through their prompting, the public too, expected to see the uncovering of buried treasure, but instead they saw a series of buried land-surfaces and construction features within the hill (Atkinson 1967; 1968; 1969; 1970; 1978; and see Whittle 1997: 5–49 for final report). More recently, the discovery of a series of three timber palisaded enclosures of mid 3rd-millennium BC date around West Kennet Farm has completely changed understanding of the area (Whittle 1991; 1997: 53–138; and see Section 4) and perhaps allows more sense to be made of the flint scatters and monument distributions in the area described by Holgate (1987).

The landscape of Stonehenge and Avebury cannot, and should not, be seen as restricted in time or in space. The use of sets of monuments and distributions of finds in defining relict cultural landscapes has been discussed in ANTIQUITY with the Stonehenge area as a case-study (Darvill *et al.* 1993: 568–70). This work emphasized the infinite scale needed when trying to understand the working and use of individual components that tend to be the focus of archaeological attention. Thus the person buried in the Upton Lovell G2a barrow discussed by Colin Shell (2000) would no doubt have known both Avebury and Stonehenge, even though his final resting place lay more than 20 km from either. Indeed, his skills as a metalworker or shaman may well have been called upon by communities over a wide area.

Stuart Piggott defined the early Bronze Age Wessex Culture of central southern England, typified by a series of richly furnished burials and monuments such as Stonehenge (Piggott 1938). He believed that these communities were closely tied to groups in northern France, and certainly there is evidence for typological similarities in certain aspects of material culture and perhaps even the transfer of a small number of prestige items between the two areas (Gerloff 1975; Needham 2000). Aubrey Burl proposed that links could be seen in the structure of the inner horseshoe settings at Stonehenge and in the rock-art motifs used on some of the stones (Burl 1997), views that were challenged in ANTIQUITY by Chris Scarre (1997), who suggested that the supposed analogies were misleading.

Still wider links have also been suggested for Stonehenge and related structures. Writers in the early 20th century, including Gordon Childe (1925), suggested that the architecture of Stonehenge has similarities with the fortified citadels of Mycenean Greece, with parallels between the rich grave-goods of the Wessex Culture barrows and those from the Shaft Graves of Mycenae itself (and see Piggott 1938: 94–6; Atkinson 1979: 165–6). This Aegean view, and the diffusionist perspective that it represented, were called into question by Colin Renfrew (1968; 1973) when it became apparent from radiocarbon dating that the main features of Stonehenge were more than 1000 years older than the supposed prototypes in Greece. Discussion and debate has continued because further dating has made the picture still more complicated (see Selkirk 1972 for useful summary; also Coles & Taylor 1971; Barfield 1991). Here it is important to separate Stonehenge from the rich graves around it. The construction and associated primary use of Stonehenge can now be placed within the 3rd millennium; there is very little evidence for constructional work after 2000 BC (although it may of course have continued in use in the form that it had reached at that stage). This date is clearly too early for Mycenean connections, and Renfrew's argument stands. The rich graves of Piggott's Wessex Culture belong mainly to the first half of the 2nd millennium BC and thus appear to post-date the main constructional activity at Stonehenge. Within the broad span of the early 2nd millennium BC, however, the dating of Wessex Culture burials remains difficult, with uncertainty about the extent to which the conventionally recognized Wessex I and II should be seen as successive, partly overlapping in duration, or essentially contemporaneous. The Mycenean Shaft Graves and associated material culture date from *c.* 1600–1200 BC, so there is clearly potential for links, whether through the exchange of actual objects or the transfer of knowledge. Following an exhaustive review of the evidence, however, Harding concludes that the idea of direct contacts should be rejected (1984: 265 & 279; but *cf.* Branigan 1970). Given the links between southern England and northern France, however, wider contacts with the Mediterranean world and beyond could have been indirect through much wider networks of relationships with communities falling within the Reinecke A1–B1 horizons of central Europe (and see Gerloff 1975: 245–6 and Needham 2000).

Despite all the discussion of monument form, classifications, and local and long-distance contacts, very little attention has been given to the question most commonly asked of Stonehenge and Avebury: what were they for? An exception is the paper published in 1998 by Mike Parker Pearson & Ramilisonina entitled 'Stonehenge for the ancestors: the stones pass the message', which is reproduced here (Parker Pearson & Ramilisonina 1998a). Their arguments were based on comparative studies and emphasize the need to take a broad landscape-based view of the past, rather than restrictive site-based narratives. Their contention that the stones of Stonehenge were representations of the ancestors, while the wooden structures of Woodhenge and Durrington Walls were monuments for the living, drew a number of comments on the methodology employed and the interpretations made, notably by Barrett & Fewster (1998) and Whittle (1998), some of which were answered by the original authors (Parker Pearson & Ramilisonina 1998b). Wrigley's discussion of 'Stonehenge from without' (1989) is also relevant to debates about the nature of interpretation, in his case looking at archaeological writing about Stonehenge from the perspective of an historian.

Just as controversial as the interpretation of Stonehenge and Avebury is the question of how to look after them. Both are popular monuments with the public, and have been for more than a century. Quite apart from their intrinsic interest as strange and curious places, it is hardly surprising that people want to see what the fuss is all about when archaeologists constantly trumpet their importance in the unfolding of the story of European prehistory and hold them up as exemplars of the achievements of early communities. And here is the essential conflict: numerous demands — academic, aesthetic, tourism, economic, political — are placed on these sites by contemporary society, but many carry with them conflicting priorities. A snap-shot picture of all this can be glimpsed from comments made in the first volumes of ANTIQUITY. Crawford as editor laments threats to the Stonehenge landscape and enjoins subscribers to contribute to an appeal for funds to buy additional land to be brought within the National Trust's considerable estate in the area (Crawford 1927: 259). At Avebury, a different and rather innovative approach was taken whereby a preservation plan constructed under the terms of the *Town and Country Planning Act 1932* would provide a blueprint for future development within and around the site, with compensation available to prospective developers whose schemes were blocked under certain circumstances (Wills *et al.* 1937). It was one of the first initiatives involving archaeological remains to be brought within the planning system. Keiller's excavations at Avebury proved very popular with the public, and on 1 June 1938 the Museum of the 'Morven Institute' was opened with 6000 people visiting in the first five months (Keiller 1939: 233). Preservation by direct control did come to Avebury, as it had to Stonehenge, when in March 1943 the National Trust secured the purchase from Alexander Keiller of 300 acres and a further 650 acres from Manor Farm using funds from the Pilgrim Trust (Anon. 1943). Later additions at Avebury included the acquisition of West Kennet Farm (see Chippindale 1989: 7–8).

The extent of reconstruction and restoration at both Stonehenge and Avebury is often overlooked by visitors and scholars alike. At Avebury, Keiller and his team replaced the stones along the northern section of the West Kennet Avenue in 1934–35 (Keiller & Piggott 1936: 418) while in 1937 to 1939 attention focused on restoring the eastern sectors of the outer circle within the Avebury Henge and marking the positions of some of the central settings with concrete blocks (Smith 1965: 187–91). At Stonehenge, restorations by the Ministry of Works followed the excavations of Richard Atkinson and colleagues between 1950 and 1958 (Piggott 1959). Interestingly, it is estimated that some 90,000 people visited Stonehenge during the restoration works especially to see the works in progress (Piggott 1959: 51): even then archaeological resource management was a popular spectator sport! It is perhaps a reflection of the quality of the restoration works at both sites that they are unnoticed now. The same cannot be said of the 1930s restorations at Woodhenge and The Sanctuary (see Cunnington 1929: 2 for a discussion of the philosophy applied).

After a period of relative quietude, the issue of enhancing the conservation and management of Stonehenge and its landscape resurfaced again in 1977 when the Department of the Environment set up a Stonehenge Working Party, whose report, and a Memorandum of Dissent by some members of Salisbury District Council, was completed in 1979 (DoE 1979). The government decided not to act upon its recommendations, but instead established the Historic Buildings and Monuments Commission for England (popularly known as English Heritage) in April 1984 as the new agency. They established a Stonehenge Study Group to 'consider the possible options for a long-term improvement of the setting of Stonehenge and the way that visitors are received and the monument is shown to them' (SSG 1985: 2). Their report was published in 1985 (SSG 1985) by which time the debate had spread widely with reports and suggestions included in ANTIQUITY and elsewhere. In 1983 Chris Chippindale published a wide-ranging general account of the way Stonehenge had been managed through the early 20th century, and in asking the question 'What future for Stonehenge?' usefully put his finger on many of the key issues that needed to be faced at the time (Chippindale 1983b). Paul Ashbee (1984) argued that four things were essential for the proper presentation of Stonehenge: closure of the A344; the presentation of the supportive landscape with its related monuments as an entity; the establishment of a Centre, the focus of which would be a full-sized replica of the monument; and the dispersal of the irrelevant and perverse elements for which Stonehenge has become the focus. Following the publication of the Stonehenge Study Group's report, Chippindale contributed a critical piece on the report and its proposals (Chippindale 1985). Work continued, focusing on three key aspects: the removal of the visitor facilities from their present position near the monument to a site further away; the closing of the A344 and the restoration to downland of the immediate environs of Stonehenge; and the upgrading of the A303 to the south of Stonehenge, preferably by 'undergrounding' all or part of it. These were widely accepted in principle, but the detail of how they could be achieved to the satisfaction of all has caused many proposals to be outlined and then scrapped amidst almost perpetual heated debate. In 1996, Geoffrey Wainwright outlined the various options for the upgrading of A303; the short paper entitled 'Stonehenge saved' argues the case for a solution that involved a tunnel to take the road south of Stonehenge (Wainwright 1996). Several different kinds of tunnel are possible, however, and the debate about which kind, how long it should be, and the costs, provided another area of debate (see Malone & Stoddart 1998: 731–7 for discussion). But things change, especially the government's plans for the upgrading of the A303, and in 2000 Wainwright came back into the pages of ANTIQUITY with a further set of proposals under the title 'The Stonehenge we deserve' (Wainwright 2000), which is reprinted here. This paper discussed not only the roads but also plans for a new visitor centre, well to the east of Stonehenge at Countess Road. Not unexpectedly, the plans drew a series of sharp responses from Baxter & Chippindale (2000), Kennet & Young (2000) and Fielden (2000). The last two focus on procedural issues and what they see as conflicting policy statements. There is still a long way to go with the development of these plans, and it is more complicated now that English Heritage and the National Trust are carrying forward proposals for a new visitor facility and the 'tidying-up' of the monument, while the Government has appointed contractors to carry forward plans for improvements to the A303.

Alongside these plans for improvement have been questions of access and the use of Stonehenge during the summer solstice. There is a long tradition of folkgames at Stonehenge and around Silbury Hill as reported by Goulstone (1985). The character of the events changed drastically in the latter 20th century. René Cutforth was at Stonehenge for the solstice in 1970 when 50–60 Druids assembled (Cutforth 1970). A decade later their activities had been supplemented by a 'Stonehenge Festival' that spanned weeks rather than days. Glyn Daniel reported on the events using text from an article by Tony Rocca in the *Daily Mail* in his editorial in the November issue of ANTIQUITY (Daniel 1981: 170–71). By 1985 he reported that English Heritage had banned the festival, and quoted newspaper reports telling the story of the events that followed (Daniel 1985: 161–2. See also Chippindale 1986).

Avebury has been beset by similar problems, although not on the scale of Stonehenge. Mike Pitts (1990) reviewed the situation up until the late 1980s, but various proposals for development followed and provoked Fielden to ask the question 'Avebury saved?' (Fielden 1996). Both monuments have working landscapes and communities, needing a balance between the extremes of total conservation (the so-called BANANA approach: Build Absolutely Nothing Anywhere Near Anything) and extreme *laissez-faire*. This need was cogently presented by Christopher Gingell (1996), the manager of the National Trust's Avebury Estate.

Detailed management plans have been published for both Avebury (English Heritage 1998) and Stonehenge (English Heritage 2000) as befits any World Heritage Site, and more recently Research Frameworks have been published for each site (for Avebury see AAHRG 2001; for Stonehenge see Darvill forthcoming and http://csweb.bournemouth.ac.uk/stonehenge). Together, all these documents will set the scene for the next phase of archaeological and managerial action at the two sites and their hinterlands.

Stukeley, Avebury and the Druids
by STUART PIGGOTT
ANTIQUITY 9 (33), 1935

THERE HAVE BEEN few tendencies in the history of English culture with so profound a contemporary influence as the so-called Romantic Movement of the 18th and early 19th centuries, and still fewer with such a strangely assorted progeny. That toying with 'the Gothick', which produced such early *jeux d'esprit* as Walpole's Strawberry Hill or Beckford's Fonthill, led, on the one hand, to the Albert Memorial, and, on the other, to the sculpture of Eric Gill; in literature, while the Romantics founded an honourable poetic tradition extending from Collins through Wordsworth to Blunden, it is surely not fantastic to see in such works as Lewis' *Bravo of Venice* the genesis of the modern thriller. Most strange of all, one outcome of the Romantic Movement was a new branch of science. For prehistoric archaeology in England was not the product of the classical lore so eagerly absorbed from Italy in the 16th and 17th centuries, but originated in those eccentric gentlemen of the 18th century who perambulated the countryside studying at first hand the antiquities of their own forefathers.

Easily the greatest of these early antiquaries was William Stukeley, and few individuals have left posterity such a mass of potential biographical material. While his published works are relatively few, he zealously kept every scrap of his own manuscript writings, his drawings, the proofs of his published engravings; his correspondence with antiquaries of the day; numerous notebooks, and 20 volumes of his diary, as well as two autobiographical essays. The main bulk of these papers was preserved by his descendants, the St Johns of Dinmore Court, Herefordshire, and, with some additional material from other sources, were utilized by W.C. Lukis in his edition of *The Family Memoirs of the Rev. William Stukeley, M.D.* prepared for the Surtees Society in 1882–7. In 1924, some of the Dinmore Court MSS were presented to the Bodleian[1] (which already possessed, in the Gough topographical collections, several important Stukeley MSS); others were purchased by that Library and by Mr Alexander Keiller, who has since acquired additional MSS from time to time.[2] With such a plethora of material it is obviously impossible, in the space of a single article, to do more than indicate the main outlines of Stukeley's life, and to deal in detail with a single, but extremely important aspect of his archaeological work — the apparent mixture, in his published account of Avebury, of sound field-work with so much fantastic theorizing that in popular estimation the second characteristic has swamped the first. Most archaeologists today would probably endorse Tom Hearne's opinion of Stukeley — 'He is a very fanciful man, and the things he hath published are built upon fancy' — but those who have had occasion to check his field-observations know him as an accurate and careful observer. A study of his life and thought as reflected in his own writings shows that this paradox is capable of explanation.

---

1   *Bodleian Quarterly Record* October 1924 (43): 149.
2   The writer owes a debt of gratitude to Mr Keiller not only for indicating in the first place the possibilities of the MSS, and suggesting the research of which this paper is an outcome, but for placing them unreservedly at his disposal and giving every facility for their study.

William Stukeley was born in 1687[3] at Holbeach in Lincolnshire, his father, John Stukeley, being a lawyer in partnership with his elder brother Adlard. Engaging glimpses of his boyhood days can be gathered from his memoranda — his learning to write at the age of seven 'of Mr Coleman who taught us in the Quire of the Church'; or later, being taught to dance 'among the other young Fry of the Town'; and playing the flute, an accomplishment of which evidence exists today in a volume of flute music which he copied out in 1714.[4] We see him listening behind a screen to the conversations between his father and Mr Belgrave — 'an ingenious Gent' — on astronomy, and writing an essay to controvert their arguments; making maps of the country round Holbeach, or a puppet theatre in imitation of one he had seen. In 1700 he was apprenticed in his father's office, but his inclinations did not lie in the study and practice of the law, and in response to his entreaties he was sent to Cambridge to study medicine, where he was admitted a pensioner at Corpus Christi in November 1703.

At Cambridge, Stukeley found himself in a congenial atmosphere. He attended Vigani's lectures on chemistry, went botanizing in the country around to collect material for a new edition of Ray's *Catalogus Plantarum,* and 'began to conceive a passionate Love for Antiquitys'. He gives a description of his room at Corpus:

> which had a very strange appearance with my furniture in it, the wall was generally hung round with guts, stomachs, bladders, preparations of parts and drawings. I had sand furnaces, Calots, glasses, and all sorts of chymical implements. Here I and my Associats often dind upon the same table as our dogs lay upon. I often prepard the pulvis fulminans and sometimes surprized the whole College with a sudden explosion. I cur'd a lad once of an ague with it by a fright.

One suspects that he was not wholly popular with those who inhabited rooms adjacent to his.

Stukeley's father died in 1705, his mother two years later, and on his taking his MB in 1709 he went to London to study at St Thomas' hospital. Before this, however, he paid a visit to friends in Northamptonshire, where it appears that he was not insensible to the charms of his host's daughter Martha, who

> had somewhat of an airy temper, and accompanyd me in several of my Rambles in that Country to view Antiquitys, Roman Camps, and the like. We traveld together like Errant Vertuosos, and when we came to an old ruind Castle, etc., we climbd together thro' every story and staircase, mutually helping one another, and pulling each other over the gaping arches and rugged heaps of rubbish, and when I had occasion to draw a view of them out, as we sat upon a stone or the grass, she held my ink horn or my paper, and was very serviceable and assistant in taking my designs, and all without any reserve or immodesty; nor could any aged Philosophers have conversd together with more innocent familiarity or less guilt even in thought or intention. Nor could travailing curiosity or Antiquarian Researches be rendered so agreeable as with a fair and witty Companion and Fellow laborer, and when we returnd home my young Disciple could entertain the Family with so very curious Relation of the curiositys we had seen, that it would be difficult to say whether so nice taste in the Remains of Ancient Time most recommended a young Lady, or that Refined study became more lovely and delightful for her sake.

---

3   Where the source is not otherwise given, the details of Stukeley's life are derived from Lukis' published work referred to above.
4   AK MSS.

There is a faint tang of bitterness and regret in that brief sentence which closes the episode in his 'Commentarys' — 'She is since marryd to a Gentleman in Wales'.

For the next 10 years Stukeley practised medicine; in Lincolnshire at first, but from 1717 in London, where he was in 1720 elected a Fellow of the College of Physicians, reading the Gulstonian Lecture to that body in 1722. His wide range of scientific interests had already secured him a Fellowship of the Royal Society in 1717, but archaeology was rapidly becoming his principal pursuit. His interest in the antiquities of his own country was symptomatic of the feeling among the intelligentsia of his day, for already for some time 'a number of gentlemen residing in and about London, of like inclination . . . used to meet weekly, on a Wednesday evening, as a club, at the Mitre Tavern in Fleet Street. Their conversation turn'd on matters of learning, chiefly Antiquitys'.[5] On his coming to London in 1717 he was introduced to the club by Maurice Johnson and the next year was largely instrumental in forming the dining club into a more formal body; this in his account of its founding he calls indifferently the Antiquarian Society or The Society of Antiquaries, and under the latter title it has continued to the present day.

The foundation of the Society of Antiquaries, of which Stukeley was the first secretary, marks the real beginning of his archaeological career, during the first 10 years of which he made a very considerable contribution to British archaeology. For it was between 1718 and 1725 that he carried out his monumental series of field-observations at Avebury and Stonehenge, without which our knowledge of those great megalithic structures would be materially less. At Stonehenge little destruction took place after his day, but Avebury was wrecked to such a degree that, without his record of its appearance 200 years ago, we could glean but little from its shattered remnants. Before we come to consider his work on these monuments in some detail, it is well to emphasize one point. Since his entering Cambridge, his training and environment had been essentially that of a scientist. His medical work, coupled with a genuine bent for scientific research so far as it was known at the beginning of the 18th century, would naturally cause him to bring to bear upon the study of antiquities an acute and observant eye; a mind accustomed to diagnosis would grasp the salient points and make cautious deductions from them; while he would appreciate the value of an accurate record of fact both in words and in drawings, the latter made easier by his own considerable talent in sketching (a talent, alas, to which the engravers of his published plates rarely did justice). In fact, Stukeley was one of the first of that large band of medical men who have turned their scientific training to the study of archaeology with excellent effect.

It is commonly thought that Stukeley started his Avebury fieldwork, and to some extent that at Stonehenge, with a preconceived theory dominating his mind — that Hydra-headed, tortuous monster of perverse ingenuity which, in the published accounts of these monuments, is so much in evidence that the solid basis of fieldwork is almost stifled, Laocoon-like, by its involved coils. We shall see, however, that there is no evidence that this was the actual state of affairs.

In the newly founded Society of Antiquaries, Stukeley met and rapidly formed a close friendship with Roger Gale, son of the master of St Paul's School. Gale had had access to, and had transcribed some of the manuscript of John Aubrey's *Monumenta Britannica,* which at that time was in the hands of Awnsham Churchill, the bookseller and publisher (Long 1862: 61), and it seems more than likely that Aubrey's description of Avebury fired Stukeley and Gale to make an expedition to this site and to Stonehenge in 1718. At all events the journey

---

[5] MS History of the Society of Antiquaries (AK).

was made, and in December of that year Stukeley copied Aubrey's account of Avebury, and his plan, from Gale's transcript, into his commonplace book.[6]

As Mr T.D. Kendrick has shown (1927: 8), in the only sane book on Druids ever written, Aubrey was the first to claim Stonehenge, Avebury and other megalithic monuments for the Druids, and it seems that from this 'humble submission to better judgment' as Aubrey himself styled his hypothesis, Stukeley ultimately built his incredible structure of fantastic theory. But in the years immediately following 1718, theory occupied a secondary place: Stukeley was working as a scientist. About this time he was attacked by gout, and rode 'on horseback in the spring, for recovery of his health. By this means, he indulged his natural love of antiquitys, especially those of his own Country'. In 1721, and 1723, he undertook lengthy tours of southern and midland England with Roger Gale, making numerous notes and drawings which were published as *Itinerarium Curiosum, Centuria I,* in 1724. But his main work was the fortnight or so of each year devoted to Avebury and Stonehenge, and sufficient material remains (thanks largely to his habit of dating most of his drawings) to reconstruct a journal of his work on the former site, in which his change of mental outlook can be clearly traced.

In May 1719, he made his first 'rude general sketch' of the Avebury circles,[7] and part of the Kennet Avenue; in 1720 and 1721 he again visited the site, the second time with Roger Gale. In 1722, he made a first draft of a large scale-plan of the circles[8] as well as other drawings, and discovered the problematical Beckhampton Avenue.

It is in 1722 and 1723 that for the first time we can detect some hint of Stukeley's searching for a theory to account for the lay-out of the circles and avenues. On the manuscript plan of the circles of 'The Remains of the BRITISH Temple in the village of AUBURY Wilts, Ao. 1722' to which we have referred, the two double concentric circles within the main circle are called 'The Lunar Temple' and 'The Solar Temple'; subsequently altered to 'Northern' and 'Southern' temples respectively. On 8 July 1723, he made his well-known drawing of the stone circles of 'The Sanctuary' on Overton Hill, and in its original form called it the 'Temple of Ertha';[9] on 19 July he made the drawing of 'A view from the spot of the Temple at the end of Bekampton Avenue'.[10] His original plans of the sanctuary described below were also in the first instance called 'The Temple of the Earth'. To this year also must belong a great panoramic view of the whole Avebury complex,[11] although it is undated. On this drawing, probably Stukeley's finest piece of draughtsmanship, there is indicated a hypothetical circle at the end of the Beckhampton Avenue to balance those on Overton Hill, and against it is written (and subsequently heavily crossed out) 'Temple of the Infernal Regions'.

A cosmic theory was obviously in his mind, and this is amplified with regard to the circles at Stanton Drew, which Stukeley visited on 23 July 1723, after he had been working at Avebury for nearly a fortnight. The engravings made from his drawings of Stanton Drew were published posthumously in *Centuria II* of the *Itinerarium Curiosum,* where one is called the 'Solar Circle', and in his account of the circles, published in the same volume under the title of 'The Weddings', and which we know from the manuscript[12] to

---

6 Commonplace Book 1717–1748, in the library of the Wiltshire Archaeological Society at Devizes.
7 In the Commonplace Book at Devizes.
8 *Avebury Drawings* (AK).
9 *Proof Plates,* no. 62 (AK).
10 *Proof Plates,* no. 61 (AK).
11 *Avebury Drawings* (AK).
12 AK MSS.

have been written in March 1724, the theory of Solar and Lunar Temples, and the Temple of the Earth, is set forth and compared with Avebury.

It is clear therefore, that when first Stukeley began to theorize, it was not his famous Serpentine ideas that filled his head, nor, in fact, does he seem to have regarded his celestial theory with any great seriousness, for he abandoned it in 1724. It is necessary to explain at this point that it appears to have been his custom to have his drawings engraved directly after each yearly visit, and on his next visit he would correct proofs on the spot; increasing shading here, deleting a tree there, or altering the title. The proof engraving of what eventually became Tab. XXI of his *Abury*, (the view of the Sanctuary), was, as we have seen, originally entitled 'the Temple of Ertha', but on 18 May 1724, when he was again at Avebury, he altered this to the sensibly non-committal 'Temple on Overton Hill', fortunately dating the correction on the proof. A similar correction was also made on his original plans of the site. The Beckhampton 'Temple' being no longer needed — 'The Infernal Regions' being unnecessary with no 'Temple of Ertha' — the proof of this view, mentioned above, was altered from 'Spot of the Temple' to 'Near the Spot of the Termination of the Bekampton Avenue' *(Abury*: Tab. XXV). It is probable that the alterations to the main plan, of 'Northern' and 'Southern' for 'Lunar' and 'Solar' Temples were made at the same time.

This year, 1724, was the last at Avebury. Stukeley, unhampered by theories, completed his magnificent detailed record, both in notes and illustrations, of a monument which was being destroyed before his eyes. We owe him a deep debt of gratitude for his Avebury work, and scarcely less for that on Stonehenge which he carried on during the same years, 1718–24. Stukeley discovered the Avenue and the Cursus, and, incidentally, it is to him that we owe the term 'trilithon' for the megalithic units at Stonehenge. The dramatic recovery of the Avenue, lost for 200 years, by air-photography in 1921, was a vindication both of the accuracy of Stukeley's observations and of the utility of this recently adopted adjunct to archaeological research.

Any modern archaeologist who has had occasion to test the accuracy of Stukeley's field-work during the decade 1718–27, will have proved the complete reliance that can be placed upon it. In 1725 Stukeley and Roger Gale made a tour in northern England, the journal of which, entitled *Iter Boreale*,[13] was not published until after Stukeley's death, in the second part of the *Itinerarium Curiosum*. Mr Crawford has recently shown, in the pages of ANTIQUITY (1934), the use to which he was able to put a drawing of the stone circle of Long Meg and her Daughters, made during this tour, in identifying the site of a now destroyed adjacent circle. Instances such as this might be multiplied indefinitely.

In February 1727, Stukeley wrote to Roger Gale:

> I begin now and then to peep over my old papers and drawings, and among antiquity matters Abury seems to touch my fancy the most at present, and probably, if business does not too much encroach upon my time, I shall publish it in a year or two.

Had Stukeley acted on this worthy resolution his reputation today as an archaeologist would have been very different. But, unfortunately, other matters did encroach upon his time, with lamentable results. Neither his leaving London and going to live in Grantham in 1725, nor his marriage in 1728 to Frances Williamson (FIGURE 1), were likely to prejudice his archaeological judgment; but in June 1729 he took a step of which the consequences profoundly coloured his whole subsequent outlook.

---

13   The original MS is in the AK Collection.

FIGURE 1. *William Stukeley and his wife Frances. (Drawing by Stukeley in a MS Genealogy (c. 1730) in the possession of Alexander Keiller.)*

Despite his scientific training, it is clear that there had always been a strong underlying vein of mysticism in Stukeley's character, increasing as the years went by. A love of elaborate symbolism and allegory probably accounts for his entry into Freemasonry in 1721 (for Stukeley's masonic career see R.F. Gould in *Ars Quatuor Coronatorum* VI), and once he had begun to think about Druids his fancy led him into strange paths. He laid out a 'Druidical grove and temple' in his garden at Grantham, and in 1728 he buried a still-born child

> ... under the high altar in the chappel of my hermitage vineyard; for there I built a niche in a ragged wall overgrown with ivy, in which I placed my roman altar, a brick from Verulam, & a waterpipe lately sent me by my Lord Colrain from Marshland ... there we entered it, present my wives mother & aunt, with ceremonys proper to the occasion.

It is perhaps surprising, after this semi-pagan ritual, to find him writing in June 1729, to his friend Dr Wake, Archbishop of Canterbury, asking his advice and help in the matter of ordination for the church, and hinting darkly that his Druidical researches had led him to 'some notions about the Doctrine of the Trinity, which I think are not common'. He was apparently more explicit in a letter to Roger Gale, to such a degree that that worthy man was seriously alarmed at his friend's decision, for he wrote back urging a reconsideration. 'Your reconciling Plato & Moses', he goes on, '& the Druid & Christian Religion may gain you applause, & perhaps a Patron; but it is good to be sure of the latter upon firmer motives than that scheme may inspire people with at present'. But Stukeley was not to be deterred. He had decided that every pagan religion, particularly that of the Druids, was a foreshadowing, not only of Christianity, but of the doctrine of the Trinity, and with this weapon he was going to battle against the sceptics in 'this age of epidemical infidelity'. And so we see him ordained in November 1729, and appointed to the living of All Saints, Stamford.

Fired with all the misguided enthusiasm of the religious revivalist, Stukeley's first task was to utilize his field-work of the last 10 years as ammunition in his holy war. Poor Avebury was the first victim of this transforming process. Gale writes in June 1730 to congratulate Stukeley on his resumption of work on the Avebury book, and declares himself 'much pleased with the plan of your theologicall enlargements upon it'. Enlargements they certainly were, and in a letter in reply on 25 June, Stukeley reveals their true nature.

> The form of that stupendous work [Avebury] is the picture of the Deity, more particularly of the Trinity. . . . A snake proceeding from a circle is the eternal procession of the son from the first cause. . . . My main motive in pursuing this subject is to combat the deists from an unexpected quarter, and to preserve so noble a monument of our ancestors' piety, I may add orthodoxy.

Stukeley had indeed plunged deeply into the waters of religious controversy. Scepticism was at this time becoming fashionable under Hume and the younger Dodwell, having developed out of the early forms of Deism of Chubb, Tindal and Toland. Now Toland, in addition to his more obviously controversial religious works, had written a diffuse and involved *History of the Druids,* containing scarcely veiled attacks on 'priestcraft' in general, which was published posthumously in 1726, and is more than once referred to by Stukeley in his published accounts of Avebury and Stonehenge. It is possible that Stukeley's attack on Deism through the Druids may have been tinged with some personal feeling against the unfortunate Toland, more particularly when we find that about 1710 Toland had published his *Origines Judaicae,* in which he ridiculed one Huetius, who in a work entitled *Demonstratio Evangelica,* had sought to prove that various Old Testament characters were allegorized in heathen mythology (including, rather unexpectedly, Moses as Bacchus) — a scheme not unlike Stukeley's own theories.

After this we are less surprised than we might be to find that, when *Stonehenge* was finally published in 1740 it was graced with a preface explaining that it, and the forthcoming *Abury,* were to be considered merely as parts of a great work entitled 'Patriarchal Christianity, or a Chronological History of the Origin and Progress of true Religion, and of Idolatry'. He had decided, he says, to publish *Stonehenge* and *Abury* first, 'and proceed to the speculative parts afterwards; reserving them, God willing, to the maturer time of my life'. 'My intent is', he goes on

> to warm our hearts into that true sense of Religion, which keeps the medium between ignorant superstition and learned free-thinking, between slovenly fanaticism

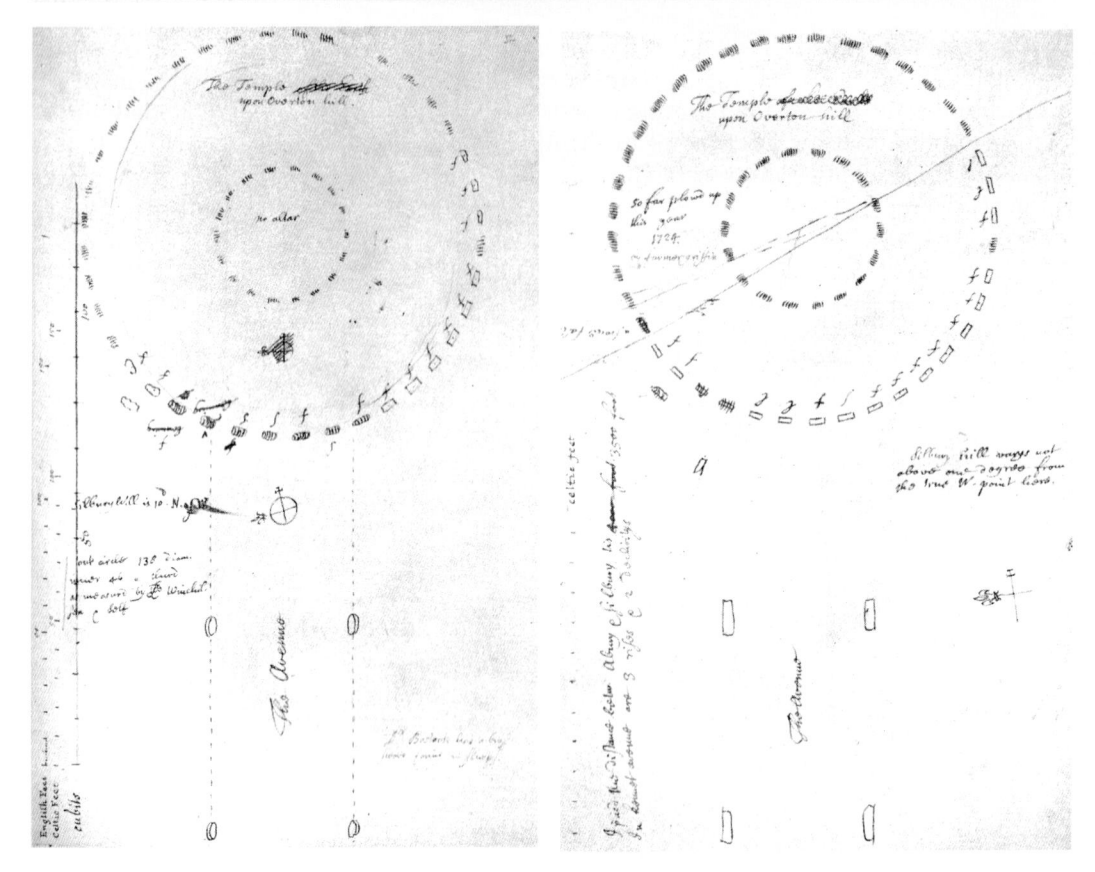

FIGURE 2. *Stukeley's original field-sketch of the plan of the Overton Hill stone circles (1724). (Bodleian Library, MS Gough Maps, 231, f. 54r.)*

FIGURE 3. *Stukeley's original field-sketch of the plan of the Overton Hill stone circles (1724). (Bodleian Library, MS Gough Maps, 231, f. 9v.)*

and popish pageantry, between enthusiasm and the rational worship of God, which is no where upon earth done, in my judgement, better than in the Church of *England*.

And so we find that odd and incongruous mixture in the published accounts of Stonehenge and Avebury — sound field-work and careful observation side by side with the wildest imaginative flights, according to whether Dr William Stukeley or the Rev. William Stukeley was the dominant mental character at the moment. So far as can be seen, enough remained of his scientific conscience to prevent him from materially altering the facts to fit his theories, but in one instance at all events he was guilty of a very grave crime in this direction.

His published plan *(Abury*: Tab. XX) of the destroyed stone circles on Overton Hill, known as 'The Sanctuary', shows them not as circles, but as ovals (FIGURE 5). As Captain and Mrs Cunnington's excavations of 1930 proved, they were in fact true circles (Cunnington 1931: 300). After this discovery, Stukeley's reputation as a field-archaeologist seemed likely to wane, but it is fortunate that in the Bodleian there are two original field-sketches of this plan (FIGURES 2, 3), and in both the circles are drawn *as* circles, and even some of the 'extra' stones near the junction with the Kennet Avenue, the sockets for which were found in 1930, are shown. The intermediate link between these excellent

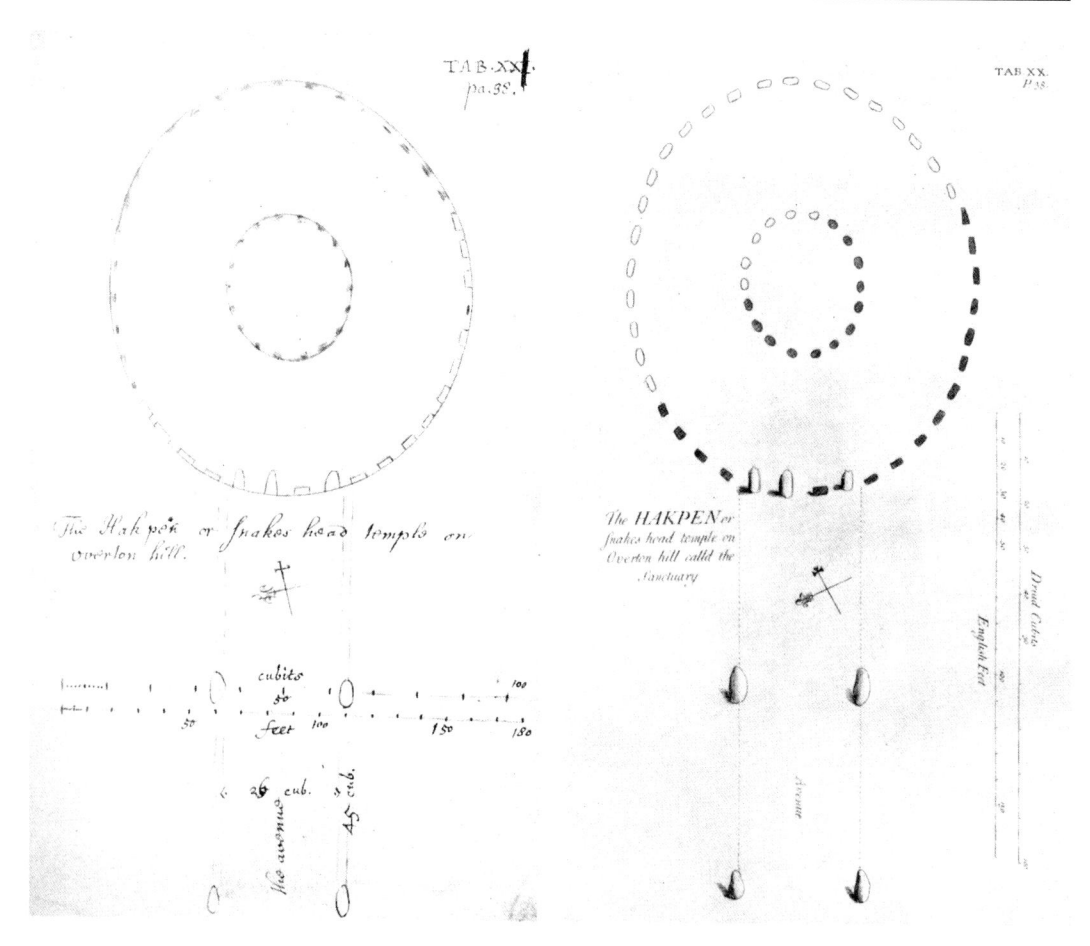

FIGURE 4. *Drawing (c. 1740) for the published plate of the Overton Hill stone circles, though not the final version, showing the circles altered to ovals. (MS in the possession of Alexander Keiller.)*

FIGURE 5. *Overton Hill stone circles: plan published in Stukeley's* Abury, *Tab. XX (1743).*

plans and the misleading published record of the site is provided by an original drawing c. 1740 which, while not that from which the plate was engraved, comes very close to it in detail[14] (FIGURE 4). In this the stones (or stone-holes) are arranged as ovals in grey wash, but are superimposed on a faint pencil outline showing them as circles, while in one of the original plans a rough oval outline has likewise been sketched. We can only feel that Stukeley, by now completely theory-ridden, thought how desirable it would be to give his snake an oval, more naturalistic, head, and so committed the serious offence of altering his original survey.

After the publication of *Stonehenge* in 1740 and *Abury* in 1743, Stukeley's archaeological career, though pursued with enormous vigour, is the melancholy record of the decay of a once-sound mind. It was in 1747 that he received the letter from Charles Bertram of Copenhagen, which ultimately led to his accepting as genuine the famous

14 *Avebury Drawings* (AK).

forgery of Richard of Cirencester, the story of which has been told in these pages by Mr H.J. Randall (1933). His subsequent archaeological productions were a most involved farrago of far-fetched hypotheses, coupled with an almost infantile credulity. The career of Carausius had long interested him, but unfortunately he misread FORTVNA on a coin as ORIVNA, and thereupon in a moment of inspired lunacy produced a wife of this name for his hero, announcing his momentous discovery in print in 1752. Windmill Street near Piccadilly he concludes quite rightly to have been called after an actual mill — but he goes on to assume that as windmills sometimes stood on barrows, a barrow therefore existed in Piccadilly Circus in which the king of the Trinobantes was buried![15] Such instances may have an almost pathological interest to the student of mental aberrations — to those who respect Stukeley's earlier work they are pathetic.

He died in 1765 at the age of 78, being at that time rector of St George's, Queen's Square, Holborn. His work during the 10 years from 1718 shows him to have been the finest field-archaeologist that England had so far seen or was to see for a century; for the next 35 he was instrumental in propagating theories the very imbecility of which seems to have endeared them for ever to the public mind. Who shall apportion praise or blame to so contradictory a character?

References

Ars Quatuor Coronatorum VI.
CRAWFORD, O.G.S. 1934. Long Meg, *Antiquity* 8: 328–9, plates I, II.
CUNNINGTON, M.E. 1931. The 'Sanctuary' on Overton Hill, near Avebury, *Wiltshire Archaeological & Natural History Magazine* 45: 300–35.
KENDRICK, T.D. 1927. *The Druids: a study in Keltic prehistory*. London: Methuen.
LEWIS, M.G. 1805. *The bravo of Venice: a romance*. London: printed by D.N. Shury for J.F. Hughes.
LONG, W. 1862. *Abury Illustrated*. Devizes. (Reprinted from *Wilts Arch. Mag.* IV and VII, but with additions not published elsewhere.)
LUKIS, W.C. 1882–7. *The Family Memoirs of the Rev. William Stukeley, M.D.*
RANDALL, H.J. 1933. Splendide Mendax, *Antiquity* 7: 49–60.
STUKELEY, W. 1740. *Stonehenge: a temple restor'd to the British Druids*. London.
    1743. *Abury: a temple of the British Druids*. London.
TOLAND, J. 1726. *History of the Druids*. London: Lackington, Hughes, Harding.

---

15 MS entitled *Knaves Acre*, written *c.* 1760 (AK).

Stonehenge: a review

by **R.S. NEWALL**

ANTIQUITY 30 (119), 1956

AN UP-TO-DATE BOOK on Stonehenge[1] by Mr Atkinson is indeed a great acquisition; it is a book for the intelligent reader as well as for the archaeologist, and is by far the best book on the subject that has so far been written.

The author explains how a potsherd or stone, when carelessly thrown away, will gradually sink owing to the action of earth worms, through the earthy top-soil till it reaches an impermeable layer, so that where, as here, the soil is shallow a layer is formed containing objects of all periods. Such a statement made in the 1920s was laughed at. Further, he goes on to say (p. 168): 'The one thing about Stonehenge upon which everyone is agreed is that it is primarily a "temple," a structure in which it was possible for man to establish contact and communication with extra-mundane forces or beings'. No one in the 1920s could have made such a statement and survived. Abercromby said it in his book *(Bronze Age Pottery,* 1912), and his chapter on Stonehenge is still well worth reading, but it is never quoted or referred to. It was Abercromby, not the present reviewer, who first pointed out the importance of the southwestern end of the axis. The only obvious error noticed (p. 195) is the statement that Colonel Hawley was Director of the Society of Antiquaries. However, this slight error is amply made up for by the 40 photographs, all but six of which reveal some feature never before published and probably not even photographed; one of them (plate II: Stonehenge from the north[2]) has an artistic quality that no other photograph I can recall has ever had. The effect of light and shade is most beautiful.

Mr Atkinson describes the excavations of the last few years, carried out in co-operation with Professor Piggott and Dr J.F.S. Stone with great care. No one of course will question statements of facts about the excavations; but some of the inferences drawn from them are open to discussion, and no one will welcome such discussion more than the author of the book, for it is through that that the story of Stonehenge unfolds. This remark applies particularly to Chapter 3 ('The Sequence of Construction'), a very difficult chapter to write and well done. Early in the book the author says that an archaeologist's eyes are too often buried ostrich-like in the ground; I feel that in order to understand Stonehenge one's eyes must be not only below ground but also above it and directed to the heavens; of this more anon.

Bearing this in mind, let us consider the first period of construction to which he assigns the Heel Stone, the bank and ditch and the post-holes on the original narrow causeway. But he does not mention the fact that these post-holes are radially arranged with six or more holes in line, and that they are also placed in arcs which are concentric with the centre, stone-holes D and E, the timber structure at A and the Aubrey-hole cremations. To his second period he assigns the double circle of blue stones, the widened causeway, the Heel Stone ditch, the Avenue, the dismantling of stones D and E and

---

1   *Stonehenge,* by R.J.C. Atkinson, Hamish Hamilton, London, 16s. The Editor wishes to thank the publishers for the loan of the block from which the plan has been printed.
2   Nearly northeast would have been more correct.

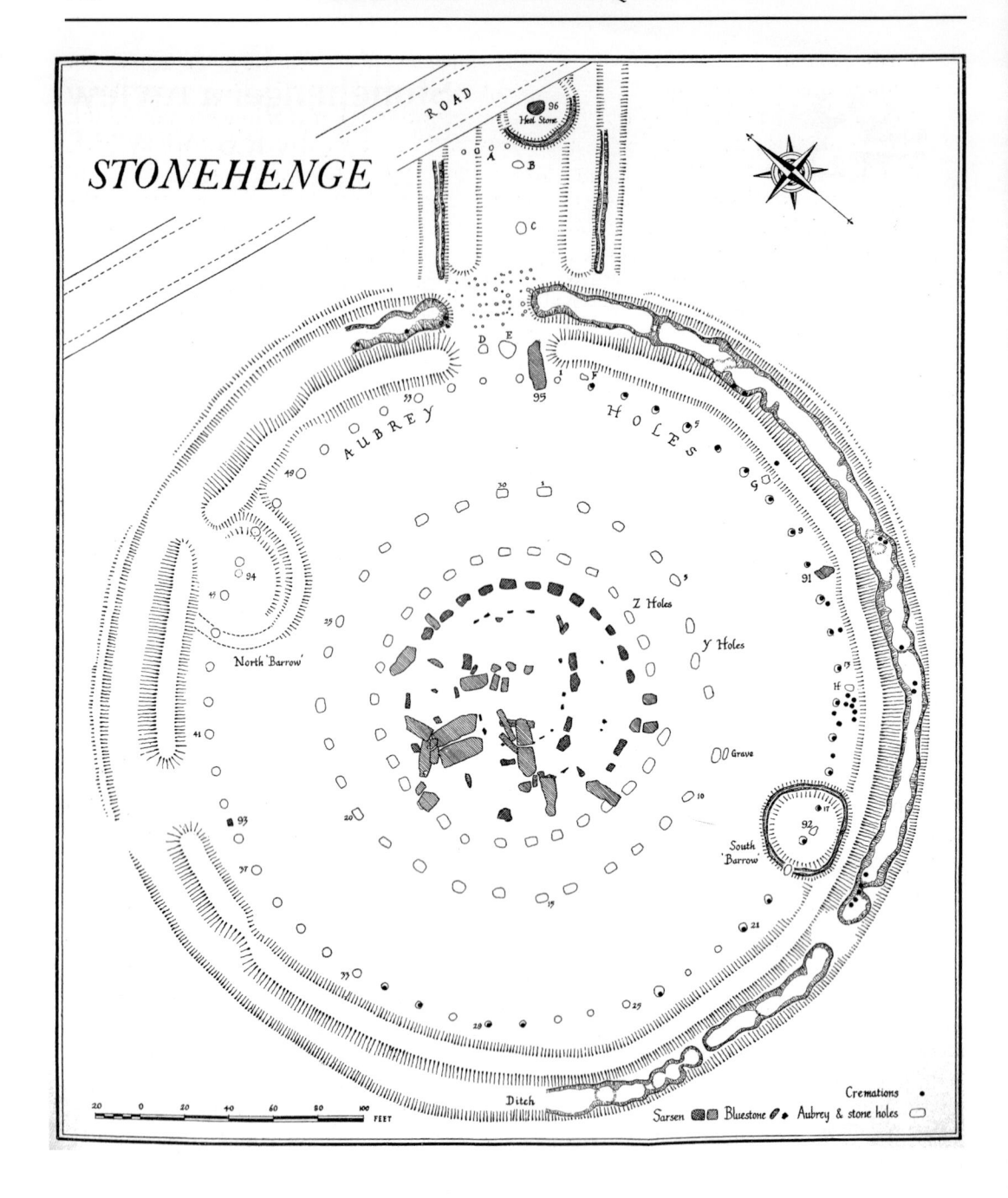

STONEHENGE

the erection of stones B and C. He says (p. 15) that the Heel Stone ditch must be more or less contemporary with the erection of the Heel Stone, or later (p. 60). This ditch belongs to Period II, therefore the Heel Stone belongs to Period II or I. If it belongs to Period II it would be contemporary with the Avenue and would then have been placed centrally on it, which it was not; therefore it is earlier than the Avenue and belongs to Period I; and this, he says, is confirmed by the Beaker sherds found in the earth filling between the outer face of the Heel Stone and the edge of the stone-hole. The outer face of this stone is now about 20° out from the perpendicular; it is not known when it began to lean. A Beaker burial could perhaps have been placed against the stone at any time in that period, but the accidental fall of some of its pieces down to a deeper level in slipping soil cannot be used as evidence of a period of construction. The reason given on p. 66 for putting the Heel Stone ditch in Period II is that a flake of rhyolite was found on the bottom of the ditch, which evidently means that the ditch is contemporary with the introduction of rhyolite into the monument, or very little later than that. No known rhyolites were present in Period I. One feels that the ditch must belong to the same period as the stone. Beaker sherds or rhyolite chips were in the refilled stone-holes of the double circle. Further, the asymmetrical position of the Heel Stone in relation to the axis of Period I is against it being of that period.

None of the finds, and none of the inferences drawn from them would be against the theory that in Period I Stonehenge was a wooden henge with some central wooden structure whose post-holes might be discoverable. The post-holes on the narrow causeway, the four A holes and the D and E holes all on one alignment (though these are more doubtful), are most suggestive, whereas the Heel Stone is some 5° to the east of this line. If, on the other hand, any part of the central area could be found still intact and unviolated by treasure hunters, there is just a possibility that excavation might reveal stone-holes which were the original holes of the dressed and spotted dolerites of the Horseshoe and the two lintels of the Blue Stone circle. This would belong to Period I and would be a very suitable setting indeed for these stones. The author says (p. 73) it is possible that stone-holes J and L may even be two of the holes for these stones, but that the holes belong to Period III b; why III? (The eight photographs showing details of these stones are most excellent). Their present position can now be explained only by recourse to that very unsatisfactory phrase, 'change of plan'. One wonders whether all the blue stones were imported at one period. In the 19th century there was a theory that a blue stone monument, not just rough boulders, had been brought from somewhere. We do not know whether there was one importation or several. If it was a monument of dressed stones that was imported, that might mean that the Stonehenge layer of blue stones is composed rather of destruction fragments than of dressing chips. The discovery of blue stones in Boles Barrow (a long barrow) suggests that there was more than one importation. On p. 104 only one such stone is mentioned, but Cunnington says in a letter that he found more than one. It is possible that the Blue Stone circle is due to a second importation in Period II.

It was during Period III a, that all the sarsens (except the Heel Stone) were transported and erected, and the carvings made. In order that this might be done the double circle was removed and the stone holes were rammed tight; in these holes were found a few Beaker sherds. Next came the erection of the five trilithons (p. 68). 'The building of the outer circle came next, followed by the erection of the four station stones and the Slaughter Stone and its companion'. Here, as I said before, the archaeologist must raise his eye — or at any rate his mind — to the sky. As stated in the guide-book, stones 91 and

93 of the four stations are very carefully placed with relation to the sunrise and the sunset at four dates in the year, namely, 45 days between the Solstices and the Equinoxes. But as there seems nothing to indicate the Equinoxes, these two stones may be regarded as dividing the year into four equal periods; with the two missing stones 92 and 94 they again duplicate the Solstitial alignment of the later sarsen monument and that of the earlier double Blue Stone circle. If these stones were intended for this use they must be earlier than the sarsen monument, because they cannot be seen either from its centre or from each other; therefore they must be either the earliest feature in Period III a or earlier than it. The author admits (p. 69) that they may belong to Period II, and that the ditches round the two barrows closely resemble the ditch round the Heel Stone, though not so deep. One cannot help feeling that these stones and their ditches, together with the Heel Stone and its ditch, all belong to Period II or the very beginning of Period III a; but since their dressing is either slight or absent one favours Period II. The author suggests (p. 18) that 'they formed symbolic memorials of an operation of field geometry' to find the centre of the circle. That their diagonals cross at the centre tells in favour of both this and the other theory, and a combination of the two is probably the correct solution. Nor does the author disregard the solar aspect of Stonehenge (p. 172). 'In Stonehenge II there is indeed specific evidence that the sun played some part, and perhaps the central one, in the beliefs of the builders'. It is curious to think that 30 years ago most members of the general public would have believed this and said so, though few archaeologists would have dared to.

Let us now go back to the Heel Stone and its ditch, remembering that the author says that the Heel Stone belongs to Period I and its ditch to Period II, and look at the Avenue. The plan shows that the distance between this stone and the Avenue bank is about 25 feet. Is it possible that just over 80 huge sarsens could be brought in Period III a through this gap without damaging either the stone or the bank? Stones B and C must necessarily belong to the end of Period II or be even later; but since they are centrally placed on the Avenue and on the axial line of the sarsen monument, they must belong to III a or be later, and it is reasonable to place the Avenue late in III a, for it is governed by the width of the wider causeway of Period II, with its bank overlying the Heel Stone ditch (assigned to the end of II or early in III a). Against this reconstruction is the absence of blue stone dressing chips in the silt and the presence of destruction fragments above the silt in the Avenue ditches. Apart from this it would be more reasonable to assign the Avenue and stones B and C to Period III than to II.

The holes D and E are said to have held stones in Period I. Their position suggests that they belong to this period. Hole D did not look like a post-hole, but from the plan only one might favour posts here. Was it a stone-hole? One cannot rely upon one's memory to decide that. E is stated to have been re-used in III a, 'but of this stone nothing remains'. It is true that nothing remains above ground, but there is still a large sarsen flake standing upright on the bottom of the hole, and above it on the side of the hole is the impression of the stone; obviously two Slaughter Stones once stood here, probably not later than the end of Period II, contemporary with the four stations and the Heel Stone. They must have been removed before III a, to allow for the bringing in of the sarsens. If they were erected after the sarsen monument, then they must have been removed soon after, because the Slaughter Stone, if standing, would have hidden the Heel Stone from the centre. The author also thinks that the Y and Z holes belong to this Period III b. It is entirely due to his careful excavations that these holes are now better understood; but it is doubtful whether these 59 (doubtless originally 60) holes were ever intended to hold blue stones, as the author suggests, pointing to the correspondence in numbers — 82 in the double blue stone circle corresponding to 60 in the Y and Z holes plus 19 in the Horseshoe plus 2 blue stone lintels and the Altar Stone. 'This correspondence cannot be dismissed as a chance coincidence; and it may accordingly be accepted (as a working hypothesis which covers the observed facts in the simplest way) that the dressed blue stones and the Y and Z holes are associated with each other and form part of the same phase of construction' (p. 72). This reminds one of Sir Flinders Petrie's theory of the Blue Stone Circle: he wrote that its stones are arranged in pairs, in which one stone is diametrically opposite the other. 'The probability of 11 out of 18 stones being by chance opposite to each other in a set of 44 places is about 5000 to 1'. If 44 paired with 34 it would increase the improbability of chance to 30,000 to 1. Thus it appears that the betting against there having ever been any more than there are now is very strong, because it is most unlikely that only stones opposite each other would have been removed. The excavations of 1954 show that many stones *were* removed or broken off above ground level.

Mr Atkinson is probably more pleased at finding the incised dagger and axes than at anything else. The axes can definitely be identified as belonging to the Middle Bronze Age, and the largest is nearly the same size as the largest known Irish bronze axe. The tapering butt of the two axes on Stone 4 may represent an unrecognized type or more probably be an error in marking out; compare the axes on plate XII a, with those on plate XII b. As for the dagger, it is doubtful, owing to the weathering of the surface, whether it can really be regarded as a Mycenaean dagger. The same may be said of the symbol on Stone 57; it cannot be regarded as certain that it represents the Mother Goddess. But to return to the dagger; seen in a certain light it gives one the impression that it began as an axe, and that the handle and about one third of the blade — the pointed end — were added later. There seems as yet to be no proof that these symbols are contemporary with the erection of the stones. Nor does there seem to be any significance in the stones selected for the symbols, except perhaps that all are made on the softer sarsens. The author says (p. 136) that it is impossible to use flint chisels on sarsen. Very many flint mauls were found during the earlier excavations, used no doubt on the softer sarsens. The general reader will be most interested in Chapter 4 ('The Technique of Construction') which gives the man-power required for transport and erection; but only an engineer could discuss this chapter. When one remembers that far larger stones have been moved by man-power alone, it is rather the skill shown in the placing of the stones in their exact positions than the transport of them that amazes one.

Mr Atkinson says that the earlier excavations of 1920–26 were not carried out as they should have been. As one who took a large part in them I freely admit this;[3] but Colonel Hawley very often complained of the lack of interest shown. No advice was ever offered, and when he read his annual report his careful work was praised. One can never imagine that 30 years hence Mr Atkinson's work will be so criticized. It is a pity that more archaeologists were not able to see it. Let me conclude by again recommending very strongly this most enlightening book.

---

[3] As one who remembers those excavations and visited them I must agree; but I would point out (what many of us knew at the time) that it was entirely due to Mr Newall's share in them that they were not worse. His observations and sectional drawings recorded much that would otherwise have been lost; and his timely removal of the objects found from the wooden hut, where — incredible as it may seem — they were just left to look after themselves, to a place of temporary safety should now be put on record. For further details and confirmation of these remarks see *A History of the Society of Antiquaries*, by Joan Evans, p. 398. O.G.S.C.

After reading the above review, Mr Atkinson sends us the following comments:
Since Mr Newall's review was written before the Stonehenge excavations of 1956, he has most generously suggested that I should comment upon it in the light of the latest work. In doing so I am delighted to have a further opportunity of acknowledging the debt which I and my colleagues owe him as the recorder and interpreter of the earlier excavations.

In criticizing my suggested sequence of construction Mr Newall has dwelt particularly on the features for which the evidence of relative date is least satisfactory, namely the Heel Stone and its ditch (assigned by me to Periods I and II respectively) and the dressed bluestones and Y and Z holes (constituting my Period III b).

The recent excavations have shown that the Heel Stone's ditch is later than an ancient disturbance extending to the west of the stone, which according to Col. Hawley was later than the innermost post-hole of the wooden structure at A, itself apparently of Period I and certainly earlier than the bank of the Avenue of Period II. The Beaker sherds (not part of a burial) found against the southeast side of the stone in 1953 are admittedly not mandatory evidence for an earlier date for the Stone, though they were not in the area disturbed by its subsequent movement. But in any case the Heel Stone and its ditch *must* be earlier than the Avenue; and the latter, from the evidence of the widening of the entrance which it matches (pp. 63–5) *must* be earlier than the period of the sarsen mauls (III a). Mr Newall's argument that the Heel Stone, not being on the axis of Period I, must be later than that period, applies with the same force to all the subsequent periods. Nor is it *necessary* to assign stone-holes B and C to Period III a, or later, on the ground that they lie on the sarsen axis ; for this is the same as the axis of Period II.

The objection that these stones, or the Heel Stone, would obstruct the passage of the sarsens up the Avenue is one which I have anticipated (pp. 116–17). The recent work suggests that the gap in the earthwork close to stone 93 was made deliberately in ancient times and may well provide the answer to this problem.

Of the existence at Stonehenge of the dressed bluestone structure (III b) we now have evidence in the form of five stone-holes not otherwise accounted for. Of these, two are the holes J and L and two others lie between them, athwart the inner ends of the extended entrance stone-holes of Period II. They were excavated, but not recognized, by Col. Hawley and the evidence of their relationship was unfortunately destroyed beyond recovery. The fifth hole lies between stones 59 a and 70, and had been dug into the filling of a still earlier hole (apparently of Period II) sealed by filling characteristic of Period III a, and had itself been re-used in Period III c for a stone of the present horseshoe (70 a) whose stump was found *in situ.*

We now know also that the double bluestone circle of Period II was never finished, since we have found a gap of unknown extent on its west sidew; and this raises the possibility mentioned by Mr Newall, of two separate importations of these stones. (Incidentally, it should be made clear that the important letter from Cunnington, to which Mr Newall refers, is an unpublished one of which I was previously unaware. It happily clears up the ambiguity of the published letter *(Wiltshire Archaeological Magazine* 42 (1924): 432) about the number of bluestones found in Boles Barrow). None the less, it is clear that *as planned* Stonehenge II consisted of upwards of 80 stones; and the known plan of the present bluestone setting (III c) shows that little short of 80 stones were still present in the last phase. Since the dressed bluestones must have numbered at least 22, there remains a residue of about 60 to be accounted for in Period III b. If the Y and Z holes were not intended for them, what were they for? Structural phases, like other entities, must not be multiplied *praeter necessitatem.*

Stonehenge: creating a definitive account
by ANDREW J. LAWSON
ANTIQUITY 66 (253), 1992

IT APPEARS that at each solstice Stonehenge, England's most famous prehistoric monument, becomes the focus of debate over public access, protection and interpretation. In 1992 the debate is poised to become more forceful as English Heritage and the National Trust appeal against the refusal of planning consent to construct better visitor facilities on a new site 1 km from the stones. English Heritage has the unenviable task of balancing the various and frequent claims for direct access to the stones with the need to protect and preserve the ancient monument which is the focus of attention. The National Trust, landowner of the surrounding area with its wealth of archaeological remains both visible and buried, has a similar task, but both bodies are united in the most laudable aim of enhancing the visitor's understanding and enjoyment of the Stonehenge landscape. Theories about the motivation behind the construction of Stonehenge and its enduring or changing role abound. However, what archaeological evidence we have about how and when it was built is derived from a large number of excavations conducted throughout the 20th century (FIGURE 1). It is known that earlier digging took place, and in some instances it may be possible to locate these attempts, but because no detailed contemporary records were made they are of little academic value. Virtually all modern guidebooks and displays which describe the sequence of construction reiterate or plagiarize Richard Atkinson's book, first published in 1956.

Unrivalled in its usefulness and clarity, this work lacks the detailed presentation of the observations recorded at the time of excavation to support the thesis advanced. In the intervening decades professional archaeology has adopted high standards, and now many of those who wish to reconsider the chronology of Stonehenge hope, perhaps over-optimistically, that a similar standard can be applied retrospectively.

Atkinson had the benefit of first-hand excavation experience at the site and, hence, had a rare opportunity to reassess the descriptions of earlier workers there. Much of his book is a careful selection of earlier conclusions presented in a logical, understandable and accessible form: such is the skill of many authors of best-selling works, but a skill elusive to most archaeologists. Re-reading earlier publications it is possible to suggest how ideas on the phased construction of the site developed.

Surveys of the monument had been conducted by Inigo Jones (in 1655), William Stukeley (1723) and John Wood (1740), and doubtless others also, but the most accurate was that of W.M. Flinders Petrie (1877) which claimed to be accurate to within one-tenth of an inch in any direction. This has remained the basis for many subsequently published plans. (It might be argued that this is a better basis for comment on the positions of stones because subsequently the majority of them have been re-positioned during consolidation works.) The numbering of the stones also originates in Flinders Petrie's (1880) publication, although additional stones have been discovered and the current numbering is now somewhat cumbersome. From the survey, Flinders Petrie plotted different centres for the earthen and stone circles and proposed four phases of construction, namely circular earthwork, Avenue, sarsen stones and the bluestones which were added at various times. The four peripheral station stones were added 'probably not earlier than the sarsen circle'.

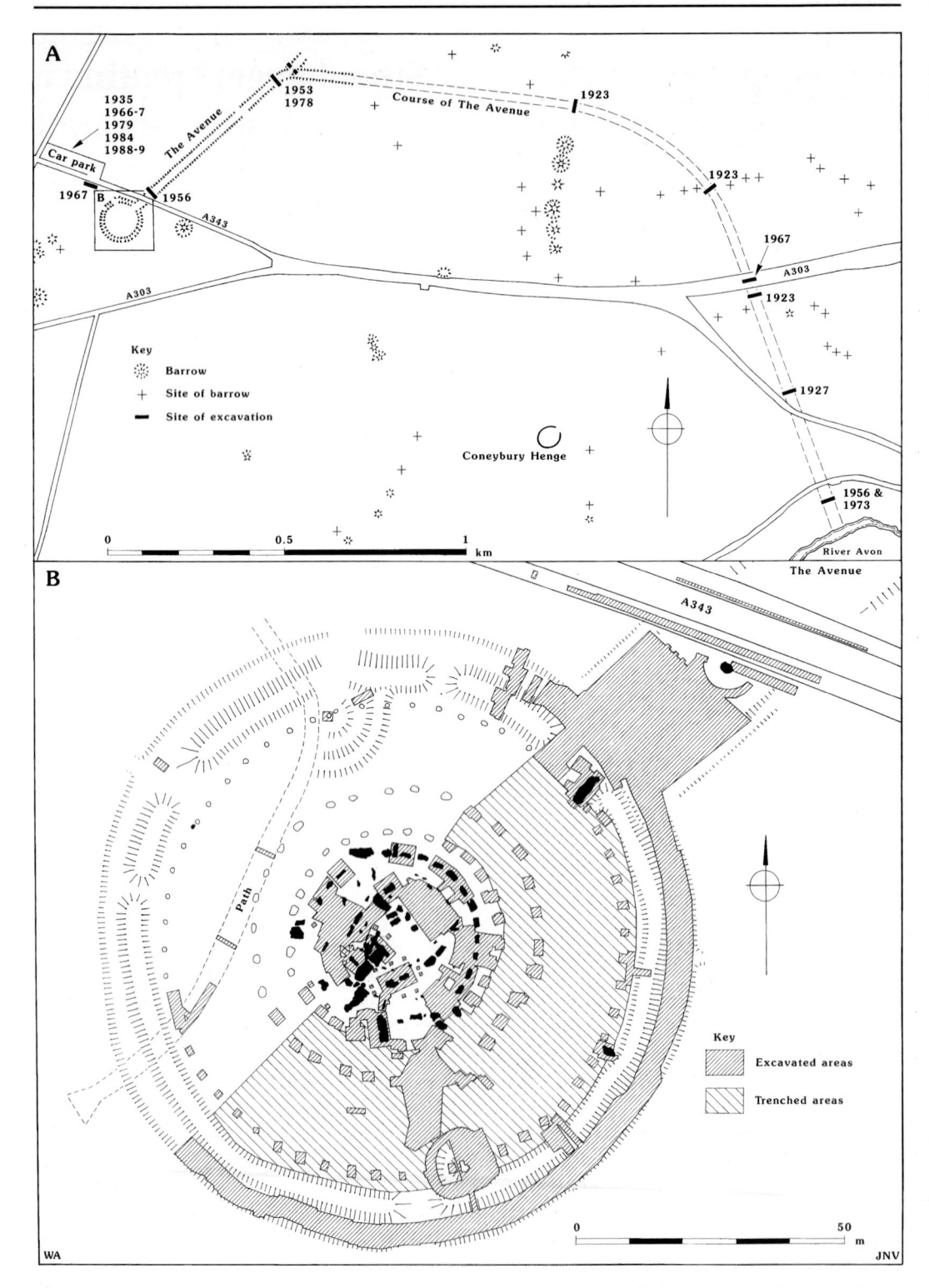

FIGURE 1. *Stonehenge*. A *schematic location of dated excavations on the Avenue and its extension.* B *area of all recorded 20th-century excavations and trenching (by Hawley) at the monument.*

In 1901 William Gowland excavated in the vicinity of the tallest stone, no. 56, which was leaning at a perilous angle and which, in the interest of public safety, was to be re-erected. His limited excavations were carefully controlled, well recorded and promptly published, a standard which declined with later excavators. He observed that the bluestone (no. 68) set within the horse-shoe of trilithons had been erected in the backfilled construction ramp of the sarsen, thus providing stratigraphic proof of a sequence. On the basis of the artefacts recovered (mainly flint tools), he concluded that Stonehenge belonged 'to an age antecedent to the full development of the use of bronze'. Aided by Lockyer and Penrose's astronomical calculations of the correlation between the monument's axis and the contemporary midsummer sunrise he concluded that the sarsens had been erected at the start of the Bronze Age about 1800 BC. Atkinson could not put forward any evidence to alter this perceptive pronouncement substantially, and only the recent recalibration of radiocarbon dates suggests a slightly older date for the erection of the stones.

The most ambitious campaign of excavations was that of William Hawley between 1919 and 1926, undertaken at the request of the Ministry of Works and described in annual reports published by the Society of Antiquaries. Hawley's perseverance was stoic. In June 1921 he wrote to Gowland (Society of Antiquaries Library):

> I am here all alone and am doing the work myself without labour but shall have a man later for filling in. I do not least mind the loneliness and am perfectly happy with the work and a comfortable little compartment in a hut.

Hawley excavated half the perimeter of the ditch and the Aubrey Holes within. In 1920 he was confident in saying 'the ditch and rampart were made at a time considerably anterior to Stonehenge'. The following year he collected 'a great quantity of small snail shells from the ditch fill and took these to signify 'a long period of neglect and and desuetude when vegetation sprang up unchecked'. A period of abandonment prior to the introduction of the stones was similarly identified from the molluscan evidence in 1978 by John Evans (1984).

In 1922 and 1923 Hawley's investigation of the entrance demonstrated its remodelling about the monument's realigned axis, additional stoneholes in the entrance area and the addition of the Avenue after these modifications. His excavations also revealed groups of post-holes in the entrance, between the stone circle and bank and within the circle. When Hawley began to investigate the area around the sarsens (nos. 8 & 9) of the outer circle he found that 'the ground was honeycombed' and admitted 'I doubt if anybody will ever be able to explain it satisfactorily'. The previously unknown Y and Z holes were also discovered, but the precise arrangement of his trenches between the circle and bank is not known because no plan survives.

By the time the work was called to a halt he had stated that 'the innumerable post holes are the earliest structures on the site'. 'The site is older than the monument standing upon it ... chips of the stones forming the latter occurring only above the silt [of the ditch] and never in it.

Because Beaker pottery was sometimes embedded in the top of the silts', it would place the building of the stone monument about the overlap of the Neolithic and Bronze Ages. Various other conclusions were reached, but in effect the suggestions of Flinders Petrie and the results of Gowland's work were reinforced.

An independent view of the sequence at Stonehenge was published in 1929 by Robert Newall, who had been responsible for recording in the field much of Hawley's work and had dug his own trenches as Hawley laboured. He pointed out that the Station Stones would need to have pre-dated the sarsen circle whose axis they shared if there was to be intervisibility between them; the Altar Stone would have been upright; the bluestone circle must have been pegged out before the erection of the sarsen trilithon because of its accuracy, yet executed after; and he said that a partner to the Heel Stone 'is to be expected', (a prediction which was confirmed by Pitts in 1979). Thus a firm foundation was laid for Atkinson's account.

Hawley recognized the Aubrey Holes as an early feature and was in no doubt that they had held uprights. Although he originally thought that they contained stones, the excavations between 1926 and 1928 at Woodhenge led the Cunningtons to conclude: '. . . judging from the size and shape of the Aubrey Holes it seems not improbable that they once held timber uprights' (1929: 24). But it was uncertainty over the function of the Aubrey Holes and of the Y and Z holes which started the next series of excavations by Atkinson, Piggott and Stone, Piggott's excavations at Cairnpapple Hill reaching the conclusion that the circle of peripheral pits there were not for uprights.

Although Atkinson was the author of what has become the standard work on Stonehenge, he was at the time the most junior of the team who began an intermittent campaign of excavations between 1950 and 1964. Initially Stuart Piggott, Marcus Stone and Richard Atkinson undertook small-scale excavations in an attempt to resolve specific questions concerning the Aubrey Holes, the Heel Stone

FIGURE 2. *Stonehenge: axe carvings on the eastern (outer) face of Stone 4 (based on a drawing by Newall, 15 January 1954).*

and the Y and Z holes. At a later lecture in Devizes, Atkinson made reference to Stuart Piggott as the 'leader' and himself as 'follower'. As the Ministry of Works' need to consolidate the monument emerged larger excavations became necessary. The majority of these were undertaken in advance of the need to place stones in secure (concrete) foundations, and hence may be regarded as rescue recording. The urgency required was amply demonstrated by the collapse of Stone 23 in 1963.

Atkinson's book was written in 1955 after three seasons of work and was published in 1956. It was written in response to an invitation from the publishing firm Hamish Hamilton following a radio broadcast which described the work of 1953 and Atkinson's discovery of the first of the celebrated carvings. In addition to the infamous carvings of Stone 53, other carvings were noted on Stones 3, 4, 5, 23, 29, 57 and 120, and Robert

Newall began a detailed study of them (FIGURE 2), although his work was never fully published. More than 35 years after the production of Atkinson's book it is easy to assess its contribution. First, it made available to a very wide audience the sum of current knowledge on the monument carefully selected from earlier writers. It would be difficult to overstate the importance of this, not least in its clarity of expression. The second was in the use of radiocarbon dating. The first dates confirmed the approximate age of the monument, but the relative inaccuracy of the dates, the complexity of the constructional sequence and the limited number of determinations to date now limit the value of this analysis. The contribution is reviewed by Pitts (1982). The third contribution was the deduction of the way in which the stone monument had been assembled. Stratigraphic relationships are infrequent: excluding the relationship between the Heel Stone and neighbouring features, and those between the ubiquitous post-holes, the main complexity is in the bluestone settings where, in the northeast quadrant at least, earlier dumbbell shaped sockets (the Q and R holes) underlie the current circle (see below also). The only relationships between bluestone sockets and those of the sarsens are that Stone 68 is set in the ramp of 56 (as noted by Gowland) and the ramp of Stone 3 cuts an early stone hole (Q4) outside Stone 32. The latter observation was crucial for the relative dating of the earliest bluestone setting. Key to the sequence and Atkinson's innovative contribution is the recognition and disentangling of the various bluestone settings, his mathematical skills being put to good use in considering various combinations and permutations of stones and stone-holes. The full extent of the double bluestone setting (Phase II) cannot be fully traced because of the limits of excavation. Evidence for its presence on the south-west side is apparently lacking and Atkinson considered it unfinished.

Although Atkinson said that the evidence of a short-lived resetting of some of the bluestones in an internal ellipse (IIIb) following the erection of the sarsens (IIIa) is 'almost wholly inferential', six stone-holes can be attributed to the structure. Two of these cut the internal ends of the elongated stone-holes which flank the axis of the double bluestone setting (Phase II). A further, but more complex stratigraphical sequence was revealed in 1956 when an area on the west side of the monument between Stones 58 and 59 was excavated. Here the stump of bluestone 70A belonging to the final (IIIc) setting was discovered, supported on a stone plinth, itself placed within an earlier, infilled stone-hole with a stone impression on its base. The inference is that the earlier hole was for a bluestone of Phase IIIb. However, this cutting shows greater complexity because the Phase IIIb stonehole cuts an even earlier curving trench with stone impressions at its base.

The 1979 edition of *Stonehenge* includes the statement, 'Excavations now provide some slight and tantalising evidence that the double circle of bluestones enclosed an inner setting' although much of the central area has not been excavated this century. The record of the 1956 cutting prepared by Richard Atkinson (FIGURE 3) provides part of the evidence for this inner structure. Apparently the curving trench contained no chips of foreign stone and hence, once again, it can only be inferred that the stone impressions were those of bluestones. Further evidence for internal structures was revealed in 1964 in small (2 ft square) cuttings in front of Stones 53 and 54, at a depth of over seven feet. These cuttings were required by the engineers engaged in straightening the adjacent trilithon.

Newall had argued that the Y and Z holes post-dated the collapse of Sarsen Stone 8, and the presence of later prehistoric pottery in their fills might argue that they represent one of the last phases of activity on the site. Newall's archival notebooks (Alexander Keiller Museum, Avebury) contain contemporary excavation drawings 'showing Z9 cut into the incline of No. 29 stone' and Z7 cutting the 'incline to Stone 7'. Nonetheless, Atkinson maintains (pers. comm.) that through probing he had located the apparently

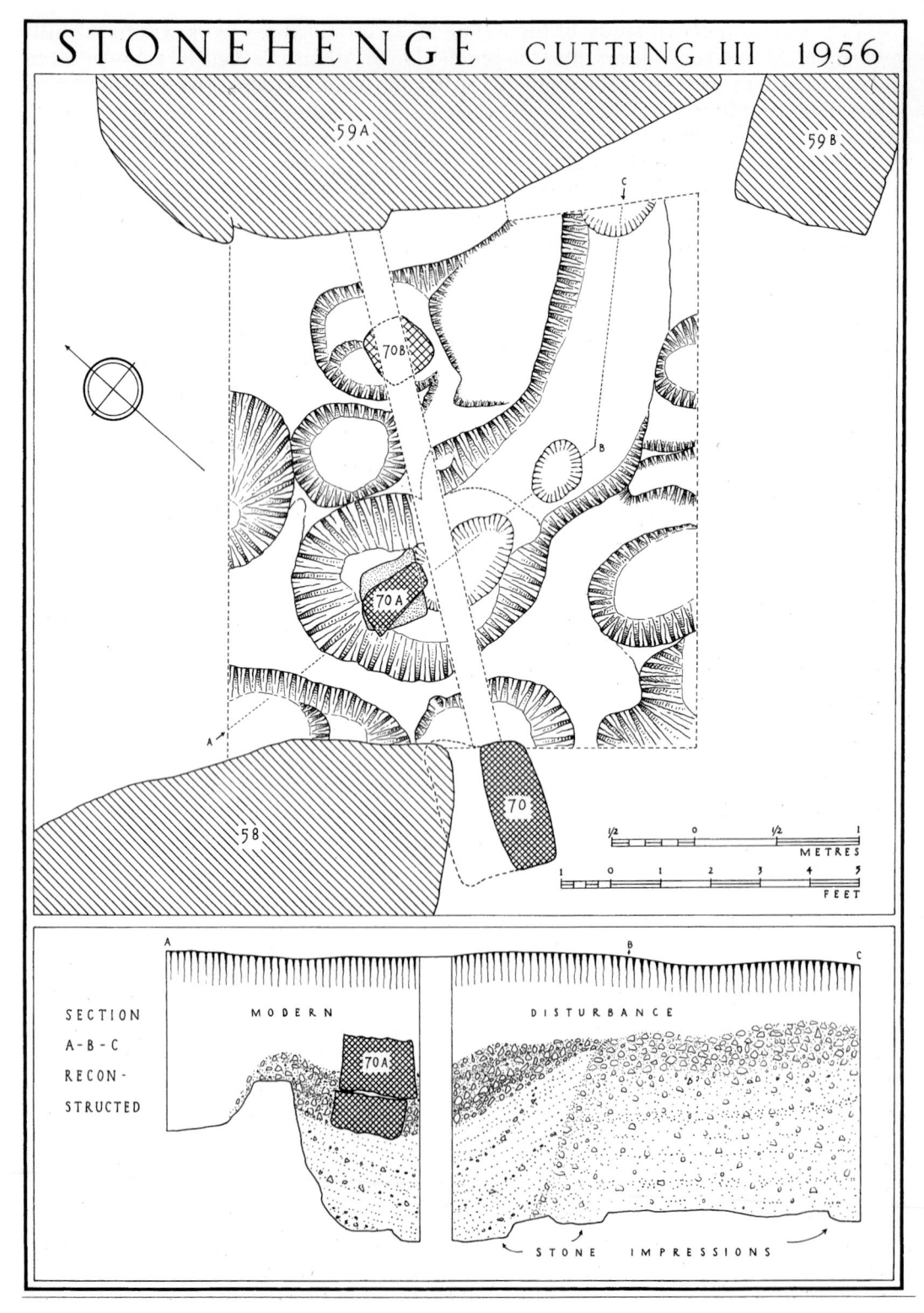

FIGURE 3. *Stonehenge: plan and section of excavation in 1956 prepared by Richard Atkinson.*

missing Z8. Therefore, the long intervals between the erection and collapse of Stone 8, and the subsequent cutting of the Y and Z holes, assumed by Newall, may not have occurred. Furthermore, the cutting of the construction ramps of the sarsen circle (IIIa) by the Z holes, which Atkinson attributes to IIIb, would be used by him to support the idea that the latter were dug to take the bluestones not used in the internal ellipse of that phase.

Although it may appear to some that Atkinson's scheme was predicated on the belief that the number of stones could not be altered — additional stones could not be commissioned or others removed (or fragmented) — it was the striking similarity in the number of stones used in the different phases that compelled him to pursue the observation rather than dismiss it as coincidence.

What appears crucial in the phasing of the archaeological features is the time at which the bluestones were worked. The final setting re-uses architectural fragments (an observation made much earlier by Herbert Stone). Either these came from a different site and were 'secondhand' or they were from a different setting within the monument. At a relatively late date in the sequence bluestones were either heavily worked or broken up, as witness the ubiquitous fragments. When this took place and where the fragments occur in the fills of negative features may be crucial to the unravelling of events. At the moment, the statements from different excavators seem inconsistent.

A superficial view of the recorded evidence within the excavated areas reveals a palimpsest of features of different sizes and depths (e.g. FIGURE 3). It may be that a number of different interpretations are possible, or Hawley may have been correct that it will be impossible to explain. Atkinson's 1956 account was a 'veritable *tour de force* of applied logic' (Pitts 1982: 126) and presented an elegant model for an elegant monument. His sophisticated interpretation reflects the architectural sophistication of the structure and he wrote with first-hand experience of the site. Unfortunately, any subsequent analysis will not have the benefit of the excavator's eyes. Marcus Stone died in 1957. In 1978 Atkinson said graciously of Piggott 'You have most generously allowed me . . . to act as spokesman' (Devizes Museum transcript), but having adopted this role his career and latter ill-health have prevented him from bringing the excavations to a fuller publication as he would wish. Many projects initiated in the 1950s, '60s and '70s had little provision for post-excavation analysis. Having learnt the hard way, professional expectations have altered and strategies are advocated to take full account of the burden that excavation places on their managers and to ensure that planning, resources and contingency underpin admirable intention (English Heritage 1991).

A number of other investigations contribute to our knowledge of Stonehenge. Atkinson's final excavation was in 1978, when the position of the socket for Station Stone 94 was confirmed. At the same time John Evans recorded a Beaker-style burial in the ditch and assessed the changing environment of the monument. His brief mention (three lines) of the counterscarp bank provides the only archaeological description of the internal structure of the remnant of this rather ignored element of the monument. Between 1979 and 1980 Mike Pitts recorded both the predicted partner to the Heel Stone and the complex deposits in that area, which include early stoneworking debris. Both of these interventions are well published. Various excavations have been conducted on the Avenue and its extension to West Amesbury (FIGURE 1A) and other, apparently unrelated features within the vicinity have been recorded. In the car park and current visitor centre area is a series of large pits attributable through radio-carbon dating and environmental evidence to a mesolithic episode, while the underpass crosses a buried palisade and accompanying bank thought to be of later Bronze Age date (FIGURE 4). The record of all these known features merits clear presentation.

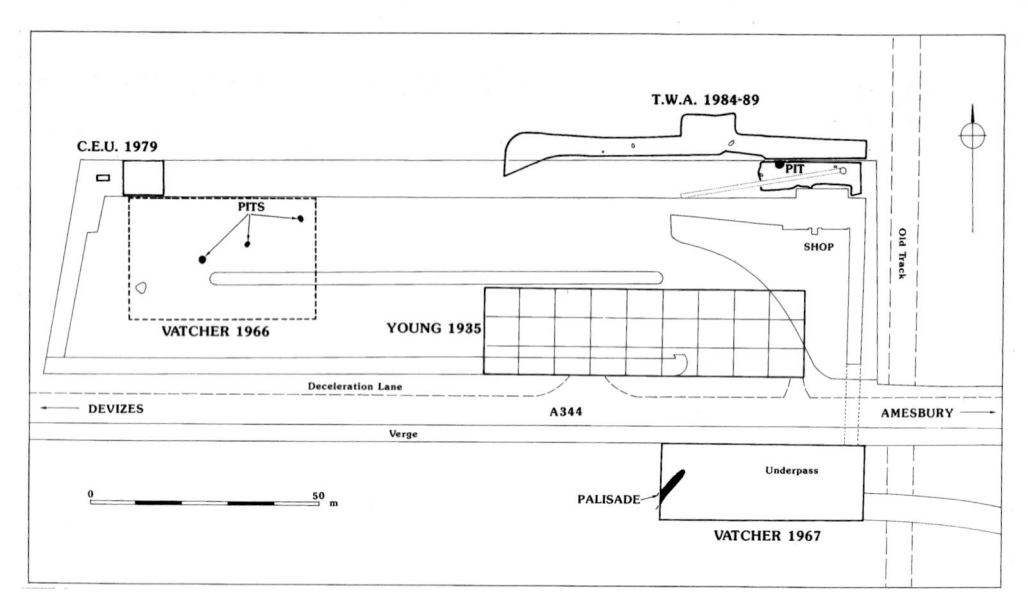

FIGURE 4. *Stonehenge: location of archaeological recording and identified features in the car park and underpass.*

Atkinson's ambition of seeing the full publication of 20th-century excavations at Stonehenge may still be realized. English Heritage has recognized this as an academic imperative and wish to see the successful conclusion not reached during the life of its predecessor, the Inspectorate of Ancient Monuments. Although work to this end is already under way, the desire to improve the facilities at the site has added urgency to the need to present the 'facts'. The interpretations of the monument required for a new visitor centre must be based on the best evidence available. Consequently, the Trust for Wessex Archaeology has been commissioned by them to create a site archive which will contain as much primary excavation evidence as can be found. Professor Atkinson has already contributed all his records and site photographs. A consistent and integrated record will be created, then analysis will begin. It is hoped that the end product will present the archaeological evidence to support Professor Atkinson's account, or, if appropriate, to suggest alternative views. Although a clear structural sequence may not emerge, a priority must be to present the evidence clearly so as to end speculation and to provide the raw material for those who wish to advance their own ideas.

Acknowledgements. I am most grateful to Professor R.J.C. Atkinson for his valuable contribution to this paper, and to Professor Stuart Piggott, Brian Davison (HBMC) and Dr Julie Gardiner (WA) for their comments on the draft. The illustrations were prepared by Julian Cross, Rob Read and John Vallender (at various times for WA).

References
ATKINSON, R.J.C. 1956. *Stonehenge*. London: Hamish Hamilton. (Revised and reprinted 1979. Harmondsworth: Penguin).
CUNNINGTON, M.E. 1929. *Woodhenge*. Devizes: George Simpson.
ENGLISH HERITAGE. 1991. *Management of Archaeologicol Projects*. 2nd edition. London: Historic Buildings and Monuments Commission for England.
EVANS, J.G. 1984. Stonehenge — the environment in the Late Neolithic and Early Bronze Age and a Beaker-Age burial, *Wiltshire Archoeological and Natural History Magazine* 78 (1983): 7–30
FLINDERS PETRIE, W.M. 1880. *Stonehenge: plans, description and theories*. London: Edward Standford.
NEWALL, R.S. 1929. Stonehenge, *Antiquity* 3: 75–88.
PITTS, M.W. 1982. On the road to Stonehenge: report on the investigations beside the A344 in 1968, 1979 and 1980, *Proceedings of the Prehistoric Society* 48: 75–132.

The myth of long-distance megalith transport
by R.S. THORPE & O. WILLIAMS-THORPE
ANTIQUITY 65 (246), 1991

MEGALITHIC MONUMENTS (stone circles and alignments, standing stones and chamber tombs) are widespread within western Europe and provide an important and often spectacular source of information on prehistoric ritual and funerary customs. They are built from varied igneous, metamorphic and sedimentary rocks, and occur in a variety of geographical and geological provinces (e.g. Mohen 1989). The distribution and structure of such monuments have been used to make inferences regarding the organization of the societies responsible for construction (e.g. Renfrew 1983a). Further inferences have been drawn from the location and structure of Stonehenge, concerning the social organization involved in stone-circle construction and in possible long-distance transport of the bluestones (e.g. Atkinson 1979). The validity of these inferences is complicated by the possibility of natural (glacial) transport of megalithic stones in the glaciated part of northwestern Europe. However, the widespread occurrence of megalithic monuments in glaciated and non-glaciated regions of Europe may be used to evaluate the likely rôle of human transport (and therefore degree of social organization required) in megalithic construction. Kempe (1983: 100–106) has summarized the rock types used for construction of megalithic stone circles, standing stones and chamber tombs. However, little attention has been paid in published discussions of megaliths to the relationship between rock types and the geological sources utilized. The aim of this paper is to explore these factors from an examination of megalithic monuments in northwest Europe, using data particularly from Britain, northwest France and the Netherlands.

FIGURE 1 summarizes the distribution of chamber tombs, stone circles and alignments in relation to the limits of the Quaternary glaciation in western Europe. For the areas to the north of the glaciation limit, glacial transport of megalith stones is possible and must be assessed, for example by study of stone provenance, local glacial deposits and likely ice-movement directions, before any proposal for human transport may be made. Conversely, to the south of the glaciation limit, human transport may be quantified by exact petrological and/or geochemical provenancing of megalith stones. FIGURE 2 shows the locations of individual sites referred to in the text.

Before assessing the possible scales of regional transport, we emphasize that small-scale transport is essential to account for the geometric features of megalithic monuments. Noting the sizes and scales of construction of these monuments, such transport may have been on the scale of 1–2 km. For example, the longest stone alignment at Carnac is *c.* 1100 m (Burl 1985: 144), and the West Kennet avenue between Avebury and the Sanctuary is *c.* 2 km in length. Such a scale for transport during construction is consistent with evidence for stone selection and transport such as:

1 movement of stones during monument reorganization (e.g. bluestone movement between Stonehenge phases II and III, Atkinson 1979);
2 selection of megalith shapes and sizes (e.g. the West Kennet Avenue, Smith 1965; recumbent stone circles (RSC), Burl 1976: 216);

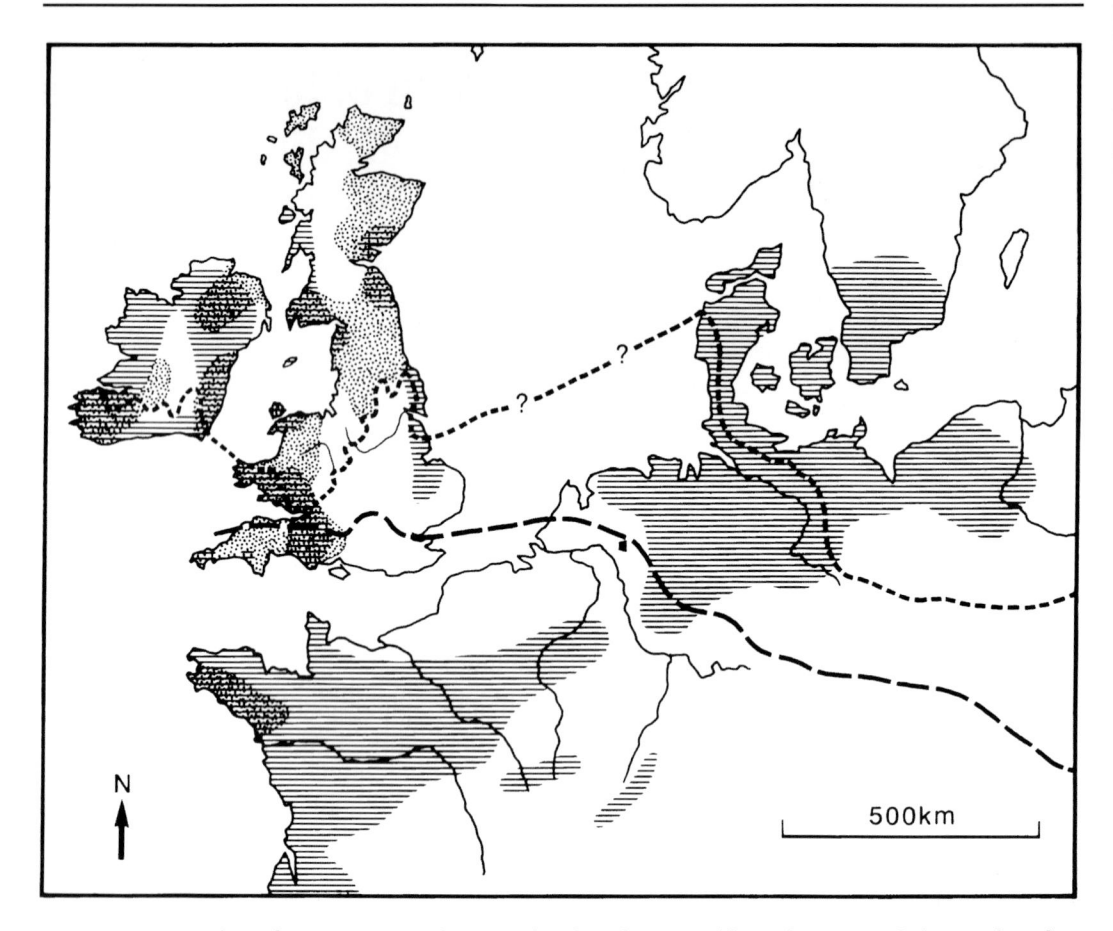

FIGURE 1. *Map of northwest Europe showing the distribution of burials in megalithic and timber chambers (horizontal lines; Mackie 1977b: 148, 149) and of contemporaneous stone circles and alignments (stippled ornament; Mackie 1977b: 97). The short broken lines indicate the approximate limit of the latest (Devensian) glaciation and the long broken lines indicate the approximate maximum limit of earlier glaciation in northwest Europe. (The glaciation limits are modified from Flint 1971, Institute of Geological Sciences 1977, and Dunning et al. 1978.)*

3   alternation and arrangement of stone rock types (e.g. Machrie Moor, Circle I, Mackie 1975: 126; Newgrange chambered tomb, O Riordain 1965; Mohen 1989; RSC, Burl 1976: 174); and

4   the siting of megaliths for astronomical purposes (e.g. Ballochroy, Heggie 1981: 190; Kintraw, Mackie 1975; 1977b: 102).

These lines of evidence clearly imply skill in stone selection and megalith construction, and suggest that 'the choice of rocks, often very precise and dictated by the exact function of each stone (covering slab, pillar, kerb) indicates the great mastery of prehistoric quarrymen' (Mohen 1989: 166). However, they do not provide evidence for human transport of megalith stones exceeding c. 1–2 km. We therefore examine possible evidence for larger-scale stone transport within northern France (unglaciated) and glaciated parts of Britain, the Netherlands, northern Germany and Scandinavia.

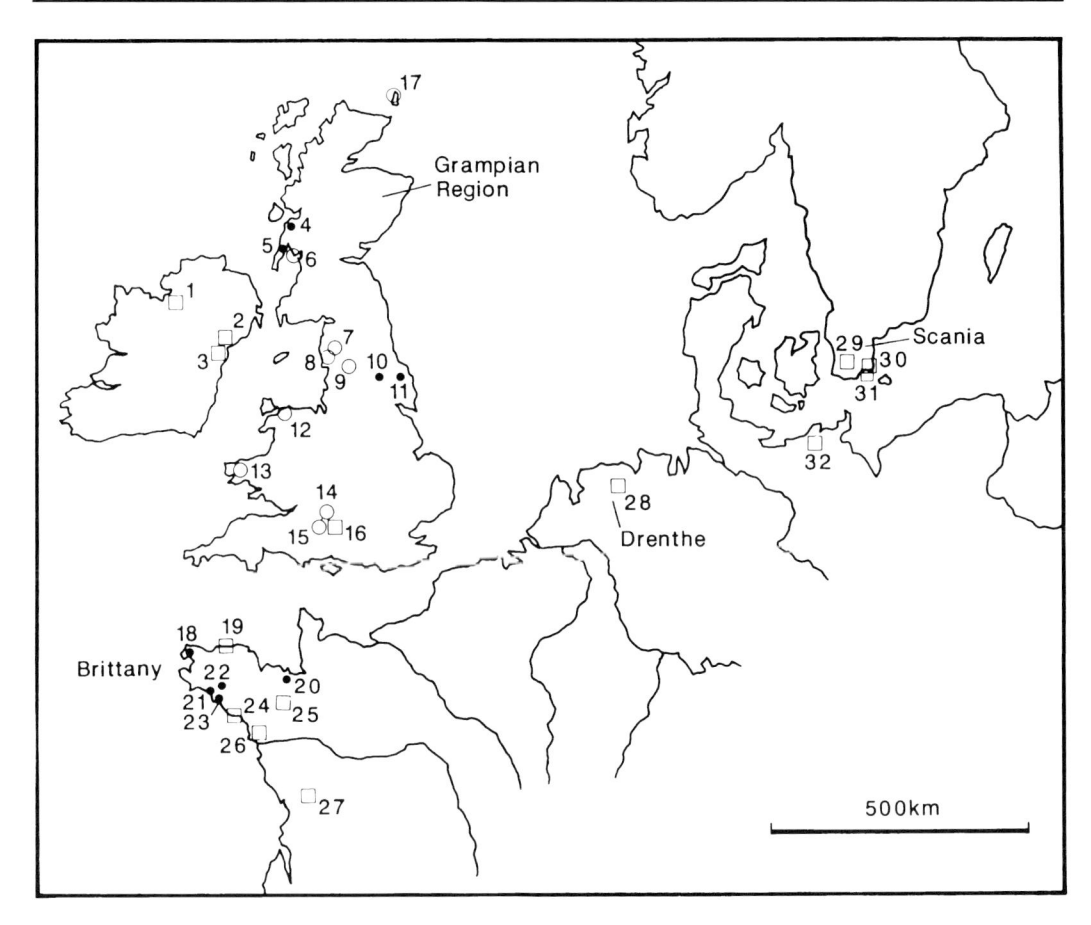

FIGURE 2. *Locations of important megalithic sites and key locations mentioned and discussed in the text.*

  Open circle = stone circle
  Filled circle = standing stone or stones/alignments
  Open square = chamber tomb

1 Carrowmore
2 Newgrange
3 Brennanstown
4 Kintraw
5 Ballochroy
6 Machrie Moor
7 Shap
8 Grey Croft
9 Yockenthwaite
10 Devil's Arrows
11 Rudston
12 'Druid's Circle'/
    Penmaenmawr
13 Gorsfawr
14 Avebury/West Kennet
    Avenue
15 Stonehenge
16 West Kennet burial
    chamber
17 Brogar and Stenness
18 Kerloas
19 Barnenez
20 Dol
21 Carnac
22 Kermarquer
23 Locmariaquer (Le Grand
    Menhir Brisé)
24 Gavrinis
25 Essé
26 Dissignac
27 Bougon
28 Borger
29 Araslov
30 Kivik
31 Ramshog
32 Gnewitz

Northern France

The archaeological characteristics and possible sources of megalithic monuments in northwest France (Brittany) have been described by Burl (1985). Burl described 216 sites (numerated 1–216; some sub-divided) which include over 350 megalithic structures. The rock-types used are dominated by granite but include sedimentary rocks (e.g. sandstone) and metamorphic rocks (e.g. schist).

Mohen (1989: 161) described many megalithic monuments from France and notes that megaliths are absent from the sands and clays of the Landes (southwest France) and Sologne (north central France) whereas chamber tombs are more abundant in other areas of western France (e.g. Touraine, Beauce in west central France) which have local supplies of hard rocks such as sandstone and limestone.

For the 28 megalithic monuments ascribed by Burl (1985) to an identified source, 18 are described as being from local stone sources (or 'close by'). However, 8 monuments provide evidence of possible human transport of between 1–5 km. These include the Kerloas menhir (c. 100–150 tonnes, 'the tallest prehistoric stone now standing . . . in the whole of western Europe' (Burl 1985: 62)) which was transported c. 2·5 km. Stones from the Barnenez passage graves may have been transported up to 1–2 km. The longest proposed transport distances (Burl 1985) are for the Dol menhir (c. 50–125 tonnes; 4 km), the Essé dolmen (c. 4 km), the Dissignac passage graves (c. 5 km), the Kermarquer menhir (c. 5 km) and Le Grand Menhir Brisé (Locmariaquer, c. 4 km). Mohen (1989: 162) notes that the covering stone on the Gavrinis tomb was brought from c. 5 km away in the Locmariaquer Peninsula. The other slabs of the monument comprise granite from the Gavrinis island (Mohen 1989: 162). These data indicate that in an area of outstanding megalithic culture (c. 4800–2100 BC; cf. Burl 1985: 14), there is no evidence for human megalith transport exceeding c. 5 km.

The evidence for megalith transport in non-glaciated areas is amplified by studies of the Bougon burial complex (necropolis) described by Mohen (1989). This complex is built from Jurassic and Tertiary limestone blocks which were quarried from within the area of the necropolis (Mohen 1989: 160–62) and were also transported from other locations within c. 5 km of the site (Mohen 1989: 163–5). A map of the sources of rock quarried and transported in the Bougon region is shown by Mohen (1989: 215).

The British Isles

The evidence for possible megalith transport by human agency within the glaciated areas of northern Europe (cf. FIGURE 1) is more difficult to interpret because of the possibility of glacial transport of apparently non-local rocks used in megaliths. However, most British stone circles appear to have been constructed from local materials (whether quarried by human activity or glacially transported).

The comprehensive study of Burl (1976) notes that (apart from Stonehenge, see below) as far as present knowledge can tell, no circle in the British Isles contains stones that were brought more than a few miles (kilometres) at the most (Burl 1976: 308). 'Many circles are built of glacial boulders common locally' (Burl 1976: 71). There are examples of stone circles built from local rocks and/or glacially-transported erratics in south Wales (e.g. Gorsfawr; Thorpe et al. in press), in north Wales (e.g. 'Druid's Circle', Penmaenmawr; Griffiths 1960), in the Lake District (e.g. Shap; Thomas 1976: 72, 69–70; Clare 1978: 5, 6), in southwest England (e.g. Thomas 1976; Kempe 1983) and in Scotland (e.g. Machrie Moor; MacKie 1975; authors' observations).

An account of prehistoric sites in England (Thomas 1976) provides comments on the stone types used in megalithic monuments. Thomas refers to rock types and possible sources for stones in 29 megalithic monuments (including the Rudston and Devil's Arrows, see below). The rock types are identified as being of local derivation (less than c. 2 km) (also Kempe 1983: 100–101), sarsen stones (see below), glacial erratics (e.g. Grey Croft, Thomas 1976: 69–70) and river boulders (e.g. Yockenthwaite, boulders from the River Wharfe; Thomas 1976: 250).

Recumbent stone circles (RSCs) provide evidence for preferential stone selection and orientation (Burl 1976: 174–5). As noted above, many RSCs have a recumbent stone which is petrologically distinct from the other stones (Burl 1976: 174). Burl shows that for the northeast Scotland RSCs (in the Grampian Region; FIGURE 2), e.g. Dyce, Hatton of Ardoyne, Old Keig, Auchquhorthies, Whitehill), the recumbent stones are of local derivation (e.g. an outcrop 45 m from the Hatton of Ardoyne RSC). However, the recumbent stone is of 'foreign' derivation at the Dyce, Loanend Auchmacher, and Easter Aquorthies RSCs. The Old Keig recumbent stone (sillimanite gneiss of dimension 4·9x2·1x2·0 m, weighing 53 tonnes) is presumed to be from an outcrop in the Don Valley c. 10 km away (Burl 1976: 174). However, the Grampian area has experienced repeated extensive glaciations; the case for human transport, rather than selection from locally-deposited glacial till, is unproven.

A possible exception to local stone derivation is the identification at the West Kennet long barrow (built on Cretaceous chalk) of (non-megalithic) blocks of oolitic limestone from Upper Jurassic outcrops (*cf.* Piggott 1962; Malone 1989). The barrow is built mainly of locally-derived sarsen stones (Piggott 1962: 57–8) but has drystone walling blocks of oolitic limestone from the Upper Jurassic (Corallian) scarp at Calne, c. 11 km to the west (Piggott 1962: 14; Malone 1989: 73, 74). However other oolitic limestone blocks, assigned by W.J. Arkell (in Piggott 1962: 14) to the Middle Jurassic Hinton Sands/Forest Marble of the Great Oolite, were derived from outcrops c. 32 km away, between Bradford-on-Avon and Frome. Such material occurs in five other local barrows and at Windmill Hill. (Piggott 1962: 58). These small (non-megalithic) blocks may have been transported by glaciation or by human agency.

Finally, a recent study of 26 megalithic monuments in south Wales, including standing stones, circles and chambered tombs, showed that all were made of rocks available at the place of construction or within c. 1 km of it (Thorpe et al. in press).

The Yorkshire monoliths: Rudston and the Devil's Arrows
The well-known monoliths of Rudston and the Devil's Arrows (Boroughbridge) in Humberside and North Yorkshire respectively (Elgee & Elgee 1930: 87) provide a case-study for the interpretation of megalith transport. Neither monument is composed of the local solid rock type and, as noted by Burl (1976: 287), 'the very existence of the monstrous stones at Rudston and Boroughbridge is a contradiction as though to emphasize the scarcity of stone'. Since these stones must have been transported either by natural (glacial) processes or by human agency (e.g. Burl 1976: 286), they provide a good opportunity for the examination of these contrasted hypotheses.

The geological structure and glacial history of Yorkshire/Humberside have been summarized by Kendal & Wroot (1924), Rayner & Hemingway (1974) and Kent (1980). The youngest (Devensian, c. 18,000 BP) glaciation was dominated by ice flow around the Cleveland Hills and Yorkshire Wolds, such that North Sea ice to the east of this area flowed clockwise from the north and northeast towards the south and southwest. Earlier ('pre-Ipswichian') glacial deposits are known from the Vale of Pickering (e.g. Kent 1980: figure 27), and these contain glacial erratics from the Lake District, Pennines or northeast England (Kent 1980: 120). To the west of the Cleveland Hills a

Devensian ice lobe advanced from northwest to southeast down the Vale of York (Kent 1980: figure 27).

The Rudston monolith (Humberside, FIGURE 2.11), the tallest British standing stone at 7–8 m, possibly extending 3–4 m below ground, is composed of a non-marine Middle Jurassic sandstone, probably of the Ravenscar Group derived from coastal outcrops around Cayton Bay and Carnelian Bay (respectively c. 20 km and 30 km northwest of Bridlington), between Scarborough and Filey (e.g. Kendall & Wroot 1924; Thomas 1976). A second block of similar sandstone c. 1·0x0·9x0·2 m is also present in the churchyard at Rudston (cf. Elgee & Elgee 1930: 87). Noting the directions of Devensian ice flow, the location of the Rudston stones is clearly consistent with glacial transport of Jurassic sandstone from c. 15–20 km to the north, either by clockwise Devensian ice movement around the east of the Wolds, or by more direct north–south transport during pre-Devensian glaciations. Although Rudston is c. 2 km outside of the limit of Devensian glaciation (Institute of Geological Sciences 1977; Kent 1980), the occurrence of earlier glaciations and the proximity to limits of Devensian glaciation indicate that it is not necessary to invoke human transport (e.g. Dymond 1966; Burl 1976) to account for the present location of the Rudston monolith.

The Devil's Arrows are three standing stones 6–7 m in height located near to Boroughbridge (FIGURE 2.10). (John Aubrey referred in 1669 to a fourth monolith 'that was taken down, and a bridge made of it': Aubrey 1980: Part 1: 110.) They are composed of coarse-grained sandstones ('grits') of presumed Namurian ('Millstone Grit') age (Kendall & Wroot 1924). Although sources have been suggested from the Knaresborough area c. 10 km to the southwest of Boroughbridge (e.g. Elgee & Elgee 1930: 87; cf. Burl 1976: 286; Thomas 1976: 244), other likely source rocks in the northern part of the Namurian outcrop are consistent with the directions (northwest to southeast) of Devensian glacial transport or earlier pre-Devensian glaciations. Glacial transport of the Devil's Arrows from c. 15–20 km to the northwest is also consistent with the occurrence of a wide range of Carboniferous lithologies present as glacial erratics in the fields surrounding the megaliths (authors' observations).

The evidence summarized for these sites is therefore consistent with glacial transport of c. 20 km of the Rudston and Devil's Arrows megaliths, followed by local rearrangement on a smaller scale (less than 1–2 km) at the individual sites.

Orkney

A further example in which previously-advocated human transport of megaliths may not be valid is provided by the stone circles of Brogar and Stenness in Mainland Orkney (described in Burl 1976: 99–102). These are composed of Middle Old Red Sandstone (Devonian) Stromness Flags for which a geological source has been suggested from Arion or Vestra Fjord/Field, respectively c. 4 km north-northwest and 11 km northwest of the Brogar/Stenness stone circles (Collins 1976: 44–5). The south slope of Vesta Field has an 'ancient quarry from which slabs *similar* [our emphasis] to those forming the Standing Stones of of Brogar and Stenness were obtained' (Mykura 1976: 122; cf. Collins 1976). Although the Devensian till (boulder clay) of Orkney contains 'abundant polished and striated boulders' of 'local material' (Mykura 1976: 113), the southeast-to-northwest glacial transport movement (Mykura 1976: figure 29) is contrary to the transport direction indicated from the proposed geological sources. However, Collins (1976: 45) suggests that a possible source (for the stones of Stenness) 'may be the circular ditch surrounding the henge, for the excavation shows that the bed-rock around the henge had been quarried and it may well have yielded blocks large enough for erection as monoliths'. This is supported by evidence reported by Renfrew (1979: 41) who notes that the Ring of Brogar is surrounded by a deep rock-cut ditch, cut into tough, laminated bedrock: 'It may be that this was also the quarry for the stones used for the stone circle.' Therefore, in view of the widespread outcrop of the Stromness Flags around the site of the Stenness/Brogar stones (e.g. Mykura 1976: figure 3), the uncertain antiquity of the Vestra Field quarry and the evidence for contemporaneous local quarrying, the hypothesis of human transport of megalith stones from this location to the Stenness/Brogar sites (*c.* 11 km) is implausible.

Ireland
The evaluation of human transport of megaliths in Ireland is complicated by the widespread glaciation (FIGURE 1). A summary of Irish megaliths (Ó Riordain 1965) comments on the use of 'field stones' in megalithic tomb construction (Ó Riordain 1965: 64) and the construction of 'boulder dolmens' and boulder circles (Ó Riordain 1965: 73–4, 87) implies the use of locally available (probably glacial) materials. Ó Riordain (1965: 71) notes that the Carrowmore megalithic tombs are constructed from 'big glacial blocks . . . easily available in the locality'. Further, Ó Riordain (1965: 73) comments that (in relation to the Brennanstown portal dolmen) 'the availability of . . . a great glacial erratic to provide the capstone without the necessity of long transport could have exercised an influence in the siting of individual tombs'.

Northern Europe
The geographical distribution and setting of megalithic monuments in northern continental Europe is summarized in Mackie (1977a), Service & Bradbery (1981) and Renfrew (1983a). The abundance of such monuments and of earth/stone-built mounds in glaciated areas has long been noted. For example, de Luc (1811: 492) noted 'masses of granite scattered on the sandy hills of Holstein, and on the tops of some hills in other parts of the north of Germany, but certainly intended as Stonehenge has probably been, for places of worship; for near them have been found instruments of sacrifice, axes, and knives made of flint; and around them are every where seen some of the tumuli known in England by the name of barrows; which were the tombs of the persons of the highest distinction in those distant ages'.

The geological features of these glacial deposits and their later clearance have been described, for Mecklenberg in Germany, by Geinitz (1886). He describes thickly scattered deposits of boulders up to several metres in diameter. He notes that the local inhabitants try to dispose of the stones by addition to drystone walls, burial in trenches and pits, as building stones and by breaking down for use as road metal. Such districts, Geinitz says, are noted for prehistoric stone buildings. Dolmens, barrows, stone circles and altars are often present in the glacial deposits areas in surprising numbers (Geinitz 1886: 221).

Megalithic monuments in northern Germany, Denmark and southern Sweden have been widely described (FIGURE 1, *cf.* Service & Bradbery 1981; Renfrew 1983a). The Funnel Beaker megaliths of northern Germany and Scandinavia (Kaelas 1983) are abundant in glaciated areas (Kaelas 1983: figure 5: 81) where long barrows are associated with constructions of erratic boulders (Kaelas 1983: 78–9), and some passage graves are built in an area of 'moraine clays' (Kaelas 1983: 87). Mohen (1989: 161) notes the use of local erratic blocks and comments that such 'moraine blocks' were used to cover many of the burial chambers of northern Germany, Denmark and southern Sweden. Examples of such material may include the megalithic chamber tombs at Ramshog (Scania; Mohen 1989:

177), Kivik (Scania; Mohen 1989: 275–7), Borger (northern Netherlands; Mohen 1989: 151) and Araslov (Scania; Kaelas 1983: figure 1). Similarly, the stones of the Gnewitz chamber tomb (Kaelas 1983: 83) comprise apparently unworked rounded boulders. The morphological features of these megalithic monuments are consistent with construction from local glacial erratic material. The location and frequency of megalithic monuments in areas of abundant glacial debris cannot therefore be used as evidence for human transport on a scale larger than that deduced elsewhere (*c.* 5 km).

A study of the derivation and construction of Neolithic megalithic tombs (termed 'hunebedden') on the Drenthe Plateau (northeast Netherlands) has been provided by J.A. Bakker and is summarized in Bakker & Groenman-van Waateringe (1988). The hunebedden are from the Trichterbecher (TRB) west culture (Bakker 1979). Bakker & Groenman-van Waateringe argue that the locations of hunebedden are determined by the local availability of glacial erratics. These erratics include igneous, metamorphic and sedimentary rocks of presumed Scandinavian origin. The hunebedden are concentrated on a north-northwest/south-southeast-trending end moraine, termed the Hondsrug, between Groningen and Emmen. Bakker & Groenman-van Waateringe (1988) note that many hunebedden have been destroyed as a result of subsequent land clearance (see comment above). They note that the location of hunebedden on dry sand locations with specific soil characteristics (type HD/21/VII; *cf.* Bakker & Groenman-van Waateringe 1988: 160) indicates small-scale transport to favoured locations. However, Bakker & Groenman-van Waateringe (1988) propose that the hunebedden are derived from local glacial erratics. For the 74 hunebedden on the Drenthe Plateau the authors argue that 78% were constructed less than 350 m from areas where glacial boulder deposits (stonefields) lay in the subsoils; for a further 8 tombs the builders must have 'resorted exclusively to boulders lying on top of the partially eroded boulder clay' (Bakker & Groenman-van Waateringe 1988: 153). These authors conclude that 'on the sandy Drenthe Plateau the presence of boulders dictated the place of the tombs' (1988: 155); and this detailed study therefore indicates relatively small-scale, less than *c.* 350–400 m (*cf.* 1988: 175), megalith transport for the Neolithic TRB West tombs (hunebedden) of the northeast Netherlands.

Monument location, geology and territory

The distribution of megalithic monuments has been repeatedly interpreted (e.g. Renfrew 1973; 1976; 1979; 1983a) in terms of 'territorial markers' for segmentary Neolithic societies. For example, Renfrew states that 'the construction of the monuments represents a *serious, coherent indeed patterned activity*' (1983a: 9; original emphasis). This concept has been developed from the distribution of megalithic monuments in the glaciated areas of Arran and Orkney (Rousay) (e.g. Renfrew 1973: 133–60) and has widespread implications for the geographic development of prehistoric societies.

However, this model is inconsistent with the distribution of middle TRB megaliths, where 'the presence of boulders dictated the place of the tombs' (Bakker & Groenman-van Waateringe 1988: 155). These authors conclude: 'nothing was found to show that hunebeds actually lay *in the centre* of the territories of local communities (as Renfrew suggested for other megalithic landscapes). Alignment along traffic routes seemed, however, often probable' (original emphasis, Bakker & Groenman-van Waateringe 1988: 174).

The evidence summarized above indicates that the locations of megalithic monuments are likely to reflect the local availability of building materials rather than the delimitation of contemporaneous territorial areas.

Stonehenge, its bluestones and sarsens

From the data summarized above, long-distance megalith transport over a distance greater than 5 km is clearly unlikely. However, this has been proposed and widely accepted for the bluestone circle and horseshoe at Stonehenge. The first erection of the bluestones in c. 2100 BC formed a monument analogous in scale to roughly contemporaneous circles in Britain (compare Burl 1979: 48). The post-Beaker sarsen constructions, c. 2000–1550 BC, which made Stonehenge unique had not yet been undertaken. Atkinson (1979: 105–16), reflecting contemporary archaeological opinion, proposed that the igneous bluestones were transported by boat/craft and rollers from a source in the Preseli Hills, c. 240 km in a direct line from Stonehenge. The evidence for this proposition has been re-evaluated, using new petrological and chemical data for bluestone samples (Thorpe et al. in press).

The new data reported and a new review of the evidence for the human or glacial hypotheses favour glacial transport of the bluestones from varied sources in southwest Wales to Salisbury Plain. The evidence includes the varied rock types and structural properties of the bluestones, and the large number of outcrops, more than seven, from which the bluestones are derived. Further, megalithic monuments in southwest Wales show no preferential use of bluestone rock types, and frequently use local glacial erratics (above). Glacial erratics of similar rock types to the dolerite and (varied) rhyolites from Stonehenge were transported as far east as Cardiff and the Bristol Channel (cf. Donnelly et al. in preparation). With the possible exception of the Boles Barrow bluestone (probably present on Salisbury Plain before being utilized by man perhaps 1000 years before the first bluestone use as monoliths in Stonehenge), there is an apparent absence of glacial erratics between the Bristol Channel and Salisbury Plain; however, this is consistent with the irregular distribution of glacial erratics at the margins of large continental ice sheets, and with later field clearance as described by de Luc (1811) and paralleled in the Netherlands (Bakker & Groenman-van Waateringe 1988) and in north Germany (Geinitz 1886). The erection of the pre-existing, mainly unworked boulders in the bluestone circles of Stonehenge II represented a much smaller input of labour than has been suggested.

The use of sarsen stones in the construction of Stonehenge has been used as evidence for megalith transport (Atkinson 1979: 116–22). Atkinson (1979: 116) rejects earlier suggestions that the sarsens may have originated from a small deposit, now worked out, on Salisbury Plain and states that it is now 'generally agreed' that the origin of the sarsens must lie on the Marlborough Downs (near Avebury), c. 40 km to the north of Stonehenge. He writes that the 'method of transport to Stonehenge must certainly have been by sledge-hauling over land all the way, for there is no possible water route' (1979: 116). Such transport may have involved 1500 men (persons) working for 5·5 years (Atkinson 1979: 121). This represents more effort than is implied for human transport of the smaller mass of bluestones from the more distant source in southwest Wales (Atkinson 1979: 115–16).

Sarsens are a variety of Cenozoic silicified deposits (silcrete) which are widely distributed in southern England (Bowen & Smith 1977; Summerfield & Goudie 1980). They are the silicified remnants of a Cenozoic sediment which formerly covered a larger area than now represented by present-day outcrops of Cenozoic sediment, summarized in Bowen & Smith (1977: figure 1) and Summerfield & Goudie (1980: figure 1). These data show large concentrations of sarsen stones in northeast Wiltshire (on the Marlborough Downs), but there are scattered concentrations within south Wiltshire (including Salisbury Plain) and Dorset.

Summerfield & Goudie (1980: 72) note, 'the present distribution of sarsen stones reflects, to a large extent, their removal by man, and those remaining are only a vestige of the numbers in existence prior to man's arrival in Britain'. This is consistent with the geological observations of J.A. de Luc (1811) who noted the field clearance of 'blocks of granulated quartz' (presumed to be sarsen stones) between travels across Salisbury Plain in 1780 and 1809 (de Luc 1811; Bartenstein & Fletcher 1987; Thorpe *et al.* in press). Since sarsen is not prominent in buildings now visible on Salisbury Plain, it must be concluded that such blocks were broken up, buried or otherwise removed (compare above, and Geinitz's (1886) descriptions of burial of erratics). In view of the wide distribution of sarsens in the southern UK and the evidence for subsequent field clearance, the elaborate model of human transport proposed by Atkinson (1979) is less plausible than collection of local sarsen blocks from within a few kilometres of the present site of Stonehenge (*cf.* Bartenstein & Fletcher 1987; Thorpe *et al.* in press).

The discussion of Stonehenge in relation to both bluestones and sarsens weakens the case for this monument providing an exception to the small scale of megalith transport (below *c.* 5 km) established above.

Discussion

In conclusion, the data summarized here demonstrate that megalith stone movement on the scale of 1–2 km took place during monument construction, and that local stone transport occurred up to 5 km as a result of human agency. We are not aware of any megalithic monument that requires stone transport from a rock outcrop or a local glacial deposit from a distance exceeding *c.* 5 km. There is therefore no evidence of long-distance Neolithic/Bronze Age megalith transport. The megalith builders utilized the simplest and most obvious methods for stone selection, transportation and construction, employing local materials, including rock outcrops and glacial erratics, collected within *c.* 5 km of the megalith site and generally much closer. The siting of megalithic monuments was therefore determined by local availability of building materials. Interpretation of the spatial distribution of the monuments in terms of social organization should therefore be discussed within this geological framework.

Acknowledgements. We are grateful to Drs A. Burl and G.D. Gaunt, Professor R. Bradley, and other colleagues and correspondents for valuable information and discussion. However the conclusions here are entirely the responsibility of the authors. The manuscript was typed by Marilyn Leggett and the diagrams drawn by Andrew Lloyd.

References

ATKINSON, R.J.C. 1979. *Stonehenge*. Harmondsworth: Penguin.
AUBREY, J. 1980. *Monumenta Britannica I*. Milborne Post: Dorset Publishing.
BAKKER, J.A. 1979. *The TRB West Group*. Amsterdam: Instituut voor Prae- en Protohistorie. *Cingula* 5.
BAKKER, J.A. & W. GROENMAN-VAN WAATERINGE. 1988. Megaliths, soils and vegetation on the Drenthe Plateau, in W. Groenman-van Waateringe & M. Robinson (ed.), *Man-made soils*: 143–81. Oxford: British Archaeological Reports. International series S410.
BARTENSTEIN, H. & B.N. FLETCHER. 1987. The stones of Stonehenge — an ancient observation on their geological and archaeological history, *Zeitschrift fur deutsche Geologische Gesellschaft* 138: 23—32.
BOWEN, H.C. & I.F. SMITH. 1977. Sarsen stones in Wessex: the Society's first investigations in the evolution of the landscape project, *Antiquaries Journal* 57: 185–96.
BURL, A. 1976. *The stone circles of the British Isles*. London: Yale University Press.
 1985. *Megalithic Brittany*. London: Thames & Hudson.
CLARE, T. 1978. Recent work on the Shap 'Avenue', *Transactions of the Cumberland & Westmoreland Archaeological & Antiquarian Society* 78: 5–15.

COLLINS, G.H. 1976. Appendix 5: geology of the Stones of Stenness, Orkney, in J.N.G. Ritchie, The Stones of Stenness, Orkney, *Proceedings of the Society of Antiquaries of Scotland* 107: 44–5.
DE LUC, J.A. 1811. *Geological travels III: Travels in England*. London: F.C. & J. Rivington.
DONNELLY, R., R.A. BEVINS & R.S. THORPE. In preparation. *The Storrie Erratic Collection: a re-appraisal of the status of the Pencoed 'Older Drift' (South Wales)*.
DUNNING, F.W., I.F. MERCER, M.P. OWEN, R.H. ROBERTS & L.M. LAMBERT. 1978. *Britain before man*. London: Institute of Geological Sciences.
DYMOND, D.P. 1966. Ritual monuments at Rudston, E Yorkshire, England, *Proceedings of the Prehistoric Society* 32: 86–95.
ELGEE, F. & H.W. ELGEE. 1930. *The archaeology of Yorkshire*. London: Methuen.
FLINT, R.F. 1971. *Glacial and quaternary geology*. Chichester: John Wiley.
GEINITZ, E. 1886. Der Boden Meckenburgs, in R. Lehmann (ed.), *Forschungen zur deutschen Lands- und Volkskunde* 1: 1–32. Stuttgard: J. Engelhorn.
GRIFFITHS, W.E. 1960. The excavation of stone circles near Penmaenmawr, north Wales, *Proceedings of the Prehistoric Society* 26: 303–39.
HEGGIE, D.C. 1981. *Megalithic science*. London: Thames & Hudson.
INSTITUTE OF GEOLOGICAL SCIENCES. 1977. *Geological Survey Ten Mile Map, South Sheet (Quaternary)*. London.
KAELAS, L. 1983. Megaliths of the Funnel Beaker culture in Germany and Scandinavia, in Renfrew (1983b): 77–91.
KEMPE, D.R.C. 1983. The petrology of building and sculptural stones, in D.R.C. Kempe & A.P. Harvey (ed.), *The petrology of archaeological artefacts*: 80–153. Oxford: Clarendon Press.
KENDALL, P.F. & H.E. WROOT. 1924. *Geology of Yorkshire*. Vienna: printed privately.
KENT, P. 1980. *British regional geology, eastern England from the Tees to the Wash*. London: HMSO.
MACKIE, E.W. 1975. *Scotland: an archaeological guide*. London: Faber & Faber.
  1977a. *Science and society in prehistoric Britain*. London: Elek.
  1977b. *The megalith builders*. Oxford: Phaidon.
MALONE, C. 1989. *Avebury*. London: Batsford/English Heritage.
MOHEN, J.-C. 1989. *The world of megaliths*. London: Cassell.
MYKURA, W. 1976. *British regional geology, Orkney and Shetland*. Edinburgh: HMSO.
Ó RIORDAIN, S. 1965. *Antiquities of the Irish countryside*. London: Methuen.
PIGGOTT, S. 1962. *The West Kennet Long Barrow, excavations 1955–56*. London: HMSO. Ministry of Works Archaeological Reports 4.
RAYNER, D.H. & J.E. HEMINGWAY. 1974. *The geology and mineral resources of Yorkshire*. Yorkshire Geological Society.
RENFREW, C. 1973. *Before civilisation: the radiocarbon revolution and prehistoric Europe*. Harmondsworth: Penguin.
  1976. Megaliths, territories and populations, *Dissertationes Archaeologicae Gandenses* 16: 198–220.
  1979. *Investigations in Orkney*. London: Society of Antiquaries. Reports of the Research Committee 38.
  1983a. Introduction: the megalith builders of western Europe, in Renfrew 1983b: 8–17.
  (Ed.).1983b. *The megalithic monuments of western Europe*. London: Thames & Hudson.
SERVICE, A. & J. BRADBERY. 1981. *A guide to the megaliths of Europe*. Frogmore: Granada.
SMITH, I.F. 1965. *Windmill Hill and Avebury: excavations by Alexander Keiller 1925–1939*. Oxford: Clarendon.
SUMMERFIELD, M.A. & A.S. GOUDIE. 1980. The sarsens of southern England: their palaeoenvironmental interpretation with reference to other silcretes, in D. Jones (ed.), *The shaping of southern England*: 71–100. London: Academic Press. Institute of British Geographers Special Publication 11.
THOMAS, N. 1976. *A guide to prehistoric England*. London.
THORPE, R.S., O. WILLIAMS-THORPE, D.G. JENKINS & J.S. WATSON. In press. The geological sources and transport of the bluestones of Stonehenge, Wiltshire, UK, *Proceedings of the Prehistoric Society*.
WILSON, V. 1948. *British regional geology, east Yorkshire and Lincolnshire*. London: HMSO.

Stonehenge for the ancestors: the stones pass on the message

by M. PARKER PEARSON & RAMILISONINA

ANTIQUITY 72 (276), 1998

MEGALITHIC STONE MONUMENT CONSTRUCTION in Madagascar has close associations with the honouring of the ancestors. Through the use of probability, piecemeal and relational analogies, and a consideration of the materiality of stone, a case can be made for certain structuring principles linking the ancestors with stone and the living with wood which can be found, in their own specific manifestations, to be relevant to historical and contemporary Madagascar and to Late Neolithic Britain. As a result Stonehenge can be interpreted as belonging to the ancestors, a stone version for the dead of the timber circles used for ceremonials by the living. By extension, Avebury and many other stone monuments of this period can be understood as built for the ancestors in parallel to the wooden monuments constructed for the living.

Introduction

That most enigmatic monument on Salisbury Plain continues to resist our attempts at understanding whilst, at the same time, it provides fertile ground for countless speculations and theories from all corners of archaeology's broad church. It has been conceived of as an astronomical observatory, a computer, and a centre of earth energies amongst many other interpretations (Hawkins 1966; Hoyle 1966; Chippindale 1983; Chippindale *et al.* 1990). All of these notions are grounded in some way or another in our own British and western 20th-century concerns and imaginings of Late Neolithic and Early Bronze Age society, as a distorted mirror of the present (Ruggles 1997). There have been attempts to draw on the knowledge of monumental architecture in traditional societies in other parts of the world, such as Colin Renfrew's use of Polynesian analogies of chiefdom organization to explain the conditions which gave rise to Stonehenge's construction (1973). With the full publication of excavations at Stonehenge (Cleal *et al.* 1995) and the publication of other volumes on the monument (Cunliffe & Renfrew 1997; Bender 1998), we should now be in the best position to think about the meanings embodied in the megalithic architecture of Stonehenge and associated monuments in Wessex (Barrett 1997). We may well be able to say much about *how* the monument was erected (Startin & Bradley 1981; Richards & Whitby 1997) but there is no satisfactory overall view as to *why* it was built.

The perspectives of indigenous scholars on their colonial and pre-colonial pasts have been a welcome and significant development in recent years (e.g. Gathercole & Lowenthal 1989; Layton 1989a; 1989b), yet there has been little opportunity for such commentary on the archaeological remains of the European heritage. At the 1986 World Archaeological Congress in Southampton, there was a relatively informal move to do so with Edward Matenga from Zimbabwe providing an alternative view of the Avebury monuments. Such an approach has also been possible through the preparation of a television documentary on Stonehenge in which both of us participated (FIGURE 1). Not only have we been working together on issues of monumentality in Madagascar since

FIGURE 1. *Ramilisonina at Stonehenge during filming. (Photo M. Parker Pearson.)*

1991 but Ramilisonina has lived his life in communities which regularly erect standing stones and which have a complex knowledge and understanding of stone's symbolism and significance.[1]

Ethnographic analogy: wood and stone

Analogy can be considered to work in four different ways: as formal or piecemeal analogy; as cross-cultural generalization; as relational analogy between structuring principles in different societies; and as analogies of materiality, appreciating the physical tangibilities of the world as experienced. Each *schema* has its contribution to make in developing an appreciation as to what is the most appropriate understanding of monumental stone architecture in Late Neolithic/Early Bronze Age Britain.

Formal analogies between present-day societies and the remains from the past are generally predicated on the notion that precise parallels can be drawn between the two. As a result, these types of analogy are often limited to relatively simple observations. In this particular case there is a formal analogy between contemporary Madagascar and Neolithic Britain in the erection of standing stones by both societies. Throughout Madagascar, stones, known as *vatolahy* ('man stones'), are erected in many places in many different circumstances. These *vatolahy* are explicitly identified with ancestors. Despite the occurrence of standing stones in both societies, the problems of extending this formal analogy are self-evident: Madagascar cannot be conceived of as a society parallel to that which existed in Britain over 4000 years ago. There is, of course, no monument in Madagascar which provides a direct comparison for Stonehenge. We cannot take any single Malagasy social context, such as the belief that the hardness of stone constitutes the essence of men as opposed to women, and present it as the mirror image of prehistoric Wessex. And yet the power of analogy opens avenues of new understanding, enabling us to explore the articulation of links between stone and ancestors, and perhaps uncover the expression of such links in the megalithic architecture of Britain.

We employ cross-cultural generalizations as a means of assessing the likelihood of certain aspects of social organization being shared between different cultural contexts. We may define these generalizations as probability analogies since they work on the principle that, if a certain relationship is found amongst most traditional societies today, then there is a probability that this relationship probably obtained in most societies in the past. A related approach can be termed the 'social typology analogy'. An example of

---

1 Ramilisonina is Bezanozano and many of the observations and sayings used in the text derive from this ethnic grouping.

this is Renfrew's use of social evolutionary typologies for characterising Late Neolithic Wessex as a chiefdom on the basis of matching certain archaeologically visible traits with a list of social traits which are deemed indicative of ethnographically documented chiefdoms (Renfrew 1973; Service 1962; Sahlins & Service 1960; Earle 1991). Criticized for its 'catch-all' definitions (Whittle 1997a: 147), the chiefdom model is not particularly pertinent to this investigation since monumentality in Madagascar is not restricted to 'chiefdom' societies; indeed, in the southern lands of Androy, megalithic funerary architecture only commenced after the collapse of chiefly authority (Parker Pearson *et al.* 1996).

Cross-cultural generalization is relevant in one area, that of the social significance of ancestors, a phenomenon found in many societies. Formal worship of ancestors is a feature of many societies, primarily in East Asia (Watson & Rawski 1988; Ahern 1973; Chidester 1990: 125–36). Lehmann & Myers claim that a universal belief in the immortality of the dead exists in all cultures whilst Steadman, Palmer & Tilley have revised Swanson's results to argue that ancestor worship is a universal aspect of religion (Lehmann & Myers 1993; Steadman *et al.* 1996: 63–4; Swanson 1964). They include ghosts, spirits and ancestral totems as ancestors and define worship broadly as reverence or respect and cast doubt on the conclusion of Swanson's cross-cultural study that, in 24 out of 50 societies, dead ancestors do not influence the living (Steadman *et al.* 1996). Although we might question the merits of defining ancestor worship so loosely and also retain a scepticism of both the sample size and the ethnographic basis of such knowledge, Steadman *et al.*'s study highlights the power of tradition in kinship-based societies in which 'the way of the ancestors' provides an unquestioned authority and truth. The role of the ancestors is very marked throughout the many ethnic groups within Madagascar (Mack 1986). Cross-cultural generalization thus suggests that the people of Late Neolithic Wessex would have engaged in particular relationships with their ancestral dead.

We may consider a relational analogy as that which links different manifestations through a common structuring principle. Hodder's work on the notion of pollution and purity in structuring relationships between men and women shows how different material outcomes stem from the same underlying ideas in Moro and Mesakin Nuba society, and in British Gypsy society (1982). Hodder is never clear as to whether his structuring principles have cross-cultural universal validity; if so, then it is hard to see exactly how his notion of relational analogy differs from the laws of human behaviour presupposed by the probability analogy. It is better to assume that structuring principles are not universal and to work on the assumption that we require a certain level of inter-contextual analysis in order to establish whether they are relevant for the purposes of analogy. In this particular case, looking at Madagascar and prehistoric Wessex, we have standing stones as the main formal analogy. We know from cross-cultural generalizations that ancestors are an intrinsic part of the social world in many kinship-based societies. In Madagascar, the ancestors are associated with standing stones in an intimate relationship with complex meanings. If we take this entwined co-presence of stones and ancestors to be a structuring principle, we can examine its different manifestations in the Later Neolithic and Bronze Age as compared to Madagascar. The manifestations will be specific to each cultural context and what is required for the relational analogy to work is a demonstration that the archaeological facts of Neolithic Wessex can be read acceptably in terms of the structuring principle of stones and ancestors. In other words, we need to construct a hermeneutic bridge between the analogy and the data. Another structuring principle might be the concept of worship of the sun and the moon, linked with ancestors, made visible through monumental constructions. We are now able to explore prehistoric Wessex for itself rather than placing Madagascar's known present and recent past lock, stock and barrel into the long-forgotten past of Britain.

There is a further reason why we consider this relational analogy of stone for the ancestors, explored below, as more than just a plausible 'just-so' story. Whilst the meanings of things can be arbitrary and open to continuous reinterpretation, the physical properties of materials such as stone, wood, water and fire are such that they resist certain interpretations and understandings and invite others. In such cases, their materiality may be a significant element of their metaphorical associations. In comparison to wood, stone has physical properties of durability, hardness, solidity and weight, the latter implying unity in the physical labour of moving a large stone. In terms of materiality, as opposed to linguistics, the sign is not arbitrary. Stone's durability and enduring nature places it at a different temporal level to the lifetimes of wood or people. Monuments of stone transcend the transience inherent in more perishable materials such as vegetal matter and wood.[2] They express the eternal in material form. This concern with materiality has been recently raised in the context of the British Neolithic and Bronze Age (Richards 1996; Tilley 1996: 168; Whittle 1997b: 152) and Whittle has even suggested that stone may have stood metaphorically for the ancestors at the time of Stonehenge (1997b: 152). This is a relationship which we can now consider in more detail through the examination of the use of stone in Madagascar.

Madagascar: ancestors and stones

Madagascar is twice the size of the British Isles. Subsistence practices vary enormously from wet rice cultivation in the central highlands and on the north and east coasts, to hunting and gathering in the forests of central southern Madagascar, to dry agriculture in the west, to semi-nomadic pastoralism in the arid south and southwest. There is also considerable diversity in political histories, from the formation of the Merina and Betsileo states in the highlands in the 17th and 18th centuries to the replacement of chiefdom societies by egalitarian yet hierarchical (in terms of clan organization) communities in Androy in the south.[3] Whilst Malagasy language and certain broad conceptions about house organization and orientation, cattle symbolism and economy, and ancestral respect are shared, Madagascar is a cultural mosaic of regional and ethnic interpretations and reworkings of these central themes. In spite of ecological and social organizational differences, the many ethnic groups in Madagascar are united in sharing cultural practices centred on elaborate funerals, monumental funerary architecture, and recognition of the power of the ancestors. It is the island of the ancestors (Mack 1986).

The significance and use of standing stones

Stone has been a fundamental component of tombs in the highlands since the 14th century AD (Lebras 1971; Joussaume & Raharijaona 1985: 540) though stone tombs have only been constructed in areas such as Androy since the mid 19th century (Parker Pearson

---

2   We also need to bear in mind that, as we shall see, wood can stand in for stone in certain contexts. Equally, earth can also be considered as durable and enduring; in Madagascar, for example, it is sacred like stone.

3   The Tandroy, the inhabitants of Androy, have a fiercely egalitarian ethos yet the structuring of asymmetrical marriage alliance relations between wife-givers and wife-takers produces a series of hierarchical relationships between the different clans and between lineages within the clans. For societies of this type, the simple distinction between egalitarian and ranked is not sufficient to describe their social structure.

FIGURE 2. *A standing stone (*vatolahy*) in the highland region of Betsileo country. (Photo M. Parker Pearson.)*

1992; Parker Pearson *et al.* 1996). Traditionally, houses in the highlands were constructed of wood and other perishable materials. They were never built out of stone since this was reserved solely for the housing and commemoration of the dead. Similarly, in Imerina (the dominant kingdom in the highlands) soil was considered to have sacred properties and, though it belonged to the king, even he could not build his house out of it. This material symbolism began to change in the 1870s in the highlands when Welsh Protestant missionaries encouraged the building of houses in brick and stone. Today the distinction between wooden houses and stone tombs is still strongly maintained by the Tandroy in the region of Androy.

Standing stones are known as *vatolahy* ('man stones') and are erected for many reasons (FIGURE 2). Traditionally, stone is reserved for the dead in the form of tombs and commemorative standing stones but the extent and nature of the association of standing stones with the dead varies from region to region.[4] For highland groups such as the Bezanozano, a *vatolahy* may represent a deceased individual or group of dead (Ndema 1973: 168–74). The stone is put up after death to commemorate a man whose body has not returned to his ancestral tomb or, alternatively, to celebrate a well-known individual who is buried in his ancestral tomb. Very occasionally a gifted wise woman will be similarly commemorated though normally all women, and men under 30 years, are ex-

---

[4] In certain regions where stones are not available, the hardest of woods are used for standing 'stones' (*vatolahy hazo*; 'wooden man stones'). The tree named *ambora* is used for symbolic stones in eastern Madagascar by groups such as the Betsimisaraka, the Bezanozano, the Tsimihety and the Antembahoaka, where it is, like stone, reserved for the ancestors.

FIGURE 3. *A Tandroy tomb with* vatolahy *at its east and west ends. (Photo M. Parker Pearson.)*

cluded from this honour. Among the Tanosy of the southeast, the *vatolahy* are erected at a short distance from hidden forest tombs. For the Tandroy, they are incorporated in the tombs of men at the east and west ends except when they are erected in isolation as cenotaphs to men or as the result of ancestral visitation in dreams (FIGURE 3). Standing stones are also used to mark the boundaries of different groups' territories, or to deflect the malign influence of a tomb whose position with respect to a house or village might affect the living. In Imerina stone came to have a legitimatory purpose in inaugurating and underwriting the establishment of state power in the 18th century. The great king Andrianampoinimerina's succession to power was established, in part, through his procession to three sacred stones in 1787 (Kus & Raharijaona in press). Kings erected stones as a mark to show that they had passed that way. Standing stones were used to mark important events such as the winning or losing of a battle. Within the kingdom of Imerina, royal palaces and residences were linked by lines of standing stones along which messages would pass; a runner would wait at each stone to pass on the message.

    The association of stone with the passing on of messages has a deeper, polysemous meaning, expressed in one of the many metaphorical proverbs: *vato namelan-kafatra* ('the stone passes on the message'). The commemorative stone is a text which informs about the person remembered. It is also the nexus of communications and exchanges between living and ancestors. Requests for supernatural help can be made to the ancestor at his stone. If the request is followed by good luck, the living leave gifts at the stone for the benevolent ancestor. In Bezanozano and Betsimisaraka country *vatolahy* are occasionally wrapped in white *lamba* (shawls) in response to communications from the ancestor to the living. Standing stones may also bring good fortune or grant wishes in other ways, by touching them for example. The asking of the ancestors' blessing prior to ceremonies of circumcision, marriage and *famadihana* (secondary burial) may also be directed to a standing stone or tomb though it is more normally requested from the living elders. The stone's passing on of messages also refers to the position of the elders who are metaphorically like stones, passing on the messages of the ancestors to the young. This links to a further metaphor in which human growth, especially that of males, is a process of hardening.[5] Babies are soft and fluid, like water, and dead infants are excluded from the ancestral tomb. Male circumcision is a significant stage in men's process of hardening, culminating in death when, as ancestors, people become hard, resistant and eternal. Tombs must also be hard, coherent and dry. If the tomb becomes unsound and is breached, its integrity is threatened by the entry of water and damp: if the ancestors become wet, their *angatra* ('ghosts') cry out. Finally, stone is not only eternal but it is also binding: *izay mitambatra vato fa izay misaraka fasika; fa ny firaisana no hery* ('as stone we are united but as sand we are separated; there is strength in togetherness'). *Vatolahy* actually embody this concept in the very activity of their quarrying, moving and erection since many people are required to act together in unison.

In summary, stone has a number of important associations which are mobilized slightly differently among the various ethnic groups of Madagascar and which have become modified in different ways through time. Yet there are certain coherent themes which have endured for over 500 years across the mosaic of the many ethnicities. These are the association of stone with the ancestors (for tombs and standing stones), the metaphorical hardening of the living to become like stone, the eternal durability of stone, and the unity symbolized by stone and mobilized in its erection.

Ancestors in Madagascar
Ancestors continue to inhabit the world of the living, though predominantly within their tombs or at the *vatolahy*. They are one of four sets of entities which may be found in most parts of Madagascar: *Zanahary* (the creator), *Andriamanitra* (God — a recent Christian concept), the *razana* (the ancestors), and other invisible spirits such as *Vazimba* (the original inhabitants of Madagascar), *kalanoro* and *zazavavy-ndrano*. Spirit possession is a feature of life in Madagascar and the living may be possessed by the spirit of an ancestor as well as by the other supernatural forces. Spirits inhabit the trees, the hills, the grass, the earth and the animals — all is sacred. Before breaking the ground for use as a rice paddy, prayers to the spirits are necessary for permission to be given.[6]

Places where the ancestors may be contacted, other than at the tombs and *vatolahy*, are located within three spatial scales: the house, the village and the territory. The northeast corner of the house, the *jorofirariazana*, where the sun rises, is the corner of the ancestors. The ancestors may be approached in the northeast corner only during the morning when the sun is in that direction, except in the afternoon of the day before a

---

[5] Certain hardwoods, the *valanirana* and the *arahara*, are also linked to the process of masculine and ancestral hardening. A song containing the words *arahara tsy zanakazo dilony avy* ('the arahara is not a baby wood but is always hard') is sung at Antembahoaka circumcision ceremonies and at Bezanozano funerals, emphasising the hardening of both men and the dead. *Teza*, the hardwood beneath the sapwood, has similar connotations (Bloch 1995a; 1995b).

[6] For groups that practice *tavy* (slash and burn), such as the Betsimisaraka, the spirits' permission is required before forest clearance. The summits of hills are, however, never cleared and these remain as domains of those spirits.

famadihana when the dead are requested to be present for the next day. In many regions, villages have sacred places at their centre, marked by a small stone, a bush or a pointed post, where the ancestors can be approached, thanked and sacrificed to. At the territorial level of large lineages or clans, ceremonial gatherings are held around a pointed wooden post (or occasionally a tomb or *vatolahy*) on level, high ground.

Concepts of the relationship between living and ancestors also involve the sun and moon, and the circularity that they embody in their shapes and in their movement. Life is conceived of as a circle from birth to ancestorhood (*mihodinkodina ny fiainana* ('life turns in a circle')) whilst the earth is considered as round and as turning in a circle. Respect for the elders is summarized in the title of grandparents: they are *masoandro amambolana* ('the sun and the moon') and should be respected in the same way as we respect the sun and the moon and their movements. Both sun and moon are important for the timing of ceremonial activities. Circumcision is held during the full moon while house-building and inauguration take place during the new moon. Marriages should never be performed during the 'dead' moon. *Famadihana* in the highlands are held between July and early October, centring on the lunar months of August and September, whereas the Tandroy forbid any activities concerned with the dead during the lunar month of September. Dancing and singing should be conducted *fari-bolana* ('round like the moon') and the direction of dancing is always sunwise (anti-clockwise since the turning of the sun is in the opposite direction in the southern hemisphere).

Stonehenge as a ceremonial circle of the ancestors

Alasdair Whittle's recent discussion of the meaning of Stonehenge (1997b) utilizes the example of the Zafimaniry of central Madagascar to emphasize the properties of wood as a metaphor for people and ancestral bones (1997b: 152) though he does not pursue the Zafimaniry's linking of stone with the ancestors (Bloch 1995a; 1995b). However, this is a theme which he develops separately, concluding that circular sites of this type, including the stones themselves, were connected with spirits, ancestors and the dead (1997b: 163). Whittle's observations on the possible meanings of Stonehenge are perhaps the most perceptive yet but they do not go far enough in spelling out the specific metaphorical associations embodied by Stonehenge, especially in relation to its wooden counterparts at Durrington Walls and Woodhenge (FIGURE 4).

The recent programme of radiocarbon dating of material from Stonehenge has resulted in a reconsideration of its overall chronology and phasing. It is currently divided into three phases (Cleal *et al.* 1995): Phase 1 (2950–2900 BC) is the construction of a circular ring of posts (known as the Aubrey Holes) within a circular earthwork, consisting of a bank and external ditch, with openings to the south and northeast. These orientations have been tentatively associated with symbolism of the rising moon (Ruggles 1997: 225). In Phase 2 (2900–2400 BC) a large number of wooden posts were erected in the interior and at the northeast entrance. Towards the end of this phase, cremation burials were placed throughout the monument. Phase 3 (2550–1600 BC) is the period of stone construction and building of the avenue. The earliest of these stone phases is a semi-circle of Welsh bluestones[7] brought from southwest Wales and the Preseli mountains (sub-phase 3i). This was dismantled and replaced by the sarsen circle and the five sets of trilithons (sub-phase 3ii), possibly with a setting of bluestones (sub-phase 3iii). The bluestones were again dismantled and set up as a bluestone circle within the sarsen

---

7   'Bluestone' is used here as a catch-all term for all of the Welsh rocks at Stonehenge, including not only the dolerites, rhyolite, and volcanic ash or tuff but also the sandstone rocks.

circle and as a bluestone oval within the trilithons (sub-phase 3iv). An arc of these bluestones was removed to form the bluestone horseshoe (sub-phase 3v). Finally, two concentric circles of stoneholes (the Y and Z holes) were dug outside the sarsen circle but they were never filled (sub-phase 3vi).

Four radiocarbon dates from the sarsen stoneholes suggest that the sarsens were erected around 2400 BC (Allen & Bayliss 1995: 524–5), several centuries earlier than had previously been thought. The significance of this is that the major stone-building period at Stonehenge was broadly contemporary with the construction of large timber post circles within the henge enclosures at Woodhenge (c. 2500–2000 BC) and Durrington Walls (c. 2500–2100 BC) (Cunnington 1929; Wainwright & Longworth 1971). Archaeological opinion is divided as to whether these concentric circles of timber posts were roofed or simply lintelled (see Musson 1971; Parker Pearson 1993: figure 58; Gibson 1994) but the large diameter of the timber circle recently detected by magnetometry at Stanton Drew in Somerset precludes the likelihood of roofing. Whether these timber circles were roofed or not, their quantities of associated finds, especially pig bones and Grooved Ware pottery, from within the post circles and from the midden areas outside them are indicative of considerable activity, involving feasting and structured deposition (Richards & Thomas 1984). There continues to be much speculation about the timber circles' purpose since they are monumental in size and massively bigger than the insubstantial remains of the few Late Neolithic houses, constructed with organic materials, which have been found in southern Britain. The presence of many thousands of relatively unfragmented pig bones within these monumental timber circles has been interpreted as evidence of an élite or a priestly caste (Wainwright 1989; MacKie 1977) though many other interpretations are possible. What is particularly important here is the relationship between the timber circles and the stone circle of Stonehenge (Darvill 1997: 189–91).[8] The structural features which link Stonehenge to the Durrington and Woodhenge timber monuments are: the six concentric rings (if we include the Y and Z holes at Stonehenge); the use of both the circle and the oval (both incorporated into the same monument at Stonehenge), the similar sizes (between 39 m and 53 m), and the solstice sunrise axes (midsummer at Stonehenge

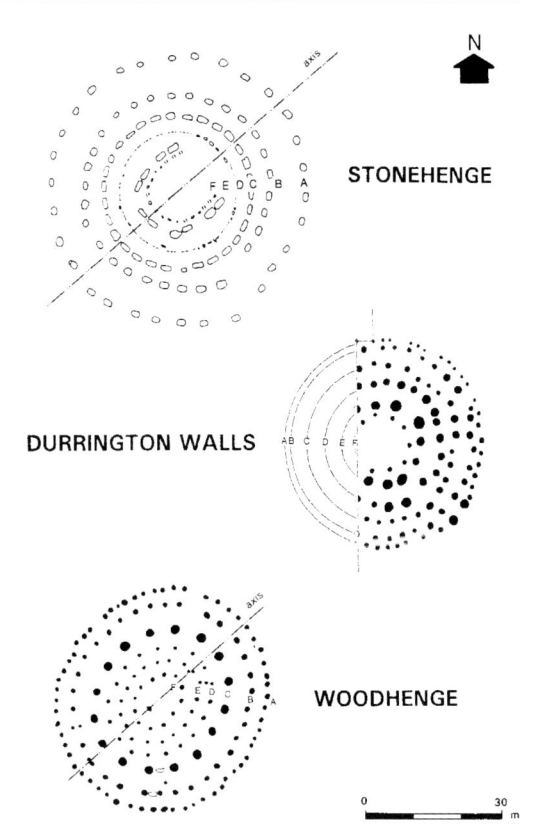

FIGURE 4. *Ground plans of Stonehenge (sub-phase 3vi), Durrington Walls Southern Circle and Woodhenge. (From Darvill 1997, courtesy of the British Academy.)*

---

[8] Coneybury henge should also be mentioned here. Lying about a mile southeast of Stonehenge, it is a small oval-ditched enclosure containing a circle of posts, inside which is a circle of pits which held either stones or posts (Richards 1990: 123–58; 1991: 89–96). Despite the many stakeholes and two large pits, the quantities of Grooved Ware and other refuse were slight. Coneybury henge dates to c. 2750 BC and, prior to its abandonment, can be compared to Stonehenge in Phase 2.

FIGURE 5. *Mortice and tenon and tongue and groove jointing at Stonehenge. (From Atkinson 1987: 16, courtesy of English Heritage.)*

and Woodhenge and possibly midwinter at the Southern Circle at Durrington Walls).

It has been noted for some time that the dressing of the Stonehenge stones, the provision of mortices and tenons,[9] and the use of tongue and groove joints for the lintels in the sarsen circle are reminiscent of techniques of woodworking (Atkinson 1979: 39; Gibson 1994: 211; FIGURE 5). Although the postholes of the Durrington and Woodhenge timber circles provide no indication whether these posts were similarly dressed with rectangular sections above ground, there appears to have been an intention to dress and erect the Stonehenge stones as if they were wooden. If stone was the medium associated with the ancestors (or simply the spirit world) then Stonehenge can be understood as a 'ceremonial circle' used and occupied by the ancestors (and/or spirits) in the same way that the timber circles were 'ceremonial circles' used and occupied by the living. The distinction can be followed up in three ways.

Firstly, Stonehenge's isolation and invisibility from Durrington Walls and Woodhenge, where three timber circles are known and other circular features are inferred (David & Payne 1997: 91–4), suggests a spatial dislocation such that the ancestors occupied the same world as the living but were given their own distinct place within it (FIGURE 6). The two monument complexes, though separate, may have been complementary. Both are linked by the flow of the River Avon, since Stonehenge's avenue leads down to the river and Durrington Walls' main entrance faces directly onto it. Whilst further work is needed to establish whether there was an avenue leading from Durrington Walls to the river, there is evidence throughout Britain of a strong association in this period of henge monuments with rivers and streams (Richards 1996).

Secondly, the quantities of rubbish at Stonehenge are far fewer than those from the timber circles. The Stonehenge finds assemblage includes sherds from only a few vessels and about 1000 animal bones. The 11 sherds of Grooved Ware and 229 Beaker sherds, most of them small, suggest that deposition was limited. Although we must bear in mind the inadequate retrieval methods of the early excavations and the limited depositional contexts for bones and pottery, the 3675 pieces of bluestone, 2173 pieces of sarsen and 1285 pieces of flint from the excavations suggest that the retrieved quantities of pot and bone are indicative of their restricted deposition. At Durrington Walls, the 5861 sherds of Grooved Ware and 71 Beaker sherds, and the 8500 animal bones attest to a different scale of deposition, interpreted as the remains of feasting (Wainwright & Longworth 1971: 189–90). About half of this material came from the Southern Circle and its environs. There were smaller but still significant quantities from the Northern Circle and from Woodhenge (Wainwright & Longworth 1971: 188; Cunnington 1929; Pollard 1995). The material record from Stonehenge presents us with two possibilities. Either little ceramic or faunal rubbish was discarded here or the monument was kept clean, with the refuse being deposited outside the earthwork in some place as yet unlocated. The latter

---

9   Technically these are ball and socket joints (Alex Gibson pers. comm.).

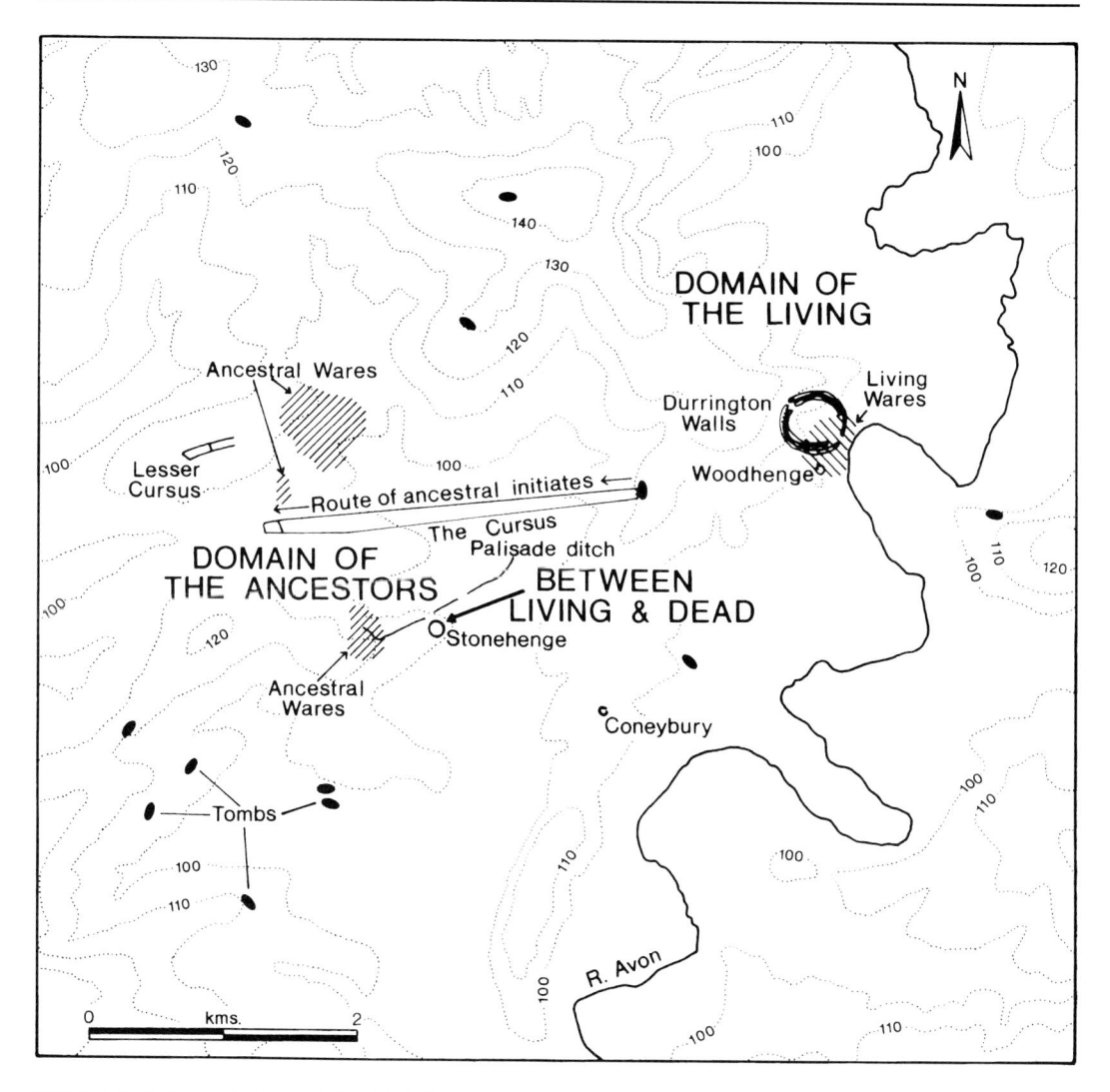

FIGURE 6. *Interpretation of the Middle to Late Neolithic landscape around Stonehenge in phases 1–2. (Adapted from from Cleal* et al. *1995: figures 252–4, drawn by Colin Merrony.)*

interpretation is less likely, given the many thousands of pieces of stone and flint recovered during excavation. The lack of ceramic and faunal debris suggests that this ceremonial place of the ancestors was probably never the scene of feasting by the living.

Thirdly, there is an unusual visual relationship between Stonehenge and the Early Bronze Age (*c.* 2200–1700 BC) round burial mounds in its vicinity (FIGURE 7). Although this part of Salisbury Plain contains one of the densest and largest groups of round barrows in Britain, only about 20 are located within Stonehenge's 'envelope of visibility' (Cleal *et al.* 1995: figure 21). The most impressive round barrow cemeteries, on Normanton Down, King Barrow Ridge and the Cursus, are all located so as to be just visible from Stonehenge, placed at the limits of visibility. The remainder, numbering several hundred, are placed so as to lie further outside this area of visibility from Stonehenge. This 'envelope of visibility' from Stonehenge provides a zone which was largely free of the physical remains of the Early Bronze Age dead except at its margins which we may

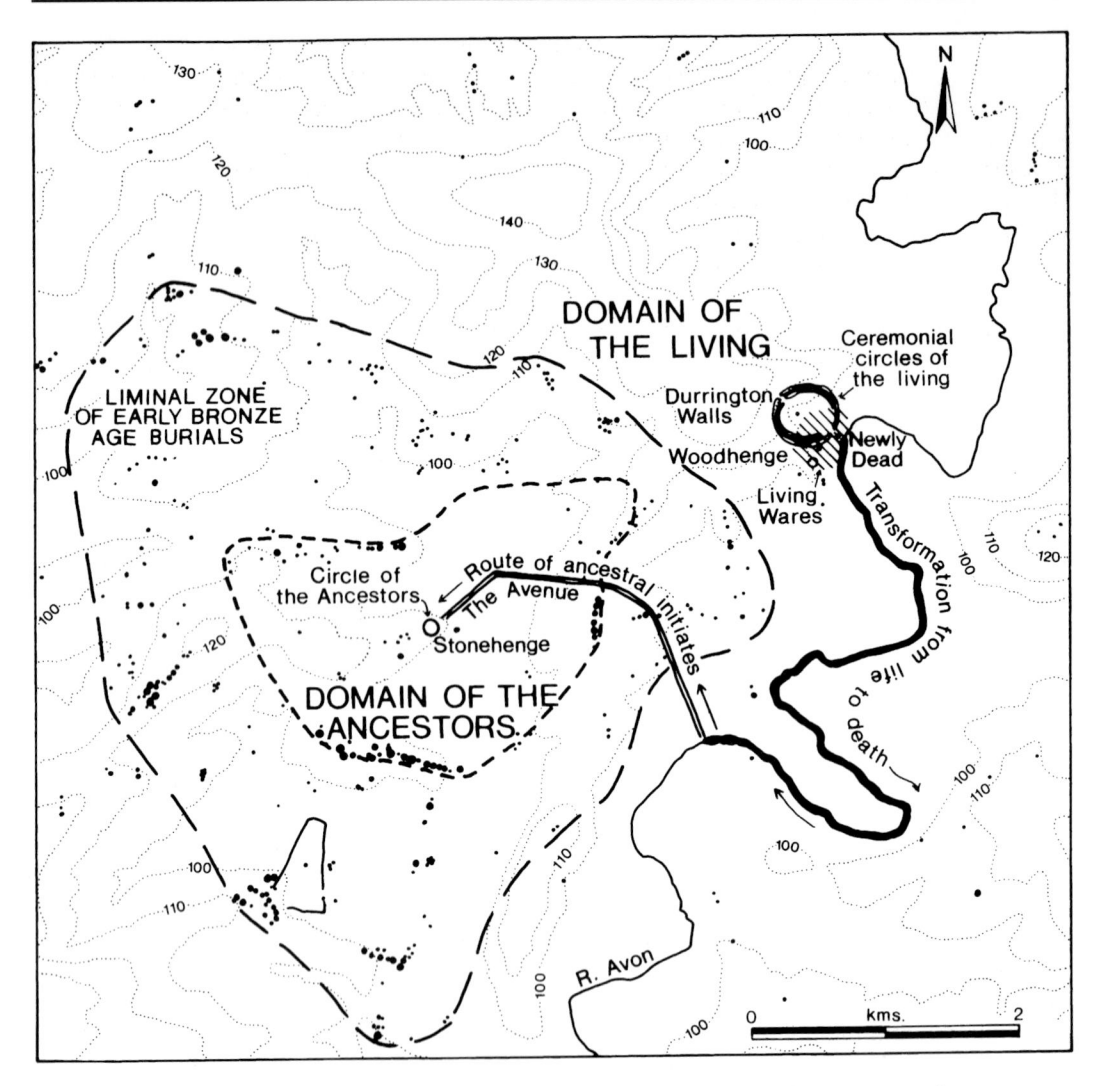

FIGURE 7. *Interpretation of the Late Neolithic to Early Bronze Age landscape around Stonehenge in phase 3. (Adapted from from Cleal et al. 1995: figures 21, 254–5, drawn by Colin Merrony.)*

interpret as liminal zones between the landscape of the living and the landscape of the ancestors. The world of the ancestors was thus a physical domain, a place which, for over 500 years after the Late Neolithic, was separate from the places where the physical remains of the dead were put.[10] It was also cut off from the domain of the living by a liminal circular zone containing the corporeal remains of the Early Bronze Age dead (Woodward & Woodward 1996).

---

10 Whilst some of the Beaker burials around Stonehenge date to the later 3rd millennium BC, we have little idea about the placing of the remains of the dead during the time when Grooved Ware was in use. The associations with water raise the possibility that corpses, defleshed skeletons or cremated bones were disposed of in rivers (Richards 1996). The encroachment into the ancestors' domain by round barrows may have happened towards the end of the Early Bronze Age, judging by the presence of a Collared Urn in the barrow immediately east of Stonehenge.

The living will have visited Stonehenge, no doubt, at certain moments to meet the ancestors, to communicate directly with them. Yet, outside the moments of building, the monument and its immediate surroundings were probably left largely alone. In other words, in terms of human action, little or nothing happened within Stonehenge in Phase 3 other than its various periods of construction work.[11] Once built, its inhabitants were the spirits of the ancestors, using it for incorporeal feasting ceremonies and calendrical rituals which mirrored those corporeal ceremonies held by the living in the timber circles of the region, specifically at Durrington Walls.

Avebury, the West Kennet enclosures and beyond

It is difficult to talk of Stonehenge without mentioning Avebury and, if our notion has any validity, then it should be equally applicable here. Avebury is a large earthen henge with four entrances, within which is a large stone circle containing two adjacent stone circles associated with unusual stone edifices; the 'Cove' in the north circle and the 'Obelisk' in the south circle (Smith 1965; Malone 1989: figure 85). Running southeast out of the south-southwest entrance of the henge is the West Kennet avenue, a double row of standing stones which culminates over 2 kilometres away at the Sanctuary, a round building which was constructed in both timber and stone (Cunnington 1931).[12] Radiocarbon dates suggest two phases of ditch-digging between c. 3490–3280 and 3150–2630 BC (Pitts & Whittle 1992). The dating of the erection of the stones rests on two dates, c. 2840–2590 and 2510–2230 BC (Pitts & Whittle 1992) which Whittle rationalizes as falling within the period c. 2800–2400 BC (1997a: 140). Though no radiocarbon dates are available for the Sanctuary, it is considered to be broadly contemporary (Pollard 1992: 213).

One of the most exciting discoveries near Avebury in recent years has been the complex of palisade enclosures at West Kennet, dated to c. 2400–2000 BC (Whittle 1997a). Here we find a modified and smaller version of Avebury but created in wood rather than in stone (FIGURE 8). There is only a short stretch visible of an outer palisade[13] to match the outer stone ring at Avebury but otherwise the adjacent circles, the southeast-running avenue and the Sanctuary are all replicated. Spatially and structurally, the south circle at Avebury can be matched with Palisade Enclosure 1 at West Kennet, the north circle with Palisade Enclosure 2, the West Kennet avenue with Outer Radial Ditch 1 (though the latter is shorter and appears to have only the southern side), and the Sanctuary with Structure 4 (Whittle 1997a: figure 28). The Avebury Cove and the stone arrangements in the south circle may equate to the simple concentric post circles such as Structures 1, 2 and 3. Although excavations of the West Kennet complex were limited in extent, over 5000 animal bones and large quantities of Grooved Ware indicate large-scale feasting within the enclosures.[14]

---

11 The living, or certain persons amongst them, may have accompanied the ancestral spirits or come to meet them at particular moments but they would have needed no razor wire to keep them outside the circle and to either side of the avenue. As we will see below, a similar situation can be envisaged at Avebury where Keiller noticed slight depressions in the chalk bedrock running along either side of the West Kennet avenue (Ucko et al. 1991: 189), and where a gap in the standing stones on the southwest side of the avenue was used for the offering of stones, flint and stone-tempered pottery (Smith 1965: 210–12).
12 A second avenue, the Beckhampton avenue, was thought to have led out of the west-southwest entrance of the henge but geophysical survey has failed to reveal any certain trace of it (Ucko et al. 1991: 199).
13 This is visible in one aerial photograph (Whittle 1997a: figure 26) as a 150-m long crop-mark which appears to be a wide ditch containing large, widely spaced post-holes. Unfortunately it has not yet been investigated.
14 The animal bones are, like other timber circle assemblages, dominated by pig. More peculiarly there is a strong preponderance of right-side portions.

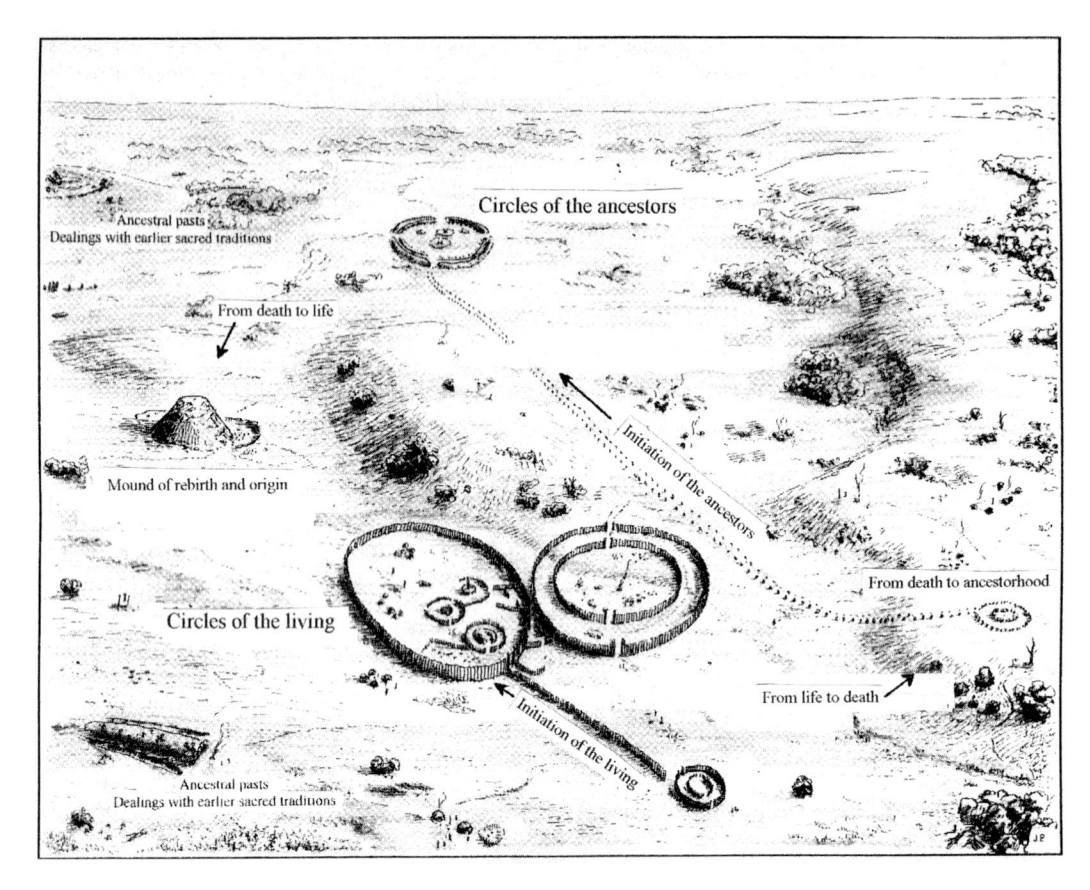

FIGURE 8. *A reconstruction of the parallel stone and timber monuments at Avebury and West Kennet. (Adapted from the drawing by Josh Pollard from Whittle 1997a: figure 87.)*

Not only does the Avebury–West Kennet evidence replicate the spatial segregation of the ancestors' stone-built space from the timber domain of the living but it also provides a set of relationships similar to those for the Stonehenge–Durrington monuments. The paired circles at Avebury and West Kennet are not intervisible; both sites have a close association with water; and the distribution of round barrows is markedly sparse within a 1-km radius of Avebury yet it lies within another major concentration of barrows.[15] We know relatively little about the interior of Avebury henge except that there is a dearth of pottery and animal bones that might be construed as feasting debris (Barclay et al. 1995: 113). Cunnington's extensive excavations of the Sanctuary produced little more than 80 sherds of Grooved Ware and a small assemblage of animal bones, though Pollard advises that surface accumulations could have been substantial (1992: 221). The

---

15 As Colin Richards has indicated (1996), water is very significant for the placing of henges. At Avebury the entry point (the Sanctuary) to the 'henge' of the ancestors lies downstream from the palisade enclosures, the 'henge' of the living, just as the beginning of the Stonehenge avenue is similarly located with respect to Durrington Walls. However, Avebury has a potentially unique monument in the form of Silbury Hill, which intercepts passage upstream from the palisade enclosures to Avebury henge (FIGURE 8). In terms of the flow of water and spiritual procession in a counter-clockwise direction, Silbury Hill marks the transition point where death turns to life, a monument of renewal and rebirth as Whittle has suggested on other grounds (1997a: 151). Its links with rebirth were also noted by Dames (1976).

geometric arrangement of post-holes and standing stones at the Sanctuary raises the possibility that wood and stone may have been in contemporary use here although it might also have begun as a timber monument and finished as a stone one (Pollard 1992). If the former is the case then we have the possibility that the Sanctuary was constructed as a place where the worlds of the living and the dead coincided, perhaps where the physical remains of the Late Neolithic dead were put, possibly immediately northwest of the Sanctuary, prior to the initiate ancestors' path up the avenue to Avebury.[16] If the latter then the Sanctuary is one of a small number of sites where wooden monuments were replaced in stone during the Later Neolithic (Pollard 1992: 218–19; Gibson 1994: 205).

If stone constructions are for the dead as opposed to timber for the living, we can use this principle to begin to understand transformations in the use of ceremonial sites over time. Timber structures which become 'lithicized' in later reworkings may be revealing in their material form a shift in their role in the social universe. We might interpret these sites as removed from the realm of the living into the realm of the ancestors as they were remodelled schematically in stone. The West Kennet enclosures, which appear to be later than the Avebury circles, may never have reached this stage of 'lithicization', of being transferred from the realm of the living to the realm of the dead. This was presumably because the ancestors' ceremonial site at Avebury was already in place. Likewise, the timber circles within Durrington Walls were never 'lithicized'. Stonehenge itself went through this wood-to-stone transformation between its Phases 2 and 3, significantly when it was used as a place of burial. It was precisely during this transition, and at no other time, that Stonehenge was used as a cemetery.[17] Other timber circles, such as Woodhenge and Mount Pleasant at Dorchester (Wainwright 1979), appear to have been replaced by token markers in stone. Mount Pleasant can also be regarded as potentially forming a wood–stone pair in that the timber circle (Site IV) is located adjacent to an unusual enclosure at Flagstones (Smith et al. 1997). The latter is, like Stonehenge's Phase 1, perfectly circular and, in contrast to Mount Pleasant, contains very few artefacts. Irregular hollows within the interior may have held stones.

The configuration of Later Neolithic stone and timber monuments in Wessex was undoubtedly different to those in other regions of Britain, yet there is a possibility that the same structuring principle of stone for the ancestors was in use throughout the British Isles, albeit expressed through regional variants. For example, the change from wood to stone can be seen to have occurred in Scotland. On sites at Machrie Moor, Arran (Haggarty 1991), at Moncrieffe (Stewart 1985), Temple Wood, Argyll (Scott 1988–89), Cairnpapple (Piggott 1947–48), probably Balfarg (Mercer 1981) and Croft Moraig on Tayside (Piggott & Simpson 1971), excavations of stone rings have revealed that they replaced timber predecessors. Precisely why some wooden monuments were lithicized and others were not is not clear but we might assume that the conferring of ancestral status was something which was largely dependent on local human agency and regional variation. The Wessex pattern of wood-and-stone paired

---

[16] Burl (1979: 127) records an observation in 1678 by Dr Robert Toupe, the physician who sought out human bones to grind into medicinal powder, about human remains near the Sanctuary '. . . soe close by one another that scul toucheth scul . . . I really believe the whole plaine, on that even ground, is full of dead bodies', and another by John Aubrey: 'About 80 yards from this monument, in an exact plain round it, there were some years ago great quantities of human bones and skeletons dug up.'

[17] The Beaker burial in Stonehenge's outer ditch (Evans 1984) now looks, in this new light, suspiciously like a clandestine killing (rather than a sacrifice pace Gibson 1994: 187). He was shot in the back and, other than the arrows that killed him, is accompanied only by a wristguard.

monuments appears to be very different to this southern and eastern Scottish example of stone-for-timber replacement.[18]

Within the Neolithic context of southern Britain we may broadly equate the use of large stones with the architecture of the ancestors, in contrast to the wooden and organic structures inhabited and used by the living.[19] The previous direct association of most Early Neolithic stone monuments with human remains, as in chambered tombs such as West Kennet, Wayland's Smithy and the Cotswold–Severn group in particular, provides us with some understanding of the contexts wherein the dead were associated with stone, a point also noted by Whittle (1997b: 163). Our general inability to locate the remains of the vast majority of the dead in the Late Neolithic presents a problem as to how that relationship between ancestors and stone might be conclusively demonstrated. Yet the prior associations between ancestors and stone provide a series of preconditions for the Late Neolithic: specific manifestations had changed, such as different means of disposal, yet there will have been threads of continuity in the more significant structuring principles of material life. Houses for the living continued to be built out of perishable materials and thus stone remained reserved for those transcendental aspects of the world associated with the ancestors. With the exception of treeless Orkney, stone was generally not incorporated into dwellings until the Middle Bronze Age. Yet not all Neolithic mortuary structures incorporate stones since many are built in regions where large stones are simply not available. In such circumstances we might expect similar solutions to those found in the stone-free regions of Madagascar where the hardest woods are substituted for stone. We should also remember that regional adoption of stone as a medium of the ancestors will have happened at different times and rates, by recalling the chronological variations in adopting raised stones as metaphors for the ancestors in different regions of Madagascar, with a 500-year gap between its adoption in Imerina and in Androy for instance.

Implications for the future

There are many avenues which the Madagascar analogy opens up. If stone was the material of the ancestors then our understanding of its modification for rock-art (Bradley 1997), its context in cave and rock-shelter burials (Chamberlain 1996) and its quarrying and shaping for stone axes (Edmonds 1995) takes on a new dimension. Equally the use of stone temper in pottery such as Peterborough Ware had ancestral associations different from Grooved Ware pots tempered with shell, grog or other materials.[20] The perfectly circular forms of Stonehenge 1 and Flagstones, along with the timber circles and Stone-

---

18   The henge at Marden in Wiltshire (Wainwright et al. 1971) contains a modest timber circle but there is no adjacent stone monument. We can only surmise that the ancestors of those celebrating at Marden were in residence at Stonehenge or Avebury.
19   It would also appear that, in the Earlier Neolithic, earth (or chalk) dug from the ground also had a certain degree of metaphorical equivalence with stone, being other materials associated with the ancestors, utilized in long-barrow construction. The ancestral significance of earth and chalk appears to have diminished in the Later Neolithic whereas that of stone was emphasized.
20   In this respect, we should rename Peterborough Ware and other Later Neolithic impressed wares, generally tempered with flint, chert, sandstone and quartz (Cleal 1995: 187–90), as 'ancestor ware'; pottery made for interactions specifically with the ancestors. Gibson (1995: 29) has noted that the quartz tempering probably had a deep significance whilst Thomas has recognized Peterborough Ware's contextual associations with the ancestral dead (1991: 92) and with continuity from the distant past (1991: 98). Peterborough Ware dominates the small assemblage from Avebury and the sherd scatter immediately west of Stonehenge. The large scatters of this pottery either side of the west end of the Stonehenge cursus lead us, additionally, to infer that this and other cursuses were built as pathways of initiation for the ancestors.

henge 3, are specifically features which are first found in the Late Neolithic; perfect circles are found in nature in the form of the sun and moon, the human eye[21] and ripples in still water. We would suggest that the former are more likely metaphors for the circular monuments since their correlations with solar and lunar movements are broadly accepted. Although there are no such round monuments today in Madagascar,[22] metaphors link the sun, moon and earth with respect for the ancestors and with the timing of rites of passage and other ceremonials.

The constitution of the Late Neolithic cosmological universe is also something which we can begin to explore. We are not dealing with ancestor worship as such. Our proposed model places the community of ancestors in an incorporeal world which they inhabit in a human fashion, a world parallel to the corporeal world inhabited by the living. Given existing interpretations of the timber circles as ceremonial centres, involving feasting — presumably calendrical celebration and sacrifice — and given the scarcity of bones and sherds at the stone circles, we suggest that the ancestors too were feasting and celebrating in their own intangible parallel world. This model suggests the presence of a third entity — an object of worship by all humans, living and dead. This 'third party' may have been a creator similar to the Malagasy's *Zanahary* but the architectural concern with precise circularity suggests that this transcendental entity was manifested in the heavenly bodies of the sun and the moon. We may invest Late Neolithic society, then, with at least two axes of transcendence, between the living and the ancestors and between people, both living and dead, and the object of their worship.

This interpretation of stone monuments as being for, or belonging to, the ancestors throughout much of Britain during this period may cause us to question Renfrew's model of chiefdom evolution in which Stonehenge is the central place of a confederacy of powerful chiefdoms in southern Britain (1973). As we have seen from Madagascar, the putting-up of stones for the ancestors is something which is found in states, chiefdoms and relatively egalitarian communities. There is no doubt that the size of the Avebury and Stonehenge stones is greater than those erected anywhere in Madagascar and that the sustained construction of these Late Neolithic composite monuments hints at a very high level of co-operation. We might heed the Malagasy metaphorical associations between stone and unity.

With the re-dating of the Stonehenge sarsens to *c.* 2400 BC, the gold-rich barrow burials of Bush Barrow, the Normanton Down cemetery and others in Britain now date to the sub-phases after the stones had been erected. With these probable 'chiefly' burials no longer dating to the relevant time frame, the copious barrow burial record of the later part of the 3rd millennium BC (associated with the Beaker period) reveals no certain social differences between individuals which might be indicative of a ranked society. Even the Beaker burials in the Cursus barrows immediately north of Stonehenge contain no exceptional collections of grave goods nor reveal any outstanding expenditure of effort in funerary rituals. Although small single items of gold occasionally appear in Beaker burials throughout Britain, these are not sufficient to indicate a chiefdom society. In fact, the funerary record of this period is far more akin to that found today amongst the competitive egalitarian Tandroy where women and children are the bread-winners whilst men are free to take part in monument construction. It may well be that the mobilization of labour for monument building in the Late Neolithic was orchestrated not by

---

21 In Malagasy the sun is *masoandro* ('the eye of the day').
22 Though tombs attributed to the Vazimba, the earliest inhabitants, are small circles of stones, hence the saying *mitangorongorona tahaky ny Vazimba* ('to be grouped tightly in a circle like Vazimba').

secular chiefs but by charismatic spiritual leaders and ritual specialists. In this respect, Whittle draws attention to the building of an enormous mound by the Nuer of eastern Africa in the 1890s (Whittle 1997a: 148–9). In a strongly egalitarian society, a charismatic war leader and prophet was able to mobilize the community in the construction of a great mound to bury all the bad things associated with smallpox and rinderpest (Whittle 1997a: 148–9; Evans-Pritchard 1956; Johnson 1994). What we might call egalitarian or even egalitarian yet hierarchical societies are capable of united mobilization to construct large monuments. What matters most is not the attainment of a certain level of social evolutionary complexity but the strength of the motivation and the ideology which drive people from their own volition to construct the world in new ways and build cosmic order on earth.

Finally, Stonehenge retains some of its mysteries. Why was it constructed where it is? Why were the Welsh bluestones brought all the way from the Preselis? We can suggest some possible answers. Associations between people and land in Madagascar are very strong[23] and links are maintained across hundreds of miles with the *tanin'drazan* ('land of the ancestors') in both rice-cultivating and cattle pastoralist regions. Perhaps the Preseli mountains were the place of origin for the founding ancestors of the people who built Stonehenge. Thus the ancestors from that place, embodied as stones, were fetched and physically incorporated into the landscape of Wessex, the new homeland. By the time that Stonehenge 1 was constructed, around 3000 BC, this part of Wessex had been the focus for much monumental activity in the form of long barrows and the Cursus. Yet Allen's synthesis of the remarkable post-holes beneath the carpark at Stonehenge establishes that they were constructed to hold *c.* 0·75-m diameter pine-tree trunks in the Early Mesolithic, *c.* 8500–7000 BC, about three or four millennia before even the earliest Neolithic monuments in Britain (Allen 1995; 1997). There is the possibility that more such post-holes may lie within Stonehenge Bottom, to the north of the monument, perhaps forming a ceremonial focus of some sort. Transmission of oral traditions over so many millennia is extremely unlikely but the post voids were visible as pits when Stonehenge was constructed, as indicated by their Late Neolithic/Early Bronze Age tertiary fill (Allen 1995: 51).[24] Thus there is the possibility that these unusually ancient diggings into the land were recognized as the work of human agency belonging to a time remote from the Neolithic. In this connection, Stonehenge Bottom is unusual in being an apparently empty space lying at the centre of one of the most densely constructed ceremonial landscapes in prehistoric northern Europe. This apparent absence of features may relate not only to the 'dead zone' set apart for the ancestors but perhaps also to as yet undiscovered pre-Neolithic structures.

Conclusion

The complex metaphorical associations between ancestors and stones in different parts of Madagascar incorporate, or are linked to, structuring principles of hardness increasing with age. These are especially associated with men, with stone as a symbol of eternity and unity, and stone (and certain hardwoods) thus being reserved for the ancestors, and which signify the sun and moon and their links with elders and with rites of passage. We can use cross-cultural or probability analogies to indicate that all traditional societies place significance on the ancestors and their role in the world of the living.

---

23   *Tsy tany mandeha fa olon' belona* ('it is not land which moves but people').
24   This might seem highly improbable but we should remember that negative features from 5000 years ago can still be seen clearly on the surface, such as ditch fills at Knap Hill amongst others.

Secondly, there is a formal analogy with Madagascar, where stones are linked to ancestors. Thirdly, relational analogies enable us to identify the structuring principles which work in both societies but to different ends. For example, the same principle can generate stones as identifiable individual ancestors in Madagascar and stones as ancestral replacements of timber in Britain, even though each outcome may be unknown in the other country. Finally, this relational analogy can be strengthened by reference to ideas about the materiality of stone as a durable and permanent marker, in contrast to the changing nature of wood, emphasizing the eternal as opposed to the transitory.

Whereas the Madagascar case-study provides a basic analogy, it also helps to highlight specific and important differences with Neolithic Wessex. These include the identification of individual *vatolahy* with individual ancestors, as opposed to the Neolithic collective stone monuments which gave the ancestors a place in which to dwell and celebrate. In Madagascar the bones of the ancestors are carefully kept in the visible stone tombs where they reside, whilst in Wessex the remains of the Late Neolithic dead were disposed of and leave little trace. The ancestors appear to have inhabited places largely separate from those where their physical remains ended up.

The efficacy of any persuasive analogy is that it not only explains the context under investigation but also opens up understanding of associated contexts. In this case, we have explained Stonehenge as a ceremonial circle built for the exclusive use of the ancestors. As a result, it appears that other stone monuments and their wooden counterparts, such as Avebury and the West Kennet enclosures, can be similarly understood as parallel ceremonial monuments, the former for the ancestors and the latter for the living. This further helps to explain the process of 'lithicization' whereby certain of the timber monuments are reworked in stone, thereby acknowledging their passing from the realm of the living to the realm of the ancestors. Thus the changing of a monument from wood to stone is a marking of the movement of the living through death to ancestorhood, as the ceremonial places which were once associated with the living became places devoid of living people where the ancestors now reside. Late Neolithic Britain was essentially shared by two communities living side by side, the living and the spirits of the dead. Contrary to recent speculations by archaeologists, New Agers and other groups, the great stone monuments, once built, were largely the domain of the spirit world into which the living rarely entered.[25]

Acknowledgements. This paper came about as a result of collaboration in association with the making of a BBC documentary on Stonehenge. The working through of this idea and the realization that it is actually applicable to Stonehenge was captured on film on Tuesday 3 February 1998. We are particularly indebted to the programme's director, Jean-Claude Bragard, for arranging for Ramilisonina's visit to Britain and for helping us towards these conclusions through his acute and perceptive questions. Susan Crighton of the BBC is also to be thanked for her administrative support. We have also benefited from discussions with and advice from Mike Allen, John Barrett, Richard Bradley, Andrew David, Jane Downes, Mark Edmonds, Alex Gibson, Karen Godden, Georges Heurtebize, Dai Morgan-Evans, Colin Renfrew, Retsihisatse, Colin Richards, Niall Sharples, Geoffrey Wainwright and Alasdair Whittle. FIGURES 6 & 7 were drawn by Colin Merrony. The Androy project has been the basis of our own collaboration and resulted in this 'spin-off'. We thank its team members and the people of Androy who have helped us further to understand about living and working with stones. That project has been funded by the British Academy, the National Geographic Society, the Nuffield Foundation and the Society of Antiquaries of London.

---

25 We come full circle in remembering that the earliest surviving written interpretation of Stonehenge, that recorded by Geoffrey of Monmouth around 1136 (Chippindale 1983: 22), is that it was a cenotaph, a monument for the ancestors, commemorating 460 British lords massacred by the Saxon king Hengist at Mount Ambrius (Amesbury).

References

AHERN, E. 1973. *The cult of the dead in a Chinese village.* Stanford (CA): Stanford University Press.
ALLEN, M.J. 1995. Before Stonehenge, in Cleal *et al.*: 41–62.
    1997. Environment and land-use; the economic development of the communities who built Stonehenge (an economy to support the stones), *Proceedings of the British Academy* 92: 115–44.
ALLEN, M.J. & A. BAYLISS. 1995. Appendix 2: the radiocarbon dating programme, in Cleal *et al.*: 511–35.
ATKINSON, R.J.C. 1979. *Stonehenge.* Revised edition. Harmondsworth: Penguin.
    1987. *Stonehenge and neighbouring monuments.* London: English Heritage.
BARCLAY, A., M. GRAY & G. LAMBRICK. 1995. *Excavations at the Devil's Quoits, Stanton Harcourt, Oxfordshire, 1972–3 and 1988.* Oxford: Oxford University Committee for Archaeology.
BARRETT, J.C. 1997. Stonehenge, land, sky and the seasons, *British Archaeology* 29: 8–9.
BENDER, B. 1998. *Stonehenge: making space.* Oxford: Berg.
BLOCH, M. 1995a. People into places: Zafimaniry concepts of clarity, in E. Hirsch & M. O'Hanlon (ed.), *The anthropology of landscape: perspectives on place and space*: 63–77. Oxford: Clarendon Press.
    1995b. Questions not to ask of Malagasy carvings, in I. Hodder, M. Shanks, A. Alexandri, V. Buchli, J. Carmen, J. Last & G. Lucas (ed.), *Interpreting archaeology: finding meaning in the past*: 212–15. London: Routledge.
BRADLEY, R. 1997. *Rock art and the prehistory of Atlantic Europe: signing the land.* London: Routledge.
BURL, A. 1979. *Prehistoric Avebury.* New Haven (CT): Yale University Press.
CHAMBERLAIN, A.C. 1996. More dating evidence for human remains in British caves, *Antiquity* 70: 950–53.
CHIDESTER, D. 1990. *Patterns of transcendence: religion, death, and dying.* Belmont (CA): Wadsworth.
CHIPPINDALE, C. 1983. *Stonehenge complete.* London: Thames & Hudson.
CHIPPINDALE, C., P. DEVEREUX, P. FOWLER, R. JONES & P. SEBASTIAN. 1990. *Who owns Stonehenge?* Cambridge: Cambridge University Press.
CLEAL, R.M.J. 1995. Pottery fabrics in Wessex in the fourth to second millennia BC, in Kinnes & Varndell (ed.): 185–94.
CLEAL, R.M.J., K.E. WALKER & R. MONTAGUE. 1995. *Stonehenge in its landscape: twentieth-century excavations.* London: English Heritage. Archaeological report 10.
CUNLIFFE, B.W. & A.C. RENFREW (ed.). 1997. Science and Stonehenge, *Proceedings of the British Academy* 92.
CUNNINGTON, M.E. 1929. *Woodhenge.* Devizes: Simpson.
    1931. The 'Sanctuary' on Overton Hill, near Avebury, *Wiltshire Archaeological and Natural History Magazine* 45: 300–35.
DAMES, M. 1976. *The Silbury treasure: the great goddess rediscovered.* London: Thames & Hudson.
DARVILL, T. 1997. Ever increasing circles: the sacred geography of Stonehenge and its landscape, *Proceedings of the British Academy* 92: 167–202.
DAVID, A. & A. PAYNE. 1997. Geophysical surveying within the Stonehenge landscape: a review of past endeavour and future potential, *Proceedings of the British Academy* 92: 73-113.
EARLE, T. (ed.). 1991. *Chiefdoms: power, economy, and ideology.* Cambridge: Cambridge University Press.
EDMONDS, M. 1995. *Stone tools and society: working stone in Neolithic and Bronze Age Britain.* London: Batsford.
EVANS, J.G. 1984. Stonehenge — the environment in the Late Neolithic and Early Bronze Age and a Beaker-age burial, *Wiltshire Archaeological and Natural History Society Magazine* 78: 7–30.
EVANS-PRITCHARD, E.E. 1956. *Nuer religion.* Oxford: Oxford University Press.
GATHERCOLE, P. & D. LOWENTHAL (ed.). 1989. *The politics of the past.* London: Unwin Hyman.
GIBSON, A. 1994. Excavations at the Sarn-y-bryn-caled cursus complex, Welshpool, Powys, and the timber circles of Great Britain and Ireland, *Proceedings of the Prehistoric Society* 60: 143–223.
    1995. First impressions: a review of Peterborough Ware in Wales, in Kinnes & Varndell (ed.): 23–39.
HAGGARTY, A. 1991. Machrie Moor, Arran: recent excavations at two stone circles, *Proceedings of the Society of Antiquaries of Scotland* 121: 51–94.
HAWKINS, G.S. 1966. *Stonehenge decoded.* London: Souvenir Press.
HODDER, I. 1982. *The present past: an introduction to anthropology for archaeologists.* London: Batsford.
HOYLE, F. 1966. Speculations on Stonehenge, *Antiquity* 40: 262–76.
JOHNSON, D.H. 1994. *Nuer prophets: a history of prophecy from the Upper Nile in the nineteenth and twentieth centuries.* Oxford: Clarendon Press.
JOUSSAUME, R. & V. RAHARIJAONA. 1985. Sépultures mégalithiques à Madagascar, *Bulletin de la Société Préhistorique Française* 82: 534–51.
KINNES, I. & G. VARNDELL (ed.). 1995. *'Unbaked urns of rudely shape': essays on British and Irish pottery for Ian Long-worth.* Oxford: Oxbow.
KUS, S. & V. RAHARIJAONA. In press. Between earth and sky there are only a few large boulders: sovereignty and monumentality in central Madagascar, *Journal of Anthropological Archaeology* 17.
LAYTON, R. (ed.). 1989a. *Conflict in the archaeology of living traditions.* London: Unwin Hyman.
    1989b. *Who needs the past?: indigenous values and archaeology.* London: Unwin Hyman.
LEBRAS, J.-F. 1971. *Les transformations de l'architecture funéraire en Imerina.* Antananarivo: Musée d'Art et d'Archéologie.
LEHMANN, A.C. & J.C. MYERS. 1993. Ghosts, souls, and ancestors: power of the dead, in A.C. Lehmann & J.C. Myers (ed.), *Magic, witchcraft, and religion: an anthropological study of the supernatural*: 283–6. Palo Alto (CA): Mayfield.
MACK, J. 1986. *Madagascar: island of the ancestors.* London: British Museum.
MACKIE, E. 1977. *The megalith builders.* Oxford: Phaidon.
MALONE, C. 1989. *Avebury.* London: Batsford & English Heritage.

MERCER, R.J. 1981. The excavation of a Late Neolithic henge-type enclosure at Balfarg, Markinch, Fife, Scotland, 1977–8, *Proceedings of the Society of Antiquaries of Scotland* 111: 63–171.
MUSSON, C.R. 1971. A study of possible building forms at Durrington Walls, Woodhenge and the Sanctuary, in Wainwright & Longworth: 363–77.
NDEMA, J. 1973. *Fomba Antakay (Bezanozano)*. Fianarantsoa: Ambozontany.
PARKER PEARSON, M. 1992. Tombs and monumentality in southern Madagascar: preliminary results of the central Androy survey, *Antiquity* 66: 941–8.
  1993. *Bronze Age Britain*. London: Batsford & English Heritage.
PARKER PEARSON, M., K. GODDEN, G. HEURTEBIZE, RAMILISONINA & RETSIHISATSE. 1996. The Central Androy Project: fourth report. Unpublished manuscript, Universities of Sheffield and Antananarivo.
PIGGOTT, S. 1947-48. Excavations at Cairnpapple Hill, West Lothian, 1947–8, *Proceedings of the Society of Antiquaries of Scotland* 82: 68–123.
PIGGOTT, S. & D.D.A. SIMPSON. 1971. Excavation of a stone circle at Croft Moraig, Perthshire, Scotland, *Proceedings of the Prehistoric Society* 37: 1–15.
PITTS, M. & A. WHITTLE. 1992. The development and date of Avebury, *Proceedings of the Prehistoric Society* 58: 203–12.
POLLARD, J. 1992. The Sanctuary, Overton Hill, Wiltshire: a re-examination, *Proceedings of the Prehistoric Society* 58: 213–26.
  1995. Inscribing space: formal deposition at the later Neolithic monument of Woodhenge, Wiltshire, *Proceedings of the Prehistoric Society* 61: 137–56.
RENFREW, A.C. 1973. Monuments, mobilization and social organization in Neolithic Wessex, in A.C. Renfrew (ed.), *The explanation of culture change: models in prehistory*: 539–58. London: Duckworth.
RICHARDS, C. 1996. Henges and water: towards an elemental understanding of monumentality and landscape in Late Neolithic Britain, *Journal of Material Culture Studies* 1: 313–36.
RICHARDS, C. & J. THOMAS. 1984. Ritual activity and structured deposition in Later Neolithic Wessex, in R. Bradley & J. Gardiner (ed.), *Neolithic studies: a review of some current research*: 189–218. Oxford: British Archaeological Reports. British series 133.
RICHARDS, J.C. 1990. *The Stonehenge environs project*. London: English Heritage. Archaeological report 16.
  1991. *Stonehenge*. London: Batsford & English Heritage.
RICHARDS, J.C. & M. WHITBY. 1997. The engineering of Stonehenge, *Proceedings of the British Academy* 92: 231–56.
RUGGLES, C. 1997. Astronomy and Stonehenge, *Proceedings of the British Academy* 92: 203–29.
SAHLINS, M. & E.R. SERVICE (ed.). 1960. *Evolution and culture*. Ann Arbor (MI): University of Michigan Press.
SCOTT, J.G. 1988–89. The stone circles at Temple Wood, Kilmartin, Argyll, *Glasgow Archaeological Journal* 15: 53–124.
SERVICE, E.R. 1962. *Primitive social organization: an evolutionary perspective*. New York (NY): Random House.
SMITH, I.F. 1965. *Windmill Hill and Avebury: excavations by Alexander Keiller 1925–1939*. Oxford: Clarendon Press.
SMITH, R.J.S., F. HEALY, M. ALLEN, E. MORRIS, I. BARNES & P. WOODWARD. 1997. *Excavations along the route of the Dorchester by-pass 1986–1988*. Salisbury: Wessex Archaeology.
STARTIN, D.W.A. & R. BRADLEY. 1981. Some notes on work organisation and society in prehistoric Wessex, in C. Ruggles & A. Whittle (ed.), *Astronomy and society in Britain during the period 4000–1500 BC*: 289–96. Oxford: British Archaeological Reports. British series 88.
STEADMAN, L.B., C.T. PALMER & C.F. TILLEY. 1996. The universality of ancestor worship, *Ethnology* 35: 63–76.
STEWART, M.E.C. 1985. The excavation of a henge, stone circles and metal working area at Moncrieffe, Perthshire, *Proceedings of the Society of Antiquaries of Scotland* 115: 125–50.
SWANSON, G.E. 1964. *The birth of the gods: the origin of primitive beliefs*. Ann Arbor (MI): University of Michigan Press.
TILLEY, C. 1996. The power of rocks: topography and monument construction on Bodmin Moor, *World Archaeology* 28: 161–76.
THOMAS, J. 1991. *Rethinking the Neolithic*. Cambridge: Cambridge University Press.
UCKO, P.J., M. HUNTER, A.J. CLARK & A. DAVID. 1991. *Avebury reconsidered: from the 1660s to the 1990s*. London: Unwin Hyman.
WAINWRIGHT, G.J. 1979. *Mount Pleasant, Dorset: excavations 1970–1971*. London: Society of Antiquaries.
  1989. *The henge monuments: ceremony and society in prehistoric Britain*. London: Thames & Hudson.
WAINWRIGHT, G.J., J.G. EVANS & I.H. LONGWORTH. 1971. The excavation of a Late Neolithic enclosure at Marden, Wiltshire, *Antiquaries Journal* 51: 177–239.
WAINWRIGHT, G.J. & I.H. LONGWORTH. 1971. *Durrington Walls: excavations 1966–1968*. London: Society of Antiquaries.
WATSON, J. & E. RAWSKI (ed.). 1988. *Death ritual in late imperial and modern China*. Berkeley (CA): University of California Press.
WHITTLE, A. 1997a. *Sacred mound, holy rings: Silbury Hill and the West Kennet palisade enclosures: a Later Neolithic complex in north Wiltshire*. Oxford: Oxbow Monograph 74.
  1997b. Remembered and imagined belongings: Stonehenge in its traditions and structures of meaning, *Proceedings of the British Academy* 92: 145–66.
WOODWARD, A.B. & P.J. WOODWARD. 1996. The topography of some barrow cemeteries in Bronze Age Wessex, *Proceedings of the Prehistoric Society* 62: 275–91.

What future for Stonehenge?
by CHRISTOPHER CHIPPINDALE
ANTIQUITY 57 (221), 1983

LIKE MANY RESEARCHERS SINCE, William Stukeley in the mid-18th century wondered why the site of Stonehenge had been selected for the Britons' most sublime temple. It was chosen, he decided, according to the ancient notion of placing temples 'in clean and distinct areas, distant from profane buildings and traffic' (Stukeley 1740: 11, plate XXIIa). Two hundred years on, Stonehenge is set about with traffic, busy main roads running past on both north and south sides, and profane buildings have appeared — the Larkhill military complex on the northern skyline, and the Stonehenge car-park and visitors' facilities close by on the northwest.

For several centuries now, Stonehenge has been among the most visited of British ancient monuments. Records of tourist day-trips from Salisbury via Old Sarum (still a favourite outing) go back more than 400 years (Folkerzheimer 1562), and Stukeley (1740: 5) talked of its 'infinite number of daily visitants'. Their numbers have certainly become many times greater since. Accordingly Stonehenge has, over the last century and a half, seen a series of measures to ensure its physical survival and to cope with the press of sightseers in the busy summer months. In 1978 these culminated in the closure of the central area among the stones, so that it was no longer possible for the visitor to see Stonehenge properly, a move which understandably caused dismay (e.g. Dyer 1978).

Stonehenge, of course, is far from being the only British site in danger of destruction from enthusiastic visitors. Hadrian's Wall has been battered for decades. Other sites on the Wessex chalklands, like West Kennet, are suffering, and Silbury Hill is now also closed. But Stonehenge is the worst single case, where the disease has been chronic for more than 100 years and has threatened at times to overwhelm the patient. Five stages in the development of the illness can be identified. The first two, under private ownership, are:
1   a long period of *minimal supervision* (to 1901), and then
2   a policy of *private restrictions* (1901–18).
After the gift of Stonehenge to the nation, and its control by successive government departments beginning with the Office of Works and now the Department of the Environment (DoE), there have been three further stages:
3   an effort to return to rural peace (1918–34), which proving unworkable gave way to
4   an attempt at accommodating the numbers (1935–75).
In the end, this has been overwhelmed also, giving rise to
5   a crisis (1976–), which continues.

1. *Minimal supervision* (to 1901)
In medieval times, Stonehenge was known, but it barely figures in the extensive land-records of Amesbury parish, in which it stands (Pugh 1947). Neither a source of profit nor a boundary marker, it was simply a worthless curiosity. Occasionally, a stone may have been removed to make a bridge or when builders needed an especially hefty block. Certainly, some smaller bluestones and at least one larger stone (presumably a sarsen) disappeared in the 17th century (Jones & Webb 1655: 42; Aubrey 1685).

Thereafter, few if any complete stones were removed. Instead, visitors attacked the stones with hammers to hack off souvenir chips. Initially, they were encouraged by the lingering superstition that the stones had magical healing properties, and later, by learned attention to the petrology of Stonehenge. On a busy day right up to the 1870s 'a constant chipping of stone broke the solitude of the place' ('Vacation Rambler' 1871). R.S. Newall's story (Atkinson 1960: 191) of a hammer kept at Amesbury expressly to be hired out to Stonehenge visitors has no foundation that I have been able to find, but there is ample evidence for many a private hammer at work (Chippindale 1983a: chapter 10).

In the 17th century, Stonehenge must usually have been deserted, except during the annual fair held there, though a shepherd might materialize to hold the horses and cadge a few pennies (e.g. Pepys 1668). About this time, nevertheless, a flint layer was laid between the stones, presumably a deliberate, artificial surface to reinforce the most-trafficked areas (Atkinson 1979: 213). And by 1740, even before the passion for Druids, the picturesque and tourism took hold, there was sufficient trade for 'Gaffer' Hunt, an ancient Amesbury carpenter, to set himself up as guide-cum-liquor-seller with a lean-to hut and a cellar dug under a sarsen (Wood 1747: 32, 34). The fall of a trilithon in 1797 was said to result from gipsies digging a shelter by it (Browne 1833: 18).

In 1824, the Amesbury estate, and with it Stonehenge, was bought by the Antrobus family, who took an active interest in its upkeep. Henry Browne, a self-styled lecturer in ancient history and disciple of Buckland's diluvial geology, was soon installed as the first of a series of Stonehenge guardians. He was unpaid, but entitled to earn a living as a guide and by selling souvenirs in return for ensuring no damage was done. The physical evidence of 19th-century carvings visible on the stones confirms contemporary records that the guardians were ineffective, but Sir Edmund Antrobus, third Baronet, stoutly resisted all pressures on him to safeguard better the 'Frontispiece to British History'. He was the proprietor of Stonehenge, and no one was to tell him what to do with it (Chippindale 1983b). General Pitt-Rivers, trying to negotiate its protection under the 1882 Ancient Monuments Act, made characteristically vigorous plans — to restore inclining stones to the perpendicular, to supply foundations of concrete or masonry, and to install a resident policeman (Pitt-Rivers 1893). Sir Edmund would have none of this, or of any other lunatic suggestions for iron fences or encircling moats (Antrobus 1894). He did what he thought fit, instructing his game-keeper to evict the Stonehenge rabbits and his architect to prop any stones that seemed in danger.

The Antrobus policy did permit much surface damage to continue, but his resistance to several attempts at large-scale restoration and/or excavation was fortunate. If contemporary expert advice had been followed, the archaeology of Stonehenge would have been quarried away wholesale. The other side of the landowner's absolute right was shown by the attitude of the fourth Baronet: he encouraged the rumour that Stonehenge might, if the government would not find £125,000 to purchase it, go to the highest bidder, most likely some American who would ship it overseas (Le Gallienne 1900: 185–6; Chippindale 1978: 113). No law seemed to exist that would have prevented such a fate.

Stonehenge on a Victorian public holiday was a busy place: 'The pilgrim who goes there with his reverent mind full of Druids . . . undergoes a series of electric shocks . . . He never bargained for van-loads of uproarious humanity, dressed in all the colours of the rainbow, and in many others of aniline origin. They come, they crack jokes, they feast, and they sing the latest sweet things from the music-hall repertoire . . . while a fusillade of ginger-beer adds to the general rudeness' (Chippindale 1983a: chapter 10). Busiest of all in the last decade of the nineteenth century was the night before the summer solstice, when watching the sun rise (supposedly directly behind the Heel Stone) became the fashion. It was neither a sober nor a reverent affair. The crowds would spend a long evening fortifying themselves for the vigil in the Amesbury pubs, and walk, up to 3,000 strong, along the dusty roads to Stonehenge, where the sun usually declined to rise visibly to the occasion (Harper 1899: 209–10).

2. *Private restrictions* (1901–18)
The persistent fears for the safety of Stonehenge were shown to have some basis when, on 31 December 1900, an upright of the sarsen circle fell inwards, bringing a lintel down with it. At last Sir Edmund took effective action, both to control access and to prevent further stone-falls. Stonehenge had until then stood on the open downland, with a scatter of tracks running to it. Now a wire fence was put up, a shilling admission fee charged, and a policeman installed to prevent misbehaviour. Opposition was intense, both locally since a well-established habit of access had been abruptly cut off, and nationally. The National Trust, the Footpaths and Commons Preservation Society and other amenity groups saw it as arbitrary interference by an arrogant squire in the public's rights to something that should have belonged to the nation. The protestors sued in the High Court and lost, with justice as they were in effect arguing for the continuation of the pre-enclosure free-for-all (Chippindale 1978).

For archaeological advice Sir Edmund consulted an expert committee (from which John Lubbock, Lord Avebury, resigned because it was 'not sufficiently insistent on the rights of access of the public' (Hutchinson 1914: 136–7)). No restoration was attempted, and the only stone thought to be in danger was stone 56, the surviving upright of the great trilithon, whose angle of lean was large and increasing. This was pulled upright in autumn 1901, and its base set in concrete. The small area round its base was excavated to the very best standards by William Gowland of the Royal School of Mines, South Kensington, whom the the Society of Antiquaries nominated as supervising archaeologist (Gowland 1902).

The restricted admission gives the first clue to actual numbers of visitors, 3,770 paying for entrance between May and October 1901. This figure seems very low, and contrasts sharply with the accounts, so numerous and strongly worded, of large and rude crowds for many years before.

These measures sufficed for the time. Stonehenge itself was now closed to vehicles and to horses (it is easy nowadays to forget that motorcars, for all their unloveliness, at least do not drop steaming excretions where they are parked); visitors were prevented from lighting fires or obviously interfering with the stones. The wire fence was visually inoffensive, though it did break the open landscape; an earlier suggestion had been for a sunken ditch or ha-ha which probably would have given no visual intrusion at all (Wiltshire Archaeological Society 1886).

3. *Return to rural peace* (1918–34)
In 1915 Stonehenge was for sale, auctioned with the rest of the Antrobus estate and bought by Cecil Chubb, a local landowner, who presented it to the nation in 1918. As soon as the war ended, The Office of Works took command, ordering engineer's survey of all the stones, and then straightening and concreting the six sarsen rights whose stability was in doubt.
Responsibility for the archaeology was again entrusted to the Society of Antiquaries, which embarked, not on the minimal excavation required by the works, but on an aimless campaign of wholesale clearance under the direction of Colonel William Hawley.

That disaster apart — for which the Office of Works can scarcely be given principal blame — the policy was admirably modest, and 'anything that could possibly be considered as "smartening up" of this venerable monument carefully avoided' (Peers 1919).

The last road across Stonehenge, an admitted right of way, was finally closed, with local people being granted free admission in recognition of their lost rights.

The surroundings of Stonehenge presented greater problems. Long before 1914, cultivation had crept across the grassland, and a pair of cottages had been built close by. The war saw the downland taken over by the military, and left Stonehenge hemmed in by the rotting remains of aircraft hangars, stores and barracks, a water tower. light railways, and so on. The Office of Works urged the War ministry to have these relics cleared up (Office of Works 1919–20), but the land for the airfield had been requisitioned, not bought, and was therefore returned in 1927 to its pre-war owners, who turned its buildings into a pig-farm' A Stonehenge Café was being put up, and there was talk of colonies of bungalows. The Office of Works was not empowered to buy the land itself instead its permanent secretary, Sir Lionel Earle helped to organize an appeal committee, which by 1930 raised the money to buy 1,500 acres of the surrounding land and, it was thought, to protect Stonehenge for ever by vesting the land in the National Trust. The aerodrome buildings were torn down, and so, in due course, were the cottages, the Stonehenge Café, and various hoardings

Further eyesores remained in the form of the two wooden huts just south of Stonehenge, where Colonel Hawley's finds were left after he stopped digging. Alexander Keiller offered in 1927 to build a Stonehenge Museum for them, on a site a distance to the east, in Stonehenge Bottom, and out of sight. Two designs were offered, and the drawings for one survive; it is hard to tell if its neo-Egyptian style is the one said to be 'possible but not wholly appropriate' or the alternative Utopian and simply produced as an experimental essay in idealism' (Keiller 1927–9). Opposition to a site museum came from B.H. Cunnington of the Devizes museum and from O.G.S. Crawford, who asked, 'Why multiply these wretched little museums which are a plague to the student and not much good to the general public which is generally ignorant of their existence?' (Crawford 1929). The huts were removed, and the finds went mostly to Salisbury museum. There had to be a building of some kind for a ticket-office but it could, thought the Office of Works architect, be slight, made of weathered oak and even deliberately temporary-looking. A below-ground shelter was considered as an alternative, 'but it would always make its presence felt and might appear "clever", and invite more attention than the purely temporary erection' (Office of Works 1929).

One major intrusion survived, the A344 Amesbury to Shrewton road running close by on the north, only a few feet from the Heel Stone. (The Winterbourne Stoke road, the A303 further away to the south, was not then thought a nuisance.) The Office of Works (1933a) pressed for the closure of this road 'which shaves past the Circle so that the Circle itself seems almost submerged by the congestion, vulgarity, speed and noise'. But in this case they were defeated, with the Road Fund declining to pay for the diversion, and worries that an Act of Parliament might be needed to authorize it.

Apart from this setback, the Office of Works had by the mid-1930s achieved its aim of restoring to Stonehenge 'a measure of isolation' (Office of Works 1933b). That was a notable success, when it had been close to submergence under a clutter of building and sprawl, and when the numbers of Visitors, about 20,000 annually just after the First War, were rising. Certainly there are many fond memories (e.g. Fowles & Brukoff 1980: 5) of childhood visits in the 1930s and even in the 1950s, when the stones seemed to stand, free, uncluttered and unsuburban on the open down — in appearance almost as they had been centuries before.

4. *Accommodating the numbers* (1935–75)
Even before the last of the old clutter had gone, the backtracking began. The 1930s was the decade of the baby Austin and booming charabanc, and uncontrolled parking on the road verge by the Heel Stone, the most conspicuous place possible, became a nuisance. So a patch of the National Trust land was leased, and early in 1935 a car-park was made west of Stonehenge and north of the road, where the land drops away. (Pressure for lavatories was resisted: 'after all, the whole Plain is available for the convenience of the public' (Office of Works 1934.)) There were two responses to the car-park. The visitors parked by the Heel Stone as before; and the car-park became a separate focus of its own, proving a good pitch for AA patrols and ice-cream vendors (Office of Works 1935).

In post-war years, the numbers of visitors grew and grew. As the figure reached a quarter-million, then half a million annually, one measure after another was thought necessary. Underground lavatories were dug, the car-park tarmacked and very much enlarged, an entrance tunnel laid under the road with semi-subterranean ticket-office and café; more recently, overflow lavatories and an extra car-park have blossomed, first as temporary now as enduring features. (All these, it may be remembered, stand on land bought by public subscription expressly to prevent cafés and other buildings being put on it.)

Traffic on both roads grew, making the A344 more obnoxious than ever and the A303 increasingly audible and visible. Intermittent vandalism, usually slogans painted on the sarsens, was particularly bad in the early 1960s. Precautions have included a system of 'Vigilante' geophones, underground microphones laid like a minefield once it had been programmed to take no notice of the sound of moles (whose control is also a problem), this proved quite effective. Stonehenge is never left unsupervised now, with two custodians on duty every night of the year.

Inside Stonehenge, drastic measures were taken. Atkinson and Piggott's excavations and the discovery of the prehistoric carvings brought more publicity, and more crowds. The stones which fell in 1797 and 1901 were restored, in part to save them from further damage by scrabbling shoes, and more concrete foundations put in. (Only seven sarsens now stand in original chalk sockets.) The grass in the centre died under the pressure, was reduced to a 'sea of mud' (Ancient Mouments Board 1962: 3), and was replaced with orange gravel over a clinker foundation. It was ugly, abrasive, dusty in dry weather and before long spotted with puddles in wet; but it might be able to take a million pairs of feet. Each of these measures was defensive in character, a small retreat in the face of the relentless growth in numbers.

Over the years, the summer solstice celebrations became larger, more drunkenly rowdy and eventually dangerous. Dr MacGregor Reid's bogus Druids (one of several groups whose connexions with the would-be Druids of the eighteenth-century Romantics, still less with the real Druids of Classical times, are extremely tenuous) had been granted admission by Cecil Chubb. In the 1920s, the Office of Works, after some nasty episodes of forcible entry, ritual cursing of the defending custodian, and accusations of religious intolerance, also gave way and let Dr Reid in. That was a mistake. The precedent was set that a group could acquire special rights over Stonehenge, if it was sufficiently aggressive in demanding them. Gawping at or teasing the white-robed devotees soon became a principal feature of the attractions. From the early 1960s, admission for the solstice dawn has been severely restricted. Only the officially sanctioned band of genuine bogus Druids, the press and Amesbury residents go in, and the ordinary fence is reinforced annually from late May to late June with great barbed-wire entanglements much taller and wider than a man, to ensure nothing goes inside more untoward than the DoE chooses to authorize.

The summer solstice, already a bizarre event (Cutforth 1970, is a restrained account), has become quite surreal since the Stonehenge Free Festival got going about eight years ago. This is now an established annual event, lasting ten days or so over the solstice period and dedicated (in the words of its own publicity) more to 'sex and drugs and rock'n'roll' than to earth mysteries or dreams of Logres. Although unofficial and unlawful, the festival has achieved a *modus vivendi* with the DoE, whose superior fortifications deflect it from Stonehenge proper into an undefended field on National Trust land west of the car-park. The police supervise it from a full-scale temporary Stonehenge Police Station.

5. *Crisis* (1976–)

The petrol shortage of 1973 brought some respite in the growth of numbers, but 1975 — with two-thirds of a million visitors, the usual solstice nonsense, and the first full-scale festival — was a bad year.

It was dawning on the DoE that somewhere along the line their Stonehenge policy might have gone a little wrong. For 1976 the admission charge in summer, when numbers go as high as 7000 per day (Stonehenge Working Party 1979: paragraph 2.8), was raised to 40p as a deliberate discouragement, though it was reduced to only 10p off-season. (It was only a shilling (5p) as late as 1970.) Numbers in 1976 went down marginally, but were up to a new record 815,000 in 1977. For 1978 more drastic measures were taken. The centre was closed entirely and restored to turf. Visitors were kept to a circular path right round the outside of the ditch. The grass there, despite protective matting, quickly turned to mud. The final solution has been to lay a permanent path in green tarmac, which runs inside the ditch but still several metres from the central stones. Special access to the centre is allowed early in the morning, one day a week. For such groups as archaeological students on field trips, and also for all visitors on Tuesdays in the winter, from November to February only. Otherwise it is not possible to see clearly those features — bluestone settings, sarsen masonry-work, prehistoric carvings — that make Stonehenge unique, unless you know exactly what to look for.

The summer solstice ritual continues as before, inside the heaped coils of barbed-wire that look like something from the Battle of the Somme. The festival shows no sign whatever of fading away. It is especially deplored by the National Trust, whose land it occupies, but no action has been taken actively to discourage it. The fear has been voiced (e.g. Hamilton 1978; Atkinson 1978) of the '1 per cent of troublemakers' who may be ready with their brushes and pots of fluorescent paint; if those fears are well founded, Stonehenge is effectively held hostage by the festival in case the authorities do anything to offend.

The DoE, though nominally hostile, makes two concessins to the festival. First, it compensates the National Trust for the damage caused to the crops and fences of the Trust's tenant. Secondly, it allows the festival to take control of the centre of Stonehenge for the solstice afternoon; no attempt is made to discourage climbing about on the stones, which at all other times is strictly forbidden.

For 1983 the DoE decided its barbed wire was 'provocative' to the festival and put up only light-weight crowd barriers. On 21 June about 1000 festival-goers climbed them and occupied the stones at dawn. On the solstice itself (the 22nd), about 1500 again saw no reason to be shut out when the officially approved Druids and pressmen were let in, climbed the barriers and celebrated the sunrise with good humour at the centre of Stonehenge. There was no aggravation, no arrests and no immediate sign of damage, but the DoE's inability to manage midsummer events at Stonehenge was rather publicly underlined.

These general arrangements seem likely to continue, and to provoke more criticism. The growth of facilities goes on gradually also. Arrangements for the Stonehenge garbage give an example. It was only in 1956 that enough rubbish was generated to require organized collection at all; in the 1980s it requires a special enclosure of jumbo-sized bins, which makes its own little eyesore at one end of the car-park.

Is there an alternative?
All in all, the immediate surroundings of Stonehenge are wholly unworthy of it. A leader in *The Times* sums it up: 'To continue to allow this marvellous relic of prehistoric ages to be ruthlessly disfigured and perish inch by inch would be an eternal disgrace to this country'. Those words, written in 1886 to describe the decay of the stones themselves (*The Times* 1886), apply equally to their environment today (FIGURE 1b). There have been decades of piecemeal accommodation to various pressures — from the Druids, from the rising tide of tourists, from the festival — without any long-term strategy or coherent plan of management and containment. Many examples could be given of the curious results that have followed space allows mention of only a few.

As the first experience with the car-park in 1935 showed, the provision of even minimal facilities generates more people and more traffic. According to 1972 figures, 32 per cent of people using its car-park do not go in to see Stonehenge at all (Stonehenge Working Party 1979: Appendix D). The car-park, in fact, has itself become an attraction; it makes a convenient place for long-distance drivers on the A303 to stop for a stroll, a sandwich and the use of a lavatory.

The café and bookstall, squeezed into cramped premises in the underground building, make quite a contrast. The café, let to an energetic private contractor, is open long hours and sells a wide range of refreshments. The bookstall, run by the DoE itself, is often shut and sells a miserably restricted range when it manages to be open. L.V. Grinsell's excellent and very cheap booklet on *The Druids and Stonehenge*, for instance, is not stocked lest considerations of balance might be thought to compel the DoE also to sell publications put out by the bogus Druids.

Perhaps the worst single feature is the insensitive design of the car-park and buildings, which 'recalls that of a motorway pull-in' (Binney 1977). Take the sloping approach to Stonehenge from the entrance tunnel for instance. Part of the astonishment of Stonehenge is in its materials, the great elephant-grey slabs of stone that seem alien in a chalk landscape. But the walls of the sunken path are not made of the local building materials — timber, chalk or flint; they are faced instead with monolithic slabs of rough-cast grey concrete (chosen presumably on the simple grounds of cost), which make a shoddy echo of Stonehenge itself (FIGURE 2).

Certainly, managing Stonehenge presents great problems; there are now more visitors in a single high-summer week than there were in a whole pre-war year. But Stonehenge has survived too many threats in the past to be lightly let go, and examples elsewhere show what might be salvaged. The summit of Snowdon, the highest mountain in Wales, is a tourist focus with striking similarities to Stonehenge. It is a 'honey-pot' attraction everyone wants to visit and has therefore been 'irreversibly popularized'; its facilities were inadequate to cope with the numbers, and failed to match the quality of their surroundings. A consultant's report (Manasseh 1978) for the Countryside Commission made strong and positive recommendations for improvement. The proposed new summit buildings have

a

b

FIGURE 1. a *Approach to stonehenge, Midsummer solstice 1716: barrow and open downland. A shepherd waits by the stones ready to shear the visitors' sixpences.* b *Approach today, off-season: tarmac and portable lavatories. In midsummer the carts spill over the grass, more huttery goes up, and the foreground field is occupied by the Free Festival.*

FIGURE 2. *The present tunnel entrance to Stonehenge: concrete at its grey nastiest. The bookshop, characteristically, is shut.*

proved too expensive, but more modest measures of management and discreet visitor control are successfully going ahead. On Hadrian's Wall, a comparable study is also leading to coherent management plans to spread the impact of visitors.

No such independent study has been made of Stonehenge. In 1976, Peter Lloyd Jones, the head of three-dimensional design at Kingston Polytechnic, proposed on his own initiative a plan for a 'prehistory discovery park' round Stonehenge. It would encourage visitors, as they set out from a new visitor centre well away from Stonehenge, to go instead along trails to other monuments, the barrows, cursus, and so on. The details of his scheme can be questioned; however important archaeologically, these chalk-built monuments are not immediately exciting to look at, and they are very vulnerable to erosion. But it does show how valuable a fresh approach to the whole Stonehenge question might be.

The Stonehenge Working Party
Lady Birk, the minister responsible when the crisis blew up in 1976, promised wide consultation. Alternative schemes were to be exhibited in London and Salisbury for public comment. A Stonehenge Working Party (1979: preface) was set up to 'consider means of improving the setting of Stonehenge and facilities for visitors', with representatives from interested parties. While the DoE went ahead with immediate measures, the Working Party tried to plan for the long term. Its majority report recommended closing the Shrewton road and erasing the present car-park and facilities, as had the Ancient Monuments Board (1997: 9). A new car-park, at least three times the size of the present one, would be made much further away, and there would be fuller facilities for visitors, who would walk up paths from Stonehenge Bottom. This plan, in several variants, was unacceptable to representatives of the district council, whose memorandum of dissent (Stonehenge Working Party 1979: Appendix 0) argued for retention of the Shrewton road and the existing car-park site. Understandably but regrettably, the report did not say whether there should be a future for the festival.

On the central question, the matter of numbers, the working party was cautious. It thought that people 'should not, and probably could not, be deterred' from visiting Stonehenge, by high admission prices or other means (paragraphs 4.1–4.5). Therefore, the new facilities should provide for a further substantial increase in numbers, perhaps 50 per cent over the next decade (though no figure is stated). But it declined to endorse the Department of Transport's belief that parking for 1000 cars should be allowed for (paragraph 4.14).

In short, the working party recommends accommodating the numbers, as before, and hopes they will not drift too high.

An alternative approach, explored by Professor R.J.C. Atkinson and other archaeological members of the working party, takes as its starting-point not the demand but the supply: that is, the maximum number of people who can see Stonehenge properly without harming it. 'Properly' may be taken to mean 'allowed to walk freely on grass among the stones', and the limiting factor is the survival of the turf. The experience of the 1950s suggests it can take at the most 200,000–250,000 visitors annually — or less than a third of the numbers in recent years. There is everything to be said for this policy. Unfortunately it would require such drastic discouragement to keep the numbers down that it is not thought politically practicable.

In any case, by the time the working party submitted its report in 1979, the politicians had moved on. The Conservative government remained silent until the autumn of 1981, when it became known that the report would not be acted upon, because of the expense and the local opposition. It has not even been published, and the consultation that was promised has not taken place. Nevertheless the DoE insists that the report has

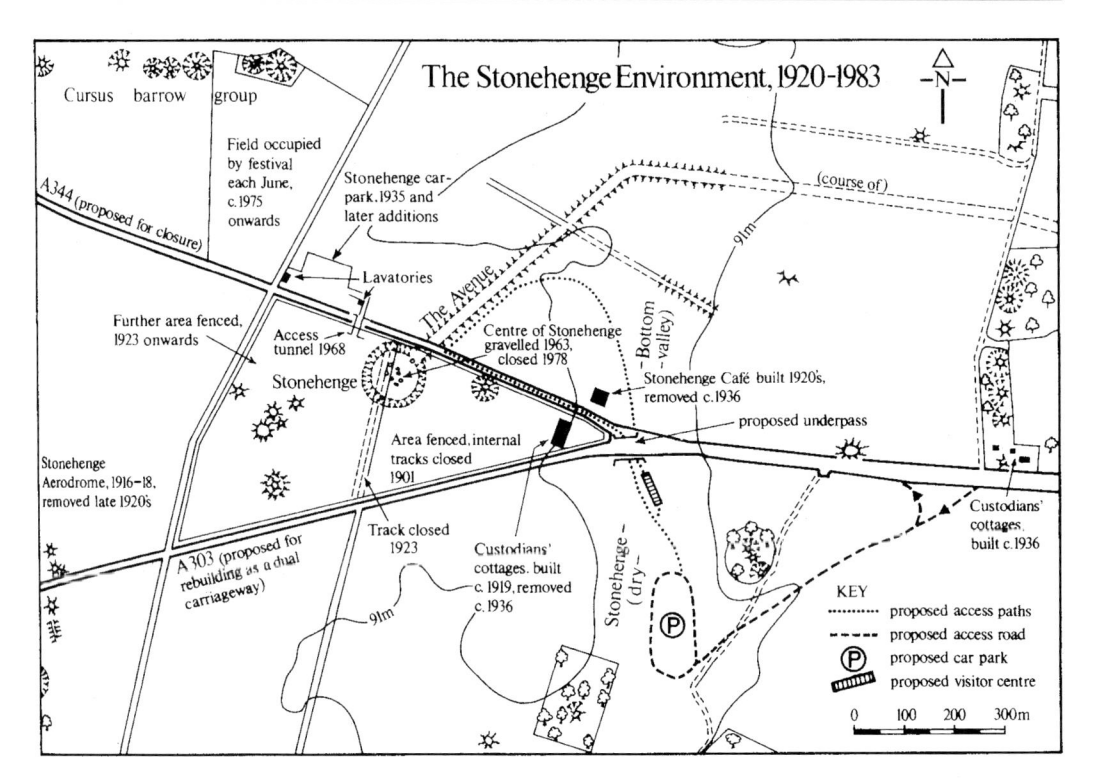

FIGURE 3. *Recent changes in the immediate Stonehenge area, with one of the working party's proposals for new access facilities. The map excludes changes in the more distant landscape such as military buildings on north and east horizons, nor can it show the visual effects of busier roads and changed farming practices.*

not been suppressed, merely that its publication would not be 'cost-effective'. This is a strange claim, since the report is a typed document of less than 50 A4 pages, and one may think that behind it lies a reluctance to tackle head-on and in public the intractable problems presented by the future management of Stonehenge.

There matters rest. As the land round Stonehenge is held inalienably, the National Trust has an effective right of veto over any proposals for change. The DoE has since decided it wants to enlarge the facilities on the existing site. The Trust rightly insists that the present site (chosen in 1935 after no great thought and with only a few parked cars in mind) is far too close to Stonehenge. It is therefore firmly resisting these new DoE proposals, whose existence has not been made public. In the next few months we shall discover if the new organization responsible for ancient monuments will push ahead with the scheme it inherits or if it has other ideas; certainly there should be the promised public consultation. If the facilities are to be improved, they cannot be left 'on the threshold of the temple', which once more should be distanced from 'profane buildings and traffic'. That must mean closing the road by the Heel Stone, and abandoning the present car-park site for one at proper distance, in Stonehenge Bottom or elsewhere. It could also mean an imaginative scheme to show Stonehenge to visitors in the proper context of its ancient landscape, restored to open unfenced downland.

Certainly there is no point in building again and ruining more downland if the result is another ugly, short-term botch. But even with the present facilities, a start can be made. A certain number visitors can be allowed among the stones without unfair discrimination (e.g. by opening the centre for the first hour each day). The bookstall can open longer hours. Non-visitors can be discouraged from using the car-park. The festival can be found a more suitable site. These kinds of measures may not, probably will not, suffice — but they should be tried.

Perhaps no agreed way forward can be found that does not involve intolerable restrictions, expense, danger to the survival of Stonehenge, or archaeological damage. The best long-term answer might, alas, be to steer people instead towards a concrete replica in, say, Longleat safari park. But it would be wrong to acquiesce in the further ruin of its environment, universally agreed to be unworthy of Europe's most famous ancient monument, without really determined efforts to provide it with something better.

References

ANCIENT MONUMENTS BOARD FOR ENGLAND. 1962. *Report for 1961*. London.
   1977. *Report for 1976*. London.
ANTROBUS, E. 1894. Letter to Commissioner of Works in Public Record Office, PRO Work/14 213.
ATKINSON, R.J.C. 1960. *Stonehenge*. Harmondsworth: Penguin.
   1978. Letter, quoted in *Antiquity* 52: 178.
   1979. Appendix II to *Stonehenge* (1979 reprint).
AUBREY, J. 1685. Monumenta Britannica, in W. Long. (ed.): 35.
BINNEY, M. 1977. Stonehenge under siege, *Country Life* 8 September.
BROWNE, H. 1833. *An illustration of Stonehenge and Abury*, 2nd edition. Birmingham: Smiths & Greaves.
CHIPPINDALE, C. 1978. The enclosure of Stonehenge, *Wiltshire Archaeological and Natural History Society Magazine* 70–71: 109–23.
   1983a. *Stonehenge Complete*. London: Thames & Hudson.
   1983b. Stonehenge, General Pitt-Rivers, and the first Ancient Monuments Act, *Archaeological Review from Cambridge* 2: 59–65.
CRAWFORD, O.G.S. 1929. Letter in Public Record Office (PRO) Work/14 489.
CUTFORTH, H. 1970. Stonehenge at midsummer, *Antiquity* 44: 305–7.
DYER, J. 1978. Letter, quoted in *Antiquity* 52: 178.
FOLKERSHEIMER, H. 1562. Letter to Josiah Simler, in H. Robinson (ed.): letter 39.
FOWLES, J. & B. BRUKOFF. 1980. *The enigma of Stonehenge*. London: Cape.
GOWLAND, W. 1902. Recent excavations at Stonehenge, *Archaeologia* 68: 38–119.
HAMILTON, M. 1978. Letter, *The Times*, 21 June.
HARPER, G.C. 1899. *The Exeter road*. London: Chapman & Hall.
HUTCHINSON, H.G. 1914. *The life of Sir John Lubbock*, II. London: Macmillan.
JONES, I. & J. WEBB. 1655. *The most notable antiquity of Great Britain, vulgarly called Stonehenge*. London: Pakeman & Chapman.
KEILLER, A. 1927–9. Letters in PRO Work/14 489.
LE GALLIENNE, R. 1900. *Travels in England*. London: Grant Richards.
LONG, W. 1876. *Stonehenge and its barrows*. Devizes: H.F. & E. Bull. Wiltshire Archaeological and Natural History Magazine 16
MANASSEH, L., & Partners. 1978. *Snowdon summit*. Cheltenham.
OFFICE OF WORKS. 1919–20. Correspondence in PRO Work/14 488.
   1929. Memorandum from Chief Architect in PRO Work/14 489.
   1933a. Memorandum in PRO Work/14 838.
   1933b. Minutes after visit to Stonehenge in PRO Work/14 837.
   1934. Memorandum in PRO Work /14 840.
   1935. Memoranda in PRO Work 14/840.
PEERS, C.H. 1919. Memorandum in. PRO Work/14 485.
PEPYS, S. 1668. Diary, 11 June, in R. Latham & W. Matthews (ed.), 1976. *The diary of Samuel Pepys* IX. Berkeley: University of California Press.
PITT-RIVERS, A. 1893. Report on Stonehenge in PRO WORK/14 213.
PUGH R.A. (ed.). 1947. *Calendar of Antrobus deeds before1625*. Devizes: WANHS.
ROBINSON, H. (ed.). 1845. *The Zurich letters* (2nd series). London.
STONEHENGE WORKING PARTY. 1979. Report to Department of the Environment (unpublished).
STUKELEY, W. 1740. *Stonehenge*. London: Innys & Manby.
The Times. 1886. Editorial, 18 August.
'VACATION RAMBLER'. 1871. Stonehenge, *The Times*, 14 September.
WILTSHIRE ARCHAEOLOGICAL SOCIETY. 1886. Report of deputation to examine into the present state of the stones at Stonehenge, *Wiltshire Archaeological & Natural History Magazine* 23: 102–7.
WOOD, J. 1747. *Choir Gaure*. . . . London.

The Stonehenge we deserve
by GEOFFREY WAINWRIGHT
ANTIQUITY 74 (284), 2000

Introduction

Stonehenge is Britain's greatest prehistoric archaeological monument and one of the most powerful landmarks in the world. It stands at the centre of over 2000 hectares of ancient landscape which contains 196 scheduled monuments — mainly prehistoric burial mounds — and a dense concentration of buried archaeological sites which combine to create a unique cultural landscape of international importance. For England it is a national heritage icon — extensively used in advertising and the media as a readily recognized and accessible image, which conveys a compelling sense of power and mystery. The management of the monument and its setting therefore provides a litmus test for millions of people across the world as to how we care for our heritage. In 1986, Stonehenge, Avebury and its associated sites were inscribed as a single cultural World Heritage Site (WHS) under the UNESCO World Heritage Convention of 1972. The 630 sites on the UNESCO World Heritage List, of which 20 are within the UK and its overseas territories, are internationally recognized for their outstanding universal value. There is an international obligation under the World Heritage Convention for the careful protection and management of these sites and the production of Management Plans which will ensure their survival for future generations.

The UK Government therefore has ultimate responsibility for what happens within the Stonehenge WHS, but exercises that in partnership with others. English Heritage is responsible for the Stones and the five hectares of land immediately surrounding them on behalf of the nation. In 1927, 587 ha of the surrounding land (about a quarter of the WHS) were purchased by the National Trust following a national public appeal. The National Trust recently acquired Countess Farm within the WHS, bringing a further 172 ha within its Stonehenge estate. This land now links Woodhenge near the A345 with Stonehenge *via* King Barrow Ridge, under National Trust ownership. The Ministry of Defence owns Larkhill and its surrounding farmland in the northern part of the WHS and the majority of the WHS is owned by six private owners and is used for farming. At Amesbury, Durrington and along the Woodford Valley, there are a number of private houses within the WHS boundaries. The existing visitor facilities at Stonehenge are operated by English Heritage on land to the northwest of Stonehenge leased from the National Trust. The business provides access to Stonehenge with a car park, small shop, a pedestrian subway under the A344 and light catering facilities.

It will be apparent that a number of Government Departments, statutory bodies, agencies, landowners and tenants have responsibilities and interests which should influence the future management of Stonehenge and the World Heritage Site. They are the Department for Culture, Media and Sport (DCMS), the Department of the Environment, Transport and the Regions (DETR), the Highways Agency, the Ministry of Defence (MOD), the Ministry of Agriculture, Fisheries and Food (MAFF), English Heritage, the National Trust, Wiltshire County Council, Salisbury District Council, Amesbury Town Council, English Nature and the Countryside Agency. Add to these the landowners, local communities and their representatives, the Wiltshire Constabulary and special interest groups and clearly there is a challenge for anyone wishing to channel the energies of such a large and volatile group towards a solution which will reconcile the sometimes conflicting demands of international legislation with local aspirations.

The problems confronting the proper management of Stonehenge and its landscape are well known and have been rightly described by the Public Accounts Committee of the House of Commons as a 'national disgrace'. The present visitor facilities are too small for the existing numbers of visitors to Stonehenge and are too close to the monument. These difficulties are compounded by the large number of motorists and tour coaches who use the free Stonehenge car park as a roadside stop with refreshments and lavatories. Stonehenge is adjacent to the trunk road A303 which cuts through the WHS and carries 26,000 vehicles per day on average — rising to over 40,000 within 10 years. The A344 road runs close to the Stones and separates them from its ceremonial avenue and the inadequate car park. The setting of the monument is therefore marred by the continuous stream of vehicles passing along the A303 and A344. The free car park is a hideous intrusion on the landscape and 833,000 visitors each year trudge through a concrete underpass to reach the monument whilst unknown numbers (?200,000) risk life and limb to rush across the A344 in order to get a free view of the monument and to stroke the Heelstone just inside the wire fence. Although the land owned by the National Trust is largely down to pasture, tracts of the core of the WHS are ploughed annually and important groups of burial mounds survive as fenced conservation ghettos in a sea of arable, where scrub and rodents flourish in an anachronistic display of how such monuments should not be managed.

It is truly a cause for national shame that we have allowed one of the most important prehistoric landscapes in the world to be so degraded.

To rectify this state of affairs presents an enormous challenge given the large number of interested parties and the variety of viewpoints they represent. A solution took 16 years to emerge and involved numerous conferences, hundreds of meetings and many hours of consultation. The objective was relatively straightforward. It was (English Heritage/National Trust 1996):

> To create a setting an environment for Stonehenge appropriate to its status as a World Heritage Site, with the minimum disturbance to the surrounding downland landscape, to the archaeology it contains and the lives of people who live in the area

The route to achieving the simple objective was difficult and placed great strains on the partnerships which were essential to the success of the enterprise. The plan which has emerged will take a decade to implement at a total cost of some £200 million but it contains a degree of unanimity which will ensure its ultimate success despite objections from those who will disagree with some parts of the package. The purpose of this paper is to describe the background, history and solution to what must be the most complex heritage problem yet to be encountered.

Researching the issues

Throughout the development of the proposals the need to document and understand the archaeological remains in the World Heritage Site was given high importance. This began with a study around Stonehenge which was commissioned by English Heritage and published by them in 1990 (Richards 1990). This was followed by a much needed reorganization of the Stonehenge archive and a report on the 20th-century excavations at the monument. This was also commissioned by English Heritage and published in 1995

(Cleal et al. 1995). These publications made it possible to move forward to formulate new programmes of research. To stimulate debate, the Royal Society, British Academy and English Heritage organized a conference entitled 'Science and Stonehenge' which was held at the Royal Society in March 1996 and published in 1997 (Cunliffe & Renfrew 1997). In 1994 the Central Archaeology Service of English Heritage, working in conjunction with the Archaeology Section of Wiltshire County Council, developed a consolidated database and assessment of the recorded archaeology for 135 sq. km around Stonehenge, including the WHS and surrounding areas (Blore et al. 1995). The database and mapped information is maintained on a GIS system by the Central Archaeology Service of English Heritage and is an essential reference document for any project which concerns itself with the cultural heritage of the WHS (Batchelor 1997).

The later history of the landscape is also important and a survey commissioned by English Heritage identified the general military land-use patterns throughout the modern era, within the World Heritage Site and its immediate environs (Wessex Archaeology 1998). The study confirmed that the modern military remains are part of the archaeological record, and that they should be treated as such.

The Visitor Centre

Proposals to improve the condition of Stonehenge and its landscape can be traced back several decades (Chippindale 1983a; 1983b). The current initiative began when English Heritage was established in 1984 and appointed a Study Group to see how matters could be improved. The Study Group produced its report in 1985 (English Heritage 1985) and at the launch of the report the then Chairman of English Heritage, Lord Montagu, announced that the proposals favoured by English Heritage involved the closure of the A344 and the resiting of the Visitor Centre at Larkhill West, about 1 km north of Stonehenge. These plans were developed between 1985 and 1990 and included the appropriate archaeological assessments, negotiations for the assembly of the necessary land and detailed plans for the layout of the site (e.g. Golding 1989).

Outline planning permission for a comprehensive scheme was applied for in May 1991, but the proposals did not find favour locally and in December 1991 the application was turned down by the Planning Committee of Salisbury District Council. An appeal against that decision was lodged. A detailed planning application relating to landscaping works along the line of the A344 and the construction of a new approach road was submitted to Salisbury District Council in September 1992. This application was accompanied by an Environmental Statement (Darvill 1991) which incorporated an extensive archaeological evaluation of the proposed Larkhill Visitor Centre Site and the western approach road corridor which was considered necessary to service it.

In April 1992 Jocelyn Stevens became Chairman of English Heritage and it is largely due to his drive and determination and the emergence of strong political support after the General Election in 1997, in particular from Chris Smith (Secretary of State DCMS) and Lord Whitty (DETR), that a solution has emerged. Both planning applications were withdrawn and Sir Jocelyn took personal charge of a review of all available options including what must be the largest public consultation exercise ever undertaken in respect of a heritage project (English Heritage 1993). The code of practice suggested by ICOMOS were used to guide the assessment of the options (ICOMOS 1991) and particular emphasis placed on the following criteria:
- the Visitor Centre should be on the edge of the World Heritage Site;
- no archaeological damage should result from its construction;
- it must not be seen from Stonehenge;

- the approach to Stonehenge should be dramatic;
- the building should form a gateway to the landscape.

Eight site options were the subject of a public consultation involving the distribution of 100,000 leaflets during the summer of 1993 and each was subjected to an archaeological assessment (Darvill 1997). They were:

1. Countess Road west of the A345
2. Countess Road east of the A345
3. Fargo North, south of Fargo Plantation and north of the A344
4. Fargo South, south of Fargo Plantation and south of the A344
5. Larkhill, south of Durrington Down Farm
6. New King Barrows, north of the A303 on King Barrow Ridge
7. Old King Barrows, north of the Stonehenge Avenue on King Barrow Ridge
8. Strangways, south of Fargo Road at the western end of the Stonehenge Cursus.

As a result of the extensive consultation process four additional sites were added to the list:

9. Stonehenge Bottom
10. Pedigree Stock Farm north of the A303
11. Stonehenge Down
12. A303 Roadline site east of King Barrow Ridge

Following the review, four potential sites for the new Visitor Centre emerged and each was subjected to an archaeological evaluation.

(i) Larkhill was the public's preferred choice but access to the site through MOD land to the north proved too difficult and was strongly opposed on archaeological grounds as it required a new access road and car park to be constructed within the WHS. In November 1997, English Heritage and the National Trust put forward scaled-down proposals for a smaller Visitor Centre at Larkhill with access from the north *via* a new road from the Packway. A meeting convened by the Secretary of State (DCMS) at Amesbury with local authority leaders and other representatives of the local community confirmed local concerns about the traffic impacts associated with the scheme.

(ii) A site on King Barrow Ridge which utilized the foot bed of the A303 and a narrow strip of land immediately south of the present A303 was considered but discarded due to access problems.

(iii) A site at Fargo North, south of Fargo Plantation and north of the A344 was a strong candidate but the archaeological evaluation showed this to be a particularly sensitive site (Wessex Archaeology 1998a) and it would have required substantial development within the WHS. The proposals were presented by the Secretary of State (DCMS) to a meeting of local authority leaders and local community representatives in April 1998. The proposals received widespread local support but were rejected on archaeological and landscape grounds.

(iv) Countess East to the north of the A303 was particularly attractive because of its situation outside the WHS, its apparent low archaeological significance as demonstrated by an evaluation in 1994 (Darvill 1995), and its general availability for development and access. In consequence, the Countess Farm Site was selected as the preferred location for the Visitor Centre and associated facilities. In 1995 and 1996 work progressed with planning a connection between Countess Road East and King Barrow Ridge. Further archaeological assessment was carried out, mainly to identify usable corridors where archaeological remains had previously been disturbed by military works, road and tracks (Reilly *et al.* 1996).

In 1996 a Planning Brief incorporating these proposals was submitted on behalf of English Heritage and the National Trust and was endorsed by both Salisbury District and Wiltshire County Councils. The Brief was prepared as a framework document to guide the development of a Visitor Centre at Countess Road East and the implementation of a major landscape restoration project called the Stonehenge Millennium Park (English Heritage/National Trust 1996). The Stonehenge Millennium Park concept failed due to the rejection of a grant application by the Millennium Commission in July 1997. This rejection caused a review of the project, particularly options at Larkhill in 1997 and Fargo North in 1998. These options were rejected for reasons already given and the Secretary of State (DCMS) confirmed Countess East as the preferred site at a public meeting in Amesbury in September 1998. The Planning Brief for Countess East was amended and updated in 1999 to take into account material changes in circumstances — particularly the A303 improvements announced in July 1998 (see below). This was adopted by Salisbury District Council and Wiltshire County Council as Supplementary Planning Guidance in October and December 1999 (English Heritage/National Trust 1999b).

The highway issues
The A303 Trunk Road cuts across the WHS from east to west and is a strategic link to the southwest, providing an alternative to the M4/M5 between London and the West Country. Towards the end of 1992 the Department of Transport announced that it was considering upgrading the A303 between Amesbury and Berwick Down. In March 1993 the first public consultation was held (Highways Agency 1993) on a number of possible routes which included an on-line scheme (Yellow route) and a southern detour (Grey route) for the eastern section, and two detour options for the western sector (Red and Blue routes). In July 1994 English Heritage and the National Trust jointly organized a one-day international conference in London (English Heritage/National Trust 1994). During the Conference the Minister for Roads and Transport withdrew the Yellow and Grey routes because of their effect on Stonehenge and on land held inalienable by the National Trust.

A planning conference to discuss these issues was held at Amesbury in 1995 (Highways Agency 1995; Wainwright 1996) which supported the objectives of English Heritage and National Trust in seeking restoration of Stonehenge to its landscape through the closure and restoration to downland of the A303 between Stonehenge Cottages and Longbarrow Cross Roads, and the A344 between Stonehenge Bottom and Airman's Corner and the resiting of the present visitor facility (Wilson 1996). The conclusions of the conference also supported in principle the proposal by English Heritage and the National Trust for a 4-km long bored tunnel under the WHS but recognized that the cost of that tunnel at £300 million was far in excess of the funds likely to be available from the current transport budget.

In August 1996 the Department of Transport announced that the long bored tunnel option was too expensive and that it would not be pursuing any of the proposed options for upgrading the A303 in the vicinity of Stonehenge in the near future. In November 1996 the Stonehenge section of the A303 Amesbury to Berwick Down Improvement was withdrawn from the Trunk Road Programme.

From 1997 the new Government reviewed all Trunk Road schemes and strenuous negotions were undertaken with the Highways Agency and DETR to reinstate in the Programme an environmentally acceptable dualling of the A303 near Stonehenge. These discussions with ministerial involvement resulted in the announcement by the DETR in July 1998 that the scheme to dual the A303 from Countess Roundabout and to bypass

Winterbourne Stoke had been included in the Government's Targeted Programme of improvements as an 'exceptional environmental scheme'. At a meeting with local authorities and other interests in Amesbury in September 1998, Chris Smith (DCMS) confirmed that the DETR would contribute two-thirds of the £125-million cost of the A303 road improvements — including the cost of a 2-km cut-and-cover tunnel past Stonehenge — and that the other third will come from heritage sources via the DCMS. DETR Minister, Lord Whitty stated that the A303 scheme would not have been included in the National Road Programme if it had not been for the importance of the heritage issues at stake. The Highways Agency has now completed a public consultation on the preferred route for the Winterbourne Stoke Bypass and the A303. The results of the public consultation, the views of the Highways Agency and the decision of the Secretary of State were announced in June 1999 (Highways Agency 1999). The decision to incorporate the scheme in the new roads programme is an unprecedented commitment by the Government to the nation's heritage. In March 2000 the Highways Agency announced that the design commission for the development of the A303 scheme, including the Winterbourne Stoke Bypass, had been awarded to Mott MacDonald Ltd. This £2·3-million commission will develop the proposals for the road improvement in more detail and will include comprehensive environmental surveys and impact assessment work. The Environmental Statement and a Public Exhibition of more detailed proposals are scheduled for the summer of 2002. A Public Inquiry is likely in 2003 and construction works are programmed to start in 2005.

Stonehenge World Heritage Site Management Plan
As a signatory to the World Heritage Convention (UNESCO 1972), the UK Government has an obligation to provide Management Plans for all of the country's World Heritage Sites. A Management Plan for the Stonehenge WHS was prepared after extensive consultation in 1998 and 1999 and will provide a framework — agreed with all interested parties — within which management decisions can be taken on a whole spectrum of issues over time. It represents the strategic framework within which the Master Plan for Stonehenge (described below) has evolved. Government policy in respect of World Heritage Sites is set out in PPG-15 *Planning and the Historic Environment* (September 1994). This confirms that no additional statutory controls follow from the inscription of a site onto the World Heritage List. Inscription does, however, highlight the outstanding international importance of the site as a key material consideration to be taken into account by local planning authorities in determining planning and listed building consent applications and by the Secretary of State in determining cases on appeal or following call-in.

The Plan was developed through an interactive process co-ordinated by consultants Chris Blandford Associates. The process was overseen by a Working Party chaired by Lady Gass, an English Heritage Commissioner, which represented many organizations and individuals. This group met on 10 occasions during the 12 months that the Plan was in preparation. This included four Topic Discussion Group workshops and a site visit . A consultation draft of the Management Plan was circulated during September and October 1999 and 13,000 leaflets distributed to households in the Stonehenge area. The Plan was finalized in January 2000 and during that month was adopted as Supplementary Planning Guidance by Salisbury District Council and approved by the Secretary of State (DCMS). It was published in April 2000 (Stonehenge World Heritage Site Management Plan).

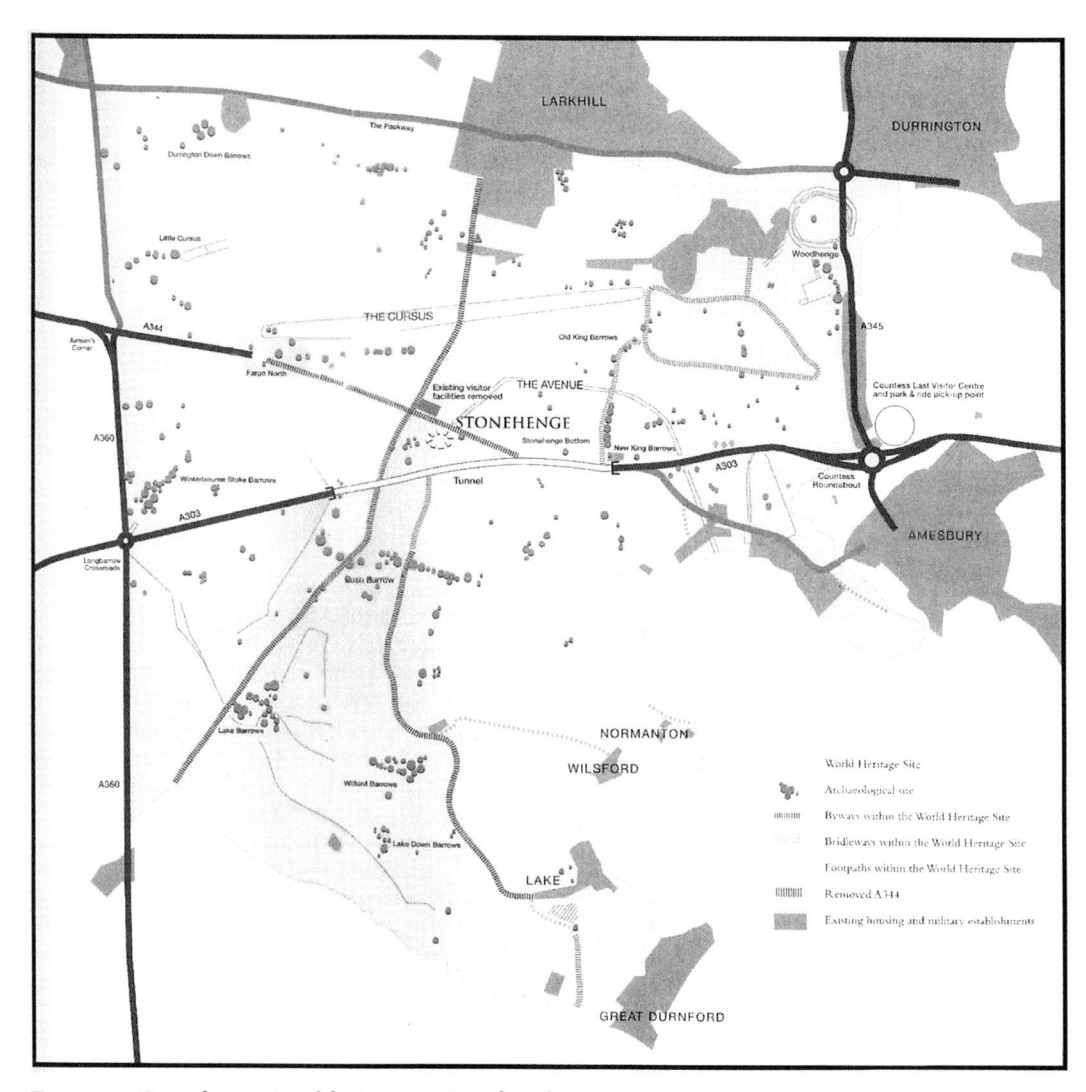

FIGURE 1. *Stonehenge World Heritage Site: key features.*

The Plan provides an assessment of the significance of the whole WHS and evaluates the management issues which affect it. There are 26 substantial objectives embracing a vision for the future; the statutory and policy framework of the area; landscape and heritage conservation; sustainable tourism; sustainable traffic and transportation; and archaeological research. The Plan identifies the need to extend the permanent grassland in the core zone surrounding Stonehenge and to balance the major benefits that would result from the removal of roads and the reunification of the landscape, with the loss of some archaeological remains. The Plan also recognizes the balance which needs to be maintained between the development of tourism in the WHS and its conservation. The Plan recognizes the need for the Visitor Centre to be outside the WHS and the consequent need for a sustainable means of access by visitors to Stonehenge and the wider landscape. The Plan is in essence an ordering of the documentation which the Stonehenge project has produced over the past 16 years into a strategic framework for landscape management and future initiatives which may arise.

Stonehenge: the Master Plan
The Stonehenge Master Plan announced by English Heritage and the National Trust in April 1999 runs in parallel to, but independently of the Management Plan, by which it was influenced. It brings together the long process of consultation and negotiation surrounding the Visitor Centre and Highway issues and was only made possible through the determination of Sir Jocelyn Stevens and the political support it received at ministerial level from several government departments.

The Master Plan provides a coordinated and managed approach to the delivery of the key elements of the A303 road improvements, A344 closure and development of the new Visitor Centre. To confirm their commitment to the Master Plan, the main partners in the project — English Heritage, the National Trust, the Department of the Environment, Transport and the Regions, the Department for Culture, Media and Sport, English Nature, the Highways Agency and Salisbury District and Wiltshire County Councils — issued a joint Mission Statement which was:

> To restore the dignity and isolation of Britain's greatest prehistoric monument, and enable people to enjoy and appreciate it fully by:
> - removing the visual impact and noise of roads and traffic from the vicinity of the Stones;
> - reuniting Stonehenge and its surrounding monuments in their natural chalk downland setting;
> - creating the conditions for improved bio-diversity with flowers, butterflies, birds and insects flourishing;
> - providing improved access, enabling people to roam freely and at no cost throughout the World Heritage Site;
> - building a new world-class Visitor Centre outside the World Heritage Site at Countess East.

The lynch-pin of the Master Plan is the scheme to remove the roads and traffic from within site and sound of Stonehenge. Transport Minister Lord Whitty announced the preferred route for the duelled A303 and the 2-km cut-and-cover tunnel on 25 June 1999. Junction improvements at Long Barrow Crossroads will respect the importance of the archaeology and a full programme of archaeological evaluation and mitigation will be developed in conjunction with the engineering design details. Support for the 2-km cut-and-cover tunnel from partners in the scheme and many archaeology bodies is conditional on the planning, design and implementation strategy bringing substantial environmental improvements to the setting of Stonehenge. It seems probable that following the successful completion of statutory procedures, work will commence in 2005. It is expected that the existing A303 will remain open during construction until the westbound tunnel is completed. Traffic will then be transferred to the west-bound tunnel whilst the east-bound tunnel replaces the existing carriageway. As part of the Master Plan, the Highways Agency and Wiltshire County Council have agreed that the A344 will close when construction work begins on the east-bound tunnel of the A303. These changes are crucial to the future management of Stonehenge and its setting and fundamental to plans for public understanding and enjoyment and access to the landscape.

The second stage of the Master Plan is the management of the landscape within the Stonehenge core zone and in the WHS as a whole, in a way which is appropriate to its international importance and to the lives of people who live and work in the area. The framework for future action is the Management Plan which has identified a set of objectives which are considered necessary for the effective future management of the Site as a whole in the short and long term. The Plan sets out the recommended mechanisms and actions required to achieve these objectives. The roles of relevant agencies, sources of funding and administrative arrangements are reviewed in the Plan and a suggested programme of action is set out. Mechanisms for monitoring and reviewing the Plan are also explored. Work on implementing the Plan must be pursued with vigour and enthusiasm by all the stakeholders to secure the benefits of its vision.

A new Visitor Centre is needed to enhance public understanding and enjoyment of one of the world's great heritage sites. The Management Plan recommends that this should be outside the WHS so as to relieve people and traffic pressure on the monument and its setting so that the current facilities and car park can be removed and grassed over. The new Visitor Centre will be developed to the east of Countess Roundabout, within the guidelines set out in the 1999 Planning Brief prepared by English Heritage and the National Trust and endorsed by Salisbury District and Wiltshire County Councils. A full range of interpretation, education, catering and retail facilities for visitors will be included. Car parking will be located at the new Visitor Centre and the Master Plan proposes that visitors will be transported to a drop-off point at Fargo North. The Management Plan recognizes the benefits of a drop-off point at King Barrow Ridge where the best views of the Stonehenge bowl may be obtained and the Stones are 20 minutes' walk away. For elderly and disabled people transport to Fargo North could be made available, from where vehicles would take them along the grassed-over footprint of the A344 to the Stones. Anyone who wishes to walk from the Visitor Centre, or into the WHS from another direction, will be encouraged to do so without charge. It will be clear from the concept that visitors will be offered a completely different experience from that currently on offer. The nature of the experience at the Visitor Centre will be vastly improved but in order to reach the Stones a 20-minute walk will be necessary. This provides an opportunity to diversify visitor activity within the World Heritage Site and dependent on the numbers of those who wish to walk to Stones it may be possible to allow appropriately supervised access to them once more.

Conclusion

At last, after so many years of debate, the Master Plan and its companion Management Plan provide a framework for action. The defining moment in the story was the decision by the DETR to incorporate the Stonehenge A303 road scheme into their roads programme and to route it underground where it passes through the Stonehenge core zone. Such co-ordination between Government Departments would have been unthinkable in the recent past and the political support for the project has been essential to its success. The partnership between government, national bodies, local authorities and the resident population inevitably created tensions but was essential to the ultimate success of the enterprise. We must now seize this opportunity and bring the plans to reality so that by the end of the decade we will truly have the Stonehenge we deserve.

References
BATCHELOR, D. 1997. Mapping the Stonehenge World Heritage Site, in Cunliffe & Renfrew (ed.).
BLORE, F., M. HITCHEN & J. VALLENDER. 1995a. *Archaeological assessment of the Stonehenge World Heritage Site and its surrounding landscape.* English Heritage Central Archaeology Service.
BLORE, F., M. HITCHEN & R. CANHAM. 1995b. *Appendix B. Gazetteer of survey and evaluation work undertaken within the*

Stonehenge World Heritage Site and its surrounding landscape. English Heritage Central Archaeology Service.
BLORE, F., M. HITCHEN, R. CANHAM & V. GRIFFEN. 1995c. *Appendix A. Gazetteer of the recorded archaeology within the Stonehenge World Heritage Site and its surrounding landscape*. English Heritage Central Archaeology Service.
CHIPPINDALE, C. 1993a. *Stonehenge Complete*. London: Thames & Hudson.
    1983b. What future for Stonehenge? *Antiquity* 57: 172–80.
CLEAL, R.M.J., K.E. WALKER & R. MONTAGUE. 1995. *Stonehenge in its landscape. Twentieth century excavations*. English Heritage.
CUNLIFFE, B. & C. RENFREW (ed.). 1997. *Science and Stonehenge*. Oxford: Oxford University Press. *Proceedings of the British Academy* 92.
DARVILL, T.C. (ed.). 1991. *Stonehenge conservation and management project: Environmental statement*. London: Debenham, Tewson & Chinnocks.
    1995. *Stonehenge visitor centre, Wiltshire, Countess Road and King Barrow Ridge Site: Field evaluations*. London: DTZ Debenham Thorpe & Bournemouth: Timothy Darvill Archaeological Consultants.
    1997. *Stonehenge conservation and management programme: a summary of archaeological assessments and field evaluations undertaken 1990–1996*. London. English Heritage.
ENGLISH HERITAGE. 1985. *The future of Stonehenge*. London: English Heritage.
    1993. *Stonehenge: the present, the future*. London: English Heritage.
ENGLISH HERITAGE/NATIONAL TRUST. 1994. *Stonehenge: the great debate*. Conference Papers, London 8 July 1994.
    1996. *The Stonehenge millennium park and visitor complex. Planning Brief*. London: DTZ Debenham Thorpe.
    1999a. *Stonehenge — the Master Plan*. London: English Heritage/National Trust.
    1999b. *A new Visitor Centre for Stonehenge at Countess Road East, Amesbury. Planning Brief*. London: DTZ Pieda Consulting.
GOLDING, F.N. 1989. Stonehenge past and present, in H. Cleere (ed.), *Archaeological heritage management in the modern world*: 256–71. London: Unwin Hyman.
HIGHWAYS AGENCY. 1993. *Trunk road improvement scheme: A303 trunk road Amesbury–Berwick Down*. (Leaflet circulated in March 1993 for first public consultation.)
    1995. *Trunk Road improvement scheme: A303 trunk road Amesbury–Berwick Down*. (Leaflet circulated for the Planning Conference held in September 1995).
    1999. *A303 Stonehenge (incorporating the Winterbourne Stoke Bypass): Preferred route announcement June 1999*.
HALCROW. 1998. *Review of English Heritage 2KM tunnel and comparative options*. Highways Agency.
ICOMOS. 1991. *Management of World Heritage Sites Seminar Papers*. London: ICOMOS.
POST. 1997. *Tunnel Vision? The future role of tunnels in transport infrastructure*. London: Parliamentary Office of Science & Technology.
RICHARDS, J. 1990. The Stonehenge environs project. London: English Heritage.
REILLY, S., N. BURTON, T. DARVILL & J. TIMBY. 1996. *Stonehenge World Heritage Site, Wiltshire. Countess Road to King Barrow Ridge — proposed visitor transportation routes; Archaeological assessment*. English Heritage Central Archaeology Service.
STONEHENGE 2000. *World Heritage Site Management Plan*.
WAINWRIGHT, G.J. 1996. Stonehenge saved? *Antiquity* 70: 9–12.
WESSEX ARCHAEOLOGY. 1998a. *Stonehenge Military Installations. A desk-based study*. Report reference 44411.
WESSEX ARCHAEOLOGY. 1998b. *Stonehenge Visitor Centre, Fargo North, Wiltshire Stoke: archaeological evaluation*. Report reference 45044.03.
WILSON, R. 1996. *A303 trunk road Amesbury to Berwick Down*. Planning Conference. Chairman's report.

Appendix: the tunnel

Finding a solution to the problems of Stonehenge is a priority for the Government, English Heritage and the National Trust. The number of conflicting interests impacting upon the World Heritage Site have made the decisions and negotiations very difficult and compromises have been necessary. In the area of cultural heritage the most difficult compromise negotiated by the principal partners was the £125-million scheme which will put the A303 in a cut-and-cover tunnel 2 km long under the Stonehenge Bowl, out of sight and sound of Stonehenge.

Roads and road traffic have long had serious impact on the World Heritage Site. In particular, the A303 trunk road and A344 county road are highly visible routes that cut through the heart of the World Heritage Site landscape and adversely impact on the character of the immediate setting and public enjoyment of the Stones themselves. The strategy put forward in the Management Plan to achieve objective 23 (reduction of traffic movements and congestion within the World Heritage Site, improve safety and enhance the historic environment) includes:

> Placing the A303 (T) in a tunnel, closure of the A344 and related restoration schemes within the Stonehenge 'Bowl', including the removal of the A344 in the longer term. Although tunnelling may inevitably have some detrimental effect on existing archaeology along the route corridor of the A303 (T), this should be balanced against the major benefits for the World Heritage Site which would result (para 4.6.4)

These benefits include the reunification of the landscape in the Stonehenge Bowl which together with the related and dependant closure of the A344 will give the public freedom to roam within the prehistoric landscape; the reduction of the impact of the visual, noise and air pollution around the Stones and the provision of safer public access to the Stones and their immediate environs. The archaeological compromise resides in the partial or total destruction of 16 plough-damaged archaeological sites and find-spots (including four scheduled sites) that the cut-and-cover tunnel will entail. The Environmental Impact Assessment and detailed design will attempt to reduce this impact still further and the scheme will be the subject of a Public Inquiry based on a full assessment of all aspects of the scheme. Nevertheless, the advocates of the 2-km cut-and-cover tunnel are firmly of the view that the advantages to be derived from the scheme are such as to justify the damage to the cultural heritage. In keeping with the principles of sustainability one form of environmental capital will have been substituted for another with greater benefits to the landscape as a whole.

At this stage in the debate there are advocates of a 4-km bored tunnel across the full width of the World Heritage Site which would add £170 million to the £125 million which the Government is committed to invest in the scheme. Although superficially attractive — if the finance could be found — a long bored tunnel would have its own adverse effects. There would be an adverse impact on the local water table as a result of dewatering during construction. Unlike the 2-km tunnel, the 4-km tunnel would require ventilation shafts with forced ventilation which would impact both visually and audibly on the World Heritage Site. The greater depth of the tunnel would require much greater excavation at the two portals which would be on the eastern and western edges of the World Heritage Site, with greater visual impact and — particularly on the western edge at Long Barrow Crossroads — greater archaeological impact (Halcrow 1998). Great care will need to be taken at the design state of the preferred option and the Public Inquiry — probably in 2003 — will be hotly contested.

3 Circles and rings; posts and stones
by TIMOTHY DARVILL & CAROLINE MALONE

SINCE THE PROPOSAL to classify archaeological objects and structures in terms of the material used in their production emerged through the work of Christian Thomsen in early 19th-century Denmark (Trigger 1989: 78), the archaeological records of many periods have been portrayed and described in prejudicial, sometimes confusing, and often inappropriate ways. Nowhere is this more apparent than in the way that timber and stone appear to have been used interchangeably in the construction of many Neolithic monuments in the British Isles, yet archaeological classifications tend to sub-divide rather than join together: split rather than lump. As stressed by many scholars, especially Richard Atkinson, Stonehenge is the stone version of the timber building that it pretends to be (Atkinson 1956: 176). The timber-built tombs, circles, alignments and palisade enclosures that competed with their stone counterparts across the Neolithic and Bronze Age landscape are just as significant. It is a fact that the former are easy to overlook; Neolithic people were builders in wood as well as stone of some very complex and sophisticated constructions.

The selection of articles in this section serve to challenge established notions about prehistoric 'megalithic' sites by adding what should perhaps be called 'megaxylo' sites. Papers published in ANTIQUITY over the years have assisted in our growing appreciation of prehistoric multi-phased and multi-material monuments. This recognition is now so well established, that were potential prehistoric ceremonial monuments — be they tombs or circles or henges — routinely excavated (which by and large they are not), then the project design would identify as a key objective the search for, and careful recording of, every phase of construction regardless of the materials employed, and may well identify as a special quest the search for the timber phases.

Stonehenge and Avebury were considered in detail in Section 2, but ANTIQUITY has presented papers, notes and observations on many other stone circles and their timber relatives over the decades. In the first volume a classic paper by Maud and Basil Cunnington entitled 'Prehistoric timber circles' upset many preconceptions (Cunnington & Cunnington 1927). In this, the two doyens of Wiltshire archaeology reported their findings at Woodhenge, which had come to light only the previous year in 1926 (Insall 1927). Although there would be more to explore and explain later on, this paper was revolutionary in showing how timber structures preceded stone structures and in offering a new vision of the components hidden under megalithic monuments. Within a few years, the Cunningtons had tackled the Sanctuary at Avebury (pursuing Stukeley's original records of the 1720s (Cunnington 1931), and William Hawley was still struggling to understand Stonehenge after five seasons of work there (1928). At both sites, timber structures were seen to pre-date stone structures. Although these findings were not published in ANTIQUITY, Keiller and Piggott's work on the Avenue that connected the Avebury henge with the Sanctuary provided a link to these developments (Keiller & Piggott 1936) and a contribution to the wider debate. In East Anglia, Grahame Clark was exploring the 'Norwich Woodhenge' as it was dubbed in ANTIQUITY, a double-ditched enclosure with a central timber setting (Clark 1935). Twelve years after Woodhenge was discovered, Stuart and Margaret Piggott added to the growing understanding of timber and stone monument associations at ceremonial monuments with their paper 'Stone and earth circles in

Dorset' (Piggott & Piggott 1939). The piece was a systematic report, suggesting possibilities and illustrating how the topography of the monuments was potentially significant. The paper was illustrated with engaging plans, but cast around desperately for a chronology using Grooved Ware pottery in the absence of excavation or scientific dating. For example (Piggott & Piggott 1939: 142):

> Whatever may be the absolute dating, there seems every likelihood that the stone and earth circles represent distinct allied strains, and that the series cannot be earlier than the Early Bronze Age in inception, although their use and possibly their construction may last into the Middle and even into the Late Bronze Age.

The Piggotts' paper, when added to the work of the Cunningtons (Cunnington 1929; 1931) and of Grahame Clark (Clark 1935; 1936) showed that there were free-standing stone circles, free-standing timber circles, stone circles enclosed by earthworks, timber circles enclosed by a earthworks, and, most important of all, where a succession could be established stratigraphically, timber structures were generally replaced by stone structures.

By the late 1940s something of the multi-phase nature of many Neolithic ceremonial sites was being well recognized. One site which stands out as critical to the development of this thinking is Cairnpapple Hill, Lothian, in southeastern Scotland. It had come to notice through work by Gordon Childe, and was excavated by Stuart Piggott in 1949. His report in ANTIQUITY of the same year (Piggott 1949) is reproduced here, for it is a classic exposition of structural succession and complexity. Piggott's final report on the site was published a few years later (Piggott 1950), but it is a testament to the quality of the work that various reinterpretations have subsequently been possible (Barclay 1999). The sequence includes Neolithic pits, timber and stone circles, a henge, Bronze Age burials and later disturbances. Cairnpapple now has parallels with North Mains (Barclay 1983) and Balfarg in Scotland (Mercer 1981; Barclay & Russell-White 1993), but in 1949 it proved to be an important stimulus to the continuing development of study into multi-phased monuments.

Not all timber structures forming part of later Neolithic monuments were replaced by stone structures. In some cases several phases of timber structure on the same spot came to light, as with the structures found inside the massive henge-enclosure of Durrington Walls, Wiltshire (originally described by O.G.S. Crawford (1929) in an early volume of ANTIQUITY). Extensive open-area excavations that were as innovative as they were controversial took place in 1966–68 in advance of realigning a major road. Directed by Geoffrey Wainwright, the initial interim report is reproduced here (Wainwright 1968; see also Wainwright (2000: 913) for personal reminiscences on the background). Two large timber structures, both multi-phase, were found inside along the new road-line together with a midden, fence-lines, and a range of other smaller features (Wainwright & Longworth 1971). What it showed was the potential for exploring these vast sites on a large scale.

The later 1960s and 1970s were a critical period in the development of excavation technique, and a number of important later Neolithic monuments were investigated through large-scale open area excavation; several were reported in ANTIQUITY. At Llandegai in North Wales, Chris Houlder excavated a small ceremonial complex on a gravel terrace between 1966 and 1967 (Houlder 1967; 1968). The story of its discovery and loss is a familiar one. Aerial photography by Kenneth St Joseph in 1960 located the site and recorded it as a series of remarkably clear cropmarks (St Joseph 1961: 264-5). With the expansion of settlement on the coastal plain during the mid 1960s the area was given over to industrial uses and the site was excavated as a rescue operation in advance of new factories being constructed. The excavations revealed two different kinds of henge, a mini-henge, a cursus, and various ring-ditches and burials. Much the same story can be seen elsewhere: at Maxey near Peterborough, for example, where gravel extraction revealed two henge monuments and a cursus. Two decorated antler objects and a painted rib of a deer were found in the fills of the ditches of the henges (Simpson 1967). Maiden's Grave, East Riding, was another henge discovered through aerial photography in an area well-known for Neolithic monuments, sampled through excavated by the East Riding Archaeological Society and Hymers College students in spring 1964 (McInnes 1964). More recently, Alex Gibson reported on a series of timber circles and related monuments at Sarn-y-Bryn Caled in Mid Wales, a paper reproduced here, as it shows what can be achieved through combining the opportunities provided by modern rescue excavation with a research interest in the problem of timber circles (Gibson 1992; and see Gibson 1994 for full report). The details from this site offered opportunities to explore the nature of the timber superstructures, and a curiously 'Stonehenge-like' monument emerged. Various reconstructions were attempted on the site itself at the conclusion of the excavation, while a more lasting version has been built at the Welsh Folk Museum at St Fagans on the west side of Cardiff.

Ceremonial sites that include stone and timber settings have also been reported fromIreland, most notably at Ballynhatty, where Barry Hartwell investigated an extraordinary series of timber circles and alignments that clustered close to the Giant's Circle henge with the remains of what appears to be a small passage-grave in the centre. His report is reproduced here (Hartwell 2002).

In some coastal areas erosion and changing sea-levels make the recognition of individual monuments and whole complexes much more difficult. In the Isles of Scilly, much of the lower ground of what was once an extensive land-mass is now drowned, and stone alignments and related structures can be seen part-submerged (Crawford 1927; Fowler & Thomas 1979). The same applies on the other side of the English Channel where the stone circles at Er Lanic in Brittany are now partly submerged (Crawford 1927: plate I).

Discovery made through aerial photography is an important theme that crops up time after time with reference to the sites already discussed, and a number of photographs published in the 50 'Air reconnaissance: recent results' reported by Kenneth St Joseph between 1964 and 1980 mark the discovery of important unrecorded later Neolithic and early Bronze Age sites. The re-examination of familiar sites can also be important, as illustrated by the work of Graham Soffe and Tom Clare for the stone circles of Long Meg and her Daughters in Cumbria (Soffe & Clare 1988; cf. Crawford 1934). Their paper is reproduced here because it reports an unsuspected (and still unexcavated) ditched enclosure adjacent to, and probably pre-dating, the main stone circle on the site. Another familiar landscape that continues to spring surprises is around Avebury in Wiltshire. Here, in the valley of the River Kennet and within sight of Silbury Hill, West Kennet, and The Sanctuary, Alasdair Whittle followed up the hints recorded in pipeline watching briefs at West Kennet to reveal a wholly unsuspected series of massive palisade enclosures. His initial report is reproduced here because it shows how original research can open up new fields of inquiry and define classes of monument that had previously been poorly known (Whittle 1991; and see Whittle 1997 for the main report on the work). Further south, the construction of the Dorchester Bypass, Dorset, provided the opportunity to examine a transect through land to the west of Mount Pleasant, an area with a high density of later Neolithic monuments. Here, in the garden of Flagstones House, part of a circuit of interrupted ditch very similar in size and appearance to the earthwork enclosure at Stonehenge, Wiltshire, came to light (Woodward 1988). The remainder of the monument lies in the garden of the adjacent house which is Max Gate, formerly home to Thomas Hardy. On the walls of the excavated portions of the enclosure ditch were four pictograms.

Fieldwork and aerial photography are important, but excavation is really a necessary part of understanding these stone and timber monuments by testing what extensive survey suggests. As Grahame Clark remarked with reference to his work at Arminghall: 'The spade, like the surgeon's knife, serves increasingly to confirm diagnosis' (Clark 1935: 465). One recent example of this is represented by the recumbent stone circles of northeast Scotland. For decades little has really been known about the date and relationships of these structures. Excavations by Richard Bradley at the Tomnaverie stone circle show that the ring of stones was built on top of an existing rubble bank which itself surrounded a low cairn with internal radial divisions (Bradley 2000). Like so many later Neolithic ceremonial monuments, they developed their ultimate appearance over a long period of time with many stages of addition and re-modelling. It seems quite likely that those involved in their initial construction had no idea of how the site would eventually look.

Simple observation and the revisitation of early records and archives is another major source for new insights into megalithic monuments especially. Many stone monuments were the subject of antiquarian speculation and record long before the era of ANTIQUITY. An entire section could have been filled here with papers dealing with this rich source of material, which at times has contained important, and now lost, hints of structural components of the sites. As the recently published paper on Carnac shows (Roughley *et al.* 2002), new survey, old records and careful observation can reveal much about well-known megaliths, even examples as well studied as Carnac. It is republished here, and shows what could be done at many other sites that have antiquarian records. The revelation that even visible monuments have much about them to discover has periodically reminded the readers of ANTIQUITY of the hidden potential. In 1954 O.G.S. Crawford reported the 'discovery' of the famous carved axes at Stonehenge (Crawford 1954), while more recently Chris Scarre and Paul Raux described newly discovered decoration on a well-known menhir at La Bretellière, Maine-et-Loire, Brittany (Scarre & Raux 2000), a repeat of the situation experienced by Aubrey Burl nearly 30 years earlier at another Breton menhir near St-Samson-sur-Rance (Burl 1986).

The excavations at Cairnpapple Hill, West Lothian 1947–8
by STUART PIGGOTT
ANTIQUITY 23 (89), 1949

IN ANTIQUITY (1948: 35), a brief account was given of the first season's work on a Bronze Age sanctuary and burial site on Cairnpapple Hill, near Torphichen in West Lothian. With the co-operation of the Ancient Monuments Department of the Ministry of Works, excavations were continued in the summer of 1948. The site was completely stripped, and revealed a complex series of structures indicated by the sockets of once-standing stones or by stones still extant. It will be laid out and conserved by the Department as an Ancient Monument under guardianship. The following account of the main results of the 1947–8 excavations is intended as a preliminary to the full excavation report, which will appear in due course in the *Proceedings* of the Society of Antiquaries of Scotland, who financed the first season's work.

Cairnpapple Hill, the summit of which is within the 1000 feet contour, is a part of the Bathgate Hills, which form a compact block of high land between the main road to Stirling on the north and from Glasgow to Edinburgh on the south. On the summit, the site before excavation was chiefly distinguished by the grass-grown cairn which gives its name to the hill, but most maps and the earlier antiquarian literature indicated a fort on the same site. Field-work in 1946 had shown that the cairn stood eccentrically within a low roughly circular earthwork (the 'fort') which on surface showing was almost certainly a member of the 'Henge Monument' class of structure. The site was confused by an octagonal turf dyke which had been made round the cairn in the late 18th or early 19th century to enclose a plantation of trees, now vanished.

The excavations in 1947 showed that the surface survey did indeed represent the actual state of affairs, and that a Henge consisting of an external bank and internal rock-cut ditch, surrounding a circle of stone-holes, was overlaid by a later cairn set within the area, but west of its approximate centre. It was therefore clear that the further excavation would involve two separate problems — the stripping of the whole area of the Henge within its ditch, and the complete excavation of the large cairn which, though robbed of stones in many places, seemed essentially intact. Both operations were carried out in 1948, and the site was found to contain further complexities of structure, involving in all at least five phases of ritual or burial performances on the hill-top. Fortunately the relation of one phase to another was in almost every instance stratigraphically fixed, and although small finds were few, they served to date the structures and to give a coherent chronological framework. The accompanying plan (FIGURE 1) shows these features as finally revealed.

Phase I

The first monument erected on the site appears to have consisted of an irregular arc of standing stones, facing west and with a chord of about 55 feet. In or against all but one of the seven stone-holes were deposits of cremated human bone, and five additional similar deposits were found in the immediate area of the arc, two carrying on its line west-

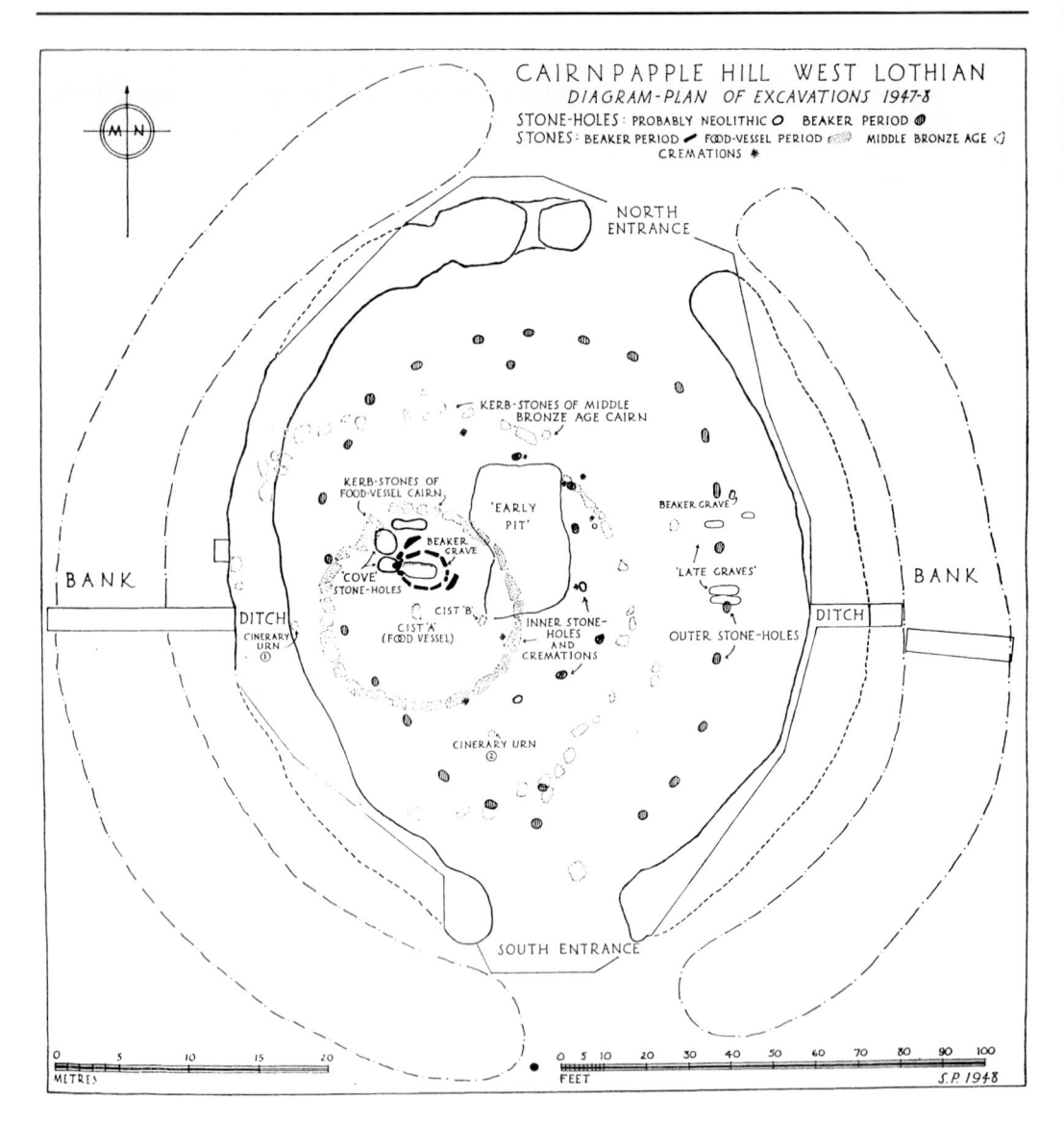

FIGURE 1.

ward at the north and south ends. No stones remained standing or identifiable, and stratigraphically the arc could be dated only by the fact that the stone-holes were beneath a late Middle Bronze Age enlargement of the main cairn: two cremations were however overlaid by the earlier phase of the cairn, of Food Vessel date.

By analogy, however, stone-holes with cremations in or by them should belong to the class of monuments represented by those recently excavated near Dorchester-on-Thames (with wooden uprights) and the first phase of Stonehenge (ditch, bank, Aubrey Holes and cremation-cemetery). With one of the Cairnpapple cremations was a broken bone pin of a type exactly matched at Stonehenge and Dorchester, and in several late Neolithic contexts elsewhere. There is good reason for thinking that the Dorchester sites, and Stonehenge I, are of late Neolithic date and affiliations, and to this period I would assign the Cairnpapple arc and its cremations. On the old ground surface under the Food Vessel cairn were found two pieces of polished stone axes, petrographically identified as being products of the Graig Lwyd and the Langdale Pike axe-factories respectively, and a sherd of Western Neolithic pottery, while another similar sherd came from the filling of a Beaker grave nearby — all these might plausibly be connected with Cairnpapple Phase I. There is no evidence when the stones were removed from the stone-holes, save that this had taken place, and the holes had become filled up, before the end of the Middle Bronze Age.

Opposite the open end of the arc, though not quite central to it, were three huge stone-holes which had become deprived of their stones and filled up by the time the Food Vessel cairn was built. Furthermore, the southernmost of these stone-holes had been re-used for a smaller stone than that for which it had been dug, forming the end-stone of a setting round a rock-cut grave of Beaker date. The setting of three large stones, then, must be pre-Beaker in date, and so likely to be contemporary with the arc. They can only be interpreted as having held the stones of what Stukeley called a 'Cove', and for which no alternative name has ever been put forward. Such 'coves' exist within the North Inner Circle at Avebury and (freestanding, as one assumes that at Cairnpapple to have been) at Stanton Drew in Somerset. It is more than probable that there was a similar structure within the Arbor Low Henge, now represented by fallen stones.

Phase I at Cairnpapple then seems to have consisted of a Cove of three large standing stones, facing east, and an Arc of smaller stones with the open end towards the Cove and the west. Deposits of cremated human bones had been made in and around the area of the arc. The date of this phase should be pre-Beaker, and is likely to have late Neolithic connexions.

Phase II

Here, fortunately, the evidence is clearer and the structures less unusual, though nevertheless there are some surprising features. The main elements of the phase are the bank, ditch and stone-holes of a Henge Monument very similar to Arbor Low. The bank measures 200 feet crest-to-crest on its east–west diameter, and within it is a quarry-ditch separated from it by a marked berm. The ditch is broken by two entrances, roughly north and south and 30 feet wide, and encloses an oval area 145 by 125 feet. It is irregularly dug in the rotted rock subsoil and at the time of excavation was silted up nearly level.

Within the area enclosed by this ditch was an oval setting of standing stones, represented by stone-holes with packing-blocks in most instances. The oval measures 115 by 92 feet and consists of 24 stone-holes forming the main setting, with two 'inliers' to north and south, making up 26 stones in all. The spacing between stones is not quite regular, but averages about 14 feet, and although the stones continue in even spacing across the northern entrance through the ditch, at the south there is a gap of 25 feet constituting an entrance to the stone setting nearly opposite that in the ditch. There was no evidence (in the form of stone chips, etc.) to suggest that the stones had been destroyed in or near the stone-holes, but they had been bodily removed.

Against one of these stone-holes on the east was a rock-cut grave for a crouched inhumation, completely destroyed by the acid soil, but accompanied by a surviving beaker of class C. No other graves were found associated with the stone-holes, but scraps of undecorated Beaker pottery were found in the silt of the ditch on the west.

Within the Henge area to the west, however, was found a remarkable burial of Beaker date (FIGURE 2). In the southernmost of the three stone-holes of the Cove an upright

FIGURE 2. *Cairnpapple Hill: Beaker grave with stone setting of Phase II, incorporated within Food Vessel cairn of Phase III.*

stone, nearly eight feet high, had been set in such a way as to occupy only the easternmost part of the large hole: there were no packing blocks and the hole was filled with rubble only. This stone formed the westernmost (and by far the largest) member of an oval setting 11 by 9 feet, the other stones being set up on or just in the old surface, and enclosing a large grave 7 by 4 feet dug in the rock. Outside the oval setting three stones appeared to have formed part of an outer ring. The whole of these features had been incorporated within the Food Vessel cairn, which had originally covered even the standing stone, though at the time of excavation the top of this projected through the robbed cairn surface.

In the grave was found evidence of an inhumation at full length. The body was represented only by a slight staining on the rock floor of the grave, and by the fragmentary remains of the enamel crowns of the teeth 5 feet 6 inches from the standing stone, which must have stood at the foot of the burial. These teeth were found under, and partly embedded in, an area of carbonized oak wood about 8 inches across and three-quarters of an inch thick, which must have been lying over the face of the corpse. On the north side of the grave were the broken remains of two beakers, one at the foot of class C and the other (of class A) above the position assumed for the head of the interment. Between them, along the side of the grave, lay the carbonized remains of a large oaken object, perhaps a club, 3 feet 6 inches long, expanding to a width of nearly one foot at the upper end. A layer of carbonized oak wood was also found over the beaker at the foot of the grave.

The whole burial is very remarkable: the full-length inhumation, the two beakers and the wooden objects all being unusual features. The wood over the face is even more curious and difficult to explain, but one cannot wholly dismiss the possibility that it represents the remains of a wooden mask worn over the features of the deceased. Such an elaborate burial within the area of the Henge, and against the site of the former Cove, can hardly be classed as anything but ritual in secondary, if not primary, intention. So far as the Henge can be claimed to have a ritual or liturgical centre, this burial must occupy the most likely position for such a focus.

It seems clear that the grave and its oval setting with tall foot-stone must have been incorporated within a small cairn as a part of its original structure. The setting could not have stood free without some support and it could not have taken the thrust of a small cairn within its circumference, but the two larger stones outside the oval setting may well have formed part of such a kerb. Direct evidence of the former presence of such a mound should have been visible in section within the later Food Vessel cairn, but by an unfortunate chance that part of the cairn had been heavily robbed, and such stratification as remained was confused and disturbed.

Eastwards of this grave was a large shallow pit dug in the rock to a general depth of not more than a foot, but going down into oval scoops up to two feet deep in three places. This seems only to be explained as a quarry: the filling showed that it had been left open to silt naturally from the outer edges, and when the cairn was built partly over this pit in Food Vessel times, it was deliberately filled up level for the required distance. Two scraps of undecorated Beaker in the silt show the pit to be approximately of this date, and one can only tentatively explain it as the quarry from which came the rubble to make the small cairn over the Beaker grave and its stone setting just described.

To sum up: Phase II saw the building of a Henge Monument similar in many respects to that of Arbor Low, enclosing the older Arc and Cove. There is no evidence to show whether the Arc stones were still allowed to stand, but it does seem inevitable that the southern Cove stone at least must have been removed from its socket before the foot-stone of the Beaker grave was set up — although both could conceivably have stood touching each other in the capacious stone-hole. The whole of the Henge structure, and the surely ritual burial in its little cairn, is securely dated by the three Beakers found. It is difficult to understand why the ritual burial was so 'off-centre' to the west: the presence, actual or ritual, of the Cove seems the only explanation, with a desire to re-hallow the older liturgical centre when the later monument was erected.

Phase III
With the third phase at Cairnpapple comes a significant change of intention. The interest shifts from the ritual to the funerary aspect, and a large burial cairn is built on the site within, and largely at the expense of, the earlier structures. The cairn visible before excavation was found on excavation to be of two dates, the second an enlargement to twice the diameter of the first mound (FIGURE 3).

The earlier cairn had an approximate diameter of 50 feet and was bounded by a massive kerb made of large stones laid on their sides on the old ground surface. These stones, like all others surviving on the site, are of local origin and could have been

FIGURE 3. *Cairnpapple Hill: cairn completely excavated, showing kerb and cists of Phase III (Food Vessel) and grave of Phase II (Beaker) (looking east).*

dragged from anywhere on the hill-top or nearby, but in view of the complete disappearance of the Henge stones, it seems extremely likely (though of course unproven) that they were taken down and re-used to form this cairn kerb. There are 21 stones in the kerb, and taking into account the Cove, the Arc and the Henge oval, there could have been 36 stones to choose from. There is no doubt that some at least of the Henge stones must have been removed at or before the time of building the cairn, for it overlies their filled-in stone-holes on the west, as it does those of the Cove. On the whole it seems most probable that the Henge was depleted, if not destroyed, to form the kerb of the cairn and perhaps some of its internal structures.

The precise position of the cairn seems to have been determined by a necessity felt by its builders for incorporating within its kerb and mound the earlier Beaker grave. This involved building part of the cairn, with its heavy kerb-stones, over the quarry-pit east of this grave: the pit seems to have been open with the exception of a small deposit of silt against its outer edges, and on its western edge, where the kerb overlies it, it was filled up deliberately with stiff blue boulder-clay brought from the foot of the hill.

The cairn was mainly built of large stones without earth, though on the east and south a thick layer of the same blue clay as that used to fill the pit was incorporated in the body of the cairn between two layers of stones: it had been trampled down and iron-pan had formed on it, as it had over that rammed down into the pit. But the precautions taken were in vain. The kerb over the made soil in the pit gave way, and the whole body of the cairn slipped disastrously to the northeast, spilling out over and partly into the pit, which seems, however to, have been filled or silted by the time the collapse took place.

Centrally within the kerb was a large cist, constructed by setting upright slabs to line a rock-cut pit, and then building up horizontal dry-stone walling to take the single massive capstone. The collapse of the cairn northeastwards had caused this cap to be wrenched aside, and the walling and cairn material on the west had tumbled in, half-filling the cist. When the situation was observed during excavation, little hope was held out of intact or even recognizable grave-goods beneath this tumble of heavy stones, and it was with considerable astonishment that an intact Food Vessel was found lying among the uppermost stones in the cist. Below the stones, smashed fragments of unburnt human bones were found on the floor of the cist, pounded to smears and scraps. The intact pot on top of the filling was difficult to understand until a more careful study of the construction of the cist walls showed that on the east wall, immediately adjacent to the spot where the Food Vessel was found, the stones had been set back so as to form a shelf on which the pot must have stood, to fall only a few inches when the cairn material shifted and the upper part of the western wall of the cist collapsed inwards.

Between this cist and the kerb on the east, was another with a very large and heavy capstone, but built only of small boulders enclosing a rectangular space only eight inches deep and containing in its centre an unaccompanied human cremation. There seems no doubt of the contemporaneity of the two cists, and the whole cairn must be of Food Vessel date.

In the stones filling the central cist was one squarish block, almost certainly part of the walling on the west, with three cup-marks 'pecked' deeply on one face. Elsewhere scattered in the body of the cairn were three or four other stones bearing each a shallow 'pecked' cup-mark.

Phase III marks the first specifically funerary use of the site, with a large cairn having a central cist containing a Food Vessel inhumation, a second cist with a cremation, and a massive kerb almost certainly formed of the re-used stones of the Henge Monument, whose destruction probably dates from this time.

Phase IV
The kerb of the Food Vessel cairn was completely invisible on the surface when the excavations were begun, though an irregularly circular kerb of boulders with a diameter of about 100 feet was conspicuous round the periphery of the visible mound. It was apparent at an early stage of the work that this outer kerb was that of an enlargement to the original, 50-foot, cairn, in which the mound had been increased to twice the diameter, though probably with little addition to the height, of the earlier structure.

This enlargement consisted of smaller stones and a greater proportion of rubble and earth than the Food Vessel cairn, and on the west it overlay the now silted-up ditch of the Henge for a distance of over 80 feet of its inner edge. The kerb was of smaller and rounder boulders than the long stones of the earlier tomb, and these were irregularly placed on the old ground surface without any form of bedding or packing into place. Within the circuit of this kerb, and under the mound of the enlarged cairn, were the Arc stone-holes of the first phase, as well as the quarry-pit probably of Phase II, and seven stone-holes of the Henge in addition to two more under the Food Vessel cairn as well.

Two burials referable to this enlargement were found, one on the west and one on the south, and both in inverted Overhanging Rim cinerary urns. The west burial (no. 1) was in a shallow pit in the old surface, and the pot had collapsed and telescoped over the cremated human bones. There were no grave-goods except a large pin of Red Deer antler, also burnt. The second burial, on the south, was similarly in a shallow pit, but the pot was almost intact, inverted over cremated human bones with a burnt bone pin with eyed head. A feature of interest however was that in the shallow pit and against the sides of the urn had been placed a quantity of dark soil containing fragments of charcoal, tiny sherds of cord-ornamented pottery, and fragments of flint implements splintered by fire. The whole appearance was strongly suggestive of soil from a hut floor and hearth. Both urns are typologically late in the cinerary urn series, and should on conventional nomenclature be late Middle Bronze Age.

Phase IV, the enlargement of an earlier burial mound for the deposition of new burials, with the provision of a new outer kerb, follows a well-known Bronze Age precedent in this country as well as on the Continent. It implies continuity in tomb-building and a continued veneration of an ancient burial.

Phase V
The final phase at Cairnpapple is curious, and not easy to understand. On the eastern side of the Henge, four graves were found cut in the rock, one destroying the greater part of a stone-hole of the Beaker period monument. There was no trace of skeletons or grave-goods in them, but they were clearly intended to accommodate bodies at full length. Their relationship to the stone-hole shows that they cannot be earlier than the phase at which the Henge stones were removed from their sockets — presumably Food Vessel times — and their presumptive purpose for full-length inhumations in a small group or cemetery suggests a date late in the prehistoric period. Elongated graves are known in North Britain in the Iron Age, and within this rather vague period covering the first few centuries before and after Christ the Cairnpapple 'Late Graves' may be placed. Although they are orientated east and west, it is very improbable that Early Christian graves would be made on a remote hill-top within an ancient pagan sanctuary.

The Cairnpapple excavations have revealed a remarkable sequence of structures related to religious or funerary rites on the same site. Continuity over a thousand years is virtually proven, from the late Neolithic to the end of the Middle Bronze Age: if the Late Graves are indeed Iron Age this would imply that after an interval of many centuries the site was still regarded as a sacred place suitable for burial at the dawn of the Christian era. For a parallel in continuity we have to turn to Stonehenge, spanning almost exactly the same period, from the late Neolithic Aubrey Holes to the Iron Age Z and Y Holes of the 1st century BC.

Continuity in barrow-building, with the enlargement and rebuilding of the cairn and its related features, has become well-known to us since the brilliant excavations of Sir Cyril Fox in Wales, but the mixed religious feelings that could desecrate a Henge by taking down its standing stones, and yet carefully build a tomb within its area in such a way as to incorporate one of the earlier features, seem unattested elsewhere in Britain. The relationship of the Food Vessel people to those of the Beaker culture, at Cairnpapple at least, was not one of direct continuity. Whatever part the Henge played in the spiritual life of the Beaker folk in the Lothians, the Food Vessel people approached it from a different point of view. Perhaps it possessed a certain sanctity, enough to render it a desirable place for the burial of a chieftain, but its standing stones were regarded as nothing more than a convenient quarry for kerb-stones.

Not only is the sequence and the continuity of Cairnpapple arresting and unusual, but the individual elements in the various phases of building and reconstruction have peculiar interest. The Arc of Phase I is a feature without apparent parallels in Britain, but it sets us on our guard against accepting all allegedly half-destroyed stone circles as incomplete monuments. The cremations, and the characteristic bone pin found with one of these, add to the rapidly growing list of cremation cemeteries that can be shown to be pre-Beaker, and provide welcome confirmation of the connexions already suspected between the cultures of Skara Brae and Ronaldsway in North Britain and those represented at Dorchester-on-Thames, Woodhenge and Stonehenge in the south (*cf.* Stone's (1948) analysis). The two axe-fragments of imported rocks, if they belong to this phase, stress the southern connexions.

The finding of the stone-holes of an authentically Stukeleian 'cove' in Scotland was as unexpected as it is important. Here again is a link between Wessex and the Forth basin — the only extant 'coves' are at Avebury and Stanton Drew: undated at the latter site and at least no later than Beaker at the former. It seems almost certain that the now prostrate stones in the centre of Arbor Low are another such 'cove' in ruin, and one recalls that by these stones an extended inhumation burial was in fact found in Mr St George Gray's excavations (1903). Here Cove and Henge seem parts of an indivisible whole, but at Cairnpapple the Cove seems the earlier feature.

But Arbor Low certainly provides the parallel for Cairnpapple in Phase II. The Derbyshire Henge is not only geographically the nearest, but in its general proportions it closely resembles Cairnpapple, though slightly larger, and significantly enough the stones, so far as can be judged from their present fallen condition, were set in an oval and not a circle — a curious feature shared, incidentally, by the posts at Woodhenge. Arbor Low, too, is one of the few Henge monuments set on a hill-top in such a way as to command a wide view, and at Cairnpapple this dominating position is such that from the site can be seen the Bass Rock on the east, and the mountains of Arran on the west, while to north and south the view is bounded by the Highlands and the Lammermuirs.

The construction of Phase II at Cairnpapple gives one the immediate impression of the work of people unaccustomed to a land of hard rocks. It was indeed lucky for its builders that the rock of the hill-top was sufficiently rotted to be, in its way, not much more difficult than hard chalk to dig into — the digging of the Cairnpapple ditch cannot have been such a task as the sheer quarrying in the limestone necessary at Arbor Low. But at Arbor Low the stones seem to have been set up in the shallowest of sockets, if these were dug at all, whereas at Cairnpapple the stone-holes were always well-cut and often surprisingly deep. The two graves containing Beaker interments, too, were dug in a manner peculiarly reminiscent of graves of similar date in southern England, and seem to be unique in Scotland, where the stone-slabbed cist is ubiquitous among the recorded Beaker burials.

In both Phase I and Phase II, in fact, connexions with the south are apparent. But with the change to funerary intent on the site, and the building of the Food Vessel cairn of Phase III, we are clearly dealing with a people familiar with the country and building in the traditions proper to it. If, as seems inevitable, the Henge was dismantled in this phase, it can only be as the result of a decisive break in religious tradition. If the Food Vessel folk have claims to be regarded as the inheritors of an ancient Neolithic culture within the Peterborough family (as their pottery and certain of their flint types so strongly suggest), then at Cairnpapple at least they are establishing themselves after a relatively short period of Beaker domination has come to an end. The Food Vessel cairn built on top of the Henge bank at Arbor Low suggests a similar state of affairs. Like the early Christian missionaries, they destroyed the *fana idolorum,* but re-consecrated the site to their own ends, and, pulling down the old temple, used its stones to wall in the tomb of a chieftain built over the dedicatory burial of the earlier and alien shrine.

The enlargement of this cairn follows a practice familiar to us from many sites in both the Lowland and the Highland Zones of Britain. Barrow IV at Beaulieu (Piggott 1943) in the New Forest is a good example from the south, with an original ditched mound of turves, 40 feet in diameter and covering a Food Vessel burial, later enlarged to 85 feet in diameter at some undetermined period before the Early Iron Age. At Sutton, Glamorganshire (Fox 1943) and Talbenny, Pembrokeshire (Fox 1942), barrows of the Beaker period were enlarged to accommodate each a single Middle Bronze Age cremated interment: at the latter site the new kerb was made by removing the stones from the earlier mound, and Fox comments on 'the decay of the fine traditions of craftsmanship in the structural use of unwrought stone . . . as the Bronze Age developed'. Such a remark is very apposite when comparing the two kerbs at Cairnpapple, with the massive carefully placed stones of the Food Vessel cairn contrasting with the haphazard collection of boulders that grace the edge of the Middle Bronze Age enlargement.

The two cremated burials call for little comment, except for the deposit of occupation soil made over and around the pot in No. 2. This feature recalls the deposit of 'occupation soil' recognized by Phillips (1936) in the Giants Hills Long Barrow in Lincolnshire, and may well have occurred elsewhere in Bronze Age burials, and lurk disguised under the familiar 'black unctuous earth' of early barrow-digging accounts.

If the graves of Phase V are to be attributed to the Iron Age, one can only note, with all reserve, other evidence of an interest in Henge Monuments at this period to which Mr C.E. Stevens first drew attention (1940; *cf.* Piggott 1941), and of which Stonehenge affords the most striking example. The Geographer of Ravenna, copying, in the Dark Ages, lists of names off a map of the Roman Empire, included among those upon or near the line of the Antonine Wall, *ubi et ipsa Britania plus angustissima de Oceano in Oceano esse dinoscitur*, a *Medio Nemeton* — the Middle Sanctuary (*Cosmographia* 1860: 434–5. The identification of the sites, 10 in number, said to be *recto tramite una alteri connexae* is by no means easy. *Cf.* Macdonald (1934: 189–90), for the problem). Standing on Cairnpapple Hill on a clear day, with a view that virtually does stretch across Britain from sea to sea, one is tempted to wonder whether the 2000-year-old shrine still retained some vestiges of sanctity among the Iron Age Celts who may have been buried within its hallowed circuit.

References
Cosmographia. 1860. M. Pinder & G. Parthey (ed.). Berlin.
Fox, C. 1942. A Beaker barrow enlarged in the Middle Bronze Age at South Hill, Talbenny, Pembrokeshire, *Archaeological Journal* 99: 1–32.
     1943. A Bronze Age barrow (Sutton 268) in Llandow Parish, *Archaeologia* 89: 89–126.
Gray, H. St George. 1903. On excavations at Arbor Low, *Archaeologia* 58: 461–98.
Macdonald, G. 1934. *Roman Wall in Scotland* (2nd edition). Oxford: Clarendon Press.
Phillips, C.W. 1936. The excavation of the Giant's Hill Barrow, Skendleby, Lincs., *Archaeologia* 85: 37–106.
Piggott, C.M. 1943. Excavations of fifteen barrows in the New Forest, *Proceedings of the Prehistoric Society* 9: 1–27.
Piggott, S. 1941. The Stonehenge story, *Antiquity* 15: 305–19.
     1948. An Early Bronze Age sanctuary site in Scottish Lowlands, *Antiquity* 22: 35–6.
Stevens, C.E.. 1940. The Frilford site: a postscript, *Oxoniensia* 5: 166–7.
Stone, J.F.S. 1948. The Stonehenge cursus and its affinities, *Antiquaries Journal* 28: 149–56.

Durrington Walls: a ceremonial enclosure of the 2nd millennium BC

by G.J. WAINWRIGHT

ANTIQUITY 42 (165), 1968

DURRINGTON WALLS lies one quarter of a mile to the north of the outskirts of Amesbury in Wiltshire and 9 miles north of Salisbury (SU 150437). Stonehenge is situated 2 miles to the southeast, and 80 yards to the south of the enclosure is Woodhenge, which was excavated by Mrs Cunnington in 1926–8. The much ploughed bank, which encloses a dry valley opening on to the River Avon, was initially recorded by Sir Richard Colt Hoare in the early 19th century (1812: 169), but until the recently completed series of excavations the only digging on the site was that carried out by Professor Stuart Piggott in 1952, despite recognition of the enclosure as being one of the largest henge monuments in the country. The 1952 excavations were in the nature of an exploration on both sides of a pipe trench where it intersected with the bank in its southern sector (Stone, Piggott & Booth 1954). A double row of post-holes was recorded along the outer edge of the bank and a quantity of animal bones, flints and sherds of Grooved Ware was found on top of the old land surface which was preserved beneath it. Sherds of Grooved Ware and two small fragments of Beaker were recorded from domestic refuse overlying the bank talus. Radiocarbon dates of 2620±40 and 2630±70 BC were obtained from charcoal under the bank in its southern sector (Piggott 1959: 289). These determinations were described by Professor Piggott as 'archaeologically unacceptable' as two small scraps of Beaker pottery were found in association with the abundant Grooved Ware.

The external bank of the henge is very degraded as a result of centuries of ploughing and the eastern half of the interior is crossed by the A345. The bank is best preserved in its northeast sector where it is visible as a broad chalky mound 110 ft. wide with an internal ditch 40 ft. wide. This comparatively well-preserved sector of bank and ditch terminates in an original entrance at the bottom of the combe at a point 200 ft. from the erosional cliff of the River Avon. The southern, western and northwestern sectors of bank and ditch are either ploughed out or masked by subsequent lynchets. A west entrance is masked by a lynchet 10 ft. high and until recently the only evidence for its existence was an aerial photograph published by O.G.S. Crawford (1929: plate 30), on which the rounded ditch terminals could be clearly seen. The existence of this entrance has now been established by means of a geophysical survey carried out in October 1967 by A.J. Clark from the Ancient Monuments Laboratory of the Ministry of Public Building and Works.

It will be seen, therefore, that up to 1966 the very plan of the monument was conjectural, the ditch of the enclosure had never been sectioned and no excavation had been undertaken in the interior. In that year the Inspectorate of Ancient Monuments received notice of a new road alignment of the A345 from the Stonehenge Inn to Totterdown Clump which would cross the eastern half of the interior to the east of the old road. It was decided to excavate along the route of the proposed road prior to its construction and the author directed these operations in 1966 and 1967. Full cooperation was received from the Wiltshire County Council who, as owners of the land, permitted the excavation of the threatened areas. As a result of these excavations the route of the road was completely excavated where it crossed the bank and ditch and the interior of the site, with a few minor exceptions where areas were required for a spoil-heap and a machine run. In addition, the route of the road to the south of the henge, including a slip road to Woodhenge, was completely excavated as far as Totterdown Clump (FIGURE 1). The total length of the excavation was some 900 yards and the width of the strip varied from 27–50 yards. Mechanical excavators (JCB 3C types) were used to remove the ploughsoil which was transported by dumper trucks — a technique initiated by the Inspectorate for the total excavation of an Iron Age enclosure in Cranborne Chase in 1965 and successfully employed since that time.

The 1966 excavations
The excavations in 1966 were confined to the area north-west of the old road, where the new route was to cross the bank and ditch, and to the area immediately south of the bank of the henge in its southern sector. The results of these excavations are the subject of an interim report in the *Antiquaries Journal* (Wainwright 1967: part 2) and will be only briefly touched on here.

Some 200 ft. to the south of the henge a sub-rectangular timber structure was located with overall dimensions of 54 ft. and 30 ft. Some Grooved Ware and domestic rubbish were found in the post-holes. The ditch in its northern sector was 41 ft. wide and 18 ft. deep from the modern surface, with a flat bottom 18·5 ft. wide. Very little pottery was obtained from its rapid silts, but a hearth on top of these silts produced sherds of a rusticated beaker. Rim sherds of Ebbsfleet type occurred above this hearth whilst Bronze Age and Iron Age material was recorded from the upper silts. The distance from the outer lip of the ditch to the inner edge of the bank was 115 ft. There were indications that the inner part of the bank had been ploughed away but even so we cannot assume a berm less than 60–70 ft. wide. In the east sector of the excavation the bank had been completely destroyed. Elsewhere it was preserved to a height of some 12 in. and rested on a fossil soil. On top of this soil was a rich occupation layer which produced pottery, flints, bone and charcoal. The pottery is mainly of Middle Neolithic character and of forms that can be paralleled in the ditches of the Windmill Hill causewayed camp, but it was associated with three sherds of Grooved Ware. There was no stratigraphic difference between these two ceramic styles and sherds of both groups rested directly on top of the fossil soil. If we interpret the Middle Neolithic material as a relic occupation much earlier than the building of the bank (certainly the flint implements are patinated), then a possible explanation is provided for the radiocarbon determinations from the 1952 excavations, namely that the samples used were relics from a Middle Neolithic occupation which was not represented ceramically. Such a date in the middle of the 3rd millennium BC is acceptable for the Middle Neolithic material, but not, in the present state of knowledge, for Grooved Ware. However, radiocarbon determinations from the 1966–7 excavations will have to be obtained before taking this matter further.

The 1967 excavations
Apart from the sub-rectangular structure located in 1966 the area excavated from the henge south to Totterdown Clump was devoid of any signs of human habitation except for a few widely spaced pits which produced no dating evidence. Woodhenge and the crest of the Avon valley lie to the west of this strip which is on an eastward facing slope. The timber structures and ditched enclosures excavated by Mrs Cunnington at the same time as Woodhenge appear to be confined to this higher ground.

FIGURE 1. *Durrington Walls:* a *general view of the excavation from the north.* b *the southern circle at the completion of the excavation with Woodhenge to the south.*

The bank and ditch

Before the excavations, the bank and ditch in their southern sector were not visible as the result of ploughing and there was some dispute over the alignment of the ditch (Crawford 1929). Excavation showed that the ditch was sited in part in the bottom of the combe and that the bank was sited some 90 ft. outside the ditch. The remarkable width of this berm corroborates the evidence from the 1966 excavations. The bank was some 100 ft. wide and best preserved under a plough lynchet which crosses the southern boundary of the henge, where it was preserved to a height of 2·5 ft. Elsewhere it was only some 6–12 in. high. The bank material of chalk lumps derived from the ditch was removed over large areas to reveal the old land surface underneath it. From the top of this fossil soil was obtained a little Grooved Ware similar to that recorded from the 1952 excavations. There was no trace of any earlier ceramic material similar to that recorded underneath the bank in the 1966 excavations, although a few scattered post-holes clearly pre-dated the building of the henge bank by a considerable margin.

A major result of the excavation of the ditch is that the causeway of the south-east entrance was located (FIGURE 2). It was quite simple with no post-holes for a gateway or barrier. In addition, the entire contents of the ditch were removed for a distance of 112 ft. from the terminal. At the top of its weathering cone the ditch was 59 ft. wide; it was 20 ft. deep from the modern surface, with steep sides and a flat bottom 22 ft. wide. A large quantity of pottery was found on the rock bottom of the ditch and in the primary silts. It consists mainly of Grooved Ware ornamented with slashed cordons together with a few sherds of Beaker pottery. The lenses of occupation refuse became appreciably richer as the ditch terminal was approached and produced quantities of pottery, bone, antler and flints which included one fragmentary chipped axe. Some 60 ft. from the terminal and resting on the rock bottom of the ditch was found a pile of 57 antler picks which presumably had been used to excavate the ditch into the natural chalk and which had been thrown into a pile when the terminal was completed. The enclosure ditch was also located at the extreme north end of the excavation immediately to the south of the old road. It was crossed by a pipe trench and was merely committed to plan.

The southern circle (FIGURES 1, 2 & 3)

The post-holes of a complex circular timber structure were located 90 ft. northwest of the causeway into the main enclosure, on a comparatively flat piece of ground at the foot of the northern slope of the combe. These post-holes and their associated features were excellently preserved by 3–4 ft. of plough-soil which had silted down the slope into the valley bottom. Rather more than one half of the structure lay within the line of the proposed road; the remainder occurred to the west of it and was not excavated. The excavation of these post-holes revealed a complex sequence of timber structures — four of the Late Neolithic period and one of the late Iron Age. Of the former, three building phases are represented in a remarkable timber structure of Woodhenge type with an overall diameter of 127 ft. This sequence has been determined largely on the basis of post-hole intersections and comparison of post-hole sizes.

Phase 1

A series of four concentric circles of post-holes whose diameters from the outer circle are as follows: 75 ft., 50 ft., 26 x 24 ft. and 7·5 ft. At a distance of 19 ft. to the southeast of the outer circle the structure is fronted by a nearly straight palisade of timber posts, aligned northeast–southwest, which has a known length of 129 ft. The size and depth of the post-holes decrease towards the northeast, possibly as a result of ploughing, although the height of the palisade may originally have been reduced towards its terminals. The post-

FIGURE 2. a *The southern circle and enclosure ditch in the course of excavation.* b *Pottery from the southern circle and enclosure ditch (not to scale). (Photos: a RCHME, b A.L. Pacitto.)*

DURRINGTON WALLS
GENERAL PLAN OF SOUTHERN CIRCLE

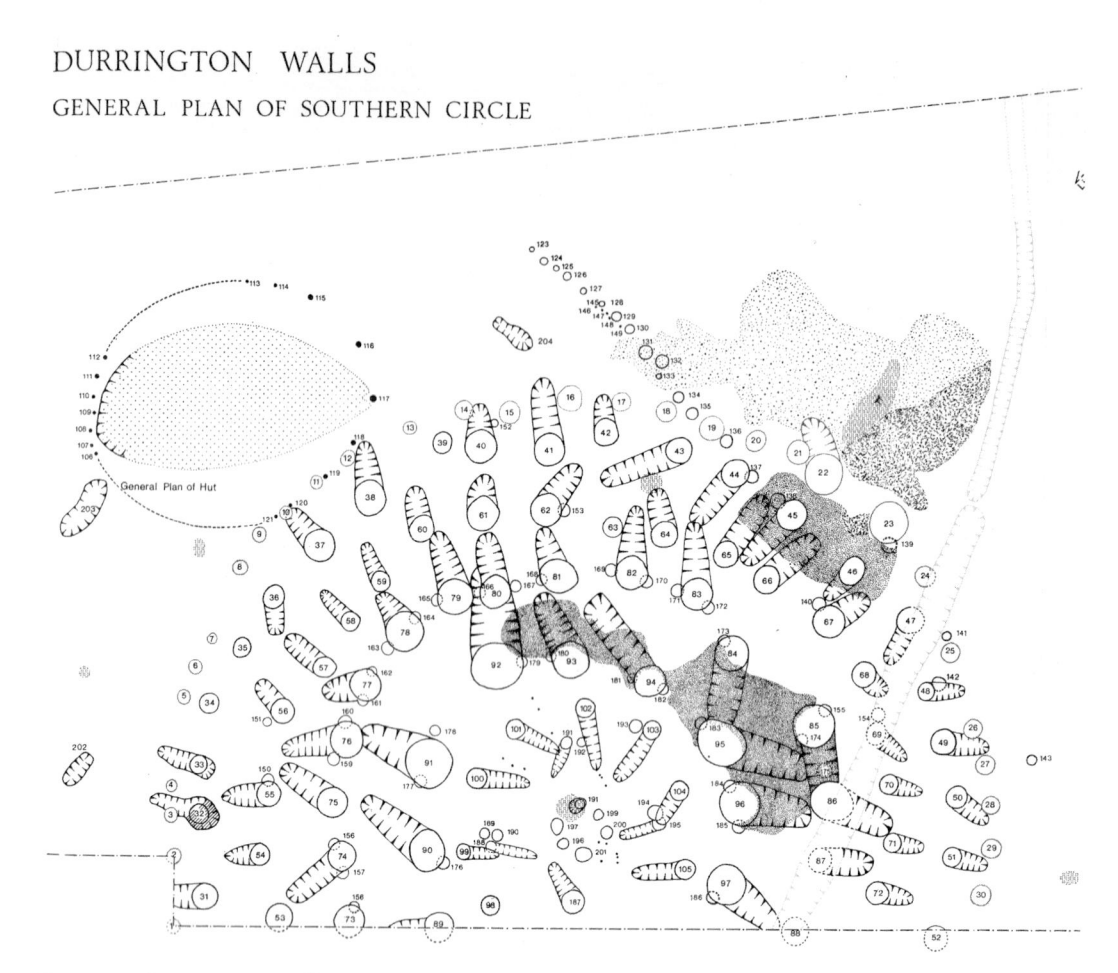

FIGURE 3. *Durrington Walls: general plan of southern circle (drawn by Mrs C. Boddington).*

holes of the circles average 2 ft. in diameter and in many cases have been cut through by the much larger post-holes of Phase 2. It is clear that several of the gaps in the circles are due to the post-holes having been destroyed in this reconstruction but also that spacing of the posts was never very regular. In the outer circle the average spacing (from centre to centre) is 4·5 to 5·5 ft. and on average the post-holes are from 3–4·5 ft. deep. The post-holes of circle 2 are more widely spaced and deeper (5–9 ft.) and there is a suggestion that they were grouped in pairs. Circle 3, slightly elliptical in plan, consists of only four post-holes and occurred totally within the excavated area. The post-holes of this circle differ from the others in that they were provided with ramps to facilitate the raising of the posts and they may have supported a canopy over the central area. Two of these posts (nos. 191 and 195) were replaced once, and no. 188 was replaced twice. The inner circle of six posts, although it is the heart of the structure at this stage, did not encircle any burial or ritualistic feature. It is of importance to note that none of the posts at this stage was packed with chalk blocks but that rammed earth and powdered chalk were used and that the circles do not have common centres.

The palisade or façade to the southeast is of interest as it appears to restrict access to the circles from the quarter where the causeway across the enclosure ditch is situated. Unfortunately the façade is much destroyed where the ramps of Phase 2 intersect with it. Nevertheless it is clear that an original gap existed in the façade at this point and that it corresponds with a gap in the outer circle of Phase 1. There is some suggestion of a double row of timber uprights passing through this gap, but in view of the subsequent disturbance this is not certain. What does seem certain is that the Southern Circle originated as four concentric circles of slender uprights which were shielded from the southeast by a façade. The entrance through this façade points in the general direction of the main causeway but is not aligned exactly upon it. A small quantity of Grooved Ware and Beaker sherds were in post-holes of this Phase.

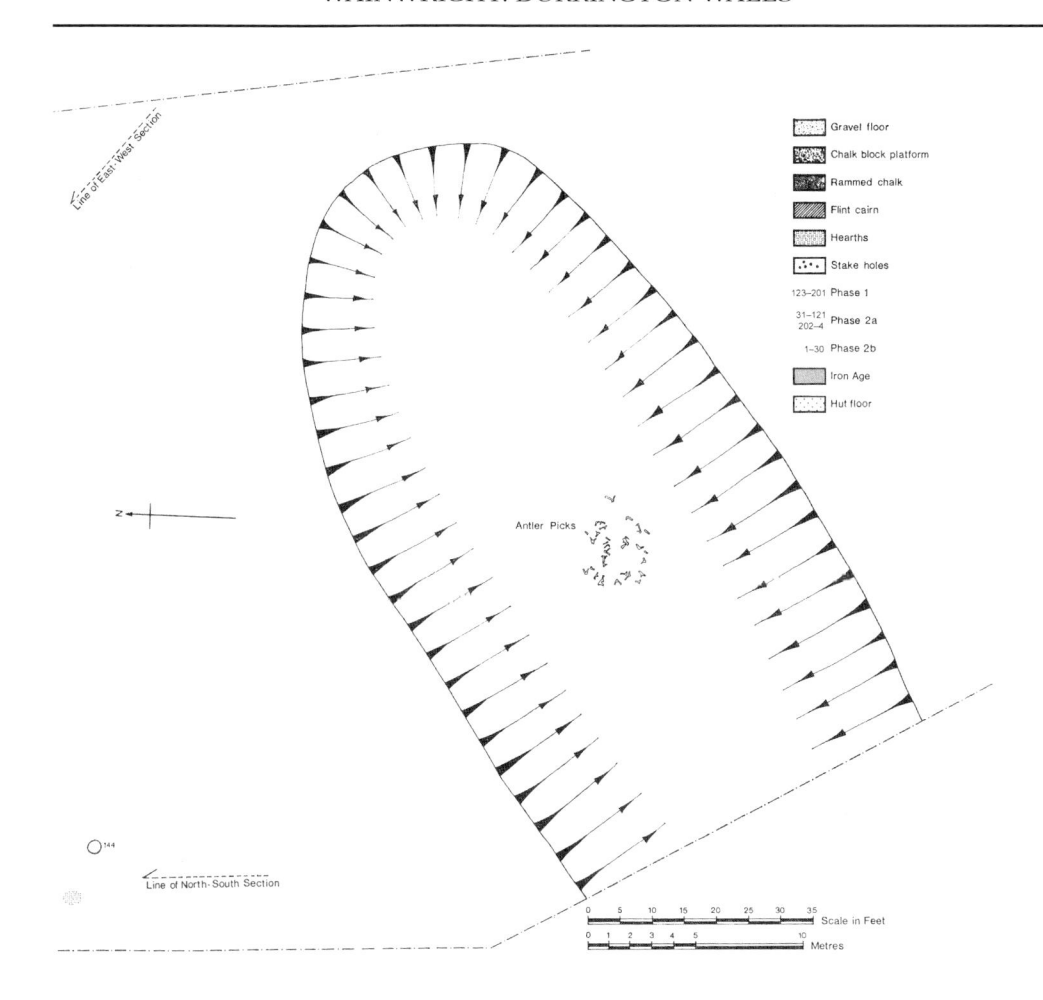

Phase 2A
The four circles of Phase 1 were replaced by a larger structure represented by a series of five concentric circles of more massive posts. These do not radiate from a common centre and have localized deviations from true circle alignments. The plan of this phase is complicated by the ramps of the post-holes which interlock and sometimes intersect. Although in the latter case a local building sequence could be determined there is no reason to extend this sequence to the whole structure as a certain amount of ramp intersection would have occurred naturally when the circles were constructed. In every case the ramps were deliberately filled with rammed chalk which was frequently found to rest on a thin humic layer. This suggests that the ramps were exposed for a while before they were levelled off.

A feature which appears for the first time in Phase 2A is the use of chalk blocks for

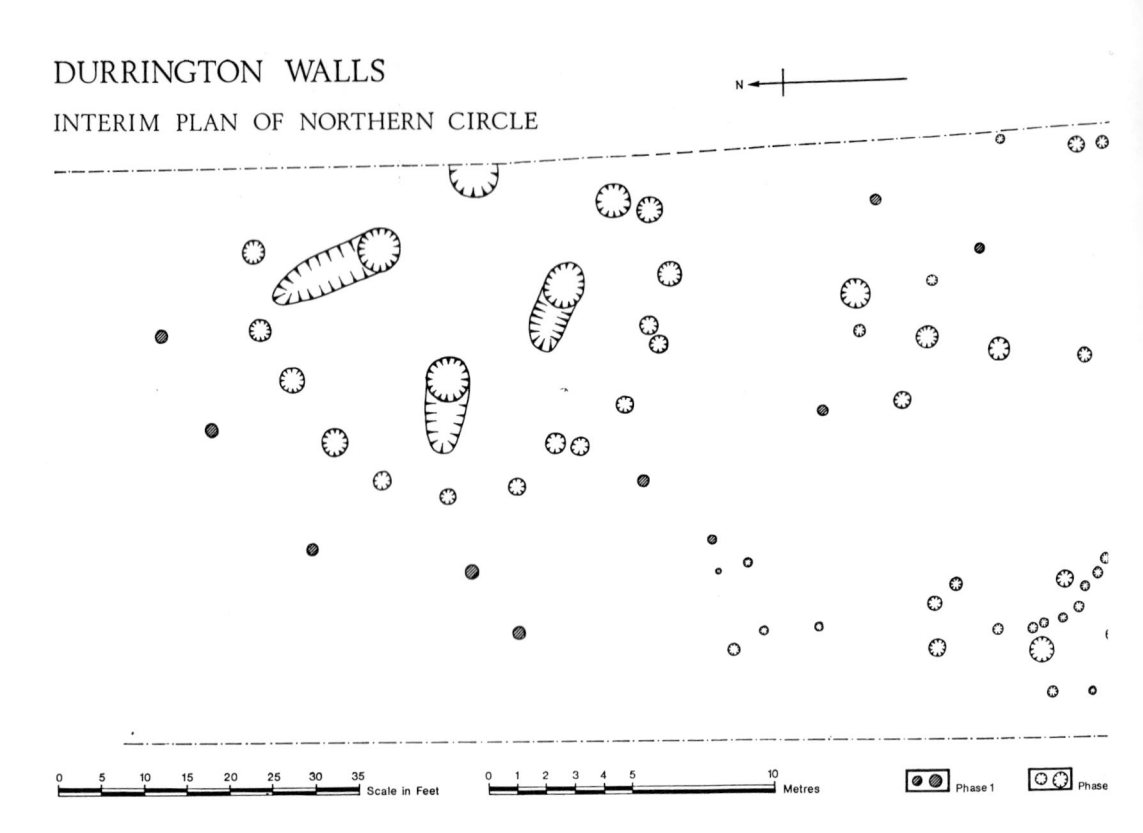

FIGURE 4. *Durrington Walls: interim plan of northern circle (drawn by Mrs C. Boddington).*

packing the posts. The preservation of the ground surface of the time was such that in the course of the excavation the packing blocks were found still to project above the level of the natural chalk, whereas on a normal ploughed site they would long since have been destroyed. In some cases the chalk blocks retained in plan the impression of the post they had supported. The lumps of chalk used for packing were large and fresh: one lump had preserved the marks of an antler pick on its surface, and it seems unlikely that such material could have been derived from anywhere but the deep levels in the enclosure ditch.

In addition to the packing of chalk blocks in the actual post-holes, the deliberate infilling of the ramps was carried to much greater lengths in the southeast sector of circles 1 and 2 and around the east and southeast circuit of circles 3 and 4. In the former area the rammed chalk filling the ramps was extended to cover an area some 24 × 12 ft. In the latter area the ramps and some of the post-hole packing were sealed by a 'platform' of rammed powdered chalk and chalk blocks, which also extended to cover the areas between the ramps. In the latter a thin fossil soil was preserved on the natural chalk but only a few sherds of pottery were obtained from it.

The outer circle of Phase 2A is slightly flattened along its north–south axis and has estimated diameters of 120 ft. and 117 ft. The diameters of the post-holes range from 3 ft. to 5 ft. and their depths from 6 ft. to 8 ft. The majority are approached by ramps which in the main are aligned out from the interior. Exceptions to this rule occur in the SE sector in the vicinity of a probable entrance. Circle 2 is also slightly flattened along its north–south axis and has estimated diameters of 100 ft. and 97 ft. The diameters of the post-holes range from 4 ft. to 5 ft. and their depths from 4 ft. to 6 ft. The ramps for these post-holes are aligned outwards. Circle 3 is 76 ft. in diameter and the post-holes range from 4–6 ft. in diameter with depths of from 5–8 ft. The ramps are aligned outwards. Circle 5 is slightly flattened along its north–south axis with diameters of 37 ft. and 35 ft. The post-holes average 3 ft. in diameter and are from 3 ft. to 6 ft. deep. There were no features in the central area apart from an area of burning which sealed post-hole 198 of Phase 1. In the majority of cases the 'pipe' of the decayed wooden post was clearly visible and it will be possible to provide estimates for the size of each timber upright.

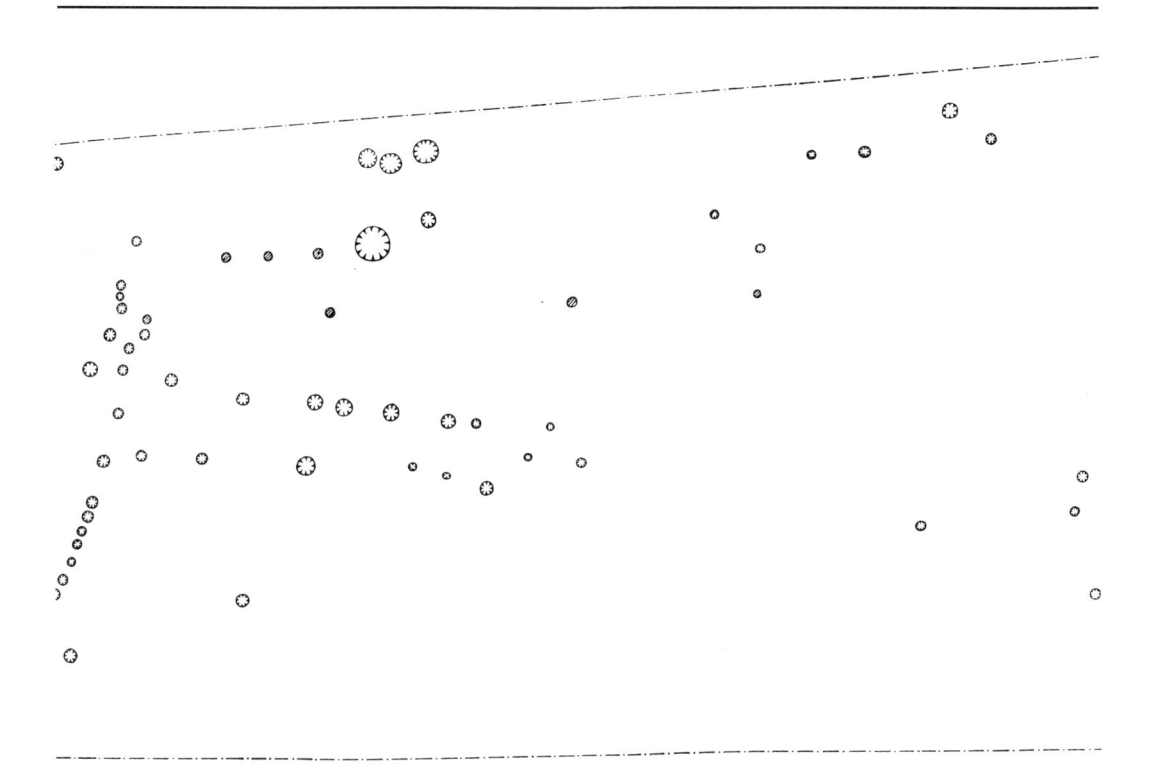

A remarkable feature was the large number of antler picks found in the packing of the post-holes — an estimated total of 400 picks in all. These had presumably been used to dig the holes and had been rammed back into the filling around the posts. A very great quantity of pottery and stone tools was recorded from the post-holes. This pottery is consistently of Grooved Ware type with an admixture of Beaker sherds. One large rim-sherd was decorated with an impressed spiral — a motif hitherto unknown in the south and best known in the Megalithic Carvings from the north and west. The flint tools include petit-tranchet-derivative arrowheads, plano-convex knives and the usual complement of scrapers and re-touched flakes. No flint axes were recorded and only one fragmentary axe of igneous rock. The absence of 'heavy' tool types must mean that the wooden uprights were trimmed and dressed away from the site. A few scraps of foreign stone were recorded, including two blocks of sarsen used as packing in post-hole 96. These blocks are quite heavy and one of them appears to have a dressed surface. The only human skeletal remains were a few skull fragments from post-hole 50.

Phase 2B
A single circle of post-holes, 127 ft. in diameter, encloses the five concentric circles of Phase 2A. These post-holes were dug subsequently to those of that phase as in several cases (nos. 3,

FIGURE 5. a *The northern circle looking north with its avenue and façade.* b *Pottery from the enclosure ditch. (Photos: a RCHME, b A.L. Pacitto.)*

10, 14) they cut through the ramps of the latter. The post-holes vary from 2 ft. to 2·5 ft. in diameter and in depth from 1 ft. to 3 ft. and they do not have ramps. They tend to increase in size towards two large post-holes 6 ft. in diameter and 7 ft. deep (nos. 22 and 23) in the southeast sector which appear to mark the position of an entrance into the precincts of the circle. In plan, these two post-holes, and those immediately to the north of them appear to be cut through a platform of rammed chalk lumps and flinty gravel. This platform extends mainly to the southeast of the entrance but a small portion of similar material occurs adjacent to post-hole 23. However the flinty gravel of this platform seals the ramp of post-hole 22 with which it must therefore be subsequent or contemporary. It is, however, surprising that the platform was not carried through the entrance gap between post-holes 22 and 23.

This platform is therefore assigned tentatively to Phase 2B. From the surface of it was obtained a very great quantity of pottery, bone, stone tools and antler which was mainly distributed around an elongated area of ash and burnt chalk immediately to the southeast of post-hole 22. The platform sealed a thin fossil soil from which a few sherds of pottery were obtained.

It is difficult to determine how much time elapsed between Phases 2A and 2B and the true position may be one of a gap of a few days rather than a deliberate reconstruction at a later date. On the whole the author tends to favour a very short interval owing to the unusual behaviour of the ramps of the outer circles of Phase 2A in their southeast sector and an unusually wide gap associated with an inset post-hole between 83 and 85. It seems likely that these anomalies are due to the presence of an entrance in the southeast sector and as the only outward signs of an entrance are post-holes 22 and 23 it follows that its erection immediately succeeded the building of the other five circles. In this case, the intersections of the post-holes of the circle of phase 2A are to be regarded as being Phase 2B circle with the ramps of the outer of local significance only — a suggestion which is supported by the intersection of post-hole 21 with the ramp of entrance post-hole 22. If this is so then Phases 2A and 2B are to be regarded as parts of a single structure 127 ft. in diameter with an entrance defined by two large post-holes in its southeast sector. This entrance, like that of Phase 1, is aligned on the main enclosure causeway.

The use of blocks of chalk for packing the posts in Phase 2A and the probability that this chalk was obtained from the enclosure ditch should indicate that these two structures are contemporary. It follows that Phase 1 with simple unramped post-holes and no chalk-block packing may antedate the enclosure ditch. It is clear, however, that no great interval separated Phases 1 and 2A as the latter was built along the alignments of the former.

The Palisade Trench
A palisade trench of late Iron Age date cuts across the southern sector of the circle. It is continuous save for one deliberate gap but was much destroyed by erosion in its eastern sector. It is not associated with any structures but it may have enclosed a considerable area of the north side of the combe if a much eroded linear feature at the extreme north end of the excavation represents its ploughed-out remains. A group of pits and a cluster of post-holes to the north of the northern circle are also to be associated with this phase on the basis of the pottery.

The Hut
A hut floor was recorded to the northeast of the timber circles and consists of an oval area 43·5 x 37 ft., surrounded by stake-holes and with its northern end terraced into the slope of the hill. The stake-holes are missing in the northeast and northwest sectors of the circuit and may have been ploughed away. Abundant domestic debris consisting of pottery, bone and stone tools was found in the centre of the hut floor in a black, ashy deposit. In its southwest sector the line of stake-holes intersects with the outer ring of the timber circle. Unfortunately, in no case do post-holes and stake-holes coincide and so their relative age cannot be ascertained. It seems clear, however, that the hut must either antedate or postdate Phase 2B of the timber circle as the two structures cannot be contemporary.*

The occurrence of an apparently purely domestic structure within the confines of a ceremonial enclosure is of some interest. It is just possible that the hut may postdate the sanctity of the enclosure but a decision on this must await a full ceramic study and the arrival of radiocarbon determinations. It is clear from the great quantity of pottery, stone tools and bone found in the area of the southern circle that human debris was not removed from the site as has been suggested at Avebury.

The northern circle (FIGURES 4, 5a)
Considerable erosion as a result of ploughing and normal weathering processes had taken place on the northern crest of the combe and only the bases of the post-holes had survived in the case of the Northern Circle and its attendant structures. This circle, similar in structure to the Southern Circle but on a smaller scale, was located on the northern crest of the combe. Well over half the post-holes were excavated, the remainder lie to the east of the threatened area. The post-holes appear to represent a two-phase structure consisting of a double timber circle, an avenue, and in the case of Phase 2, a façade.

Phase 1
The structures of Phase 1 are ephemeral owing to the erosion referred to above and consist of an outer circle of which four post-holes survive and an inner circle represented by five post-

---

* Later reconsideration of the evidence suggests that this structure is most probably a midden and not a roofed building.

holes. The estimated diameters of these circles are 90 ft. and 62 ft. respectively but it should be stressed that the post-holes do not exceed 4 in. in depth. The outer circle is approached from the south by an avenue of post-holes of which only eight have survived the centuries of ploughing — four irregularly spaced along each alignment. This largely conjectural avenue is 6·5 ft. wide and has a known length of 95 ft. but its original extent is unknown.

Phase 2
The circles of Phase 1 were replaced by two concentric circles, smaller in diameter but consisting of larger timbers, and the avenue was succeeded by another along a different alignment. In addition a façade of closely set timber posts was built across the avenue. The outer circle has an estimated diameter of 48 ft. and consists of post-holes ranging in diameter from 1·5 ft to 3 ft. and from 0·5 to 2·5 ft. deep. The inner circle consists of four large ramped post-holes averaging 4 ft. deep and has an estimated diameter of 21·5 ft. These circles are approached from the south by an avenue represented by a double row of post-holes which pass through a façade of closely set post-sockets set 55 ft. from the outer circle of Phase 2. The eastern half of the façade has been badly damaged by ploughing but the western half is well preserved and, assuming that the avenue is central to it, one can suggest that its original length was some 60 ft. and that it was straight in its central portion with its terminals pointing in towards the circle. The average width of the avenue is 7·5 ft. but where it passes through a gap in the façade it broadens to 10 ft. It continues through the façade towards the circles for a distance of 35 ft. but cannot be traced closer to the latter than 20 ft. In the centre of the avenue, at what must be called the entrance through the façade, is a single post-hole which may represent the siting of a gate. It appears from the closely set post-holes of the façade that it provided a clear demarcation line between the area to the south of it and the space immediately to the north in front of the circle. The only access through this barrier was by means of an avenue of timber uprights which was closed by a gate at the point where it crossed the façade. A small quantity of pottery, bone, antler and stone tools was found in the post-holes for the Phase 2 circles. The pottery includes sherds of a long-necked Beaker and Grooved Ware.

Conclusion
Considerable labour must have been expended in excavating an enclosure ditch of the Durrington dimensions (which has a total length of 1460 yards), transporting the chalk out of its depths and across a berm 90 ft. wide to pile up a bank over 100 ft. across. Such an undertaking implies a large labour farce belonging to a society whose beliefs necessitated the building of enclosures on this scale, and who could afford to deflect labour from the necessities of food production in order to provide for the non-material aspects of their existence. The timber structures found in the interior have clear analogies with those at Woodhenge itself, the Sanctuary, Arminghall and Great Bleasdale, but possibly of greater value are the quantities of domestic debris found in the excavations and the information that will thus be gained concerning the material culture and domestic economy of the time. Finally, these results were obtained in the excavation of an arbitrary strip across the eastern half of the interior and it is difficult to believe that similar timber structures do not occur within the enclosure ditch.

References
CRAWFORD, O.G.S. 1929. Durrington walls, *Antiquity* 3: 49–59.
HOARE, R.C. 1812. *Ancient Wiltshire* 1. London: W. Miller.
PIGGOTT, S. 1959. The Radiocarbon Date from Durrington Walls, *Antiquity* 33: 289–90.
STONE, J.F.S., S. PIGGOTT & A.ST J. BOOTH, 1954. Durrington Walls, Wiltshire: recent excavations at a ceremonial site of the early second millenium B.C., *Antiquaries Journal* 34: 155–7.
WAINWRIGHT, G.J. 1967. Interim report on 1966 excavations at Durrington Walls, *Antiquaries Journal* 47 part 2:

The timber circle at Sarn-y-Bryn-Caled, Welshpool, Powys: ritual and sacrifice in Bronze Age mid-Wales

by ALEX GIBSON

ANTIQUITY 66 (250), 1992

THE SARN-Y-BRYN-CALED pit circle, lying about two miles (c. 3 km) south of Welshpool at the junction of the A483 with the A490 (SJ 21930491), was discovered from the air by St Joseph in 1975 (St Joseph 1980) as a circle of 20 pits, c. 20 m in diameter around a central feature or pit c. 5 m in diameter. It forms one component of a ritual complex near the northeast terminal of the Sarn-y-bryn-caled Cursus (also known as the Welshpool or Lwyn Wron cursus), comprising in addition a penannular ring ditch, a ditched hengiform site and two ring-ditches (FIGURE 1). A possible barrow lies in the field to the north of the cursus, just west of the settlement of Sarn-y-bryn-caled, and Beaker pottery has been recovered from the plough-soil in the field.

Excavation of this scheduled ancient monument was prompted by the current construction of the Welshpool by-pass. Accordingly the Clwyd–Powys Archaeological Trust was commissioned to undertake the excavations, funded by Highways Department of the Welsh Office, from November 1990 till February 1991.

The pit circle lies on the first river terrace above the present flood plain of the River Severn, on a gravel peninsula which protrudes into the valley bottom. Palaeo-channels, weaving through the valley and skirting the eastern edge of this peninsula, indicate the constantly changing meanderings of the river. The terrace itself, composed of fine to medium river gravels, is pitted with geological features. The terrace is also slightly crested and the pit circle lies on the top of this undulation.

An area of c. 1·2 ha was stripped mechanically over and around the pit circle and then cleaned by hand. Among a small number of archaeological features located outside the pit circle were two pits containing Peterborough pottery and a few undated charcoal-filled pits. The pits of the circle itself showed as patches of pink, silty soil in the rounded-gravel matrix. Occasional charcoal flecks were noted in the fills of the pits at surface levels; the quantity of charcoal often increased with depth.

Excavation of the post-pits belonging to the circle showed them to be c. 1·0–1·2 m deep and c. 1 m in diameter (FIGURE 2) forming a true circle 18 m across to the centre of the pits. The pits had held wooden posts c. 30–40 cm in diameter. Charcoal from the edges of the post-pipes suggested that the post-butts had been charred, perhaps as a deliberate attempt to arrest decay. In all cases the post-pipes were circular or near circular, and no traces of square or rectangular post-pipes were noted. Traces of gleying in the bottoms of most of the pits indicated the bases of the posts; where recorded, these gleyed areas were invariably smaller than the post-pipes at a higher level suggesting, perhaps, that the posts were narrowed at their bases, possibly as a result of axe-felling. In all cases the posts were nearly central to the post-pits. Furthermore, the post-pits were regularly spaced and arranged to form a perfect circle. The absolute depths of each pit were all within c. 10 cm of each other, despite the natural 30-cm high ridge of the gravel terrace.

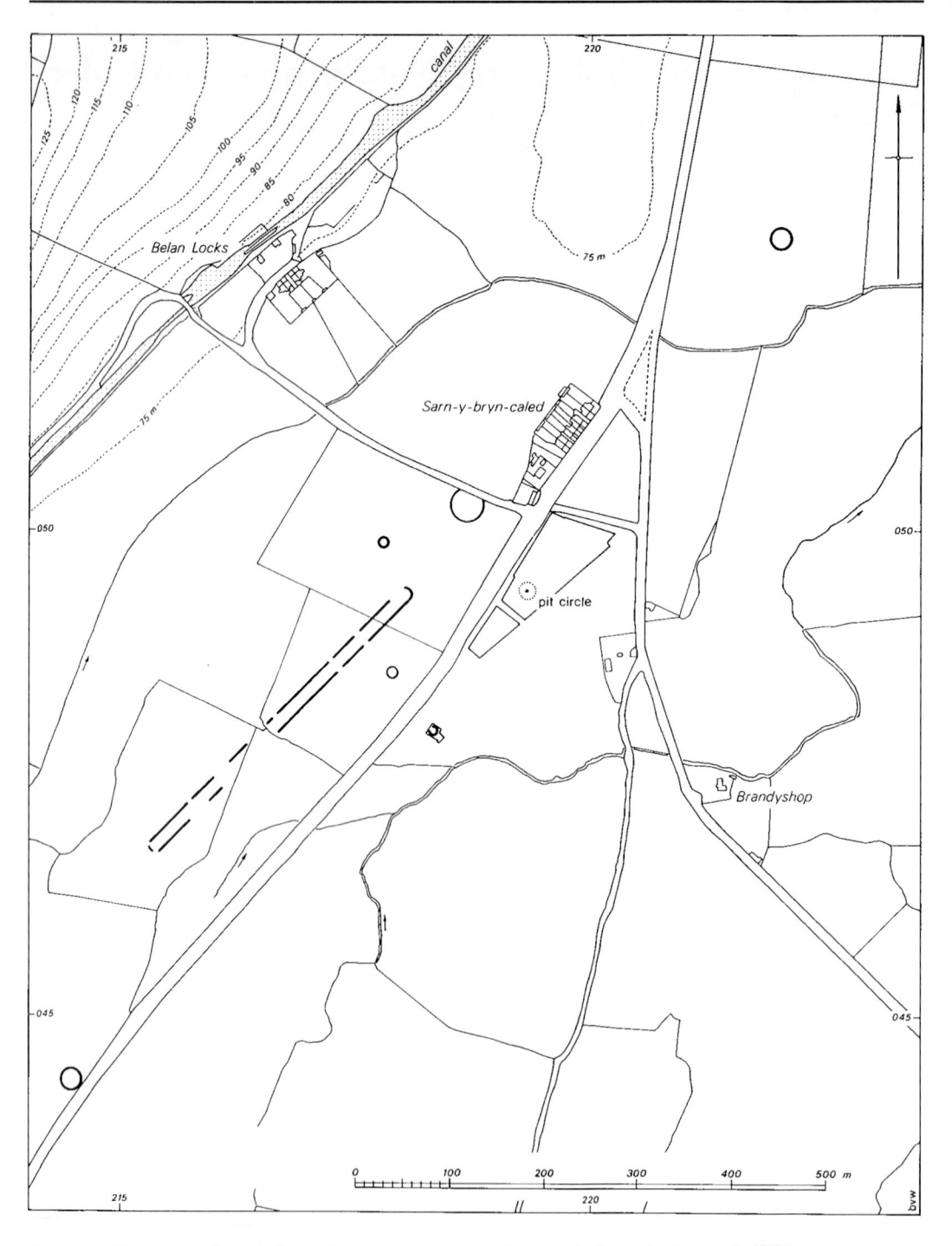

FIGURE 1. *Location plan of the timber circle at Sarn-y-bryn-caled in relation to the cursus complex.*

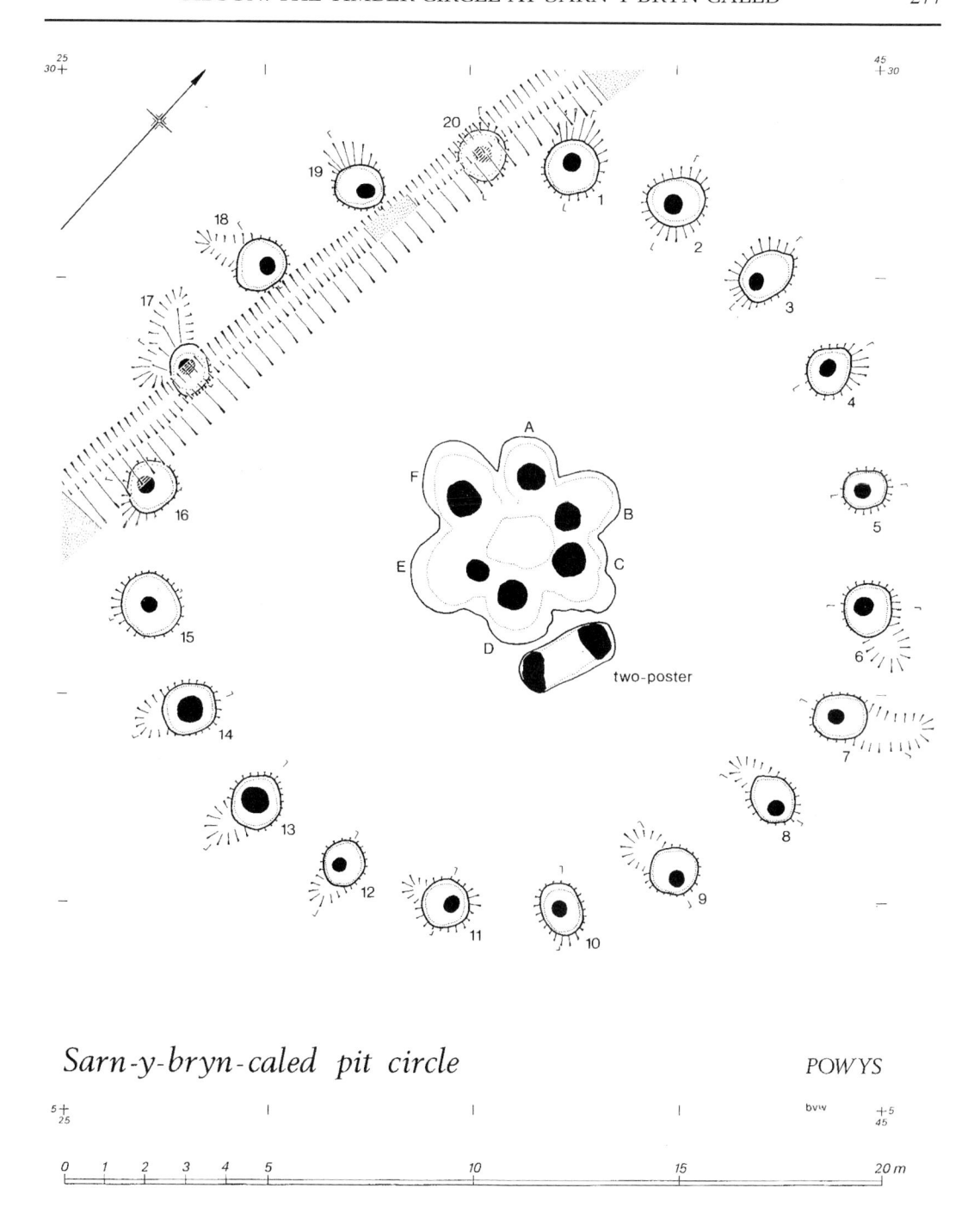

FIGURE 2. *Sarn-y-bryn-caled: plan of the post-pits.*

Some of the pits were approached by ramps, presumably to facilitate the raising of the timbers; most of the ramps faced outwards from the circle. Some of these 'ramps' were so impractically short that in these cases the effect seems to result from accidental damage to the pit edges caused during the erection of the posts rather than a deliberate easing into place of the uprights.

Exceptions to these general observations were noted in pits 13 and 14 in the SSW arc of the outer circle. Here the pits were deeper, *c*. 1·25 m, and had contained larger posts, reaching 70 cm in diameter (FIGURE 3). It seems that larger posts stood in these two pits, giving the circle an entrance or focus.

The central pit, visible on the aerial photographs, proved to be composed of six substantial post-pits spaced so closely as to be intersecting. These contained post-pipes indicating central or near-central posts *c*. 50 cm in diameter and arranged in a circle 3·5 m across to the centres of the posts (FIGURE 2). These posts, larger than the posts of the outer circle but smaller than the two 'entrance' posts, measured *c*. 50 cm in diameter. No entrance gap in this inner circle was immediately apparent, though a slight causeway on the western side of the circle may indicate a marginally wider gap at this point. If this is an 'entrance', it is not aligned on that of the outer circle though there is no reason why this should be expected.

To the east of the inner circle, the only archaeological feature discovered in the 5·5-m wide space between the outer and inner rings was a structure comprising two shallow (55 cm) 'D'-shaped post-pits set within an elongated depression. Traces of burning were located in the upper fills of this depression. The nature of this two-poster must remain uncertain. The shallow post-holes suggest that the posts were low, probably no more than 1 m high. It is tempting to see this as an altar-like structure but this must necessarily remain subjective. The interior of the circle was otherwise empty.

FIGURE 3. *Sarn-y-bryn-caled: post shadow in outer pit no. 13.*

All the post-pits had been backfilled with excavated gravel. There were no finds other than charcoal from any of the pits, and tip lines were only noted in a few instances. Through the back-filled pits of the central area, however, had been cut a roughly rectangular pit with sides measuring *c.* 2 m long at the top but narrowing to 0·75 m square at the base. It had been dug to the same level as the bases of the inner circle of post-pits. Charcoal staining indicated that this central pit had been lined with wood, perhaps as shoring; the sides of the pit had been distorted to a lozenge-shape, probably by the pressure of the re-deposited soil and gravel filling the inner post-pits. The fill of the area inside this lining was composed of soft, pink, clayey sand, free of gravel and with little charcoal.

Finds and dating

At the base of this central pit lay a cremation deposit (as yet unstudied) in a compact heap which suggested that it had originally been in some bag or perishable container. Four fine barbed-and-tanged arrowheads of Green's Conygar type (Green 1980: 138–9) were recovered from it. Above this primary cremation, at about two-thirds the depth of the central pit, a secondary cremation was associated with an undecorated bipartite vase food vessel. Small fragments of copper or copper alloy recovered from the uppermost fill of the central pit probably represent a much later episode of bronze-working.

The outer pits were of sufficient depth to hold timber uprights standing 2·5–3 m above ground by the commonly accepted ratio of 3:1 for the above- and below-ground sections of free-standing posts. The uniform absolute depths of the post-pits of both inner and outer circles, irrespective of the natural rise and fall of the gravel, suggest they may have been designed to hold pre-cut timbers standing to a uniform height.

Absolute dating of the timber circle awaits radiocarbon assay from suitable material. In the meantime, Peterborough ware from pits outside the circle and the near-by cursus suggest a possible origin for the monument in the late 3rd millennium BC. The barbed-and-tanged arrowheads from the primary cremation in the central pit and the secondary burial accompanied by a food vessel indicate use of the site into the early 2nd millennium. The monument is therefore contemporary with the henge monuments and timber circles of the Late Neolithic and Early Bronze Age, another variant in this complex tradition of circularity within the ritual monuments of the period (Clare 1986; 1987; Harding & Lee 1987).

The wooden structure and its analogues

It seems unlikely that the circle was roofed. The span of 7 or 8 m on the level, *c.* 9 m on the slope, seems too great for the size and presumed height of the original posts. Compare this, for instance, with phase 2 of the southern circle at Durrington Walls, where a distance of 15 m between the innermost and outermost circles is occupied by six concentric post rings (Wainwright & Longworth 1971: figure 84) giving average spans of only *c.* 2·5 m.

The care taken in levelling in the bases of the pits surely indicates a high degree of precision in the construction of the monument and this must have had a structural, visual or ritual purpose. It is not inconceivable that the posts were cut to length, and possibly even carved or decorated before their erection; the stones at Stonehenge were dressed before being set upright. This might suggest that the heights of the posts were also pre-determined and, if so, then taken in conjunction with the absolute and relative depths of the post-pits, their tops would have been level.

If this was the case, then it is worth considering whether the posts might have carried lintels. Lintels may be inferred from the example at Stonehenge. Here, the lintels of the sarsen circle and horseshoe were carefully fitted to the uprights using mortice-and-tenon and tongue-and-groove joints (Atkinson 1979: 39); bluestones had been used in an earlier lintelled arrangement (Atkinson 1979: 51–3). Tongue-and-groove and mortice-and-tenon joints are, in essence, carpentry techniques unnecessary in such a stone monument where the sheer weight of the lintels (about 6 or 7 tons) would have kept them in place. The implication is that the builders at Stonehenge were familiar not just with wood-working techniques but also with building the monument type itself in wood. Stonehenge may be unique amongst these timber circles only in its lithicization — its survival due to its translation of the basic form into stone rather than timber.

Indeed, there is growing evidence for the replacement of wooden circles by stone phases. A timber circle within Stonehenge I has been suggested by Burl (1987: 54–5), and timber settings replaced by stone have been excavated at the Sanctuary, Wiltshire (Cunnington 1931), Balfarg, Fife (Mercer 1981) and Croft Moraig, Perthshire (Piggott & Simpson 1971), to name but three.

As long ago as 1929, Cunnington demonstrated how the ground-plans of the multiple timber circle at Woodhenge coincided with the sarsen and bluestone circles and horseshoes at Stonehenge (Cunnington 1929: plate 18). This similarity of ground-plan prompted the Cunningtons to name their site 'Woodhenge', an otherwise philologically meaningless name. Since then, timber circles, enclosed and unenclosed, single and multiple, have been widely recognized in Britain. Simple, single, unenclosed post-pit circles have been excavated in Northumberland at Milfield North (phase 1) (Harding 1981: 101–5); at Ferrybridge, West Yorkshire, two single post circles, c. 16 m in diameter, were arranged around a central post (inf. J. Hedges); at Hungerford, Berkshire, a circle of seven posts 6 m in diameter was associated with fragments of Aldbourne cup (inf. S. Ford); and in Oxfordshire at Standlake (site 20) a timber circle enclosed a ring ditch (Catling 1982: 97–9). A double circle similar to Sarn-y-bryn-caled has also been found at Oddendale in Cumbria (Turnbull 1991). And large, complex, unenclosed multiple circles have been investigated at Newgrange, Co. Meath (Sweetman 1985) and The Sanctuary (Cunnington 1931).

Enclosed post circles are far more common and vary from single circles such as Bleasdale, Cumbria (Varley 1938), Goldington, Bedfordshire (Mustoe 1988), Whitton Hill 1, Northumberland (Miket 1985), Conygar Hill, Dorset (Woodward & Smith 1987) and Springfield are enclosed by causewayed ditched circles (Conygar) or henges. Springfield lies in the northeast terminal of a cursus.

Multiple unenclosed timber circles are the most common. Those at Woodhenge, Wiltshire (Cunnington 1929), Durrington Walls, Wiltshire (Wainwright & Longworth 1971), Mount Pleasant, Dorset (Wainwright 1979) and Balfarg (Mercer 1981) are well known. Like the simpler monuments, enclosed or unenclosed, they consistently have henge associations and are datable to the Later Neolithic/early Bronze Age.

Was Sarn-y-bryn-caled roofed? Or were the posts free-standing? The arguments that these large, multiple sites were roofed are far from clear-cut (see Musson in Wainwright & Longworth 1971). In his study, Musson (in Wainwright & Longworth 1971: 363) was clear to point out that 'the study produces no conclusive evidence that the . . . structures were originally . . . roofed buildings; indeed, the . . . deductions which can be made from the archaeological evidence allow equally convincingly for other interpretations'. Throughout this paper Musson stresses that his study is a feasibility study; it *may* be *possible* that the circles were roofed and *if* so, they *may* have been roofed in the following ways. Yet, in the main report, the hypothesis becomes fact: 'the structures from these four sites [Marden, The Sanctuary, Durrington Walls southern circle and Woodhenge] represent the range of roofed circular buildings of Late Neolithic date as known at present' (Wainwright & Longworth 1971: 212).

Musson's provisional reconstructions have become accepted in much of the archaeological literature; the illustration of the southern Durrington circle reconstructed as an impressive timber hall with massive protruding entrance posts and central oculus has been reproduced and redrawn almost *ad infinitum*. However, the negative arguments, given equal weight by Musson, have not generally received corresponding attention (a notable exception is Burl, who preferred to see the Sanctuary as a 'free-standing circle of wooden posts' (1976: 31–2). Musson writes that some of the spans on the southern Durrington circle (phase 1) may have been excessive, and the central quartet of posts too flimsy to have stood the 9 m required (Wainwright & Longworth 1971: 366). In the southern circle (phase 2) the posts of ring 2F, which could not be fitted into a roofed reconstruction, had to be left as free-standing 'ritual' posts (Wainwright & Longworth 1971: 367). At the same site, the concentric posts are rarely arranged radially, although long straight timbers were clearly available for the uprights, and a radial arrangement would certainly have saved much effort in the roof construction (Wainwright & Longworth 1971: 367). Perhaps it is better to envisage a ring-beam or purlins but no roof so that the site appeared as multiple lintelled timber rings.

The sequence at the Sanctuary is best seen as phases of free-standing timber posts, replaced, aggrandized and finally converted into stone as a stone circle which, had it existed at the same time as the timber posts, would, in Musson's intentionally ironic footnote, have 'formed a fairly effective barrier for anyone seeking a dignified entry to the central area' (Wainwright & Longworth 1971: 370 and Musson pers. comm.). The depths of the phase 1 post-holes, far in excess of what a hut would need, suggest they may well have formed simply a ring of tall, free-standing or lintelled posts; free-standing posts paradoxically need deeper foundations than those bound into a multi-timbered, load-bearing structure.

In purely structural terms, Musson's interpretation of Woodhenge as a two-phased roofed structure is more acceptable than Piggott's single-phased reconstruction (Piggott 1939: 209) or Musson's own single-phased reconstruction which necessitates removing ring D from the structural elements (Wainwright & Longworth 1971: figure 115). However, the inwardly sloping roof — channelling rainwater into the central area — seems impractical in a climate such as ours, even allowing for climatic amelioration. The interpretation of a smaller triple-ringed structure (represented by rings D, E and F) later replaced by a more elaborate and larger structure of the same basic form (represented by rings A, B and C) seems a more logical development. But, in presenting arguments *against* the roofed hypothesis, Musson points out the mathematical progression involved in the post-rings at several sites and suggests quite specifically that numerical arrangements may have had more importance than simple structural considerations, there being 'no compelling logic in terms of beam spans or column distribution' (Wainwright & Longworth 1971: 375).

Sarn-y-bryn-caled reconstructed

The timber circle at Sarn-y-bryn-caled was reconstructed for a public open day in February 1991 (FIGURE 4). Oak logs 4 m and 4·5 m long, slightly narrower than the original posts, were placed in the original holes of the outer and inner rings. Two larger posts, 4·5 m long, were erected in the outer pits to distinguish the putative entrance or focal point.

FIGURE 4. *Sarn-y-bryn-caled: reconstruction of the timber circle.*

The uprights were linked by lintels *c.* 3 m long, seated onto their tops. While the posts were free-standing, they appeared from ground level as an unintelligible forest of posts; only when the lintels were placed on the uprights did the circularity of the monument become apparent. This visible consequence of lintels is relevant to how we envisage Sarn-y-bryn-caled and lintels would give added stability to otherwise free-standing posts.

Discussion

The dates for phase 2 of the southern Durrington circle lie between 2050 and 1900 BC and the Grooved Ware associations from the other Wessex timber circles suggest that they are broadly contemporary. These sites are, therefore, as much as 300 radiocarbon years earlier than the presently accepted date for the Stonehenge sarsen circle (Stonehenge III) (Atkinson 1979: 216). Stonehenge III therefore must represent the climactic development of an already well-developed tradition of wood-working and timber construction. As has already been inferred from the carpentry techniques used at Stonehenge, these wooden multiple circles may indeed have provided the timber antecedents for this otherwise unique monument, ritual and tradition being inseparably connected.

The earliest burial in the central pit included four prestige arrowheads amongst the cremated bone. Heat-spalling visible on the surfaces of the arrowheads is much less severe than would have arisen had the flints been in contact with the naked flames for a prolonged period or exposed to a temperature of over 400°C (the temperature at which the water of chemical composition in flint is converted to steam and explodes violently, causing the disintegration of the artefact (inf. Ann Woods)). It might be reasonably concluded that the arrowheads had been actually in the body, being most probably the cause of death, and had therefore been protected to some degree from the naked flames of the cremation pyre. An obvious parallel for this event is the secondary burial in the Stonehenge ditch which was associated with two more-or-less complete Conygar type arrowheads, a Sutton D type and the tip of a fourth (Evans 1984: 19), similar to those at Sarn-y-bryn-caled. The latter, lodged in the rear of the sternum, was almost certainly the fatal shot, having entered the body from behind and passed through the heart.

Human sacrifice is always an emotive and sensational topic. Evidence for it is almost always likely to be inconclusive in normal soil conditions. Lindow Man, if buried in a grave rather than in a bog would, at best, only have provided evidence of having been axed. This situation could have been interpreted equally well as a ritual killing, a murder or a casualty of war. Only the preservation of the organic remains indicates that ritual killing was the most likely explanation (Stead *et al.* 1986). Similarly, the child burial at Woodhenge (Cunnington 1929: 13), roughly central to the timber ovals, had had its skull split in two with a sharp object, presumably a stone axe. This act, taken in consideration of the context of the burial, again suggests ritual killing.

There is no conclusive proof of human sacrifice at Stonehenge or Sarn-y-bryn-caled, but the context of both burials combined with the prestige nature of the well-made Conygar type arrowheads is certainly suggestive and adds up to more than a murder, hunting accident or casualty of war. An execution is perhaps plausible, but why should a criminal receive burial in such a prestigious position? For all the uncertainties, the examples of St Sebastian and St Edmund in a later age clearly show that religion and execution may be inextricably intertwined.

Acknowledgements. The writer extends his thanks to Welsh Office Highways for funding the excavation of Sarn-y-bryn-caled and to Powis Estates, particularly the chief forester Mr B. Barker, for facilitating the reconstruction. Mr C. Musson, Mr B. Britnell and Dr H.A.W. Burl all made valuable comments on an earlier draft of this article. The photographs were printed by Mr R. Hankinson and the site excavation plan is by Mr B.V. Williams.

References
ATKINSON, R.J.C. 1979. *Stonehenge, archaeology and interpretation.* Revised edition. Harmondsworth: Penguin Books.
BRADLEY, R. & R. CHAMBERS. 1988. A new study of the cursus complex at Dorchester on Thames, *Oxford Journal of Archaeology* 7(3): 271–89.
BURL, H.A.W. 1976. *The stone circles of the British Isles.* London: Yale University Press.
  1987. *The Stonehenge people.* London: Dent.
CASE, H.J. & A.W.R. WHITTLE (ed.). 1982. *Settlement patterns in the Oxford region; excavations at the Abingdon causewayed enclosure and other sites.* London: Council for British Archaeology and the Ashmolean Museum. Oxford. Research Report 44.
CATLING, H.W. 1982. Six ring ditches at Stanlake, in Case & Whittle: 88–102.
CLARE, T. 1986. Towards a reappraisal of henge monuments, *Proceedings of the Prehistoric Society* 52: 281–316.
  1987. Towards a reappraisal of henge monuments: origins, evolutions and hierarchies, *Proceedings of the Prehistoric Society* 53: 457–77.
CLARK G. 1936. The timber monument at Arminghall and its affinities, *Proceedings of the Prehistoric Society* 2: 1–51.
CUNNINGTON M.E. 1929. *Woodhenge: a description of the site as revealed by excavations carried out there by Mr and Mrs B.H. Cunnington, 1926–7–8.* Devizes: Simpson.
  1931. The 'Sanctuary' on Overton Hill near Avebury, *Wiltshire Archaeological and Natural History Magazine* 45: 300–35.
EVANS J.G. 1984. Stonehenge — the environment in the late Neolithic and early Bronze Age and a Beaker-age burial, *Wiltshire Archaeological and Natural History Magazine* 78: 7–30.
GIBSON, A.M. (ed). 1989. *Midlands prehistory.* Oxford: British Archaeological Reports. British series 204.
GREEN, H.S. 1980. *The flint arrowheads of the British Isles.* Oxford: British Archaeological Reports. British series 75.
HARDING, A.F. 1981. Excavations in the prehistoric ritual complex near Milfield, Northumberland, *Proceedings of the Prehistoric Society* 47: 87–136.
HARDING, A.F. & G.E. LEE. 1987. *Henge monuments and related sites of Great Britain: air photographic evidence and catalogue.* Oxford: British Archaeological Reports. British series 175.
HEDGES, J.D. & D.G. BUCKLEY 1981. *Springfield cursus and the cursus problem.* Chelmsford: Essex County Council. Occasional paper 1.
MERCER R.J. 1981. The excavation of a late Neolithic henge-type enclosure at Balfarg, Markinch, Fife, Scotland, *Proceedings of the Society of Antiquaries of Scotland* 111: 63–171.

MIKET, R.F. 1985. Ritual enclosures at Whitton Hill, Northumberland, *Proceedings of the Prehistoric Society* 51: 137–48.
MUSSON, C.R. 1971. A study of possible building forms at Durrington Walls, Woodhenge and The Sanctuary, in Wainwright & Longworth: 363–77.
MUSTOE, R.S. 1988. Salvage excavation of a Neolithic and Bronze Age ritual site at Goldington, Bedford: a preliminary report, *Bedfordshire Archaeology* 18: 1–5.
PIGGOTT, S. 1939. Timber circles: a re-examination, *Archaeological Journal* 96: 193–222.
PIGGOTT, S. & D.D.A. SIMPSON 1971. Excavation of a stone circle at Croft Moraig, Perthshire, Scotland, *Proceedings of the Prehistoric Society* 37: 1–15.
ST JOSEPH, J.K. 1980. Air reconnaissance: recent results, 49, *Antiquity* 54: 47–51 & plate VII.
STEAD, I.M., J.E. BOURKE & D. BROTHWELL. 1986. *Lindow Man — the body in the bog*. London: British Museum Publications.
SWEETMAN D.P. 1985. A late Neolithic/early Bronze Age pit circle at Newgrange, Co. Meath, *Proceedings of the Royal Irish Academy* 85 C: 195–221.
TURNBULL, P. 1991. *Excavations at Oddendale, 1990: interim summary*. Kendal: Cumbria County Council, County Planning Department.
VARLEY, W. 1938. The Bleasdale circle, *Antiquaries Journal* 18: 155–71.
WAINWRIGHT, G.J. 1979. *Mount Pleasant, Dorset: excavations 1970–1971*. London: Society of Antiquaries. Research report 27.
WAINWRIGHT, G.J. & I.H. LONGWORTH. 1971. *Durrington Walls: excavations 1966–1968*. London: Society of Antiquaries of London Research report 29.
WOODWARD, P.J. & R.J.C. SMITH 1987. Survey and excavation along the route of the southern Dorchester by-pass, 1986–87 — an interim note. *Proceedings of the Dorset Natural History and Archaeological Society* 109: 79–89.

A Neolithic ceremonial timber complex at Ballynahatty, Co. Down
by BARRIE HARTWELL
ANTIQUITY 76 (292), 2002

BELFAST LOUGH is a deep indent of the Irish Sea into the coastline of Northern Ireland. Its southwestern continuation is the Lagan Valley, which separates the steep scarp of the Antrim Plateau (height $c.$ 300 m) from the hills of Co Down ($c.$ 120 m) to the southeast. The River Lagan flows along this broad, undulating valley floor through thick deposits of glacial sands and gravels before emptying into the Lough at Belfast. Eight kilometres southwest of Belfast, the river passes the townland of Ballynahatty, a sandy plateau 100 ha in extent. This was the site in the 4th millenium BC of a small passage tomb, orientated to the northwest (Collins 1954: 48; Lawlor 1918: 16–19). Though now denuded of its covering mound, it provided the subsequent focus for a series of atypical passage tombs utilizing ever smaller settings of stone (Hartwell 1998: 33–6). Shortly after 3000 BC this was followed by a complex of large and elaborate east-facing timber structures (Ballynahatty 5 and 6). These in turn were eventually replaced by the earth and stone hengiform enclosure of the Giant's Ring, built around the original passage tomb. At over 200 m in diameter and 4 m in height this is one of the largest and best-preserved henges in Ireland and dominates the southeast corner of the plateau (Hartwell 1998: 36–9). A low, broad ridge ($c.$ 5 m high) runs east–west less than 100 m to the north of the Ring. At its western end is a large boulder, the only other visible archaeological feature. A number of sites were removed from the townland in the 18th and 19th centuries including standing stones, elaborate cists and two unmarked cemeteries which produced 'many cartloads of human bones' (MacAdam & Getty 1855: 364).

The timber enclosures
Following their identification from crop marks in 1989, the eastern end of Ballynahatty 5 (BNH5) and the whole of Ballynahatty 6 (BNH6) were excavated over 10 seasons from 1989 to 2000 by the School of Archaeology & Palaeoecology at Queen's University Belfast with grant aid from the Environment and Heritage Service — Built Heritage. The air photographs had shown a large oval palisaded enclosure (BNH5) sitting on the edge of the ridge overlooking the Ring and spreading down the more gentle slope to the north, at the bottom of which is the remains of a small glacial kettle lake. BNH5 consisted of a double line of substantial pits 100x70 m containing the smaller enclosure, BNH6 (16 m diameter), at its eastern end. Excavation showed these to be the postholes of complex timber structures with elaborate entrances carefully sited to take maximum advantage of local relief. Excavation of the features was particularly difficult in the glacial sands and gravels and plough damage was at its most severe on the top of the ridge. Most of the original ground surface and any shallower features have been destroyed and many of the flint artefacts, for example, were recovered from the top soil. Detailed phasing and dating must await further analysis and the full excavation report but the substantial nature of the postholes, averaging 2 m in depth, allow preliminary interpretation of the more substantial structures.

BALLYNAHATTY 5 and 6, Co. Down

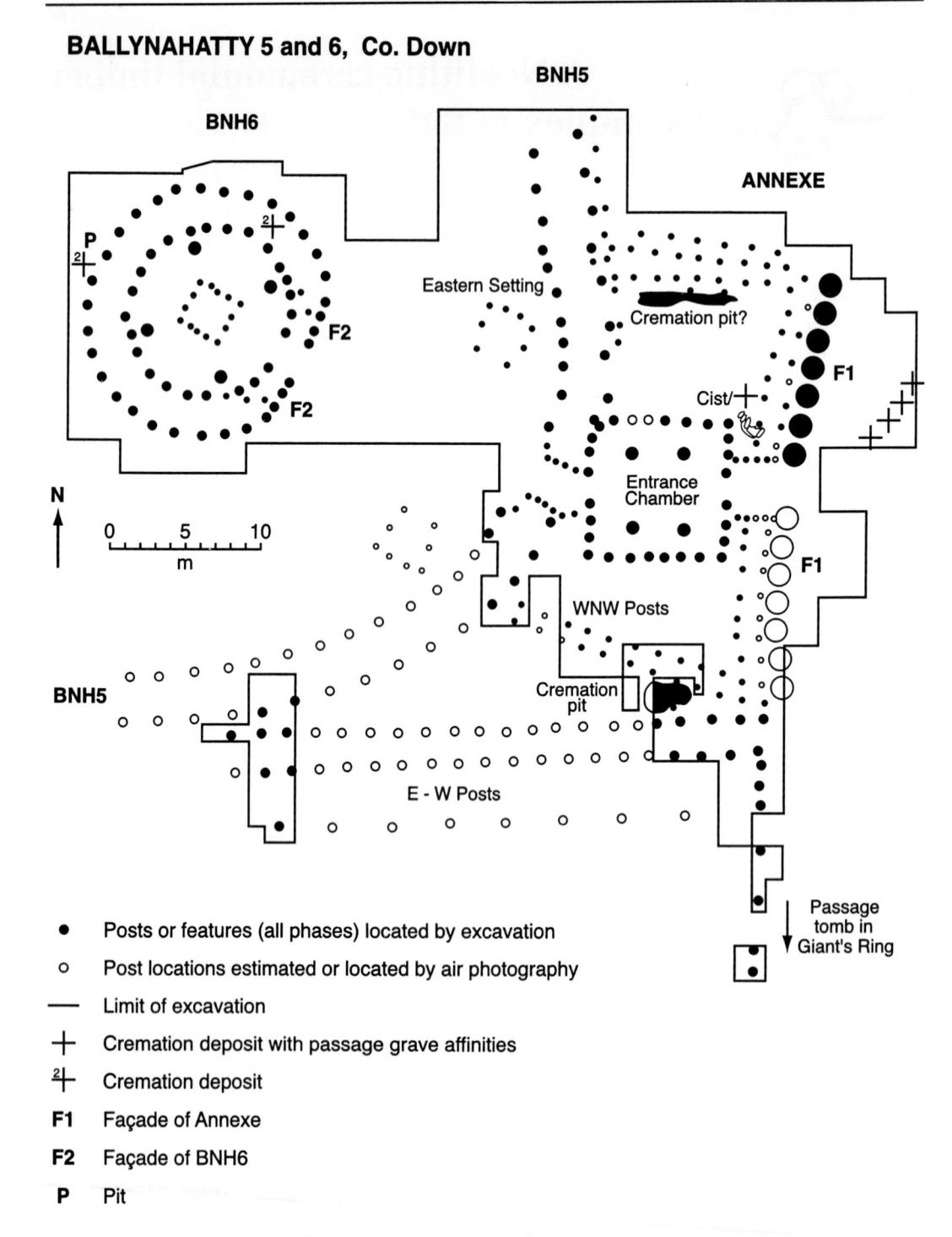

FIGURE 1. *Ballynahatty 5 and 6: location of posts and features.*

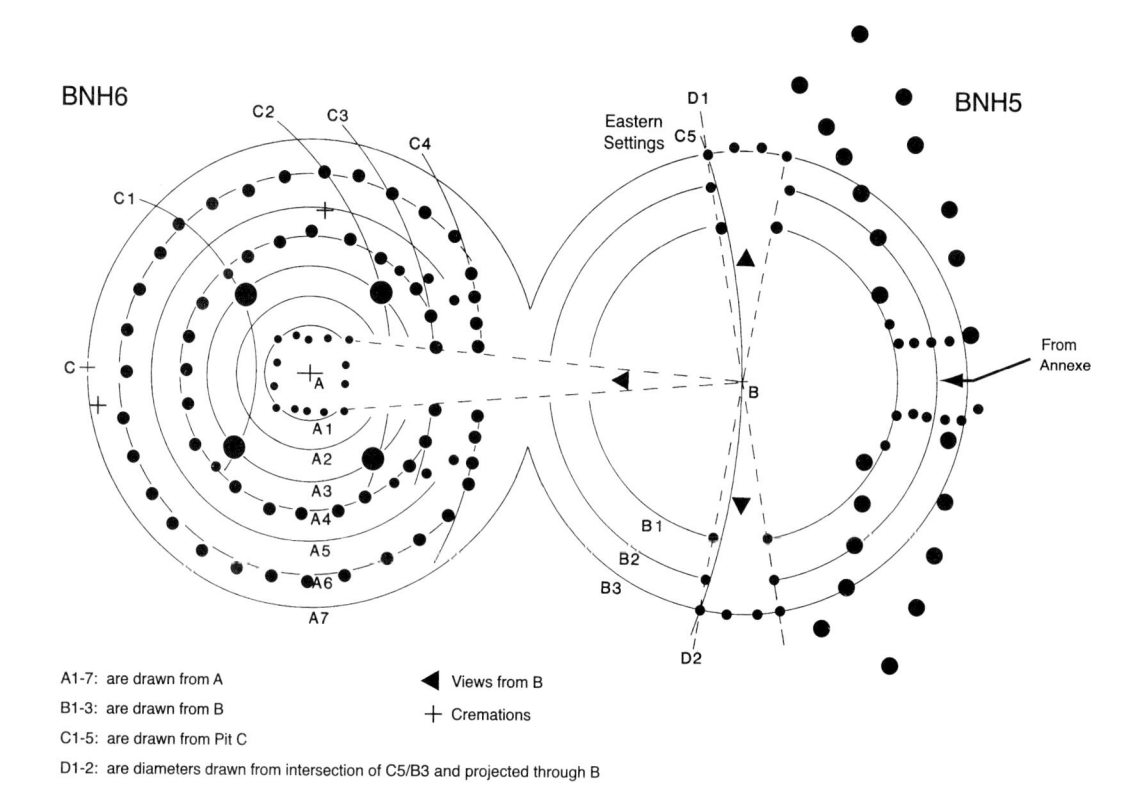

FIGURE 2. *The construction of BNH6, the Eastern Settings and entrance in BNH5.*

The dominant pottery type is Grooved Ware. Carrowkeel ware comes from the earlier passage tombs and possibly from an early stage of the timber structure — if a line of four cremations is assumed to align with the entrance (FIGURE 1). Part of a Beaker pot was recovered but the context was uncertain. Of the worked flint, end scrapers predominate and there are substantial amounts of burnt flint.

The earliest focus of activity on the ridge area seems to have been at the BNH6 enclosure. Two postholes either side of the entrance between C3 and C4 (FIGURE 2) may be all that is left of an earlier and simpler enclosure similar to that found at Knowth (Eogan & Roche 1997: 101–23). If so, this has been destroyed in large part by the inner ring (A4) of BNH6.

BNH6 is a double concentric circle of posts, 16 m in diameter, set in 2-m deep postholes with radiating ramps. The outer circle has been flattened on either side of the entrance to create an impressive façade. There is excavation evidence for planking linking the entrance timbers and a short section of a charred oak plank was found in the secondary fill. The façade was probably constructed of vertical timbers, about 6 m high, down which grooves had been cut to take horizontal oak planks. Much of the discussion which follows assumes that the areas between the posts were infilled or at least had some horizontal elements. Infilling can be inferred because otherwise, behind the façade, the carefully designed complex becomes a mass of posts without visual order — rather like a Hollywood film set. The effect of adding lintels can be seen at the Sarn-y-bryn-caled timber circle reconstruction (Gibson 1994: 212) and how this may have looked at Ballynahatty in Hartwell (1998: 41). Apart from the planking there is little direct archaeological evidence for infilling, although modern ploughing would have removed any signs of more ephemeral structures at ground level such as wattle-and-daub — although this has been suggested elsewhere (Gibson 1998: 89). Aerial structures, such as horizontal bracing between the posts or lintels, would leave no trace at all (Gibson 1998: 108, 119). There is no evidence that any of these structures were roofed, although this possibility has been investigated at Knowth, Brú na Bóinne (Eoghan & Roche 1997: 283–94).

Immediately within the inner circle were four large posts (A3). These were bigger and taller than the BNH6 enclosure posts, being supported in 2·3-m deep holes, but set very close to them so that the postholes run together. Within this was a centrally placed square setting of 14 posts. The postholes were relatively shallow (c. 0·5 m), the implication being that this part of the structure was secured together in some way to provide rigid support, unlike the other posts on the site which required deep postholes because they were probably self-supporting. As there was no space around its perimeter for a door this has been interpreted as a platform. The precisely aligned Eastern Settings came next (FIGURE 2). Presumably the passage through BNH5 was laid out at the same time as it also conforms to the circles B1-3. There are differences though, the Eastern Settings are defined by projections D1-2, providing two opposing sectors focussed on B. The entrance is wider — much closer to that of the entrance into BNH6 and is probably laid out on projections from pit C. It is also constructed of posts in two slots whereas the Eastern Settings are in individual postholes (Hartwell 2000: 45).

The larger enclosure, BNH5, came next, built as a double-post structure reflecting that of BNH6 (A4 and A6). Again, parallels come from Brú na Bóinne at Newgrange (Sweetman 1984: 195–221). The excavated section clearly swings out to include the Settings (FIGURE 2) and the placement of its posts is less precise. The architect clearly had problems when faced with setting out the Entrance Chamber because of the necessity of realigning the passageway to the east–west orientation of the ridge. Effectively it was pivoted on the BNH5 enclosure post at the northeastern end of the entrance passage. This required inserting an extra post in an easterly extension to the south slot of the passage and a double post at the northwest corner of the Chamber. The chamber is 9 m square and defined by 28 posts, 30–40 cm in diameter, set in c. 1·8-m deep postholes. A gap on the east side, 1·5 m across and matching that on the west, leads to another slot-defined passage and to a further gap in the two lines of posts of the eastern façade. The area between this façade and BNH5 constitutes an elaborate annexe with double lines of posts closing the north and south sides (the west-northwest posts). The function of the two areas in the northern and southern parts of the annexe is difficult to determine but it was here, spread over the surface of the north area and in the postholes of the entrance chamber, that a number of sherds of Grooved Ware were found. Though BNH6, BNH5 and the Annexe have been built sequentially, evidence points to a single unified plan and any interruptions to the construction may just have been seasonal. At some stage the west-northwest posts were deemed inadequate and a much more substantial double line of posts was constructed along the brow of the ridge (the east–west posts). Presumably this provided a more impressive-looking structure when viewed from the bottom of the ridge to the south and may additionally have blocked views and access to the interior structures to add to its exclusivity. The final construction comes with the erection of a third set of posts around the enlarged annexe, which on the eastern side takes the form of a massive façade, with seven posts either side of the entrance. Each post was at least 1·2 m in diameter and set less than 20 cm apart. If a 3:1 ratio of height to depth is assumed, the façade would have been over 6 m high.

The end of BNH5 and 6 must have been quite spectacular. Most of the posthole fills contain large amounts of charcoal so there is little doubt that the complex was burnt. However, the evidence for the burning comes in the form of a mixture of sandy fill, charcoal and cobbles filling the postmould. This indicates that the timbers had not rotted *in situ* but had been levered out of the ground, presumably burnt, and then deliberately replaced by the mixed secondary fill. In some cases a conical pit had been dug around the post to facilitate its removal. At its most developed, the secondary fill took the form of a sandwich with alternating layers of charcoal and stone in the precise shape of the original post.

The Ballynahatty experience
Having briefly discussed the principal structural evidence of Ballynahatty 5 and 6, it is worthwhile considering its regional situation, function and how the complex could have been experienced in the Neolithic period. To do this we must return to the coast. Medieval Belfast grew at the mouth of the Lagan, taking advantage of a ford to allow north–south passage. Towards the end of the Neolithic this ford would have been covered by a rise in the sea level which caused the inundation of a low-lying area on the northwest side of the Lagan Valley known as the Bog Meadows. Coring in the Meadows has shown the presence of a thick blue estuarine clay. This area, through which the River Blackwater now flows, would have separated the light, sandy and habitable Malone ridge, which runs like a spine down the Valley, from the steep basalt slopes of the Antrim Plateau and, more importantly, the flint quarries along the underlying chalk exposures. The effect would have been to push north–south routes some 7 km further west to the next fording point of the River Lagan at Shaw's Bridge. This area then took on a new importance as the focus of north–south land routes along the coast and east–west river routes from the coast to the interior. A kilometre upstream, the river flows along the western flank of the undulating Ballynahatty plateau (height 40 m). Access to the plateau, though possible from anywhere around its edge, is naturally facilitated from the river by an approach up the Purdysburn, a shallow tributary of the Lagan, which defines the northern edge of the plateau.

Continuing the upward journey, a trackway climbs from the stream to the northeast corner of the plateau and then passes south along the exposed steep, eastern side. In their fully developed forms, the timber enclosures would have been approached from this eastern edge across a small natural depression which emphasized the steepness of the eastern end of the ridge beyond it (FIGURE 3). Looking up could be seen the imposing façade of timbers straddling the crest of the ridge on the skyline. From the River Lagan therefore, the progression was ever upwards, culminating in this final climb to the site where the tall narrow entrance would have visually linked the earth with the sky.

Passing through the massive timber wall, a short passage lead to the Entrance Chamber. Characteristic of most of the complex, the posts were over 5 m high. With no view of the horizon and the outside world, the sky would have dominated the interior. Crossing the chamber to reach the exit on the far side meant passing through a setting of four posts. Unlike the Chamber walls, these posts had not been erected as a square and were more substantial and taller. The entrance chamber can probably be viewed as two separate cells, north and south of the passage, each with two carefully centred posts. Passage through it was therefore facilitated, but the opening out of this space also provided a punctuation in the journey, perhaps a halfway-house for the performance of ceremonial activity flagged by the posts which, if high enough, may even have been seen outside the complex. If a procession was involved, this chamber may have acted as a waiting-room for followers, allowing only the privileged to continue. The exit from this chamber is also the entry point to the larger enclosure BNH5.

Effectively, this elaborate and imposing annexe functioned as a venue for preliminary rituals — a zone of transition. The importance of this is underlined by the later construction along the line of the ridge, at the break of slope, of the longer and larger line of east–west posts on the south side of the annexe. This prevented much of the interior of the Annexe from being visible from the south, but together with the southern side of BNH5 — which also sweeps along the edge of the ridge — the combined effect when seen from the passage-tomb must have been awe-inspiring. That there is a link between BNH5 and the passage tomb can be demonstrated by the alignment of the Annexe façade. The southward projection is aimed directly at the tomb and may physically have been joined to it by another line of posts, some of which have been located at the southern end of the façade (FIGURES 1 & 3).

The view along the passageway through the entrance chamber was contrived to reveal only the interior of BNH5. Only when standing on the threshold of the BNH5 enclosure would it become obvious that the route had been angled to the northwest to pass between the two wedge-shaped settings of posts before finally arriving at the inner enclosure, BNH6. The Eastern Settings and the passage through BNH5 have clearly been conceived and constructed together. FIGURE 2 shows how carefully these structures were laid out and emphasizes that this was the product of sophisticated planning — designed by an architect. However, rope, stakes and a measuring stick were all that was required to set out this elegant structure (Hartwell 1998: 39–41). Passing between the two settings a crucial point is reached (B in FIGURE 2). Because of the way that these timber structures have been laid out as opposing sectors of a circle, the centre is the only point from which it is possible for their full interiors to be seen and their contents revealed. Looking forwards it is also the first point at which a complete view can be had of the square platform at the centre of BNH6. At such close quarters, BNH6 would have towered above point B, again emphasizing links between the earth and sky and the façade would have focused attention on the entrance and the central and most exclusive part of the whole complex.

Passing through the façade into the interior, the arrangement of four posts reappears. This is almost square as this time the posts do not define a passage, but the rear two posts are slightly closer together than the front two. Bearing in mind the precision with which the site is laid out this is unlikely to be an error. The effect of these posts towering above the enclosing circle when viewed from 'B' would have been to emphasize perspective and provide more visual depth. These posts must also have acted as the visual markers for the core of the whole complex — the central platform. Though 2 m square, this structure had a distinct orientation, being five posts long in line with the entrance by four posts wide — again playing with perspective and emphasizing depth.

The function of the platform defines the function of the complex as a whole. The association with death is pronounced both from the orientation on the earlier passage tomb and the two cremations incorporated within BNH6. In one case the ramps of two of the inner ring posts diverge to protect the integrity of a primary cremation, that of a young women placed in a herringbone setting of split stones. The other, to the west, was of a child. The annexe, north and south of the entrance chamber, also contains the remains of two possible cremation pits. Though one was severely plough damaged, the other showed evidence of being used on a number of occasions. Together with the strongly

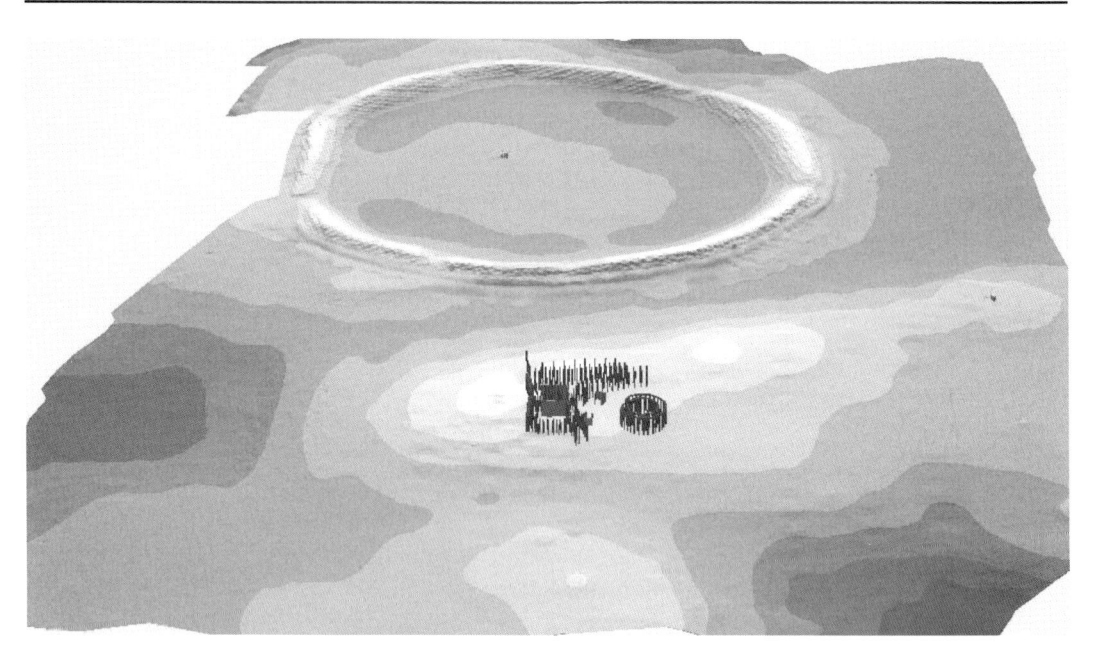

FIGURE 3. *A GIS model of the Ballynahatty landscape from the north (by Brian McDonagh) showing BNH6 and the Annexe sitting on the eastern end of the ridge. The approach is from the east across a depression. The slope to the northwest runs down to a small lake. At the western end of the ridge is a large stone and to the south is the Giant's Ring containing the passage-grave. The façade of the Annexe is aligned on the tomb.*

implied association between earth and sky, the square structure may best be interpreted as an excarnation platform. To return to the pivotal position (B) between the Eastern Settings, looking forward into the inner enclosure would have revealed the process of bodily decay and transformation from a person with identity to the anonimity of ancestral bone. Perhaps the two Eastern Settings were ossuaries, where the physical manifestation of the ancestors could be seen and crossing the line between them was passing from the realm of the present and temporary into the unending parallel world of the ancestors. These processes were reflected in the final conflagration of the complex. The burning was not an act of destruction but one of change in which the decaying posts, the transient, 'fleshy' parts of the structure, were transformed into a permanent state. It mirrored the process of excarnation of the body. Charcoal and stone thus replaced wood to become the permanent skeleton of the site and there is some evidence to suggest that the major posts were marked by low cairns of stones.

The interior of the large enclosure BNH5 was not excavated, though the air photographs show areas of disturbance scattered across it. Air photographs also show three concentric bands inside the Giant's Ring and these may represent another timber enclosure centred on the passage-tomb. If so, this complex may also have functioned as a conduit to the earth as well as the sky.

Conclusion
The plateau is therefore a set of contrasts — regionally accessible from land and sea by its location near routeways, yet physically isolated; in the valley floor, yet above it; centrally placed, yet, with its concentration of ritual sites, on the spiritual edge. Both the

siting and architecture of the Ballynahatty enclosures seem to have focused on links between earth and sky with excarnation in the form of 'sky burial' and cremation being the principle functions. The passageways and rooms were necessary to carefully choreograph movement and progressively restrict, reveal or enhance views of the ceremonial journey from life to death. The architecture had to give formal structure to preconceived ritual (Rappaport 1999: 32) and the elegance of the architectural solution is as impressive now as it must have been in the 3rd millennium BC.

References

COLLINS, A.E.P.C. 1954. Excavations at the Giant's Ring, Ballynahatty, *Ulster Journal of Archaeology* (3rd series) 17: 44–60.
EOGAN, G. & H. ROCHE. 1997. *Excavations at Knowth* (2). Dublin: Royal Irish Academy.
GIBSON, A. 1994. Excavations at the Sarn-y-Bryn-Caled cursus complex, Welshpool, Powys, and the timber circles of Great Britain and Ireland, *Proceedings of the Prehistoric Society* 60: 143–223.
   1998. *Stonehenge and timber circles*. Stroud: Sutton.
GIBSON, A. & D. SIMPSON (ed.). 1998. *Prehistoric ritual and religion. Essays in honour of Aubrey Burl*. Stroud: Sutton.
HARTWELL, B. 1998. The Ballynahatty complex, in Gibson & Simpson (ed.): 32–44.
   2000. Ballynahatty 5, Ballynahatty, in I. Bennett (ed.), *Excavation 1999, summary accounts of archaeological excavations in Ireland*: 44–6. Bray: Wordwell.
LAWLOR, H.C. 1918. The Giant's Ring, *Proceedings of the Belfast Natural History & Philosophical Society* 1917–1918: 13–28.
MACADAM, R. & E. GETTY. 1855. Discovery of an ancient sepulchral chamber, *Ulster Journal of Archaeology* (1st series) 3: 358–65.
RAPPAPORT, R.A. 1999. *Ritual and religion in the making of humanity*. Cambridge: Cambridge University Press.
SWEETMAN, P.D. 1984. A Late Neolithic/Early Bronze Age pit circle at Newgrange, Co. Meath, *Proceedings of the Royal Irish Academy* 85C: 195–221.

New evidence of ritual monuments at Long Meg and her Daughters, Cumbria

by GRAHAME SOFFE & TOM CLARE

ANTIQUITY 62 (236), 1988

THIS NOTE records the recognition of a remarkable pear-shaped ditched enclosure attached to the well-known stone circle, Long Meg and her Daughters in Hunsonby parish, Cumbria (NGR NY 571374). A number of other interesting monuments in the immediate vicinity of the stone circle were also recorded. None of these features are clearly visible on the ground. The large enclosure was first recognized by RCHME on RAF photographs in its care (NAR NY53NE 21; Challis & Harding 1975). It was again recorded together with a group of other smaller enclosures as crop and parch marks during RCHME's 1984 season of air photographic reconnaissance (PLATE 4 (page 448)), and by the Cumbria County Council. The air photographs provide accurate plans of the individual elements and allow an assessment of their significance in terms of prehistoric activity in the immediate area (FIGURES 1, 2, 4).

The site lies on a wide flat terrace of sandstone above the east bank of the Eden, sloping down northwards from about 167 m OD at Long Meg to 160 m on the north side of the circle. Much of the area has been cleared and enclosed for arable cultivation over the past 300 years, although the stone circle and large enclosure are now in pasture. The great henges of Mayburgh and King Arthur's Round Table, near Penrith (RCHME 1936: 252–3), are sited 9 km away across the river.

Just over 50 years ago in these pages, Crawford referred to the Long Meg circle as 'one of the major monuments of its kind in Britain, and one of the most perfect' (Crawford 1934: 28). So it remains. Indeed, it is the largest stone circle in Britain after Avebury and Stanton Drew, 109·4 x 93·0 m, 68 massive igneous boulders set out in an oval, flattened on its north side. Twenty-seven stones remain upright, with a portal of double-stones on the southwest perimeter and a second entrance on the northwest. Very slight traces of an earth bank can be detected along the southwest circumference, but whether this indicates some affinity with henges or is the result of soil being embanked against the stones by post-medieval rig cultivation is uncertain. At 18 m beyond the southwest entrance stands Long Meg, a menhir of tabular red sandstone, 3·7 m high, bearing prehistoric carvings on its eastern face (Harvey 1948). Full descriptions of the stone circle are given by Dymond (1881: 40–7, with the first accurate plan), Burl (1976: 89–92) and Waterhouse (1985: 99–102). One of us has discussed it in the context of other Cumbrian stone circles (Clare 1973; 1975); Thom (1967) and Hutchinson (1972) discuss geometric and astronomical interpretations, although their views on the flattened north side will need modification in respect of the 'new' enclosure.

Large enclosure (FIGURES 1A & 2)
The parch mark revealed by air photography indicates a ditch of variable thickness enclosing a pear-shaped area 220 x 190 m. There is an entrance on the south side where the ditch terminals thicken, and a less distinct gap, possibly a second entrance, on the north side. Evidence for the ditch circuit and other possible entrances to the northwest has been concealed by the modern farmyard. In several places a faint lightening inside the ditch *may* be interpreted as an internal bank.

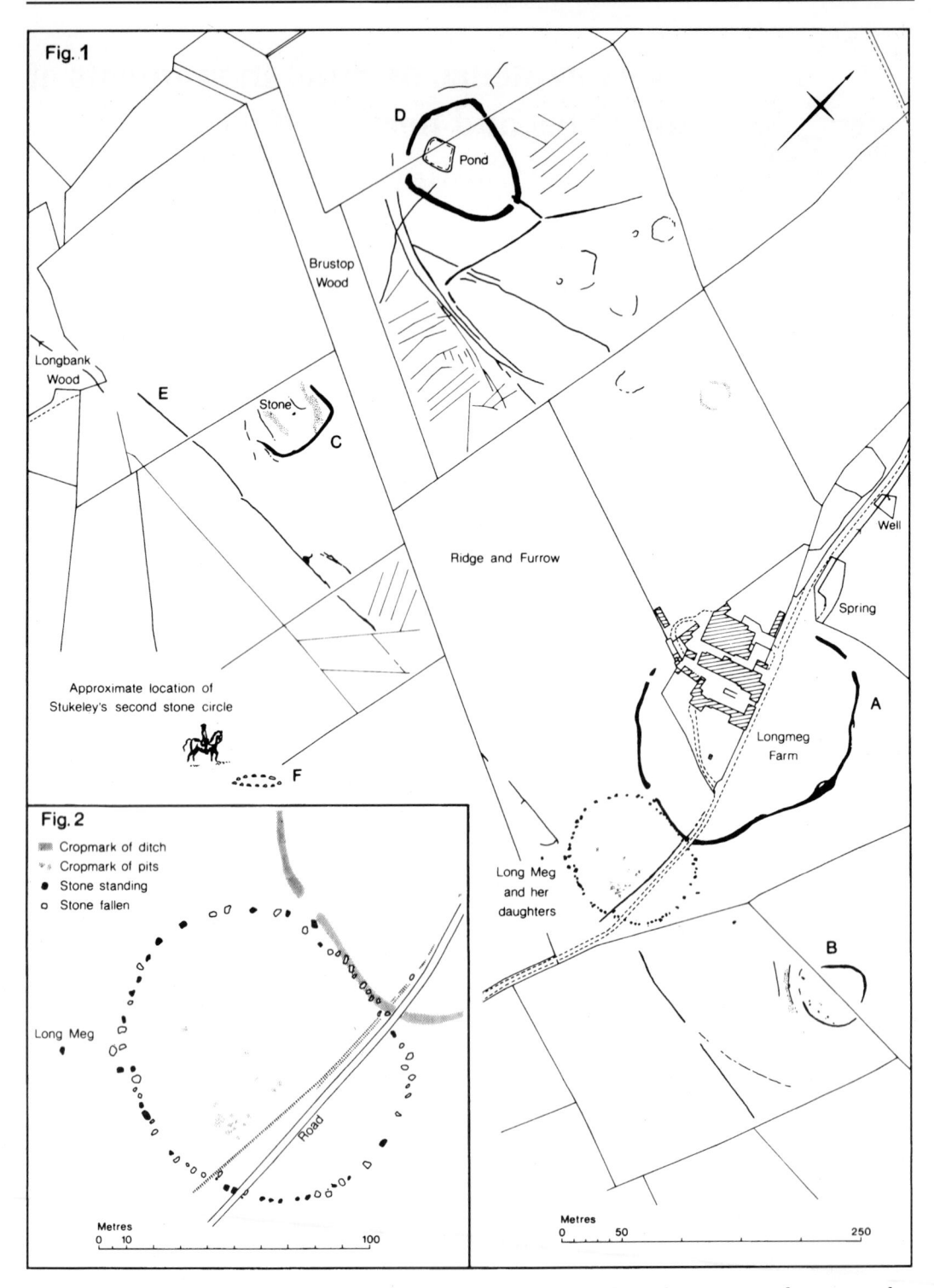

FIGURE 1. *The Long Meg monuments.* A *Large enclosure* B *Small enclosure* C *Enclosure south of Brustop Wood* D *Pond enclosure* E *Linear ditches* F *Lesser stone circle.*
FIGURE 2. (inset) *Detail of the ring and adjacent portion of the large enclosure.*

Of particular interest is the area where the southern length of enclosure ditch joins the flattened side of the stone circle (FIGURE 2). Remarkably, here also the north portal of the stone circle appears to turn slightly east to open directly into the enclosure entrance. Presumably a western outer stone stood here originally, in parallel with the south portal of the circle, although the air photographs give no indication of its former position.

The flattening of the stone circle finds numerous parallels in other British sites such as Castlerigg (Cumbria), and Avebury, whose geometry Thom discusses at length (1967: 66–7, etc.). He concludes their shapes 'were controlled by factors unknown to us today'. At Long Meg, however, we can suggest the flattening was occasioned directly by the presence of the ditched enclosure. Several other factors are also relevant here. All the stones on the flat side are generally closer together, shorter and narrower than those forming the remaining circuit. Moreover at least ten of these appear to have stood on the lip of the enclosure ditch when it was still open, and all have subsequently fallen or slipped into its upper fill. Indeed, where probable packing stones are visible, indications are that stones fell northwards, with three examples almost buried in the ditch fill. We must record the likelihood of some stones having been moved in historic times. Stukeley noted stones being displaced by 'blowing them in pieces with gunpowder' (1776: 47). About 1800 Colonel Lacy attempted to move stones by blasting. The resulting storm was said to be 'so terrible that the workmen fled for their lives' (Sullivan 1857: 127–8, Whellan 1860: 502). At about the same time stones were removed, and after the failure of a crop, replaced (Hodgson 1935: 79). Crop marks do not indicate the presence of empty stone holes around the circumference of the circle, but this interference probably accounts for some fallen stones and gaps in the perimeter. The northern sequence of stones, nevertheless, seems fairly complete and few stones here lie significantly distant from the line of circumference.

This combination of factors demonstrates a close functional relationship between the stone circle and the enclosure. It also implies near- contemporaneity, with the construction of the stone circle following that of the enclosure, for which a Neolithic to Early Bronze Age date might be suggested. None of these points can be proven, and it is impossible to argue further without more fieldwork and excavation. Whilst the enclosure does not appear to have a close morphological affinity with Neolithic causewayed enclosures or larger henges such as Marden and Durrington Walls, it has characteristics reminiscent of the Neolithic enclosures at Bury Hill, West Sussex (Bedwin 1981), Duggleby Howe, Yorkshire (Kinnes *et al.* 1983) and Lyles Hill in Ireland (Gibson & Simpson 1982). Bury Hill was associated with disposal of human dead whilst internal tumuli were present at Duggleby Howe and Lyles Hill. Significantly, Camden (in 1586) recorded two stone tumuli in the middle of the Long Meg circle (1695: 831), which were illustrated by Aubrey after Dugdale in the late 17th century (Aubrey 1980: 115, plate XIIII). Stukeley's description (1776: 47), shows them to have been almost destroyed by 1725, and now they have completely gone. Although these mounds may have been clearance cairns as Gibson suggests (Camden 1695: 831, note hh), the possiblity of barrows should be seriously considered, particularly when viewed from the position of the now-denuded monument of Little Meg, 580 m northeast of Long Meg. This, Dymond described in 1875 as 'a cist inclosed in a ring of 11 stones, formerly covd. with a mound' (1881: plan memoranda). The air photographs show no clear trace of the mounds, only a number of pits. These may be tree-holes, the sites of former stones like the three earth-fast boulders situated inside the circle along the old ditch, or the sites of burials.

The enclosure completely encircles the buildings of the present farm of Longmeg and so the relationship between the two might be considered. The siting of the enclosure may have been influenced by Stukeley's 'very fine spring, whence, no doubt, they [the builders of the stone circle] had the element of water, used at their religious solemnities'. The spring may also have influenced the siting of the farm. Stukeley makes no mention of the farm, however, and the existing buildings appear entirely post-medieval, built in two main phases, 1785–1826, and 1855. They are directly related to the enclosure of commons in Little Salkeld township after the disappearance of Addingham village and parish (Cumbria Record Office: Donald's Survey (1770) D+C/2/15, QRE/1/31; Parson & White (1829); and dated buildings).

As the site was unencumbered in Stukeley's day we must assume the enclosure (which we have already argued as being prehistoric) was already silted and ploughed flat. This too would seem to have been the fate of some of the other interesting monuments surrounding the great stone circle which were revealed by crop and parch marks in 1984, nearly all new discoveries.

Small enclosure east of the stone circle (FIGURE 1B)
An egg-shaped enclosure, bounded by a thin ditch, contains several possible pits.

Enclosure south of Brustop Wood (FIGURE 1C)
The east half of the ditch circuit of a small sub-rectangular enclosure is revealed as a crop mark; it surrounds a single earth-fast stone. Only one other similar stone occurs in the immediate neighbourhood, just to the northeast in the cleared wood, and there may be a parallel here with other enclosed stones such as the Menhir de Guérande in France (information: J. Meissonier).

Pond enclosure (FIGURE 1D)
To the north of this last enclosure lies another enclosure of similar size and shape but with a very wide ditch and an east entrance. It sits on the very edge of the terrace overlooking the Eden and surrounds a large pond. The site is now heavily ploughed and there is no trace on the ground of the ditch which Stukeley observed in 1725. He described the site as 'a large spring, intrenched about with a *vallum* and foss, of a pretty great circumference, but no depth' (1776: 47). The juxtaposition of enclosure and pond is not coincidental; similar enclosures of prehistoric and Roman date are known to be sited near tarns or other water sources elsewhere in Cumbria (Bewley 1984: chapter 5), although a concentric arrangement is rare. Several linear ditches fan out from the entrance area; immediately to the south a double ditched trackway funnels out into the valley and seems to underlie a number of ditches running at right angles to it.

Parallel linear ditches (FIGURE 1E)
Two other linear ditches run *nearly* parallel to one another east from Longbank Wood toward Long Meg. The idea of a prehistoric cursus or an avenue analogous to Stonehenge is attractive but must be discounted on the evidence. The course of the northern ditch runs through and beyond the stone circle. It has an irregular character and is probably prehistoric in origin, although its association with the stone circle or a bank in Longbank Wood is unclear. The other ditch is straighter and thinner and is clearly part of a 19th-century herring-bone drainage system.

Lesser stone circle (FIGURES 1F & 3)
The air photographs help little in the quest for the circle that was observed and drawn by Stukeley southwest of Long Meg. In a close comparison of these observations with his own fieldwork, Crawford (1934) argued convincingly that it was sited just north of another tarn and two derelict barns (NY 568370). It was in this area in 1986 that the farmer cleared a large number of boulders. Interestingly, three earth-fast stones remain *in situ*;

FIGURE 3. *William Stukeley, A View of the Celtic Temple calld Long Meg Aug. 16 1725. (Bodleian Library MS Top. Gen. b. 53 fo. 13ᵛ. Photo © the Bodleian Library, Oxford.) The great circle is in the foreground, the taller stone of Long Meg behind it at rear left, and the lesser circle beyond.*

they may have formed part of a 15-m diameter lesser circle, which was possibly similar to those in the Burn Moor complex at Eskdale, Cumbria, and illustrated by Burl (1976: 96–7).

Conclusion

The site of Long Meg and her Daughters now takes on a fresh appearance. With the aid of air photography and ground observation, important advances have been made. The well known stone circle can be seen to have been constructed adjacent to an earthwork enclosure and some contemporaneity of use is to be inferred. As such it can be suggested that these sites, and perhaps some of the others immediately surrounding them, represent a complex which served as the focus for Late Neolithic peoples in the Eden Valley. The existence of a similar focal point 9 km to the southwest at Mayburgh and King Arthur's Round Table (RCHME 1936: 252–3) would, however, imply we are dealing not with *the* focal point for the Eden Valley but one of several complexes, each of which must have served a discrete terri-

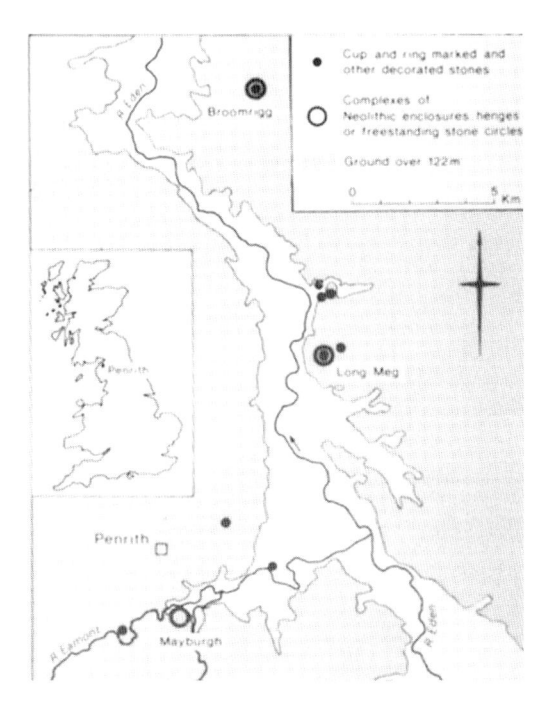

FIGURE 4. *Distribution of cup- and ring-marked and other decorated stones in relation to henge/stone-circle complexes in Cumbria.*

torial area. In seeking to identify similar foci attention is drawn to the complex of sites at Broomrigg, 10 km north of Long Meg.

Such foci imply Neolithic settlement in the Eden Valley was — whether permanent or seasonal — more extensive than the paucity of long barrows suggests. Whether formal boundaries existed between the postulated territorial units is, however, unclear. Nevertheless, it is interesting to note that the Mayburgh complex lies immediately south of the River Eamont which was historically a frontier and a county boundary, whilst immediately to the north there have been several finds of cup- and ring-marked stones with motifs similar to those on Long Meg (FIGURE 4: Frodsham forthcoming). As any natural boundary between the Long Meg and Broomrigg sites would have to be at right angles to the Eden — as the River Eamont is — it seems that the inferred territorial units embraced resource areas not dissimilar from those which can be postulated for later multiple estates.

Little more can now be learnt about the Long Meg monuments until fresh revelations are made through further fieldwork. The significance of the new evidence should be seen against recent wider discussion of henges and similar dated enclosures elsewhere (e.g. Clare 1987; Harding & Lee 1988). Here, however, we should like to know the probability that some sites previously suggested as belonging to later prehistory and the Roman period (Challis & Haridng 1975: 135; Bewley 1984), may well be earlier in date and now require re-evaluating.

Acknowledgements. G. Soffe wishes to thank Dr R. Whimster, Ms G. Stout, Dr R. Bewley, Ms C. Stoertz and Mr J. Edis for useful discussion, and Messrs K. and S. Morton and Mr R. Mark for their interest and permission to visit sites on their farms. T. Clare thanks Miss Clare Fell for her comments on an earlier draft of his part of this note. Both thank P. Sinton for his help in producing the final versions of FIGURES 1, 2 & 4, which are the copyright of RCHME.

References

AUBREY. J. [1980] (ed. J. Fowles). *Monumenta Britannica* 1. Sherborne: Dorset Publishing.
BEDWIN O. 1981. Excavation at the Neolithic enclosure on Bury Hill, Houghton, West Sussex 1979, *Proceedings of the Prehistoric Society* 47: 69–86.
BEWLEY, R.H. 1984. Prehistoric and Romano-British settlement in the Solway Plain, Cumbria. Unpublished Ph.D thesis, University of Cambridge.
BURL, A. 1976. *The stone circles of the British Isles.* New Haven : Yale University Press.
CAMDEN, W. 1695 (ed. E. Gibson). *Britannia.* Oxford.
CHALLIS A.J. & D.W. HARDING 1975. *Later prehistory from the Trent to the Tyne.* Oxford. British Archaeological Reports. British series 20.
CLARE T. 1973. Aspects of the stone circles and kindred monuments of North West England. Unpublished MA thesis, University of Liverpool.
    1975. Some Cumbrian stone circles in perspective, *Transactions of the Cumberland & Westmorland Antiquarian & Archaeological Society* (new series) 75: 1–16.
    1987. Towards a reappraisal of henge monuments: origins, evolution and hierarchies, *Proceedings of the Prehistoric Society* 53: 457–78.
CRAWFORD, O.G.S. 1934. Long Meg, *Antiquity* 8: 328–9.
DYMOND, C.W. 1881. A group of Cumberland megaliths, *Transactions of the Cumberland & Westmorland Antiquarian & Archaeological Society* (1st series) 5: 39–57.
FRODSHAM, P. Forthcoming. *On two newly discovered cup and ring marked stones from Penrith and Hallbankgate, with some general observations on all megalithic carvings in Cumbria.*
GIBSON, A.M. & D.D.A. SIMPSON. 1987. Lyles Hill, Co. Antrim, *Archaeology Ireland* 2: 72–5.
HARDING, A.F. & G. LEE. 1988. *Henge monuments and related sites of Great Britain: air photographic evidence and catalogue.* Oxford: British Archaeological Reports. British series 175.
HARVEY, J.H. 1948. A note on Long Meg, Salkeld, *Archaeological Journal* 105: addendum.
HODGSON, K.S. 1935. Notes on stone circles at Broomrigg, Grey Youlds, etc., *Transactions of the Cumberland & Westmorland Antiquarian & Archaeological Society* (new series) 35: 77–9.
HUTCHINSON, G.E. 1972. Long Meg reconsidered, *American Scientist* 60: 24–31, 210–19.
KINNES I., T. SCHADLA-HALL, P. CHADWICK & P. DEAN. 1983. Duggleby Howe reconsidered, *Archaeological Journal* 140: 83–108.
PARSON, W. & W. WHITE 1829. *History, directory and gazetteer of Cumberland and Westmorland.* Leeds.
RCHME. 1936. *An inventory of the historical monuments in Westmorland.* London: HMSO.
STUKELEY, W. 1776. Iter Boreale [written 1725, first published in *Itinerarium Curiosum*].
SULLIVAN, J. 1857. *Cumberland and Westmoreland, ancient and modern.* London: Whittaker.
THOM, A. 1967. *Megalithic sites in Britain.* Oxford: Clarendon.
WATERHOUSE, J. 1985. *The stone circles of Cumbria.* Chichester: Phillimore.
WHELLAN, W. 1860. *History and topography of Cumberland and Westmoreland.* Pontefract: Whellan.

A late Neolithic complex at West Kennet, Wiltshire, England

by ALASDAIR WHITTLE

ANTIQUITY 65 (247), 1991

AN IMPORTANT COMPLEX of Late Neolithic sites is emerging in the Kennet valley, Wiltshire, under the nose of the Avebury region's celebrated Neolithic sites. These new sites — two large palisade enclosures, attached fence lines, and a double circular timber structure — have significant implications for the Neolithic record of the Avebury region.

Palisade enclosure 1

Palisade enclosure 1, under investigation since 1987, straddles the present course of the Kennet (FIGURES 1–2). In 1987 it was possible, as part of a university research project, to follow the leads provided by an aerial photograph of St Joseph in 1950 and by summary recording by Faith Vatcher of the Avebury Museum of a pipeline along the south side of the Kennet valley in the early 1970s. Sample excavation found, on the terrace south of the Kennet and east of the Gunsight Lane, two concentric ditches which contained substantial palisades (cuttings C, D, E and F on FIGURE 1). Both ditches were 2 m or more deep, the inner one reaching 2·7 m in F; while the inner ditch was about 2 m broad, the outer was as little as 1 m broad in places. In the base of these ditches or bedding trenches were slots cut to receive close-set oak posts. The posts were seen through the ditch fills as charcoal-rich post-pipes, around 30 cm in diameter on average. There were two to three per linear metre. The posts were originally held upright by backfilled spoil from the ditch digging, with the addition of substantial sarsen stones as further packing; in cutting F, the middle and upper parts of the deep inner ditch were literally stuffed with sarsen packing stones. This constructional overkill immediately made one think of 'loony late Neolithic' activity. The posts had decayed *in situ*, and abundant charcoal suggests that they may well have been burned down. A very fine oblique ripple-flaked flint arrowhead was found in the outer ditch, and two antler samples from the same outer ditch cutting (D) gave uncalibrated radiocarbon determinations of 3810±50 BP (BM-2597) and 3620±50 BP (BM-2602). The obvious analogy was with the single-circuit palisade enclosure inside (and replacing) the large henge at Mount Pleasant, Dorset (Wainwright 1979). That too had been burned, and was associated with Beaker pottery and uncalibrated radiocarbon determinations of 3645±43 BP (BM-665) and 3637±63 BP (BM-662).

In 1989 the Trust for Wessex Archaeology undertook a surface evaluation in the yard of the West Kennet Farm, north of the Kennet and opposite the eastern part of the enclosure revealed in 1987. This was in advance of proposals to build on the farmyard. The work showed, with little doubt, the existence north of the river of a curving ditch circuit, which had to be a further part of the roughly circular layout of enclosure 1. Excavation, however, was not attempted (Whittle & Smith 1990). The new circuit in the farmyard was promptly scheduled in advance of the ensuing planning enquiry, which has led to permission to develop being refused (Pitts 1990; Chippindale 1991: 5).

In 1990 was dug one cutting immediately adjacent to the farmyard, north of the river (O on FIGURE 2). This confirmed the existence of the ditch circuit north of the river,

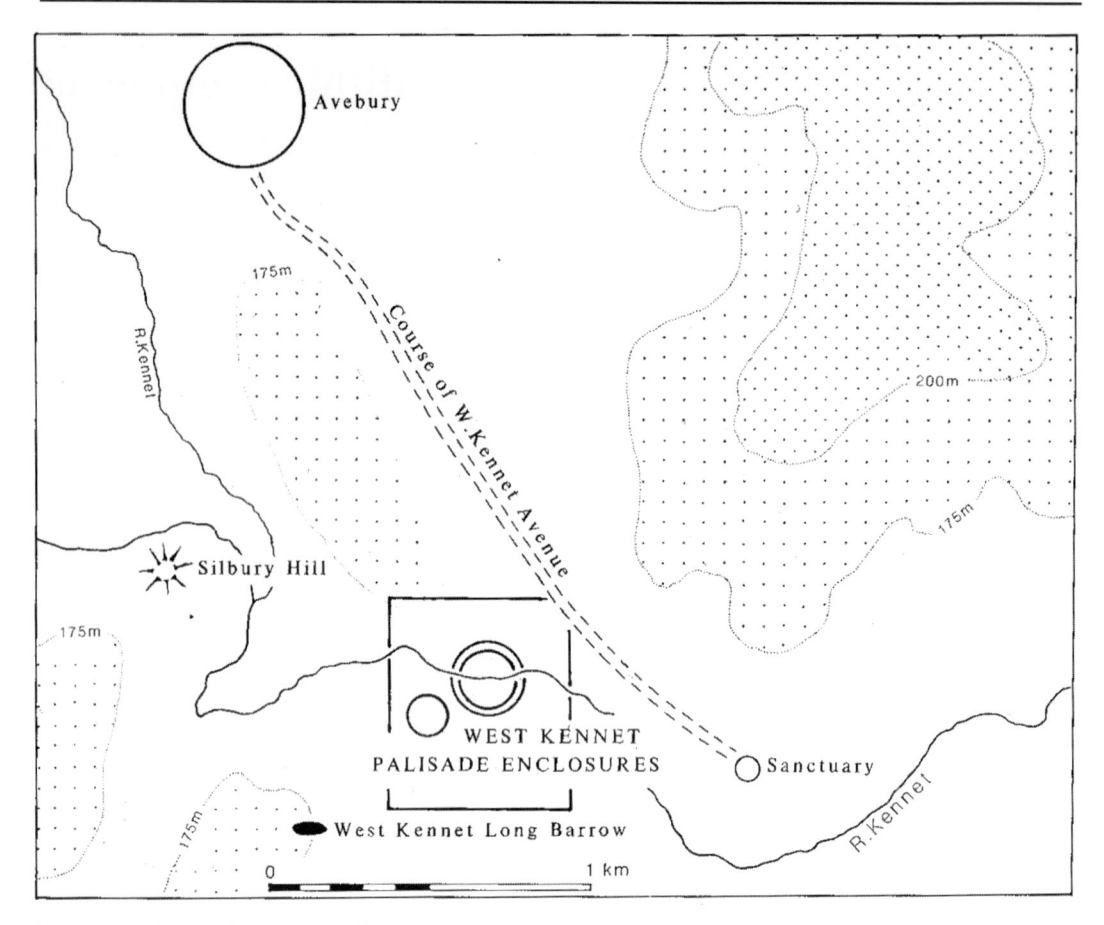

FIGURE 1. *Simplified map of the Avebury area, showing the West Kennet palisade enclosures in relation to Avebury and other sites.*

as all the recurrent features were there: ditch over 2 m deep, close-set post-pipes, basal sockets, deliberate backfill, and sarsen packing stones. What remains unclear is whether there was another ditch circuit north of the river, which would affect the shape of enclosure 1, and this will require further investigation.

South of the river, it was possible in 1990 to pinpoint where the ditches entered the floodplain meadows of the Kennet. To the west, we were led by superb aerial photographs taken by the Royal Commission on Historical Monuments (England) in the dry spring of 1990 (cuttings H and P), and to the east (cutting N) we followed on from the 1987 work. The inner ditch (cutting J) was found by dead reckoning; this had also been seen in further pipeline work in 1989, at the junction between terrace and floodplain. Recurrent features turned up again, including magnificent post-pipes in the outer ditch in cutting H (FIGURE 2), and there was evidence for the deliberate placing of animal bone around the posts within the backfill of the ditch. There were scraps of Grooved Ware in the ditches, and sherds of the same Late Neolithic pottery in a deposit of animal bone on the surface of the interior within the outer ditch. This deposit survived just below the modern ploughsoil. Faith Vatcher (Avebury Museum records) also recorded various scoops and hollows east of the Gunsight Lane. Area excavation might reveal extensive deposits and perhaps structures, but the nature of survival on the long-cultivated terrace south of the Kennet is variable.

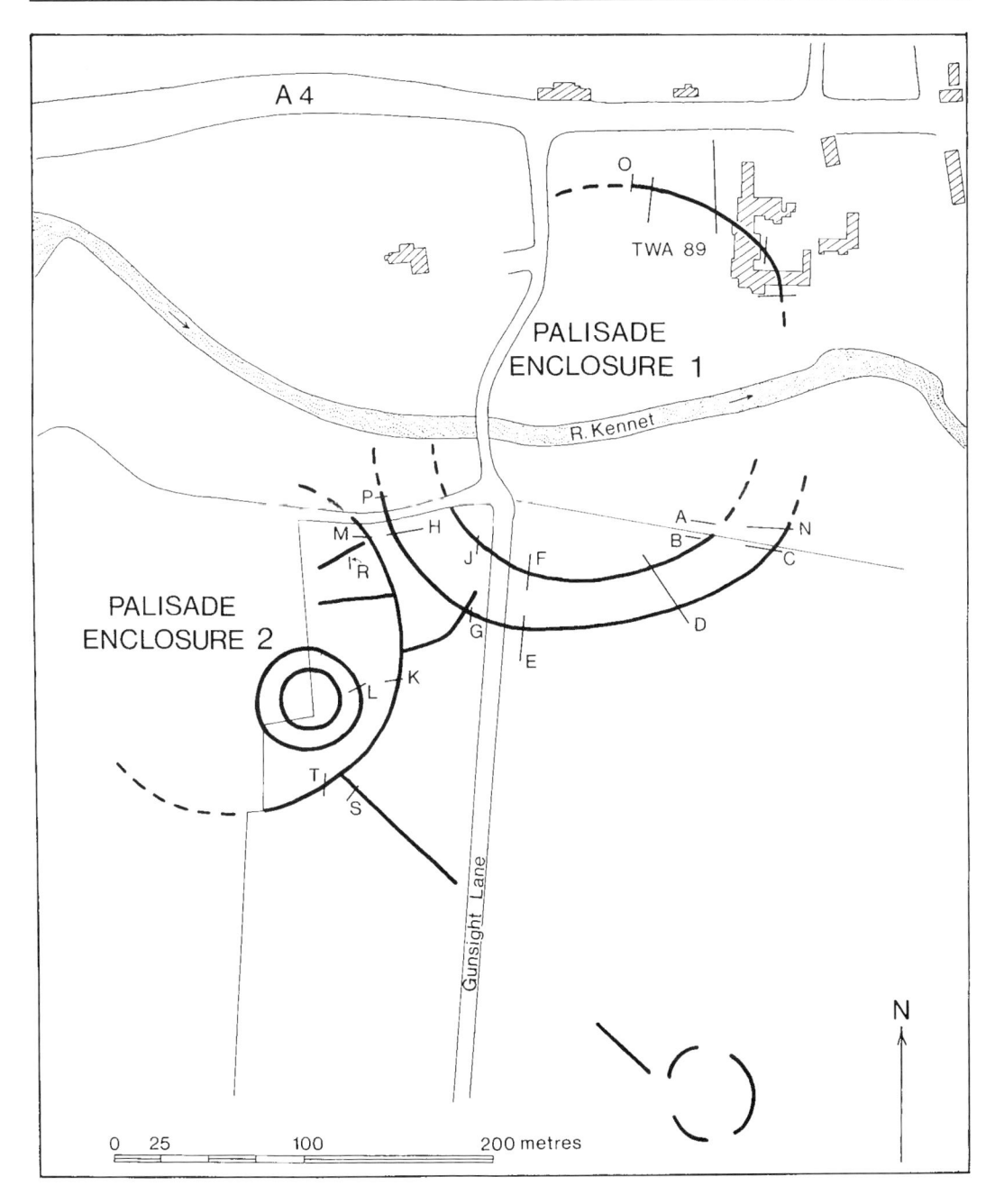

FIGURE 2. *Interim plan of enclosures 1 and 2. Cuttings are marked A–F (1987), TWA 89 (1989), and G–T (1990).*

Palisade enclosure 2

In 1989 it began to become clear that enclosure 1 was not in isolation. Amateur aerial photographs of the field west of the Gun Road began to show further features to the south-west of enclosure 1, which were confirmed by a magnetometer survey carried out by Mike Hamilton of UWCC in 1989 and again by the RCHM(E) air photos of spring 1990. These features included a double concentric ring over 40 m in diameter, a long

FIGURE 3. *Post-pipes in plan and section during excavation of the outer ditch of enclosure 1 (cutting H). Note also sarsen packing stones.*

curving ditch and various straight and curving ditches apparently butted on it (FIGURE 1). The second aim in 1990 was to see whether enclosure 1 had attracted around it other sites such as ring ditches.

The outer ring of the double concentric feature was located by excavation (cutting L, FIGURE 1); cultivation prevented testing the inner as well. The outer ring proved not to be a ditch but a close-set row of post holes, about a metre deep and 40 cm in diameter. The posts had probably rotted in situ. There were no finds apart from quite abundant charcoal and pieces of bone. It is hard to see this as other than Late Neolithic or Early Bronze Age in date. It recalls the timber 'wossit' at Street House, Cleveland (Vyner 1988), though that was much smaller. Many timber structures of Late Neolithic date have diameters around 40 m, including the Sanctuary, the South Circle inside Durrington Walls, and site IV inside Mount Pleasant.

It had been anticipated that the long curving ditch would be of later date. Excavation proved otherwise. Within the first week Grooved Ware sherds in Durrington Walls style had turned up in cutting M, and more were found in T and S. The ditch in fact forms an arc of nearly circular form; its presumed continuation must lie in the next field west, on the lower ground below the ridge rising to the West Kennet long barrow, where it is hoped to trace its course by geophysical survey in 1991. At this stage, it can tentatively be projected as a near-circular shape some 180 m in diameter. The ditch which defines palisade enclosure 2 was again some 2 m deep by 2 m broad, and other familiar features emerged. There were basal sockets for posts. There were charcoal-rich post-pipes; these were rather bigger, around 50 cm or more in diameter, and a little more spaced than in enclosure 1. Animal bone had been packed around their upper parts in some cases. The posts had again remained in situ and the charcoal, especially in M, may reflect a story of burning. The posts had been held by deliberate backfill, with some sarsen packing stones, particularly in M (FIGURE 3).

The ditch of enclosure 2 was not, however, completely backfilled, and a shallow hollow was left at its top. In this hollow in cutting M was deposited a considerable quantity of dark soil, rich in charcoal and animal bone, though this was largely unburnt. Probably this was deposited while posts were standing, though it is possible that it represents a secondary phase of activity. The impression during excavation was of a series of dumps of animal bone; identification of species and body parts will refine this picture.

The last striking feature of enclosure 2 is the radial lines apparently butted on it. No relationships were examined, since the first task was to understand the individual structures. Two inner radial lines appear to converge, perhaps aligned on the putative centre of the enclosure, recalling the very orderly layout of the Late Neolithic circular enclosure at the Flagstones site, Dorchester (Woodward 1988). Unfortunately, the first cutting attempted (R) failed to locate the northern inner radial seen clearly on the geophysical survey and the aerial photographs, and time ran out before the feature could be pursued further. The southeastern external radial was firmly located in cutting S; it consisted of post-pipes about a metre deep and 25 cm in diameter, set in an irregular, narrow bedding trench and held by earth packing. Animal bone was packed around the tops of posts, and there were again small sherds of Grooved Ware. It looks as though the radial lines were fence lines of some kind, and part of the unitary layout of enclosure 2. A curving line on the east side, which intersects enclosure 1, is intriguing. The southeastern radial continues, as seen on older air photos researched by Rowan Whimster of RCHM(E), for over 200 m and appears to terminate on another ring mark east of the Gunsight Lane.

FIGURE 4. *Post-pipes and sarsen packing stones in the upper part of the ditch of enclosure 2 (cutting M).*

The structural similarity of enclosure 2 to enclosure 1 is striking. Enclosure 2 finds echoes in the layout of the Flagstones enclosure, of around 100 m diameter, or the much larger post-pit circle at Greyhound Yard, Dorchester, which has an estimated diameter of nearly 400 m (Wainwright 1989: 88). The two enclosures at West Kennet are presumably not contemporary, but we will have to wait for further radiocarbon dates to see if the relationship can be resolved by that means.

Archaeological implications

To have missed one enclosure so near other major monuments may have been bad luck, but to have missed two begins to look like carelessness. The history of research in the Avebury area goes back to Aubrey in the 17th century, and probably before him, since it was in Aubrey's interests to dramatize his 'discovery' in 1648/9. The roll-call of great names is impressive, and there have been many excavations. Plotted out, the list appears formidable (Pitts 1990: table 1). Yet, most excavations have been episodic at best in duration. Knowledge of surface assemblages of flints relies heavily on collections made from the 1910s to 1930s. Aerial photographic cover has also been extremely patchy (Rowan Whimster pers. comm.). The existence of some sites is known (or suspected), like small stone circles at Langdean, Falkner's near Avebury, Clatford and Winterbourne Bassett, but too little of their details. Other sites have been claimed on the basis of insufficient evidence. A supposed enclosure on Overton Hill near West Kennet is seen irregularly on air photographs since the 1930s (Malone 1989). Geophysical survey in 1989 and test excavation in 1990 showed nothing but very minor surface geological irregularities. One could go on. The full extent and nature of the archaeological record in this flagship area are not known, simply because we have not systematically examined them. Other parts of this research project, at Windmill Hill in 1988 and the ruined chambered tomb at Millbarrow, Winterbourne Monkton, have offered unexpected results, such as the pre-enclosure grave at the former (Whittle 1990) and two pairs of ditches flanking the latter. I think it unlikely that the whole area is covered in undiscovered sites, since pattern is part of the nature of landscapes dominated by ritual monuments, but the possibility cannot now be ignored that other important sites are still to be recovered. This must lead now to further systematic survey of known sites, cropmark evidence and lithic scatters, as well as to further test excavation at major and minor monuments.

More radiocarbon dates are required to be sure of the sequence. My present belief, following the first results from enclosure 1, is that both enclosures will post-date Avebury and the phase of obscure monumentalism represented at Silbury Hill. Radiocarbon dates from Avebury may indicate a major construction phase around 4050 BP (Pitts & Whittle 1992) and I believe that Silbury Hill came soon after, at say 3950 BP, using one reliable date on organic matter from the primary core (4095±95 BP: I-4136) and two dates on antler from near the base of the final ditch (3849±+43 BP: BM-842, and 3752±50 BP: BM-841) (Whittle 1997). It is possible to regard the palisade enclosures as sacred precincts, defensive strongholds or stockades around prominent settlements. There are arguments for and against each possibility. The more or less circular enclosures can be seen as redefining the tradition of earthwork enclosures which had endured since the Earlier Neolithic, and placed deposits of animal bone around their perimeters also as part of a by-now ancient tradition. It remains to be seen, however, whether the circuits are a true guide to the nature of the interiors. The great wooden walls could be seen as defensive, and may have ended by being burned. Finds of arrowhead tips in skeletons have shown the Earlier Neolithic as not wholly peaceful, and raiding or warfare could have been endemic in the Later Neolithic (*cf.* Carneiro 1990); inter-group competition need not just have been played out in the abstractions of ideology or ritual. Yet the circumferences of the enclosures are considerable, and their position low-lying. These may be modern objections. Carneiro (1990: 197) has noted how palisade fortifications in the Cauca valley in Colombia could be abandoned in the face of impending severe attack for more defensible positions. One view of the development of Neolithic occupation, based on the changing character of lithic remains, holds that settlement was not well established till the Late Neolithic (Bradley 1987). If this is so, one might expect the first substantial or well-defined settlements in the Later Neolithic. The enclosures could mark such sites, though they need not have been crammed within by palisade-to-palisade occupation. Were this the general case, one might expect more such sites in southern England (unless we have missed them all!).

One can combine these explanations. In every case, if the enclosures belong to a very late phase of the Neolithic, transformations can be seen taking place. The considerable labour involved in construction could have been broken down into manageable units and carried out by much smaller gangs than are implied by the great earthwork enterprises of the Later Neolithic. A continuous ditch only 2 m broad does not allow a large workforce, and timbers could be handled more easily than vast sarsens. A reduced scale of participation may be significant in view of what follows in the burial record of the Early Bronze Age.

The enclosures contribute vividly to understanding the environmental setting of the Avebury area. Posts sunk some 2 m deep could have stood 6 or 8 or more metres high above ground (Mercer 1983), as bare wooden walls or covered with cob or daub. Suppose each post to have been only 8 m long (2 below ground, and 6 above, in a reasonable ratio of 1:3); bring in 2 to 3 posts per metre of the palisade, and estimate a total ditch circumference of around 1000 m for enclosure 1. The result is a lot of timber — perhaps 20,000 linear metres. The figure is smaller for enclosure 2, where there are roughly 2 posts per metre. The average diameters of the posts, around 30 cm and 50 cm in enclosure 1 and 2 respectively, suggest secondary rather than primary woodland. It is not difficult to envisage this woodland resource as managed and controlled. It is not known where it lay, whether in the valley or on the high chalk downland or on the clay-with-flints of Savernake. It need not have been far away. While the turf-line under Avebury showed mature grassland (Evans *et al.* 1985), the pollen under Silbury Hill includes woodland species in some numbers (Whittle 1997). There is much still to learn.

Acknowledgements. My thanks to the landowners Richard Hues and David Hues; to the British Academy, The Society of Antiquaries, The Prehistoric Society, and the Wiltshire Archaeological Society for financial support; and to John Evans, Mike Hamilton, Caroline Grigson, Caroline Cartwright, Roland Smith and Rowan Whimster for specialist cooperation.

References

BRADLEY, R. 1987. Flint technology and the character of Neolithic settlement, in A. Brown & M. Edmonds (ed.), *Lithic analysis in later British prehistory*: 181–6. Oxford: British Archaeological Reports. British series 162.
CARNEIRO, R. 1990. Chiefdom-level warfare as exemplified in Fiji and the Cauca valley, in J. Haas (ed.), *The anthropology of war*: 190–211. Cambridge: Cambridge University Press.
CHIPPINDALE, C. 1991. Editorial, *Antiquity* 65: 3–11.
EVANS, J.G., M.W. PITTS & D. WILLIAMS. 1985. An excavation at Avebury, Wiltshire, 1982, *Proceedings of the Prehistoric Society* 51: 305–10.
MALONE, C. 1989. *Avebury*. London: Batsford.
MERCER, R. 1983. The excavation of a Late Neolithic henge-type enclosure at Balfarg, Markinch, Fife, Scotland, 1977–78, *Proceedings of the Society of Antiquaries of Scotland* 111: 63–171.
PITTS, M. 1990. What future for Avebury? *Antiquity* 64: 259–74.
PITTS, M. & A. WHITTLE. 1992. The development and date of Avebury, *Proceedings of the Prehistoric Society* 58: 203–12.
VYNER, B. 1988. The Street House Wossit: the excavation of a Late Neolithic and Early Bronze Age palisaded ritual monument at Street House, Loftus, Cleveland, *Proceedings of the Prehistoric Society* 54: 173–202.
WAINWRIGHT, G. 1979. *Mount Pleasant, Dorset: excavations 1970–71*. London: Society of Antiquaries.
1989. *The henge monuments*. London: Thames & Hudson.
WHITTLE, A. 1990. A pre-enclosure burial at Windmill Hill, Wiltshire, *Oxford Journal of Archaeology* 9: 25–8.
1997. *Sacred mounds, holy rings. Silbury Hill and the West Kennet palisade enclosures: a late Neolithic complex in North Wiltshire*. Oxford: Oxbow Monograph 74.
WHITTLE, A. & R. SMITH. 1990. West Kennet, *Current Archaeology* 118: 363–5.
WOODWARD, P. 1988. Pictures of the Neolithic: discoveries from the Flagstones House excavations, Dorchester, Dorset, *Antiquity* 62: 266–74.

Past records, new views: Carnac 1830–2000

by CORINNE ROUGHLEY, ANDREW SHERRATT & COLIN SHELL

ANTIQUITY 76 (291), 2002

THE MEGALITHIC MONUMENTS of Carnac, Brittany, in the Département of the Morbihan, are amongst the most famous in France, indeed in the world. This region has not only the densest concentration of such sites in Europe but also retained its importance as a centre of monument-building from the late 5th to the 3rd millennium BC, giving it a unique significance in the study of Neolithic landscapes (Sherratt 1990; 1998). Its menhirs, stone alignments, and megalithic tombs have attracted the attention of scholars since the 18th century, and there is thus an unusually full record, both written and pictorial, of the nature of these monuments as they were perceived over 300 years. This documentation is of interest not only for the history of archaeology, but also because it contains information about these sites which cannot be otherwise ascertained. Such early records have two advantages: first, they show the sites before changes which resulted from the accelerated pace of destruction (and reconstruction) in more recent times, and secondly they were made at a time when the landscape was more open than it is today, so that it was easier to see the larger relationships between groups of stones. Their disadvantage is of course that standards of accuracy in recording have improved more or less continuously over this time, so that the most accurate records apply to the most altered states of the sites, and only relatively simple records were taken when the monuments were at their most complete. The following discussion illustrates how these two advantages of completeness and accuracy can be combined, so that an optimal record of these world-famous monuments may be obtained.

The historical record

The work presented here is a small sample of a current project[1] under the auspices of the AREA network, concerned with early records of the megalithic monuments of the Morbihan. It uses both archival materials and published sources to provide documentation of these sites, with the aim of illuminating the development of Neolithic funerary and ceremonial monumentalism over more than two millennia. Early records of these sites are critical in reconstructing the nature of both the megalithic chamber-tombs and the later stone rows, and constitute a resource of exceptional value for European archaeology (Sherratt 1987). Such records were compiled both by French scholars (either from

---

1 This project *The Neolithic Landscape of the Carnac Region* under the direction of Andrew Sherratt, is based in the Ashmolean Museum, Oxford, and uses the catalogue of megalithic sites in the Morbihan and their archaeological documentation prepared between 1986 and 1990 with the assistance of Sue Robinson and Shirley Collier, which incorporates all archival documentation in British collections, together with published French sources. Corinne Roughley, who is now a member of the project, has recently completed her doctoral thesis at the Department of Archaeology, University of Cambridge on the use of GIS and Visualisation in investigating the Neolithic landscapes of the Morbihan (funded by the NERC); Colin Shell supervised the technical aspects of this work and was instrumental not only in obtaining the NERC aerial photographs used in this article but in helping to georeference them by GPS for orthorectification and mosaicking.

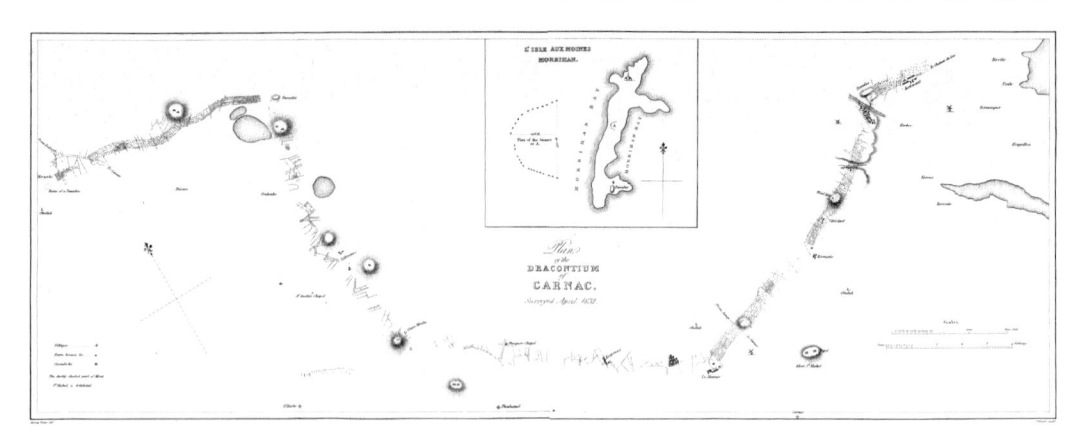

FIGURE 1. *Reduced image of the fold-out plan from Bathurst Deane's report in* Archaeologia *1833. (Original compiled by M. Vicars at 15 feet to the mile [1:352]: the printed version is c. 1 m in length). A portion is reproduced in greater detail in* FIGURE 2.

Brittany itself, or from metropolitan France) and also by British visitors who were drawn by their observations. The monuments were well known to 18th-century antiquarian writers in France (notably de Caylus 1764: 369–89), familiar with Caesar's account of this area in the *Gallic War*, but they took on a new interest in the context of the Romantic Movement and their assumed association with the Celts. Brittany, like Wales and Scotland, became the object of scholarly tourism. While notions of the significance of their stone monuments was often couched in terms of Druidism and serpent-temples, the desire to depict these constructions led to important observations. The work of Stukeley in England provided a common inspiration both for local investigations in Brittany and for a succession of British antiquarians who, after the end of the Napoleonic War, were able to see these monuments for themselves, reporting their discoveries to the Society of Antiquaries. During the 1820s the first systematic descriptions of French megalithic monuments appeared in English, beginning with Alexander Logan's account of Carnac in the *Archaeologia* for 1825, making known the work of French scholars such as Maudet de Penhouët, himself a Celtophile and an enthusiastic admirer of Stukeley and Colt-Hoare and author of several descriptive works.

Although both British and French antiquarians produced a variety of records of the Morbihan megaliths (of which the most readable is undoubtedly Prosper Merimée's *Notes d'un voyage dans l'ouest de la France* of 1836), the contribution of British visitors was most notable for the plans which they took of the chambered tombs and alignments. While there are many useful and often accurate views among the multitude of engravings generated in the genre of the *voyage pittoresque* (such as the carefully observed paintings of megalithic tombs in the Morbihan made by Jorand in 1829, lithographed by Engelmann for inclusion in Sébastian Bottin's *Mélanges d'archéologie* of 1832), there are few representations of the spatial layout of the stones. British visitors, on the other hand, consistently provided measured diagrams on various scales — in part reflecting the topographic tradition of Stukeley, but perhaps also arising from the importance of land-surveying in the process of enclosure and agrarian intensification that accompanied early industrialization in Britain. In consequence, the British contribution from 1830 onwards is distinctively characterized by maps of the relationships between monuments, and plans of the sites themselves. This tradition began with the visits of the

FIGURE 2. *Portion of the Bathurst Deane 1833 map (shown in totality as FIGURE 1) covering the Kermario and Kerlescan alignments (in red), georeferenced and overlain on the orthophoto mosaic.*

Reverend John Bathurst Deane in 1831–2 to meet Maudet de Penhouët. He was accompanied by a professional land surveyor, Murray Vicars, who produced an extensive plan of the area), published in the *Archaeologia* for 1833 (FIGURE 1). He was followed in 1834 by Alexander Blair and Sir Francis Ronalds (inventor of the electric telegraph), who amplified Bathurst Deane's map and took views with the aid of a *camera lucida*, publishing their work privately in 1836. This phase of investigation was followed later in the century by visits from the Reverend William Collings Lukis (Rector of Wath in Yorkshire, and a member of a Guernsey family famous for its megalithic interests) and Sir Henry Dryden of Canons Ashby, Northamptonshire, a distinguished amateur architectural historian and accomplished surveyor (Atkinson 1976). This phase of systematic data-collection parallels contemporary work on the typology of prehistoric artefacts and monuments being carried out at the time (Sherratt, this volume). The extensive plans and notes made by Dryden and Lukis, unpublished at the time for lack of financial sponsorship, are being prepared for publication within the scope of the AREA III project.

The tradition of field recording was continued by James Miln, who took up residence at Carnac in 1873, recruiting Zacharie Le Rouzic to be his assistant: on his death in 1881, Le Rouzic became curator of the Museum (now the Musée Miln-Le Rouzic) in the house which contained his collections. Le Rouzic was responsible for extensive campaigns of excavation and restoration between 1897 and 1939, designed to arrest the growing deterioration of the monuments by agricultural work and road-building (Le Rouzic

1939). There was renewed interest in these monuments at the turn of the 20th century in connection with the possible geometric and astronomical significance suggested by Sir Norman Lockyer, and this phase of work was given precision by the plans of the alignments and enclosures taken by Professor Alexander Thom in the 1970s (Thom & Thom 1978).

Contemporary perspectives

During the last three decades, understanding of Neolithic Brittany has been put on a new footing by the pioneering work of Pierre-Roland Giot and Jean L'Helgouach, and by recent campaigns of excavation by Charles-Tanguy Le Roux and Joel Lecornec on the chambered tombs at the centre of the complex and by Boujot and Cassen on the earlier phase of earthen long-mounds (see Bailloud *et al.* 1995). These have provided a chronological framework and detailed reconstruction of some of the key sites. It remains, however, to make full use of the accumulated observations of the topography and typology of these monuments within the landscape as a whole, and to maximize the value of earlier observations. This involves situating the monuments in relation to the contemporary landscape, identifying fixed points, and calibrating the older surveys by reference to more accurate plans — bearing in mind the extent to which sites have been altered both by depredation and reconstruction. In this way the early records can be made more precise by comparison with later ones, and the latter can be amplified with information otherwise missing.

This objective is being achieved through the construction of a spatial database integrating early plans with a topographic model of the Carnac landscape. The georeferencing of individual archaeological features has been achieved by use of an orthophoto map created from 66 aerial photographs flown in March 2000 by NERC's Airborne Remote Sensing Facility. These were rectified to remove the horizontal displacement using a photogrammetrically generated terrain model produced from the photographs, and the resulting images were then mosaicked to produce a single orthophoto map covering an area of 15×16 km. This is ideal for rectification and georeferencing of earlier surveys, and the results are illustrated here by reference to the plan published in the *Archaeologia* by Bathurst Deane in 1833 (reproduced in miniature as FIGURE 1). Individual stones are visible in both the orthophoto map and Bathurst Deane's survey, and field boundaries surveyed in 1832 can be identified as crop marks in the orthophoto map, providing additional control points and allowing a more accurate georeferencing of the 1833 map than would otherwise be possible. Comparison of the 1833 map with the contemporary landscape confirms the accuracy of Vicars' extensive survey, and allows this to be used to provide further information on the original courses and extents of the alignments. The extent of the alignments at this time can be demonstrated by overlaying the section of Bathurst Deane's map covering the Kermario and Kerlescan alignments on the contemporary orthophoto map, as shown in FIGURE 2. There is a good correspondence between the 1833 map of the Kermario alignments and their modern extent. However, the Kerlescan alignments (while less heavily robbed than some other examples) can be seen to have undergone significant alteration in the last 170 years. Many of the stones recorded by Bathurst Deane at the western end of the Kerlescan have been removed, transforming both the extent and shape of the monument. In particular, the 1833 plan does not show the apparently fan-shaped appearance of the monument as it is represented in later plans (e.g. Thom & Thom 1978), which seems to have resulted from the differential removal of stones. Moreover the alignment can be seen to continue across the road to La Trinité-sur-Mer, towards the lines of Petit Ménec (where the 1833 survey ends). This demonstrates the exceptional value of this early information, recorded (despite the fantastic theories of its archaeological initiator) by a professional surveyor, before the major attrition of the monuments in the later 19th century.

Greater detail of the disposition of individual stones can be supplied from the work by Lukis & Dryden in the 1860s and '70s, when some stone-removal had already occurred (their surveys show fewer stones present in the alignments than in 1832), but which preceded the large-scale reconstruc-

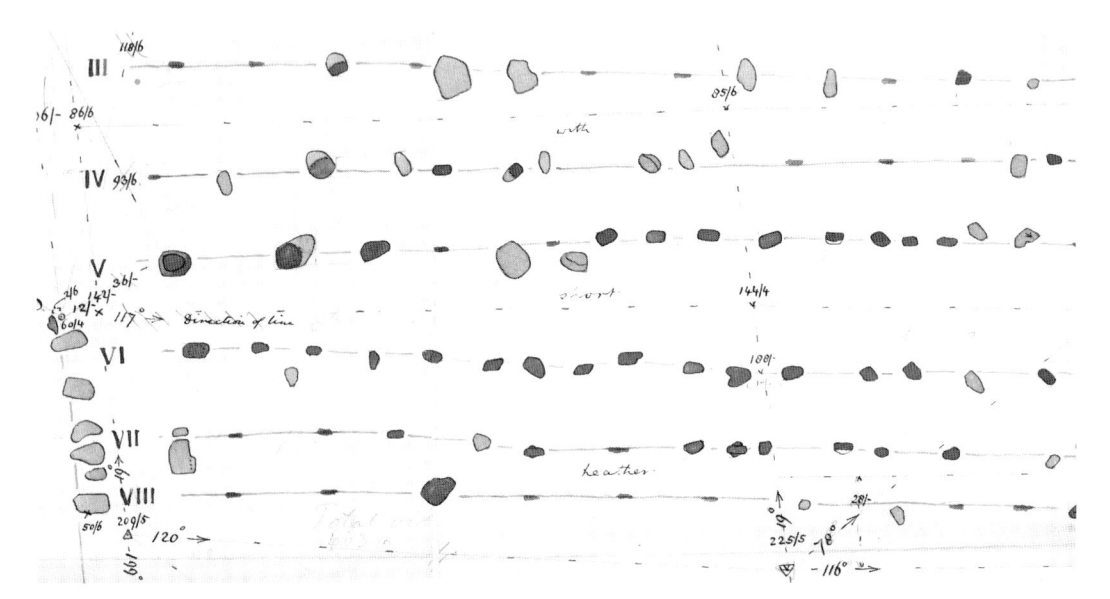

FIGURE 3. Above. *View of the Kerlescant alignments, looking northeast from the head of Line VIII, by H. Dryden (August 1869, copy by CH): Ashmolean Museum.*
Below.*Section of two joining sheets of the Dryden/Lukis survey (1867–9) of the Kerlescant alignments (original 1·70x0·78 m): Ashmolean Museum.*

tion which began towards the end of the century, when many fallen stones were re-erected — not always in their original positions. The Lukis and Dryden plans and elevations provide measurements of individual stones, and are an important record both of the alignments and the large number of passage graves which they also recorded. Moreover, the plans were sometimes accompanied by sketches and watercolours, taken with the aid of a *camera lucida*. The visual fields of these records can be identified on the measured plans, as demonstrated by a watercolour of Kerlescan which depicts stones that can be identified on the corresponding plan (FIGURE 3). The identification of key stones which have remained in position throughout the period of recording allows further calibration by reference to the most accurate current plans, those produced by Alexander Thom in the 1970s.

This iterative procedure, using both current records and the accumulated historical documentation, not only allows the recovery of lost information but also permits the calibration and rectification of earlier records. When the project is complete, it will permit the interrogation of this cumulative record and the comparison of successive generations of plans and views. In this way it is possible to make use of information which has survived, either in published form in the earlier literature or as archival material in museums, so that it has a contemporary relevance — thus perpetuating a tradition of concern for the major monuments of prehistoric Europe which has been continuously amplified across three centuries.

References

ATKINSON, R.J.C. 1976. Lukis, Dryden and the Carnac megaliths, in J.V.S. Megaw (ed.), *To illustrate the monuments*: 111–24. London: Thames & Hudson.
BAILLOUD, G., C. BOUJOT, S. CASSEN & C.-T. LE ROUX. 1995. *Les prèmieres architectures de pierre*. Paris: CNRS Editions.
BATHURST DEANE, J. 1833. Observations on Dracontia, *Archaeologia* 25: 188–229.
BLAIR, A. & F. RONALDS. 1836. *Sketches of Carnac (Brittany) in 1834*. (Privately printed).
BOTTIN, S. (ed.). 1832. *Mélanges d'archéologie*. Paris: Bureau de l'almanach du commerce.
CAYLUS, A.C.P., Comte de. 1764. *Receuil d'antiquités egyptiennes, etrusques, greques, romaines et gauloises*. Vol. 4. Paris: Desaint et Saillant.
LE ROUZIC, Z. 1939. Les monuments mégalithiques du Morbihan: cause de leur ruine et origine de leur restoration, *Bulletin de la Société préhistorique francaise* 1939: 234.
LOGAN, A. 1825. Account of a visit to a monument usually considered Druidical, at Carnac, Brittany. *Archaeologia* 22: 190–203.
MERIMÉE, P. 1833. *Notes d'un voyage dans l'ouest de la France*. Paris: Fournier.
SHERRATT, A. 1987. 'Of men and megaliths', *The Ashmolean* 12: 2–5.
    1990. The genesis of megaliths: monumentality, ethnicity and social complexity in Neolithic north-west Europe, *World Archaeology* 22(2): 146–67.
    1998. Points of exchange: the Later Neolithic monuments of the Morbihan, in A. Gibson & D. Simpson (ed.), *Prehistoric ritual and religion*: 119–38. Stroud: Sutton.
THOM, A. & A.S. THOM. 1978. *Megalithic remains in Britain and Brittany*. Oxford: Oxford University Press.

4 Beyond the megaliths
by TIMOTHY DARVILL & CAROLINE MALONE

FROM THE VERY earliest antiquarian interest in megaliths, speculative and even visionary interpretations have been rife and to some audiences very influential. Going beyond the megaliths into a world of myth, fantasy, and interpretation began with Henry of Huntingdon and Geoffrey of Monmouth's views about Stonehenge (Atkinson 1979: 184–5; Chippindale 1983: 20–28). As described in Section 2 above, William Stukeley took a Romanticist view of the ancient past with his attempts to restore the great stone circles and rings to the British Druids, in part a reaction to the Enlightenment views of Inigo Jones and others, who just decades earlier had suggested that Stonehenge was essentially of classical inspiration and set up by the Romans (Chippindale 1983: 48–60). During the 20th century, interpretations have been driven by changing philosophies and social trends: the importance of engineering; the technological revolution; the discovery of the cosmos; and at the extreme end of the scale the widely held idea that extra-terrestrial beings visited planet earth in the distant past. It was this kaleidoscope of overlapping ideas spinning around some of the core values of archaeological understanding that led Jacquetta Hawkes to pen her memorable and oft-quoted line (1967: 174):

> Every age has the Stonehenge it deserves — or desires

Over the years, ANTIQUITY has sought to document these trends, while publishing authoritative and scientific debates, occasionally venturing close to the edge of pure theory and originality! Glyn Daniel in particular amongst the editors of ANTIQUITY had his own way of introducing, sometimes saluting, and occasionally mildly poking fun at some of the more unconventional interpretations of megalithic remains. In his editorial for the September 1970 issue he draws readers' attention to an article entitled 'why flying saucers followed the Leys', published in *The Ley Hunter*, concluding (Daniel 1970: 174):

> How sad it is that so many obviously intelligent and interested people these days should spend their time writing and thinking dottinesses while the whole world of man's past endeavour and achievement is theirs to appreciate, understand and admire.

The papers published by Glyn Daniel and the other editors have avoided 'dottinesses' and ranged wide, exploring past ideas and their context, as well as current research. Some of this has been based on excavation and survey, other work on experimental archaeology, and yet more on understanding the visionary effects and sensations of monuments. This section presents a selection of papers to offer a flavour of the changing interests and methods of study. What stands out is the way that archaeologists, and others who are interested in the interpretation of megaliths, keep returning to similar themes and debate: how were the megaliths built? How did they function? How did they connect to the wider physical and social world? And what might they have meant in prehistoric society? In this latter, the debate and development of archaeoastronomy is particularly significant, since it was in the pages of ANTIQUITY that some of the most clearly presented and argued assessments of the astronomical potential of prehistoric megalithic monuments were aired and became established areas of inquiry.

The construction of megalithic and other large prehistoric sites has been an enduring theme of 20th-century archaeology. The inverse relationship between modern monster machines and recognition of apparently futile human and animal muscle power to raise the great earthworks of Avebury or the trilithons of Stonehenge is salutory. Simple practical issues of engineering and scale are important, and can really only be tested through experimental work. Richard Atkinson presented his view on methods of 'Neolithic engineering' and construction in an influential paper that we reprint here (Atkinson 1961). He examined several classes of prehistoric monument, and stressed the importance of cultural, chronological and human logistics as fundamental in the archaeologist's assumptions about moving and assembling building materials. Since then, others have continued the debate (although invariably focused on Stonehenge) through practical experiment and experience; for example Garfitt's (1979) 'Moving the stones at Stonehenge' and his 'Raising the lintels at Stonehenge' (Garfitt 1980); Pavel's experimental work in the Czech Republic (1992), Osenton's 'Megalithic engineering techniques: experiments using axe-based technology' (2001), and Adamson's (2002) account of the craft of the stone mason all serve to extend the discussion and present possibilities, but by their very nature leave the problem wide open. Although the principles of ancient engineering and stone moving are broadly understood, there is still much that remains unknown, for example the number of people involved; the precise methods used and the tricks of the trade that were applied; the routes taken to transport stones; and so on.

Construction naturally involves design work and site layout, and here we enter an archaeological minefield. The debate ranges from accepting that there were preconceived designs for monuments to archaeological evidence for cumulative and successive rebuilding. Standardized units of measurement have their origins a long way back, but it was Alexander Thom who suggested the existence of a 'Megalithic Yard', or 'MY'. Thom's initial calculations were set out in the early 1960s (Thom 1963), showing the existence and widespread use of a precise unit of length in Neolithic and early Bronze Age Britain; but in 1966 he developed the arguments further with a paper in ANTIQUITY entitled 'Megaliths and mathematics' which we reproduce here. In it he provides a classification of stone circles based on the way he believed they were set out: 'circles', 'flattened circles', 'eggs', and 'ellipses'. Along the way there is a clear discussion on the limitations of prehistoric geometry, plus a consideration of astronomical principles embodied in a range of solar, lunar and celestial movements and calendrical solstices that might have been used by prehistoric communities to give order and meaning to the design of their monuments. Since Thom's studies there have been various views expressed on the way circles and rings were physically set out, most favouring simple pragmatic solutions (see for example Barnatt & Herring 1986). More enduring, however, is the interest in astronomy and what has become known as 'archaeoastronomy'.

Astronomy, and the part played by observing celestial bodies in the building of megalithic monuments, has been a favourite theme since at least Sir Norman Lockyer's recognition of astronomical possibilities at prehistoric sites early in the 20th century (Lockyer 1906). The prominence given to the debate by Gerald Hawkins in his book *Stonehenge decoded* (1965) triggered a spate of new papers focused on applying complex mathematics and astronomical theory to ancient sites. Glyn Daniel as Editor of ANTIQUITY promoted the seductive theme. He made excellent use of his scholarly contacts, persuading researchers to comment and explain the possibilities and limitations of archaeoastronomy. One was Richard Atkinson's (1966) review of Hawkins' book in a paper catchily entitled 'Moonshine on Stonehenge'. Another was the Cambridge astronomer and cosmologist Fred Hoyle, whose 'Speculations on Stonehenge' (Hoyle 1966) provided a commentary on the work of Hawkins and Atkinson. In place of extravagant theories he offered a practical approach by examining how Stonehenge, and by implication other circles, could work as observatories. He also raised the perennial question of predicting solar changes and seasons that are assumed to have so engaged prehistoric people's attention. Hoyle credited prehistoric societies with considerable sophistication (Hoyle 1966: 274):

> I have formed several cultural hypotheses concerning the builders of Stonehenge. It seems to me that the three essential requirements for high intellectual achievement are

availability of food, leisure and social stability, and good communications. It must be possible for people in one district to know what is being done in other districts. Outstanding individuals must be able to get together. The young must be taught. Preferably the brightest youngsters should be brought together into a 'university'. There seems no reason why the society in S. England around 2000 B.C. did not meet all these requirements.

Needless to say, the responses that the paper provoked were detailed, and, as Hawkins and others showed in their comments (Hawkins *et al.* 1967), individual theories and their own explanations were closely guarded from criticism or change. In many ways the last word in this particular round went to Jacquetta Hawkes, who concluded (1967: 180) that:

> nothing of any great moment has been established by the astronomical *nouveau vague* flowing over Stonehenge.

In 1980 Moir, Ruggles & Norris continued the analysis of Hoyle and Thom, in particular in relation to Scottish sites in their paper 'Megalithic sciences and some Scottish site plans'. They claimed that greater precision and observation was often needed in the primary survey of sites if they were to be properly analysed by precision mathematics. All too often the studies were proved pointless, since the actual surveys on the ground were simply unable to render the detail required. Another paper in the same vein was by Douglas Heggie, a Cambridge astronomer. In his contribution 'Megalithic lunar observatories — an astronomer's view' (Heggie 1972), reprinted here, he discussed Alexander Thom's book, *Megalithic lunar observatories* (Thom 1971). This offered a practical and accessible appraisal of what astronomy really meant for archaeologists, and where some of the limitations lay between geometry and reality. His conclusion (Heggie 1972: 48) was that

> Thom's evidence that megalithic man observed the moon is so strong that it may be accepted without hesitation. That he also used extrapolation in the interpretation of his observations seems to be indicated by the evidence of the stone fans of Caithness and elsewhere. The data on which Thom bases his assertion that the builders of the monuments established accurate sight-lines for several interesting declinations, implying a knowledge of its motions that was not to be improved on for over three thousand years, may have been interpreted incorrectly.

With this sane damper on the enthusiasm for complex astronomy, it is not surprising that the excitement died down. Sites beyond Britain became a focus instead for reappraisal, such as Hadingham's (1981) paper on 'Carnac as a lunar observatory'. The parameters of the accuracy needed for explanation had been clearly established, and scholars, at least in Britain, went back to thinking and surveying. Some slightly different approaches were presented by Thom *et al.* (1988) suggesting that the decorated gold lozenge from Bush Barrow was a calendar used by engineer–surveyor–astronomer–priests as an *aide mémoire* in setting out the astronomical orientations of the phase 3 stone monument (See also Kinnes *et al.* 1988; Shell & Robinson 1988).

The late 1990s saw a resurgence of interest in possible astronomical alignments embodied in the design of megalithic monuments and in 1997 Euan MacKie's 'Maeshowe and the winter solstice: ceremonial aspects of the Orkney Grooved Ware culture' re-opened the debate. Working in the emerging genre of post-processual archaeology, MacKie recognized the importance of setting the broader cultural and landscape context of particular sites, as part of his ceremonial, calendrical and sensational interpretations. His theme included the idea of controlling religious élites specialized in astronomical observations, much in the style suggested by Hoyle (1966). Mackie examined alignments and their relationship to solstices, and to certain monuments — Kintraw, Newgrange and Maeshowe, which seemed well designed as observatories. Descriptions of angles, declinations and calendrical possibilities show that the central debates in archaeoastronomy and megaliths are still very much alive — if modified. But such ventures do not go uncriticized, and MacKie's work prompted a lively response from Ruggles & Barclay (2000) in their paper 'Cosmology, calendars and society in Neolithic Orkney — a rejoinder to Euan MacKie', reproduced here. They request that the apparently simplified interpretations and linkages between assumed types of social hierarchy, sites, dating, alignments and landscape geometry (and much else in the new field of landscape cognition and cosmology) be considered as parts of the complex archaeoastronomical evidence of prehistory. It is a debate that continues at the time of preparing this volume, the most recent salvos being a retort from Mackie (2002) and a further response from Barclay & Ruggles (2002).

Looking to the heavens is one way of looking outwards from megalithic monuments. In recent years there has been an increasing concern for what some have scholars have boldy dubbed 'touchy-feely' archaeology, or, perhaps more properly, the 'archaeology of the perceptive senses'. Exploring the sensations (sight, sound, smell, feel and taste) that might have been experienced by ancient human encounters with places, people and events provides many new insights, even though it is impossible to gauge what individuals in the past might have been thinking. Their dramatic form, and the sensory effects resulting from ceremonial activities within and around megaliths, provide much opportunity for speculation. For example, the intervisibility of monuments and views out to distinctive landscape features, framed in some cases by structural elements of a monument, have long been discussed and widely recognized as potentially significant. Paul Devereux (1991) followed through such interests with reference to the Avebury area in his paper 'Three dimensional aspects of apparent relationship between selected natural and artificial features within the topography of the Avebury complex', reproduced here. He continued this work in a short paper written jointly with Robert Jahn 'Preliminary investigations and cognitive considerations of the acoustical resonances of selected archaeological sites', also reproduced here (Devereux & Jahn 1996). Sound, like visibility, is a tangible phenomenon that can be measured and mapped in various ways, and work in this field has been followed up by Aaron Watson and David Keating (1999) in a study entitled 'Architecture and sound: an acoustic analysis of megalithic monuments in prehistoric Britain'. Here, the study focuses on Scottish circles and cairns, where the combination of careful survey combined with precise measurements of controlled sounds provides interesting patterns of acoustic effects and explains, in part, why and how they occur. Such work opens up new vistas in the rather silent world of archaeology, and other sensory studies will doubtless follow.

When discussing the working of the human senses in the ancient past, assumptions inevitably have to be made, and these are open to challenge. Appropriately, therefore, the final paper in this section provides a cautionary tale, told in this case by Henry Chapman & Benjamin Gearey in their (2000) paper 'Palaeoecology and the perception of prehistoric landscapes: some comments on visual approaches to phenomenology'. They remind us forcefully that modern-day understandings of ancient places and landscapes need to be firmly underpinned by accurate reconstructions of the natural environment. Trees can block the view, demolishing an apparently powerful argument about intervisibility between sites, and showing it to be deeply flawed. The same is true, as Watson and Keating note (1999), about ancient sites which have been restored and changed — if stones are moved or reset the original prehistoric effects may not be the same, just as the precision of celestial–lunar–solar movements also change over great spans of time. The moral perhaps of all the papers in this section is that archaeology can approach ancient function, meaning and sensory effect, but still only at a distance.

Neolithic engineering
by **R.J.C. ATKINSON**
ANTIQUITY 35 (140), 1961

IN HISTORIES of technology the subject of early engineering is usually discussed mainly with reference to the achievements of the literate civilizations of the Ancient East. The contemporary or even earlier feats of our own more barbarous ancestors in the west, in their way no less remarkable, have been passed over largely in silence, or at best with a brief reference to Stonehenge.

There are, of course, good reasons for this disparity of treatment. From the ancient east we have a body of reliable evidence for engineering processes, in the form of carved reliefs and tomb-paintings; whereas in Europe we are compelled to infer the processes from their end-products. The reliability of such inference is not increased by the virtual absence of surviving specimens of tools and equipment made from perishable organic materials, and particularly from timber. Moreover, it is obvious that some engineering operations, such as the movement of heavy stones, will leave few traces for the archaeologist to identify and interpret.

Any discussion of Neolithic engineering must thus confine itself more to problems than to their solution. None the less, it is perhaps worth while to pay some attention to the technological aspects of such products of Neolithic engineering as flint-mines, earthworks and megalithic structures. We are inclined perhaps too much to regard these monuments merely as cultural indicators, or as components in some hypothetical scheme of morphological development, and to forget that they are also the products of skills which, as the restorers of Stonehenge well know, we should find it difficult to emulate even with our own vastly greater resources. Moreover, it is in the last resort only these monuments which provide us with positive evidence for the existence of social aggregates larger than the individual family, acting in concert for a common purpose.

It is essential to realise from the start that for all the operations of early engineering the only source of power was human muscle. The use of animals can be ruled out. The horse became an efficient means of heavy traction only with the invention of the horse-collar in early medieval times. Oxen, though certainly available, are slow, deliberate and ruminative in a metaphorical as well as a literal sense; and their reactions to words of command, or even to more painful stimulation, are notoriously sluggish, so that for any operation which required precise timing and strict control they would be inferior to man-power, in spite of their greater strength. The basic problem of the Neolithic engineer was thus to find devices by which human muscle-power could be transmitted, by which loss of power in friction could be reduced, and by which the rate at which work was done could be adapted to the most efficient rate at which human muscles can expend their energy.

In the first category, the transmission of power, we have chiefly to consider ropes. Apart from finds in the lakeside settlements of the Alpine region of Europe, few actual Neolithic ropes survive, though the existence of suitable rope-yarns is amply attested by cord-impressions on pottery. The raw materials are likely to have been either leather, animal hair, or vegetable fibres such as flax, nettle or bast (the inner bark of certain trees, usually lime or willow)

Leather and animal hair are still used today for the transmission of power, in the form of industrial belting. Both have an ultimate *breaking* strength of about 4000 lb. per sq. in. A safe *working* load for a 3-in. (circumference) rope of these materials would be around 180 lb., or about one-quarter of that for a standard quality modern Manila rope of the same size. Since a rope of more than 6 in. in circumference is difficult to grip, it follows that the largest Neolithic ropes would have a working strength of about one-third of a ton, and that where heavy stones had to be moved, weighing up to several dozens of tons, the number of ropes required would be correspondingly large.

In the second category come devices for the reduction of friction, chiefly in the moving of heavy stones. Undoubtedly the most efficient method of transport is by water, as was sufficiently demonstrated by the now-vanished spectacle of a single horse towing a loaded coal barge along a canal; and this remains true today, if one neglects the time factor. The decline of our inland waterways is due not least to the fact that speeds on canals have to be kept low to prevent erosion of their banks. Where time is relatively unimportant, as it was in prehistory, a slow rate of progress is a positive advantage, because the drag on the hull of a vessel rises exponentially with its speed.

Even where it was possible, as it may have been in the transport of the Stonehenge bluestones from Pembrokeshire, to use a water route for 90 per cent of the journey, the problem of moving heavy masses on land still remained. As Heyerdahl's experiment with one of the Easter Island statues has shown, (Heyerdahl 1958: 150–1) it is *possible* to drag a 12-ton stone directly over the ground; but it is also very wasteful of manpower. By mounting the stone on a timber sled, and hauling the sled on a track of rollers, the tractive effort required can be reduced to about 100 lb. per ton on level ground. If we assume that a man can keep up a pull of 50 lb. on a rope throughout a working day, it follows that the *minimum* hauling party required to move a heavy stone is two men per ton.

In the third category we have to consider simple forms of machine, giving some mechanical advantage,* whereby the limitations of human strength directly exerted can be circumvented. The range of such machines available in Neolithic times is exceedingly small, since most of the basic forms incorporate principles of much later invention, such as the screw and the differential pulley.

The simple lever was undoubtedly used for the raising of heavy stones, and for moving them laterally when recumbent, by alternately lifting each end and swinging it sideways a few inches at a time. By way of example, the largest stone at Stonehenge, which is 30 ft. long and weighs 50 tons, could be raised at one end with three levers, each giving a mechanical advantage of ten, and each manned by eighteen men.†

For straight pulls on ropes it is conceivable, though extremely unlikely, that some kind of capstan or windlass was used. Of the two the capstan allows the greater mechanical advantage, since the length of the capstan-bars is limited only by the strength of their material. But both these machines require strong and well-turned bearings which

---

* That is, broadly speaking, 'leverage'. A rigid lever on which the load rests at 1·5 ft. from the fulcrum on one side, and the effort is exerted at 15 ft. from the fulcrum on the other, gives a mechanical advantage of 10 (i.e. 15 ÷ 1·5), and allows the lifting of, say, 500lb. by an effort of 50 lb. To counterbalance this gain, of course, the effort must be exerted through ten times the distance that the load is lifted.

† The maximum downward pull or push that a man can exert on a lever is of course equal to his own weight, or say 150 lb. But with his feet off the ground he can exert no control. I therefore assume here a maximum effort of 100 lb. per man.

could not be made without the use of a lathe, and would in any case be unable to withstand the stresses involved, if built wholly of timber.

The employment of the so-called Spanish Windlass, however, is a good deal more probable. In this very simple but effective device, a skein of ropes or cords is anchored firmly at one end, and attached at the other to the load to be moved. A lever (or two levers at right-angles in the form of a cross) is then inserted transversely at the centre of the skein, and rotated in order to twist up the skein and convert the rotary torque into a longitudinal tension. This is the means still adopted for tensioning the blade of a carpenter's bow-saw; and it was certainly used to brace together the bow and stern of papyrus-reed boats on the Nile in the third millennium BC (Singer *et al.* 1954: 735 figure 535)). In any case, so simple a device could easily have been invented by any one fiddling idly with a stick and a loop of string. The mechanical advantage obtainable depends, of course, on the length of the levers used; while the pull developed, and the distance through which it can be exerted, is a function of the cross-section and the length of the skein of ropes.

These, then, are the principal devices available to the Neolithic engineer. The three main fields of activity in which they were applied are mining, the building of earthworks and the erection of megalithic structures.

Mining, apart from the unique workings for metamorphic rock at the stone axe factory on Mynydd Rhiw, Caernarvonshire (Notes in *PPS* 1959; 1960) appears to have been confined to the exploitation of seams of flint stratified in chalk. The typical flint-mining area, with its multiplicity of filled shafts encircled by annular spoil-heaps, resembling nothing so much as an abandoned bombing-range, at first sight gives an impression of great activity combined with an incredible wastefulness of effort. The individual shafts, averaging 20 ft. in diameter, are usually very close to each other, and in many cases are simply shafts, with no galleries radiating from their bases to follow the seams of flint. Moreover, even where galleries do exist, their length is short, and small compared with the depth of the shafts.

It must be remembered, however, that in modern mining, particularly for coal, there is a critical depth, above which the difficulties of underground excavation and transport, and the instability of rock strata near the surface, make it more economic to adopt opencast methods of working. It seems likely that in Neolithic mining also there was an empirical recognition of a corresponding critical depth (which appears to be of the order of 15 ft.). Above that depth it would be cheaper, in terms of foot-pounds of work per pound of flint extracted, to sink a fresh shaft alongside than it would be to tunnel from the base of an existing shaft, since tunnelling in a confined space must always be more difficult (and in the absence of timbering, more dangerous) than removing an even larger volume of material from a vertical shaft of larger cross-section open to the sky.

The tools used — antler picks, bone wedges and occasionally stone axes — are well known and require no further discussion. What we do not know is the method used to transport the spoil to the surface. It has been suggested that it was carried in baskets on mens' backs (like those still used in Ireland for turf) by way of ladders made of notched tree-trunks. The principal argument for ladders relies on the presence in the galleries of the skeletons of voles, the marks of those teeth have been found on discarded antler picks. The voles must have reached the bottom alive and, it is claimed, by ladders, since the fall from the top would have killed them. But in fact these small rodents are a great deal more resilient than this. I have myself rescued them, alive and biting, from the dry bottom of a Romano-British well far deeper than any known flint mine. It is probable, of course, that ladders were used by the miners for access in any case; but their use also for the removal of the spoil would have been very inefficient, since the carriers would have to raise their own weight as well as their load. The use of baskets hauled to the top by ropes is attested by occasional scored marks on the walls of the shafts; and it must be remembered that frost-weathering of the mouths of the shafts and their margins will have destroyed any possible traces of timber structures at the pit-head.

The problems of constructing Neolithic earthworks, such as causewayed camps, long barrows, henge monuments and cursuses, have recently been discussed in the light of the experience gained in building the experimental earthwork on Overton Down, near Avebury (Ashbee & Cornwall 1961). The calculation of the human effort involved in these undertakings, even with this experimental basis, is still full of uncertainties; but it is perhaps a little too simple, in estimating, say, the effort needed for the building of the Avebury earthwork, merely to scale up linearly the output per man/hour attained at Overton Down. In all earthworks the process of construction can be divided into two groups of operations: the loosening of subsoil and the filling of baskets *in the ditch,* and the transport and dumping of the basket-loads *on to the bank.* In the former the rate of production is independent of the size of the ditch, and will vary only with the hardness of the material excavated; whereas the latter is clearly related directly to the scale of the earthwork concerned. If allowance is made for this in calculation, a revised estimate for the effort required at Avebury would be 156,000 man-days, or 100 men for three years and three months.*

The plans of many of these earthworks, and particularly those of a ritual character, raise the interesting question of their builders' knowledge of plane geometry. Circular earthworks could of course be set out very simply, by means of a taut cord of fixed length rotated round a peg at the centre. An elaboration of the same method was doubtless used for certain British stone 'circles' of non-circular plan, such as Boscawen-un and Rough Tor in Cornwall, which have been discussed by Professor A. Thom (1961). These anomalous settings appear to be made up of several circular arcs of differing radii, symmetrically disposed, a smooth transition from one arc to the next being achieved through the choice of centres lying on a common radius.

It is possible too that some of the henge monuments which approximate in plan to ellipses, such as the Devil's Quoits in Oxfordshire (Grimes 1939–45: I; 1960: 149, figure 60) and Cairnpapple in West Lothian, (Piggott 1949: 32, figure 1) were set out in the same way, as a combination of circular arcs. Pending detailed analysis, it seems at least as likely, however, that they were planned as true ellipses, by means of a cord fastened at its ends to two separated pegs (located at the foci of the ellipse) and stretched taut by a moving stick which would trace out the circumference. The same method is used for drawing ellipses in school geometry exercises, using two pins, a length of thread and a pencil.

For rectilinear monuments, such as the mounds of long barrows and chambered tombs, the boundaries were presumably fixed by means of lateral offsets from an axial base-line. There is some evidence, however, that the offsets were not arbitrarily chosen,

---

* As a first approximation I have arrived at the empirical formula $H = V(120 + 8L + 2F)/1000$, where H equals the total man-hours required, V is the volume of solid chalk excavated in cu. ft., and L and F are respectively the vertical and horizontal distances in feet between the centroids (the 'centres of gravity') of the cross-sections of the ditch and bank as originally constructed. I shall be glad to discuss the derivation of this formula with any interested reader.

but were related to a basic geometric figure of simple proportions. The truncated wedge-shaped outline of the chambered cairn of Parc-le-Breos Cwm in Gower,* (Lacaille & Grimes 1961) for instance, appears to be based on an isosceles triangle with sides in the ratio of 4:1 and the chamber and forecourt of the West Kennet Long Barrow (Piggott 1963) on a similar triangle with a ratio of 2:1.

The method of offsets seems to have been used also in monuments of the cursus type, one side of which is sometimes noticeably straighter and more regular than the other,† and was presumably taken as the base. The same monuments also occasionally have their ends accurately squared off at right-angles,‡ as are the corners of parallel-sided chambered tombs such as Wayland's Smithy in Berkshire or Tinkinswood in Glamorgan. The problem of setting out such right-angles is of course amenable to solution by trial and error, through successive approximations based on the measurement of the diagonals of a parallelogram; but this in itself implies some theoretical understanding of plane geometry. We cannot rule out the possibility that the Pythagorean method used by field archaeologists today, of laying out a triangle with sides in the ratio 3:4:5, was known to our Neolithic ancestors.

Of possible Neolithic units of measurement I propose to say nothing, if only for lack of incontrovertible evidence and because the contemporaneous use of variant standards is extremely probable. The detection of such units is in any case a matter of fairly rigid statistical analysis, based on data which should for preference be taken in the first instance only from sites whose basic geometric framework exhibits simple proportions of the kind already mentioned.

I turn now to the final category of Neolithic engineering, the building of tombs and ritual circles of large stones. The work involved can be divided into three basic operations: the transport of the stones from their source to the site; the erection of upright stones; and the raising of the capstones of chambered tombs (and, by an illegitimate extension of the term 'Neolithic', the lintels of Stonehenge).

For transport, a water route is to be preferred for economy of effort; but it is probably only in the exceptional case of the bluestones of Stonehenge that full advantage could have been taken of this method. In Neolithic times, when the width, depth and course of rivers and streams was determined wholly by natural agencies, and not by man, it is very doubtful if a load of more than 10 tons could be carried satisfactorily by water. Moreover, the majority of megalithic constructions, at any rate in Britain, are on high ground, away from running water, and are built of materials available close at hand, within a few miles at most. The main problem is thus that of transporting overland stones weighing up to about 50 tons.

For this the most economical method is the use of a sled and rollers, hauled by a party of men. The strongest form of sled would be one whose main longitudinal members were formed of a natural pair of forked tree-trunks, in the shape of a modern tuning-fork, joined by nature at their bases and braced transversely by cross-members morticed and pegged. Such sleds have been used by the Naga peoples of Assam in modern times for precisely the same purpose.

The rollers were presumably selected lengths of cylindrical tree-stems, with the bark and any small branches carefully trimmed off. Since the rollers would have to be

---

* Re-excavated and restored for the Ministry of Works by the writer in 1960 and 1961.
† e.g. the Dorset Cursus (Atkinson 1955: 9) and the Benson (Oxon.) Cursus (Leeds 1934: 414, plate LVII).
‡ e.g. that at Benson cited above, and the neighbouring site at Sutton Courtenay (Berks.) Leeds 1934: 414, plate LVIII)

wider than the width of the sled-runners, and would form a tiresome series of obstacles for a hauling-party on an axial line, it seems reasonable to suppose that ropes were attached to a draw-bar which projected on either side of the sled far enough to clear the ends of the rollers, even though the advantages of such an arrangement would be offset by the necessity of maintaining an even tension on both sides (Hope-Taylor 1960). Alternatively, the hauling party must have been sufficiently far in advance of the stone to leave a space in which the roller track could be laid, behind the rear rank and in front of the advancing sled. In either case the limited working load on a single rope demands that the hauling party should be disposed either in parallel files or in the form of a fan of narrow angle.

On flat, ground the *minimum* hauling party would be two men per ton, or 100 men for a 50-ton stone. In the latter case, we may assume at least another hundred men for shifting the rollers and steering the sled. A single roller of hardwood, 10 ft. long and 1 ft. in diameter, weighs about 4 cwt. and would need a team of six to eight men to carry it. A softwood roller of the same size weighs a little more than half this figure, but is more easily damaged and more rapidly abraded by the runners of the sled.

On slopes, whether up or down, the minimum size of the hauling party increases rapidly. For a gradient of 1 in 6·5, or about 9°, nine men per ton are required, as against two on flat ground.

For the methods used in the erection of upright pillars or slabs we have hardly more evidence than for their transport; but such as there is suggests that the same basic method (HMSO 1959: 62, diagrams) was used in all cases, though with some important modifications at Stonehenge.

Once the position of the hole had been decided, it was dug to a suitable depth with three sides approximately vertical and the fourth, facing the direction from which the stone was to approach, in the form of a sloping ramp. The side opposite the ramp was then lined with close-set wooden stakes, to protect it from being crushed by the toe of the stone during its erection.

The stone would then be rolled along the ground, base foremost, to a position in which the toe was nearly touching the stakes, and the centre of gravity was a short distance behind the leading roller, while the latter was just short of the edge of the ramp, in which position it could be held by stakes to act as a fulcrum in the next operation. The necessary starting-positions for the stone and the leading roller, in relation to the hole and ramp, could be found without difficulty by previous trial and error.

The next step would be to lever up the outer end of the stone, so that the toe gradually dipped into the hole. Since the weight of the stone would be very nearly balanced on the leading roller, the amount of leverage, even for a very heavy stone, would be small, and the degree of control proportionately large. In this way, as model experiments have shown, the toe of the stone could be brought to within a few inches of the bottom of the hole before the centre of gravity passed in front of the fulcrum, allowing the stone to slip a short distance and to come to rest leaning on the ramp and the leading roller, at an angle of up to 50° from the horizontal, depending on the depth of the hole.

A suitable crib of crossed timbers would then be built beneath the outer (top) end of the stone, to provide support for the fulcra of levers whereby it could be raised a few inches at a time. Temporary support would be given by timber struts when the crib had to be rebuilt at intervals closer to the stone.

At an inclination of about 70° from the horizontal the levers would become ineffective; but from this position the stone could be pulled upright by hauling on ropes attached to the top. The heaviest stone at Avebury, standing 17 ft. high and weighing about 47 tons, would require an initial pull of about 9·5 tons from an inclination of 70°. This could be exerted by a team of slightly more than 200 men, if each is assumed to be able to exert a pull of 100 lb. over a short period of time. The raising of a stone is thus in general within the capacity of the total number required to transport it on flat ground.

It is true that today the stone-holes at Avebury and elsewhere are extremely shallow — too shallow, indeed, to allow the stone to be tipped in under control and to come to rest in a stable leaning position. But it must be remembered that during the course of the last four or five millenia soft rocks such as chalk and limestone have been dissolved to depths of up to 2 ft. by chemical weathering, (Atkinson 1957) so that the original depth of the holes was correspondingly deeper. At Stonehenge the holes appear to have been unusually deep in the first instance, presumably to allow for the narrow proportions and greater length of the uprights, which result in the centres of gravity being further from the bases than is common elsewhere.

The raising of the capstones of chambered tombs presents few difficulties, if it is assumed that the mound surrounding the chamber was first built up to the level of the tops of its walls, to provide a sloping ramp up which the capstones could be hauled and levered, resting on rollers. The main necessity would be the very careful strutting of the chamber walls to resist lateral pressure; and indeed it seems probable that the interior of the chamber was packed solid, either with rammed earth or with lengths of timber wedged in place, the packing being removed, not perhaps without some trepidation, only after the capstones were all in place.

The uprights forming the walls of many chambered tombs stand in very shallow holes, often no more than 9 in. in depth, which at first sight give an impression of criminal optimism on the part of the builders. It must be remembered, however, that once in place the weight of the capstones provides sufficient friction to prevent relative movement of the component slabs. This is well demonstrated by tomb-chambers which have subsequently lost their supporting mounds, like Kits Coty House in Kent and many of the *allées couvertes* of France.

The raising of the lintels of Stonehenge presents another problem altogether, but one on which I have nothing to add (Atkinson 1960: 134–9).

In conclusion, I would stress again that it is worth while considering the technological aspects of the products of Neolithic engineering, as well as their significance in cultural or chronological terms. These monuments are after all the only direct evidence that we have for the existence of prehistoric *communities,* which otherwise we can infer only from the repetitive occurrence of similar artifacts in individual graves or habitation-sites, which we interpret (no doubt rightly; but it is still a matter of inference) as the expression of a communally acceptable pattern of behaviour.

Moreover, considerations of a purely mechanical type may occasionally lead to conclusions about the social or economic structure of our prehistoric communities, on which evidence of any kind is all too rare and too equivocal. It is a fact, for instance, that the capstone of the burial chamber at Tinkinswood in Glamorgan weighs approximately 50 tons, and that not less than 200 able-bodied persons, representing a total population of not less than 300, would be needed to get it into its present position with the means currently available. The chamber itself contained 'at least fifty' individuals — an abnormally high number. Even so, if we assume, as we safely can, a crude death rate of 40 per 1000 per annum, a population of 300 souls would incur that number of deaths in just over *four years,* an impossibly short period of use for a structure of this character. We may thus assume that this tomb; and by inference many others, are not the mausolea of a whole local population, but only of one small fraction of it; from which it follows that the structure of Neolithic societies in Western Europe may have been a great deal less egalitarian than the lack of differentiation in their artifacts might lead us to suppose.

References
ASHBEE, P. & I.W. CORNWALL. 1961. *An experiment in field archaeology*, Antiquity 35: 129–34.
ATKINSON, R.J.C. 1955. The Dorset Cursus, *Antiquity* 29: 4–9.
    1957. Worms and weathering II: the weathering of natural subsoils, *Antiquity* 31: 228–33.
    1960. *Stonehenge*:134–9. Harmondsworth: Penguin.
GRIMES, W.F. 1960. *Excavations on Defence Sites, 1939–45* I. London: HMSO.
HMSO. 1959. *Stonehenge and Avebury*.
HEYERDAHL, T. 1958. *Aku Aku*. London: Readers Union.
HOPE-TAYLOR, B. 1960. *National Geographic Magazine* 117: 850–51
LACAILLE, A.D. & W.F. GRIMES. 1961. The prehistory of Caldey, part 2, *Archaeologia Cambrensis*: 110: 30–70.
LEEDS, E.T. 1934. Recent Bronze Age discoveries in Berkshire and Oxfordshire, *Antiquaries Journal* 14: 264–76.
PIGGOTT, S. 1949. The excavations at Cairnpapple Hill, West Lothian 1947–8, *Antiquity* 23: 32–9.
    1963. *The West Kennet Long Barrow excavations 1955–6*. London: HMSO.
PPS NOTES. 1959. Mynydd Rhiw, Caernarvonshire: notes on excavations, *Proceedings of the Prehistoric Society* 25: 280.
PPS NOTES. 1960. Notes on excavations, *Proceedings of the Prehistoric Society* 26: 349.
SINGER, C., HOLMYARD & HALL. (ed.) 1954. *A History of Technology* I. Oxford: Clarendon Press.
THOM, A. 1961. The geometry of megalithic man, *Mathematical Gazette* 45: 83–93.

Megaliths and mathematics
by ALEXANDER THOM
ANTIQUITY 40 (158), 1966

IT IS BECOMING APPARENT that megalithic man possessed and used a considerable knowledge of geometry. As more of his constructions are unravelled, we obtain an increasing appreciation of his attainments. Undoubtedly he also observed the heavenly bodies and used them to tell the time of day or night and to tell the day of the year. To take geometry first, let us look at the various shapes which, in his hands, a ring of stone could take. To understand these rings fully it is necessary to appreciate that he used extensively a very precise unit of length — the megalithic yard (MY). The exact length of this unit has become known to us by an examination of simple circles and flattened circles. When the author produced the first batch of circle diameters there was no universally accepted statistical analysis for the determination of the reliability of a quantum such as the suggested value for the megalithic yard. Then Broadbent produced two papers providing exactly the methods required to find, from a set of measurements, the most probable value of the quantum and the probability level at which it could be accepted (Broadbent 1955; 1956). This last is very important because Hammersley had shown that almost any random set of (say) diameters will yield an apparent unit of some sort.

Logically a sound approach would be to use the measurements to test an *a priori* value of the quantum, but in the case of the megalithic yard we have no *a priori* value. The unit must come from the data themselves and Broadbent's second paper provides for this case. It is sufficient to say that the accumulated data, much of which I set out in 1962, stands up to Broadbent's analysis, thus establishing definitely that the unit exists and that its value is just over 2·72 ft. (Thom 1962). The result is the same whether the unit is derived from the English or the Scottish circles. The analysis gives us two interesting by-products: (a) the precision of the measurements does not decrease with length, and (b) the builders of the circles measured to the centres of the stones in a ring. Exceptions to this rule occur in those cases where the ring was of closely spaced stones forming a retaining-wall holding rubble filling. Then it would only be natural to measure to the more or less regular side of the wall outside the tumulus or to the inside of a wall forming a cell inside. It has also been shown that half and perhaps quarter yards were often used in alignments (3). Later work supports this subdivision of the yard, but no trace of a subdivision into three is apparent.

In their desire to use integral multiples of the yard the incommensurability of π posed a problem. One soon notices how many of the smaller circles have a diameter of about 22 ft.

These are 8 megalithic yards in diameter and so with $\pi = 3\cdot125$ the circumference would be 25. The importance of 25 lies in megalithic man's use of a larger unit of 10, subdivided again into halves and quarters. It seems likely that for longer distances he used measuring rods 2·5 yd. (6·80 ft.) long.

Some of the types of rings used are shown (FIGURE 1). There are at least 25 examples of 'flattened circles' Types A and B still in existence, many of which have been surveyed (Thom 1955; 1961). There are 9 sites known with egg-shaped rings Type I and II. Type I is the commonest but both are based on Pythagorean triangles or triangles which are

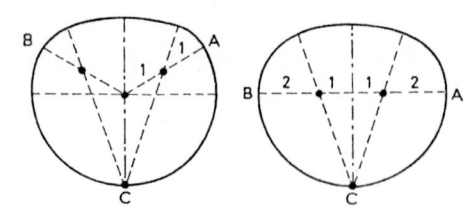

Flattened circles, type A and B.

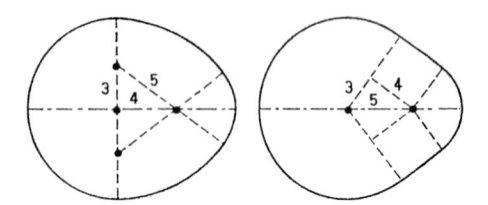

Egg shapes, type I and II

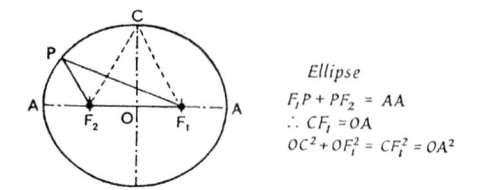

Ellipse
$F_1P + PF_2 = AA$
$\therefore CF_1 = OA$
$OC^2 + OF_1^2 = CF_1^2 = OA^2$

FIGURE 1. *Classes of megalithic rings.*

nearly Pythagorean. The favourite is the 3,4,5 triangle which, from earliest times, has been used to set out a right-angle. Having laid out two of these triangles back to back we have established 4 points on the ground (FIGURE 1). The egg shape can now be constructed by scribing four arcs centred on these four points. Type II differs in the placing of the triangles and in having only two arcs joined by straight lines parallel to the side of the triangle. It will be evident in both types that once the first arc is drawn the others follow, their radii being determined by that of the first. Further, if the radius chosen for the first arc drawn is an integral number of yards then, since the sides of the triangle are integers, the other radii will also be integers. An example is given which shows the inner ring at 'The Druid Temple' near Inverness (FIGURE 2).

When the triangles have been drawn any desired value can be chosen for the radius of the first arc, so a large variety of egg shapes can be drawn. It appears that the value actually chosen was such as to make, in nearly all cases, the perimeter of the ring as closely as possible a multiple of $2^{1/2}$ yd.

The most important of the egg-ring sites is Woodhenge (FIGURE 3). Here the triangle was 12, 35, 37, an exact Pythagorean triangle, set out in units of the half yard. By a little trigonometry we can show that with this triangle the relation between the radius chosen for the large end and the perimeter P is:

$$r = (P-9\cdot 08)/2\pi$$

Using this, the values of r were found corresponding to P = 40, 60, 80, 140 and 160 yd. To check that the above was the construction actually used at Woodhenge a careful large-scale survey was made and tested with a steel tape. The geometrical design, with the values of r as found above, was drawn carefully on tracing-paper and superimposed. The result is shown to a small scale in the figure. Further details regarding Woodhenge geometry and other egg-shaped rings have been set out elsewhere (Thom 1961).

These triangles were also used for constructing ellipses. The easiest way to draw an ellipse on the ground is to drive two stakes at the points F_1 and F_2 chosen for the foci. A rope having a length equal to the required major axis has its ends tied to the stakes. The outline can then be drawn by a third stake slid round the rope. When the third stake is at C (FIGURE 1) we see that the semi-axes major and minor and half the focal distance OF_1 form a right-angled triangle. So if all the dimensions are to be integers we again require a Pythagorean triangle.

As an example take the 'circle' above Penmaenmawr (FIGURE 4). Here the major axis is 31 MY and the distance between the foci is 9·5 MY. This makes the minor axis equal to $\sqrt{(870\cdot 75)}$ or 29·508, which on the ground is indistinguishable from 29·5. It can be

Bases shaded
Heights in feet

Lat. = 57° 27'·0
Long. = 4° 11'·4
NH 685420

Perimeter = 47·28 MY

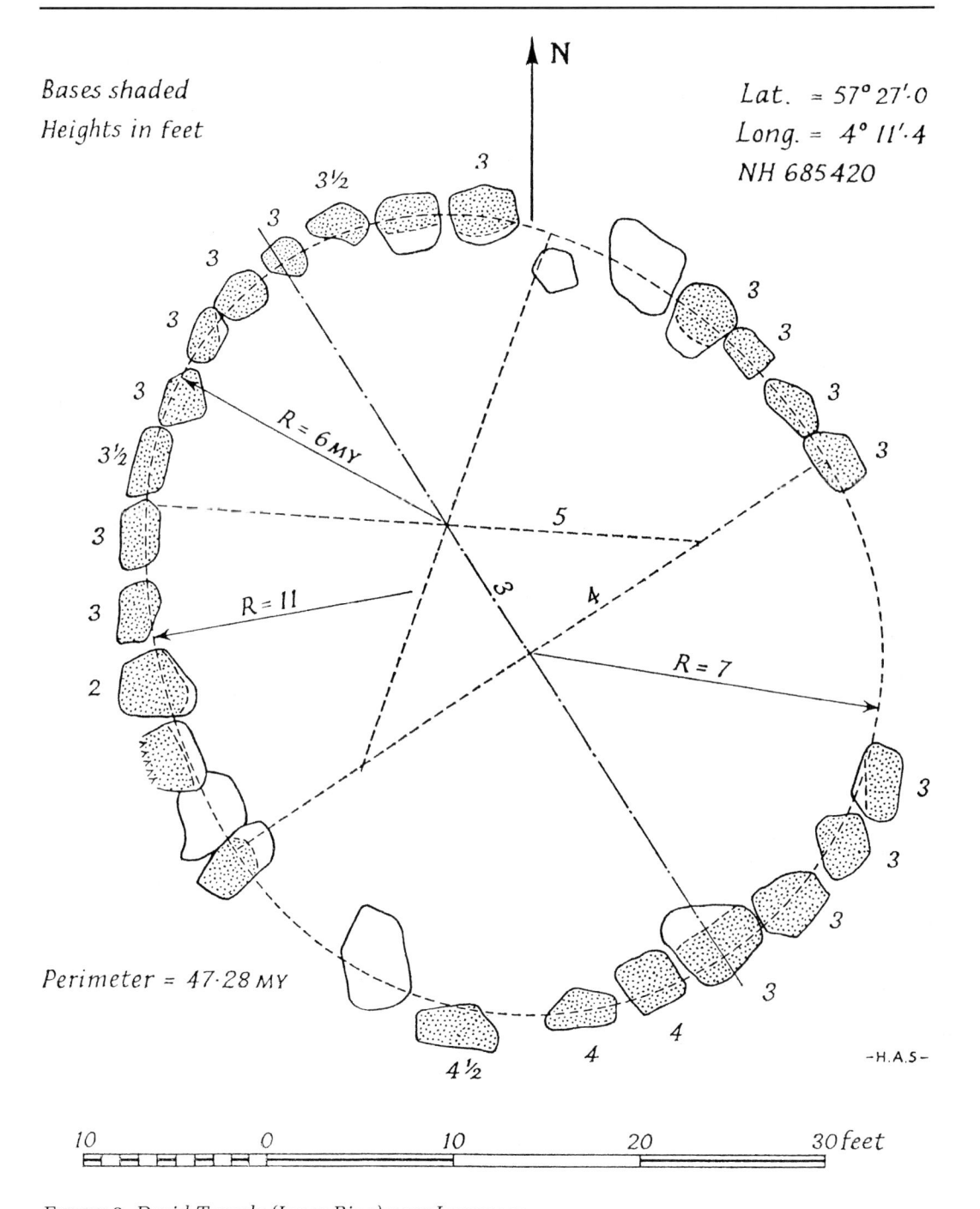

FIGURE 2. *Druid Temple (Inner Ring) near Inverness.*

shown by calculation that the perimeter of the ellipse so drawn is 95·06 which is remarkably near 95. By a study of this circle we have, in fact, found another triangle which is almost Pythagorean since $19^2 + 59^2$ is 3842 and 62^2 is 3844. But how did they get at the same time dimensions which made the perimeter 95?

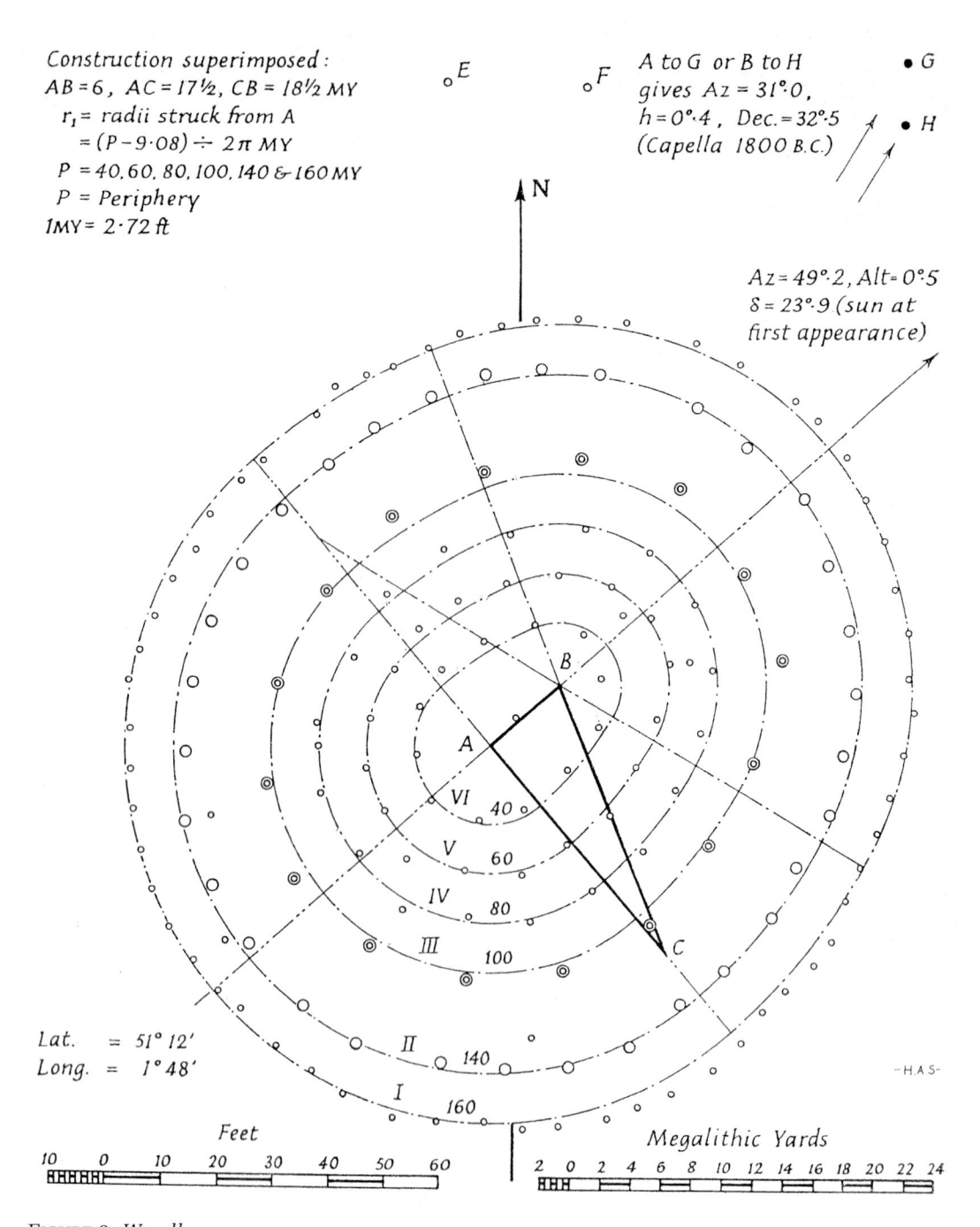

FIGURE 3. *Woodhenge.*

Of the nine ellipses surveyed up to the present by the author, only one fails to have its perimeter close to a multiple of 2·5 MY. Today we would use a digital computer to discover ellipses with these properties. To do it by trial and error must have been a prodigious task.

A very interesting ring of compound type occurs in Wales at Moel Ty Ucha (FIGURE 5). The details of the geometry are given (FIGURE 6). With the radii of the two construction circles 4 and 7 MY the radius of the long arcs will be found to be 13·5 MY. Trigonometry shows that the exact length is 13·503 and that the perimeter is 42·85. It is remarkable that with this beautiful construction these people succeeded in finding dimensions which made all radii integral and made the perimeter so close to 42·5. The construction is superimposed on an accurate survey (FIGURE 5). The agreement is much too close to be accidental. Note also the position of north relative to the construction lines of the figure and note the outlier A on the cross-axis produced. Other compound rings might be described but enough has been said to demonstrate the advanced state of megalithic man's geometry and his determination to spare no pains, to get, if possible, all the dimensions of his figures multiples of the yard or half yard. One can only surmise that, having no pen and paper, he was building in stone a record of his achievements in geometry and perhaps also in arithmetic.

Upright stones shaded
Heights in feet

N

Main circle to small circle
Az = 60°·9   h = −0·2   Dec = 16°·3

Distance between centres
820·9 ft (304·8 MY)

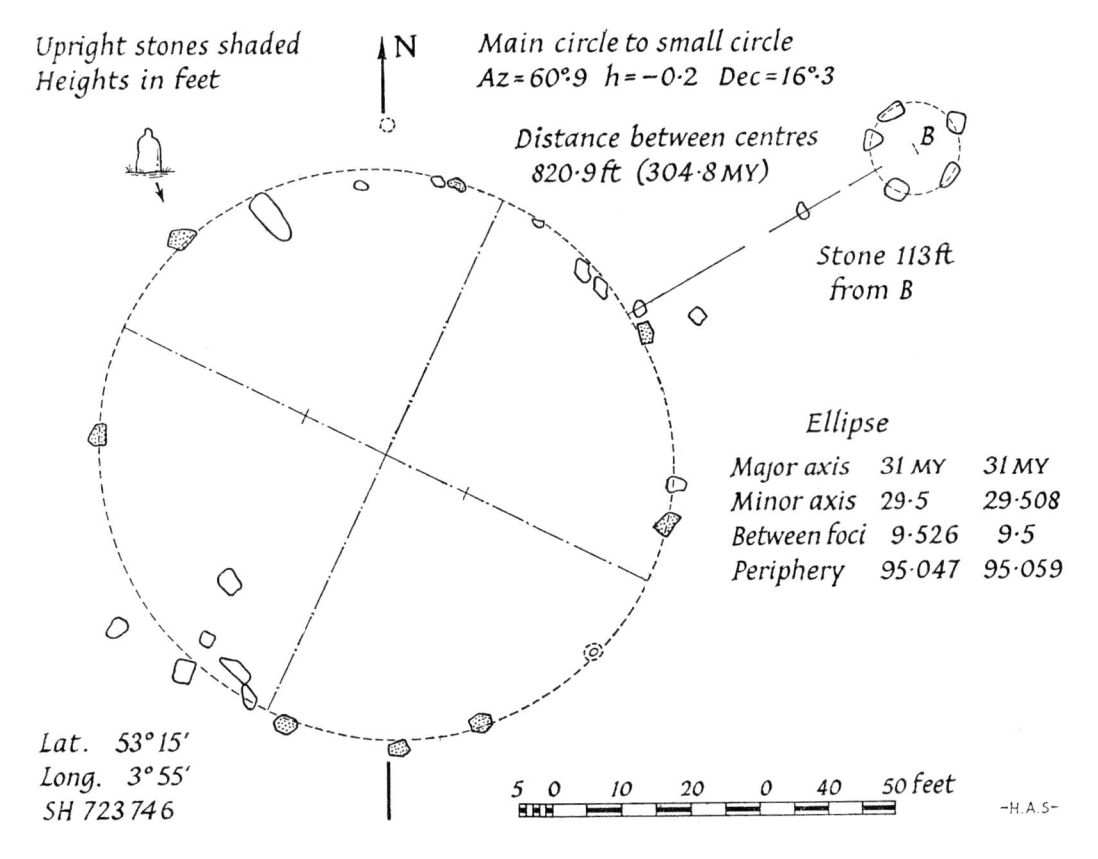

Stone 113 ft
from B

Ellipse

Major axis	31 MY	31 MY
Minor axis	29·5	29·508
Between foci	9·526	9·5
Periphery	95·047	95·059

Lat. 53° 15′
Long. 3° 55′
SH 723 746

5 0   10   20   0   40   50 feet

−H.A.S−

FIGURE 4. *Penmaenmawr.*

Lat. 52° 55′·4
Long. 3° 24′·2
SJ 057 371

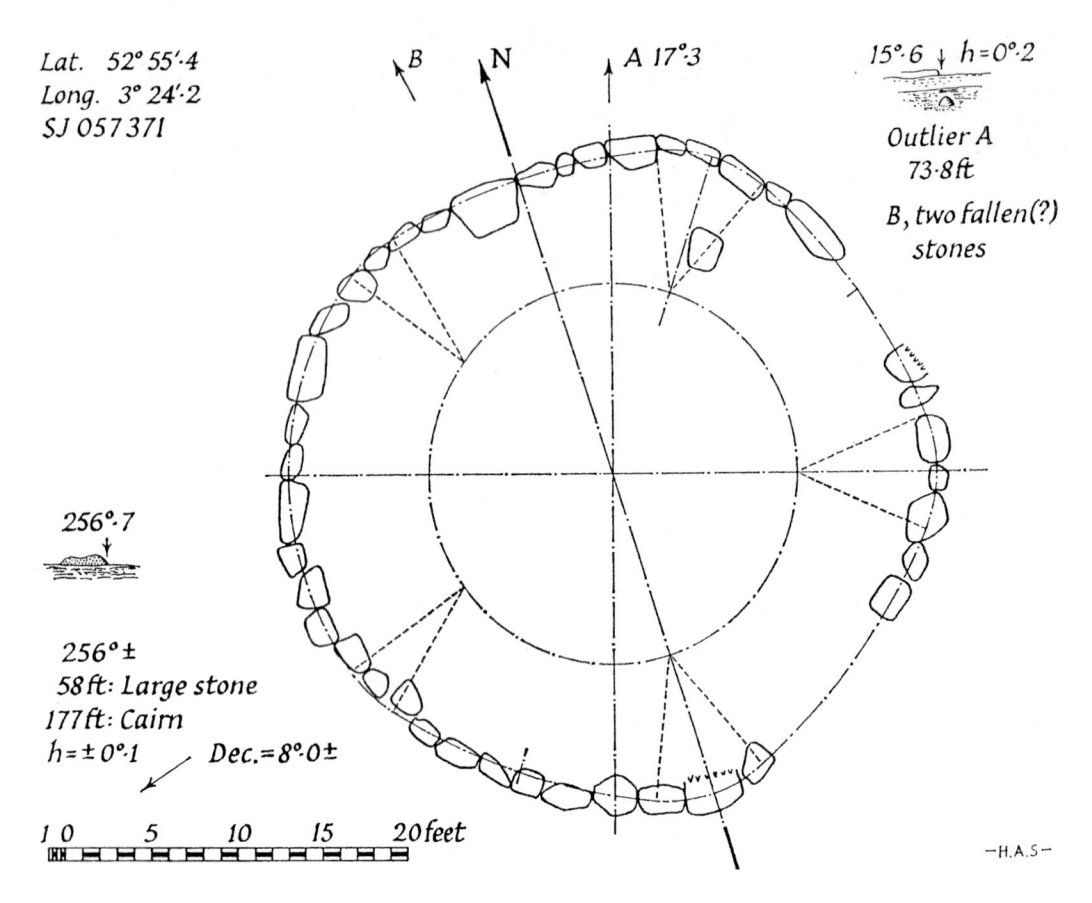

B   N   A 17°·3   15°·6 ↓ h=0°·2

Outlier A
73·8 ft

B, two fallen(?)
stones

256°·7

256° ±
58 ft: Large stone
177 ft: Cairn
h = ±0°·1   Dec. = 8°·0 ±

1 0   5   10   15   20 feet

—H.A.S—

FIGURE 5. *Moel Ty Ucha.*

Astronomy

Consider now the evidence that these people observed and used astronomical phenomena. A number of the most impressive sites such as Callanish, Temple Wood and Duncracaig can only be explained astronomically. Such things as outliers and straight alignments seem to have little purely geometric significance. Do they fit into an astronomical picture? Consider the boulder at Moel Ty Ucha assumed above to be an outlier. Its azimuth from the circle centre is about 17·3° (N 17·3° E). On this line the horizon is low and a rising star would not be visible until it had attained what is called its 'extinction angle' (Neugebauer 1912). In megalithic times the first magnitude star Deneb would, in this sense, rise when its altitude was about 1·4° and it would then be exactly on the line indicated. This isolated example is perhaps by itself unimpressive and might be accidental and so as many sites as possible have to be examined and the data subjected to strict statistical tests to find the probability that outliers and alignments were associated with first magnitude stars. This was attempted by the author in 1955 (Thom 1955). Using severe terms of reference for selecting the material the result was definite — there was a strong probability that stars were used as well as the sun. Unfortunately the importance of the extinction angle was not realized with the result that too early a mean date was found for the country as a whole. A repeat calculation taking into account the extinction angle and many new data shows a later date, but is not yet complete. It has shown that the relation between extinction angle and magnitude derived from megalithic sites agrees with that given by Neugebauer (1912).

In megalithic times there were two methods available of telling the time: by the rising and setting of certain stars uniquely indicated by outliers, and by the transit of the sun or stars over the meridian. For the second method great slabs or sometimes rows of slabs, were erected truly north and south. One can today watch the sun's shadow on these stones and so determine local apparent noon to within a few minutes. There are over a dozen such sites still capable of being used.

Because of the remarkable accuracy with which the site at Ballochroy can be operated one thinks of it as easily the best megalithic solstitial observatory (Thom 1954)). This is only one of the large number of sites with indications for the solstitial sun, but other dates in the calendar were also important. It seems that the year was divided into 8 equal parts. In this connexion the most impressive evidence is the number of indicators for a declination between + 0·4° and + 0·8°. If these are equinoctial indicators why do we not find zero declination? The reason given below is completely convincing. If we calculate the two dates in the year when, in megalithic times, the sun had a declination of + 0·5° we find that these are separated by exactly half a year. Thus megalithic man's 'equinox' occurred when the sun's declination was + 0·5°. These dates, with the solstices, divide the year into 4. To subdivide again we need for example indicators for May Day, 46 days, i.e. one eighth of a year, before the summer solstice, and for Candlemas, 46 days after mid-winter. We find many lines giving the required declinations. This matter is to some extent discussed (Thom 1954), but since this was written much more confirmatory material has turned up, together with a group of lines for delineations ± 21·5°. These are not explained satisfactorily by star positions but they are approximately the sun's declination 23 days before and after the equinoxes. This is not so well established as the May Day, Candlemas dates but support comes from the 5 or 6 lines showing a date 23 days before or after the equinoxes. These taken together indicate that the year was divided into 16 parts. Perhaps it should be pointed out that the accuracy with which a date may be determined from the position of the setting sun is in Scotland nearly twice as great as that in the tropics. But the solstices are the most difficult dates to determine in this way. The sun has then its maximum declination north or south and so its setting position is changing so slowly that only with a site like Ballochroy is there any hope of picking the exact day. It can however be shown that the sophisticated calendar which was in use, by linking the solstice with the more easily determined equinox, would determine midsummer day exactly. The calendars in the outlying districts could have been synchronized by signal fires such as were still being lit this century on midsummer night on the hilltops in various parts of Europe.

In the sense that *solstice* means a standing still of the sun's declination the moon might be said to have four solstices. The plane of the lunar orbit is inclined at some 5° to the ecliptic which is the path of the sun amongst the stars. The line of intersection of the two planes (the line of nodes) rotates slowly completing a revolution in about 18·6 years.

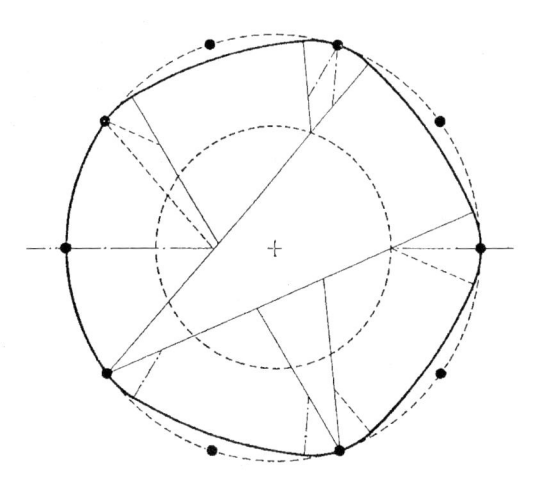

Construction: Set out outer circle with radius 7MY. Divide this circle into ten equal arcs. Set out inner circle with 4MY and draw the five 'corner-arcs' with crs. on the inner circle. Draw the four flat arcs with crs. on the large circle. The radii of these arcs will be found to be 13½ MY.

FIGURE 6. *Moel Ty Ucha — the geometrical construction.*

This means that we sometimes see the moon 5° north of the sun's path and sometimes 5° south. It follows that the rising point of say the full moon nearest to midwinter oscillates back and forward along the horizon by some 20°. The extremes of this oscillation, the lunar solstices, are marked at some 30 places in Britain. Some of these sites are arranged like Ballochroy and give the maximum lunar declination with such great accuracy that we can be perfectly certain that they were set up as lunar observatories. They give an entirely independent mean date of 1800 ± 100 BC.

Hawkins (1964) points out that a 56-year cycle is better for eclipse prediction than an 18-year cycle, 56 being close to 3 x 18·6. Thus the 56 Aubrey holes at Stonehenge could have been used for markers to keep track of the position of the current year in the eclipse cycle. Since there was free communication among the communities why did each have to do its own eclipse prediction? Was this work eventually centred on Stonehenge?

We need more information. We need many more accurate surveys particular attention being paid to hill horizons. With our present lack of knowledge of cup and ring marks we cannot exclude these from the study. The existing sketches must be replaced by accurate plans accurately orientated. It is useless to make inferior surveys of the work of a people whose linear metrology was of a very high order.

References
BEER, A. (ed.). 1966. *Vistas in astronomy* 7.
BROADBENT, S.R. 1955. Quantum Hypothesis, *Biometrika* 42: 45.
   1956. Examination of a Quantum Hypothesis Based on a Single Set of Data, *Biometrika* 43: 32.
HAWKINS,G.S. 1964. Stonehenge: a Neolithic Computer, *Nature* 202: 1258.
NEUGEBAUER, P.V. 1912. *Tafeln zur Astronomischen Chronologie*. Leipzig.
THOM, A. 1954a. The Solar Observatories of Megalithic Man, *Journal of the British Astronomical Association* 64, no. 8: 396.
   1955. A Statistical Examination of the Megalithic Sites in Britain, *Journal of the Royal Statistical Society* A. 118: 275–98.
   1961a. The Geometry of Megalithic Man, *Mathematical Gazette* 45: 83–93.
   1961b. The Egg-Shaped Standing Stone Rings of Britain, *Archives Internationale d'Histoire des Sciences* 14: 291–302.
   1962. The Megalithic Unit of Length, *Journal of the Royal Statistical Society* A. 125, part 2: 243.
   1966. Megalithic Astronomy: Indications in Standing Stones, in A. Beer (ed.), *Vistas in Astronomy* 7: 1–58.

Megalithic lunar observatories: an astronomer's view
by D.C. HEGGIE
ANTIQUITY 46 (181), 1972

ALTHOUGH SEVERAL STUDIES along broadly similar lines have been attempted by other authors in the past, it will benefit any archaeologist approaching the work of Professor A. Thom for the first time to do so with a fresh mind. What is new about Thom's approach to this subject, which many astronomers find equally absorbing, is the care that has evidently been bestowed in the measurement of the sites themselves, the attention to detail that characterizes the reduction of this data, and finally the great volume of source material which, in his books and other writings, he has put at the disposal of others. Previous work seems by comparison to have been of lower accuracy and restricted to at most a few sites, of which Stonehenge figures most frequently.

Professor Thom's first book on this subject (Thom 1967) dealt with some 150 British megalithic sites from several points of view, and in his later work (Thom 1971), recently reviewed in this journal by Professor Kendall, he selected about 50 of these, with a few others, for the purpose of discovering how much the constructors of these fascinating monuments may have known about the motion of the moon. It is to a discussion mainly of the astronomical content of this book that the following remarks will be devoted.

Essential Astronomy
Thom's own account of the gross features of the motion of the sun and moon, which are central to the understanding of his thesis, can hardly be bettered for succinctness. An astronomer generally measures the position of any object in the sky by two angles, one of which may be what is called 'declination'. Its importance here lies in the fact that the declination of a star or planet determines the points on the horizon at which it rises and sets: the greater the declination the further to the north both points are. In summer, we are all aware, the sun rises and sets quite far to the north, and far to the south in winter. Throughout the year, likewise, the declination of the sun moves through a complete cycle, being high in summer and low in winter. It is one task of astronomers to measure its declination at midsummer (which Thom calls ϵ), although they do not adopt direct methods.

What is less well known is that the moon regularly completes a similar cycle, but takes only a month to do so. If the point at which it rises on the horizon is quite far north, then a fortnight later it will rise at a point equally far south. What have astronomers to say on its maximum declination for the month? Crude observation would show that this value, the monthly maximum declination, or MMD for short, is not much different from ϵ. It varies slowly from month to month with a period of nearly 19 years, over a range that can be described by introducing a new angle, which Thom calls i and astronomers have evaluated accurately. If for some months the MMD is $\epsilon + i$, then a little over 9 years later it will be about $\epsilon - i$, and after a similar period it will approach the number $\epsilon + i$ again. Actually the motion of the moon is much more complicated, but only one more feature need concern us: the MMD in addition varies cyclically by a small amount, called by Thom Δ, over a period of about six months. In principal all these changes in the declination of the moon can easily be detected by painstakingly studying the positions on the horizon at which it rises and sets.

Astronomical significance of megalithic sites

So much for the astronomical background. We next come to the central question: how much of this was known to the people who constructed megalithic monuments? Let us suppose that it was indeed the rising and setting positions of astronomical objects that they attempted to record. For stars there was no problem: the declination of a star changes so slowly that the point at which it rises hardly moves for many years, and it would have been worth while marking it permanently. The point at which the sun rises changes from day to day, but the rising position at, for example, midsummer changes so slowly that many years would elapse before its motion could be detected. As for the moon, its MMD changes noticeably from month to month, as already explained, mainly over a period of about 19 years. The limits of this variation are, to a certain accuracy, almost the same for some centuries, so that it would be worth recording the corresponding positions on the horizon. Is there any indication that records of some of these points still exist in the megalithic sites? This was one question which Thom answered, to my mind conclusively, in his *Megalithic sites in Britain* (1967: 94). He there remarked that the appropriate points on the horizon could be indicated by a long alignment of stones, perhaps numbering as few as two, or perhaps by a circle and a single menhir. In any case one stands at one end of the alignment — the backsight — and looks beyond the other — the foresight. In this way a location on the horizon is indicated, and it remains to find the declination of an object which rises or sets there.

The point on the horizon need be distinguished in no other way, but at some sites the alignment of a single flat menhir indicates a feature on the horizon which is somehow distinctive: it may be a valley, the top of a hill, or the apparent coast of a distant island, and so on. The advantage of such a site (the point on the horizon here being termed by Thom an 'indicated foresight') is that the rising position towards which the constructor of the site intended us to look is generally much more accurately defined than in the cases where an alignment alone was constructed. From the point of view of the student attempting to interpret them the drawback is that it may not be precisely clear which of several points on the horizon was intended, or even exactly where we ought to stand to use the foresight, if we can identify it uniquely. Such sites should therefore be set aside until it has been established that alignments in general have astronomical significance.

Although Thom did not omit them in his first analysis, his result is almost unchanged if we do so, since most of the sites he considered then were alignments: in other words both foresight and backsight were artificial structures. It was clearly demonstrated that very many of the alignments could be accommodated by the hypothesis that they were erected to indicate points on the horizon at which very bright stars rose or set, or those at which the moon or sun rose or set at one or other position of permanent interest, as described above.

If in this way we select those alignments that seem to have been constructed for the purpose of studying the motion of the moon, a detailed study of these alone (Thom 1967: figure 10.1) establishes in a definite way that they were set up to indicate not its centre, but either the upper or lower edge. The fact that the alignments fall into two such clear groups in approximately the way that would be expected if either edge were observed, is further strong evidence that one function of some of these sites was the study of the motion of the moon. This conclusion is little affected by the exclusion of sites with indicated natural features on the horizon as foresights.

Indicated foresights

As Thom remarked (1967: 121), it is not possible to establish from alignments alone that their erectors knew anything about the motion of the moon other than the large 19-year oscillation of the MMD, for they are not sufficiently accurate to show whether or not the six-month variation had been detected. Only the sites with indicated foresights are capable of the required precision, and their interpretation is subject to the difficulty of ambiguity already alluded to.

Although some remarks are directed towards this subject in *Megalithic sites in Britain*, it forms the major part of the material in Professor Thom's new book. With a suitable indicated foresight it is, in principle, possible to observe the six-month oscillation of the MMD and so in a study of these sites an attempt must be made to decide whether or not indications exist of the position in which the moon rose or set when its declination took one of the twelve values $\pm \epsilon \pm i$ and $\pm \epsilon \pm i \pm \Delta$.

Thom's answer to this question is a clear 'yes', but his evidence is explicitly signposted in only one or two places. It is clear, however, from these few remarks (1967: 125; 1971: 47; etc.) that the author intends our confidence in the truth of his assertion to follow directly from the frequency of sites in which one or more of the interesting declinations are quite accurately shown. It is important that the reader of this book now decides whether or not this is correct, for, if it is, we can proceed to examine the sites with more ambiguous foresights or backsights, and can confidently select only those combinations of foresight and backsight which most closely indicate rising and setting positions when the declination of the moon took one of the interesting values. This is Professor Thom's approach, although presented rather implicitly in his book.

In arriving at a decision, the reader should be guided by considerations of the following kind. The indicator stone or alignment generally indicates unequivocally whether the intended declination is close to $\epsilon +i$, $\epsilon -i$, $-\epsilon +i$ or $-\epsilon -i$ (although in the case of Carrach an Tarbert the stone cannot point to *both* suggested foresights), but around these values there are six interesting declinations, if we exclude the centre of the moon and assume that only one or other edge was observed. These lie in a range of declination of only 49 minutes of arc, which corresponds to some small section of the horizon where there may be a number, say N, of usable foresights. Even if these are just randomly placed on this part of the horizon, the number that may be expected to indicate one of the interesting declinations to within an accuracy of minutes of arc is about $\frac{Nx}{4}$ looking at Thom's list of reliable indicated foresights on (1971: 76), it is seen that some of the indicated declinations agree with each other to no better than 7 minutes, although this is exceptional, so that the reader may feel at liberty to take x to be about 2. He may then study the various illustrations of the relevant section of horizon given for most sites, determine N, and decide whether the number of indications is indeed impressive. If there are several possible backsights, this should be taken into account as well.

The reader must not be tempted to accept figure 7.1 as proof of Thom's assertion, for it is constructed from just those combinations of backsight and foresight that were selected because they indicate declinations close to the interesting values. It does suggest, however, the manner in which the evidence could have been presented. To establish conclusively that megalithic man did observe the interesting declinations, a calculation should be carried out of the declination corresponding to every sightline within, say, the 49-minute range already mentioned. If the interesting declinations showed up in these calculations significantly more often than others, then we should have little hesitation in accepting this part of Thom's thesis.

The same difficulties hinder any study of indicated foresights at solar sites, but if they be ignored for the moment, it is possible from these monuments to arrive at a value for ϵ. This varies slowly with time, according to a formula, versions of which have been published by various authors including de Sitter, the source used by Thom. Actually these formulae are intended for use only at times within, at most, a few hundred years of the present. However a more accurate computation reveals that the error in estimating ages by de Sitter's formula amounts to no more than about fifteen years at the epoch of interest.

In the same way Thom analyses the declinations indicated by his selected sightlines at the lunar observatories, and arrives at a value of ϵ closely agreeing with that just obtained at the solar sites, and values for i, Δ and the mean apparent size of the moon in good agreement with the values observed today. Astronomical theory predicts that these quantities do not change significantly over 4,000 years, but again the agreement is not evidence that the sites were designed to show the interesting declinations, for reasons already given.

Extrapolation

Thom does not deny that the establishment of accurate sightlines is fraught with considerable difficulties, but his discussion of how these could be overcome invites some comment. The most serious difficulty, in the sense that it is the one whose neglect would introduce the largest errors, stems from the fact that the moon rises and sets roughly only once each day. If the moon reaches its MMD between two successive risings, then when it does rise its declination will be different from the maximum value for that month. A sightline established at either moonrise would generally be in serious error, and its accurate erection depends on the knowledge by its constructors of some method of correcting for this effect, i.e. a method of 'extrapolation'.

As Professor Thom remarks, this could be accomplished by measuring out lengths on the ground related to a fundamental length, called G, which depends on the site. Since this quantity would be used repeatedly, there seems a high likelihood that, at least in some sites, it would be permanently laid out on the ground. Evidence for this is given in part of figure 9.14, which shows that the overall size of certain sites is comparable to the theoretically ideal value of G. This evidence, though weak by itself, finds support in Professor Thom's analysis of a type of monument which has not so far been mentioned.

Extrapolation requires, as well as G, another quantity that can be obtained from it by any one of several geometrical methods. Thom's ingenious suggestion is that the stone fans of Caithness may have served this purpose, a hypothesis that can be checked in the following manner. From the dimensions of the fan one can estimate the value of G for which it is appropriate, and the horizon is studied for possible foresights in the usual way. The value of G for a foresight, if one is found, may then be compared with that used in the construction of the fan. The agreement (figure 9.14 again) is good. It must be remarked that, in one case at least (Dirlot), the remains of the fan are vestigial, rendering G uncertain, while in this and in others, the indications of the foresights are rather weak. However, because conspicuous indicators were erected in other parts of the country does not imply that the men in Caithness need have done so. After all, this method of extrapolation seems to be peculiar to Caithness, at least in Britain. More recently Thom and his colleagues have obtained quite similar results for two fans in north-west France (*Chronicle*, BBC2, 21 August 1971; Thom & Thom 1971).

The effect of the distance of the moon

Before continuing this discussion of extrapolation it is appropriate to make mention of the other serious difficulty that might have hindered attempts to erect accurate sightlines. Because the moon is, relatively speaking, a nearby object, the point on the horizon at which it rises depends not just on its declination but on its distance as well, which varies over a period of about one month. As Thom shows, however, its distance on that day of the month when the moon reaches its MMD and during the few months when this is close to an interesting value, varies with a period of about 180 years.* Since some of the sites show the rising and setting positions corresponding to the average distance or, more precisely, the average of the reciprocal of the distance, their erection must have taken not less than about 90 years. All the sites in fact show on average the positions corresponding to the average inverse distance, and it is again, possible that this is almost entirely due to the selection of sightlines close to these positions.

Thom's theoretical derivation of G can be substantially improved. First, the value of the quantity k used in equation (2.2) is more correctly

$$k = \frac{2\pi}{P} \tan g$$

as is shown in an appendix. This implies that values of G should be increased by about 9 per cent when the declination is $\pm(\epsilon + i)$ approximately, and by about 4 per cent when it is about $\pm(\epsilon - i)$. This correction reduces the agreement between the ideal values and those measured from the stone fans, but only in the case of Mid Clyth would it lead to errors of as much as a minute of arc.

The values of k and G depend with surprising sensitivity on the distance of the moon, a point that appears not to be discussed in Thom's book. As is shown in an appendix, k and G vary on this account by over 20 per cent on either side of their mean values. If the workers at these sites had used one value always, errors of at least 2 minutes of arc would have occurred frequently. They might have determined G afresh on each occasion it was required, but the method by which, Thom suggests, this could be done (p. 101) demands observations on three consecutive nights.

Feasibility

Such considerations suggest a study of the visibility of rising and setting phenomena, a point that is scarcely considered by Thom. Even when most of the sky is free from cloud, by a simple effect of perspective it is at the horizon that the cloud appears to be thickest. Even when the sky is completely unobscured by cloud, there is often sufficient haze near the horizon that daylight moonrise is difficult to observe. (Thom's diagrams of the horizon are presented according to conditions prevailing at night.) If we suppose that the probability that two particular successive moonrises take place over a sufficiently clear horizon is one half — and today it would be substantially less than this[†]— and take account of the fact that about half occur in daylight, we see that at most in only one month out of four would it be possible to observe both moonrises on either side of the time when the moon reached its MMD. Since erection of a sightline corresponding to, say, the declination $\epsilon + i + \Delta$ requires this to be done for two consecutive months, of the periods when the MMD is near this value, only at about one in eight will it be possible to set up a sightline. Since there are at most two such periods every 18 years, a new sightline can be erected only once every 70 years on average. If G is to be evaluated every so often, so that observations on three consecutive days are required, the position is still more difficult, and in any case several sightlines must be erected before it is possible to construct one corresponding to the mean distance of the moon. By the time sufficient

---

* Thom's discussion of this period is slightly incorrect, for the average time between successive declination maxima is not the draconic month (p. 80) but the tropical month. This does not affect the value of the period, however, since 250 draconic months almost exactly equals 249 tropical months.

† Data published by R. J. Livesey (1971) show that it does not exceed 1 in 10.

observations had accumulated, the slow change of ϵ would have become sufficient to interfere seriously with this project. It is considerations of this kind which might compel us to search for some alternative explanation of the apparent high accuracy of some of the sites.

Conclusion

To the reader who has successfully followed the previous paragraphs it will come as no surprise if the views there expressed are summarized as follows. Thom's evidence that megalithic man observed the moon is so strong that it may be accepted without hesitation. That he also used extrapolation in the interpretation of his observations seems to be indicated by the evidence of the stone fans of Caithness and elsewhere. The data on which Thom bases his assertion that the builders of the monument established *accurate* sightlines for several interesting declinations, implying a knowledge of its motion that was not to be improved upon for over three thousand years, may have been interpreted incorrectly. This view is supported by a consideration of the feasibility of the prject which, according to Thom, megalithic man successfully completed.

Much interesting material for feeding research in this subject may be found in Professor Thom's writings. The fact that few others have repeated his work should be understood as a symptom, not of doubts as to its value, but of the enormous effort that must be expended if Thom's standards are to be maintained.

Appendix

Let δ be the declination of the moon at a short time, t, after it achieves its MMD, called g. Let ω be the angular velocity of the moon across the sky. Then, using the cosine formula of spherical trigonometry,

$$\sin \delta = \sin g \cos \omega t \quad \text{so that} \quad \delta - g \doteq -\tfrac{1}{2} \tan g \cdot \omega^2 t^2. \quad (1)$$

If r is the distance of the moon, a and e respectively the semi-major axis and eccentricity of its orbit around the earth, and P the value of the sidereal month, from celestial mechanics

$$r^2 \omega = \frac{2\pi}{P} a^2 \sqrt{1-e^2}. \quad (2)$$

Introducing Thom's quantity k, (1) and (2) imply that

$$k = \frac{2\pi^2}{P^2} \tan g \left(\frac{a}{r}\right)^4 (1-e^2).$$

Thom's expression for k corresponding to the monthly motion of the moon should be multiplied by

$$\frac{\tan g}{g} \left(\frac{a}{r}\right)^4 (1-e^2).$$

Putting for the moment $r = a$, we see that Thom's values of k and G should be increased approximately by 9 per cent when $g \doteq \epsilon + 1$ and by 4 per cent when $g \doteq \epsilon - i$. $\frac{a}{r}$ varies about its mean value by over 5 per cent, and so k and G may differ from their mean values by at least 20 per cent.

References

LIVESEY, R. J. 1971. The distribution of cloud and its effect on observing, *Journal of the British Astronomical Association* 81: 292–4.
THOM, A. 1967. *Megalithic sites in Britain*. Oxford: Clarendon Press.
    1971. *Megalithic lunar observatories*. Oxford: Clarendon Press.
THOM, A. & A.S. THOM. 1971. The astronomical significance of the large Carnac menhirs, *Journal for the History of Astronomy* 2: 147–60.

Cosmology, calendars and society in Neolithic Orkney: a rejoinder to Euan MacKie

by CLIVE RUGGLES & GORDON BARCLAY

ANTIQUITY 74 (283), 2000

> You can't measure time in days the way you can money in dollars because every day is different.
> JORGE LUIS BORGES

IN A RECENT ARTICLE in ANTIQUITY Euan MacKie (1997) has presented new material to support a modified version of his long-standing contention (MacKie 1977a; 1977b) that there existed in later Neolithic Britain and Ireland theocractic élites who possessed what seems astonishingly precise and sophisticated astronomical and mathematical knowledge. He uses new archaeoastronomical data obtained at Maes Howe passage tomb in Orkney, combined with archaeological evidence from the nearby Neolithic settlement of Barnhouse, to reaffirm a number of earlier ideas (e.g. MacKie 1969; 1976; 1977a; 1977b; 1981; 1982; 1983; 1986; 1994). In particular, he suggests that certain pre-Christian calendrical festivals, some of which survive into modern times, could derive from a 'Neolithic solar calendar' in widespread use in later Neolithic Britain and Ireland in which the solar year was divided into 8 or even 16 parts of equal length measured to the nearest day, starting from one of the solstices. Further arguments in support of these ideas, extending the origin of the 'calendar' back to the earlier Neolithic, are also presented in a subsequent article on Neolithic and later structures at Howe, Orkney (MacKie 1998).

Some of these ideas are important because of their clear, and radical, implications for our understanding of aspects of prehistoric cognition and cosmology, social organization and the factors determining patterns of continuity and change. In considering the new evidence, it is helpful to separate three overlapping, although not necessarily mutually dependent, fundamental ideas. The first is that the theocracies occupied a powerful and influential place in a strongly hierarchical social structure present throughout Britain, using 'national' forms of monument and pottery (MacKie 1997: 339). The second is that precise relationships existed between monuments, points of reference on the distant horizon, and sunrise or sunset on significant days in the calendar year. The third is that an 'elaborate and accurate' ceremonial calendar was in widespread use from Orkney to southern England and even Brittany (*cf.* MacKie 1997: 340, 358).

MacKie refers back repeatedly to the 1977 proposition of his ideas in the book *Science and society in prehistoric Britain* (MacKie 1977a — hereafter *S&S*). He dismisses critical reviews and commentaries (e.g. Hawkes 1977; Piggott 1978; Daniel 1980; Ritchie 1982) as 'not finding favour' and accuses others of lacking the courage to deal head-on with his views (MacKie 1994). The propensity of this topic to generate more heat than light is undeniable, but in view of the continued propagation of these ideas the present authors felt it necessary to attempt to provide — if not the detailed refutation that MacKie (1983) has demanded — at least the main threads of such a case, both from an archaeological and an archaeoastronomical point of view, together with pointers to some of the many relevant publications which, in our view, support that refutation.

Social hierarchy and theocracy
MacKie's basic belief is stated clearly on p. 22 of *S&S*:

> as in the Classic period Maya, a dominating class of priests and chiefs emerged of whom at least the former lived in special ceremonial centres supported by food surpluses grown by the rural population. Its members thus had plenty of time to engage in intellectual activities and to develop systematically a variety of skills — astronomy, mathematics, an accurate calendar, writing, a legal system, elaborate religions and so on.

By 1997 *S&S* is retrospectively described as arguing (MacKie 1997: 339) that

> the Grooved Ware sites in Orkney were a sign of the penetration into the far north of a society dominated by a religious élite with advanced skills . . . [which] had already been responsible for the late Neolithic earthworks and stone circles on Salisbury Plain.

MacKie (1997: 339) sees the discovery of the Barnhouse settlement 'as a vivid confirmation of his earlier reinterpretation of Skara Brae as a settlement of a religious elite'.

Not only does he take no account of the fact that the largest, clearly non-domestic structure at Barnhouse was built late in the life of, or even after the abandonment of, the settlement (Richards 1996: 200), but in presenting his case again he ignores a number of other developments: for example, that further settlements of the period have been discovered and excavated in Orkney (Barclay 1996 and references) and continue to appear (*Discovery and Excavation in Scotland (DES)* 1995: 10; 1998: 70), confirming that the architectural forms seen at Skara Brae and Barnhouse are typical rather than exceptional; that the Grooved Ware radiocarbon dates for northern Britain are now comparable with or even earlier than those for the south (MacSween 1992: 269; Ashmore 1998); that the henges of northern Britain may be built before those of Wessex (Parker Pearson 1993: 72); and that such a strongly diffusionist model for a homogenous 'British' Neolithic (early or late) is no longer sustainable. Significant studies have been published in the last decade that undermine the assertion (MacKie 1997: 339) that other archaeologists continue to interpret 'Skara Brae and allied sites . . . as peasant villages' (e.g. Richards 1990a; 1991; 1993; Parker Pearson & Richards 1994). That much recent work has been overlooked in the preparation of MacKie (1997) is shown by the supposed recent confirmation (1997: 338) of the distribution of Grooved Ware in two widely separated areas, in the far north and northwest of Scotland, and in southern England and East Anglia. Manby's work in Yorkshire, which pre-dates *S&S* (Manby 1974), and the results of a series of excavations in southeastern Scotland since the 1970s (Mercer 1981; Barclay & Russell-White 1993; Stevenson 1995; and now Barclay & Maxwell 1998) surely cannot be dismissed in this way.

S&S was set out in three main parts: an introduction, a section entitled 'The Achievement' and a third entitled 'The Society'. In the introduction it is made clear that MacKie based his argument on three foundations that he felt were firm:
1 the calibration of radiocarbon dates, which many archaeologists then used as if it provided calendar year determinations accurate to a few tens of years; it was also assumed that relatively few dates could provide a secure dating sequence for a site;
2 Alexander Thom's ideas about prehistoric astronomy, geometry and mensuration; and

3   the results of the excavations at Durrington Walls, in particular the interpretation of the circular timber settings as roofed buildings — the dwellings of an élite (Wainwright & Longworth 1971).

Time has dealt harshly with all three, or at least the way in which they can be used.

Radiocarbon

In the last 20 years the calibration of radiocarbon dates has been shown to be far less cut and dried than was at first believed (Aitken 1990: 98–101; Ashmore 1996; 1998), and MacKie's use of calibrated dates in *S&S*, the norm in the 1970s, as though they allowed exact relative dating, is no longer tenable. His assertions of the contemporaneity of key sites are therefore no longer sustainable.

Astronomy, geometry and metrology

The work of Alexander Thom has been subjected to detailed scrutiny. While the last 20 years have seen a broad archaeological acceptance of a prehistoric interest in the cosmos and the movements of the sun and moon, Thom's claims for high-precision astronomical alignments have not been substantiated, quite apart from his ethnocentric interpretations of them (Ruggles 1999: chapter 2) (see below). Thom's hypotheses on geometry and mensuration have also been challenged, and largely dismissed, from both archaeological and statistical perspectives (Ruggles 1999: 82–3 and references).

In brief, Thom (1955; 1967) had argued for the existence of a prehistoric unit of measurement — the 'megalithic yard' or MY — which was defined so precisely that 'standard' measuring sticks would have had to be used to communicate it from one end of Britain to the other (Thom & Thom 1978: 177). He also concluded that many non-circular stone rings were laid out using certain constructions, some of considerable complexity, which involved knowledge of the techniques of Euclidean geometry. The latter conclusion was challenged mathematically by authors such as Angell (1977), who showed that a number of different multi-parameter shapes, some less complex to construct in practice than Thom's, could be fitted equally well to the groundplans considered by Thom. It was also challenged by archaeologists such as Barnatt & Moir (1984) who concluded that the majority of stone circles could simply have been laid out by eye to appear circular. Barnatt & Herring (1986) documented an experiment in which over 100 circles were set out by eye by a range of individuals; it was found that these 'circles' could then all be described by the 'complex geometries' of Thom, even though they had not been set out using them. MacKie's quotation (1977a: 16) from Dingle (1972) is particularly resonant:

> the greatest danger is the fallacy to believe that 'everything that is mathematically true must have a physical counterpart; and not only so, but must have the particular physical counterpart that happens to accord with the theory that the mathematician wishes to advocate'.

It is as well to remind ourselves that any shape may be *described* by complex geometry, but that there is no evidence that the shape was *laid out* using it (Angell 1977).

The dataset used by Thom to deduce the existence of the MY comprises the diameters of best-fit circles imposed on over 100 roughly circular stone rings. Even if the data are taken at face value, the statistical evidence for a common unit of length is, at best, marginal, and even if it is accepted as existing, our knowledge of its value is only of the order of centimetres, far poorer than the 1-mm precision claimed by Thom (Kendall

1974; Freeman 1976; Angell 1979). The evidence is adequately explained by, say, a common practice of pacing (Heggie 1981: chapter 3). Huxley's wise comment (1869), ironically also quoted by MacKie (1977a: 16), sums up our view:

> this seems to be one of the many cases in which the admitted accuracy of mathematical processes is allowed to throw a wholly inadmissible appearance of authority over the result obtained by them . . . pages of formulae will not get a definite result out of loose data.

Durrington Walls and the Neolithic of Wessex
Finally, MacKie's use of the evidence from Durrington Walls and the other multiple timber ring sites is selective. In all his papers he presents as acknowledged fact that the timber structures were roofed, and disregards Musson's conclusions in the final report (Musson 1971). MacKie states (1977a: 164–5) that

> consideration of the problem by a professional architect led him to the conclusion that there was no evidence against . . . roofed buildings but that size, spacing and general arrangements were consistent with the hypothesis that they had once supported fairly massive, conical superstructures.

However, Musson makes it clear that the patterns of posts at Durrington Walls, Woodhenge and the Sanctuary allow equally well for unroofed as well as roofed interpretations. He states clearly (1971: 375) that the explanation seems 'more closely related to a purely numerical or dimensional reasoning than to any structural logic' and that 'it must be stressed again that no conclusive evidence has been produced that these monuments *were* in fact roofed buildings'. Gibson (1998: 104) has recently noted that 'the negative arguments which Musson produced . . . have largely been ignored' by subsequent writers.

Barrett's perceptive re-analysis of the southern circle at Durrington Walls (1994: 20–24), not referenced by MacKie, has demonstrated a far more complex construction sequence and simultaneously provided a more convincing interpretation of the structures — the 'steady embellishment of [a] *locale*' through a 'lengthy and piecemeal programme of construction', rather than two phases of massive roofed building. The subsequent discovery of vast complexes of concentric rings of posts clearly far too large to roof (as recently at Stanton Drew, where nine concentric rings between 23 m and 95 m in diameter have been located (David 1998)), must cast further doubt on MacKie's assertions. In Scotland Mercer (1981: 159) proposed a convincing interpretation of the concentric circles of posts within the henge at Balfarg (Fife) as a series of barriers.

Social theory
There is surely irony in MacKie's (1977a) criticism of archaeologists for avoiding social theory before that time, as it is the subsequent development of a complex body of social theory by archaeologists (e.g. in the context of archaeoastronomy, Thorpe 1983) that exposes the weaknesses of his own cultural-historical approach to the later Neolithic. In the main body of *S&S*, and more recently (1997: 339) MacKie always offers a limited choice to the reader: either his preferred Maya-style hierarchy or a 'barbarian' or 'simple peasant' society that only undertook construction for utilitarian purposes. For example, the interpretative choices for henges are either

1 the site of 'barbarian rituals concerned with economic needs' or
2 (as MacKie would wish) 'ceremonial centres of skilled learned orders'.

Or again: society is either 'predominantly homogeneous, segmented and rural' or a 'complex, highly stratified hierarchical organisation with advanced political structure and many specialised groups, almost a proto-urban society in fact'. In contrast to the offering of 'barbarian peasants', Richards and others (Richards 1990a; 1991; 1993; Parker Pearson & Richards 1994) have demonstrated the complexity of the society that built and used the later Neolithic settlements, perhaps even involving 'ritual specialists', without resorting to MacKie's model.

Regional archaeologies
But there are broader problems. The 1977 study is a product of its period: there were very limited amounts of reliable excavated data in most parts of the country, and the creation of a coherent 'story' required the pulling together of material widely separated geographically. This process tended to create homogenous, broad brush prehistories that underemphasized regional variation and promoted a diffusionist approach. It is possible to see now that the sites drawn together to create a 'British Neolithic' are probably parts of different regional 'Neolithics' throughout Britain and Ireland (Kinnes 1985; Harding *et al.* 1996; Cooney 1997; Barclay 1997a; in press). We must also consider the extent to which Orkney's supposed prominence in the Neolithic (e.g. as a destination for pilgrimage — MacKie 1994) is an accurate reflection of prehistory, or whether it is, to some extent, a product of the recent history of investigation (Barclay in press).

We therefore believe that MacKie's 1977 consideration of Neolithic society has not stood the test of time. The excavations at Durrington Walls cannot be interpreted now as directly applicable to material many hundreds of kilometres away, as it was believed they could 20 years ago; there is a far greater understanding of regional diversity in the Neolithic in Britain. It is significant, for example, that MacKie draws such diverse monuments as the henges and recumbent stone circles into his homogenous cultural, astronomical and geometrical structure; it can be seen that the distribution of henges and RSCs is almost mutually exclusive (FIGURE 1), and it has been suggested that, if the monument types are broadly contemporary, their very different nature and the ways that members of the classes inter-relate may indicate considerable differences in ceremonial practice and indeed in social structure (Barnatt 1989; Barclay 1997a). MacKie's reliance on the evidence of Wessex to interpret material in the rest of Britain, and the identification of Stonehenge and Silbury Hill as drawing on resources from a British-wide base, rests on a view of British prehistory that few would now find acceptable.

A further fundamental weakness of MacKie's approach, both in 1977 and 20 years later, is the assumption that the data he has to work with is complete (*cf.* Barclay 1997b). For example, his assumption that the three later Neolithic settlements known in Orkney at that time — Skara Brae, Rinyo and Links of Noltland — were all there ever were of their kind, and could therefore be seen as rare, élite, settlements, has been shown to be erroneous by later work. We can see that other excavated settlements display broadly similar characteristics, and further discoveries continue to come to light (Barclay 1996 and references).

Problems with MacKie's interpretation
In summary, the problems with MacKie's hypothesized social structure are as follows:
1. the Megalithic Yard is not supported by the statistical evidence, and simple 'by eye' construction can explain the shapes of stone rings just as well as complex 'laying out geometries';
2. as will be discussed below, the precise astronomy proposed by Thom can be seen as a modern scientific imposition upon an intense, but different, interest in the sky;

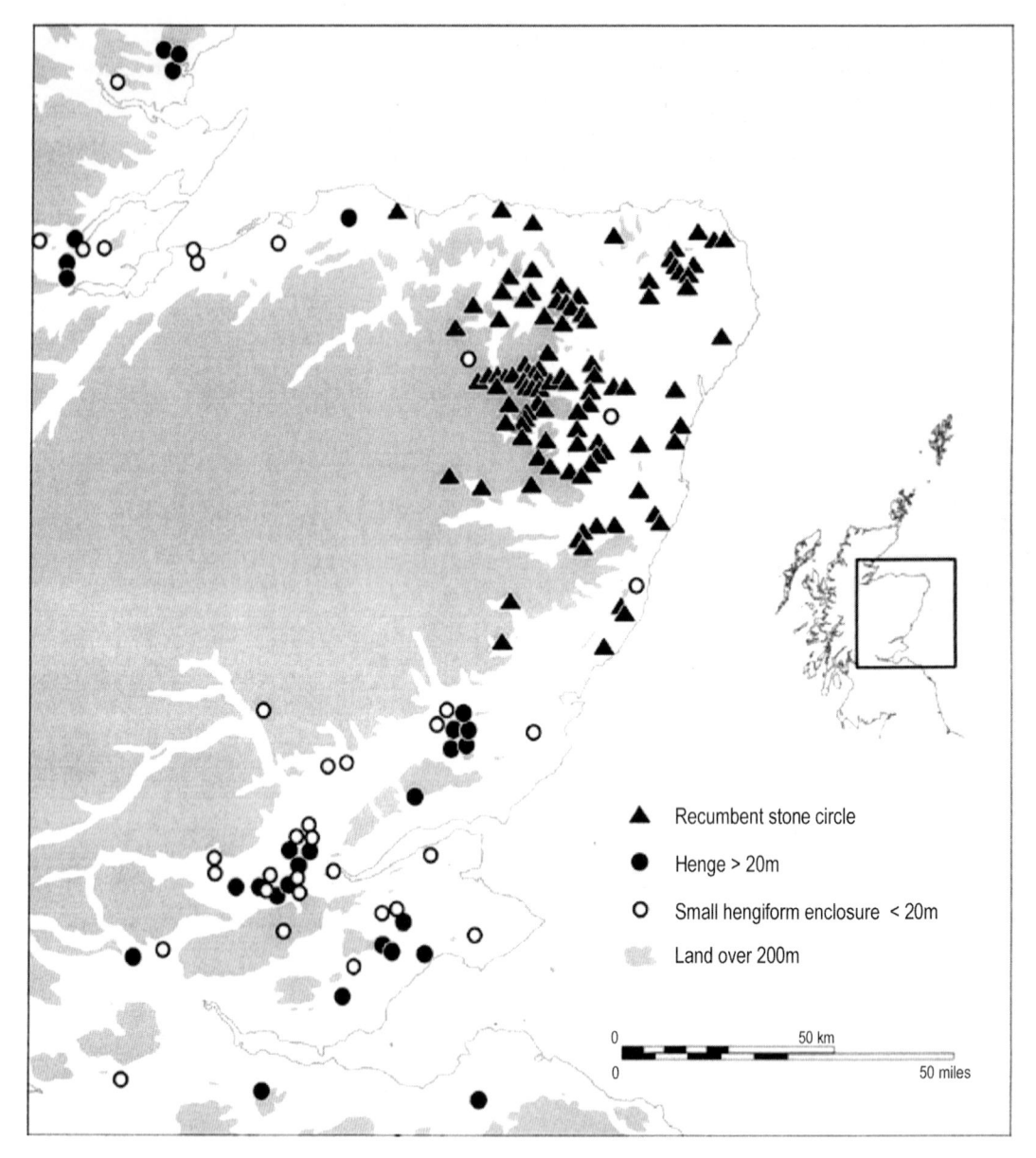

FIGURE 1. *Distribution map of henges, small hengiform enclosures and recumbent stone circles in eastern Scotland, apparently indicating strong regional traditions in the distribution of ceremonial structures in the later Neolithic.*

3   the contemporaneity of events suggested by MacKie (1977a) based on a common 1970s view of ^{14}C calibration is no longer demonstrable;
4   it is no longer believed possible to make up deficiencies in evidence in one area by drawing on material from another, that may have different meanings;
5   there is no evidence that the 'roofed buildings' at Durrington Walls and other sites were in fact roofed; it seems very unlikely that they were the élite dwelling places claimed by MacKie;
6   the societies of later Neolithic Orkney need not necessarily lie at one of the two extremes ('barbarous peasant' and 'wise man') offered by MacKie.

Solar alignments, cosmologies and calendars
Solstitial alignments and cosmology

The tendency to measure prehistoric astronomy — along with mensuration and geometry — against the yardstick of modern science has, it seems, finally been laid to rest (Ruggles 1999: 80–81; Ruggles in press and references). However, there is no doubt that architectural alignments with celestial bodies and events are potentially of considerable importance within broader investigations of ways in which of the location and form of monuments served to express meaningful cosmological relationships, and the ways in which such relationships were exploited (Ruggles & Saunders 1993; Ruggles 1999: chapter 9). A variety of local groups of similar monuments in Britain and Ireland from the early Neolithic through to the middle Bronze Age show striking consistencies in orientation (Ruggles 1998; 1999: chapter 8), which suggest that celestial referents were used in the broadest sense to determine direction. Furthermore, many of these are confined to sectors of the horizon roughly demarcated by the cardinal directions or the directions of sunrise or sunset at the solstices (which from here onwards, we shall refer to simply as the 'solstitial directions'). In specific cases, such as the recumbent stone circles of northeast Scotland and the short stone rows of the Irish southwest, there is apparently a strong relationship to the moon (Ruggles 1999: chapters 5, 6). What these studies show perhaps most importantly is there is no overall pattern of development but rather various regional patterns of continuity and change.

In this context, the suggestion that the great passage tomb at Maes Howe may have been engineered in relation to the midwinter sunset is certainly not surprising in itself; there are other specific cases of the orientation of public monuments upon solstitial sunrise or sunset, examples now well known in the archaeological literature ranging from the Dorchester and Dorset cursus monuments (Bradley & Chambers 1988; Barrett *et al.* 1991: 56–7) to Wessex henges (Ruggles 1999: 138 and references), Newgrange (O'Kelly 1982) and Balnuaran of Clava (Bradley 1998). Some argue that harmonizing a monument with the cosmos in this way helped to affirm its place at the centre of things (e.g. Renfrew 1984: 178–80); others that this helped to place its operation above challenge and thereby reinforced political control (e.g. Barrett *et al.* 1991: 56). Yet others point out that astronomical alignments served to place a monument in time, empowering it perhaps with special meanings on certain regular occasions (*cf.* Bradley 1993: 68; Darvill 1996: 177–8; Ruggles 1999: 154). There is also much evidence from historical and modern indigenous communities of the widespread importance of the solstitial directions in schemes of sacred geography (Ruggles 1999: 148 and references).

In fact, there has been considerable confusion in the literature as to whether the passage at Maes Howe is in fact oriented such that the light from the setting sun at midwinter does illuminate the rear wall of the chamber (e.g. Ritchie 1985: 127; Parker Pearson 1993: 59) or whether this actually occurs a few weeks earlier and later (Burl 1981: 251). One must also consider the shift in the position of midwinter sunset since the time of construction (about half a degree). MacKie's discussion of the bent shape of the passage (MacKie 1997: 345–56) and clear presentation of the horizon profile information do a great deal to clarify the basic data. MacKie shows that the outer straight section ('axis B') is more or less aligned upon the setting point of the solstitial sun in the early 3rd millennium BC whereas the inner straight section ('axis A') is aligned more than 5° further round to the west.

But such matters should be interpreted in context. We cannot ignore the fact that the orientations of central hearths in Orcadian houses fall into four clearly separate, although wide, bands centred roughly upon the four solstitial directions (Richards 1990a: figure 5.5; Parker Pearson & Richards 1994: figure 2.3). This is strongly suggestive that they were constrained according to quadripartite cosmological principles associated with the solstices. The structural similarity between Maes Howe and the principal building at Barnhouse, and the approximate orientation of the latter upon midwinter sunrise (Richards 1990b: 312–13), is suggestive of a dichotomy between houses for the living and monuments for the dead which is reflected in a symbolic dichotomy between the rising and the setting sun. These modest interpretations are consistent with the wider archaeoastronomical evidence concerning houses for the living as well as those for the dead, but are suggestive of broad cosmologies rather than exact calendars. Furthermore, they are not affected by the subtleties of the exact play of sunlight in the Maes Howe passage at or close to midwinter.

Using video evidence and three-dimensional computer models, Victor Reijs has recently demonstrated that sunlight strikes the back of the chamber shortly before sunset for some 35 days on either side of the solstice, and did so for perhaps 40 days either side 5000 years ago (http://www.geniet.demon.nl/maeshowe/ see also Ashmore in press). This in itself also suggests that the orientation of that tomb was designed without great precision of alignment in mind.

The horizon at Maes Howe
MacKie, however, goes considerably further in insisting that Maes Howe was an 'observing instrument'. Even though he now distances himself from claims of 'scientific' astronomy, he continues strongly to endorse Thom's claim that prehistoric people set up alignments of high precision, using features on the distant natural horizon as foresights (MacKie 1997: 340–41). He also maintains that they provide evidence of 'scientific capability', Maes Howe functioning as a 'solar temple/observatory' (1997: 343).

On a factual level, the data relating to certain points on the southwestern horizon are in almost complete agreement with an unpublished theodolite survey of Maes Howe undertaken by one of the present authors (CR) in August 1979 (from a point 10 m from the present entrance on axis B). The results for three common points are shown in TABLE 1.

There are therefore no reasonable grounds for doubting the azimuth, altitude and declination figures quoted by MacKie for these and other points in the southwestern horizon as viewed from Maes Howe.

It is in the interpretation of these data that we are in strong disagreement with MacKie. His claim is that Maes Howe is a 'multiple calendar site' incorporating two precise alignments upon horizon features marking sunset at two epoch dates in Alexander Thom's 16-month solar calendar. Before examining these specific conclusions it is necessary to review the wider interpretative context in which they have been formulated.

Calendars and continuity
MacKie (1997: 340) states that 'the reality of . . . solar calendar alignments is shown by independent archaeological and historical evidence which supports also the existence of the sixteen "month" calendar inferred statistically by Thom'. He also strongly contends that this solar calendar was not only widespread in Britain in Neolithic times but that the solstices, equinoxes and mid-quarter days continued to be important through to the Iron Age, where they were incorporated in the ancient Celtic calendar as festivals such as Beltane and Samhain, and hence survived through to modern times (MacKie 1997: 355).

Despite the support for this idea that has been shown by some other archaeologists (e.g. Burl 1988: 197) and archaeoastronomers (e.g. Krupp 1994: xi), it rests upon the assumption that dividing the year into 8 or 16 precisely equal parts was likely to have

	Az	Alt	Dec
Ward Hill, left slope, junction with nearby ground	217°·1 [217°·0]	1°·3 [1°·3]	−23°·4 [−23°·4]
Ward Hill, right slope, junction with nearby ground	222°·9 [222°·9]	1°·0 [1°·0]	−21°·6 [−21°·6]
Cuilags, left slope, junction with nearby ground	225°·7 [225°·6]	0°·9 [0°·9]	−20°·7 [−21°·0]

TABLE 1. *A comparison of horizon data from independent surveys at Maes Howe by Ruggles (1979, previously unpublished) and MacKie (as reported in MacKie 1997). MacKie's data are shown in square brackets.*

been important to prehistoric people. This may seem natural from a modern European perspective where time is seen as an abstract 'axis', but is unconvincing in the context of a non-Western world-view where notions of (space and) time are likely to have been highly contextualized (Shanks & Tilley 1987: chapter 5; McCluskey 1998: 4–5). In any case, the evidence to support it is slight.

1   The evidence for Thom's solar calendar derives from accumulations of declinations corresponding to the upper limb of the sun rising or setting at dates at intervals of one-eighth (and possibly one-sixteenth) of a year measured from either solstice (the 'epoch' dates). It is important to realize that the evidence — from Thom's (1967) large-scale analyses of 145 'megalithic sites' — comes from a variety of 'indications' from many different types of megalithic structures scattered throughout Britain (*cf.* Ruggles 1999: 52). This wide variety is worrying in itself if there really was uniformity of astronomical and calendrical practice throughout Britain (Fleming 1975). It is also important to realize that the declination targets are 'fuzzy' because the number of days in a year is neither integral nor divisible by 16 (Ruggles 1999: 54–5). This increases the flexibility of being able to interpret any particular alignment as calendrical. Thom's data were thoroughly re-examined and reassessed by one of the present authors (CR) in the course of a major survey project between 1975 and 1981. Thom's results could not be reproduced once strict attention was paid to the demonstrably fair selection of data, and the inescapable conclusion was that the apparent accumulations of declinations at the calendrical epochs can easily be accounted for as data selection effects (Ruggles 1984; 1999: 70, figure 3.3).

2   Once Thom's own data are discounted, no evidence from coherent local groups of monuments supports the idea of an 8- or 16-part calendar; there are only isolated and scattered examples of putative alignments upon 'calendrical' epoch dates (Ruggles 1999: 142).

3   The geometric designs on the Bush Barrow gold lozenge have been interpreted by A.S. Thom and colleagues as a device for implementing Thom's solar calendar (Thom *et al.* 1988) and are cited by MacKie (1997: 340) as further evidence in support of the idea of the Neolithic solar calendar. By holding the lozenge horizontally and in a certain orientation, Thom *et al.* argue that the directions of sunrise and sunset at the calendrical epoch dates are marked on the lozenge. However, the regularity of the decorative design, the fact that only a small and apparently arbitrary subset of the lines actually appear to correlate with epoch directions, and the fact that the majority of the directions do not fit with lines on the artefact at all (*cf.* Ruggles 1999: figure 8.10) all argue strongly against this. The arbitrary nature of the theory is highlighted by North's (1996: 508–9) criticisms of it and the fact that he manages to impose an equally complex but completely dif-

ferent interpretation of his own (1996: 511–8). There is also the problem, acknowledged by North, that other lozenges exist, similar in form and decoration but with different angles, which do not appear susceptible to his own arguments or those of Thom *et al.* The Bush Barrow lozenge, like the others, is certainly a very fine decorative artefact, representing a high order of technological achievement, but its interpretation as a calendrical device is speculative.

4   The evidence to support the idea of a ubiquitous 'Celtic' calendar existing in later Iron Age times, with its seasonal festivals dividing the year into eight precisely equal parts, is itself very much weaker than is generally assumed (for detailed arguments see Ruggles 1999: 141–2 and references).

Attractive as it may be to envisage threads of continuity from early Neolithic through to Iron Age and even modern times, there is however a great deal of evidence that contradicts this conclusion, and we cannot agree with MacKie (1997: 340) that the existing evidence provides any support, let alone strong support, for the idea of 'calendrical' alignments.

High-precision alignments

Thom's 1967 analysis was followed by a succession of publications in which he argued the case for the existence of astronomical alignments of ever greater precision, finally claiming the existence of some which were precise to a single minute of arc (*cf.* Ruggles 1999: chapter 2). These claims were subjected to detailed reassessments by one of the present authors (CR) during the early 1980s (Ruggles 1981; 1982; 1983; 1999: chapter 2). It is misleading for MacKie to assert (1997: 340) that the statistical arguments against alleged high-precision alignments 'have been shown to be circular'. The article quoted in support of this (MacKie 1986) states that high-precision alignments were not found in a large independent survey of evidence from western Scotland by CR (Ruggles 1984) because they were not looked for. In claiming this MacKie himself ignored, and continues to ignore, an existing body of earlier published work directly addressing the very question of high-precision alignments and reassessing Thom's data in detail (Ruggles 1981; 1982; 1983). The earlier publications by Ruggles show beyond any reasonable doubt that all Thom's putative astronomical sightlines of a precision greater than about half a degree can be quite adequately accounted for as chance occurrences. Even the existence of deliberate high-precision solstitial foresights at 'classic' sites such as Ballochroy and Kintraw (*cf.* MacKie 1997: 342) is questionable (Ruggles 1999: 19–29 and references therein).

In sum, the case in favour of high-precision astronomy is completely unproven. And to say that 'there is increasing evidence . . . that . . . the sixteen "month" Neolithic solar calendar was a reality' (MacKie 1997: 355) ignores an overwhelming range of evidence to the contrary.

The alignment evidence from Maes Howe

Returning to the alignment evidence from Maes Howe, we must bear in mind the definition of the calendrical alignments set out by MacKie (1997: 340):

> To be plausible the structure must have some built-in direction indicator which points to [a] . . . distant natural mark on the horizon like a notch or hill slope which is the foresight.

To achieve adequate precision, we should expect to find alignments upon places on the horizon where the upper limb of the sun rises or sets on dates at some multiple of 1/16-year from either solstice. These should be marked by conspicuous horizon features such as notches between distant hills, and 'indicated' by archaeologically evident structures.

We can now examine the specific alignments listed in MacKie 1997: table 1.

1. Axis B, as already discussed, was approximately aligned upon the upper limb of the solstitial setting sun. There is no horizon foresight at this point; the horizon is relatively close and featureless, a little over 1° to the left of the point where the left slope of Ward Hill disappears behind the closer ground.

2. Axis A is aligned on a point some 1°·5 to the left of where the right slope of Ward Hill disappears behind closer ground. It is thus a plausible, though not precise, indicator of the latter point, whose declination, −21°·6, does correspond (within the margins of uncertainty mentioned above) to the upper limb of the setting sun at a time 1/16 of a year before or after the winter solstice. The upper limb of the sun would actually reappear at this point, so this is a classic Thomian foresight.

3. The right-hand end of Cuilags is not indicated. According to MacKie it yields a declination −17°·0, corresponding to a centre disc declination of −17°·3. The declination of centre of the sun on the appropriate mid-quarter days would be between −16°·8 and −16°·0 (Ruggles 1999: 55). MacKie proposes that a bump at the top of the slope, rather than the extreme right-hand end, might have been the foresight, but its declination −16°·6, corresponding to a centre disc declination of −16°·9, is still marginal if it is to be interpreted as a precise mid-quarter day alignment.

Only (2) fits MacKie's own criteria for a calendrical alignment, and only then if an indication 1°·5 to the left of the target is thought to be acceptable. (1) has no foresight. (3) has no indication, and is also only marginal as a indicator of the appropriate calendar date, and then if one makes the assumption that a secondary feature, rather than the right-hand end of the slope itself, was the intended foresight.

In view of the fact that there is no convincing background evidence for calendrical alignments, we would be inclined to put down the precise calendrical alignments proposed at Maes Howe to chance. On the other hand, we would be inclined to accept the idea that the outer axis (Axis B) was aligned upon midwinter sunset, to 'good' but not to 'calendrical' precision. The argument that the solstitial sun itself may originally have shone down the passage after passing through a light-slit above the door (MacKie 1997: 356) has been published before (Welfare & Fairley 1980: 93, quoted in Ritchie 1982) and certainly seems plausible and worthy of further investigation. We would also be inclined to accept that the general alignment of the tomb passage upon 'the most conspicuous natural foresights on the southern mainland of Orkney' (MacKie 1997: 357) might also have been deliberate, and meaningful, in itself.

The general alignment upon the standing stone at Barnhouse and the Hills of Hoy, as well as roughly with the midwinter sunset, accords with other instances where monuments are aligned upon conspicuous features in the landscape, man-made and natural, and/or celestial bodies and events, all as part of organizing the landscape according to the principles of a cosmology that does not separate people, land and sky into separate categories but in which they are intimately tied together. This is very different from the sort of view of time as abstraction, strongly redolent of a modern Western world-view, which encourages thoughts of dividing the solar year into exactly equal parts.

The alignment evidence from Howe

In a separate paper, MacKie (1998) has examined a sequence of structures from Neolithic times through to the Iron Age at Howe, some 4·5 km west-southwest of Maes Howe and 3 km southwest of the Ring of Brodgar across the Loch of Stenness. Unfortunately he has not referred to Hingley's more wide-ranging survey of the re-use of Neolithic monuments in Scotland in the Iron Age, in which the relationship between the features at Howe is placed in a broader context (Hingley 1996).

On a factual level, MacKie is to be congratulated on determining the correct orientation of the passage of the Neolithic tomb at Howe from confused earlier reports and on his clear presentation of the orientation and horizon profile data (MacKie 1998: table 1 & figure 3). The problem is once again in the interpretation. The reader should recall that the nature of the evidence invoked to support a precise Thomian calendar is supposed repeated alignments upon precise epoch dates at 1/8 or 1/16-year intervals from either solstice, marked by the upper limb of the sun rising or setting behind conspicuous horizon features such as notches between distant hills, 'indicated' by archaeologically evident structures (*cf.* MacKie 1998: 10, 12).

In fact, none of the potential alignments listed and illustrated by MacKie (1998: table 1 & figure 3) fulfils these criteria.

1. To judge from MacKie 1998: figure 2, the axis of the stalled cairn or rectangular house S seems to be somewhat (perhaps as much as 4°) to the right of the azimuth (123°) marked. The chosen orientation appears to have been selected because it corresponds approximately to the azimuth of the upper limb of the Quarter Day rising sun. However, this event occurs on a featureless stretch of horizon, so there is no horizon foresight to mark it.

2. The orientation of the passage tomb points at a saddle between the conspicuous hills of Mid Hill and Ward Hill, but the declination (−10°·6) has no obvious astronomical interpretation — and certainly none in terms of Thom's 16-month calendar, for which the closest epoch declination is around −8°·5 (Ruggles 1999: 55).

3. What is interpreted as an open-ended cross-passage between the 'stalled cairn' and mortuary house aligns in the southwest upon a dramatic cleft between the distant hills of Hoy. For a few days around midwinter, the disc of the setting sun would have passed across this cleft (whose lowest point has a declination −25°·0). But note that the whole sun appeared here — this was a dramatic affirmation of the relationship between the setting sun on days close to midwinter, and the visible horizon at that place. The top limb of the midwinter setting sun did *not* appear in a notch or twinkle down a hillslope, so there is no evidence of the use of the horizon as an observing 'instrument' to pinpoint the solstice. A similar argument applies to the appearance of this same cleft from the nearby Ring of Brodgar (MacKie 1998: figure 3d), from which the declination of the base of the cleft is only slightly greater (−24°·9).

Additionally, no information is given regarding the northeasterly alignment of the cross-passage, and there is no apparent reason (other than the astronomical potential of the southwesterly alignment) for selecting this direction in preference as the one that was meaningful to the builders.

4   The Keelylang Hill profile (MacKie 1998: table 1 & figure 3b) is not indicated. A shallow dip in the horizon at this point, whose declination according to MacKie is $-0°·1$, corresponds roughly to equinoctial sunrise, although the upper limb of the equinoctial sun would actually appear approximately 1° (two solar diameters) to the left. There is no reason other than its astronomical potential to mark it out for special attention from a large number of possible horizon features of equal prominence in other directions.

These data provide no compelling evidence for an interest in Thom's calendar in Neolithic times. This is not to say, however, that certain alignments upon conspicuous features in the landscape, and important celestial events, might not have been significant. Indeed, the general orientation of the passage tomb upon a conspicuous set of hills, as at Maes Howe, may well have been intentional. Furthermore, the apparent alignment of a cross-passage both upon a dramatic cleft between the distant hills of Hoy, and approximately upon midwinter sunset, does suggest that there was a deliberate encapsulation of a dramatic relationship between a spectacular terrestrial feature and the setting sun on days close to midwinter, which would have passed directly through the cleft, appearing to stand in it shortly before starting to disappear below the horizon.

Plausible as these relationships are, it is impossible to agree that the evidence from Howe gives any support to MacKie's contention (1998: 37) that 'concern with ... Quarter Day festivals now seems likely to go back into the earlier part of the Neolithic period in Orkney'. The calendrical explanation derives from a reading of the evidence that falls into all the methodological traps identified by one of the present authors (CR) many years ago (*cf.* Ruggles 1999: chapters 1–3) — criticisms that are ignored, and are certainly not addressed, in these new papers.

Conclusions
As questions of landscape cognition and cosmology take their proper place in archaeological thought it becomes important to look for astronomical referents, since meaningful associations between celestial bodies and events and objects and actions in other parts of the perceived world are an important feature of non-Western world-views. Astronomical associations encapsulated in architecture, serving perhaps as metaphors for perceived properties of the cosmos, may give important insights into such perceptions in the past. Well-established archaeoastronomical approaches, seeking to correlate the locations of monuments or houses in the landscape with celestial objects or events, are relevant as part of broader investigations. So also are novel approaches such as Bradley's (1998) exploration, at the passage tombs at Balnuaran of Clava, of apparent conflicts between the requirements of sound structural design and the desire to conform to certain cosmological requirements, in this case a broad solstitial alignment.

There remains considerable confusion in the archaeological literature about matters astronomical. A relevant example is the erroneous claim that the latitude of Orkney is especially favoured because only here do the four directions of the rising and setting solstitial sun fall at right-angles to one another (Parker Pearson 1993: 59; Souden 1997:

122). In fact, the azimuths of solstitial sunrise and sunset are dependent upon the horizon altitude, and the most favourable latitude is in fact around 55°. Certainly it is impossible to achieve at the latitude of Orkney (59°) (Ruggles 1999: 250).

Archaeoastronomy has the potential to clarify such confusions, and has an important role to play in broader studies of sacred geography and cosmology. The practice of presenting reliable and quantitative orientation and horizon profile data, as MacKie has done at both Maes Howe and Howe, is thus to be applauded and encouraged. It is crucial, though, to ensure that the interpretation of such data is in tune with wider developments in archaeological thought relating to the relevant social and cognitive issues.

This means abandoning a vision of a Mayan-type late Neolithic which rests upon Wessex-oriented diffusionist prehistories and which ignores so much that has been written about the period and about some of its most significant monuments in the last decade. It also means moving beyond simplistic interpretations featuring universal calendars which rest implicitly upon modern Western-style abstract conceptions of space and time, and which themselves ignore a weight of contrary archaeoastronomical evidence from the last two decades.

Acknowledgements. We are grateful to Patrick Ashmore, Richard Bradley and Roger Mercer for comments on the draft text. FIGURE 1 was prepared by Michael Middleton.

References

AITKEN, M.J. 1990. *Science based dating in archaeology*. London & New York: Longman.
ANGELL, I.O. 1977. Are stone circles circles?, *Science and Archaeology* 19: 16–19.
    1979. Arguments against the existence of the 'megalithic yard', *Computer Applications in Archaeology* 1979: 13–19.
ASHMORE, P.J. 1996. *Neolithic and Bronze Age Scotland*. London: Batsford.
    1998. Radiocarbon dates for settlements, tombs and ceremonial sites with Grooved Ware in Scotland, in A. Gibson & D. Simpson (ed.), *Prehistoric ritual and religion*: 139–47. Stroud: Sutton.
    In press. Archaeology and astronomy: an archaeological view, *Archaeoastronomy: the Journal for Astronomy in Culture* 14(2).
BARCLAY, G.J. 1995. What's new in Scottish prehistory? *Scottish Archaeological Review* 9/10: 3–14.
    1996. Neolithic buildings in Scotland, in T. Darvill & J. Thomas (ed.), *Neolithic houses in NW Europe and beyond*: 61–75. Oxford: Oxbow.
    1997a. The Neolithic, in K. Edwards & I.B.M Ralston (ed.), *Scotland: environment and archaeology, 8000 BC to AD 1000*: 127–49. Chichester: Wiley.
    (Ed.) 1997b. *State-funded 'rescue' archaeology in Scotland: Past, present and future*. Edinburgh: Historic Scotland.
    In press. Between Orkney and Wessex: the search for the regional Neolithics of Britain, in A. Ritchie (ed.), *Neolithic Orkney in its European context*.
BARCLAY, G.J. & G.S. MAXWELL. 1998. *The Cleaven Dyke and Littleour: monuments in the Neolithic of Tayside*. Edinburgh: Society of Antiquaries of Scotland.
BARNATT, J. 1989. *Stone circles of Britain*. Oxford: British Archaeological Reports. British series 215.
BARNATT, J. & P. HERRING. 1986. Stone circles and megalithic geometry: an experiment to test alternative design practices, *Journal of Archaeological Science* 13: 431–49.
BARNATT, J. & G. MOIR 1984. Stone circles and megalithic mathematics, *Proceedings of the Prehistoric Society* 50: 197–216.
BARRETT, J.C. 1994. *Fragments from antiquity*. Oxford: Blackwell.
BARRETT, J.C., R.J. BRADLEY & M. GREEN. 1991. *Landscape, monuments and society*. Cambridge: Cambridge University Press.
BRADLEY, R.J. 1993. *Altering the earth: The origin of monuments in Britain and Continental Europe*. Edinburgh: Society of Antiquaries of Scotland. Monograph series 8.
    1998. Architecture, imagination and the Neolithic world, in S. Mithen (ed.), *Creativity in human evolution and prehistory*: 227–40. London: Routledge.
BRADLEY, R.J. & R. CHAMBERS. 1988. A new study of the cursus complex at Dorchester on Thames, *Oxford Journal of Archaeology* 7: 271–89.
BURL, H.A.W. 1981. 'By the light of the cinerary moon': Chambered tombs and the astronomy of death, in Ruggles & Whittle (ed.): 243–74.
    1988. 'Without sharp north': Alexander Thom and the great stone circles of Cumbria, in C.L.N. Ruggles (ed.), *Records in stone*: 175–205. Cambridge: Cambridge University Press.
COONEY, G. 1997. Images of settlement and landscape in the Neolithic, in P. Topping (ed.), *Neolithic landscapes*: 23–31. Oxford: Oxbow.

DANIEL, G.E. 1980. Megalithic monuments, *Scientific American* 243: 64–76.
DARVILL, T.C. 1996. *Prehistoric Britain from the air*. Cambridge: Cambridge University Press.
DAVID, A. 1998. Stanton Drew, *Past: the Newsletter of the Prehistoric Society* 28: 1–2.
DAVIDSON, J.L. & A.S. HENSHALL. 1989. *The chambered cairns of Orkney*. Edinburgh: Edinburgh University Press.
DINGLE, H. 1972. *Science at the crossroads*. London: Martin Brian & O'Keeffe.
FLEMING, A. 1975. Megalithic astronomy: a prehistorian's view, *Nature* 255, 575.
FREEMAN, P.R. 1976. A Bayesian analysis of the megalithic yard, *Journal of the Royal Statistical Society* A139: 20–55.
GIBSON, A. 1998. *Timber circles and Stonehenge*. Stroud: Tempus.
HARDING, J., P. FRODSHAM & T. DURDEN. 1996. Towards an agenda for the Neolithic of Northern England, in P. Frodsham (ed.), *Neolithic studies in No-mans Land*: 189–201. Newcastle-upon-Tyne: Northumberland Archaeology Group.
HAWKES, J. 1977. Review of *Science and society in prehistoric Britain* by E.W. MacKie, *Sunday Times* 14 August: 35.
HEGGIE, D.C. 1981. *Megalithic Science*. London: Thames & Hudson.
   (Ed.) 1982. *Archaeoastronomy in the Old World*. Cambridge: Cambridge University Press.
HINGLEY, R. 1996. Ancestors and identity in the later prehistory of Atlantic Scotland: the reuse and reinvention of Neolithic monuments and material culture, *World Archaeology* 28(2): 231–43.
HUXLEY, T.H. 1869. Geological reform. *Quarterly Journal of the Geological Society of London* 25: xxviii–liii.
KENDALL, D.G. 1974. Hunting quanta, *Philosophical Transactions of The Royal Society of London*: A276: 231–66.
KINNES, I. 1985. Circumstance not context: the Neolithic of Scotland as seen from outside, *Proceedings of the Society of Antiquaries of Scotland* 115: 15–57.
KRUPP, E.C. 1994. *Echoes of the ancient skies: The astronomy of lost civilizations*. Oxford: Oxford University Press.
MCCLUSKEY, S.C. 1998. *Astronomies and cultures in Early Medieval Europe*. Cambridge: Cambridge University Press.
MACKIE, E.W. 1969. Stone circles: for savages or savants?, *Current Archaeology* 1: 279–83.
   1976. The Glasgow conference on ceremonial, and science in prehistoric Britain, *Antiquity* 50: 136–8.
   1977a. *Science and society in prehistoric Britain*. London: Elek.
   1977b. *The megalith builders*. Oxford: Phaidon.
   1981. 'Wise men in antiquity?' in Ruggles & Whittle (ed.): 111–52.
   1982. Implications for archaeology, in Heggie (ed.): 117–39.
   1983. From the present to the past, *Scottish Archaeological Review* 2: 187–9.
   1986. Review of *Megalithic astronomy* by C.L.N. Ruggles, *Archaeoastronomy* (Maryland) 7: 144–50.
   1994. Review of C. Renfrew (ed.), *The prehistory of Orkney*, *Glasgow Archaeological Journal* 16 (1989–90): 89–92.
   1997. Maeshowe and the winter solstice: ceremonial aspects of the Orkney Grooved Ware culture, *Antiquity* 71: 338–59.
   1998. Continuity over three thousand years of northern prehistory: the 'tel' at Howe, Orkney, *Antiquaries Journal* 78: 1–42.
MACSWEEN, A. 1992. Orcadian Grooved Ware, in N. Sharples & A. Sheridan (ed.), *Vessels for the ancestors*: 259–71. Edinburgh: Edinburgh University Press.
MERCER, R. 1981. The excavation of a late Neolithic henge-type enclosure at Balfarg, Markinch, Fife, Scotland, *Proceedings of the Society of Antiquaries of Scotland* 111: 63–171.
MUSSON, C.R. 1971. A study of the possible building forms at Durrington Walls, Woodhenge and The Sanctuary, in Wainwright & Longworth: 363–77.
NORTH, J.D. 1996. *Stonehenge: Neolithic man and the cosmos*. London: HarperCollins.
O'KELLY, M.J. 1982. *Newgrange: Archaeology, art and legend*. London: Thames & Hudson.
PARKER PEARSON, M. 1993. *Bronze Age Britain*. London: Batsford/English Heritage.
PARKER PEARSON, M. & C. RICHARDS. 1994. Architecture and order: spatial representation and archaeology, in M. Parker Pearson & C. Richards (ed.), *Architecture and order: approaches to social space*: 38–72. London: Routledge.
PIGGOTT, S. 1978. Review of *Science and society in prehistoric Britain* by E.W. MacKie, *Antiquity* 52: 62–3.
RENFREW, A.C. 1984. *Approaches to social archaeology*. Edinburgh: Edinburgh University Press.
   (Ed.). 1990. *The prehistory of Orkney*. Edinburgh: Edinburgh University Press. Reprint; first published 1985.
RENFREW, A.C. & P.G. BAHN. 1996. *Archaeology: theory, methods and practice*. 2nd edition. London: Thames & Hudson.
RICHARDS, C. 1990a. The late Neolithic house in Orkney, in R. Sampson (ed.), *The social archaeology of houses*: 111–24. Edinburgh: Edinburgh University Press.
   1990b. Postscript: the late Neolithic settlement complex at Barnhouse Farm, Stenness, in Renfrew (ed.): 305–16.
   1991. Skara Brae: revisiting a Neolithic village in Orkney, in W.S. Hanson & E.A. Slater (ed.), *Scottish archaeology: new perceptions*: 24–43. Aberdeen: Aberdeen University Press.
   1993. Monumental choreography: architecture and spatial representation in late Neolithic Orkney, in C. Tilley (ed.), *Interpretative archaeology*: 143–78. Oxford: Berg.
   1996. Monuments as landscape: creating the centre of the world in late Neolithic Orkney, *World Archaeology* 28(2): 190–208.
RITCHIE, J.N.G. 1982. Archaeology and astronomy: an archaeological view, in Heggie (ed.): 25–44.
   1985. Ritual monuments, in Renfrew (ed.): 118–30.
RUGGLES, C.L.N. 1981. A critical examination of the megalithic lunar observatories, in Ruggles & Whittle (ed.): 153–209.
   1982. A reassessment of the high precision megalithic lunar sightlines, 1: Backsights, indicators and the archaeological status of the sightlines, *Archaeoastronomy* 4 (*Journal for the History of Astronomy* 13): S21–40.
   1983. A reassessment of the high precision megalithic lunar sightlines, 2: foresights and the problem of selection. *Archaeoastronomy* 5 (*Journal for the History of Astronomy* 14): S1–36.

1984. *Megalithic astronomy: A new archaeological and statistical study of 300 western Scottish sites.* Oxford: British Archaeological Reports. British series 123.

1998. Ritual astronomy in the Neolithic and Bronze Age British Isles: patterns of continuity and change, in A. Gibson & D. Simpson (ed.), *Prehistoric ritual and religion*: 203–8. Stroud: Sutton.

1999. *Astronomy in prehistoric Britain and Ireland.* New Haven (CT) & London: Yale University Press.

In press. Palaeoscience, in G. Cimino (ed.), *History of science* 1. Rome: Enciclopedia Italiana.

RUGGLES, C. L. N. & N.J. SAUNDERS. 1993. The study of cultural astronomy, in C.L.N. Ruggles & N.J. Saunders (ed.), *Astronomies and cultures*: 1–31. Niwot (CO): University Press of Colorado.

RUGGLES, C.L.N. & A.W.R. WHITTLE (ed.). 1981. *Astronomy and society in Britain during the period 4000–1500 BC.* Oxford: British Archaeological Reports. British series 88.

SHANKS, M. & C. TILLEY. 1987. *Social theory and archaeology.* Cambridge: Polity Press.

STEVENSON, S. 1995. The excavation of a kerbed cairn at Beech Hill House, Coupar Angus, Perthshire, *Proceedings of the Society of Antiquaries of Scotland* 125: 197–235.

SOUDEN, D. 1997. *Stonehenge: mysteries of the stones and landscape.* London: Collins & Brown/English Heritage.

THOM, A. 1955 A statistical examination of the megalithic sites in Britain, *Journal of the Royal Statistical Society* A118: 275–91.

1967. *Megalithic sites in Britain.* Oxford: Oxford University Press.

THOM, A.S., J.M.D. KER, & T.R. BURROWS. 1988. The Bush Barrow gold lozenge: is it a solar and lunar calendar for Stonehenge? *Antiquity* 62: 492–502.

THOM, A. & A.S. THOM. 1978. *Megalithic remains in Britain and Brittany.* Oxford: Oxford University Press.

THORPE, I.J. 1983. Prehistoric British astronomy — towards a social context, *Scottish Archaeological Review* 2: 2–10.

WAINWRIGHT, G.J. & I. LONGWORTH. 1971. *Durrington Walls: Excavations 1966–1968.* London: Society of Antiquaries.

WELFARE, S. & J. FAIRLEY. 1980. *Arthur C. Clarke's mysterious world.* London: Collins.

Three-dimensional aspects of apparent relationships between selected natural and artificial features within the topography of the Avebury complex
by PAUL DEVEREUX
ANTIQUITY 65 (249), 1991

SILBURY HILL, the largest artificial mound of prehistoric Europe, stands 40 m tall within the Avebury complex of other major monuments of the Neolithic and Bronze Age. Nevertheless, despite its height and bulk, representing enormous labour by its late Neolithic builders, Silbury does not stand proud of the general level of the chalk ridges that surround it because it is built on very low-lying land. It declares itself in the Avebury environs not by its greater elevation but by the artificial cone of its profile. This curious fact gives some reason to suspect that the mound was not built in some casually convenient spot. If the location was special for some significance that leaves no archaeological trace, such as some kind of spiritual vision, then that reason cannot be recovered. But if part of the significance of the place contained topographical factors, in relation to natural landscape features or the ceremonial landscape of constructed monuments, then it is possible those elements may still be discernible.

Alignments between sites, and to astronomically-significant directions, are notoriously hard to prove (or disprove), as a certain number of alignments necessarily arise in crowded landscapes by chance. But one alignment in the British Isles is particularly satisfactory, that of the Newgrange passage-grave; its megalithic passage is aligned towards the horizon in such a way that the midwinter sunrise shines, not down the main entrance, but through the special 'roofbox', a slit constructed above the passage entrance. Why is Newgrange so convincing, even to those unnecessarily sceptical about ancient alignments in general? First, the alignment is in three dimensions; Newgrange is not just broadly aligned with a certain compass direction on a distant horizon, but the large and complex structure has been built at exact levels that allow the angled winter solstitial sunbeam to pass down the 19-in-long passage, which is approximately only 1·5 m high, and to reach to the back of the innermost chamber of the mound. Second, the roof-box is a deliberately-constructed feature, indicating that the structure was designed to take notice of the alignment as part of its purpose. (Another instance, closer in time and space to Silbury, of design affected by an alignment is the wider spacing of the two sarsen uprights of the Stonehenge circle that frame its axial orientation to the midsummer sunrise.)

Silbury Hill, like Newgrange, offers this third dimension: it was not just built on this spot, but on this spot and to this height. It also offers two possibly significant design features: a strikingly flat summit, 30 m in diameter, and a ledge, visible from a long distance, that runs round the mound roughly 5 m below the summit. This marked terrace' (as Atkinson described it) results from the stepped cone structure of the mound; the other ledges were filled in to form a smooth profile, but this topmost one seems to have been left unfilled. Although now most distinct on Silbury's easterly and northerly flanks, it can be detected on all sides of the mound. Atkinson found that the inner angle of the terrace had been re-cut, probably in late Saxon or Norman times, presumably as part of a defensive structure (Atkinson 1970).

Sight-lines

These two distinctive features of Silbury Hill's profile seem to come into play when the mound is viewed from certain surrounding Neolithic monuments. FIGURE 1 shows Silbury Hill as viewed from East Kennet Long Barrow, The Sanctuary, Beckhampton Long Barrow, and West Kennet Long Barrow. In each case, the skyline can be seen visually to intersect the Silbury profile between the platform-like summit and the ledge.

The sight-line from West Kennet Long Barrow is particularly interesting (FIGURE 1d). The skyline intersecting the Silbury outline is formed by Windmill Hill, a causewayed enclosure on a natural eminence, so an alignment involving Windmill Hill, Silbury and West Kennet is formed. This sight-line functions only from a limited area around the western tip of the 100-m-long mound of the barrow, and thus Richard Bradley's suggestion that an earthen 'tail' may have been added to the monument takes on added possible significance (Bradley 1983). That the surviving western end of the mound approximates its original westward extent is indicated by Stuart Piggott's observation that although it 'is now squared off by cultivation ... the contours of the untouched mound at this point suggest that its present shape is not far from the original intention' (Piggott 1962).

The fifth extant Neolithic site so far checked within the Avebury complex from which Silbury is visible is the Avebury henge itself. It is a frequently repeated fallacy that Silbury is not visible from within the henge; it is, in fact, visible from several points within the northern part of the enclosure. But there is a key location in the southern half of the henge from where a very precise sight-line to Silbury can be obtained. This is at the position of The Obelisk. This stone, which formed part of the central complex of the South Circle, is no longer extant, but was described and drawn by the 18th-century

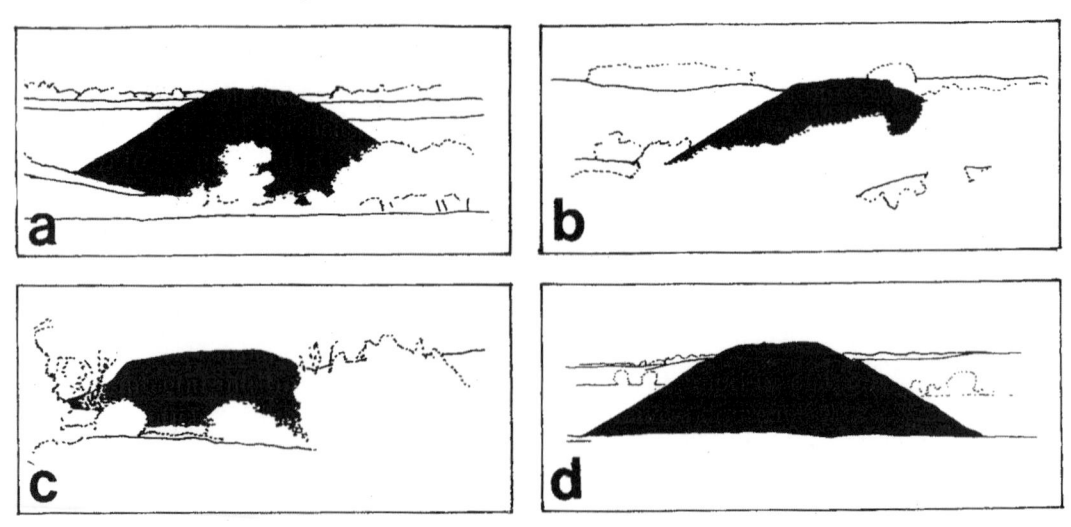

FIGURE 1. *The relationship of Silbury Hill (depicted in silhouette) with the horizon as viewed from (a) East Kennet Long Barrow; (b) the Sanctuary; (c) Beckhampton Long Barrow, and (d) West Kennet Long Barrow – in this instance the skyline is formed by Windmill Hill. It can be seen that the horizon intersects the profile of Silbury Hill between the monument's summit and ledge. (Depictions derived from telephotographs. Broken lines indicate foliage.)*

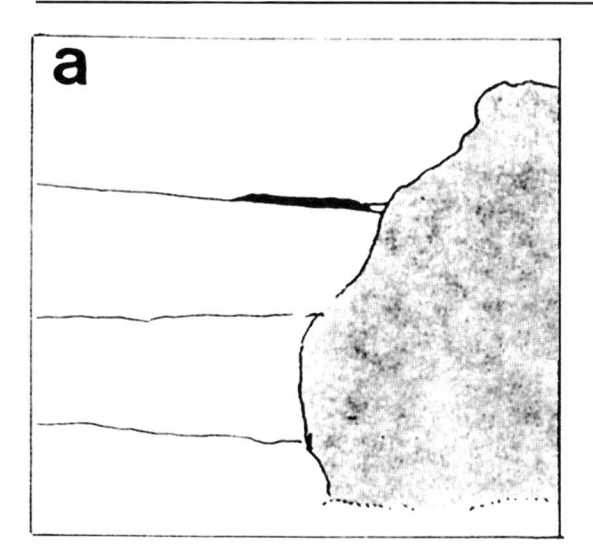

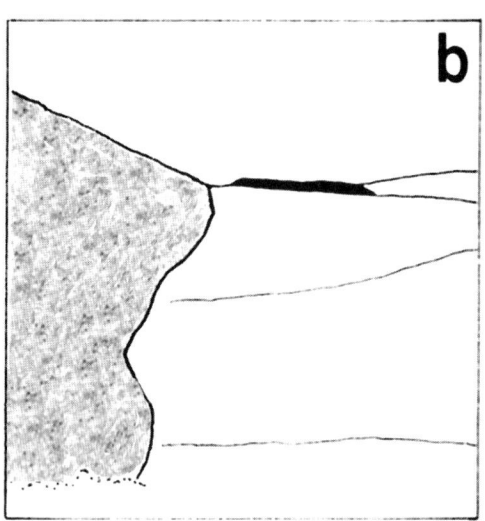

FIGURE 2. *Depiction of the view looking south-southwest towards Silbury Hill (in silhouette) from the Obelisk position in the henge: (a) from the east side of the Obelisk marker plinth looking past stone 102 (a remnant of the South Circle); (b) from the west side of the marker plinth looking past stone 102, showing the dip in the distant skyline. Most of Silbury Hill is concealed behind the slope of Waden Hill. This sight-line is effectively obscured just before harvest, when the cereal crop on Waden Hill is at its greatest height. (Depictions derived from telephotographs).*

antiquarian William Stukeley. It would have been the single largest known stone in the henge, some 6·4 m in height and 2·7 m in diameter. Its position, now marked by one of Keiller's concrete plinths, was clearly a major one in the enclosure. Viewed from there, the very top of Silbury Hill can be seen just proud of the foreground slope of Waden Hill and intersected by the distant horizon which dips sharply at this point (see FIGURE 2). If the plinth marks the centre of the stone hole, as is assumed (Stuart Piggott pers. comm.), then the view to Silbury would have been obstructed by Stone 102 from a position at the centre of The Obelisk's base; the views in FIGURE 2 are from what would have been positions touching either side of the great stone. Why this 'blocking' should occur can only be speculated upon, but it is noteworthy that the top metre or two of The Obelisk would have risen above Stone 102 (if the two features were contemporaneous), and would have been visible from the summit of Silbury Hill. The post-holes immediately to the north of The Obelisk may also have some relevance to this matter.

It is again Silbury's summit-ledge segment which is involved in the skyline connection.

The eastern skyline 'window'
It is possible that there is a particular significance to this specific aspect of Silbury Hill's morphology. Looking eastwards from Silbury's summit, one sees the ridge of Waden Hill several hundred metres away, and beyond that, several kilometres distant, the skyline formed by the Marlborough Downs and intervening ridges. It is striking how closely the contours of the far horizon and of Waden Hill match one another. There is only a small visual separation of the two as viewed from the top of Silbury. When the viewing position on Silbury is lowered by going down to the east-facing ledge, this separation becomes even more minimal. At one point, the further horizon dips out of sight behind the bulk of Waden for a short distance.

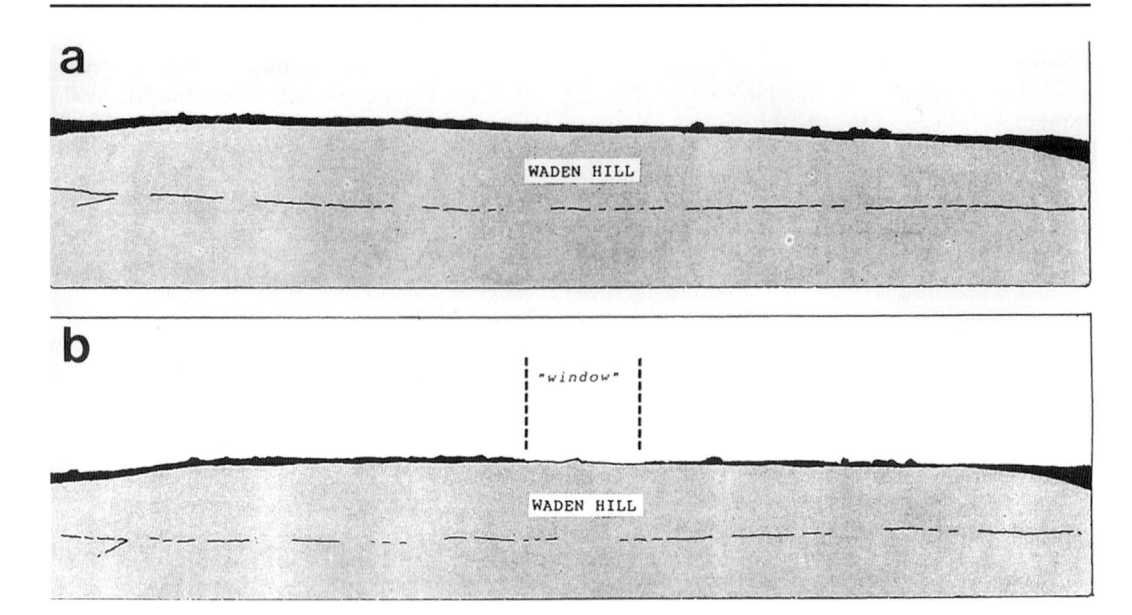

FIGURE 3. *The eastwards view from Silbury across the top of Waden Hill to the distant horizon (shown in silhouette). (a) from Silbury's summit, and (b) from the ledge, indicating the approximate length of the far skyline that dips behind nearby Waden Hill. This vertical separation of viewing positions provided by Silbury allows sets of 'double sunrises' to occur within the 'window' indicated. (derived from photographs.)*

Because of this 'double horizon' as viewed from Silbury, an interesting effect can be observed. At certain times of the year, the sun can be seen to rise once over the far skyline from Silbury's summit, and to rise a second time, a minute or two later, over the top of Waden Hill if one moves down to a viewing position on the ledge. The dip the horizon makes behind Waden as viewed from the ledge provides a window' to allow this 'double sunrise' to occur (FIGURE 3). This window accommodates early August sunrises, a cross-quarter period of traditional significance (Celtic Lughnassadh; Christian Lammas) associated with the harvest. It may be relevant that R.J.C. Atkinson's 1968–70 excavations at Silbury Hill revealed evidence (winged ants in the grass within the centre of the mound) indicating that the building of the monument commenced around that time of year. The early May period (Celtic Beltane) sunrises occur, of course, at the same points on the horizon. Preliminary work by R.D.Y. Perrett from limited topographical information suggests that these sunrises would have been accommodated within the window in 2600 BC, as would midsummer sunrise and the rising midwinter full moon at Minor Standstill (Perrett pers. comm.).

These astronomical effects would have been of a ceremonial nature rather than any form of exact astronomical observation, if deliberately employed by the builders of Silbury Hill at all. But if so used, the coincidence between the Waden Hill and Marlborough Downs skylines would have allowed the effects to have been observable only from the position in which Silbury Hill is placed, and at the height to which the mound is built; that is, its height is about the minimum at which the skyline separation could have been effected. This suggests the possibility that the north–south location of the Hill may have been governed by this. By similar reasoning, its east–west positioning could have been governed to a considerable extent by the West Kennet Long Barrow–Windmill Hill sight-line.

Concluding remarks

If all these various apparent relationships are not merely a 'mare's nest', then we are presented with some fresh ways of approaching the Avebury complex in general, and Silbury Hill in particular, a monument which is, by general agreement, most enigmatic.

It may reasonably be argued that the West Kennet–Windmill Hill alignment is rather weak, due to the size of Windmill Hill. As a sight-line, however, it is more convincing. It involves specifically the highest point of Windmill Hill, the area enclosed by the Neolithic earthworks, which does visually relate to the ledge feature of Silbury Hill. On the ground, the effect is one of precision. In assessing this line, therefore, its vertical dimension has to be taken into account — it is not just a line on a map. The Obelisk–Silbury Hill sight-line is a particularly dramatic example of this three-dimensional aspect. The visibility of the ledge-summit segment of Silbury is critically positioned with regard to the foreground and horizon skylines. It was observed that, just before the harvest in 1991, this segment was fully obscured by the cereal crop on Waden Hill. If cereals were grown there during the later Neolithic, they would similarly have obscured the view to Silbury at harvest time. In view of the time of year the first stages of Silbury appear to have been commenced, this may not be mere coincidence.

The 'double sunrise' occurs from Silbury not only because of its height, but also due to its proximity to Waden Hill. Waden's ridge fills the foreground view with its bulk. That factor would have been lost if Silbury had been placed any significant distance to the west. Whether or not a 'double sunrise' could be achieved by relating natural ridges elsewhere within the Avebury district would take considerable time to ascertain, but what really matters is that Silbury Hill, if the 'double sunrise' was intentional, monumentalizes the event. Similarly, Newgrange monumentalizes the midwinter sunrise, an event which can be seen anywhere.

It is not being suggested here that the sole *raison d'être* for Silbury was ceremonial astronomy, such as for the celebration of the harvest; the various sight-lines described above relate to Silbury from all quarters of the Avebury complex, indicating that, if the 'double sunrise' was indeed a deliberate effect, the astronomical aspect was only an integral component in some broader conceptual scheme that involved the position and height of Silbury Hill and its visibility from selected parts of the local landscape. Similarly, there is no suggestion that the apparent topographical aspects of Silbury Hill's location and morphology need have excluded other factors of perceived religious significance associated with the site by the monument's builders. It is extremely unlikely, however, that they constructed Silbury Hill where it stands without taking into consideration the other features of the ceremonial landscape which the Avebury complex comprises. This is particularly true of the obvious intervisibility existing between West Kennet and Windmill Hill which Silbury interrupts.

The various observations presented here need to be taken as a whole; to take each observation in isolation is to risk missing the possible significance of the collective picture. If valid, these observations offer fresh conceptual tools for tackling aspects of the Silbury enigma. The purpose of this note, however, is simply to draw attention to this possibility.

Acknowledgements. I appreciate the observations made at Avebury by Christopher Chippindale and Peter Fowler. I am also indebted to earlier discussion with John Barnatt, and the preliminary calculations undertaken by R.D.Y. Perrett. Finally, I thank my wife Charla for assisting me on numerous visits to the Avebury complex, usually at unsocial hours!

References

ATKINSON, R.J.C. 1970. Silbury Hill, 1969–70, *Antiquity* 44: 313–14.
BRADLEY, R. 1983. The bank barrows and related monuments of Dorset in the light of recent fieldwork, *Dorset Natural History and Archaeological Society Proceedings* 105: 15–20.
PIGGOTT, S. 1962. *The West Kennet Long Barrow, Excavations 1955–56*. London: HMSO.

Acoustical resonances of selected archaeological sites
by PAUL DEVEREUX & ROBERT G. JAHN
ANTIQUITY 70 (269), 1996

THE ACOUSTICAL aspects of archaeological sites have in the main tended to be overlooked as possible sources of information, probably because it is instinctively felt that sound is too immediate and ephemeral to have significance for archaeological investigation. Nevertheless, for those assessing 'cognitive' approaches, an exploration of various acoustical techniques holds some prospect of revealing new and useful investigative methods. This potential has already been highlighted by the observations of Frances Lynch that the use of the passage in certain passage-graves may have related to communication rather than access (Lynch 1973), and by acoustical research conducted by Steven Waller at prehistoric rock-art sites in Australia, North America and western Europe (Dayton 1992). Waller's tests have reportedly indicated that petroglyphs tend to be found on rock surfaces that yield louder echoes than adjacent ones. Echo effects produced by yelling, clapping and percussive noises also seemed to associate with some of the rock-art imagery, resembling the sound of individual running hooved animals, or, in painted deep caves such as Lascaux, animal herds on the move. Curved rock surfaces acted much like parabolic reflectors, focusing echoes at specific central images in the rock paintings.

    The present research has concentrated on the acoustical resonances of six selected prehistoric chambered structures in England and Ireland. This arose out of initial observations by Jahn concerning the relationship between Hopi ceremonial chanting and the interior of the restored Anasazi kiva at Aztec, New Mexico. The question was posed as to whether ancient ritual structures could have arrived at their proportions as the optimal result of empirical recognition of the acoustical properties of the kinds of ceremonial singing or musical sounds for which they may have provided the environment. If so, then knowing the acoustical resonance frequency of the cavity forming an ancient structure's interior could feasibly provide a guide as to whether musical/vocal activity once occurred there or not. The UK and Irish sites were chosen as they had no associated ethnology, and so provided useful 'blind' test cases. Fieldwork was conducted in the summer of 1994. Deployed at each site was an omnidirectional loudspeaker driven by a variable frequency sine-wave oscillator and a 20-W amplifier, with sound frequency verified by an external, hand-held digital multimeter. The sound amplitude patterns were mapped by a portable meter, sensitive between 55 and 105 dB sound-pressure level. Typically, the sound source was placed on the floor or on a short tripod roughly at the centre of the chamber configuration, with the acoustic axis oriented vertically. The frequency was manually swept through the lower audible range until the lowest natural resonance of the cavity was evidenced by clearly discernable reverberation of the chamber. With this established, the sound intensity was adjusted to the highest comfortable level, usually between 100 and 110 dB at the source, and horizontal surveys of standing-wave patterns were made over some accessible grid covering the chamber. Full details can be found in Jahn *et al.* (1995; 1996), but here it is sufficient to note that

---

The original title of this paper was: Preliminary investigations and cognitive considerations of the acoustical resonances of selected archaeological sites.

site	frequency
Carn Euny, Cornwall ('beehive' chamber)	99 Hz
Chun Quoit, Cornwall	110 Hz
Wayland's Smithy, Berkshire (east chamber)	112 Hz
Wayland's Smithy, Berkshire (west chamber)	95 Hz
Cairn L, Loughcrew, Co. Meath	110 Hz
Cairn I, Loughcrew, Co. Meath	112 Hz
Newgrange, Co. Meath	110 Hz

all the sites, despite individual structural differences, yielded a tight band of measured resonance frequencies (see table).

Discussion

This research is rudimentary and is not being presented as anything more than a pilot experiment at this stage. Nevertheless, it is noteworthy that the range of frequencies measured was not meaningless, varied and random, as might well have been expected, but in fact falls well within that of the male voice, which can generate a relatively high intensity in this range, and the human ear can detect it comfortably, even though it is not a range that contributes to speech intelligibility to any significant extent. The simplest conclusion to draw, therefore, is that the evidence provided by the acoustical resonance tests indicates that male chanting occurred in ritual contexts within these places. Of course, one could speculate that deep-chanting women or even musical instruments could account for sounds in that frequency range. Considerable further work will be required before this method can be seen as a cognitive tool that can be employed with confidence at appropriate archaeological sites. For this reason, it is intended to conduct further resonance frequency tests at archaeological sites where ethnological evidence can help 'calibrate' results, and at sites where it might reasonably be speculated that female officiants operated, to see if workable distinctions can be determined in the acoustical data. (The authors welcome input from archaeologists concerning sites most suitable for such further work involving this technique.)

A final observation ought to be made. If one accepts the usefulness of the above results, it can be seen that they have particular significance for the Iron Age site of Carn Euny, for there has been some debate concerning the function of such *souterrains*. Suggestions have centred on storage, refuge and ritual uses, with conservative opinion favouring the first one or two options. The acoustical evidence, however, as it stands, would support the third option, in the case of Carn Euny at least. This provides just one example of the informational potential of this acoustical approach, should it be validated in future tests in archaeological contexts.

Acknowledgements. Thanks to our colleague Michael Ibison for his contributions to the PEAR Technical Report 95002 and the paper for JASA, and to Brenda Dunne and Charla Devereux for their invaluable help with the fieldwork. We also appreciate the assistance of John Bradish in designing and assembling the field equipment. We are indebted to the National Monuments Branch of the Office of Public Works, Dublin, for special arrangements with respect to Newgrange. This research was conducted under the auspices of the ICRL (International Consciousness Research Laboratories) with funding from the Fetzer Institute.

References
DAYTON, L. 1992. Rock art evokes beastly echoes of the past, *New Scientist* 28 November: 14.
JAHN, R.G., P. DEVEREUX & M. IBISON. 1955. *Acoustical resonances of assorted ancient structures*. Princeton (NJ): Princeton University. PEAR Technical Report 95002.
   1996. Acoustical resonances of assorted ancient structures, *Jurnal of the Acoustical Society of America* 99(2): 649–58.
LYNCH, F. 1973. The use of the passage in certain passage-graves as a means of communication rather than access, in G. Daniel & P. Kjærum (ed.), *Megalithic graves and ritual: papers of the 3rd Atlantic Colloquium*: 147–62. Jutland Archaeological Society.

Architecture and sound: an acoustic analysis of megalithic monuments in prehistoric Britain

by AARON WATSON & DAVID KEATING

ANTIQUITY 73 (280), 1999

IT SEEMS UNLIKELY that the world was silent in prehistory. Sound was present in all aspects of peoples' lives — from speech to the manufacture of stone tools. Artefacts from across Europe have been interpreted as musical instruments and many of these, like carved bone pipes, may date back to the Palaeolithic (Megaw 1960; 1968). In Britain, similar evidence in later prehistory is rare and problematic (e.g. Megaw 1984), possibly as a result of the poor preservation of organic matter. The definition of musical instruments is itself unsatisfactory, and it is perhaps more appropriate to consider what Lund (1981: 246) defines as 'sound-producing devices'. These include any agency that can emit sound, from the use of raw materials such as wood, bone or stone, to the human body itself. It is possible to produce unexpectedly sophisticated sounds from very simple artefacts, and even unworked raw materials (Purser 1997). Fragmentary evidence could also be misinterpreted. For example, Lund (1981) has suggested that the remains of ceramic drums in Scandinavia may be lost amongst the mass of sherds in the archaeological record. Furthermore, it is also feasible that vessels used for storage, or other purposes, may perform as percussive devices with only simple modifications. Experimental reconstruction has demonstrated that later prehistoric ceramic containers could have been adapted to perform as effective drums (Purser 1997).

Despite the possibility that people had access to 'sound-producing devices', there has been relatively little discussion of the contexts within which sound may have been used. While archaeologists have considered the echoes present in decorated caves or rock-shelters across the world (Dams 1984; Reznikoff & Dauvois 1988 (see also Scarre 1989); Dayton 1992), there has been relatively little consideration of the acoustic qualities of artificially constructed monuments in Britain. The few studies in print are encouraging. For example, Devereux & Jahn (1996) suggest that some ancient structures may resonate in response to the human voice, and Lynch (1973) has discussed the 'roof box' at Newgrange in Ireland as means of communicating with the dead.

It is possible that the highly conspicuous nature of many Neolithic and Early Bronze Age monuments has had a substantial bearing upon their archaeological interpretation. Many of these sites physically dominate their surroundings, and research has tended to emphasize their highly visible characteristics. Consequently, there have been studies of the relationships between architecture and natural topography (e.g. Richards 1996; Bradley 1998), intervisibility and spatial relationships (e.g. Bergh 1995; Woodward & Woodward 1996), the aesthetics and meaning of construction materials (e.g. Lynch 1998; Parker Pearson & Ramilisonina 1998) and orientations upon astronomical events (e.g. Ruggles 1984). While these theories add valuable dimensions to our understanding of ancient monuments, they do not consider the possibility that the other senses may have contributed to experiences in the past.

It remained to be seen whether an understanding of acoustics at prehistoric sites could further our understanding of the ways in which prehistoric monuments may have been used. To test this possibility, the acoustic properties of two quite different prehistoric sites in northeast Scotland were explored. The first was Easter Aquorthies, a recumbent stone circle near Aberdeen, where a peculiar echo inside the ring appeared to originate from the large recumbent stone. The project then visited the enclosed space of Camster Round, a passage-grave in Caithness, where a wide range of sound effects were recognized. In combination, the results from these studies suggest that the acoustic properties of these sites should be considered alongside visual and spatial analyses.

Acoustic tests at a recumbent stone circle
The potential for acoustic phenomena at a stone circle was recognized at Easter Aquorthies, where a curious echo was heard during a visit to the site. Recumbent stone circles possess a number of characteristic features that have primarily been interpreted in visual or aesthetic terms. For example, their standing stones tend to be graded in height towards the southwest, creating a visual focus for the large recumbent block itself, which lies between the two tallest stones. The recumbent at Easter Aquorthies is elaborated by two stones which project from its inner face to form an alcove (FIGURE 1). The stones in the circle also appear to have been chosen for their colour (Lynch 1998). There may have been a cairn inside the monument, but this is likely to be a secondary addition (Shepherd 1987). In addition to these visual and spatial qualities, it appeared that the configuration of Easter Aquorthies could direct sound in rather unexpected ways. The recumbent block and its flanking stones seemed to project speech and other sounds across specific areas of the site, so that they could be heard easily in some areas, but were faint in others. Even with fairly quiet sounds this echo noticeably fluctuated in intensity relative to the position of the listener. In addition, subtler reverberations appeared to originate from different places around the circle, and these could not easily be explained.

Easter Aquorthies was acoustically surveyed on a 2-m grid, using an audio amplifier as a sound source. The amplifier was placed in the alcove created by the recumbent and its surrounding stones, and set to emit a constant pink noise at approximately 100 decibels. Pink noise, which sounds rather like a distant waterfall, was selected as the source sound because it combines a wide range of frequencies that encapsulate the range of sounds that are most likely to have been created in prehistory. Recordings made across the site using an omni-directional microphone and a digital audio tape recorder were converted into decibels using a real-time spectrum analyser. A control experiment using the same equipment was performed in a open environment to provide a comparison.

The results from Easter Aquorthies and the control are shown in FIGURE 2. The contours represent sound pressure in increments of 2 decibels. The control shows a regular decay of sound with distance from the loudspeaker that is entirely in accordance with the physical behaviour of sound. The measurements from Easter Aquorthies itself contrast markedly with the control, demonstrating that the distribution of sound energy is governed considerably by the stones. A spur of higher sound pressure that projects from the recumbent towards the centre of the ring is likely to be the echo heard within the monument. In addition to reflecting sound, the recumbent setting also constitutes an impressive visual backdrop, making this feature comparable to a stage in a theatre. Listeners outside the stone circle would have remained largely unaware of the acoustic effects within. The more complex reverberations perceived by listeners at Easter Aquorthies were too subtle to be captured in this test, although it is suggested that these may result from sound being reflected between individual standing stones in the circle.

FIGURE 1. *The recumbent and its flanking stones at Easter Aquorthies. (Photo Aaron Watson.)*

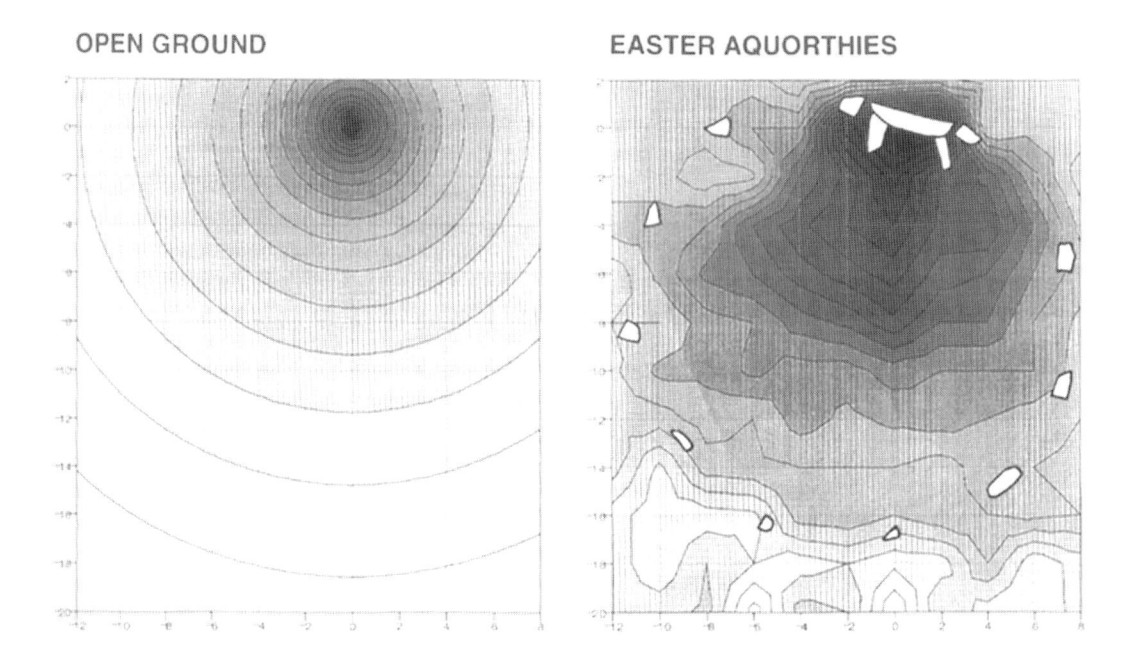

FIGURE 2. *The distribution of sound pressure across open ground and from within Easter Aquorthies. The darker greys represent louder volumes and the contours are in increments of 2 decibels. The stones of the circle are shown in outline (from Thom et al. 1980: 162).*

Acoustic tests at a megalithic tomb

The pilot study at Easter Aquorthies confirmed that it was possible to demonstrate the presence of audible phenomena within an open stone circle. As a comparative project, measurements were taken within the enclosed architectural form of a megalithic tomb where it seemed likely that the acoustics would be rather more complex. For the results to be valid it was crucial to examine an intact site, and Camster Round in Caithness was chosen (FIGURE 3). This remote tomb had been restored to its original form in the 1960s using material derived from the site (Davidson & Henshall 1991). While this renovation cannot have reproduced the tomb's precise prehistoric form, it successfully retained its essential integrity (FIGURE 4). This is not a problem, since minor architectural details would only have a negligible effect on the behaviour of sound. The only modern feature, a glass-plate skylight mounted into the roof of the chamber, was not considered to have any serious impact upon these acoustic tests. In contrast, the nearby monument of Camster Long proved to be quite unsuitable because it had been reconstructed using artificial materials in a manner which varied substantially from the original stone structure.

Camster Round is a passage-grave of the Orkney-Cromarty group (Davidson & Henshall 1991). This monument consists of a stone-built chamber that is enclosed by a cairn of boulders. A narrow passageway sealed under the cairn enables the chamber to be accessed from the outside world. The cairn is circular in plan, with the chamber placed centrally. On the eastern side of the cairn is a recess, or forecourt, where dry-stone walling enhances the external appearance of the mound to either side of the passage entrance. This façade provides a setting for people to enter or leave the tomb, and has parallels elsewhere in Britain. The first 6 m of the passageway are rather claustrophobic, being only 0·5 m wide and about 1 m high. The passage then broadens into an antechamber, from which the main chamber is accessed through a narrow portal. Within the chamber itself, dry-stone corbelling rises 3 m above the ground surface and is sealed by a large roof slab.

FIGURE 3. *View of Camster Round showing the forecourt and entrance. The neighbouring monument of Camster Long can be seen on the horizon. (Photo Aaron Watson.)*

The cave-like interior was found to have a significant influence upon the behaviour of sound. The evidence for structured deposition within the chambers of passage graves suggests that they were centres of activity, and it seemed reasonable to consider how sound may be disseminated from these innermost spaces. Initially, the interior was surveyed using the same methodology that had been employed at Easter Aquorthies. A loudspeaker was placed with a vertical acoustic axis in the central chamber and set to emit a constant pink noise. Systematic recordings were made using a microphone and digital recorder throughout the monument to assess the horizontal distribution of sound. Three main effects were noted:

1 The stone walls of the chamber reflected rather than absorbed sound waves. This amplified noises and created echoes.
2 Sound was transmitted along the passageway, but gradually softened with distance from the loudspeaker.
3 Outside the tomb, the sound could be heard emerging from the passage entrance, but its amplitude decreased markedly towards the margins of the forecourt. These effects occur because sound waves move more readily through the airspace of the passageway than the enveloping cairn material.

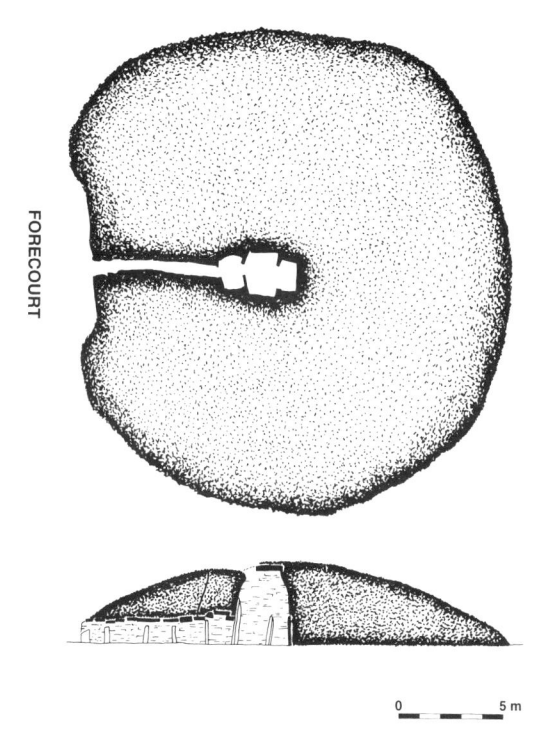

FIGURE 4. *A plan and elevation of Camster Round showing the extent of the cairn and details of the chamber and passage (from Davidson & Henshall 1991: 103).*

Walking around the outer perimeter of the cairn revealed that sound emerging from the chamber was not constant around the entire circumference. It could be heard easily in some zones, but was indistinct in others. There are no external differences in the cairn material that could explain these fluctuations, and they seemed to occur irrespective of noises in the natural environment like wind and rain. It is possible that variations in the density of the cairn material, such as internal walling, could influence the transmission of sound, although it is not known to what extent these features exist within the cairn matrix at Camster Round (Davidson & Henshall 1991). Alternatively, the fluctuations may result from interference between sound waves simultaneously travelling in both directions away from the passage entrance and recombining at different points around the perimeter.

The filtering effect of the cairn was examined in greater detail by assessing the degree to which different sound frequencies were conveyed from the chamber to the outside world. An amplifier in the chamber was set to broadcast notes which swept from high to low frequencies. By listening to the sound in different places around the monument, it was possible to perceive clear changes. The most complete range of audible frequencies was present in the chamber, along the passage, and immediately outside the entrance. Away from the passage and towards the margins of the forecourt the sound became transformed as the higher notes were lost and bass frequencies became increasingly prominent. Around the sides and back of the monument, the sounds perceived to emerge from the tomb were quite different in nature to those being generated inside the chamber. The elemental movement of sound was altered significantly by the boulders of the cairn, which blocked higher-frequency sounds so that predominantly low frequencies emanated from the monument.

Overall, these tests suggest a disparity between the experiences of people within Camster Round, and those who remained outside. Sounds generated by the occupants of the tomb will be enhanced by echoes, while those listening to these sounds from the outside will only hear a filtered rendition emerge through the cairn. Further experiments revealed that the interior was also suited to a range of peculiar sound effects, such as standing waves.

Standing waves at Camster Round

Standing waves result from the combination of two waves of equal frequency and intensity travelling in opposite directions, and can be induced if waves are reflected from a solid surface. Acoustic standing waves result from sound waves being reflected between solid walls, and these produce zones of low or high intensity as waves either cancel or combine (Morse & Ingard 1986). They can be created in any enclosed space, and were therefore expected to occur in Camster Round under certain conditions. It was not clear, however, which sounds or frequencies would be required to generate them, or what their impact upon listeners would be. Initial mathematical modelling indicated that it should be possible to generate audible standing waves inside the tomb using the human voice or musical instruments. Devereux & Jahn's (1996) assessment of standing waves at a number of ancient structures (including the passage-graves of Loughcrew and Newgrange in Ireland) also concluded that these could be evoked by vocalization. It remained to assess the physical experience of these wave effects upon participants.

An electronic tone generator and an amplifier were employed in the manner of Devereux & Jahn (1996), although it was later demonstrated that a group of people could replicate these effects by vocalization alone. A continuous note was played in the chamber at a variety of pitches until a clearly audible change was heard. A number of frequencies responded in this way, and most were accompanied by a surprising range of effects:

1   The source of the note became unclear. Rather than originating from the loudspeaker, sound appeared to issue from different directions around the chamber. Listeners occasionally perceived these sounds to be contained within their heads, which could be unpleasant.
2   Some standing-wave frequencies created an environment of sound within the monument which could be explored by physically moving around the chamber. Even small movements of the head revealed marked variations in the volume and pitch of the sound.
3   Listeners in the chamber could detect the movement of individuals along the passage, as the solid mass of their bodies created microtonal disturbances in the distribution of sound which could be heard throughout the monument.
4   A timbre that resonated inside the chamber sounded quite ordinary when heard from the exterior. Upon entering the passage, however, it soon became apparent that the sound was behaving in unusual ways. During progress towards the chamber, distinct oscillations in the volume of the note would be perceived in specific places, irrespective of the distance to the loudspeaker. In the antechamber the sound could unexpectedly intensify, change in pitch, and develop vibrato.
5   Speech within the chamber could become seriously distorted, resulting in some extraordinary harmonics.

These effects all resulted from simply playing or vocalizing a continuous note within the chamber, techniques which are unlikely to have been beyond the ability of people in the Neolithic. The possibility remained that percussive instruments in this environment may possess peculiar effects of their own. This constituted the next phase of the project.

The effects of percussion at Camster Round

While it is not possible to generate standing waves with percussive sounds, drums were found to evoke quite different results. The clarity with which percussive sounds moved between the chamber and the outside world varied according to the listeners' location. Like other sounds, drumming was transferred most effectively along the passage, and could be distantly heard in the forecourt. Away from the passage entrance, the sound became increasingly distorted as the high-frequency elements of the drum noise were filtered by the cairn, and the bass was enhanced. Around the sides and back of the tomb, the drumming sounded deep and unfamiliar, and was perceived to be rising up from the ground rather than the tomb itself, which was quite striking.

During these tests it became apparent that drumming could have been used as a form of communication between tombs which were in close proximity. In general, the sound of drumming inside Camster Round did not travel far beyond the cairn, despite the surrounding topography being open. This was due to the dampening effect of the cairn material and interference from natural background sounds like wind. On the day of these tests, drumming in the chamber could not be heard further than 100 m away from the outer perimeter of the cairn. It was remarkable, therefore, that listeners standing within the chambers of the neighbouring monument of Camster Long, which is approximately 190 m away (see FIGURE 3), did perceive the beat. Although the effect was subtle, the drum could be heard as a distant 'booming' which appeared to rise from the ground. The precise reasons for this remain uncertain, but it is probable that the calm air within Camster Long permitted distant sounds to be perceived more clearly without disturbance from natural sounds in the outside world. It is also possible that the stone shell of both monuments filtered out high-frequency noises while allowing the bass sounds of drumming to be transmitted. These low frequencies are rare in the natural world, and may be disproportionately enhanced relative to other noises in the landscape. This effect could have been exploited elsewhere, where tombs occur in close proximity. An interesting example is Knowth in Ireland, where a large tomb is surrounded by a number of smaller cairns (Eogan 1986). Many of these satellite tombs have their passages oriented towards the main mound (FIGURE 5), perhaps assisting the transmission of sound between what were otherwise separate components of a cemetery.

Many of the effects recognized during the previous tests are not unique to passage-graves. They could be recreated at other types of tomb where there is an enclosed chamber. The final series of experiments at Camster Round, however, revealed a remarkable acoustic phenomenon which is entirely reliant upon the specific format of passage-graves.

Passage-graves and Helmholtz Resonance

Despite variations in size and shape, passage-graves all possess a buried chamber connected to the outside world by a relatively confined passageway. These features encapsulate the critical components of the Helmholtz Resonator, which is recognized for its powerful ability to amplify certain frequencies (Rayleigh 1945; Turner & Pretlove 1991). To create Helmholtz Resonance, a sound of a specific frequency has to be played in the chamber. This frequency is determined by the relative volumes of the chamber and passage. Sound waves generated in the chamber cause the air to expand, pushing against the mass of air confined within the narrow passageway, and moving it towards the entrance. A critical point is reached when the elastic properties of the air overcome this outward motion, causing the air in the passage to retract back towards the chamber. Helmholtz Resonance occurs when this oscillation becomes synchronized with the pressure waves emitted by the sound source, causing these waves to increase in amplitude.

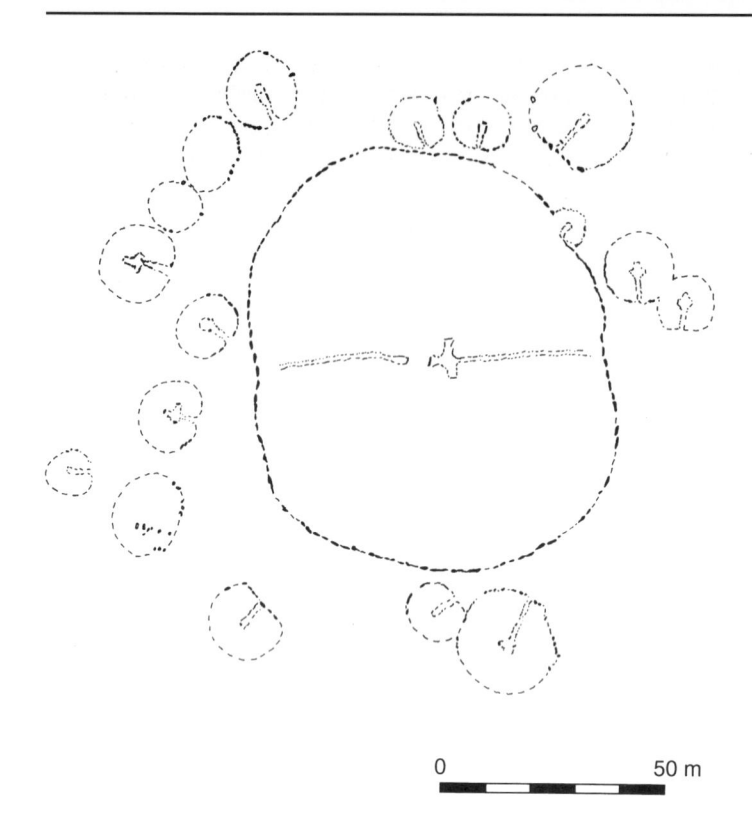

FIGURE 5. *A plan of the passage-graves at Knowth, Ireland, showing the distribution of smaller monuments around the central cairn. The approximate outlines of these tombs have been enhanced for clarity (modified from Eogan 1986: 23).*

The resulting sound becomes multiplied until it is greater than the original input. An example of Helmholtz Resonance is the sound made by blowing across the neck of a glass bottle.

To test whether passage-graves could resonate when the appropriate sound frequency was played in the chamber, the process was mathematically modelled using the Helmholtz theorem (see below). While the volume of the tomb interior could not be precisely determined due to irregularities in the stonework, it was possible to calculate these dimensions from plans within an acceptable margin of error. The results suggested that Camster Round would, in theory, resonate if continuous sounds were generated in the chamber at a frequency of about 4 Hertz. This is an infrasonic frequency, meaning that it is beneath the audible threshold for conventional human hearing. However, infrasonic sound has, in recent years, received considerable attention because of the surprising physical effects it may have on the body and mind. Helmholtz Resonance could, therefore, contribute to the experience of being inside the tomb. It remained to be demonstrated that such a low frequency could be produced.

In the modern world there are no acoustic instruments which can generate a note sufficiently low to induce Helmholtz Resonance at Camster Round. Cathedral organs can achieve some of the lowest notes of any musical instrument at around 16 Hertz (Hz), and it is unlikely that any acoustic instrument in the past or present would be capable of playing a continuous note at 4 Hz. While it is possible that a strong breeze blowing across the passage entrance with sufficient force may induce Helmholtz Resonance —

$$\text{resonant frequency} \approx \frac{\text{speed of sound}}{2\pi} \sqrt{\frac{\text{passage cross sectional area}}{\text{passage length} \times \text{main body volume}}}$$

by stimulating the movement of air within the structure — the conditions under which this would occur are unpredictable and would be infrequent. One remaining possibility was that the infrasonic frequency could be excited artificially by striking a drum at the correct rhythm. At Camster Round this rhythm would have to be a regular beat of 4 beats per second (240 bpm) in order to generate 4 Hz. It remained to demonstrate that such drumming would produce sufficient energy to excite Helmholtz Resonance, and that the resulting effect could be perceived by people within the tomb.

It was beyond the means of this project to employ specialist equipment to measure infrasonic frequencies at Camster Round. Instead, a 1:10 scale model of the passageway and chamber was constructed from medium-density-fibreboard, a material sufficiently dense to simulate stone at this scale. While the model could not completely emulate the intricacies of the real tomb, it would adequately simulate it at the frequencies under consideration. Cavities within the dry-stone walling may reduce the amplitude of Helmholtz Resonance to some extent, but would not affect the frequency. The acoustic scale model supplemented mathematical modelling by enabling the theory to be tested in three dimensions under controlled conditions. Given the size of the model, it was necessary to re-scale any acoustic response by a factor of 10. This meant that a resonance of 4 Hz would scale to 40 Hz, permitting its measurement and analysis using conventional equipment. These sounds could then be reconverted to reveal the behaviour of sound within the monument itself.

A sweep of computer-generated tones from infra- to ultrasonic were played into the scale model through a loudspeaker mounted in the chamber floor. A microphone measured the resulting responses, which were assessed by a digital sound analyser. This was repeated three times, with the microphone placed in a different part of the model. The range of frequencies that were attained from these recordings are depicted in FIGURE 6. The most substantial response was an increase in sound pressure centred upon frequencies between approximately 40 and 60 Hz. When reduced by a factor of 10, these results equate with frequencies between 4 and 6 Hz at Camster Round, and correspond closely with the theoretical prediction for Helmholtz Resonance. The complex peaks and troughs recorded in the higher-frequency spectrum probably represent standing waves within the model. Two significant peaks at 250 and 400 Hz may result from organ-pipe resonances created as standing waves are established along the length of the passage. These would give the greatest output at the tunnel entrance. The frequency and sound pressure of the narrow bands at higher frequencies vary considerably in relation to the location of the microphone, suggesting that different standing-wave resonances are established in various parts of the structure. This agrees with the results of the tests which explored standing waves at Camster Round. In contrast, the peak between 40 and 60 Hz possesses a consistently high amplitude at each microphone location within the scale model, meaning that air throughout the interior of the tomb was being excited to a similar extent. Given that this peak also reflects the frequency predicted by mathematical modelling, it seems reasonable to attribute this distinctive response to Helmholtz Resonance.

These results imply that it would be possible to produce Helmholtz Resonance in the chamber, but would this phenomenon have been noticeable? Research into the impact of infrasonic frequencies upon the human body suggests that their harmful nature has been overrated (Broner 1978), but that people exposed to sufficient levels of infrasonics under laboratory conditions can experience a variety of psychological and physiological responses (Evans 1976). While these symptoms are to some extent subjective, particularly as Nussbaum & Reinis (1985) have demonstrated that responses to infrasonics may vary between individuals, they provide a valuable reference in assessing the possible

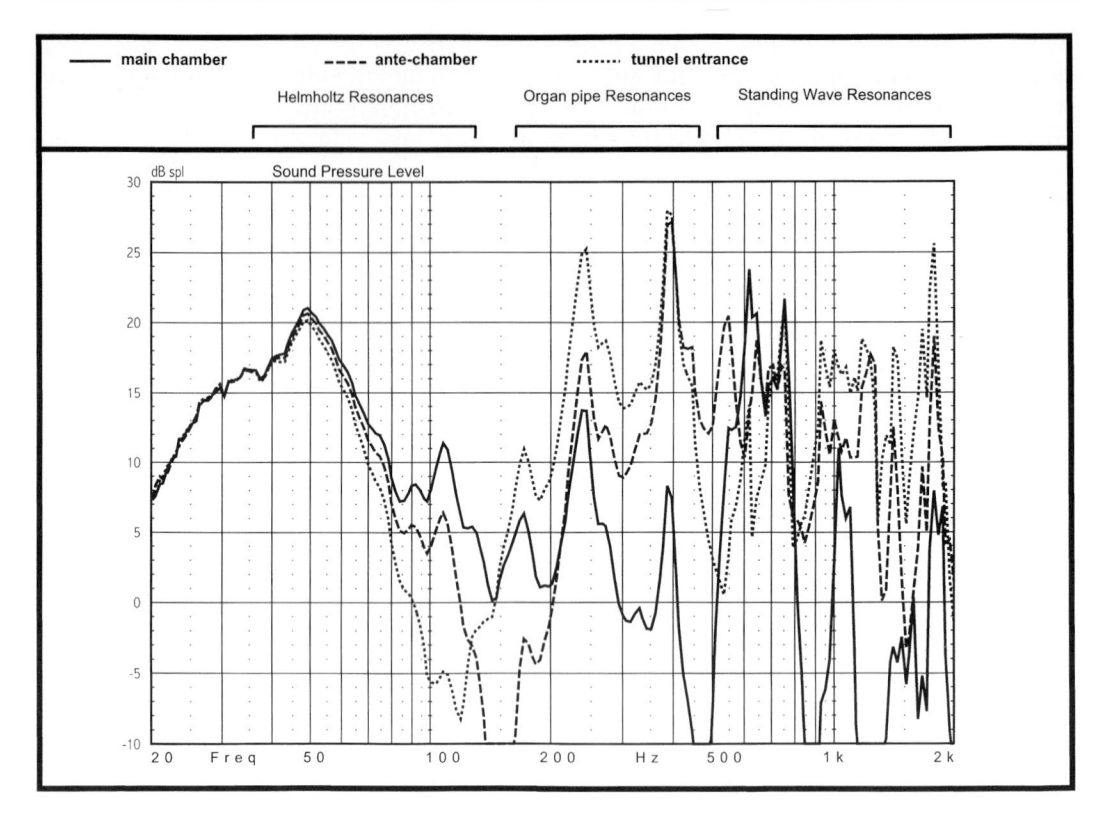

FIGURE 6. *Graph showing the frequency responses from different microphone positions within the scale model of Camster Round, illustrating the presence of Helmholtz Resonance, organ-pipe resonance and standing waves.*

influence of a 4-Hz resonance inside Camster Round. To calculate the amplitude of Helmholtz Resonance in the tomb, the decibel output of a 30-cm diameter drum was measured and calibrated against the scale model tomb. This suggested that a single drum was capable of generating approximately 4 to 5 Hz at between 120 and 130 decibels inside Camster Round. According to Evans (1976: 107), this level of exposure could result in balance disturbance, pressure on the ears, speaking difficulties, vibration, drowsiness and headaches. Any increase in either frequency or sound pressure would intensify the severity of these symptoms.

To assess whether any unusual effects could be detected at Camster Round, drumming tests of short duration were conducted within the tomb in the presence of an audience. While the experiences of these people remain broadly subjective, given that individual responses to sound may vary, many of the listeners did complain of a range of unfamiliar sensations which correlate with those which could be expected from infrasonics (Evans 1976). In particular, participants felt that their pulse and breathing pattern was being influenced, raising the possibility that long-term exposure could result in hyperventilation. While it is possible that the noise and rhythm of drumming in the enclosed environment could itself influence behaviour, there were fewer complaints during equally loud sequences at beats which were too slow to excite Helmholtz Resonance. All of the reported sensations declined rapidly when the drumming ceased. Although the presence of infrasonics in sufficient quantities to influence people could not be absolutely confirmed, it was certainly apparent that the tomb interior was conducive to the creation of unusual experiences.

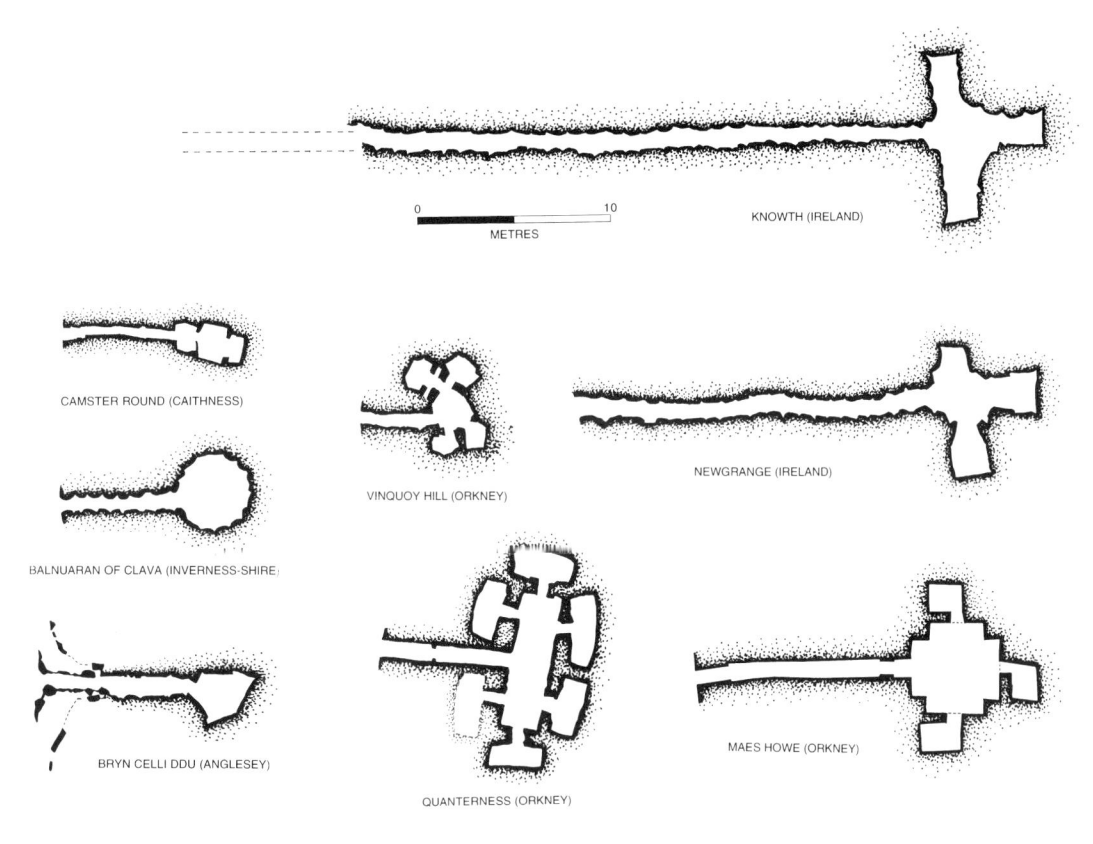

FIGURE 7. *Plans of passage-grave chambers that are sufficiently complete to allow their resonant frequencies to be calculated.*

Resonance and passage-graves across Britain

Helmholtz Resonance would not be restricted to Camster Round, and the resonant frequencies of a sample of other passage-graves were calculated by deducing their internal volumes from plans and elevations. This was only attempted if their structure was sufficiently well preserved to permit the reconstruction of their original morphology. The frequency of resonance at each site broadly reflects their size, which varies considerably (FIGURE 7):

Bryn Celli Ddu (Wales)	6–7 Hz
Vinquoy Hill (Scotland)	5–6 Hz
Camster Round (Scotland)	4–5 Hz
Balnuaran of Clava Northeast (Scotland)	3–5 Hz
Maes Howe (Scotland)	2 Hz
Quanterness (Scotland)	2 Hz
Newgrange (Ireland)	1–2 Hz
Knowth (Ireland)	1–2 Hz

In general the larger tombs have lower resonant frequencies, and would require a slower drum-beat to evoke Helmholtz Resonance. Groups of tombs with comparable internal volumes will have similar frequencies, irrespective of their precise morphology.

It was not possible, however, to demonstrate empirically the presence of infrasonics within Camster Round, or to test further the effects of drumming upon people. The effects of rhythm or noise can affect people in many different ways, both physical and psychological. Drum-beats are often associated with activities which seek to create links with the supernatural, and are often associated with ritual procedures across the world (Neher 1962; Needham 1967). In part, this may reflect the potential for drums to emit rhythms at loud volumes (Huntington & Metcalf 1991: 67), but it has also been proposed that the sound waves produced by percussive instruments may contribute to the inducement of altered states of consciousness (Neher 1962; Needham 1967; Jackson 1968). Tuzin (1984) has speculated that an infrasonic component of thunderstorms may contribute to feelings of anxiety, disquiet and, ultimately, altered states of mind.

Discussion

This project has considered a wide range of acoustic effects that are present at two quite different prehistoric monuments, a recumbent stone circle and a passage-grave. The elemental movement of sound has been considered, as well as the intriguing possibilities of standing waves and Helmholtz Resonance. Yet acoustics should not be restricted to these monuments alone. The physical scale of the earthworks and stone settings at many Neolithic and Early Bronze Age monuments makes them ideal subjects for acoustic effects. The enclosed chambers within tombs may have the most dramatic influence. While this study has focused upon passage-graves, other kinds of chambered tombs, for instance the Cotswold–Severn long barrows, are likely to exert a different influence on the movement of sound. While their configuration is unsuited to Helmholtz Resonance, phenomena like standing waves remain a possibility, as Devereux & Jahn (1996) have demonstrated at Wayland's Smithy in Berkshire.

As the results from Easter Aquorthies testify, acoustic effects need not be restricted to tombs. An open-air site like a henge, which is surrounded by an earthwork, may also interrupt the passage of sound. Like the earthwork baffles along major roads today, embankments can create considerable sound 'shadows', which may have served to isolate henge interiors from the surrounding landscape. Features like coves, which regularly consist of three large megaliths set at right angles to create an alcove (Burl 1988), have a considerable potential to direct and focus sound. This is difficult to demonstrate, since none of these sites are complete, although the flat stones used in the Cove within Avebury may have a considerable potential to create unusual echoes. Like the recumbent at Easter Aquorthies, these stones would have directed sound in one direction, while filtering it in others. The close-set standing stones at Stonehenge would also have influenced the distribution of sound. When this monument was complete, the dressed surfaces of the sarsen blocks would have created an almost continuous wall around the central area. This may have reverberated sound around the interior, and interrupted or distorted the transmission of sound between the centre and the outside world.

Despite being open to the sky, the fundamental behaviour of these monuments is similar to Camster Round in the sense that people who were outside the monument would not clearly be able to perceive, through either sound or vision, the activities taking place within. At Easter Aquorthies, it was shown that an echo created by the recumbent stone was mainly contained within the interior of the ring of standing stones. The limited internal areas of these structures may have precluded large gatherings of people, and only those permitted within certain parts of these monuments would have experienced unusual acoustics. Such effects may have been a significant contribution to the experience of participation, particularly inside megalithic tombs, where darkness, the presence of the dead and sound effects may have combined to create a memorable experience. In this sense, acoustic effects could serve to differentiate between people who were permitted access and those who were not. Participants inside a tomb would hear sounds enhanced by echoes, while those outside would only perceive filtered sound emerging from the cairn. This may have heightened a sense of mystery regarding the unseen activities within the tomb and empowered those who were able to produce such marked transformations of sound when in the presence of the dead.

The evidence for Neolithic and Early Bronze Age domestic settlements across many regions of Britain suggests that dwellings were ephemeral and may have been built of wood. The size of these dwellings, and the scale of their construction, implies that their acoustic potential was considerably less than stone-built circles and tombs. This may have further differentiated monuments from the everyday, because sound effects within these settings could not have been reproduced at domestic sites in the surrounding landscape.

Conclusion

Prehistoric monuments may not have been as peaceful during their use as they are today. While these sites can be interpreted as a means by which people in the past structured space to emphasize their social order, studies at a stone circle and a passage-grave suggest that some of these places were also ideal environments for producing dramatic sound effects. While it cannot be demonstrated that the architecture of monuments was deliberately configured to enhance acoustic performance, the behaviour of sound would have been an unavoidable factor in their use. Perhaps acoustics should be regarded as an inseparable component in the genesis of potent events, particularly as many of these compelling sound effects could not have been explained without our modern awareness of physics. In this respect, acoustics should be considered alongside the structural, spatial, or visual attributes of ancient monuments. These places may not have been simply a technology for producing visual and acoustic experiences, but a means of creating different worlds altogether.

Acknowledgements. Thanks to Richard Bradley, Nicky Clarkson, Andy Jones and Tim Phillips for their invaluable help with the fieldwork, and to Christopher Chippindale, Paul Devereux, Graeme Lawson and Howard Williams for their comments and support. John Perser kindly contributed sound recordings of ancient musical instruments. Thanks also to Brian Hayter of the Music Education Group at Bulmershe Court, Reading University, and to Andrew Colyer, for the loan of percussion instruments. We are grateful to Liam Bassett of the Department of Psychology, Reading University, for constructing the scale model of Camster Round.

References
BERGH, S. 1995. *Landscape of the monuments: a study of the passage tombs in the C'il Irra region, Co. Sligo, Ireland.* Stockholm: Riksantikvarieämbetet Arkeologiska Undersökniger, Skrifter nr 6.
BRADLEY, R. 1998. Ruined buildings, ruined stones: enclosures, tombs and natural places in the Neolithic of south-west England, *World Archaeology* 30: 13–22.
BRONER, N. 1978. The effects of low frequency noise on people — a review, *Journal of Sound and Vibration* 58: 483–500.
BURL, A. 1988. Coves: structural enigmas of the Neolithic, *Wiltshire Archaeological and Natural History Magazine* 82: 1–18.
DAMS, L. 1984. Preliminary findings at the 'Organ' Sanctuary in the cave of Nerja, Malaga, Spain, *Oxford Journal of Archaeology* 3: 1–14.
DAVIDSON, J.L. & A.S. HENSHALL. 1991. *The chambered cairns of Caithness.* Edinburgh: Edinburgh University Press.
DAYTON, L. 1992. Rock art evokes beastly echoes of the past, *New Scientist* 28 November: 14.
DEVEREUX, P. & R.G. JAHN. 1996. Preliminary investigations and cognitive considerations of the acoustic resonances of selected archaeological sites, *Antiquity* 70: 665–6.
EOGAN, G. 1986. *Knowth and the passage-tombs of Ireland.* London: Thames & Hudson.
EVANS, M.J. 1976. Physiological and psychological effects of infrasound at moderate intensities, in W. Tempest (ed.), *Infrasound and low frequency vibration:* 97–113. London: Academic Press.
HUNTINGTON, R. & P. METCALF. 1991. *Celebrations of death: the anthropology of mortuary ritual.* New York (NY): Cambridge University Press.

JACKSON, A. 1968. Sound and ritual, *Man* 3: 293–9.
LUND, C. 1981. The archaeomusicology of Scandinavia, *World Archaeology* 12: 246–65.
LYNCH, F. 1973. The use of the passage in certain passage graves as a means of communication rather than access, in G. Daniel & P. Kjærum (ed.), *Megalithic graves and ritual*: 147–61. Copenhagen: Jutland Archaeological Society. Publication 11.
– 1998. Colour in prehistoric architecture, in A. Gibson & D. Simpson (ed.), *Prehistoric ritual and religion*: 62–7. Stroud: Sutton Publishing.
MEGAW, J.V.S. 1960. Penny whistles and prehistory, *Antiquity* 34: 6–13.
– 1968. Problems and non-problems in palaeo-organology: a musical miscellany, in J.M. Coles & D.D.A. Simpson (ed.), *Studies in ancient Europe*: 333–58. Leicester: Leicester University Press.
– 1984. The bone ?flute, in W.J. Britnell & H.N. Savory (ed.), *Gwernvale and Penywyrlod: two Neolithic long cairns in the Black Mountains of Brecknock*: 27–8. Bangor: Cambrian Archaeological Association. Cambrian Archaeological Monograph 2.
MORSE, P.M. & K.U. INGARD. 1980. *Theoretical acoustics*. Princeton (NJ): Princeton University Press.
NEEDHAM, R. 1967. Percussion and transition, *Man* 2: 606–14.
NEHER, A. 1962. A physiological explanation of unusual behaviour in ceremonies involving drums, *Human Biology* 34: 151–60.
NUSSBAUM, D.S. & S. REINIS. 1985. *Some individual differences in human response to infrasound*. Toronto: University of Toronto Institute for Aerospace Studies. Report 282.
PARKER PEARSON, M. & RAMILISONINA. 1998. Stonehenge for the ancestors: the stones pass on the message, *Antiquity* 72: 308–26.
PURSER, J. 1997. *The Kilmartin sessions: the sounds of ancient Scotland*. Compact disc produced by the Kilmartin House Trust, Argyll: KHT CD1.
RAYLEIGH, J.W.S. 1945. *The theory of sound*. New York (NY): Dover Publications.
REZNIKOFF, I. & M. DAUVOIS. 1988. La dimension sonore des grottes ornées, *Bulletin de la Société Préhistorique Française* 85: 238–46.
RICHARDS, C. 1996. Monuments as landscape: creating the centre of the world in late Neolithic Orkney, *World Archaeology* 28: 190–208.
RUGGLES, C.L.N. 1984. *Megalithic astronomy: a new archaeological and statistical study of 300 western Scottish sites*. Oxford: British Archaeological Reports. British series 123.
SCARRE, C. 1989. Painting by resonance, *Nature* 338: 382.
SHEPHERD, I. 1987. The early peoples, in D. Omand (ed.), *The Grampian people*: 119–30. Golspie: The Northern Times.
THOM, A., A.S. THOM & A. BURL. 1980. *Megalithic rings: plans and data for 229 monuments in Britain*. Oxford: British Archaeological Reports. British series 81.
TURNER, J.D. & A.J. PRETLOVE. 1991. *Acoustics for engineers*. Basingstoke: Macmillan.
TUZIN, D. 1984. Miraculous voices: the auditory experience of numinous objects, *Current Anthropology* 25: 579–96.
WOODWARD, A.B. & P.J. WOODWARD. 1996. The topography of some barrow cemeteries in Bronze Age Wessex, *Proceedings of the Prehistoric Society* 62: 275–91.

Palaeoecology and the perception of prehistoric landscapes: some comments on visual approaches to phenomenology

by HENRY P. CHAPMAN & BENJAMIN R. GEAREY

ANTIQUITY 74 (284), 2000

THE NEED to obtain meaning from data is fundamental to the study of archaeology. This has been highlighted in the study of archaeological landscapes with the development of phenomenological approaches that centre on the proposition that landscapes are embodded with meaning and imbued with and recreated through changing human experience (*cf.* Meinig 1979 and Cosgrove 1989 for non-archaeological landscapes, and Tilley 1994 for archaeological landscapes). Such approaches to landscape have concentrated on the 'topography, waters, rocks, locales, paths and boundaries' (Tilley 1994: 67) and have studied landscape phenomenology by using visibility as a primary tool to measure perception in the past. Although contemporary vegetation patterns would clearly have influenced past visibility, this has often been neglected within such studies. In this short note we wish to demonstrate how this oversight may serve to render studies of past landscapes incomplete, and it is argued that, where such evidence exists, it should be embraced. Environmental data provides a broader platform from which enhanced archaeological meaning may be derived.

Landscape theory

The central themes within landscape theory are underlain by the definition of landscape (*cf.* Olwig 1993). Tilley (1996) summarized the relationship between archaeology and landscape in four ways:
1 as 'a set of relationships between named locales' (p. 161);
2 to be 'experienced and known through the movement of the human body in space and through time' (p. 162);
3 as 'a primary medium of socialisation' (p. 162); and
4 creating 'self-identity' by controlling knowledge and thereby influencing power structures (p. 162).

The key principle is that of experience, and thus studies of archaeological landscapes have been based upon attempting to replicate the experience of 'Being-in-the-world' while trying to reconstruct the dialectic of the existential 'Being' (Tilley 1994: 12). The primary method of measuring experience (if measuring is a suitable word) is through analysing visibility patterns. For example, Thomas (1993) investigated the visual impact of monuments, particularly around Avebury, suggesting themes of inclusion and exclusion (similar to Tilley's fourth point, mentioned above). Devereux (1991) analysed the spatial relationships between monuments and topography at Avebury by investigating their visual relationships. Similarly, Tilley (1994) investigated three archaeological landscapes through a photographic essay and by recording patterns of intervisibility between monuments. This technique has also been explored through digital landscape reconstruction. Fisher *et al.* (1997), for example, analysed the positioning of Bronze Age cairns, demonstrating a visual relationship between their positioning and corresponding view to/from the sea.

Leskernick and visibility analysis: a case study
At Leskernick, Bodmin Moor, Cornwall, the relationship between a Bronze Age settlement and its surrounding physical and anthropogenic landscape was explored using a very direct way of measuring visibility (Bender *et al.* 1997). This was achieved primarily by 'framing' the landscape using wooden 'door' frames held in the positions of the settlement hut entrances. From each of the 50 or so huts on Leskernick Hill the view of neighbouring tors, such as the important site of Rough Tor with its possible early Neolithic hill top enclosure (Johnson & Rose 1994), and the view of the stone row from particular parts of the settlement were explored. On the basis of this approach, the authors concluded that 'What these people saw, and what they oriented their hut doorways towards, was a nested landscape' (Bender *et al.* 1997: 169); a landscape consisting of the merged components of the anthropogenic and natural environment.

The discussions of landscape visibility in these cases are dominated by considerations of topography. Other aspects of the landscape, such as *significant* tors and water courses, are considered (e.g. Tilley 1994; 1995; 1996; Bender *et al.* 1997), but the issue of palaeovegetation is usually given a cursory or contradictory mention. In their investigation of Bronze Age cairns referred to above, Fisher *et al.* approach this issue from a methodological basis: 'In spite of the palaeobotanic record of the area, it is not possible to reconstruct vegetation with sufficient detail for visibility analysis [using Geographical Information Systems]' (1997: 587).

More often vegetation is mentioned in passing but not investigated in any detail. Tilley, for example, in his general investigation of the phenomenology of landscape on Bodmin Moor, Cornwall, refers to oak as the 'most significant . . . tree' (1995: 48) in the prehistoric period. In a later article referring to the same landscape, Tilley mentions that 'Environmental evidence . . . indicates that the landscape was dominated by grassland and heath as it is today' (1996: 165), but continues later in the same article to mention 'localized woodland destruction [on Bodmin Moor during the later Neolithic and Bronze Age]' (1995: 168); two statements which appear at best confusing and at worst contradictory. Bender *et al.* (1997) make only one explicit reference to available palaeoecological data, and this is in the context of establishing the Bronze Age as a period of local woodland clearance on the moor rather than to address the issue of the vegetation *per se*.

The site of Leskernick is particularly pertinent since there is a near-complete Holocene pollen sequence from the nearby Rough Tor area (2–3 km to the southwest) providing palaeovegetation data contemporary to the settlement (incidentally mentioned by Bender *et al.* 1997: 147, see above). Tilley's (1995; 1996) main reference for the essentially open character of Bodmin Moor during the early to mid-Holocene is Brown (1977) who concluded that the environment of the moor was essentially open, with little tree cover except in the more sheltered areas such as valleys. However, this hypothesis has since been challenged and an alternative one erected: with total tree and shrub pollen percentages accounting for over 95% of total land pollen in a sequence recovered from 280 m OD at Rough Tor south, woodland cover spread to the higher parts of the moor during the early-mid Holocene (Gearey 1996; Gearey & Charman 1996; Gearey *et al.* in press). *Corylus avellana*-type (hazel) and *Quercus* (oak) are the dominant taxa in the pollen record, indicating dense hazel-oak scrub which may have reached up to tor summits, particularly on sheltered lee slopes. Damper areas such as valley bottoms would have been more open with grass and sedge mire, but alder became established in these and other areas of high soil moisture following the *Alnus* rise at *c.* 6500 years before present. *Alnus* accounts for 80% of total land pollen identified in a core from a valley mire site on the eastern edge of Bodmin Moor (Gearey *et al.* in press). The only significant open areas on the moor would therefore have been at Dozmary Pool, an open body of water since the Late-glacial period (Brown 1977), and perhaps the more exposed tor summit areas.

It was therefore anything but an open landscape which faced the Mesolithic gatherer–hunters who probably used the moor on a seasonal basis (Herring & Lewis 1992), and the later Neolithic groups, who may have built the earliest monuments such as the hill top enclosures at Rough Tor, the Cheesering and the Long Cairns at Louden, Catshole and Bearah. The clearance of tree cover that would thus have been necessary prior to this settlement and monument construction is in fact reflected in clearance episodes in the pollen record. Evidence of Neolithic activity is dated to around 4700 cal BC at Rough Tor south and intensifies into the Bronze Age at around 3700 cal BC (Gearey *et al.* in press).

The possible importance of the more prominent craggy tors highlighted by Tilley (1995; 1996) is given an added dimension with the likelihood that the higher tors might have been the only 'naturally' open areas in the earlier Holocene prior to this anthropogenic clearance activity. Likewise, the concept of 'paths of movement' (Tilley 1995: 11), as well as the act of 'being' in the landscape, might also be viewed in a different light if the hypothesis of a largely open moor is replaced with one of a closed, woodland environment (*cf.* Evans *et al.* 1999). The significance of Dozmary Pool (situated in the centre of the moor), with its extensive collection of flint assemblages, is acknowledged by Tilley (1995; 1996) and attributed to the pool as a 'manifestation of a sea in the land' (1995: 12). The treeless setting of this location in the context of a wooded moor may also be regarded as an important aspect of the focus of early activity at this locale.

Bender *et al.*'s (1997) consideration of visibility and lines of sight is also potentially flawed by this lack of appreciation of environmental factors. For example, the visibility of the top of Rough Tor from Leskernick ('the tip of Rough Tor comes into view in the far distance' — Bender 1997: 155) would have been dependent upon the vegetation cover on the intervening ridge of High Moor. Whilst the precise spatial and temporal structure of this vegetation cannot be easily established, it cannot be immediately assumed in the manner the authors do, that the hill was entirely cleared of its probable cover of hazel-oak woodland by the time the settlement at Leskernick was occupied. The view to and from the stone row to the southeast of the settlement are also regarded as significant. This row is some 300 m in length and crosses a boggy area (since modified by tin streaming) after which it becomes more 'regular' in the arrangement of its stones. The authors regard the topographic point at which this occurs (i.e. the boggy area) as significant in this change in its construction. No consideration is made of the likelihood that alder fen woodland may have been present on such a boggy area during the Neolithic. Not only might this have affected the visibility to and from the monument, but by disregarding it the possible role of the 'natural' environment beyond that of the topography in the siting of such structures is ignored.

Conclusions

We acknowledge the inherent difficulties both in extrapolating site-specific palaeoecological data over extensive areas (*cf.* Caseldine & Maguire 1981) and in incorporating such data where available into landscape-wide syntheses of the sort attempted by Tilley, Bender and their collaborators. Similarly, we have not attempted to comment on the validity of their field data, as has been questioned elsewhere (Fleming 1999). Rather we wish to highlight that, if 'scientific' sources of data pertaining to landscapes are given a low priority by landscape theoreticians, meanings gained from them will be incomplete.

This short note has focused upon the potential influence of vegetation on visibility and therefore of palaeoenvironmental data on visibility analysis, but this is not the only area where closer integration may be fruitful. The dichotomy between environmental and landscape archaeology has been evident to certain palaeoecologists for some time (e.g. McGlade 1995) and has only recently begun to be addressed, at least in terms of more rigorous data interpretation and analysis (e.g. Brown, 1997). More collaboration between landscape archaeologists and environmental archaeologists is clearly desirable to prevent the split between the respective 'camps' becoming ever wider.

Acknowledgements. This note has benefited from the comments of J.A. Pearson and two anonymous referees.

References
BENDER, B. (ed.). 1993. *Landscape: politics and perspectives*. Oxford: Berg.
BENDER, B., S. HAMILTON & C. TILLEY. 1997. Leskernick: stone worlds; alternative narratives; nested landscapes, *Proceedings of the Prehistoric Society* 63: 147–78.
BROWN, A.P. 1977. Late Devensian and Flandrian vegetational history of Bodmin Moor, Cornwall, *Philosophical Proceedings of the Royal Society of London* B276: 251–320.
1997. Clearance and clearings: deforestation in Neolithic Britain, *Oxford Journal of Archaeology* 16: 133–46.
CASELDINE, C.J. & D.J. MAGUIRE. 1981. A review of the prehistoric and historic environment on Dartmoor, *Proceedings of the Devon Archaeological Society* 39: 1–16.
COSGROVE, D. 1989. Geography is everywhere: culture and symbolism in human landscapes, in D. Gregory & R. Walford (ed.), *Horizons in human geography*: 118–35. Basingstoke: Macmillan.
DEVEREUX, P. 1991. Three-dimensional aspects of apparent relationships between selected natural and artificial features within the topography of the Avebury complex, *Antiquity* 65: 894–8.
EVANS, C., J. POLLARD & M. KNIGHT. 1999. Life in woods: tree-throws, 'settlement' and forest cognition, *Oxford Journal of Archaeology* 18: 241–54.
FISHER, P., C. FARRELLY, A. MADDOCKS & C. RUGGLES. 1997. Spatial analysis of visible areas from the Bronze Age cairns of Mull, *Journal of Archaeological Science* 24: 258–92.
FLEMING, A. 1999. Phenomenology and the megaliths of Wales: a dreaming too far, *Oxford Journal of Archaeology* 18: 119–25.
GEAREY, B.R. 1996. Human environment relations on Bodmin Moor during the Holocene. Unpublished Ph.D thesis, University of Plymouth.
GEAREY, B. & D. CHARMAN. 1996. Rough Tor, Bodmin Moor: testing some archaeological hypotheses with landscape scale palynology, in D.J. Charman, R.M. Newnham & D.G. Croot (ed.), *Devon and East Cornwall Field Guide*: 109–19. London: Quaternary Research Association.
GEAREY, B.R., D.J. CHARMAN & M. KENT. In press. Palaeoecological evidence for the prehistoric settlement of Bodmin Moor, Cornwall: Part 1: The status of woodland and early human impacts, *Journal of Archaeological Science*.
HERRING, P. & B. LEWIS. 1992. Ploughing up gatherer-hunters on Bodmin Moor: Mesolithic and later flints from Butterstor and elsewhere on Bodmin Moor, *Cornish Archaeology* 31: 5–14.
JOHNSON, N. & P. ROSE. 1994. *Bodmin Moor. An archaeological survey* I: *the human landscape to c. 1800*. London: English Heritage. Archaeological report 24.
MCGLADE, J. 1995. Archaeology and the ecodynamics of human modified landscapes, *Antiquity* 69: 113–32.
MEINIG, D.W. 1979. The beholding eye — ten versions of the same scene, in D.W. Meinig (ed.), *The interpretation of ordinary landscapes — geographical essays*: 33–48. Oxford: Oxford University Press.
OLWIG, K.R. 1993. Sexual cosmology: nation and landscape at the conceptual interstices of nature and culture; or, what does landscape really mean, in Bender (ed.): 307–43.
THOMAS, J. 1993. The politics of vision and the archaeologies of landscape, in Bender (ed.): 19–48.
TILLEY, C. 1994. *A phenomenology of landscape — places, paths and monuments*. Oxford: Berg.
1995. Rocks as resources: landscapes and power, *Cornish Archaeology* 34: 5–57.
1996. The powers of rocks: topography and monument construction on Bodmin Moor, *World Archaeology* 28: 161–76.

References

AAHRG (Avebury Archaeological and Historical Research Group). 2001. *Archaeological Research Agenda for the Avebury World Heritage Site*. London: English Heritage & Salisbury: Wessex Archaeology.
ADAMSON, T. 2002. Stonehenge: the stone mason and his craft, *Antiquity* 76: 41–2.
ALCOCK, L. & E. ALCOCK. 1952. Ringham Low: the rediscovery of a Derbyshire chambered tomb, *Antiquity* 26: 41–3.
ANON. 1943. Avebury, *Antiquity* 17: 94–5.
ASHBEE, P. 1963. The Wilsford Shaft, *Antiquity* 37: 116–20.
  1969. Timber mortuary houses and earthen long barrows again, *Antiquity* 43: 43–5.
  1964. The radiocarbon dating of the Fussell's Lodge Long Barrow, *Antiquity* 38: 139–40.
  1966. The Fussell's Lodge Long Barrow, *Archaeologia* 100: 1–80.
  1984. Safekeeping Stonehenge, *Antiquity* 58: 217–18.
ASHBEE, P., M. BELL & E. PROUDFOOT. 1989. *Wilsford Shaft Excavations, 1960–62*. London: English Heritage. HBMCE Archaeological Report 11.
ASHBEE, P.A. & I.F. SMITH. 1960. The Windmill Hill long barrow, *Antiquity* 34: 297–9.
  1966. The date of the Windmill Hill long barrow, *Antiquity* 40: 299.
ATKINSON, R.J.C. 1956. *Stonehenge*. London: Hamish Hamilton.
  1961. Neolithic Engineering, *Antiquity* 35: 292–99.
  1965. Wayland's Smithy, *Antiquity* 39: 126–33.
  1966. Moonshine on Stonehenge, *Antiquity* 40: 212–16.
  1967. Silbury Hill, *Antiquity* 41: 259-62.
  1968. Silbury Hill, 1968, *Antiquity* 42: 299.
  1969. The date of Silbury Hill, *Antiquity* 43: 216.
  1970. Silbury Hill 1969–70, *Antiquity* 44: 313–14.
  1974. The Stonehenge bluestones, *Antiquity* 48: 62–3.
  1978. Sibury Hill, in R. Sutcliffe (ed.), *Chronicle: essays from ten years of television archaeology*: 159–73. London: BBC.
  1979. *Stonehenge* (revised edition). Harmondsworth: Penguin.
ATKINSON, R.J.C. & J.G. EVANS. 1978. Recent excavations at Stonehenge, *Antiquity* 52: 235–6.
BAKKER, J.A. 1979. Lucas de Heere's Stonehenge, *Antiquity* 53: 107–11.
BARCLAY, G.J. 1983. Sites of the third millennium bc to the first millennium ad at North Mains, Strathallan, Perthshire, *Proceedings of the Society of Antiquaries of Scotland* 113: 122–281.
BARCLAY, G.J. 1999. Cairnpapple revisited: 1948–1998, *Proceedings of the Prehistoric Society* 65: 17–46.
BARCLAY, G.J., G.S. MAXWELL, I.A. SIMPSON & D.A. DAVIDSON. 1995. The Cleaven Dyke: a Neolithic cursus monument/bank barrow in Tayside Region, *Antiquity* 69: 317–26.
BARCLAY, G. & C. RUGGLES. 2002. Will the data drive the model? A further response to Euan MacKie, *Antiquity* 76: 668–71.
BARCLAY, G.J. & C.J. RUSSELL-WHITE. 1993. Excavations in the ceremonial complex of the fourth to second millennium BC at Balfarg/Balbirnie, Glenrothes, Fife, *Proceedings of the Society of Antiquaries of Scotland* 123: 43–210.
BARFIELD, L. 1991. Wessex with and without Mycenae: new evidence from Switzerland, *Antiquity* 65: 102–7.
BARNATT, J. & P. HERRING 1986. Stone circles and megalithic geometry: an experiment to test alternative design practices, *Journal of Archaeological Science* 13: 431–49.
BARRETT, J.C. & K.J. FEWSTER. 1998. Stonehenge: is the medium the message? *Antiquity* 72: 847–52.
BAXTER, I. & C. CHIPPINDALE. 2000. The Stonehenge we don't deserve, *Antiquity* 74: 944–6.
BEWLEY, B., M. COLE, A. DAVID, R. FEATHERSTONE, A. PAYNE & F. SMALL. 1996. New features within the henge at Avebury, Wiltshire: aerial and geophysical evidence, *Antiquity* 70: 639–46.
BOADO, F.C. & R.F. VALCARCE. 1989. The megalithic phenomenon of northwest Spain: main trends, *Antiquity* 63: 682–96.
BOUJOT, C. & S. CASSEN. 1993. A pattern of evolution for the Neolithic funerary structures of the west of France, *Antiquity* 67: 477–91.
BRADLEY, R. 2000. Tomnaverie stone circle, Aberdeenshire, *Antiquity* 74: 465–6.
  2001. Orientations and origins: a symbolic dimension to the long house in Neolithic Europe, *Antiquity* 75: 50–55.
BRANIGAN, K. 1970. Wessex and Mycenae: some evidence reviewed, *Wiltshire Archaeological & Natural History Magazine* 65: 89–107.
BRITNELL, W. 1979. The Gwernvale long cairn, Powys, *Antiquity* 53: 132–4.
  1980. Radiocarbon dates from the Gwernvale chambered tomb, Crickhowell, Powys, *Antiquity* 54: 147.
BURKITT, M. 1938. Megalithic paintings and engravings, *Antiquity* 12: 235.
BURL, A. 1986. Newly recognized carvings on a Breton menhir, *Antiquity* 60: 147–8.
  1991. Megalithic myth or man the mover? *Antiquity* 65: 297–8.
  1997. The sarsen horseshoe inside Stonehenge: a rider, *Wiltshire Archaeological & Natural History Magazine* 90: 1–12.
  2000. *The stone circles of Britain, Ireland, and Brittany*. London & New Haven (CT): Yale University Press.
BURTON, N. 2000. New tools at Avebury, *Antiquity* 74: 279–80.
CHAPMAN, H. & B. GEARY. 2000. Palaeoecology and perception in prehistoric landscapes, *Antiquity* 74: 316–19.
CHILDE, V.G. 1925. *The dawn of European civilization*. London: Routledge.

CHIPPINDALE, C. 1983a. *Stonehenge complete*. London: Thames & Hudson.
 1983b. What future for Stonehenge? *Antiquity* 57: 172–80.
 1985. English Heritage and the future of Stonehenge, *Antiquity* 59: 132–7.
 1986. Stoned Henge: events and issues at the summer solstice, 1985, *World Archaeology* 18.1: 38–58.
 1989. Editorial, *Antiquity* 63: 3–12.
CLARK, G. 1935. The Norwich Woodhenge, *Antiquity* 9: 465–9.
 1936. The timber monument at Arminghall, and its affinities, *Proceedings of the Prehistoric Society* 2: 1–51.
CLAY, R.C.C. 1927. Stonehenge Avenue, *Antiquity* 1: 342–4.
CLEAL, R.M.J., K.E. WALKER & R. MONTAGUE. 1995. *Stonehenge and its landscape. Twentieth-century excavations*. London: English Heritage. English Heritage Archaeological Report 10.
CLIFFORD, E. 1966. Hetty Pegler's Tump, *Antiquity* 40: 129–32.
COLES, J. & J. TAYLOR. 1971. The Wessex Culture: a minimal view, *Antiquity* 45: 6–14.
COLLINS, A.E.P. 1973. A re-examination of the Clyde-Carlingford tombs, in Daniel & Kjærum (ed.): 93–104.
COONEY, G. 1990. The place of megalithic tomb cemeteries in Ireland, *Antiquity* 64: 741–53.
CORCORAN, J.X.W.P. 1960. The Carlingford Culture, *Proceedings of the Prehistoric Society* 26: 98–148.
 1969. The Cotswold–Severn group, in T.G.E. Powell, J.X.W.P. Corcoran, F. Lynch & J.G. Scott, *Megalithic enquiries in the west of Britain*: 13–106. Liverpool: Liverpool University Press.
 1972. Multi-period construction and the origins of the chambered long cairn in western Britain and Ireland, in F. Lynch & C. Burgess (ed.), *Prehistoric man in Wales and the west. Essays in honour of Lily F. Chitty*: 31–64. Bath: Adams & Dart.
 1973. The chambered cairns of the Carlingford Culture, an enquiry into origins, in Daniel & Kjaerum (ed.): 105–16.
CORNWALL, B. 1999. *Stonehenge. A novel of 2000 BC*. London:HarperCollins.
CRAWFORD, O.G.S. 1927a. [Stonehenge], *Antiquity* 1: 259, 387.
 1927b. Barrows, *Antiquity* 1: 419–34.
 1927c. Lyonesse, *Antiquity* 1: 5–14.
 1928. Stone cists, *Antiquity* 2: 418–22.
 1929. Durrington Walls, *Antiquity* 3: 49–59.
 1934. Long Meg, *Antiquity* 8: 328–9.
 1938. Bank-barrows, *Antiquity* 12: 228-32.
 1954. The symbols carved at Stonehenge, *Antiquity* 28: 221–4.
CRAWFORD, O.G.S. & A. KEILLER. 1924. *Wessex from the air*. Oxford: Clarendon Press.
CUNNINGTON, M.E. 1927. Prehistoric timber circles, *Antiquity* 1: 92–5.
 1929. *Woodhenge*. Devizes: George Simpson & Co.
 1931. 'The Sanctuary' on Overton Hill near Avebury, *Wiltshire Archaeological & Natural History Magazine* 45: 486–8.
CUNNINGTON, M. & B. CUNNINGTON. 1927. Prehistoric timber circles, *Antiquity* 1: 92–132.
CUTFORTH, R. 1970, Stonehenge at midsummer, *Antiquity* 44: 305–7.
DANIEL, G.E. 1937. Dolmens in Southern Britain, *Antiquity* 11: 183–200.
 1938. Megalithic tombs of northern Europe, *Antiquity* 12: 297–310.
 1950. *The prehistoric chamber tombs of England and Wales*. Cambridge: Cambridge University Press.
 1959. Some megalithic follies, *Antiquity* 33: 282–4.
 1964. The long barrows of the Cotswolds, *Transactions of the Bristol and Gloucestershire Archaeological Society* 82: 5–17.
 1967. Northmen and Southmen, *Antiquity* 41: 313–17.
 1969. Editorial, *Antiquity* 43: 169–75.
 1970a. Editorial, *Antiquity* 44: 169–74.
 1970b. Megalithic answers, *Antiquity* 44: 260–69.
 1976. Megaliths galore, *Antiquity* 50: 187–9.
 1981. Editorial, *Antiquity* 55: 165–71.
 1985. Editorial, *Antiquity* 59: 161–6.
DANIEL, G. & P. KJÆRUM (ed.). 1973. *Megalithic graves and ritual. Papers presented at the III Atlantic Colloquium, Moesgård 1969*. Moesgård: Jutland Archaeological Society. Publication 11.
DARVILL, T.C. 1982. *The megalithic chambered tombs of the Cotswold–Severn region*. Vorda: Highworth.
 Forthcoming. *Stonehenge World Heritage Site Archaeological Research Framework*. London: English Heritage & Bournemouth: Bournemouth University.
DARVILL,T., C. GERRARD & B. STARTIN. 1993. Identifying and protecting historic landscapes, *Antiquity* 67: 563–74.
DARVILL, T. & G. WAINWRIGHT. 2002. SPACES — exploring Neolithic landscapes in the Strumble-Preseli area of southwest Wales, *Antiquity* 76: 623–4.
DE VALERA, R. 1960. The court cairns of Ireland, *Proceedings of the Royal Irish Academy* 60C: 9–140.
DEVEREUX, P. 1991. Three-dimensional aspects of apparent relationships between selected natural and artificial features within the topography of the Avebury complex, *Antiquity* 65: 894–8.
DEVEREUX, P. & R. JAHN. 1995. Preliminary investigations and cognitive considerations of acoustical resonances of selected sites, *Antiquity* 70: 665–6.
DOE [Department of the Environment]. 1979. *Report of the Stonehenge Working Party*. London: Department of the Environment. Limited circulation printed report.
DONOVAN, D.T. 1977. Stony Littleton long barrow, *Antiquity* 51: 236–7.

REFERENCES

DRONFIELD, J. 1995. Subjective vision and the source of Irish megalithic art, *Antiquity* 69: 539–49.
ENGLISH HERITAGE. 1998. *Avebury World Heritage Site Management Plan*. London: English Heritage.
  2000. *Stonehenge World Heritage Site Management Plan*. London: English Heritage.
EOGAN, G. 1969. Excavations at Knowth, Co. Meath, 1968, *Antiquity* 43: 8–14.
  1977. Two decorated stones from Knowth, Co. Meath, *Antiquity* 51: 48–9.
  1983. A flint macehead at Knowth, Co. Meath, Ireland, *Antiquity* 57: 45–6.
  1998. Knowth before Knowth, *Antiquity* 72: 162–72.
EVANS, C. 1994. Natural wonders and national monuments: a meditation upon the fate of The Tolmen, *Antiquity* 68: 200–208.
EVANS, J.D., B. CUNLIFFE & C. RENFREW (ed.). 1981. *Antiquity and man. Essays in honour of Glyn Daniel*. London: Thames & Hudson.
EVANS-PRITCHARD, E.E. 1935. Megalithic grave-monuments in the Anglo-Egyptian Sudan and other parts of East Africa, *Antiquity* 9: 151–60.
FIELDEN, K. 1996. Avebury saved? *Antiquity* 70: 503–7.
  2000. Stonehenge deserves the right road solution, *Antiquity* 74: 946–9.
FITZPATRICK, A.P. 2002. 'The Amesbury Archer': a well-furnished early Bronze Age burial in southern England, *Antiquity* 76: 629–30.
FOWLER, M.J.F. 1996. High-resolution satellite imagery in archaeological applications: a Russian satellite photograph of the Stonehenge region, *Antiquity* 70: 667–71.
FOWLER, P. & C. THOMAS. 1979. Lyonesse revisited: the early walls of Scilly, *Antiquity* 53: 175–89.
FOX, C. 1931. Sleds, carts and wagons, *Antiquity* 5: 185–99.
GARFITT, J.E. 1979. Moving the stones to Stonehenge, *Antiquity* 53: 190–94.
  1980. Raising the lintels at Stonehenge, *Antiquity* 54: 1424–44.
GERLOFF, S. 1975. *The early Bronze Age daggers in Great Britain and a reconsideration of the Wessex Culture* Munich: C.H. Beck. Prähistorische Bronzefunde VI,2.
GIBSON, A. 1992. The timber circle at Sarn-y-Bryn-Caled, Welshpool, Powys: ritual and sacrifice in Bronze Age mid-Wales, *Antiquity* 66: 84–92.
  1994. Excavations at the Sarn-y-bryn-Caled cursus complex, Welshpool, Powys, and the timber circles of Great Britain and Ireland, *Proceedings of the Prehistoric Society* 60: 143–224.
  1998. *Stonehenge and timber circles*. Stroud: Tempus.
GINGELL, C. 1996. Avebury: striking a balance, *Antiquity* 70: 507–11.
GIOT, P-R. 1958. The chambered tomb barrow of Barnenez in Finistère, *Antiquity* 32: 149–53.
GIOT, P-R., D. MARGEURIE & H. MORZADEC. 1994. About the age of the oldest passage-graves in western Brittany, *Antiquity* 68: 624–6.
GORDON, D.H. 1937. The megalithic site of Burf Hama, *Antiquity* 11: 220–21.
GOULSTONE, J. 1985. Folk games at Silbury Hill and Stonehenge, *Antiquity* 49: 51–3.
GOWLAND, W. 1902. Recent excavations at Stonehenge, *Archaeologia* 58: 37–105.
GOWLETT, J.A.J., E.T. HALL & R.E.M. HEDGES. 1986. The date of the West Kennet long barrow, *Antiquity* 60: 143–4.
GRAY, H.ST.G. 1935. The Avebury excavations, 1908–1922, *Archaeologia* 84: 99–162.
GRIMES, W.F. 1960. *Excavations on defense sites* I: *mainly Neolithic and Bronze Age. 1939–45*. London: HMSO.
HADINGHAM, E. 1981. Lunar observatory hypotheses at Carnac, *Antiquity* 55: 35–42.
HARDING, A. 1984. *The Mycenaeans and Europe*. London: Academic Press.
HARTWELL, B. 2002. A Neolithic ceremonial timber complex at Ballynahatty, Co Down, *Antiquity* 76: 526-32.
HAWKES, J. 1967. God in the machine, *Antiquity* 41: 174–80.
HAWKINS, G.S. 1965. *Stonehenge decoded*. London: Souvenir Press.
HAWKINS, G.S., R.J.C. ATKINSON, A. THOM, C.A. NEWHAM, D.H. SADLER & R.A. NEWALL. 1967. Hoyle on Stonehenge: some comments, *Antiquity* 41: 91–8.
HAWLEY, W. 1928. Report on the excavations at Stonehenge during 1925 and 1926, *Antiquaries Journal* 8: 149–76.
HEGGIE, D.C. 1972. Megalithic lunar observations — an astronomer's view, *Antiquity* 46: 43–8.
HENSHALL, A.S. 1963. *The chambered tombs of Scotland* 1. Edinburgh: Edinburgh University Press.
  1972. *The chambered tombs of Scotland* 2. Edinburgh: Edinburgh University Press.
HODDER, I. & P. SHAND. 1988. The Haddenham long barrow, *Antiquity* 62: 349–52.
HOLGATE, R. 1987. Neolithic settlement patterns at Avebury, Wiltshire, *Antiquity* 61: 259–63.
HOULDER, C. 1967. The henge monuments at Llandegai, *Antiquity* 41: 58–60.
  1968. The henge monuments at Llandegai, *Antiquity* 42: 216–21.
HOYLE, F. 1966. Speculations on Stonehenge, *Antiquity* 40: 162–76.
HUNTINGFORD, G.W.B. 1935. Megaliths in Kenya, *Antiquity* 9: 219–40.
INSALL, G. 1927. Woodhenge, *Antiquity* 1: 99–100.
JONES, O.T. 1956. The bluestones of the Cardigan district, *Antiquity* 30: 34–6.
KEILLER, A. 1939. Avebury. Summary excavations 1937 and 1938, *Antiquity* 13: 223–33.
KEILLER, A. & S. PIGGOTT. 1936. The recent excavations at Avebury, *Antiquity* 10: 417–27.
KENNET, W. & E. YOUNG. 2000. The Stonehenge we don't deserve — continued, *Antiquity* 74: 949–51.
KINNES, I. 1982. Les Fouaillages and megalithic origins, *Antiquity* 56: 24–30.
KINNES, I.A., I.H. LONGWORTH, I.M. MCINTYRE, S. NEEDHAM & W.A. ODDY. 1988. Bush Barrow gold, *Antiquity* 62: 24–39.
KJAERUM, P. 1967. Mortuary Houses and funeral rites in Denmark, *Antiquity* 41: 190–96.

LAWSON, A. 1992. Stonehenge — creating a definitive account, *Antiquity* 66: 934–40.
LE ROUX, C-T. 1985. New excavations at Gavrinis, *Antiquity* 59: 183–7.
LOCKYER, N. 1906. *Stonehenge and other British monuments astronomically considered*. London: Macmillan.
MACKIE, E. 1997. Maeshowe and the Winter Solstice: ceremonial aspects of the Orkney Grooved Ware culture, *Antiquity* 71: 338-59.
    2002. The structure and skills of British Neolithic society: a brief response to Clive Ruggles & Gordon Barclay, *Antiquity* 76: 666–8.
MALONE, C. & S. STODDART. 1998. Editorial, *Antiquity* 72: 729–38.
MASSET, C. 1972. Megalithic tomb at La Chaussée -Tirancourt, *Antiquity* 46: 297–300.
MASTERS, L. 1973. The Lochhill long cairn, *Antiquity* 47: 96–100.
    1974. The chambered tombs of Scotland, *Antiquity* 48: 34–9.
MCINNES, I.J. 1964. A class II henge in the East Riding of Yorkshire, *Antiquity* 38: 218–19.
MERCER, R. 1981. The excavation of a late Neolithic henge-type enclosure at Balfarg, Markinch, Fife, Scotland, *Proceedings of the Society of Antiquaries of Scotland* 111: 63–171.
MOIR, G., C. RUGGLES & R. NORRIS. 1980. Megalithic sciences and some Scottish site plans, *Antiquity* 54: 37–43.
MOLLESON, T. 1981. The relative dating of bones from Quanterness chambered cairn, Orkney, *Antiquity* 55: 127-9.
MORGAN, F. DE F. 1959. The excavation of a long barrow at Nutbane, Hants., *Proceedings of the Prehistoric Society* 25: 15–51.
MORGAN, F. DE M.V. & P. ASHBEE. 1958. The excavation of two long barrows in Wessex, *Antiquity* 32: 104–11.
NEEDHAM, S. 2000. Power pulses across a cultural divide: cosmologically driven acquisition between Amorica and Wessex, *Proceedings of the Prehistoric Society* 66: 151–208.
NEWALL, R.S. 1929. Stonehenge, *Antiquity* 3: 75–88.
    1956. Stonehenge: a review, *Antiquity* 30: 137–41.
O'KELLY, M.J. 1964. Newgrange, Co. Meath, *Antiquity* 38: 288–91.
    1968. Excavations at Newgrange, Co. Meath, *Antiquity* 42: 40–42.
    1969. Radiocarbon dates for the Newgrange passage grave, Co. Meath, *Antiquity* 43: 140–41.
    1972. Further radiocarbon dates from Newgrange, Co. Meath, Ireland, *Antiquity* 46: 226–7.
    1979. The restoration of Newgrange, *Antiquity* 53: 205–10.
    1981. The roofing of Newgrange, *Antiquity* 55: 218–19.
OSENTON, C. 2001. Megalithic engineering techniques: experiments using axe-based technology, *Antiquity* 75: 293–8.
PARKER PEARSON, M. & RAMILISONINA. 1998a. Stonehenge for the ancestors: the stones pass the message, *Antiquity* 72: 308–26.
PARKER PEARSON, M. AND RAMILISONINA. 1998b. Stonehenge for the ancestors: part two, *Antiquity* 72: 855–6.
PAVEL, P. 1992. Raising the Stonehenge lintels in Czechoslovakia, *Antiquity* 66: 389–91.
PATTON, M. 1992. Megalithic transport and territorial markers: evidence from the Channel Islands, *Antiquity* 66: 392–5.
    1995. New light on Atlantic seaboard passage-grave chronology: radiocarbon dates from La Hougue Bie (Jersey), *Antiquity* 69: 582–6.
PIGGOTT, S. 1935. Stukeley, Avebury and the druids, *Antiquity* 9: 22–32.
    1937a. Long barrows in Brittany, *Antiquity* 11: 441–55.
    1937b. Prehistory and the Romantic movement, *Antiquity* 11: 31–38.
    1938. The early Bronze Age in Wessex, *Proceedings of the Prehistoric Society* 4: 52–106.
    1941. The sources of Geoffrey of Monmouth. II. The Stonehenge story, *Antiquity* 15: 305–19.
    1949. The excavations at Cairnpapple Hill, West Lothian 1947–8, *Antiquity* 22: 32–9.
    1950a. The excavations at Cairnpapple Hill, West Lothian, 1947–48. *Proceedings of the Society of Antiquaries of Scotland* 87 (1948–49): 68–123.
    1950b. *William Stukeley. An eighteenth-century antiquary*. London: Thames & Hudson.
    1951. Stonehenge reviewed, in W.F. Grimes (ed), *Aspects of archaeology in Britain and beyond. Essays presented to O.G.S. Crawford*: 274–92. London: Edwards.
    1953. The tholos tomb in Iberia, *Antiquity* 27: 137–43.
    1958. The excavation of the West Kennet Long Barrow: 1955–56, *Antiquity* 32: 235–46.
    1959. Stonehenge restored, *Antiquity* 33: 50–51.
    1962. *The West Kennet long barrow. Excavations 1955–56*. London: HMSO.
    1973. The Dalladies long barrow: NE Scotland, *Antiquity* 47: 32–6.
PIGGOTT, S. & C.M. PIGGOTT. 1939. Timber and earth circles in Dorset, *Antiquity* 12: 138–58.
PITTS, M. 1990. What future for Avebury? *Antiquity* 64: 259–74.
POWELL, T.G.E. 1960. Megalithic and other art: centre and west, *Antiquity* 34: 180–90.
    1963. The chambered cairn at Dyffryn Ardudwy, *Antiquity* 37: 19–24.
POWELL, T.G.E., J.X.W.P. CORCORAN, F. LYNCH & J.G. SCOTT. 1969. *Megalithic enquiries in the west of Britain*. Liverpool: Liverpool University Press.
RENFREW, C. 1967. Colonialism and megalithimus, *Antiquity* 41: 276–88.
    1968. Wessex without Mycenae, *Annual of the British School at Athens* 63: 277–85.
    1973. *Before civilization*. London: Jonathan Cape.
RENFREW, C., D. HARKNESS & R. SWITSUR. 1976. Quanterness, radiocarbon and the Orkney cairns, *Antiquity* 50: 194–204.
REYNOLDS, A. 2001. Avebury: a late Anglo-Saxon burh? *Antiquity* 75: 29–30.
RICHARDS, J. & M. WHITBY. 1997. The engineering of Stonehenge, *Proceedings of the British Academy* 92: 231–56.
ROUGHLEY, C., A. SHERRATT & C. SHELL. 2002. Past records, new views: Carnac 1830–2000, *Antiquity* 76: 218–23.

REFERENCES

RUGGLES, C. & G. BARCLAY. 2000. Cosmology, calendars and society in Neolithic Orkney: a rejoinder to Euan MacKie, *Antiquity* 74: 62–74.

SAUNDERS, P. 1981. General Pitt-Rivers and Kit's Coty House, *Antiquity* 55: 51–3.

SAVILLE, A., J.A.J. GOWLETT & R.E.M. HEDGES. 1987. Radiocarbon dates from the chambered tomb at Hazleton (Glos.): a chronology for Neolithic collective burial, *Antiquity* 61: 108–19.

SAVORY, H.N. 1973. Pen-y-wyrlod: a new Welsh long cairn, *Antiquity* 47: 187–92.

SCARRE, C. 1997. Misleading images: Stonehenge and Brittany, *Antiquity* 71: 1016–20.

SCARRE, C. & P. RAUX. 2000. A new decorated menhir, *Antiquity* 74: 757–8.

SCARRE, C., R. SWITSUR & J-P. MOHEN. 1993. New radiocarbon dates from Bougon and the chronology of French passage-graves, *Antiquity* 67: 856–9.

SCOTT, J.G. 1962. Clyde, Carlingford and Connaught cairns — a review, *Antiquity* 36: 97–101.

1973. The Clyde Cairns of Scotland, in Daniel & Kjærum (ed.): 117–28.

SELKIRK, A. 1972. The Wessex Culture, *Current Archaeology* 3.9 (32): 241–4.

SHELL, C. 2000. Metalworker or shaman? early Bronze Age Upton Lovell G2a burial, *Antiquity* 74: 271–2.

SHELL, C.A. & P. ROBINSON. 1988. The recent reconstruction of the Bush Barrow lozenge plate, *Antiquity* 62: 248–60.

SIMPSON, D.D.A. 1968. Timber mortuary houses and earthen long barrows, *Antiquity* 42: 142–4.

SIMPSON, G. 1967. Three painted objects from Maxey, nr Peterborough, *Antiquity* 41: 138–9.

SMITH, C. 1981. Trefignath burial chambers, Anglesey, *Antiquity* 55: 134–6.

SMITH, I.F. 1965. *Windmill Hill and Avebury. Excavations by Alexander Keiller 1925–1939*. Oxford: Clarendon Press.

SMITH, I.F. & J.G. EVANS. 1968. Excavation of two long barrows in North Wiltshire, *Antiquity* 42: 138–42.

SOFFE, G. & T. CLARE. 1988. New evidence of ritual monuments at Long Meg and her Daughters, Cumbria, *Antiquity* 62: 552–7.

SSG [Stonehenge Study Group]. 1985. *The future of Stonehenge*. London: English Heritage. Limited circulation printed report.

ST JOSEPH, J.K. 1961. Aerial reconnaissance in Wales, *Antiquity* 35: 263–75.

STONE, J.F.S., S. PIGGOTT & A. BOOTH. 1954. Durrington Walls, Wiltshire: recent excavations at a ceremonial site of the early second millennium BC, *Antiquaries Journal* 34: 155–77.

STUKELEY, W. 1740. *Stonehenge: a temple restor'd to the British Druids*. London.

1743. *Abury: a temple of the British Druids*. London.

TALLGREN, A.M. 1933. Dolmens of north Caucasia, *Antiquity* 7: 190–202.

THOM, A. 1996. Megaliths and mathematics, *Antiquity* 40: 121–8.

1963. The megalithic unit of length, *Journal of the Royal Statistical Society* A 125.2: 243.

1971. *Megalithic lunar observatories*. Oxford. Oxford University Press.

THOM, A.S., J.M.D. KER & T.R. BURROWS. 1988. The Bush Barrow gold lozenge: is it a solar and lunar calendar for Stonehenge? *Antiquity* 62: 492–502.

THORPE, R.S. & O. WILLIAMS-THORPE. 1991. The myth of long-distance megalith transport, *Antiquity* 65: 64–73.

TRIGGER, B.G. 1989. *A history of archaeological thought*. Cambridge: Cambridge University Press.

TRUMP, D. 1961. Skorba, Malta and the Mediterranean, *Antiquity* 35: 300–303.

VATCHER, F. DE M. 1965. East Heslerton long barrow, Yorkshire: the eastern half, *Antiquity* 39: 49–52.

1969. Two incised chalk plaques near Stonehenge Bottom, *Antiquity* 43: 310–11.

1959. The radio-carbon dates from the Nutbane long barrow, *Antiquity* 33: 289.

WAINWRIGHT, G. 1968. Durrington Walls: a ceremonial enclosure of the 2nd millennium BC, *Antiquity* 42: 20–26.

1996. Stonehenge saved? *Antiquity* 70: 9–12.

2000a. The Stonehenge we deserve, *Antiquity* 74: 334–42.

2000b. Time please, *Antiquity* 74: 909–43.

WAINWRIGHT, G.J. & I.H. LONGWORTH. 1971. *Durrington Walls Excavations 1966–68*. London: Society of Antiquaries. Report of the Research Committee of the Society of Antiquaries of London 29.

WATSON, A. & D. KEATING. 1999. Architecture and sound: an acoustic analysis of megalithic monuments in Britain, *Antiquity* 73: 325–36.

WHITEHOUSE, R. 1971. Rock cut tombs in the central Mediterranean, *Antiquity* 46: 275–81.

WHITTLE, A. 1991. A late Neolithic complex at West Kennet, Wiltshire, England, *Antiquity* 65: 256–62.

1996. Eternal stones: Stonehenge completed, *Antiquity* 70: 463–5.

1997. *Sacred mound, Holy rings. Silbury Hill and the West Kennet palisade enclosures: a later Neolithic complex in north Wiltshire*. Oxford: Oxbow. Monograph 74.

1998. People and the diverse past: two comments on 'Stonehenge for the ancestors', *Antiquity* 72: 852–4.

WILLIAMS-THORPE, O. 1993. Reply to 'Megalithic transport and territorial markers: evidence from the Channel Islands by Mark Patton', *Antiquity* 67: 120.

WILLIAMS-THORPE, O., D.G. JENKINS, J. JENKINS & J.S. WATSON. 1995. Chlorine-36 dating and the bluestone of Stonehenge, *Antiquity* 69: 1019–20.

WILLS, E., BATH, BALDWIN OF BEWDLEY, P. SASSOON, W.O. GORE, STANHOPE, ZETLAND, CRAWFORD & BALCARRES, F.G. KENYON, H.C. BRENTNALL & B.H. CUNNINGTON. 1937. The plan for Avebury. An appeal to the nation, *Antiquity* 11: 490–93.

WOODWARD, P.J. 1988. Pictures of the Neolithic: discoveries from the Flagstones House excavations, Dorchester, Dorset, *Antiquity* 62: 266–74.

WRIGLEY, C.G. 1989. Stonehenge from without, *Antiquity* 63: 746–52.

WYMER, J.J. 1970. Radiocarbon date for the Lambourne long barrow, *Antiquity* 44: 144.